Library Use Only

Library Use Only

SHORT STORIES
for Students

Advisors

Susan Allison: Head Librarian, Lewiston High School, Lewiston, Maine. Standards Committee Chairperson for Maine School Library (MASL) Programs. Board member, Julia Adams Morse Memorial Library, Greene, Maine. Advisor to Lewiston Public Library Planning Process.

Jennifer Hood: Young Adult/Reference Librarian, Cumberland Public Library, Cumberland, Rhode Island. Certified teacher, Rhode Island. Member of the New England Library Association, Rhode Island Library Association, and the Rhode Island Educational Media Association.

Ann Kearney: Head Librarian and Media Specialist, Christopher Columbus High School, Miami, Florida, 1982–2002. Thirty-two years as Librarian in various educational institutions ranging from grade schools through graduate programs. Library positions at Miami-Dade Community College, the University of Miami's Medical School Library, and Carrollton School in Coconut Grove,

Florida. B.A. from University of Detroit, 1967 (magna cum laude); M.L.S., University of Missouri–Columbia, 1974. Volunteer Project Leader for a school in rural Jamaica; volunteer with Adult Literacy programs.

Laurie St. Laurent: Head of Adult and Children's Services, East Lansing Public Library, East Lansing, Michigan, 1994–. M.L.S. from Western Michigan University. Chair of Michigan Library Association's 1998 Michigan Summer Reading Program; Chair of the Children's Services Division in 2000–2001; and Vice-President of the Association in 2002–2003. Board member of several regional early childhood literacy organizations and member of the Library of Michigan Youth Services Advisory Committee.

Heidi Stohs: Instructor in Language Arts, grades 10–12, Solomon High School, Solomon, Kansas. Received B.S. from Kansas State University; M.A. from Fort Hays State University.

SHORT STORIES
for Students

**Presenting Analysis, Context, and Criticism on
Commonly Studied Short Stories**

VOLUME 25

Ira Mark Milne, Project Editor

Foreword by Thomas E. Barden

THOMSON

GALE

Detroit • New York • San Francisco • New Haven, Conn. • Waterville, Maine • London

Short Stories for Students: Volume 25

Project Editor
Ira Mark Milne

Editorial
Jennifer Greve

Rights Acquisition and Management
Tracie Richardson, Sue Rudolph, Timothy Sisler, Robyn Young

Manufacturing
Drew Kalasky

Imaging and Multimedia
Lezlie Light, Mike Logusz

Product Design
Pamela A. E. Galbreath, Jennifer Wahi

Vendor Administration
Civie Green

Product Manager
Meggin Condino

ISBN-13: 978-0-7876-8905-6
ISBN-10: 0-7876-8905-X
e-ISBN-13: 978-1-4144-3271-7
e-ISBN-10: 1-4144-3271-2
ISSN 1092-7735

Printed in the United States of America
10 9 8 7 6 5 4 3 2 1

Table of Contents

Why Study Literature At All?

Short Stories for Students is designed to provide readers with information and discussion about a wide range of important contemporary and historical works of short fiction, and it does that job very well. However, I want to use this guest foreword to address a question that it does *not* take up. It is a fundamental question that is often ignored in high school and college English classes as well as research texts, and one that causes frustration among students at all levels, namely why study literature at all? Isn't it enough to read a story, enjoy it, and go about one's business? My answer (to be expected from a literary professional, I suppose) is no. It is not enough. It is a start; but it is not enough. Here's why.

First, literature is the only part of the educational curriculum that deals directly with the actual world of lived experience. The philosopher Edmund Husserl used the apt German term *die Lebenswelt*, "the living world," to denote this realm. All the other content areas of the modern American educational system avoid the subjective, present reality of everyday life. Science (both the natural and the social varieties) objectifies, the fine arts create and/or perform, history reconstructs. Only literary study persists in posing those questions we all asked before our schooling taught us to give up on them. Only literature gives credibility to personal perceptions, feelings, dreams, and the "stream of consciousness" that is our inner voice. Literature wonders about infinity, wonders why God permits evil, wonders what will happen to us after we die. Literature admits that we get our hearts broken, that people sometimes cheat and get away with it, that the world is a strange and probably incomprehensible place. Literature, in other words, takes on all the big and small issues of what it means to be human. So my first answer is that of the humanist we should read literature and study it and take it seriously because it enriches us as human beings. We develop our moral imagination, our capacity to sympathize with other people, and our ability to understand our existence through the experience of fiction.

My second answer is more practical. By studying literature we can learn how to explore and analyze texts. Fiction may be about *die Lebenswelt*, but it is a construct of words put together in a certain order by an artist using the medium of language. By examining and studying those constructions, we can learn about language as a medium. We can become more sophisticated about word associations and connotations, about the manipulation of symbols, and about style and atmosphere. We can grasp how ambiguous language is and how important context and texture is to meaning. In our first encounter with a work of literature, of course, we are not supposed to catch all of these things. We are spellbound, just as the writer wanted us to be. It is as serious students of the writer's art that we begin to see how the tricks are done.

Seeing the tricks, which is another way of saying "developing analytical and close reading skills," is important above and beyond its intrinsic literary educational value. These skills transfer to other fields and enhance critical thinking of any kind. Understanding how language is used to construct texts is powerful knowledge. It makes engineers better problem solvers, lawyers better advocates and courtroom practitioners, politicians better rhetoricians, marketing and advertising agents better sellers, and citizens more aware consumers as well as better participants in democracy. This last point is especially important, because rhetorical skill works both ways when we learn how language is manipulated in the making of texts the result is that we become less susceptible when language is used to manipulate us.

My third reason is related to the second. When we begin to see literature as created artifacts of language, we become more sensitive to good writing in general. We get a stronger sense of the importance of individual words, even the sounds of words and word combinations. We begin to understand Mark Twain's delicious proverb "The difference between the right word and the almost right word is the difference between lightning and a lightning bug." Getting beyond the "enjoyment only" stage of literature gets us closer to becoming makers of word art ourselves. I am not saying that studying fiction will turn every student into a Faulkner or a Shakespeare. But it will make us more adaptable and effective writers, even if our art form ends up being the office memo or the corporate annual report.

Studying short stories, then, can help students become better readers, better writers, and even better human beings. But I want to close with a warning. If your study and exploration of the craft, history, context, symbolism, or anything else about a story starts to rob it of the magic you felt when you first read it, it is time to stop. Take a break, study another subject, shoot some hoops, or go for a run. Love of reading is too important to be ruined by school. The early twentieth century writer Willa Cather, in her novel *My Antonia*, has her narrator Jack Burden tell a story that he and Antonia heard from two old Russian immigrants when they were teenagers. These immigrants, Pavel and Peter, told about an incident from their youth back in Russia that the narrator could recall in vivid detail thirty years later. It was a harrowing story of a wedding party starting home in sleds and being chased by starving wolves. Hundreds of wolves attacked the group's sleds one by one as they sped across the snow trying to reach their village. In a horrible revelation, the old Russians revealed that the groom eventually threw his own bride to the wolves to save himself. There was even a hint that one of the old immigrants might have been the groom mentioned in the story. Cather has her narrator conclude with his feelings about the story. "We did not tell Pavel's secret to anyone, but guarded it jealously as if the wolves of the Ukraine had gathered that night long ago, and the wedding party had been sacrificed, just to give us a painful and peculiar pleasure." That feeling, that painful and peculiar pleasure, is the most important thing about literature. Study and research should enhance that feeling and never be allowed to overwhelm it.

Thomas E. Barden
Professor of English and Director of
Graduate English Studies, The
University of Toledo

Introduction

Purpose of the Book

The purpose of *Short Stories for Students* (*SSfS*) is to provide readers with a guide to understanding, enjoying, and studying short stories by giving them easy access to information about the work. Part of Gale's "For Students" Literature line, *SSfS* is specifically designed to meet the curricular needs of high school and undergraduate college students and their teachers, as well as the interests of general readers and researchers considering specific short fiction. While each volume contains entries on "classic" stories frequently studied in classrooms, there are also entries containing hard-to-find information on contemporary stories, including works by multicultural, international, and women writers.

The information covered in each entry includes an introduction to the story and the story's author; a plot summary, to help readers unravel and understand the events in the work; descriptions of important characters, including explanation of a given character's role in the narrative as well as discussion about that character's relationship to other characters in the story; analysis of important themes in the story; and an explanation of important literary techniques and movements as they are demonstrated in the work.

In addition to this material, which helps the readers analyze the story itself, students are also provided with important information on the literary and historical background informing each work. This includes a historical context essay, a box comparing the time or place the story was written to modern Western culture, a critical overview essay, and excerpts from critical essays on the story or author. A unique feature of *SSfS* is a specially commissioned critical essay on each story, targeted toward the student reader.

To further aid the student in studying and enjoying each story, information on media adaptations is provided (if available), as well as reading suggestions for works of fiction and nonfiction on similar themes and topics. Classroom aids include ideas for research papers and lists of critical sources that provide additional material on the work.

Selection Criteria

The titles for each volume of SSfS were selected by surveying numerous sources on teaching literature and analyzing course curricula for various school districts. Some of the sources surveyed include: literature anthologies, *Reading Lists for College-Bound Students: The Books Most Recommended by America's Top Colleges*; *Teaching the Short Story: A Guide to Using Stories from around the World*, by the National Council of Teachers of English (NCTE); and "A Study of High School Literature Anthologies," conducted by Arthur Applebee at the Center for the Learning and Teaching of Literature and sponsored by the National Endowment for the

Arts and the Office of Educational Research and Improvement.

Input was also solicited from our advisory board, as well as educators from various areas. From these discussions, it was determined that each volume should have a mix of "classic" stories (those works commonly taught in literature classes) and contemporary stories for which information is often hard to find. Because of the interest in expanding the canon of literature, an emphasis was also placed on including works by international, multicultural, and women authors. Our advisory board members—educational professionals—helped pare down the list for each volume. Works not selected for the present volume were noted as possibilities for future volumes. As always, the editor welcomes suggestions for titles to be included in future volumes.

How Each Entry Is Organized

Each entry, or chapter, in *SSfS* focuses on one story. Each entry heading lists the title of the story, the author's name, and the date of the story's publication. The following elements are contained in each entry:

Introduction: a brief overview of the story which provides information about its first appearance, its literary standing, any controversies surrounding the work, and major conflicts or themes within the work.

Author Biography: this section includes basic facts about the author's life, and focuses on events and times in the author's life that may have inspired the story in question.

Plot Summary: a description of the events in the story. Lengthy summaries are broken down with subheads.

Characters: an alphabetical listing of the characters who appear in the story. Each character name is followed by a brief to an extensive description of the character's role in the story, as well as discussion of the character's actions, relationships, and possible motivation.

Characters are listed alphabetically by last name. If a character is unnamed—for instance, the narrator in "The Eatonville Anthology"—the character is listed as "The Narrator" and alphabetized as "Narrator." If a character's first name is the only one given, the name will appear alphabetically by that name.

Themes: a thorough overview of how the topics, themes, and issues are addressed within the story. Each theme discussed appears in a separate subhead, and is easily accessed through the boldface entries in the Subject/Theme Index.

Style: this section addresses important style elements of the story, such as setting, point of view, and narration; important literary devices used, such as imagery, foreshadowing, symbolism; and, if applicable, genres to which the work might have belonged, such as Gothicism or Romanticism. Literary terms are explained within the entry, but can also be found in the Glossary.

Historical Context: this section outlines the social, political, and cultural climate *in which the author lived and the work was created.* This section may include descriptions of related historical events, pertinent aspects of daily life in the culture, and the artistic and literary sensibilities of the time in which the work was written. If the story is historical in nature, information regarding the time in which the story is set is also included. Long sections are broken down with helpful subheads.

Critical Overview: this section provides background on the critical reputation of the author and the story, including bannings or any other public controversies surrounding the work. For older works, this section may include a history of how the story was first received and how perceptions of it may have changed over the years; for more recent works, direct quotes from early reviews may also be included.

Criticism: an essay commissioned by *SSfS* which specifically deals with the story and is written specifically for the student audience, as well as excerpts from previously published criticism on the work (if available).

Sources: an alphabetical list of critical material used in compiling the entry, with bibliographical information.

Further Reading: an alphabetical list of other critical sources which may prove useful for the student. Includes full bibliographical information and a brief annotation.

In addition, each entry contains the following highlighted sections, set apart from the main text as sidebars:

Media Adaptations: if availablee, a list of film and television adaptations of the story, including source information. The list also includes stage adaptations, audio recordings, musical adaptations, etc.

Topics for Further Study: a list of potential study questions or research topics dealing with the story. This section includes questions related to other disciplines the student may be studying, such as American history, world history, science, math, government, business, geography, economics, psychology, etc.

Compare and Contrast: an "at-a-glance" comparison of the cultural and historical differences between the author's time and culture and late twentieth century or early twenty-first century Western culture. This box includes pertinent parallels between the major scientific, political, and cultural movements of the time or place the story was written, the time or place the story was set (if a historical work), and modern Western culture. Works written after 1990 may not have this box.

What Do I Read Next?: a list of works that might complement the featured story or serve as a contrast to it. This includes works by the same author and others, works of fiction and non-fiction, and works from various genres, cultures, and eras.

Other Features

SSfS includes "Why Study Literature At All?," a foreword by Thomas E. Barden, Professor of English and Director of Graduate English Studies at the University of Toledo. This essay provides a number of very fundamental reasons for studying literature and, therefore, reasons why a book such as *SSfS*, designed to facilitate the study of literterure, is useful.

A Cumulative Author/Title Index lists the authors and titles covered in each volume of the *SSfS* series.

A Cumulative Nationality/Ethnicity Index breaks down the authors and titles covered in each volume of the *SSfS* series by nationality and ethnicity.

A Subject/Theme Index, specific to each volume, provides easy reference for users who

may be studying a particular subject or theme rather than a single work. Significant subjects from events to broad themes are included, and the entries pointing to the specific theme discussions in each entry are indicated in **boldface**.

Each entry may include illustrations, including photo of the author, stills from film adaptations (if available), maps, and/or photos of key historical events.

Citing Short Stories for Students

When writing papers, students who quote directly from any volume of *SSfS* may use the following general forms to document their source. These examples are based on MLA style; teachers may request that students adhere to a different style, thus, the following examples may be adapted as needed.

When citing text from *SSfS* that is not attributed to a particular author (for example, the Themes, Style, Historical Context sections, etc.), the following format may be used:

> "The Celebrated Jumping Frog of Calavaras County." *Short Stories for Students*. Ed. Kathleen Wilson. Vol. 1. Detroit: Gale, 1997. 19–20.

When quoting the specially commissioned essay from *SSfS* (usually the first essay under the Criticism subhead), the following format may be used:

> Korb, Rena. Critical Essay on "Children of the Sea." *Short Stories for Students*. Ed. Kathleen Wilson. Vol. 1. Detroit: Gale, 1997. 39–42.

When quoting a journal or newspaper essay that is reprinted in a volume of *Short Stories for Students*, the following form may be used:

> Schmidt, Paul. "The Deadpan on Simon Wheeler." *Southwest Review* Vol. XLI, No. 3 (Summer, 1956), 270–77; excerpted and reprinted in *Short Stories for Students*, Vol. 1, ed. Kathleen Wilson (Detroit: Gale, 1997), pp. 29–31.

When quoting material from a book that is reprinted in a volume of *SSfS*, the following form may be used:

> Bell-Villada, Gene H. "The Master of Short Forms," in *García Márquez: The Man and His Work*. University of North Carolina Press, 1990, pp. 119–36; excerpted and reprinted in *Short Stories for Students*, Vol. 1, ed. Kathleen Wilson (Detroit: Gale, 1997), pp. 89–90.

We Welcome Your Suggestions

The editorial staff of *Short Stories for Students* welcomes your comments and ideas. Readers who wish to suggest short stories to appear in future volumes, or who have other suggestions, are cordially invited to contact the editor. You may contact the editor via E-mail at: **ForStudents Editors@thomson.com.** Or write to the editor at:

Editor, *Short Stories for Students*
Thomson Gale
27500 Drake Road
Farmington Hills, MI 48331-3535

Literary Chronology

1896: Francis Scott Key Fitzgerald is born on September 24 in St. Paul, Minnesota.

1921: Patricia Highsmith is born Mary Patricia Plangman on January 19 in Fort Worth, Texas.

1922: F. Scott Fitzgerald's "The Diamond as Big as the Ritz" is published.

1925: James Salter is born James Horowitz on June 10 in Passaic, New Jersey.

1940: F. Scott Fitzgerald dies of a heart attack on December 21.

1944: Joy Williams is born on February 11 in Chelmsford, Massachusetts.

1947: Mark Helprin is born on June 28 in New York City.

1950: Peter Baida is born on July 26 in Baltimore, Maryland.

1952: Padgett Powell is born on April 25 in Gainesville, Florida.

1959: Don Lee is born in Tokyo, Japan, to parents who are second-generation Korean Americans.

1960: Marisa Silver is born on April 23 in Shaker Heights, New Jersey.

1966: Elizabeth McCracken is born.

1969: Edwidge Danticat is born on January 19 in Port-au-Prince, Haiti.

1969: Aimee Bender is born on June 28 in Los Angeles, California.

1973: ZZ Packer is born in Chicago.

1973: Anthony Doerr, also known as Tony Doerr, is born on October 27 in Cleveland, Ohio.

1980: Patricia Highsmith's "A Girl like Phyl" is published.

1993: Elizabeth McCracken's "Here's Your Hat What's Your Hurry" is published.

1993: Padgett Powell's "Trick or Treat" is published.

1995: Patricia Highsmith dies of leukemia on February 4.

1995: Edwidge Danticat's "Caroline's Wedding" is published.

1997: Aimee Bender's "The Rememberer" is published.

1998: Peter Baida's "A Nurse's Story" is published.

1999: Peter Baida dies of liver failure and post-surgical complications on December 10 within months of receiving his O. Henry Award.

2000: Don Lee's "The Price of Eggs in China" is published.

2001: Marisa Silver's "What I Saw from Where I Stood" is published.

2002: James Salter's "Last Night" is published.

2002: Anthony Doerr's "The Shell Collector" is published.

2003: ZZ Packer's "Brownies" is published.

2004: Mark Helprin's "Perfection" is published.

2004: Joy Williams's "The Girls" is published.

Acknowledgments

The editors wish to thank the copyright holders of the excerpted criticism included in this volume and the permissions managers of many book and magazine publishing companies for assisting us in securing reproduction rights. We are also grateful to the staffs of the Detroit Public Library, the Library of Congress, the University of Detroit Mercy Library, Wayne State University Purdy/Kresge Library Complex, and the University of Michigan Libraries for making their resources available to us. Following is a list of the copyright holders who have granted us permission to reproduce material in this volume of *SSFS*. Every effort has been made to trace copyright, but if omissions have been made, please let us know.

COPYRIGHTED EXCERPTS IN SSFS, *VOLUME 25, WERE REPRODUCED FROM THE FOLLOWING PERIODICALS:*

The Believer, v. 4, September, 2006. All contents copyright 2006 *The Believer* and its contributors. All rights reserved. Reproduced by permission.— *CLA Journal*, v. xl, December, 1996. Copyright 1996 by The College Language Association. Used by permission of The College Language Association.—*Collectanea*, v. 1, winter, 2006. Reproduced by permission.—*International Herald Tribune*, November 4, 2004. Copyright 2004 by The New York Times Company. Reprinted with permission.—*Los Angeles Times*, August 5,

2001; December 1, 2002. Copyright 2001, 2002 *Los Angeles Times*. Both reproduced by permission.—*MELUS*, v. 26, summer, 2001. Copyright 2001 by *MELUS: The Society for the Study of Multi-Ethnic Literature of the United States.* Reproduced by permission.—*NPR: Weekend Edition*, November 6, 2004. Copyright 2004 National Public Radio. All rights reserved. Reproduced by permission.—*Pif Magazine*, November, 1998. Copyright 1998 *Pif Magazine*. All rights reserved. Reproduced by permission.— *Poets & Writers Magazine*, May 26, 2004. Copyright 2004 Poets & Writers, Inc. Reprinted by permission of the publisher, Poets & Writers, Inc., 72 Spring St., New York, NY, 10012. www.pw.org.—*Public Libraries*, v. 40, March–April, 2001. Copyright 2001 by the American Library Association. Reproduced by permission.—*Publishers Weekly*, v. 248, August 6, 2001. Copyright 2001 by Reed Publishing USA. Reproduced from *Publishers Weekly*, published by the Bowker Magazine Group of Cahners Publishing Co., a division of Reed Publishing USA, by permission.—*San Francisco Chronicle*, March 9, 2003. Copyright 2003 *San Francisco Chronicle*. Republished with permission of *San Francisco Chronicle*, conveyed through Copyright Clearance Center, Inc.—*The Washington Post*, August 9, 2001 for "The Hidden Corners of L.A.," by Jonathan Yardley; October 13, 2002 for "Little Terrors," by James Lasdun. Copyright 2001, 2002 The Washington Post Company. Both reprinted by permission of the publisher and the respective authors.—*World Literature Today*, v. 70, winter, 1996. Copyright 1996 by *World Literature Today*. Reproduced by permission of the publisher.—*WritersMarket.com*, April, 2001. Copyright 2001 Writers Digest Books, an imprint of F&W Publications, Inc., Cincinnati, Ohio. All rights reserved. Reproduced by permission.

COPYRIGHTED EXCERPTS IN SSFS, VOLUME 25, WERE REPRODUCED FROM THE FOLLOWING BOOKS:

Dowie, William. From "James Salter," in *Dictionary of Literary Biography, Vol. 130, American Short-Story Writers Since World War II.* Edited by Patrick Meanor. Gale Research, 1993. Reproduced by permission of Thomson Gale.—Prigozy, Ruth. From "F. Scott Fitzgerald," in *Dictionary of Literary Biography, Vol. 86, American Short-Story Writers, 1910–1945, First Series.* Edited by Bobby Ellen Kimbel. Gale Research, 1989. Reproduced by permission of Thomson Gale.—Stenger, Karl L. From "Patricia Highsmith," in *Dictionary of Literary Biography, Vol. 306, American Mystery and Detective Writers.* Edited by George Parker Anderson. Thomson Gale, 2005. Reproduced by permission of Thomson Gale.—Vice, Brad. From "Padgett Powell," in *Dictionary of Literary Biography, Vol. 234, American Short-Story Writers Since World War II, Third Series.* Edited by Patrick Meanor and Richard E. Lee. The Gale Group, 2001. Reproduced by permission of Thomson Gale.

COPYRIGHTED EXCERPTS IN SSFS, VOLUME 25, WERE REPRODUCED FROM THE FOLLOWING WEBSITES OR OTHER SOURCES:

From *Contemporary Authors Online*. "Aimee Bender," www.gale.com, Gale, 2006. Reproduced by permission of Thomson Gale.—From *Contemporary Authors Online*. "Anthony Doerr," www.gale.com, Gale, 2005. Reproduced by permission of Thomson Gale.—From *Contemporary Authors Online*. "Don Lee," www.gale.com, Gale, 2006. Reproduced by permission of Thomson Gale.—From *Contemporary Authors Online*. "Edwidge Danticat," www.gale.com, Gale, 2005. Reproduced by permission of Thomson Gale—From *Contemporary Authors Online*. "Elizabeth McCracken," www.gale.com, Gale, 2002. Reproduced by permission of Thomson Gale.—From *Contemporary Authors Online*. "F(rancis) Scott (Key) Fitzgerald," www.gale.com, Gale, 2004. Reproduced by permission of Thomson Gale.—From *Contemporary Authors Online*. "James Salter," www.gale.com, Gale, 2006. Reproduced by permission of Thomson Gale.—From *Contemporary Authors Online*. "Joy Williams," www.gale.com, Gale, 2005. Reproduced by permission of Thomson Gale.—From *Contemporary Authors Online*. "Marisa Silver," www.gale.com, Gale, 2006. Reproduced by permission of Thomson Gale.—From *Contemporary Authors Online*. "Mark Helprin," www.gale.com, Gale, 2005. Reproduced by permission of Thomson Gale.—From *Contemporary Authors Online*. "(Mary) Patricia Highsmith," www.gale.com, Gale, 2004. Reproduced by permission of Thomson Gale.—From *Contemporary Authors Online*. "Padgett Powell," www.gale.com, Gale, 2006. Reproduced by permission of Thomson Gale.—From *Contemporary Authors Online*. "Peter Baida," www.gale.com, Gale, 2004. Reproduced by permission of Thomson Gale.—From *Contemporary Authors Online*. "Z.Z. Packer," www.gale.com, Gale, 2004. Reproduced by permission of Thomson Gale.—From *http://us.penguingroup.com/static/rguides/us/shell_collector.html*. "Interview with Anthony Doerr," Penguin Group (USA), 2006. Copyright 2006. Used by permission of Penguin Group (USA) Inc.

Contributors

Bryan Aubrey: Aubrey holds a Ph.D. in English and has published many articles on literature. Entry on *Brownies*. Critical essay on *Brownies*.

Jennifer Bussey: Bussey holds a master's degree in Interdisciplinary Studies and a bachelor's degree in English Literature. She is an independent writer specializing in literature. Critical essays on *Last Night* and *A Nurse's Story*.

Klay Dyer: Dyer holds a Ph.D. in English literature and has published extensively on fiction, poetry, film, and television. He is also a freelance university teacher, writer, and educational consultant. Entries on *Last Night* and *A Nurse's Story*. Critical essays on *The Girls*, *Last Night*, *A Nurse's Story*, *The Price of Eggs in China*, and *The Rememberer*.

Joyce Hart: Hart is a freelance writer and published author. Critical essay on *What I Saw from Where I Stood*.

David Kelly: Kelly is an instructor of creative writing and English literature. Entries on *Here's Your Hat What's Your Hurry* and *The Price of Eggs in China*. Critical essays on *A Girl Like Phyl*, *Here's Your Hat What's Your Hurry*, *Last Night*, and *The Price of Eggs in China*.

Melodie Monahan: Monahan has a Ph.D. in English and operates an editing service, The Inkwell Works. Entry on *The Shell Collector*. Critical essay on *The Shell Collector*.

Wendy Perkins: Perkins is a professor of American and British literature and film. Entries on *A Girl like Phyl* and *What I Saw from Where I Stood*. Critical essays on *A Girl like Phyl* and *What I Saw from Where I Stood*.

Laura Pryor: Pryor has a Bachelor of Arts degree from the University of Michigan and over twenty years experience in professional and creative writing with special interest in fiction. Entries on *The Diamond as Big as the Ritz* and *The Rememberer*. Critical essays on *The Diamond as Big as the Ritz* and *The Rememberer*.

Claire Robinson: Robinson has an M.A. in English. She is a writer, editor, and former teacher of English literature and creative writing. Entries on *Caroline's Wedding* and *Perfection*. Critical essays on *Caroline's Wedding* and *Perfection*.

Carol Ullmann: Ullmann is a freelance writer and editor. Entries on *The Girls* and *Trick or Treat*. Critical essays on *The Girls*, *A Nurse's Story*, and *Trick or Treat*.

Brownies

ZZ PACKER

2003

"Brownies" is a story by ZZ Packer, a young African American writer. It appears in Packer's short story collection, *Drinking Coffee Elsewhere*, which was published in 2003 to great acclaim. The story is about a Brownie troop of fourth-grade African American girls from suburban Atlanta, Georgia, who go to summer camp. At the camp, they encounter a troop of white girls and believe that one of the white girls addressed them with a racial insult. The African American girls resolve to beat up the white girls.

"Brownies" is a story about racism as it is experienced by young girls, but it has a twist. The African American girls discover that the situation is not as clear-cut as they had believed, and as they return home on the bus, Laurel, the African American girl who narrates the story, tells them of an incident in her family involving a white Mennonite family. As she tells the story, she comes to an unsettling realization about racism and the nature of human life.

AUTHOR BIOGRAPHY

ZZ Packer was born in Chicago in 1973. Her first name is Zuwena, which is a Swahili word meaning "good." But she has been known by the nickname ZZ for as long as she can remember, she told Richard Dorment in a March 2003 interview for *Interview* magazine. When she

ZZ Packer © *Robert Birnbaum*

was five, she and her family moved to Atlanta, where she remained until she was eleven. Then her parents got divorced, and ZZ went to live in Louisville, Kentucky, with her mother. During her early schooling, Packer was interested in math and science, but in high school a teacher had the class write short stories, and that planted a seed in Packer's mind that she might one day become a writer.

After graduating from high school, Packer attended Yale University. For a while she was unsure of whether to focus on the humanities or the sciences, but she then decided she would become an engineer. At the time she did not think writing was an activity that people could actually do in order to make a living. But after graduating from Yale, she attended the Writing Seminar at Johns Hopkins University in Baltimore. At Johns Hopkins, one of her tutors was Francine Prose, whose perspective on writing encouraged Packer to look at her own work in a new way.

After Johns Hopkins, Packer taught in a public high school for two years, determined to write during her spare time. But she found that teaching was a demanding profession, and it was difficult to find the time to write as well as teach. She took many odd jobs during the summers and then decided to apply to the prestigious Writers' Workshop at the University of Iowa. She was admitted to the program and graduated in 1997.

It was not long before she began to have success. Her story, "Drinking Coffee Elsewhere" was included in the Debut Fiction issue of the *New Yorker* in 2000, and her work also appeared in *Seventeen*, *Harper's*, *The Best American Short Stories* (2000), and *Ploughshares*. Eight of Packer's stories, including "Brownies," were collected in *Drinking Coffee Elsewhere*, which was published by Riverhead Books in 2003 to universal praise from reviewers. John Updike chose the book as the June 2003, Today Book Club selection on the NBC network's *Today Show*, and the book was also nominated for the PEN/Faulkner Award for Fiction in 2004.

Among the writers Packer most admires are Toni Morrison, especially Morrison's novel, *Beloved*. She has also been influenced by Leo Tolstoy's *War and Peace*, Mark Twain's *Huckleberry Finn*, Ralph Ellison's *Invisible Man*, Marilynne Robinson's *Housekeeping*, and James Baldwin's *Go Tell It on the Mountain*.

As of 2006, Packer lived in San Francisco, California, and taught at Stanford University. She was working on a novel about the Buffalo Soldiers, African Americans who served in the U.S. Army following the Civil War.

PLOT SUMMARY

"Brownies" takes place at Camp Crescendo, a summer camp for fourth graders near the suburbs of Atlanta, Georgia. The story is told in the first person by an African American girl named Laurel, known to the other girls by her nickname, Snot. Laurel announces that by the second day at the camp, all the girls in her Brownie troop had decided they were going to "kick the asses" of every girl in Brownie Troop 909, who were all white girls. The black girls took a dislike to the white girls when they first saw them. Arnetta, the girls' ringleader, said they smelled "like Chihuahuas. *Wet* Chihuahuas." When she adds that they were like "*Caucasian* Chihuahuas," all the black girls go into fits of laughter. They regard the word Caucasian as a hilarious term of abuse that can be used in almost any situation.

The black girls have seen whites before but have never had much to do with them. But the ten white girls they encounter at the camp are closer to them and, therefore, more real and capable of exciting envy and hatred.

At the end of the first day at camp, Arnetta reports she heard one of the white girls refer to Daphne, a black girl, as "a nigger." On prompting by Arnetta, Daphne, a quiet girl, nods her head to confirm that the derogatory term was used. Arnetta tells the other girls that they cannot let the white girls get away with using that word about them. She says they must teach the white girls a lesson. Janice suggests that they put daddy-long-legs in the white girls' sleeping bags, and when the girls awake, beat them up. Arnetta tells Janice, who is not a popular girl, to shut up. Arnetta then announces that they are to hold a secret meeting. She turns to Laurel, whom she appears not to like, and asks her whether Laurel plans to tell Mrs. Margolin, their troop leader, about the situation.

On the second day of camp, the black girls eat their sandwich lunch by a stream that borders the field hockey lawn. Arnetta eyes the white girls from Troop 909 and would like to attack them right then and there, but the white girls are with their troop leader, which makes the mission impossible. When the white girls leave, Arnetta says they must find a way of getting them when they are alone. Laurel says that the girls will never be alone, and the only time they will be unsupervised is in the bathroom. Octavia tells Laurel to shut up, but Arnetta seems to think this is a useful piece of information.

The black girls walk to the restrooms, which are messy, with leaves and wads of chewing gum on the floor. Arnetta says that when they meet the white girls there, they will be nice to them at first and then tell them what happens when they call any one of the black girls a "nigger." Janice says that she will tell the white girls, "We're gonna teach you a *lesson!*" Laurel, who is normally very quiet, asks what will happen if the white girls say they did not use the offending word. Arnetta dismisses this possibility and says that all they have to do is fight. An exception is made for Daphne, however, since they are doing this to avenge her. The girls leave the restrooms, although Daphne stays behind, picking

up the trash. When Arnetta is asked about the secret meeting, she replies that they have just had it.

That evening, just before their bedtime, Mrs. Hedy, the parent helper, comes to their cabin. The girls, knowing she is depressed about her impending divorce, sing her favorite Brownie song for her. The girls are then reluctantly persuaded by Mrs. Margolin to sing "The Doughnut Song," a religious song which they all hate. Mrs. Margolin is tired and leaves to go to the lodge. Arnetta says it is time to go to the restroom, hoping that Mrs. Hedy will not go with them. Arnetta knows that the troop of white girls will be in the restrooms soon and will not be expecting an ambush. Mrs. Hedy indicates that the girls can go to the bathroom unaccompanied. She makes Octavia promise to be good.

Daphne tells Laurel that she is not going with them, and Laurel says she is not going either. But Arnetta overhears her and insists that she comes.

They make their way to the restrooms in the darkness, using a flashlight to guide them. They do not talk about fighting; they are all frightened enough to be walking through the woods at night.

When they arrive, the white girls are already there. Arnetta and Octavia go in first, instructing the others to follow when they hear Arnetta say, "We're gonna teach you a lesson."

After about a minute, Laurel hears one of the white girls deny that they had used the offensive word. The other black girls decide to go inside, even though Arnetta has not given the signal. Inside, they see five white girls huddled up against a bigger girl. Octavia whispers to Elise that she thinks the white girls are retarded. The big girl denies it, but it is obvious to the others that she and all the other white girls are indeed mentally handicapped. Arnetta says they are just pretending, but Octavia, deflated, says that they should just leave. Octavia tells the big girl they are leaving and not to tell anyone they were there. The big girl asks why not, saying she knows the black girls will get into trouble. She threatens to tell on them.

Shortly after this, the white girls' troop leader enters the bathroom and assures the girls that everything will be all right. All the girls start crying. Then the ranger comes, then

Mrs. Margolin and Daphne. Mrs. Margolin tells the leader of Troop 909 that the girls will apologize and their parents will punish them. The white girls' leader denies that her girls are mentally handicapped but admits they are "*delayed learners.*"

The black girls are speechless, while the Troop 909 leader is full of words and energy. She tells Mrs. Margolin that some of her girls are "echolalic," which means they will repeat whatever they hear. (Echolalia, the repeating of the speech of others, is a severe communication disorder associated with childhood schizophrenia and mental retardation.) So they might have used the racial slur, but it would not have been intentional. Arnetta points to a small girl and says it was she who used the word. The troop leader says that is impossible, since the girl never speaks. Arnetta then picks out another girl as the culprit, but Laurel thinks it very unlikely that this happy-looking girl would call anyone a "nigger."

On the fourth morning, they board a bus to go home. The journey is quiet to begin with, but then the girls all try to silently imitate the expressions and mannerisms of the white girls, trying not to laugh too hard and attract the attention of Mrs. Margolin and Mrs. Hedy. Octavia wonders why they had to be stuck at camp with retarded girls. When Laurel starts to tell a story, Octavia tries to shut her up, but Daphne encourages Laurel to continue. Laurel tells her about an incident in a mall when she was there with her father. They saw a Mennonite family, dressed in their distinctive garb. Laurel's father had told her that if someone asked the Mennonites to do something for the person, they would be compelled to do it, because it was part of their religion. Laurel's father asked them to paint his porch, and the entire Mennonite family came and did so. Laurel's father explained to her that he had asked them to do this because it would be the only time he would be able to see a white man on his knees doing something for a black man for free.

Laurel now understands why her father said that, although she does not agree with the sentiment. When Daphne asks if Laurel's father had thanked the Mennonites, Laurel replies no, and she suddenly realizes that there is "something mean" in the world that she cannot stop.

CHARACTERS

Arnetta

Arnetta is the strong-minded leader of the black girls in the Brownie troop. She is a dominant personality, and after she speaks the other girls are usually quiet: "Her tone had an upholstered confidence that was somehow both regal and vulgar at once. It demanded a few moments of silence in its wake, like the ringing of a church bell or the playing of taps." It is Arnetta who says that she heard one of the white girls call Daphne a "nigger," and she is determined that the white girls must not be allowed to get away with it. She is eager to start a fight and makes sure that the reluctant Snot goes along, too. Arnetta plans out how the confrontation in the restroom is to be handled and gives instructions to the other girls. With Octavia, Arnetta is the first one to enter the bathroom. Arnetta is also a cunning girl. She makes a point of listening to Mrs. Margolin in class and giving all the right answers. Mrs. Margolin, therefore, has a good opinion of Arnetta and does not realize quite how subversive she can be. Arnetta knows how to deceive both Mrs. Margolin and Mrs. Hedy.

Daphne

Daphne is the black girl who was allegedly insulted by one of the white girls, although she does not seem to be upset by it. Daphne is a very quiet girl. When she speaks, her voice is "petite and tinkly, the voice one might expect from a shiny new earring." She appears to be intelligent and wrote a poem for Langston Hughes Day that won a prize at school. (Langston Hughes was a prominent African American poet.) Daphne's parents are poor, and she wears old but clean clothes. She has no desire to fight the white girls and is excused from doing so by Arnetta. When the girls first visit the restrooms to assess the place where they seek out the fight, Daphne busies herself by cleaning up the trash.

Elise

Elise is a black girl who plays a minor role in the story. She is a follower of Arnetta and Octavia, although on one occasion she takes the unusual step of asking Snot, who is usually ignored by the others, for her opinion.

Mrs. Hedy

Mrs. Hedy is the parent helper for the troop of black girls. She is Octavia's mother. Mrs. Hedy is worried about her impending divorce and talks about it in public, to Octavia's embarrassment. She tries in a perfunctory manner to get the girls to behave themselves, but she has little authority over them. Instead, she persuades them to sing Brownie songs to cheer her up. She is lenient and allows the girls to go to the restrooms on their own.

Octavia Hedy

Along with Arnetta, Octavia Hedy is one of the leaders in the troop of black girls. She is an aggressive girl with very long hair which "hung past her butt like a Hawaiian hula dancer's." Octavia is as determined as Arnetta that the white girls should not get away with insulting Daphne. She is scornful of Janice and keeps telling her to shut up, and she has the same attitude toward Laurel. She is also disdainful of the experience of being in camp. She says, "I mean, I really don't know why it's even called *camping*—all we ever do with Nature is find some twigs and say something like, 'Wow, this fell from a tree.'" It is Octavia who decides that the girls should leave the restroom when they discover the white girls are retarded.

Janice

Janice is the girl who comes up with a plan to put daddy-long-legs in the white girls' sleeping bags. She is a simple, country girl, "her looks homely, her jumpy acrobatics embarrassing to behold." Janice is a big fan of Michael Jackson. Arnetta and Octavia treat her with contempt, but Janice does not seem to mind or even notice. At one point, Snot and Daphne are worried that Octavia may push Janice into the stream. Janice is enthusiastic about the prospective fight and carefully rehearses the line she has thought up: "We're gonna teach you a *lesson*!" But when the time comes and she says this to the big white girl, it has no effect, and Octavia tells her to shut up.

Laurel

Laurel, the narrator of the story, is one of the black girls in the Brownie troop. She has been called Snot ever since first grade. Laurel is a quiet, studious, observant girl who tends to stand apart from the others. She is not very popular with them. No one ever asks for her opinion; Octavia tells her to shut up, and Arnetta demands to know whether she is going to tell on them to Mrs. Margolin. Laurel seems

TOPICS FOR FURTHER STUDY

- Research the history of affirmative action and the role it plays in social policy today. Is affirmative action justified as a way of helping those who have been disadvantaged, or does it amount to "reverse discrimination?" Should it be continued or abolished? Partner with one other student and make a class presentation in which one person argues for affirmative action and the other argues against it.

- How can racism in schools be addressed? Write an essay about your own school and how such issues are tackled. Have you experienced or observed any racist behavior at your school? Are relations between students of different races at your school a problem? Do white students and students of color tend to sit apart from one another in the cafeteria? Is this is so, why does it happen? What can be done to improve the situation?

- Read another story in Packer's collection *Drinking Coffee Elsewhere* and compare it to "Brownies." What role does race play in the story you have selected? Are there any parallels between the two stories? Write an essay comparing the two.

- With another student, select and interview one or more persons in your town or neighborhood who is of a different race. Ask how they feel about the topic of race and their experience with it. Try and draw them out and listen to their story. Then in a class presentation talk about your findings and draw some conclusions about issues of race generally in your school, neighborhood, city, or state.

more thoughtful than the others. She is the only girl who considers the possibility that the white girl did not use the forbidden term, that perhaps Arnetta misheard what was said. Laurel also wonders, unlike the others, what will happen if the white girls deny using the bad word, and why none of her troop considers the possibility that the white girls will not be so easy to beat up and may well fight back. But it is Laurel who observes that the only time the white girls will be unsupervised will be when they are in the bathroom, so she is in a way partly responsible for the confrontation that ensues. However, Laurel does not want to fight and tries to stay behind with Daphne, but Arnetta refuses to let her. Finally, it is Laurel who tells the story about the Mennonite family that paints the porch of their house, and it is she who understands more deeply than the other girls the origins of racism.

Mrs. Margolin

Mrs. Margolin is in charge of the troop of black girls and watches over them like a mother duck looks after her ducklings. According to Snot, Mrs. Margolin even looks like a mother duck: "she had hair cropped close to a small ball of a head, almost no neck, and huge, miraculous breasts." Mrs. Margolin is a religious woman who likes to give religious instruction to the girls in the Brownie troop.

Snot

See Laurel

Troop 909 Leader

The Troop 909 leader is a white woman who enters the restroom shortly after the confrontation between the two groups of girls. She explains to Mrs. Margolin that the white girls may have special needs, but they are not retarded.

THEMES

Racial Segregation

The racial prejudice and hostility shown in the story appears to be the product of historical circumstances combined with the current reality of racial segregation. The first noticeable fact in the story is that the Brownie troops at the summer camp appear to be either all-white or all-black. No mixed-race troop is presented. It also transpires that in the Woodrow Wilson Elementary School in the south suburbs of Atlanta, there is only one white child, a boy named Dennis. For all intents and purposes, the black girls in the story have been raised in a racially segregated environment. This is confirmed by the remark of Laurel: "When you

lived in the south suburbs of Atlanta, it was easy to forget about whites. Whites were like those baby pigeons: real and existing, but rarely seen or thought about."

Because they have had so little contact with whites, the black girls are extremely conscious of the differences between themselves and the white girls. Many of these differences are purely imaginary: "Man, did you smell them?" asks Arnetta of the other girls in her troop after they first see the white girls of Troop 909. For the black girls, the term Caucasian is an all-purpose, humorous term of abuse that can be applied in almost any situation: "If you ate too fast you ate like a Caucasian, if you ate too slow you ate like a Caucasian." It is because the black girls are so used to living in a racially segregated environment, in which they may catch only momentary sight of white people in places like clothing stores or the downtown library, that Arnetta regards the white girls as "*invaders.*"

Indeed, until the confrontation in the restrooms, Laurel, Arnetta, and their friends do not even see the white girls at the camp at close quarters. The one thing they are able to see is that the white girls' long straight hair looks like the shampoo commercials they have seen on television, and this difference alone is cause for "envy and hatred." But they cannot see "whether their faces were the way all white girls appeared on TV—ponytailed and full of energy, bubbling over with love and money." In other words, the black girls' knowledge of whites comes not from direct experience but through the distorting, homogenizing lens of mass culture.

Racial Prejudice

Given the extent of racial segregation, it is not surprising that the encounter between the black girls and the white girls should be full of misunderstandings. It is never established beyond doubt that any of the white girls actually used the racial insult, but even if they had, they would not have used it with the intention of offending the black girls. But this is not the whole story. If a white girl used the word, she must have heard it somewhere, possibly spoken in private by her parents or other white people. It is thus made clear that racial prejudice continues to exist in present-day Atlanta. This is confirmed by Arnetta in the bus returning from the camp, when she reports on her experience at the mall in Buckhead. (Buckhead is an extremely affluent area in the northern part of Atlanta, known as a shopping mecca for the entire South.) While Arnetta was there with her family, she says, "this white lady just kept looking at us. I mean, like we were foreign or something. Like we were from China." It appears that there are still places in Atlanta where black people are perceived as not belonging.

The story Laurel tells on the bus illustrates the depths of resentment that black people feel over such slights. Her father feels his resentments keenly, and that is why he asks the Mennonite family to paint his porch for free, so he can for once feel himself to be in a position of superiority over whites. Laurel now understands why her father did this: "When you've been made to feel bad for so long, you jump at the chance to do it to others." This is a great moment of realization for Laurel. She is mature enough to realize that she does not agree with her father's motivation, but she also learns that "there is something mean in the world" that she cannot stop, something that makes people dislike those who are different from themselves and also makes those who suffer discrimination harbor grudges and try to settle old scores whenever opportunity presents itself. The sad thing that Laurel realizes is that the kind act of the Mennonite family did nothing to heal the situation or remove past pain, since her father refused to thank the family for the work they had done. It is to Laurel's credit that she does not indulge in racist thoughts of her own to explain such sad incidents. She appears to attribute the painful reality to human nature rather than to one specific racial group.

STYLE

Figurative Language

Figurative language is the art of describing something in terms of something else. There are many types of figurative language. Prominent in "Brownies" are similes, in which something is compared to something else that on the surface may be dissimilar but at some other level is similar. Similes can be recognized by the presence of connecting words such as "like" or "as if." Similes seem to come naturally to Laurel, the lively, observant first-person narrator of the story. Mrs. Hedy wags her finger "like a windshield wiper," for example. The similarity between the finger and the windshield wiper is based on the

regular, repetitive, rhythmic motion of both. The leader of Troop 909 holds a banana in front of her "like a microphone," the similarity between banana and microphone based on the shape of the object and the way it is held. The shape and color of the dissimilar objects being compared are at the basis of the simile that occurs to Laurel in the bathroom: "Shaggy white balls of paper towels sat on the sinktops in a line like corsages on display." Other similes include the tree branches that "looked like arms sprouting menacing hands"; the girl who flaps her hand "like a bird with a broken wing"; and Mrs. Margolin with her Brownie troop following behind her "like a brood of obedient ducklings."

Unlike a simile, a metaphor is a figure of speech in which one object is identified with another, rather than compared with it. There are several metaphors in the story. At sunset, the leafy tops of the trees "formed a canopy of black lace," the shared qualities between leaves and black lace being the color the leaves appear to take on in the setting sun and the delicate fine patterns or designs they appear to form as the narrator looks up at them. Another metaphor occurs when the sound made by a covey of insects leads Laurel to think of them as "a throng of tiny electric machines, all going at once." Inside the restrooms, another metaphor occurs to Laurel. Noticing how the wooden rafters of the restroom come together in large V's, she observes that "We were, it seems, inside a whale, viewing the ribs of the roof of its mouth." Thus metaphorically, the interior of the restroom becomes the inside of a whale's mouth. Laurel also shows a talent for humorous metaphorical thinking. After Arnetta suggests that they sing a Brownie song about old friends being gold, while new friends are only silver (both lines employ metaphor), Laurel dryly observes, "If most of the girls in the troop could be any type of metal, they'd be bunched-up wads of tinfoil, maybe, or rusty iron nails you had to get tetanus shots for."

HISTORICAL CONTEXT

Racial Segregation in the United States

In "Brownies" the fictional Woodrow Wilson Elementary School in south suburban Atlanta has only one white student. This is a telling detail, since Atlanta, especially in the inner city, has one of the highest levels of separation between blacks and whites in the southern United States, a segregation that is also reflected in the public schools.

Since 1988, there has been a widespread trend in public schools in the United States towards more segregation. This is a reversal of a trend toward racial integration that began following the 1954 Supreme Court decision in *Brown vs. Board of Education*, which ruled that racially segregated educational facilities were unconstitutional because they were inherently unequal. Researchers at the Harvard Graduate School of Education found that the years between 1991 and 1994 were marked by the largest movement back toward segregation since the landmark 1954 Supreme Court ruling. It was estimated that two-thirds of African American children in the United States attend schools in which most of the students are members of minority groups.

A study conducted by Catherine Freeman and others at the Fiscal Research Center, Andrew Young School of Policy Studies, found that in Georgia from 1994 to 2001 there was a slight trend towards increased black-white segregation in public elementary schools. In 1994, 17.7 percent of students attended predominantly black elementary schools (defined as over 70 percent black). This increased to 19.1 percent in 2001. The highest level of black-white segregation was in the Atlanta metropolitan area, which is caused largely by segregation between school districts. Segregation within the same district is related to residential segregation. Residential segregation is apparent in the story, since Laurel states that in the south suburbs of Atlanta, it was rare to see a white person. Another factor in the reemergence of racial segregation is that in the 1990s and early 2000s there has been less pressure from the courts to integrate public schools than there was from the mid-1950s to the 1980s.

The same study found that in Georgia, schools with higher percentages of blacks had higher teacher turnover rates. Such schools also have fewer teachers with advanced degrees and more inexperienced teachers. Teacher quality has a large impact on how well students perform. Schools with high percentages of African American students also received fewer school resources.

These statistics from Georgia reflect a trend toward increased segregation amongst whites and blacks in the general population elsewhere in the United States. University of Chicago researchers, as reported by James Waller in *Face to Face: The Changing State of Racism Across America* (1998), found that middle-class blacks are less likely than Hispanics or Asian Americans to live among whites.

Persistence of Racism in the United States

Although blatant, violent racism decreased in the United States between 1965 and 2005, racism still existed in more subtle forms. During the 1940s, 1950s, and 1960s, especially in the American South, black people were subject to beatings, racially motivated murders, cross-burnings by the white supremacist group the Ku Klux Klan, as well as everyday insults and humiliations, such as having to sit at the back on buses and use separate public facilities such as water fountains. The civil rights movement of the 1950s and 1960s and changing public attitudes toward race and racism have ensured that old-style racism of this kind has been vastly reduced in the United States. However, it has been replaced by a less overt form of racism in which prejudice is not stated openly but is nonetheless discernible in different behaviors adopted by white people when dealing with blacks rather than people of their own race. Waller, in *Face to Face*, reports the comments made by a late 1990s graduate of Georgia Tech University about his experiences with racism:

> [W]hite clerks 'tailing' him in a local music store; restaurant managers checking repeatedly on the satisfaction of other patrons while ignoring him and his dining partner; people expressing surprise at how 'articulate' and 'well-spoken' he was; and white women who, when passing by him on a downtown Atlanta sidewalk, would shift their purses to the opposite side of their bodies.

This student's comments are in line with studies that have documented the regular occurrence of this kind of subtle but unmistakable everyday discrimination suffered by middle-class African Americans. Eduardo Bonilla-Silva, in "'New Racism,' Color-Blind Racism, and the Future of Whiteness in America," calls this changing face of racism the "new racism." He argues that although it appears less harmful than the older, violent form of racism, "it is as effective as slavery and Jim Crow in maintaining the racial status quo."

Brownie troops are generally non-discriminatory groups but that doesn't stop their members from being victims or perpetrators of discrimination Photograph by Ellis Neel. AP Images

CRITICAL OVERVIEW

Packer's short story collection, *Drinking Coffee Elsewhere,* was published to a chorus of praise from reviewers. The reviewer for *Publishers Weekly* comments that "the clear-voiced humanity of Packer's characters, mostly black teenage girls, resonates unforgettably through the eight stories of this accomplished debut collection." The reviewer concludes, in a comment that might be applied also to "Brownies": "These stories never end neatly or easily. Packer knows how to keep the tone provocative and tense at the close of each tale, doing justice to the complexity and dignity of the characters and their difficult choices."

Jean Thompson in the *New York Times Book Review* praises Packer's skill in characterization; she also brings attention to the youthfulness of the characters and the fact that in some cases they lack self-knowledge. "The very young characters in "Brownies" [have not] developed much insight into matters of race, adulthood or a

religion that reduces its teachings to acronyms—Satan, for example, is 'Serpent Always Tempting and Noisome.'"

Thompson's conclusion, however, is entirely positive regarding the collection as a whole:

> Young writers, naturally enough, write about young characters. *Drinking Coffee Elsewhere* is not really limited by this. Instead, there is a sense of a talented writer testing and pushing at those limits, ringing as many changes as possible within her fictional world. It is a world already populated by clamoring, sorrowing, eminently knowable people, and with the promise of more to come.

David Wiegand, in *San Francisco Chronicle*, also has fulsome praise for Packer's stories: "Packer doesn't merely tell stories brilliantly, but she also packs each one with a right-between-the-eyes moral about issues of race and black identity." However, Wiegand argues that in some stories Packer's didacticism, her desire to teach a moral lesson, "seems slightly forced." He cites as an example the incident in "Brownies," in which the learning disabled white girls innocently repeat the racial insult only because they have

WHAT DO I READ NEXT?

- Toni Morrison's *The Bluest Eye* (1970) is a novel about a lonely black girl, Pecola Breedlove, living in Ohio in the 1940s. Bombarded by white, middle-class perceptions of beauty and value, Pecola becomes obsessed with having the bluest eyes. The novel shows what it is like to be a young black girl in a culture defined by white, middle-class values.

- *How to Breathe Underwater* (2003), by Julie Orringer, is a highly praised collection of stories about adolescent girls—the difficulties they face as they grow up and their ability to survive the challenges and successfully emerge into young adulthood.

- *The Sea Birds Are Still Alive* (1982), by Toni Cade Bambara, contains ten stories about the lives of black people by one of the leading late twentieth-century African American writers.

- *Children of the Night: The Best Short Stories by Black Writers, 1967 to the Present* (1997), edited by Gloria Naylor, contains thirty-seven stories that together depict the diversity of black life. The anthology includes such well-established writers as Alice Walker, Maya Angelou, Charles Johnson, Ralph Ellison, Jamaica Kincaid, and Ntozake Shange, as well as newer writers.

heard it somewhere themselves. "It's Packer's way of reminding us, unnecessarily, that prejudice is learned," writes Wiegand.

CRITICISM

Bryan Aubrey

Aubrey holds a Ph.D. in English and has published many articles on literature. In this essay, he

> IN ADDITION TO THE THEME OF RACIAL PREJUDICE, 'BROWNIES' MAKES ANOTHER SERIOUS POINT. IT SHOWS THE POWER OF GROUP THINKING AND THE PRESSURE TO GO ALONG WITH THE ACTIONS OF THE GROUP TO WHICH ONE BELONGS, EVEN AGAINST ONE'S WISHES AND BETTER JUDGMENT."

discusses "Brownies" in the context of modern racism in the United States.

"Brownies" is a story with a great deal of humor but a serious theme and purpose. No one who lives in the United States can be unaware that in the history of the nation, relations between black people and white people have been fraught with injustice and oppression. Although the civil rights movement of the 1950s and 1960s, and later federal government policies, including equal opportunity laws and affirmative action, removed most of the egregious racist practices, racism continues to exist in the United States. This fact is plain from the story, not only in the words and actions of the little girls, but in a small but significant comment made by Laurel, the narrator, which gives a glimpse into the day-to-day world of the black girls' parents in suburban Atlanta. Laurel states, "We had all been taught that adulthood was full of sorrow and pain, taxes and bills, dreaded work and dealings with whites, sickness and death." There is an old saying that the two inevitable things in life are death and taxes, but these young girls have also learned that "dealings with whites" must be added to those unpleasant realities.

Modern racism, according to James Waller in *Face to Face*, is more insidious, subtle, and covert than the old racism. It manifests in negative, stereotypical, mistrustful attitudes that many whites have towards African Americans and other people of color. It is compounded by the fact that many whites believe that racism no longer exists in the United States, which makes them resistant to the demands by minorities for equal and fair treatment. Modern racism has measurable effects on quality of life indicators such as economic status and educational attainment, as well as self-esteem and general well being. According to Waller, the effects of such racism are "cumulative, draining, energy consuming, and, ultimately, life consuming."

Racism is not confined to adults; it can also be found in young children. Research in the late 1990s and early 2000s has shown that children develop an awareness of racial categories and society's established racial hierarchies at a very early age. Previously it had been believed that young children were color blind in this respect, with no awareness of racial differences or the meanings applied to them by adults. But Debra van Ausdale and Joe R. Feagin in *The First R: How Children Learn Race and Racism*, using experimental data on fifty-eight preschool children from age three to six in an ethnically diverse urban day-care center, demonstrate how children of this age use awareness and knowledge of race in their social relationships. These children had already learned at an early age "the desirability of whiteness, of white identity and esteem"; they knew that "whiteness is privileged and darkness is not"; they had the ability to understand and use the power of racial insults to hurt other children and to reinforce the perceived superiority of whiteness over blackness. In some cases, white children had learned to exclude others from games based on racial identity, as with the four-year-old white girl who had been pulling a wagon across the floor and told an Asian girl that "Only white Americans can pull this wagon." In another incident, a three-year-old white girl refused to let a three-year-old black boy get on a swing, telling him that "Black people are not allowed on the swing right now, especially Black boys." The authors comment: "Children hold knowledge of the power and authority granted to whites and are not confused about the meanings of these harsh racial words and actions." The children know where status and privilege lie. The authors further point out that "Black children, like Black adults, must constantly struggle to develop and maintain a healthy sense of themselves against the larger society that tells them in a legion of ways that they are inferior."

If this is indeed so, the black girls in "Brownies" seem to have done extremely well. This is not a story about the struggles of these girls to establish self-esteem. On the contrary, whatever their parents may have told them, or what they may have overheard about the

difficulties of "dealings with whites," they are not suffering from any sense of inferiority. When they hear, or Arnetta thinks she hears, the offensive racial word used by a white girl, their reaction is not to go off into a corner and cry, but to fight back, to teach the white girls a painful lesson. These are tough, confident girls, especially Arnetta and Octavia.

The African American girls in "Brownies" also know how to use language to counter any negative names or labels that whites might try to impose on them. They simply do the same in reverse. Although none of them has directly encountered many white people—whites are largely objects of curiosity to them—they have adopted the term "Caucasian" as an all-round term of abuse and ridicule. When someone does something, or wears something, they do not approve of, or acts in a clumsy or incompetent manner, the response is, "What are you? *Caucasian*?" as Arnetta said to a black boy in school who was wearing jeans considered to be unfashionable.

The behavior of the African American girls in the story is a reverse image of the way in which some white people still use language that denigrates others because of their racial or ethnic identity. In "White Fright: Reproducing White Supremacy Through Casual Discourse," Kristen Myers reports on her own experiment in tracking what she calls "casual racetalk" (talk that denigrates someone due to race or ethnicity or celebrates white supremacy) in the everyday encounters of a variety of mostly white people, including college students, family members, employers, coworkers, parishioners, and professors, as well as strangers. Myers used a covert approach because explicit racist expressions, since they are no longer considered socially acceptable, are not commonly used in public. Instead, Myers used informants to report on "casual racetalk" that occurs in contexts when people are with friends and others whom they believe think like they do. She found that the racetalk revealed whites' belief that they form a "unified, superior group whose interests were threatened by the very presence of people of color." Whites constructed language consisting of caricatures and slurs (including the word that incites the black girls to plan violence in "Brownies") that delineated an us-against-them mentality. Certain negative qualities were attributed to black people and then applied also to whites who did something that fitted the nega-tive stereotype, as in this example:

> We sat around on Saturday night, and some-times we called each other niggers because something stupid would happen. I guess we sometimes refer stupidity to black people. For example, we were playing a card game. . . . I did something wrong, and my friend asked me, "Why are you such a black person?"

In addition to the theme of racial prejudice, "Brownies" makes another serious point. It shows the power of group thinking and the pres-sure to go along with the actions of the group to which one belongs, even against one's wishes and better judgment. People tend to do things when caught up in the pressures exerted by a group of peers, or even in a crowd of strangers, that they would not do if left to themselves. The example in the story is the narrator, Laurel. Laurel is more reflective than the other girls; she is the only one who questions whether the white girl actually made the insult, and she has no desire to fight. She wants to stay back with Daphne until Arnetta forces her to join in the planned assault. But then an interesting thing happens; as the girls approach the restrooms, Laurel finds that her thinking has changed: "Even though I didn't want to fight, was afraid of fighting, I felt I was part of the rest of the troop; like I was defending something." It should be noted that Laurel does not define what she is defending; it seems to be only a vague feeling, induced by her membership of a group that has collectively decided on a certain course of action. Had the fight broken out, no doubt the normally quiet, nonviolent Laurel would have done what was expected of her.

This small example serves as a kind of inverse parable of race relations between blacks and whites up to the later twentieth century: many African Americans, especially in the South, have had good reason to fear the violence of an unthinking white mob, ready to beat and even lynch a man whose skin happened to be a different color than theirs because of some perceived racial insult. "Brownies" offers no comforting conclu-sion that this deep-seated racism, that has existed for centuries, may by overcome. Laurel's remark, that "there was something mean in the world that [she] could not stop" is a sobering reminder from a young girl of the enduring weight of racial preju-dice and the pain it continues to cause.

Source: Bryan Aubrey, Critical Essay on "Brownies," in *Short Stories for Students*, Thomson Gale, 2007.

> **FOR THOMPSON, 'PACKER'S COLLECTION REMINDS US THAT NO STYLISTIC TOUR DE FORCE—OR AUTHORIAL GAMESMANSHIP, OR FLIGHTS OF LANGUAGE—CAN GROUND A STORY LIKE A WELL-REALIZED CHARACTER. . . .'"**

Thomson Gale

In the following essay, the critic gives an overview of Z.Z. Packer's work.

ZZ Packer's debut short-story collection, *Drinking Coffee Elsewhere*, has collected consis-tently high praise from readers, reviewers, and prominent literary figures such as John Updike. The eight "finely crafted tales" in the book make up "a debut collection that cuts to the bone of human experience and packs a lasting wallop," wrote a *Kirkus Reviews* critic. Updike chose the book as the June, 2003, Today Book Club selec-tion on the NBC network's *Today* show. Packer has converted skeptical reviewers, such as Evette Porter, who observed on the *Africana* Web site, "ZZ Packer's *Drinking Coffee Elsewhere* lives up to its billing. More impressively, Packer handles the burden of being the next big thing by exceed-ing expectations."

And it is that level of quality that Packer consistently strives to maintain, or exceed. "Packer writes nearly every day and sets herself page number goals instead of time require-ments," wrote Kim Curtis in a profile of Packer on the *Monterey Herald* Web site. "You have to nurture your talent or it's going to lie fallow," Packer said in the profile. On those infrequent days when Packer doesn't practice her craft, "the guilt of not doing so gets her to write the next day," Curtis remarked.

She was born Zuwena Packer; "ZZ" is a family nickname that evolved into Packer's pro-fessional name. "I didn't come up with that [nickname]," she said in an interview on the *Seattle Post-Intelligencer* Web site. "My first name is Zuwena and my family nickname has been ZZ for ages. People say it's such a clever pen name since it's so memorable, but I've been ZZ since middle school."

Packer spent her childhood in areas around Appalachia, Atlanta, and Baltimore. She graduated from Yale and the prestigious Iowa Writers Workshop and always considered herself "bookishly uncool," she said in a profile in *Book*. She is a Jones lecturer at Stanford University in Stanford, CA, and despite her success and critical acclaim, still considers herself an apprentice in the literary world, still in awe of writers she admires. "I have not achieved what I want, but maybe I will someday," she said in the *Seattle Post-Intelligencer* profile. In an interview on the Barnes & Noble Web site, she named Toni Morrison's *Beloved* as the book that most influenced her life. "*Beloved* is a reflection of how our most horrid actions are wedded to our most noble desires," Packer remarked. "Few living authors are able to write in such a way as to give me the shivers," she commented. "I loved *The Bluest Eye*, but it was only while reading *Beloved* that I knew without a doubt that I was in the presence of greatness." Among other books she named as influences are Leo Tolstoy's *War and Peace*, Mark Twain's *Huckleberry Finn*, Ralph Ellison's *Invisible Man*, Marilynne Robinson's *Housekeeping*, and James Baldwin's *Go Tell It on the Mountain*.

In the title story of Packer's collection, Dina, a young black woman from Baltimore, is newly arrived at Yale University and is undergoing mandatory orientation games, trust-building exercises, and other trite and bland activities required of freshmen. When one such game requires Dina to decide which inanimate object she'd like to be, she chooses a revolver, a choice that guarantees her psychological counseling and status as a loner and outcast. A relationship begins to bloom between Dina and Heather, a fellow freshman who is Caucasian and unsure of herself. When Heather declares herself a lesbian, Dina flees from the relationship and the characterization it would impose on her. Dina's carefully maintained walls may be her way of coping with her mother's recent death, or they may be her way of dealing with the world when she can't escape by pretending she's drinking coffee elsewhere. Jean Thompson, writing in *New York Times Book Review*, called "Drinking Coffee Elsewhere" a "superb story, its wry and mournful tones bound together by a complex psychological portrait." Laurie Meunier Graves, writing on the Wolf Moon Press Web site, remarked that the story "is as close to perfect as a short story can be, and perfection is a rare thing."

Linnea Davis, the main character of "Our Lady of Peace," is a teacher struggling to reach her students in a rough Baltimore public school. She sees her job as teacher as little more than a way to make a living, "but finds herself drowning amid a chaotic classroom filled with angry, disruptive, and violent inner-city students," Porter wrote. Her rescuer arrives in the unlikely form of a burly student transferred from another district. The characters in "Geese," a group of young American students abroad in Japan, are unable to find work or sustenance, and slowly and bitterly lose "the all-knowing arrogance of youth" as they spiral into frustration and desperation. In "Speaking in Tongues," teenage Tia resists all attempts by her sternly religious aunt to "get saved." One day she is locked in a church closet for the dubious sin of laughing in Sunday school. Packing her clarinet, Tia heads to Atlanta to search for her mother, a drug addict who abandoned her years before. Tia fails to find her mother, but becomes involved with Marie and Dezi, a streetwise hustler. "Packer knows how to turn up the volume and invest a narrative with shocking turns of events," Thompson remarked. "Ironically, it is a sexual experience with Dezi that brings Tia a moment of ecstatic, visionary feeling that she's been unable to achieve in church," Thompson wrote. Tia emerges from the experience the type of person who won't be locked in a closet by anyone again. In "Brownies," a troop of black brownie scouts plots revenge against a perceived racial insult committed by a fellow group of white brownie scouts. Bookish Laurel watches the self-appointed leaders of the troop, Arnetta and Octavia, plan retaliation, but it turns out that neither the alleged insult, nor the hated rival troop, may actually be what they seem.

"The Ant of the Self," featuring the collection's only male protagonist, puts Spurgeon into conflict with his ne'er-do-well father, who browbeats Spurgeon into driving him to the Million Man March in Washington. Tensions erupt in a fistfight between Spurgeon and his father. The boy is left abandoned in an unfamiliar city, where a sermon from the Million Man March urges him to cast off the ant of the self, "that small, blind, crumb-seeking part of ourselves," and rise up to greater things.

Packer "has distilled her writing so that in its 100-proof potency, it goes right to the back of the throat," wrote David Abrams on the *January*

Magazine Web site. Ann H. Fisher, writing in *Library Journal*, called the collection "bright, sharp, promising, and recommended," while Allison Lynn, writing in *People*, declared it "a bottomless cup of longing, loneliness, and real, vital literature." *Drinking Coffee Elsewhere* is "truly a stunning debut," wrote Toni Fitzgerald on the *Book Reporter* Web site. "Here's hoping that Packer's next work, be it more stories or a novel, comes quickly."

"Remarkably, in the eight stories that make up *Drinking Coffee Elsewhere*, Packer manages to capture the complexity of what it is to be black in a world where race, gender, sexuality, and class are all mutable," Porter observed. For Thompson, "Packer's collection reminds us that no stylistic tour de force—or authorial gamesmanship, or flights of language—can ground a story like a well-realized character. This is the old-time religion of storytelling, although Packer's prose supplies plenty of the edge and energy we expect from contemporary fiction. The people in the eight stories here form a constellation of young, black experience."

Source: Thomson Gale, "Z.Z. Packer," in *Contemporary Authors Online*, Thomson Gale, 2004.

David Wiegand

In the following review, Wiegand notes that Packer's writing is resolute on moralizing "issues of race and black identity." He commends her on this, calling her "courageous," and praises her stories as "beautifully crafted."

Do writers create for readers of their own race? Do readers of races or ethnicities different from the writer's have similar experiences with their work as do readers of the same race or ethnicity?

Some might think those are dangerous questions even to ask, but they will become unavoidable to anyone reading ZZ Packer's extraordinary first collection, *Drinking Coffee Elsewhere*. All eight stories here are about African Americans, but what provokes the questions of audience is that Packer doesn't merely tell stories brilliantly, but she also packs each one with a right-between-the-eyes moral about issues of race and black identity. And that makes it inevitable that African American readers will have a different experience reading Packer's work than white readers, in particular.

What is also true is that the experiences will be provocative and rewarding for any category

> PACKER'S STORIES ARE, IN A SENSE, POLITICAL, IN THAT, COLLECTIVELY AND INDIVIDUALLY, THEY ARE ALL MEANT TO MAKE A POINT. SOME MIGHT CRITICIZE THE WRITER FOR PREACHING AND FOR NOT MERELY TELLING STORIES. BUT THE OBVIOUSLY CONSCIOUS DECISION TO WRITE FROM A SOAPBOX IS JUST AS BOLD AS PACKER'S STYLE AND CHARACTER DEVELOPMENT, PERHAPS EVEN COURAGEOUS."

of reader, because Packer, a Jones Lecturer at Stanford whose title story here was included in the New Yorker's debut fiction issue in 2000, has a commanding sense of character and setting, a captivating eye for detail and, most of all, a bold and often thrilling use of language and style. Consider a few random quotes from some of the stories: "We'd seen them, but from afar, never within their orbit enough to see whether their faces were the way all white girls appeared on TV—ponytailed and full of energy, bubbling over with love and money." "(S)he imagined her uterus, that Texas-shaped organ, the Rio Grande of her monthly womanly troubles, flushing out to the Gulf." "The sunset has ignited the bellies of clouds; the mirrored windows of downtown buildings distort the flame-colored city into a funhouse."

But a story needs more than style to make it successful, and most of Packer's stories have all the right stuff. "The Ant of the Self," possibly the best story in the book, finds a somewhat estranged father and son driving to the Million Man March in Washington, D.C., because the old man, Roy Bivens Jr., just out of jail on another DUI charge, has an idea that they can clean up by selling exotic birds at the march. His son, Spurgeon, knows that the idea is lame, but it's just another part of the burden he has to bear as the son of Roy Bivens Jr., a terminal loser who claims to have been part of the Black Panther movement.

There's not much to like about Roy, but is Spurgeon the real loser here? Feeling oppressed as the only black kid in his class is about as far as his African American identity seems to go. When he and his father get to Washington, they load up the birdcages and head toward the march. "Quite a few whites stop to look as if to see what this thing is all about, and their hard, nervous hard smiles fit into two categories: the 'don't mug me!' smile, or the 'Gee, aren't black folks something!' smile. It occurs to me that I can stay here on the sidelines for the entire march."

That final line is telling. In his effort to distance himself from his no-account father, Spurgeon has distanced himself from his own identity and is doomed to a life on the sidelines of being black.

Like "Ant of the Self," many of the stories are set in the past, such as "Doris Is Coming," in which a young girl stages a one-person sit-in at a soda fountain in the South. That's the simple plot summary. What enriches the story is that Doris is the only black girl in her class. Her mother cleans house for a well-to-do Jewish family whose daughter, Livia, pushes her friendship on Doris. Doris isn't really interested in being friends, but gives in, perhaps out of loneliness. She is always reminded that she is different from the other girls, however: At one point, one of Livia's friends tells them about her new "flesh-colored" prom dress.

"'You mean, the color of your flesh?' Doris said ...

"'Well, how should I say it? What should I say when describing it? Say, "Oh, I bought a dress the color of everybody else's skin except Doris's?"'"

Although the story, like others here, is about events and racial attitudes of the past, it is part of Packer's gift that she's able to make even "ancient history" credibly relevant to contemporary readers.

But what about those morals? What about the lessons Packer is clearly intent on teaching through her fiction? There are moments when the didacticism seems slightly forced. In "Doris Is Coming," for example, the young girl hears a news report about a racial demonstration that ends with the white commentator expressing hope that there will soon be an end to the "tumult." "She could not forget the radio show she'd heard earlier, how the announcer seemed to loathe the colored people of Albany when all they'd wanted was to march for decent sewage disposal without being stoned for it."

In "Brownies," in which a troop of African American Brownies encounters its white counterpart at Camp Crescendo, a dispute arises over whether one of the white girls used the "n" word. But their troop leader explains that her charges, who have what we'd call learning disabilities today, "are echolalic. . . . That means they will say whatever they hear, like an echo—that's where the words comes from. . . . (N)ot all of them have the most progressive of parents, so if they heard a bad word, they might have repeated it. But I guarantee it would not have been intentional."

It's Packer's way of reminding us, unnecessarily, that prejudice is learned. On the other hand, consider the substrata of meaning in the fact that these girls are all "Brownies" and you can easily overlook a bit of obviousness here and there.

Packer's stories are, in a sense, political, in that, collectively and individually, they are all meant to make a point. Some might criticize the writer for preaching and for not merely telling stories. But the obviously conscious decision to write from a soapbox is just as bold as Packer's style and character development, perhaps even courageous.

And that's why the issue of audience becomes interesting. Of course, the experience of reading is always individual and subjective, but when a writer makes such a point of preaching in her work, you have to ponder who her audience is. Nonblack readers might seem at first to be the target for Packer's sermons, but, in fact, African Americans will learn something from her work as well.

But don't let all this talk of preaching put you off. The fact is, Packer's stories also just happen to be beautifully crafted.

Source: David Wiegand, "Packer Blends Race, Lessons and Craft," in *San Francisco Chronicle*, March 9, 2003, p. M1.

SOURCES

Bonilla-Silva, Eduardo, "'New Racism,' Color-Blind Racism, and the Future of Whiteness in America," in *White Out: The Continuing Significance of Racism*, edited by Ashley "Woody" Doane and Eduardo Bonilla-Silva, Routledge, 2003, p. 272.

Freeman, Catherine, Benjamin Scafidi, and David Sjoquist, "Racial Segregation in Georgia Public Schools, 1994–2001: Trends, Causes and Impact on Teacher Quality," FRP Report No. 77, Fiscal Research Center, Andrew Young School of Policy Studies, December

2002, http://frc.gsu.edu/frpreports/Report_77/ (accessed November 13, 2006).

Myers, Kristen, "White Fright: Reproducing White Supremacy Through Casual Discourse," in *White Out: The Continuing Significance of Racism*, edited by Ashley "Woody" Doane and Eduardo Bonilla-Silva, Routledge, 2003, pp. 130, 132, 136.

Packer, ZZ, "Brownies," in *Drinking Coffee Elsewhere*, Riverhead, 2003, pp. 1–28.

Review of *Drinking Coffee Elsewhere*, in *Publishers Weekly*, Vol. 249, No. 50, December 16, 2002, p. 43.

Thompson, Jean, "Notorious in New Haven: This Debut Collection's Title Story Takes Place at Yale and Involves an Imaginary Handgun," in *New York Times Book Review*, Vol. 108, No. 11, March 16, 2003, p. 7.

Van Ausdale, Debra, and Joe R. Feagin, *The First R: How Children Learn Race and Racism*, Rowman & Littlefield Publishers, 2001, pp. 35, 56, 57, 104, 105, 107.

Waller, James, *Face to Face: The Changing State of Racism Across America*, Plenum Press, 1998, pp. 95, 100, 137, 166.

Wiegand, David, "Packer Blends Race, Lessons, and Craft," in *San Francisco Chronicle*, March 9, 2003, p. M1.

FURTHER READING

D'Souza, Dinesh, *The End of Racism*, Free Press, 1996.
This is a controversial study by a conservative writer of the history, nature, and effects of racism, as well as contemporary approaches to it. Most approaches, in the author's view, are misguided. He claims that racism is no longer an important factor in American life and cannot be blamed for black underachievement.

Reddy, Maureen T., ed., *Acts Against Racism: Raising Children in a Multiracial World*, Seal Press, 1996.
This anthology of essays by mothers and teachers is a resource for parents. Drawing on their own experience, the authors describe strategies by which racial prejudice can be countered in schools, colleges, and elsewhere.

Stern-LaRosa, Caryl, and Ellen Hofheimer Bettmann, *The Anti-Defamation League's Hate Hurts: How Children Learn and Unlearn Prejudice*, Scholastic Paperbacks, 2000.
This practical book offers a guide to how children learn prejudice and how it can be unlearned. The authors offer strategies, role plays, and sample dialogues for parents and teachers. Some of the sections record and discuss true stories about children of all ages who have initiated or suffered from hateful words and actions.

Wright, Marguerite, *I'm Chocolate, You're Vanilla: Raising Healthy Black and Biracial Children in a Race-Conscious World*, Jossey-Bass, 2000.
Wright argues that young children do not understand adult racial prejudice and that such color blindness must be taken advantage of in order to guide the development of a child's self-esteem. Wright discusses issues such as the age at which children understand the concept of race; how adults can avoid instilling in children their own prejudices, and how schools can lessen the impact of racism.

Caroline's Wedding

EDWIDGE DANTICAT

1995

"Caroline's Wedding," by Edwidge Danticat, is the last story in the collection *Krik? Krak!*, which was published in 1995. The story features the narrator and protagonist, Gracina (Grace) Azile, who, with her mother and sister Caroline, has immigrated to the United States from Haiti. It describes the cross-generational and cross-cultural conflicts triggered by Caroline's wedding to a non-Haitian man. Danticat introduces her readers to traditional stories, games, beliefs, and rituals from a culture that is little known or understood outside Haiti. In particular, the story explores the role of storytelling and tradition, and the relationship between mother and daughter, in creating social and family cohesion. Against the background of Haiti's violent history, the individual stories of the pain and suffering experienced by the different characters unfold and interlink. Although the focus is on Haiti's culture and history, many of the collection's themes, including memory, loss, dispossession, and the resilience of the human life and spirit in the face of extreme circumstances, have a broader relevance.

AUTHOR BIOGRAPHY

Edwidge Danticat was born on January 19, 1969, in Port-au-Prince, Haiti, to André Miracin (a cab driver) and Rose Souvenance (a textile worker) Danticat. When Edwidge was two years old, her father emigrated from Haiti to New York, to be

Edwidge Danticat Photograph by Laurent Rebours. AP Images

followed two years later by her mother. Remaining in Haiti, the young Danticat was raised by her aunt and uncle. During these years she was exposed to the Haitian tradition of storytelling. Danticat's aunts and grandmothers would call out, "Krik?" and she would reply, "Krak!" as a signal to the storyteller to begin. Her formal education in Haiti was in French, but at home Danticat spoke Haitian Creole.

Danticat joined her family in Brooklyn, New York, in 1981, at which time English became her third language. She attended junior high classes in Brooklyn but had difficulty fitting in with her peers. In her isolation, she turned to writing about the people of her native country.

Danticat's parents wanted her to pursue a career in medicine, and with the aim of becoming a nurse, she attended a specialized school in New York City. However, she soon abandoned this course and earned a degree in French literature from Barnard College, where she won the 1995 Woman of Achievement Award. She was awarded a Master of Fine Arts degree from Brown University in Providence, Rhode Island, in 1993. Her thesis at Brown was her highly acclaimed first novel, *Breath, Eyes, Memory* (1994). In 1998, the television celebrity Oprah

Winfrey picked the novel for her book club and introduced its author to a mass readership. Subsequently, Danticat published a collection of short stories, *Krik? Krak!* (1995), and the novels, *The Farming of Bones* (1998), *Behind the Mountains* (2002), and *The Dew Breaker* (2004). Danticat also edited a collection of writings by Haitian authors entitled *The Butterfly's Way: Voices from the Haitian Dyaspora in the United States* (Soho Press, 2001).

Danticat gained critical acclaim for her portrayals of the Haitian experience both in Haiti and the United States and for her lyrical use of language. After completing her master's degree, she taught creative writing at New York University and the University of Miami. She also worked with filmmakers Patricia Benoit and Jonathan Demme on projects on Haitian art and documentaries about Haiti. As of 2006, Danticat lived in the Little Haiti neighborhood of Miami and regularly returned to Haiti to visit friends and family.

Danticat's work has attracted many awards and award nominations. In 1994, her novel *Breath, Eyes, Memory* won fiction awards from the following magazines: *Essence, Caribbean Writer*, and *Seventeen*. In 1995, her short story collection *Krik? Krak!* was nominated for a National Book Award. In 1996, *Granta* magazine named Danticat one of its Best Young American Novelists. In the same year, a short story, "Between the Pool and the Gardenias," published three years earlier in *Caribbean Writer*, won a Pushcart Prize for short fiction. In 1999, Danticat's novel *The Farming of Bones* gained an American Book Award from the Before Columbus Foundation. *The Dew Breaker* was nominated for a 2004 National Book Critics Circle Award and a PEN/Faulkner Award in 2005.

PLOT SUMMARY

When "Caroline's Wedding" opens, Grace Azile is leaving a Brooklyn courtroom, having just received her certificate of U.S. citizenship. When she calls her mother (Ma) to tell her the news, Ma advises her to hurry and get her passport, as that is what is truly American. Grace has to temporarily trade in the certificate at the post office to get a passport. She feels anxious without it, since when her mother was pregnant with her sister Caroline, she was arrested in a sweatshop raid and spent three days in an immigration jail.

Grace reaches home to find her mother preparing a pot of bone soup. Ma holds the traditional Haitian belief that bone soup has the magical power to separate lovers, so she has served it every night since Caroline announced her engagement. Ma disapproves of Eric because he is Bahamian and not Haitian.

Caroline was born without a left forearm. Ma thinks the cause was a drug that was injected into her by a prison doctor after the sweatshop immigration raid and that Caroline was lucky to have been born at all. Unlike Grace, Caroline was born in the United States.

Ma calls Grace into her bedroom. She is upset that Eric's courtship of Caroline is different from how she was courted by her daughters' father, which took place in Haiti and was formal. Grace and Caroline's father (Papa) is now dead.

One night, Caroline and Grace play a traditional Haitian free association game around the word, "lost." The game was taught to them by Ma, who learned it as a girl. Ma appears and asks them to go with her to a mass for a dead Haitian refugee woman. Grace goes, but Caroline does not. The Catholic Church they attend holds services tailored to the Haitian community. The priest reads out the names of refugees drowned at sea that week. Many are known to members of the congregation. He says a prayer for the dead woman, who gave birth to a baby on board the boat. The child died, and the mother threw the baby overboard and then jumped into the sea after it, drowning herself. Grace thinks of the Haitian belief that there are spots in the sea where Africans who jumped off the slave ships rest, where those who die at sea can choose to join their long-lost relations. The priest asks the congregation to remember those they have loved and lost. As screams erupt in the congregation, Ma suddenly gets up and leaves.

Caroline and Eric plan a civil ceremony. Ma wants Eric to bring his family to their house to court her favor and to have his father ask her blessing, according to the old Haitian custom. Caroline tells Grace that she dreamt of Papa the previous night. It is ten years since he died. After Papa's death, Ma told her daughters to wear red panties, in the belief that this would ward off his spirit so that he would not mistake the daughters for his wife and try to lie with them at night. For some time after he died, Caroline and Grace had the same dream: they try in vain to catch up with him as he walks through a deserted field. They disobeyed Ma and did not wear the red panties, as they wanted Papa's spirit to visit them.

Grace tells Caroline that the son of their Cuban neighbor, Mrs. Ruiz, was recently shot by the pilot of an airplane after trying to hijack the plane to go from Havana to Miami.

Grace recalls that when she and Caroline were younger, they used to wish that one day the rest of Caroline's arm would burst out of Ma's stomach and float back to her. Caroline likes to have her stub stroked, but no one does, out of fear of giving offense. Caroline says that if she were to cut the vein that throbs below the surface of her stub, she could bleed to death.

Grace dreams that she sees her father at a masked ball but cannot get close to him. By his side is Caroline. Grace screams in protest that they are leaving her out. When alive, he remembered everything about their life in Haiti and its traditions and beliefs.

Preparations are under way for Caroline's wedding, which is a month away. Though Ma does not want to attend, she pretends that this is the "real wedding" she wants for her daughter, so that Caroline does not resent her. However, she is not going to cook a wedding-night dinner, as is the custom. Grace decides to throw a wedding shower for Caroline. Ma disapproves because to her a shower seems like begging.

Ma, Caroline, and Grace go to Eric's house for dinner. Ma is as unenthusiastic about Eric's cooking as she is about him, and Grace thinks he should have hired a Haitian cook. To save Ma's feelings, Caroline goes home with her and Grace even though she would rather stay the night with Eric. Ma warns Caroline that people are known by their stories and that she should value herself and guard against being the subject of gossip. After Ma falls asleep, Caroline calls a cab and returns to Eric's place. Grace dreams of Papa: this time, she is on a cliff and he is leaning out of a helicopter trying to grab her hand to rescue her.

Grace was born when her parents were poor and living in a shantytown in Port-au-Prince, Haiti. They called her their "misery baby," and Ma thought she might die. Desperate to find a way to leave Haiti, Papa got a visa by taking vows in a false marriage with a widow who was leaving Haiti for the United States. A few years later, Papa divorced the woman and sent for Ma and Grace. While he was alive, this was a secret that Grace and Caroline were not supposed to know.

Caroline's wedding shower takes place. After the guests leave, Ma gives Caroline her present, a silk teddy. Privately, Grace tells Ma that she did not think such things were to her taste, but Ma replies that she cannot live in the United States for twenty-five years and not be affected by it. Ma fears that Caroline is marrying Eric because she thinks he is the only man who would marry her, but Grace suggests that he may love Caroline. Ma remarks that people's hearts are made of stone. Grace suspects that this is a result of her hurt feelings when Papa married the widow. Ma brings out a bag of Papa's letters that he wrote to her from the United States while she was still in Haiti. The letters address practical matters but never mention love.

The night before her wedding, Caroline tries to make Ma understand why she and Eric are getting married in a small civil ceremony: they do not wish to spend all their money on a big wedding. Eric has a friend who is a judge, and he will perform the ceremony in his office. Ma says that such a "mechanical" affair is typically American.

Caroline puts on her wedding dress for Ma and Grace to see. She is also wearing a new false arm. She has been having phantom pain in her arm such as amputees experience, and her doctor told her that the false arm may make it go away. When Ma points out that Caroline is not an amputee, she says she feels like one because of the pressure of the wedding. Ma says, "In that case, we all have phantom pain."

Caroline wakes on her wedding day looking ill, with a pain in her arm which makes her not want to get married. Ma says she was the same on the morning of her own wedding. Ma boils a traditional concoction with leaves, gives Caroline a bath, and rubs the leaves over Caroline's body. Ma tells Caroline that she is looking forward to visiting her in her new house.

Caroline, her family, and Eric arrive at Judge Perez's office for the ceremony. Grace cannot help but feel that Caroline is divorcing her family for a new allegiance. After the ceremony, Caroline feels better. At lunch, Grace toasts Caroline, saying that she will never be gone from the family and reflecting that this is something Ma might have said. Caroline and Grace bid each other a tearful farewell.

That night, Ma receives a bunch of red roses from Caroline. She keeps sniffing them and calls her daughter "Sweet, sweet Caroline." Grace dreams that she is sitting with her father beside a stream of rose-colored blood. As they look at the stars, Papa tells Grace that wherever she is, she can see them. He tries to play a question-and-answer game with Grace, asking her what

landscapes they would paint if they were painters and what she would name a daughter. Grace does not know how to answer. He tells her that she has forgotten how to play the game. She wakes, for the first time frightened of the father who appears in her dreams. She asks her mother what she thought of the wedding. Ma tells Grace that when Papa left her in Haiti to move with the widow to the United States, she made a charm to keep his love but knew his feelings for her had changed. Then she shows Grace Papa's romantic, respectful proposal letter. She adds that Caroline's wedding was nice.

Grace's passport arrives. For the first time, she feels secure in the United States. She reflects that her whole family has paid dearly for this piece of paper. She visits Papa's grave to show him the passport.

While making bone soup, Ma reports to Grace that she has told Caroline that she will keep her bed for whenever she wants to use it, a turnaround from her previous stance that she would get rid of the bed the day Caroline got married. Grace drops a bone into the soup, and the splash leaves a red mark on her hand. Grace asks Ma the questions Papa asked her in her dream. Ma says that as the older woman, the first question belongs to her. She asks Grace one of the questions from traditional Haitian question-and-answer games, one that Papa often asked Grace: why, when you lose something, is it in the last place you look? Grace knows the answer: because once you remember, you stop looking.

CHARACTERS

Eric Abrahams

Eric is Caroline's fiancé, whom she meets while working as a teacher in a school where he is a janitor. He is originally from the Bahamas, and Ma disapproves of him because he is not Haitian. Eric has a learning disability and is slow of speech. Though Ma calls him a "retard," Grace knows that he has a good heart and sincerely cares for Caroline.

Carl Azile

See Papa

Caroline Azile

Caroline is the younger daughter of Hermine and Carl Azile and the sister of Grace. She was injected with a drug that she believed caused her daughter Caroline to be born without a forearm. When Grace receives her certificate of U.S. citizenship, she remarks that her entire family has "paid dearly for this piece of paper." Indeed, she says, "It had cost my parents' marriage, my mother's spirit, my sister's arm."

Traditional Stories, Games, and Rituals

Krik? Krak! takes its title from a Haitian storytelling tradition. In Haiti, which has experienced high levels of illiteracy, the oral tradition of storytelling is beloved. It is customary for the person who has a story to tell to ask a potential audience, "Krik?" If they want to hear the story, they shout back, "Krak!" Then the storyteller begins. As a collection of stories, *Krik? Krak!* implicitly engages the reader in this ritual.

In addition, a major theme of "Caroline's Wedding" concerns how the broken continuities wrought by the Haitian diaspora are countered by traditional stories, games, beliefs, and rituals. These stories create a cultural identity and a sense of community between individual Haitians and different generations of Haitians. When a person has lost family or relatives, those people live on in their stories. In "Caroline's Wedding," Danticat particularly emphasizes the central role of women in passing these traditions from mother to daughter. Tension arises in the story between Ma, who wants the old traditions to continue, and Caroline, who seems to be turning her back on those traditions by paying them scant attention and by marrying a non-Haitian.

Memory and Loss

In keeping with the themes of diaspora and of a dispossessed people, the concept of loss is emphasized throughout the story. Loss is highlighted in the traditional free-association game that Caroline and Grace play with the word "lost," in which Grace describes herself as "the *lost* child of the night," whose mother and father are also lost.

Many of the characters have lost people, places, and things that were cherished by them. Ma has lost her homeland and has twice lost her husband, first to a marriage of convenience and then to death; she fears that she will lose Caroline through her marriage to a non-Haitian; Caroline and Grace have lost their father; Papa lost his mother to typhoid fever; Caroline lost her forearm; members of the congregation at the mass for the drowned Haitian realize that they have lost friends and relatives as the names of dead refugees are read out; the Cuban Mrs. Ruiz lost her

son; and the Bahamian Eric has lost his family. Grace's dreams about her father are characterized by unsuccessful attempts to catch up with him, be rescued by him, or get close to him. Only in the final dream that Grace recounts does she succeed in interacting with her father, only to be rebuked by him for forgetting (losing) the old Haitian traditions.

Violence and Suffering

The violence of the history of Haiti and the suffering of its people is not explicitly shown, but it is suggested as being ever-present just below the surface of life, just as Caroline's vein throbs just below the surface of her stub: As she says, a slice through the vein would make her bleed to death. Grace is Ma and Papa's "misery baby" because of the poverty her parents suffer in their Haitian shantytown; the sweatshop raid and subsequent imprisonment in which Ma is caught up is her terrifying introduction to her adopted country, the United States. Her being injected with a drug that may have harmed the unborn Caroline is a violation comparable to rape. Haitians are not the only people who suffer such violent episodes: the son of the Cuban Mrs. Ruiz is shot when he tries to hijack an airplane from Cuba to Miami (possibly in an attempt to escape from Cuba).

Paradoxically the violence and suffering endured by the Haitian people in their scattering also brings them together as they share their stories. At the mass for the drowned Haitian woman and her baby, members of the congregation scream as they recognize people among the list of names of the refugees who have drowned at sea in just that week. This graphically confirms Ma's assertion that "all Haitians know each other" and shows how the community is held together through pain and suffering as well as love.

STYLE

Short Story Cycle

In her epilogue to *Krik? Krak!*, Danticat likens the act of writing to braiding the hair, in that it is a matter of bringing unity to a number of unruly strands. The book is a short story cycle, in which each story can be read in isolation, but it also links to other stories in the collection. In "Caroline's Wedding," Grace accompanies Ma to a mass for a drowned Haitian woman and her baby; this is the same woman whose story is told in the first story in the collection, "Children of the Sea." The effect of this linkage is to emphasize the power of storytelling to establish identity and recreate community for people who have suffered diaspora. This is confirmed by two of Ma's remarks: "all Haitians know each other," and "We know people by their stories." Ma's own story, of her broken marriage and violent pregnancy with Caroline, emerges during the course of the short story. It helps to define who she is and why she acts as she does. In a lifetime of discontinuity, she understandably wishes everything to continue as it was in Haiti.

Symbolism

Caroline's missing forearm, as well as being a believable element of the story on a literal level, also carries a weighty poetic symbolism. Caroline's forearm fails to develop as a result of an act of violence and medical malpractice (Ma is injected with a drug when imprisoned after a New York sweatshop raid). Thus the missing arm is a kind of war wound, a scar gained during a time of danger. Because Ma stresses that the unborn Caroline could have died as a result of the drug, the episode suggests a major group of themes of the entire short story cycle, having to do with aborted or violent pregnancies and infanticide. This theme in turn, as Jana Evans Braziel points out in her essay, "Défilée's Diasporic Daughters: Revolutionary Narratives of *Ayiti* (Haiti), *Nanchon* (Nation), and *Dyaspora* (Diaspora) in Edwidge Danticat's *Krik? Krak!*" symbolically enacts the arrested or aborted development that Haiti has suffered during its many periods of unrest.

Caroline's arm also represents the homeland from which Caroline has been cut off by her parents' flight to the United States. This is especially true because Caroline is the only member of the family to be born in the United States. Grace remarks that "Caroline liked to have her stub stroked... Yet it was the only part of her that people were afraid of." This circumstance reflects the dilemma experienced by many people who have lost a place or person they loved. There may be times when they want to remember the loved one and talk about the person, but other people steer clear of the subject because they do not wish to give offense or because they feel uncomfortable discussing it. Thus, the bereaved person is isolated by grief and pain. In the case of the Haitian people, including Caroline, the suffering and persecutions of the past both isolate them from society in general (when Grace receives her passport, she says, "It was like being in a war zone

and finally receiving a weapon of my own") and brings them closer to one another (as in the mass at the church). When Grace and Caroline were younger, they fantasized that one day the rest of Caroline's arm would burst out of Ma's stomach and float back to her and she would be complete. Symbolically, this dream reflects the longing for wholeness felt by the dispossessed person.

Another symbol is that of Sor Rose. According to Haitian folklore, Sor Rose was the black African slave woman who was raped by her French master and gave birth to the nation of Haiti. Danticat scatters references to the color, name, or object called "rose" and to literal or symbolic rape throughout the stories in *Krik? Krak!* These references suggest, as Jana Evans Braziel posits in her essay, "Défilée's Diasporic Daughters," that Danticat is consciously invoking the Sor Rose story. The refugee woman from the first story in *Krik? Krak!*, "Children of the Sea," who is remembered in the mass that Ma and Grace attend in "Caroline's Wedding," was raped by a soldier, gave birth on the boat to the United States, and when the baby died, she threw it into the sea, then jumped overboard after it, drowning herself. In "Caroline's Wedding," Ma is injected, while a captive, with a drug that caused a birth defect in Caroline. This may be seen as a violation akin to rape, a forced invasion of someone's body. The violence of this symbolic rape breeds death: the unborn Caroline could have died, and the adult Caroline is conscious that it would only take a slice to the vein that throbs below the surface of her stub to make her bleed to death. In the violent story of Haiti, the symbolism suggests, death is ever-present, just beneath the thin surface of life.

Grace's dream that she and her father are sitting beside "a stream of rose-colored blood" is probably another reference to Sor Rose. This interpretation is confirmed by Grace's remark that the stream of blood is beautiful, at which Papa's face begins to glow. Papa's purpose in the dream is to reconnect Grace with her roots by engaging her in the question-and-answer game, in which he asks her what traditions she will pass on to her children. While sitting by the stream of blood, they gaze at the stars, and Papa tells her, "If you close your eyes really tight, wherever you are, you will see these stars." The symbolic implication is that shared stories, by which suffering (a river of blood) is transfigured through the art of the storyteller, unify the scattered Haitian people.

COMPARE & CONTRAST

- **1970s:** Before 1971, waves of Haitian refugees flee to the United States and other industrialized countries as a result of Dr. François Duvalier's ("Papa Doc") regime of persecution. Many are middle-class and educated. After his death in 1971, the waves of refugees increase. Most refugees in this second group are poor people, fleeing the miserable conditions under the corrupt regime of François Duvalier's son, Jean-Claude Duvalier ("Baby Doc").

  1990s: After Haiti's president Jean-Bertrand Aristide is deposed in a coup in 1990, the Organization of American States, the United Nations, and the U.S. government begin to impose sanctions on Haiti. The number of Haitian refugees grows as poverty intensifies under the sanctions. Sanctions are in place from 1990 until 1994, when Aristide is reinstated as president.

  Today: According to the United Nations, in 2005, due to continuing political instability around the election, there is a steep increase in asylum seekers from Haiti to industrialized countries. As of 2006, Haiti remains one of the poorest countries in the world.

- **1970s:** The term, boat people, refers to refugees, including those from Haiti, who risk their lives on unsafe, overcrowded boats to escape oppression or poverty in their home countries. During the 1970s and 1980s, between 50,000 and 80,000 boat people arrive without authorization in Florida. An unknown number drown at sea.

  1990s: In 1990, the flow of Haitian boat people temporarily stops following the presidential election of Jean-Bertrand Aristide. By late 1991, however, following Aristide's deposition in a military coup, the flow of Haitian boat people resumes. Between 1991 and 1994, thousands of Haitians flee the country, mostly by boat. Some who flee are accorded refugee status and are resettled in the United States, but others are repatriated.

  Today: After the military regime is removed in 1994, numbers of Haitian boat people decline. As of 2006, the Haitian diaspora in the United States continues to grow, fueled by the arrival of friends and relatives of the Haitian immigrant population and by internal growth, as second- and third-generations are born into Haitian-American families. The Haitian government begins to try to attract members of the Haitian diaspora to Haiti, especially as investors.

The word "rose" also appears in the story when Caroline sends a bunch of red roses to Ma. This gesture comes after Ma has revived an ill and despondent Caroline just before her wedding, using a traditional Haitian treatment that involves giving her a bath and rubbing boiled leaves over her body. Before this incident, Caroline shows little interest in Ma's traditional Haitian attitudes and beliefs. But for the first time, she surrenders to Ma and is rejuvenated. The gift of roses is Caroline's recognition and honoring of the wisdom and loving care conveyed by the rituals and customs that Ma has preserved.

The Color Red

Red is the color of blood and therefore of life-blood, but it is also the color of violence, danger, and potentially, death. In "Caroline's Wedding," red is used symbolically to suggest the violence, bloodshed, and suffering of Haiti's history, and, ultimately, the land of Haiti itself. Ma has a red port-wine mark on her neck, which she believes stems from unsatisfied cravings during pregnancy, a reference to the hunger she suffered in Haiti. Ma tells her daughters to wear red panties after their father dies, as according to Haitian tradition, the color has the power to keep away the spirit of her dead husband. Caroline's awareness of the possibility of her bleeding to death from a sliced vein links with Grace's dream on the night of her sister's wedding.

The red symbolism recurs in the final scene. Grace, disturbed by her failure to remember how to play the ancient game with Papa in her dream, goes to Ma for help. As she drops a bone into Ma's bone soup, the splash creates a red mark on her hand. It is a fitting time for Grace to receive the blood-like mark of her homeland on her body, as she is about to learn from Ma the lesson that escaped her under Papa's interrogation.

HISTORICAL CONTEXT

Violence and Political Unrest in Haiti

Haiti's history is one of violence and political unrest, and its population has been subjected to many occupations and enslavements. Haiti is situated in the western part of an island called Hispaniola; the eastern part is called the Dominican Republic. Hispaniola was inhabited by the Taino and Arawak peoples (classed as indigenous peoples of the Americas) when in 1492, the explorer Christopher Colombus landed and claimed the island for Spain. The Spanish enslaved the indigenous people and imported African slaves to mine for gold. In the 1600s, French, Dutch, and British pirates established bases in Haiti. In 1664, France claimed control of the western part of the island, calling it Saint-Domingue. The colony prospered, growing sugar and coffee. The population was divided into ruling white Europeans, free black people, and black slaves. The majority of slaves were African-born, since harsh conditions meant that the Haitian-born slaves were unable to increase their population.

Inspired by the French Revolution, in 1790 and 1791, free and enslaved black people revolted against the French rulers of Saint-Domingue. Three black leaders of the revolution emerged: Toussaint L'Ouverture, Jean-Jacques Dessalines, and Henri Christophe. Finally, the revolutionary forces defeated the French, and in 1804, the nation declared its independence. It was named Haiti after the old Arawak name for the island, Ayiti. Dessalines became the first emperor of Haiti but was murdered in 1806, setting a pattern of violent fates for Haitian leaders, which was only broken in the 1990s. Throughout the nineteenth century, Haiti was ruled by a succession of presidents, whose periods of office ended prematurely through coups and revolutions.

In 1915, Haiti was invaded by the United States and remained under its military occupation for nineteen years. The invasion was prompted

by fears that a popular revolution against Haitian dictator Jean Vilbrun Guillaume Sam threatened the business interests of the United States and a suspicion that Haiti was too closely aligned with Germany during World War I. An unsuccessful yet popular revolt against the U.S. occupation led to the deaths of around two thousand Haitians. Thereafter, a certain order was established. However, opposition to the occupation grew among the Haitian population, prompted by the perceived racial prejudice of the occupiers. Particularly hated were the forced-labor gangs, in which roads and other infrastructure were constructed under the direction of the U.S. military. Escapees could be shot, and the gangs were seen as another form of slavery.

After World War I, the U.S. occupation of Haiti was increasingly questioned both within the United States and internationally. An incident in which U.S. Marines killed ten Haitian peasants who were marching to protest economic conditions helped to prompt the complete withdrawal of U.S. forces in 1934. For the next fifty years, Haiti was ruled by a series of dictators supported by the United States. The first waves of Haitian refugees to the United States coincided with the 1957 installment of Dr. François Duvalier ("Papa Doc") as president after an election that many believed was manipulated by the army. Duvalier maintained power through his secret police, the Volunteers for National Security, nicknamed the Tonton Macoutes. The Tonton Macoutes terrorized the population with torture, killings, and extortion. They murdered hundreds of Duvalier's opponents and sometimes hanged their corpses in public view as a warning to would-be rebels.

Upon Duvalier's death in 1971, his son Jean-Claude Duvalier ("Baby Doc") took over the presidency. His regime became known for corruption, and much of the population sank into poverty. These people formed another wave of refugees who fled to the United States in the 1970s and early 1980s. In "Caroline's Wedding," Grace and Caroline's parents belong to this wave of refugees. With the election of Jean-Bertrand Aristide in 1990, the flow of refugees briefly stopped, only to resume shortly afterwards when Aristide was deposed in a coup. Aristide returned to office in 2001 but was again deposed in 2004.

René Préval was elected president in 1996 and was remarkable for the fact that he left office after serving a complete term (he was again

Conflicts between immigrant mothers and daughters frequently arise when the younger generation adopts the cultural attitudes of their new home © *Richard Bickel/Corbis*

elected president in 2006). All previous presidents had died in office, been assassinated or deposed, overstayed their prescribed term, or been installed by a foreign power.

The country's history of forced occupations and enslavements, violent depositions or murders of its leaders, and aborted development is symbolically suggested in "Caroline's Wedding" and other stories in the cycle by references to rape, violent and aborted pregnancies, and infanticide.

Voodoo

In "Caroline's Wedding," Ma's beliefs are a mixture of Catholicism (she goes to mass) and voodoo (she invokes the magical powers of charms and bone soup), which as of 2006 remained the dominant religion in Haiti. Voodoo is a polytheistic religion that includes a belief that objects can be imbued with magical properties that can be used to affect the outcome of events. It is based on a variety of African religions, with elements of Catholicism superimposed.

Voodoo has long been viewed with fear and contempt by many white colonials, but its development was partly a reaction to the suppression by white Europeans of the religious beliefs and practices of African slaves. Rather than abandon their old faiths, the slaves created a new faith, which helped them endure the hardships of their lives and at the same time to avoid persecution by their owners.

CRITICAL OVERVIEW

When Danticat's short story collection *Krik? Krak!* was published in 1995, it cemented the reputation that Danticat had begun to build with her earlier debut novel, *Breath, Eyes, Memory* (1994). The collection was nominated for a National Book Award and was warmly received by critics, who welcomed Danticat's humanizing of Haiti, a country that had been largely ignored by writers and artists and that had mainly been the subject of

WHAT DO I READ NEXT?

- Stories by Danticat that can be read alone yet connect with "Caroline's Wedding" and that deal with Haitian and Haitian American themes are collected in *Krik? Krak!* (1995).

- Danticat's debut novel, *Breath, Eyes, Memory* (1994), explores the theme of Haitian immigrants to the United States, who struggle to adjust to their adopted culture without losing touch with the old Haitian ways.

- A number of interviews with Danticat about her work are collected at www.haitiglobal village.com/sd-marassa1-cd/d-conversations. htm (accessed October 18, 2006).

- *The Butterfly's Way: Voices from the Haitian Dyaspora in the United States* (2001), edited by Edwidge Danticat, is a collection of autobiographical literary essays and poems, alongside some pieces of social and political analysis, written by thirty-two Haitian exiles. Themes include migration, childhood, cross-generational differences, return to the homeland, and the future.

- Amy Tan's novel *The Joy Luck Club* (1989) focuses on mother-daughter relationships in families exiled from their native country—in this case, China. The novel is divided into short vignettes, which are rather like short stories.

- *The Oxford Book of Caribbean Short Stories* (2002), edited by Stewart Brown and John Wickham, is a collection of fifty-one short stories by twentieth-century Caribbean-born writers, including Gabriel García Márquez, V. S. Naipaul, Patrick Chamoiseau, Juan Bosch, and Alicia McKenzie, as well as Danticat.

- Charles Arthur's *Haiti in Focus: A Guide to the People, Politics, and Culture* (2002) provides an accessible introduction to Haiti's history, politics, economy, society, people, culture, and environment, and includes tips on what to see for those traveling to Haiti.

news reports focusing on political upheaval and violence. In her *Boston Globe* review, "Danticat's Stories Pulse with Haitian Heartbeat," Jordana Hart praises Danticat's "honest and loving portraits of Haitian people" which have "smashed the numbing stereotypes created by a barrage of media accounts of Haitian poverty, misery and death."

In an interview with Danticat for Knight-Ridder/Tribune News Service, Margaria Fichtner makes comments on Danticat's novel *Breath, Eyes, Memory* that could easily be applied to *Krik? Krak!* Fichtner notes the novel's emotional complexity and its portrayal of the burdens of history, politics, and culture upon the lives and hearts of women, adding that it has "much to say about what it is like to be young, black, Haitian and female wandering in a world too often eager to regard all of those conditions as less than worthwhile." Fichtner calls *Krik? Krak!* "a collection of interrelated stories celebrating Haitian home life, tradition and myth and the ennobled lives of people who have lost everything but a rich will to survive."

In his review of *Krik? Krak!* for *World Literature Today*, Hal Wylie singles out "Caroline's Wedding" for particular praise, on the grounds that this story is "the most penetrating in exploring the psychology of assimilation." Wylie notes that the Haitian stories featured within the story help the characters "in finding the essential values of life—the foundation for a character able to resist life's traumas." The story of Caroline's wedding, he writes, "shows the relationship of family stories to the larger social rituals, also important in people's finding their way in the urban labyrinth."

In her review entitled "Stories Resound with Haiti's Tragedy, Spirit," for the *San Francisco Chronicle*, Wendy Sheanin also notes the "legacy of pain" carried by each member of Grace's family. Against this legacy, Sheanin writes, the stories demonstrate "the healing and affirming power of storytelling," in the sense that stories "provide spiritual sustenance, whether they are told to escape harsh reality or to pass the time on board a doomed refugee boat or to fantasize about a better life." Sheanin draws attention to the story cycle structure, whereby the interrelatedness of stories reinforces the sense of community among the scattered Haitian exiles. She praises Danticat's "honesty, coupled with her wit and subtlety," which combine to yield "powerful stories that remain with us long after we close the book."

CRITICISM

Claire Robinson

Robinson has an M.A. in English. She is a writer, editor, and former teacher of English literature and creative writing. In the following essay, Robinson examines how continuity and community are sought in the Haitian diaspora in Edwidge Danticat's "Caroline's Wedding."

The central event of "Caroline's Wedding," the marriage of a young woman from a family of Haitian immigrants living in the United States, acts as the focus for a number of cross-generational and cross-cultural conflicts. While these conflicts threaten to divide the Azile family, by extension, similar conflicts also affect the wider Haitian community, whose members find themselves separated from friends, family, and homeland due to the diaspora caused by Haiti's historical instability. The story opens with Ma making bone soup, an old Haitian ritual that she hopes will separate Caroline from her fiancé, Eric. Ma disapproves of Eric because he is not Haitian and no one in her family has married outside before. In addition, Eric's courtship of Caroline has been very different from her own husband's courtship of her. It has been informal, has involved pre-marital sex, and has been lacking in the traditional romantic, respectful courtship rituals that she proudly remembers her husband following in seeking her own hand. Worst of all, Caroline's marriage will take place not in a church, but in a judge's office. Ma compares the two and finds Caroline's arrangements disappointingly "mechanical" and typically American. The conflict is a typical clash of generations and cultures.

However, throughout the course of the story, Ma slowly and reluctantly becomes used to the idea of Caroline's marriage. It is suggested, though not made explicit, that she comes to an understanding that the old ways that she has championed for so long have their limitations. This conclusion is revealed through the slow unfolding of Ma's own tragic story, which makes clear that any advantages that Ma's marriage had over Caroline's in terms of romance

> THE WORDS OF THE SONG SUGGEST THAT BEING PARTIALLY OUTSIDE ONE'S OWN CULTURE, AS HAITIAN IMMIGRANTS TO THE UNITED STATES SUCH AS GRACE NECESSARILY ARE, ENABLES ONE TO UNDERSTAND IT BETTER."

and ritual were outweighed by internal weaknesses and hostile circumstances. Ma's happiness did not last. First poverty then Papa's marriage of convenience to another woman and departure for the United States helped to destroy the fabric of the marriage. While Ma continued to love her husband, he appears to have ceased to love her. Ma never gets over the grief: "My heart has a store of painful marks . . . and that is one of them."

It is open to question whether Ma's admission of the truth about her marriage mellows her attitude toward Caroline's, but the parallels suggest that this is the case. Ma's marriage to Papa had all the traditional external formalities in place but was wrecked by betrayal, unrequited love, and grief. Caroline's wedding to Eric lacks traditional ritual, but their relationship is one of mutual trust and caring, and they almost certainly know one another better than did Caroline's parents before their wedding. The gap between Ma's expectations of her marriage and the reality prompts her late in the story to ask Grace to destroy all traces of Papa's courtship of her and their marriage after her death. Such an act would be the exact opposite of Ma's usual determination to preserve the old ways and memories at all costs.

Caroline, for her part, also subtly changes in her attitude toward Ma's traditional Haitian beliefs and practices during the course of the story. With her chemically straightened hair and non-Haitian fiancé, Caroline appears to have completely assimilated the ways of her adopted country, the United States. Her attitude toward Ma's attachments to the old rituals, such as making bone soup and attending mass, varies from good-natured tolerance, engaging in small deceptions to save Ma's feelings (such as going home after dinner at Eric's but then secretly catching a cab back to Eric's so that she can sleep with him without upsetting Ma), to plain irritation. It is clear that Caroline has no emotional attachment to Haiti's traditional beliefs—certainly not as much as Grace. Grace was born in Haiti and retains a strong sense of tradition, yet she has just been delighted to receive her U.S. citizenship. She acts as a conduit and mediator between Ma and Caroline, explaining and justifying the ways of each to the other.

The turning point for Caroline begins when she feels ill just before her wedding. This part of Caroline's journey is expressed through the symbolism of her missing forearm. When she appears in her wedding dress wearing a new false arm, she explains that she has been having phantom pain in her arm such as amputees experience, and a doctor told her that the false arm may make it go away. When Ma points out that she is not an amputee, Caroline replies that the pressure of the wedding is making her feel like one. Ma says, "In that case, we all have phantom pain." As Caroline prepares to leave Ma's home and marry the non-Haitian Eric, the pain in her arm symbolically suggests that she is more attached to her homeland and her home than she consciously realizes. Ma's comment about phantom pain underlines the symbolism. She is referring to the sense of loss that refugees and dispossessed people feel. The false arm may symbolically indicate the myriad ways that people suffering loss try to compensate and feel whole again; getting married is one way; becoming a citizen of one's adopted country is another.

Ma rescues Caroline from her pain. She takes care of her, gives her a bath, and revives her with a traditional Haitian herbal treatment. What is more, Ma knows exactly what Caroline needs because she felt the same on her wedding day. In giving herself up to Ma's care, Caroline is brought to surrender to and honor the accumulated wisdom of countless generations of Haitian women. It is evident that Ma's attitude towards Caroline's marriage has thawed when she tells Caroline that she is eager to be a guest in her new house, the first overture she has made towards the couple in their new life together. The episode shows the relationship between mother and daughter to be unique and irreplaceable. It emphasizes the continuity that will overcome their physical separation through Caroline's marriage. Each comes to understand and accept the other. Danticat's use of Haitian ritual and tradition underlines this point. At the beginning

of the story, Ma employs an old Haitian ritual—the making and serving of bone soup—against Caroline, to try to separate her from Eric. But at the story's end, she turns to the healing ritual of the herbal bath to calm and support her daughter before her marriage.

Traditions such as these enable Haitians everywhere to reconnect with lost loved ones, culture, and homeland through times of suffering and diaspora. But keeping those traditions alive depends upon memory. In Laura Jamison's review for the *San Francisco Examiner* of *Krik? Krak!*, "The Exquisite Tales of Edwidge Danticat," Danticat is quoted as saying, "In Haiti, memories are important. They give you hope for the future if present circumstances are not very good." Memory is a major theme of "Caroline's Wedding." It is also one of Grace's chief preoccupations. Grace finds that preserving the memory of Haitian traditions is not easy in the face of modern life in a very different country. She becomes upset when her father, in a dream on the night after Caroline's wedding, accuses her of having forgotten how to play the question-and-answer game. He asks her, "What kinds of legends will your daughters be told? What sort of charms will you give them to ward off evil?" For the first time, she feels afraid of him. She feels disturbed at her loss of the traditions that he kept alive in his perfect memory and of the safeguard that they offer against fear and insecurity. She intuitively knows the importance of such games in maintaining her cultural identity and her closeness to her family members, both dead and alive. Finally, she is driven by this experience to seek from Ma what she has lost.

In the Haitian tradition, Ma answers Grace's question by asking another. She asks Grace, "Why is it that when you lose something, it is always in the last place that you look for it?" On one level, this is Ma's wry reference to what she sees as her daughters' neglect of the old Haitian ways that she espouses; in their new lives in the United States, she has become the last person they consult. On a deeper level, it is a profound statement about the paradox of memory, summed up in the old Haitian proverb that provides the answer to Ma's question. Grace knows the answer to this question well: "Because . . . once you remember, you always stop looking." While memory keeps alive the history and culture of Haiti, a feat performed to perfection by Papa, once one has remembered, one ceases to seek. The absolute success of memory means the end of seeking, which ultimately means the loss of living history and culture. This paradox is summed up in the Haitian song that is playing on the radio immediately after Grace's dream in which she fails to answer her father's questions about the traditions of the country:

> Beloved Haiti, there is no place like you.
> I had to leave you before I could understand you.

The words of the song suggest that being partially outside one's own culture, as Haitian immigrants to the United States such as Grace necessarily are, enables one to understand it better.

Source: Claire Robinson, Critical Essay on "Caroline's Wedding," in *Short Stories for Students*, Thomson Gale 2007.

Thomson Gale

In the following essay, the critic gives an overview of Edwidge Danticat's work.

Fiction writer Edwidge Danticat conjures the history of her native Haiti in award-winning short stories and novels. She is equally at home describing the immigrant experience—what she calls "dyaspora"—and the reality of life in Haiti today. Danticat's fiction "has been devoted to an unflinching examination of her native culture, both on its own terms and in terms of its intersections with American culture," wrote an essayist in *Contemporary Novelists*. "Danticat's work emphasizes in particular the heroism and endurance of Haitian women as they cope with a patriarchal culture that, in its unswerving devotion to tradition and family, both oppresses and enriches them." Readers will find "massacres, rapes, [and] horrible nightmares in Danticat's fiction," wrote an essayist in the *St. James Guide to Young Adult Writers*, "but above all these are the strength, hope, and joy of her poetic vision."

Danticat's first novel, the loosely autobiographical *Breath, Eyes, Memory*, was a 1998 selection of the Oprah Winfrey Book Club, thus assuring its best-seller status. Other Danticat works have won warm praise as well, with some critics expressing surprise that such assured prose has come from an author so young. *Antioch Review* correspondent Grace A. Epstein praised Danticat for "the real courage . . . in excavating the romance of nationalism, identity, and home." *Time* reporter Christopher John Farley likewise

"BUT *MS.* CONTRIBUTOR JORDANA HART FELT THAT THE TALES IN *KRIK? KRAK!* 'ARE TEXTURED AND DEEPLY PERSONAL, AS IF THE TWENTY-SIX-YEAR-OLD HAITIAN-AMERICAN AUTHOR HAD SPILLED HER OWN TEARS OVER EACH.'"

concluded that Danticat's fiction "never turns purple, never spins wildly into the fantastic, always remains focused, with precise disciplined language, and in doing so, it uncovers moments of raw humanness."

Danticat was born in Haiti and lived there the first twelve years of her life. She came to the United States in 1981, joining her parents who had already begun to build a life for themselves in New York City. When she started attending junior high classes in Brooklyn, she had difficulty fitting in with her classmates because of her Haitian accent, clothing, and hairstyle. Danticat recalled for Garry Pierre-Pierre in the *New York Times* that she took refuge from the isolation she felt in writing about her native land. As an adolescent she began work on what would evolve into her first novel, the acclaimed *Breath, Eyes, Memory*. Danticat followed her debut with a collection of short stories, *Krik? Krak!*—a volume which became a finalist for that year's National Book Award. According to Pierre-Pierre, the young author has been heralded as "'the voice' of Haitian-Americans," but Danticat told him, "I think I have been assigned that role, but I don't really see myself as the voice for the Haitian-American experience. There are many. I'm just one."

Danticat's parents wanted her to pursue a career in medicine, and with the goal of becoming a nurse, she attended a specialized high school in New York City. But she abandoned this aim to devote herself to her writing. An earlier version of *Breath, Eyes, Memory* served as her master of fine arts thesis at Brown University, and the finished version was published shortly thereafter. Like Danticat herself, Sophie Caco—the novel's protagonist—spent her first twelve years in Haiti, several in the care of an aunt, before coming wide-eyed to the

United States. But there the similarities end. Sophie is the child of a single mother, conceived by rape. Though she rejoins her mother in the United States, it is too late to save the still-traumatized older woman from self-destruction. Yet women's ties to women are celebrated in the novel, and Sophie draws strength from her mother, her aunt, and herself in order to escape her mother's fate.

Breath, Eyes, Memory caused some controversy in the Haitian-American community. Some of Danticat's fellow Haitians did not approve of her writing of the practice of "testing" in the novel. In the story, female virginity is highly prized by Sophie's family, and Sophie's aunt "tests" to see whether Sophie's hymen is intact by inserting her fingers into the girl's vagina. Haitian-American women, some of whom have never heard of or participated in this practice, felt that Danticat's inclusion of it portrayed them as primitive and abusive. American critics, however, appreciated *Breath, Eyes, Memory.* Joan Philpott in *Ms.* described the book as "intensely lyrical." Pierre-Pierre reported that reviewers "have praised Ms. Danticat's vivid sense of place and her images of fear and pain." Jim Gladstone concluded in the *New York Times Book Review* that the novel "achieves an emotional complexity that lifts it out of the realm of the potboiler and into that of poetry." And Bob Shacochis, in his *Washington Post Book World* review, called the work "a novel that rewards a reader again and again with small but exquisite and unforgettable epiphanies." Shacochis added, "You can actually see Danticat grow and mature, come into her own strength as a writer, throughout the course of this quiet, soul-penetrating story about four generations of women trying to hold on to one another in the Haitian diaspora."

Krik? Krak! takes its title from the practice of Haitian storytellers. Danticat told Deborah Gregory of *Essence* that storytelling is a favorite entertainment in Haiti, and a storyteller inquires of his or her audience, "Krik?" to ask if they are ready to listen. The group then replies with an enthusiastic, "Krak!" The tales in this collection include one about a man attempting to flee Haiti in a leaky boat, another about a prostitute who tells her son that the reason she dresses up every night is that she is expecting an angel to descend upon their house, and yet another explores the feelings of a childless housekeeper in a loveless

marriage who finds an abandoned baby in the streets. The *New York Times Book Review* reviewer, Robert Houston, citing the fact that some of the stories in *Krik? Krak!* were written while Danticat was still an undergraduate at Barnard College, felt that these pieces were "out of place in a collection presumed to represent polished, mature work." But *Ms.* contributor Jordana Hart felt that the tales in *Krik? Krak!* "are textured and deeply personal, as if the twenty-six-year-old Haitian-American author had spilled her own tears over each." Even Houston conceded that readers "weary of stories that deal only with the minutiae of 'relationships' will rejoice that they have found work that is about something, and something that matters."

Danticat's novel *The Farming of Bones* concerns a historical tragedy, the 1937 massacre of Haitian farm workers by soldiers of the Dominican Republic. In the course of less than a week, an estimated 12,000–15,000 Haitian workers in the Dominican Republic were slaughtered by the Dominican government or by private citizens in a classic case of "ethnic cleansing." *The Farming of Bones* is narrated by a young Haitian woman, Amabelle Desir, who has grown up in the Dominican Republic after being orphaned. As the nightmare unfolds around her, Amabelle must flee for her life, separated from her lover, Sebastien. In the ensuing decades as she nurses her physical and psychological wounds, Amabelle serves as witness to the suffering of her countrymen and the guilt of her former Dominican employers. The massacre, Danticat told Mallay Charters in *Publishers Weekly*, is "a part of our history, as Haitians, but it's also a part of the history of the world. Writing about it is an act of remembrance."

Dean Peerman wrote in *Christian Century* that "*Breath, Eyes, Memory* was an impressive debut, but *The Farming of Bones* is a richer work, haunting and heartwrenching." In *Nation*, Zia Jaffrey praised Danticat for "blending history and fiction, imparting information, in the manner of nineteenth-century novelists, without seeming to." Jaffrey added: "Danticat's brilliance as a novelist is that she is able to put this event into a credible, human context." Farley also felt that the author was able to endow a horrific episode with a breath of humanity. "Every chapter cuts deep, and you feel it," he stated, continuing on to say that Amabelle's "journey from servitude to slaughter is heartbreaking." In *Américas,*

Barbara Mujica concluded that Danticat has written "a gripping novel that exposes an aspect of Dominican-Haitian history rarely represented in Latin American fiction. In spite of the desolation and wretchedness of the people Danticat depicts, *The Farming of Bones* is an inspiring book. It is a hymn to human resilience, faith, and hope in the face of overwhelming adversity." Jaffrey ended her review by concluding that the novel is "a beautifully conceived work, with monumental themes."

Behind the Mountains takes the form of a diary of teenage Haitian Celiane Esperance. Celiane is happy in her home in the mountains of Haiti, but she hasn't seen her father since he left for the United States years before. She had intended to join him in New York, along with her mother and older brother, but visa applications are inexorably slow. After eight years, the visas are granted, and the family reunites in Brooklyn. After an initially joyful reunion, however, the family begins to slowly unravel. A child when her father left Haiti, Celiane is now a young woman with her own mind and will. Her brother, Moy, a nineteen-year-old artist, does not quietly slip back into the role of obedient child. Even more universal concerns, such as the freezing New York winters, difficulties at school, and the need to make a living, chip away at the family's unity. Good intentions go awry in a book showcasing "friction among family members" exacerbated by "the separation and adjustment to a new country," but especially by the inevitable maturation of younger family members and the unwillingness of parents to acknowledge it, wrote Diane S. Morton in *School Library Journal.* Hazel Rochman, writing in *Booklist,* praised the "simple, lyrical writing" Danticat demonstrates in the novel. "Danticat brings her formidable skill as a writer and her own firsthand knowledge of Haiti and immigrating to America to this heartfelt story told in the intimate diary format," wrote Claire Rosser in *Kliatt.*

In addition to her own works, Danticat has also edited the fiction of others, including *The Butterfly's Way: From the Haitian Dyaspora in the United States.* This work is a collection of stories, poems, and essays from Haitian writers living in America and Europe, many of whom are concerned with the feeling of displacement that is perhaps an inevitable consequence of emigration. Denolyn Carroll suggested in *Black Issues Book Review* that the pieces in *The Butterfly's Way* "help paint a vivid picture of what it is like to live in two worlds." Carroll also felt that the work adds "new dimensions of understanding of Haitian emigrant's realities. This compilation is a source of enlightenment for us all." *Booklist* contributor Donna Seaman found the book "a potent and piercing collection" that will help all Americans understand "the frustrations... of Haitians who are now outsiders both in Haiti and in their places of refuge."

After the Dance: A Walk through Carnival in Haiti is Danticat's nonfiction account of her first encounter with Carnival, the boisterous, sometimes debauched, sometimes dangerous celebrations that rock Haiti every year. As a child, she did not have the opportunity to attend Carnival. Her family inevitably packed up and left for a remote area in the Haitian mountains each year to escape the celebrations, perpetuating an almost superstitious distrust of the event. At times, though, staying clear has been a good idea. During the regime of Haitian dictator François "Papa Doc" Duvalier, carnival-goers were "subject to beatings and arrest by Duvalier's infamously unregulated militamen," wrote Judith Wynn in the *Boston Herald.* Danticat therefore approaches her first experience of Carnival uneasily. Her trip, however, beginning a week before the actual event, immerses her in the rich culture and history of Haiti, the cultural importance behind Carnival, and the background of the celebration itself. Danticat's "lively narrative" describes a country with a deep history, "influenced by Christianity, voodoo, Europeans, pirates, dictators, past slavery, and an uncertain economy," wrote Linda M. Kaufmann in *Library Journal.* Donna Seaman, writing in *Booklist,* observed that "as in her fiction, Danticat writes about her odyssey with an admirable delicacy and meticulousness," while a *Publishers Weekly* critic noted that the author "offers an enlightening look at the country—and Carnival—through the eyes of one of its finest writers."

The Dew Breaker is a work of mystery and violence. It is a collection of short stories (many previously unpublished) connected by the character of the Dew Breaker, a torturer whose nickname is based on the fact that he attacks in the dawn before the dew has disappeared in the light of day. The Dew Breaker ultimately moves from Haiti to Brooklyn, becomes a barber, and raises a loving family. In Danticat's stories, the Dew Breaker reveals his secrets out of guilt, and his victims reveal their secrets, too, to ease the pain of their memories. Danticat's "spare, lyrical prose is ever present," wrote Marjorie Valbrun in the *Black Issues Book Review*, "in the gentle telling of stories that are soft to the ear even when pain and violence seem to scream from the pages." "The text presents two levels of truth," commented Robert McCormick in *World Literature Today*. In the course of reading, one comes to understand much, he hinted, but "what we don't know . . . is just as important."

Anacaona, Golden Flower: Haiti, 1490 is a novel for the upper elementary and middle school grades, written in the form of a diary. Anacaona is a young princess of the Taíno people who comes of age in the time of Christopher Columbus. She weds a royal chieftain who lives nearby and undergoes military training to defend her island home. *Booklist* reviewer Gillian Engberg predicted that "readers will connect with Danticat's immediate, poetic language, Anacaona's finely drawn growing pains, and the powerful, graphic story."

"In order to create full-fledged, three-dimensional characters, writers often draw on their encounters, observations, collages of images from the everyday world, both theirs and others," Danticat remarked in a biographical essay in *Contemporary Novelists*. "We are like actors, filtering through our emotions what life must be like, or must have been like, for those we write about. Truly we imagine these lives, aggrandize, reduce, or embellish, however we often begin our journey with an emotion close to our gut, whether it be anger, curiosity, joy, or fear."

Source: Thomson Gale, "Edwidge Danticat," in *Contemporary Authors Online*, Thomson Gale, 2005.

Rocio G. Davis

In the following essay, Davis explores Danticat's particular use of the short story cycle in Krik? Krak!, *which reflects the oral narrative and, through this narration, articulates "the process toward ethnic self-identification."*

Only when ethnic literature liberates its sources of meaning from hegemonic impositions and begins to inform theory and subvert traditional signifying strategies can it begin to

> THOUGH THE STORIES IN *KRIK? KRAK!* HAVE A CONTINUITY DERIVED FROM RECURRENT THEMES AND MOTIFS, THEY ARE MORE PROFOUNDLY LINKED BY A SPIRITUAL VISION WHERE THE BONDS BETWEEN WOMEN ARE IMPERATIVE FOR SURVIVAL."

reconfigure cultural interpretation. As though responding to this challenge, ethnic fiction demonstrates a proliferation of the short story cycle, a form until now most clearly defined within the Euro-American literary tradition, that many ethnic writers have adapted for the formulation of their processes of subjectivity. Amy Tan's *The Joy Luck Club*, Gloria Naylor's *The Women of Brewster Place*, Julia Alvarez's *How the Garcia Girls Lost Their Accents*, and Louise Erdich's *Love Medicine* emblematize how ethnic writers appropriate the specifics of this narrative genre to engage with the dynamics of meaning. This article will explore the short story cycle as a vehicle for the development of ethnic literature by analyzing Haitian-American Edwidge Danticat's *Krik? Krak!* to show how the drama of identity and community is mediated through a genre that is linked to the oral narrative, itself a way of fostering imaginative communities and developing identities.

The dynamics of the short story cycle make it appropriate for the quest for a definition of the cultural pluralism that incorporates immigrant legacies while adapting to the practices of the culture in which these works are created. A cycle may be defined as "a set of stories linked to each other in such a way as to maintain a balance between the individuality of each of the stories and the necessities of the larger unit" (Ingram 15). The term "short story cycle" implies a structural scheme for the working out of an idea, characters, or themes, even a circular disposition in which the constituent narratives are simultaneously independent and interdependent. The challenge of each cycle is twofold: the collection must assert the individuality and independence of each of the component parts while creating a necessary interdependence that emphasizes the wholeness and unity of the work.

Consistency of theme and an evolution from one story to the next are among the classic requirements of the form, with recurrence and development as the integrated movements that effect final cohesion (Ingram 20).

The essential characteristics of the short story cycle abound in the literatures of the world: Homer's *Odyssey*, Ovid's *Metamorphoses*, Boccaccio's *Decameron*, Chaucer's *The Canterbury Tales*, the Indian *Panchatantra*, the Arabian *A Thousand and One Nights*, and Mallory's *Morte d'Arthur* reflect the fundamental separation and cohesion of the form as defined by twentieth-century critics. Cycles figure prominently in twentieth-century American literature: Sherwood Anderson's *Winesburg, Ohio*, Ernest Hemingway's *In Our Time* and Raymond Carver's *Cathedral*, among others, have constituted and popularized the form within the "mainstream" canon. By appropriating and transforming this narrative genre as established and defined by "mainstream" writers and critics, Danticat, like other ethnic writers, intervenes in the dominant Euro-American literary tradition. A text such as *Krik? Krak!* challenges hegemonic discourse on several levels, as the author exploits the advantages of the established structure and theme to present her version of the immigrant story, blending cultural traditions and codes for innovative literary representation.

The short story cycle looks back to oral traditions of narrative while embodying signs of modernity. One of its most salient features is its attempt to emulate the act of storytelling, the effort of a speaker to establish solidarity with an implied audience by recounting a series of tales linked by their content or by the conditions in which they are related. The experience of the oral narrative, of telling and listening to stories, has been a vital part of the development of the body of thought and tradition that has formed culture and united diverse peoples. As Walter Ong argues, in its physical constitution as sound, the spoken word manifests human beings to each other as persons and forms them into close-knit groups: when a speaker is addressing an audience, the members of the audience normally become a unity, with themselves and with the speaker. Much of the vividness of the oral narrative comes precisely from the fact that it resists writing, preserving the spoken word as always "an event, a movement in time, completely lacking in the thing-like repose of the written or printed word" (Ong 74).

Sarah Hardy's comparison of the short story and the oral narrative is, I believe, equally applicable to the story cycle: "A single theme or episode . . . pulls in the direction of its own self-contained narrative line, towards other similar and parallel stories, and towards certain patterns of language or a particular set of symbols. . . . In other words, the presence of an audience is vital to the completion and validity of the short-story [cycle] form just as it is in an oral setting." The title of Danticat's cycle sets it clearly within the oral narrative. She invites the reader not merely to read the book but to participate in a traditional Haitian storytelling ritual. "*Krik? Krak!* is call-response but it's also this feeling that you're not merely an observer—you're part of the story. Someone says, 'Krik?' and as loudly as you can you say 'Krak!' You urge the person to tell the story by your enthusiasm to hear it" (Shea 12).

In the stories, Danticat examines the lives of ordinary Haitians: those struggling to survive under the cruel Duvalier regime and others who have left the country, highlighting the distance between people's dreams and the distressing reality of their lives. As Ethan Casey points out: "Writers will spend precious time accounting for what has happened, it is true; the *literary* challenge is to write about Haiti in the vocabulary of human tragedy and human survival." As such, the book becomes a literary response to the Haitian situation and a feeling description of the immigration of the 1980s. Importantly, Danticat's presentation of the *theme* of storytelling through the *technique* of storytelling locates her writing within what Jay Clayton has called the "narrative turn" in recent ethnic fiction, which stresses the political dimensions of form, making the pragmatics of traditional narrative a theme in the fiction. Through technical experimentation with the story cycle, Danticat heightens the power of narrative, elucidating the significance of the oral mode to her characters by positioning the theme within a genre that engages it on different levels. Importantly, the blending of the performative dimension of storytelling in form and content allows Danticat to expand the reach of her art by making the text dramatize as well as signify.

In a note distributed by her publisher, Danticat defines the challenge she set herself: "I look to the past—to Haiti—hoping that the extraordinary female story tellers I grew up with—the ones that have passed on—will choose to tell their stories through my voice. For those of us who have a voice must speak to the present and the past" (qtd. in Casey 525–26). Danticat's narrative presents the voices and visions of women, usually mothers and daughters, whose personal tragedies impel them to form community in the midst of oppression and exile. Because the practice of breaking silence has become one of the shaping myths in the writings of ethnic women, storytelling in the cycle becomes both a medium of self-inscription and subjectivity and an instrument for dialogue. The telling of stories heals past experiences of loss and separation; it also forges bonds between women by preserving tradition and female identity as it converts stories of oppression into parables of self-affirmation and individual empowerment. The manner in which Danticat links the stories with the processes of self-inscription by the different women becomes a metaphor for the negotiation of the characters' strategies of survival.

The profoundly oral character of Haitian culture is illustrated on both textual and contextual levels in *Krik? Krak!*. The epigraph to the cycle, a quote from Sal Scalora from "White Darkness/Black Dreamings," discloses the purpose of the old tradition: "We tell the stories so that the young ones will know what came before them. They ask Krik? We say Krak! Our stories are kept in our hearts." Seven of the nine stories are told in the first person, with two of them written as monologues, and the rest alternating two voices in the narration. The epilogue, "Women Like Us," is written in the second person, a technique with rich connotations in a contemporary text inspired by the oral tradition. The art of storytelling figures importantly in several of the tales. The game of "Krik? Krak!" is played in the first story as a way for the refugees on the boat to wile away the fearful hours. In "Wall of Fire Rising," the inhabitants of the town who watched a state-sponsored newscast every evening "stayed at the site long after this gendarme had gone and told stories to one another beneath the big blank screen." The night woman whispers her mountain stories in her son's ear, "stories of the ghost women and the stars in their hair. I tell him of the deadly snakes lying at one end of the rainbow and the hat full of gold lying at the other. I tell him that if I cross a stream of glass-clear hibiscus, I can make myself a goddess." "We know people by

their stories", one of the characters declares, signalling how storytelling, which educates people in imaginative history and community values, provides an organic link between the past and the lives of the people in the present.

Other stories present verbal games that serve both as entertainment and strategy for identification and survival. Among the rituals that unite the women in the stories is the verbal code established in times of trial which was used to signal belonging. When Josephine meets a woman who claims to be part of the group who went on pilgrimages to the Massacre River, she questions her in the secret way because "if she were really from the river, she would know... all the things that my mother had said to the sun as we sat with our hands dipped in the water, questioning each other, making up codes and disciplines by which we would always know who the other daughters of the river were." This question-and-answer ritual is kept alive by Gracina and Caroline in Brooklyn: "We sat facing each other in the dark, playing a free-association game that Ma had taught us when we were girls.... Ma too had learned this game when she was a girl. Her mother belonged to a secret women's society in Ville Rose, where the women had to question each other before entering one another's houses." This game, played in the United States, carries within it memories of the lost country and links to those who have died. Gracina will be charged, in a dream, with remembering the lost past through the paradigm of the game: "If we were painters, which landscapes would we paint?... When you become mothers, how will you name your sons?... What kind of lullabies do we sing to our children at night? Where do you bury your dead?... What kind of legends will your daughters be told?" The commission, which emphasizes the power of the word, implies that the daughters must be similarly creative and constructive. The words and the hidden meanings in their mothers' verbal games form a significant starting point from which they can develop their own voice and autonomy because a space is created within the inherited contest in which their own representation is possible. Drawing from a rich source of oral traditions, as well as from their own experience and imagination, the daughters can then construct and claim their own subjectivity....

On different levels, ethnic short story cycles may project a desire to come to terms with a past that is both personal and collective: this type of fiction often explores the ethnic character and history of a community as a reflection of a personal odyssey of displacement, and search for self and community. More specifically, the two principal thematic constituents of the ethnic story cycle are the presentation of identity and community as separate entities and the notion of an identity within a community, again, a common theme of ethnic fiction. In Danticat's case, the textual tension arises from the presentation of women who struggle to establish and preserve the bonds of the Haitian community in the United States through powerful links with the mother country. Her stories, centering on the politics and the people of Haiti and Haitian immigrants to the United States, illustrate the numerous and varied connective strands that serve to draw the individuals of the short story cycle into a single community. The passage from appreciation of individual stories to the whole presented in the cycle marks the shift from the individual to community, setting the individual against the social group to which he or she belongs. The connections that are established will therefore yield what J. Gerald Kennedy has called the "defining experience" of the short story cycle: a vision of community accumulated by the reader's discernment of meanings and parallels inherent in the composite scheme. This movement, witnessed in other cycles by women such as Tan's *The Joy Luck Club* and Naylor's *The Women of Brewster Place,* constitutes the collective protagonist, the community, as the central character of the cycle.

The individual stories in *Krik? Krak!* present versions of life in and away from Haiti that create a composite portrait of the Haitian and her world. Although the stories are independent and written in different styles, they inform and enrich one another. In "Caroline's Wedding," the protagonist and her mother attend a funeral service for those who died at sea in the first story. The seaside town of Ville Rose figures in the lives of many of the female characters: the young woman and her parents in "Children of the Sea" seek refuge there when she is being sought by the police; this town is also the setting of the stories "The Missing Peace," "Night Women," and "Seeing Things Simply." More importantly, a common ancestry links the women in the diverse stories. The main character of "Between the Pool and the Gardenias" is the goddaughter of Lili from "A Wall of Fire Rising" and the granddaughter of Défilé, imprisoned for witchcraft in

"1937." As Renée Shea signals, these details serve to show that the many narrators come to understand their connections and their place primarily "through the bonds of women."

The presentation of women and their relationships, specifically that of mothers and daughters, is pivotal to Danticat's narrative. In this sense, she reflects the same concerns as another emblematic mother-daughter short story cycle, Amy Tan's *The Joy Luck Club.* Both complex ensembles of stories told by mothers and daughters are innovative variations of the traditional mother-daughter plot, which focuses on the daughter's perspective and the foregrounding of the voices of mothers as well as daughters (Heung 599). The women in both cycles are primarily responsible for the perpetuation of culture and bonds with the lost homeland. The mothers play major roles in the daughters' lives and growth, a role that provides the daughters with models for self-affirmation. Although the mothers all have different names and individual stories, they seem interchangeable in that their role as mother supersedes all others. The discrete identities of the women are woven into a collectivized interchangeability through the cycle's juxtapositions of characters and motifs. Through the narrative interweaving of time frames and voices, both Danticat and Tan unite generations of women within a relational network that links grandmothers, mothers, daughters, aunts, and sisters. For these women, however, "mutual nurturance does not rise from biological connections alone; rather, it is an act affirming consciously chosen allegiances" (Heung 612–13).

In stories where the mother/daughter bond is broken by the mother's death, this loss is viewed as devastating and must be compensated for by the daughter's taking the place of the mother or finding mother substitutes. Josephine, in "1937," is taught early in life the importance of a mother and need to belong to a history of women: "Manman had taken my hand and pushed it into the river, no further than my wrist.... With our hands in the water, Manman spoke to the sun. 'Here is my child, Josephine. We were saved from the tomb of this river when she was still in my womb. You spared us both, her and me, from this river where I lost my mother.'" She joins the yearly All Saint's Day pilgrimage to Massacre River with the women who had lost their mothers there:

My mother would hold my hand tightly as we walked toward the water. We were all daughters of that river, which had taken our mothers from us. Our mothers were the ashes and we were the light. Our mothers were the embers and we were the sparks. Our mothers were the flames and we were the blaze... The river was the place where it had all begun. "At least I gave birth to my daughter on the night that my mother was taken from me," she would say. "At least you came out at the right moment to take my mother's place."

The narrator of "Between the Pool and the Gardenias" reiterates the idea of the loss of a mother and importance of the link with past generations: "For no matter how much distance death tried to put between us, my mother would often come to visit me... There were many nights when I saw some old women leaning over my bed. 'That there is Marie,' my mother would say. 'She is now the last one of us left.'" As exemplified in this story, Danticat locates subjectivity in the maternal and employs it as a axis between the past and the present.

Other daughters feel the need to complete the work their mothers had left undone. Emilie, in "The Missing Peace," comes to Ville Rose to search for her mother, a journalist who disappeared while on assignment in the area. Part of her pursuit involves an attempt to bond with her lost mother by fulfilling one of her dreams: "I am going to sew [the small pieces of cloth] onto that purple blanket.... All her life, my mother's wanted to sew some old things together into that piece of purple cloth." Her search parallels that of Lamort, named because her mother died when she was born: "'They say a girl becomes a woman when she loses her mother,' [Emilie] said. 'You, child, were born a woman.'" An epiphany comes for both women as they are forced to face and accept the loss of their mothers: "I became a woman last night.... I lost my mother and all my other dreams", Emilie says. Lamort will take her mother's name, Marie Magdalène, as her rightful heritage. Though these stories reflect loss and a sense of a lack of affiliation, the overwhelming movement is toward reconciliation and pertinence, confirming the necessity and the possibility of seeking connection even after death.

Occasions in which communication between mother and child is obstructed result in confusion and unnecessary hurt. Two stories that mirror each other present the mother leading a secret life that her offspring does not know about. "Night Women," set in Haiti, is a mother's monologue as she gazes at her sleeping son. "There are two kinds of women: day women and night women. I am stuck between the day and night in a golden amber bronze", she says. Corollary to this, the story entitled "New York Day Women" has a daughter watching, unobserved, as her mother makes her way from her home in Brooklyn to Madison Avenue where in Central Park she cares for a young child while his Yuppie mother goes jogging: "This mother of mine, she stops at another hot-dog vendor and buys a frankfurter that she eats on the street. I never knew that she ate frankfurters... Day women come out when nobody expects them." Both stories emphasize the different worlds that mothers and children inhabit while linking the mothers. Furthermore, issues of race and class oppression suggested in both stories serve as factors that complicate maternal relationships because they lead the mothers to find ways of surviving or of asserting independence that they cannot, or will not, share with their children. The second story also suggests that the rift between mother and daughter may be brought about by attitudes towards immigration. Exile, which implies the loss of an original place, banishes belonging to memory and often causes dissociation from both the old ways and the new home. The process of diasporic self-formation is presented here through the growing distance between mother and daughter who struggle to define new identities and decide what to keep and what to relinquish.

This theme recurs in "Caroline's Wedding," where conflict centers on the American-born daughter's impending marriage with a Bahamanian and her mother's reactions to it. Gracina, the daughter born in Haiti, tries to serve as buffer between the two points of view. She understands her mother's dreams: "Ma wanted Eric to officially come and ask her permission to marry her daughter. She wanted him to bring his family to our house and have his father ask her blessing. She wanted Eric to kiss up to her, escort her around, buy her gifts, and shower her with compliments. Ma wanted a full-blown church wedding. She wanted Eric to be Haitian." For Caroline, the old country's rules do not determine her obligations nor her mother's authority. The traditional role of a Haitian mother has been greatly curtailed in America, and the mother has had to learn to deal with daughters whose way of life is American:

"When we were children, whenever we rejected symbols of Haitian culture, Ma used to excuse us with great embarrassment and say, 'You know, they are American.' Why didn't we like the thick fatty pig skin that she would deep-fry so long that it tasted like rubber. We were Americans and we had *no taste buds*. A double tragedy." "In Haiti, you own your children and they find it natural", their mother would say, which explains her sense of loss at what she considers abandonment by her younger daughter. The relationships between the mother and daughters in this Haitian American family underline some of the cross-generational and cross-cultural conflicts typical of ethnic texts. At the end of the story, the relationship will rest on the daughters' recognition of the value of the mother's establishment of community that provides them with the resources they need to survive on their own.

There is an obsessive need to find and establish familial and historical connections with other Haitians. Because "Ma says all Haitians know each other", the community in America survives. The immigrants experience continued and profound nostalgia for the lost home though their children chaff at the extent of this loyalty: "Twenty years we have been saving all kinds of things for the relatives in Haiti. I need a place in the garage for an exercise bike." The song "*Beloved Haiti, there is no place like you, I had to leave you before I could understand you*" is sung by the refugees in the first story and listened to on the radio in the last.

In consequence, history also becomes a protagonist in *Krik? Krak!* as stories set in Haiti directly or indirectly involve historical events. "1937," for instance, centers on the Dominican Republic's dictator Rafael Trujillo's massacre of Haitians at the river separating Haiti from the Dominican Republic. Furthermore, Danticat has commented that the original title of the first story was "From the Ocean Floor" but that she decided to change it to "Children of the Sea" to emphasize the link to the Middle Passage. "It's a very powerful image—from the ocean floor," she explains. "No one knows how many people were lost on The Middle Passage. There are no records or graves—and the ocean floor is where our fossils are. The journey from Haiti in the 1980s is like a new middle passage. Not to romanticize it, but the comforting thing about death is that somehow all these people will meet. I often think that if my ancestors are at the bottom of the sea, then I too am a part of that. So we are all children of the sea" (Shea 12). Gracina, in "Caroline's Wedding," reflects on this ancient belief that links Haitians: "There are people in Ville Rose, the village where my mother is from in Haiti, who believe that there are special spots in the sea where lost Africans who jumped off the slave ships still rest, that those who died at sea have been chosen to make that journey in order to be reunited with their long-lost relations." The death of the people in the refugee boat in the first story will establish historical links, forging a community of Haitians that includes not only those alive in the present time but also those lost in the past.

Though the stories in *Krik? Krak!* have a continuity derived from recurrent themes and motifs, they are more profoundly linked by a spiritual vision where the bonds between women are imperative for survival. The most vivid metaphor for interconnections, echoes, and blending appears with Danticat's image of braids in the final section, "Epilogue: Women Like Us," a meditative finale to the nine stories. "When you write," she says, "it's like braiding your hair. Taking a handful of coarse unruly strands and attempting to bring them unity." Danticat uses this ritualistic image to illustrate the inseparable strands of history and the need for community:

> Your mother, she introduced you to the first echoes of the tongue that you now speak when at the end of the day she would braid your hair while you sat between her legs, scrubbing the kitchen pots.... When she was done, she would ask you to name each braid after those nine hundred and ninety-nine women who were boiling in your blood, and since you had written them down and memorized them, the names would come rolling off your tongue. And this was your testament to the way that these women lived and died and lived again.

The persona in the epilogue pays tribute to what she calls "Kitchen Poets," those voices "urging you to speak through the blunt tip of your pencil." The storytelling tradition, essential for the transmission of lives and cultures, strengthens the connections between women:

> With every step you take, there is an army of women watching over you. We are never any farther than the sweat on your brows or the dust on your toes... you have never been able to escape the pounding of a thousand other hearts that have outlived yours by thousands of years. And over the years when you have

needed us, you have always cried 'Krik?' and
we have answered 'Krak!' and it has shown us
that you have not forgotten us.

The use of the second-person narrator implicates the reader/listener, inviting her to participate in the storytelling act, commisioning her, as
with many of the characters, with the task of
telling, of participating in the process of creating
and preserving community though narrative.

Considering the urgency and implications of
the identity politics within which Danticat works
and her awareness of the dynamics of the culturally diverse audience of her story, her innovative
use of narrative perspective in the concluding
section of her cycle further challenges the construct of a monolithic "you." Ethnic writers who
use the second-person address are aware that
"assumptions that white middle and upper class
audiences bring to the act of reading are thus
foregrounded and exposed—particularly the
insidious assumption that they are, 'naturally,'
the universal you addressed by the text"
(Richardson 323–24). Opening up a possibility
for the narratee, the second-person point of view
also opens up a possibility for the reader. The use
of the narrative "you" becomes one of the more
interesting facets of literary theory and criticism
because, while in standard fiction the protago-
nist/narratee is quite distinct from the actual or
implied reader, this mode of narration often collapses this distinction because the "you" could
refer to the reader as well.

Danticat's epilogue to her short story cycle
forces the reader to face the experience of cultural betweenness and choices in the manner that
implicates most directly, pulling her into the
drama and suggesting that this is, more than
just a Haitian-American story and dilemma,
everyone's as well. Although the oral community
figured in *Krik? Krak!* is clearly distinct from the
mass readership in the US and European mar-
kets, Danticat, by identifying and contesting the
assumed "you," generates a widening of discur-
sive space, where more and more diverse voices
may be heard and similarly plural subjectivities
may be addressed. This concluding strategy is
Danticat's *tour de force,* the final touch to the
integration of theme and technique, as she
weaves the formal strands of oral narrative and
story cycle with the contextual telling of wom-
en's lives, expanding the reach of the stories and
drawing more people into the experience.

This short story cycle, as a discourse on
ethnic self-definition has recollections or personal experiences of Haiti as an important aspect
of the creation of self. The questions the characters ask themselves are answered through narratives that, in reflecting the form of the oral
narrative, articulate almost epic tales of survivors. Edwidge Danticat has turned to roots—
family, community, and ethnicity—as a source
of personal identity and creative expression. The
manner in which she, like other ethnic writers,
has appropriated the short story cycle as a metaphor for the fragmentation and multiplicity of
ethnic lives is itself an articulation of the process
towards ethnic self-identification. The subsequent narrative, in turning to past forms of narration and reflecting a tendency towards a
hybrid form, provides enriching glimpses of societies in the process of transformation and
growth. The vivid dream and aspiration that
remains at the end of the book is succinctly proclaimed by Josephine: "I raised my head toward
the sun thinking, one day I may just see my
mother there. 'Let her flight be joyful,' I said to
Jacqueline. 'And mine and yours too.'"

Source: Rocio G. Davis, "Oral Narrative as Short Story
Cycle: Forging Community in Edwidge Danticat's *Krik?
Krak!*," in *MELUS*, Vol. 26, No. 2, Summer 2001, pp. 65–80.

Hal Wylie

In the following review, Danticat's collection Krik?
Krak! *is praised as "well told and dramatic." Wylie
also notes that the author's work places particular
focus on "parental stories" passed on to instill
"essential values."*

Edwidge Danticat is a major new talent who
combines her Haitian heritage with her first-
class American education to produce stories
that transcend the quest for Haitian identity to
scrutinize the modern world. Born in Haiti in
1969, she spent her first twelve years in the new
Haiti of violence and horror, before moving to
New York City. The emotions of her childhood
made her a published writer by age fourteen, and
seem to have sharpened her vision.

Danticat is not the first Haitian to write in
English, but she *is* the first to gain attention. Her
hybrid nature reflects the no-longer-isolated Haiti
that has emerged as a pivotal crossroads of the
Third World, with large diasporas of Haitians
living in New York, Canada, and France.
Danticat is representative of the new immigrant
literatures. Her characters are haunted by their

mixed culture but often are able to transcend the problem and find ways to cope. Perhaps this is true because the lines of communication between mothers and daughters (and other relatives) remain open, even when major conflicts emerge. Danticat and her daughter protagonists are good at exploring their heritage, tradition, and current situation to locate central values.

Krik? Krak! consists of nine stories, the last almost a novella. The first five are more fictional, more sensational, and sketch in the major aspects of Haiti's social situation today: the boat people, the misery and violence, the Macoutes. They are well told and dramatic. However, I prefer the last four, which are more autobiographical. Here the author's power of transforming small everyday realities into "story," are most clearly visible; the directly observed seems more universal, the stories more gripping.

The last story "Caroline's Wedding," is the longest and best. Recalling the family drama of Danticat's 1994 novel *Breath, Eyes, Memory*, (see *WLT* 69:2, p. 417), it is the most penetrating in exploring the psychology of assimilation. There are two daughters here, both resisting the domination of a tyrannical mother. The protagonist watches her sister break away while moderating the trauma. Caroline was born without a left forearm, an existential reality that increases the impact and credibility of the story as it is woven into the frame of cross-references. She likes to have her stub stroked, even though almost everybody is afraid of it. Her mother tells its story (she has lots of stories, which explain and justify reality): pregnant, she was arrested in a sweatshop raid and given a shot to tranquilize her in prison.

In all her works, Danticat focuses on the way parental stories pass on a heritage and mold the child's character.

Source: Hal Wylie, Review of *Krik? Krak!*, in *World Literature Today*, Vol. 70, No. 1, Winter 1996, p. 224.

SOURCES

Danticat, Edwidge, "Caroline's Wedding," in *Krik? Krak!*, Soho Press, 1995, reprint, Vintage Press, 1996, pp. 155–216.

Eder, Richard, "Off the Island," in *New York Times*, March 21, 2004, http://query.nytimes.com/gst/fullpage.html?res=9507E0D6123EF9 (accessed October 20, 2006).

Fichtner, Margaria, "Author Edwidge Danticat Writes about Being Young, Black, Haitian, and Female," in *Knight-Ridder/Tribune News Service*, May 1, 1995.

Hart, Jordana, "Danticat's Stories Pulse with Haitian Heartbeat," in *Boston Globe*, July 19, 1995, "Living" section, p. 70.

Jamison, Laura, "The Exquisite Tales of Edwidge Danticat," in *San Francisco Examiner*, July 19, 1995, p. C.

Sheanin, Wendy, "Stories Resound with Haiti's Tragedy, Spirit," in *San Francisco Chronicle*, May 28, 1995, p. RV-4.

Wylie, Hal, "Haiti," in *World Literature Today*, Vol. 70, No. 1, Winter 1996, pp. 224, 225.

FURTHER READING

Aristide, Jean-Bertrand, *In the Parish of the Poor: Writings from Haiti*, translated by Amy Wilentz, Orbis Books, 1990.

> In this book, Aristide, a former president of Haiti, gives his view of the problems in Haiti and their possible solutions. The book has been used in classrooms to provoke discussions on social justice. It includes some of Aristide's sermons (he was once a Roman Catholic priest).

Chin, Pat, Gregory Dunkel, and Sara Flounders, *Haiti: A Slave Revolution: 200 Years after 1804*, International Action Center, 2004.

> Haiti's slave revolution and its resistance to occupation and dictatorship are recounted through the art, poems, and essays collected in this anthology. Topics include Haiti's impact on the United States, the effects of U.S. embargoes against the country, and reasons given for occupation.

Farmer, Paul, *The Uses of Haiti*, Common Courage Press, 2005.

> This book is an impassioned critique of U.S. policy in Haiti by a physician and anthropologist who at the time of publication had worked for twenty-five years in the country. Farmer traces the history of injustices in Haiti, from the eighteenth-century slave economy to the 1915 invasion by the U.S. Marines, and the subsequent U.S. support of dictators such as "Papa Doc" Duvalier.

Metraux, Alfred, *Voodoo in Haiti*, Pantheon, 1989.

> Metraux describes the lives and rituals of the Haitian voodoo priests and investigates the origin and development of the religion.

The Diamond as Big as the Ritz

F. SCOTT FITZGERALD

1922

F. Scott Fitzgerald's story "The Diamond as Big as the Ritz" first appeared in the June 1922 issue of *The Smart Set*, a popular magazine of the 1920s. Fitzgerald had attempted to sell it to the *Saturday Evening Post*, which had published many of his other stories, but its harsh anticapitalistic message was rejected by the conservative magazine. In September 1922, the story appeared in his second collection, *Tales of the Jazz Age*.

The story was inspired by Fitzgerald's 1915 visit to the Montana home of a Princeton classmate, Charles Donahoe, and was one of Fitzgerald's few forays into the realm of fantasy. It tells of young John Unger, who is invited to visit a classmate at his impossibly lavish home in Montana. Gradually, Unger learns the sinister origins of his host's wealth and the frightening lengths to which he will go to preserve it.

In this story, Fitzgerald begins to explore many of the themes he used later when writing his best-known work, *The Great Gatsby*. The carelessness and immorality of the vastly wealthy and the American fascination with wealth are personified by Braddock Washington and his narcississtic family, who seem to believe that all others have been put on Earth for their amusement. The cataclysmic ending, in which the family and their home are destroyed, shows the result of their single-minded pursuit.

AUTHOR BIOGRAPHY

Francis Scott Key Fitzgerald was born in St. Paul, Minnesota, on September 24, 1896, to Edward and Mary ("Mollie") Fitzgerald. In 1898, the family moved to upstate New York, where Edward worked as a salesman for Procter and Gamble. By the time the family returned to St. Paul, Fitzgerald was twelve years old, and his parents enrolled him at St. Paul Academy. Though Fitzgerald's family was by no means poor, they were not nearly as wealthy as most of the families that sent their sons to the academy, and it was here that Fitzgerald's lifelong fascination with the lives of the extremely wealthy began. At St. Paul Academy, he wrote stories for the school magazine and performed in school plays. After the academy, he went on to the Newman School in Hackensack, New Jersey, a Catholic prep school. He continued his writing at the Newman School.

In 1913, Fitzgerald entered Princeton, where he made important friendships that would last for years to come. He spent so much of his time writing stories and plays for college publications, however, that his academics suffered, and in 1916, he withdrew from Princeton due to low grades. In 1917, he entered the army but was disappointed that in his fifteen months' service, he was never sent overseas. One of the most significant results of Fitzgerald's military service was that, while stationed in Alabama, he fell in love with Zelda Sayre, the daughter of a judge on the Alabama Supreme Court. Also during this time, he wrote the first draft of his first novel, *This Side of Paradise*.

Fitzgerald was discharged from the army in 1919; in March 1920, *This Side of Paradise* was published. A week later he married Zelda Sayre. That same year, Fitzgerald's first collection of short stories was published, entitled *Flappers and Philosophers*. These two books established Fitzgerald's reputation as the official chronicler of the Jazz Age, the name used for the 1920s. He was especially known for his stories featuring flappers, young women exploring the new social and fashion freedoms and rebelling against the restrictive mores of the past.

In October 1921, Zelda Fitzgerald gave birth to the couple's first and only child, a girl named Frances Scott Key Fitzgerald, whom the couple called Scottie. Then in 1922, Fitzgerald had two more books published: *The Beautiful*

F. Scott Fitzgerald © *Bettmann/Corbis*

and Damned, a novel, and *Tales of the Jazz Age*, his second collection of short stories, which includes "A Diamond as Big as the Ritz."

Fitzgerald's relationship with his wife Zelda was a tempestuous one, even during their courtship, and the combination of their extravagant lifestyle, Fitzgerald's heavy drinking, and Zelda's gradually deteriorating mental health took a toll on their marriage. In 1924, the couple spent time in France, where Fitzgerald wrote his best-known novel, *The Great Gatsby* (1925). In France, Fitzgerald also became good friends with Ernest Hemingway.

After *The Great Gatsby*, the quality of Fitzgerald's work was erratic, affected by his continued drinking and his stressful relationship with Zelda. However, his 1926 collection of stories, *All the Sad Young Men*, garnered favorable reviews, though it did little to improve the Fitzgeralds' financial situation. Despite mounting debt, the couple lived extravagantly, much like the characters in Fitzgerald's fiction. In 1930, Zelda suffered a complete mental collapse and was hospitalized.

In an effort to get out of debt, Fitzgerald wrote dozens of short stories during this time, including many that were not up to the quality of his former work. In 1934, he finally finished his fourth novel, *Tender Is the Night*, which he had been working on sporadically since 1925. At the time of its release, critics were not fond of the book, feeling that it was a less successful treatment of the same themes explored in *The Great Gatsby*. Unsurprisingly, the antics of the fabulously wealthy were not as well received by a nation mired in economic depression. In 1935, Fitzgerald published a collection of short stories entitled *Taps at Reveille*, which was reviewed by few critics. Fitzgerald was aware of the decline of his work and wrote a series of essays on his own emotional decline as an artist, published in *Esquire* magazine.

In 1937, Fitzgerald moved to Los Angeles, California, to find work as a screenwriter. While working in the film industry, he began writing a novel set in Hollywood, to be titled *The Last Tycoon*. Before he could finish the book, however, Fitzgerald died suddenly of a heart attack on December 21, 1940. The unfinished novel was published posthumously in 1941. He was survived by his wife Zelda, who died in a hospital fire in 1948, and his daughter Scottie, who died in 1986.

PLOT SUMMARY

As "The Diamond as Big as the Ritz" opens, sixteen-year-old John T. Unger is leaving the small middle-class town of Hades to attend St. Midas School near Boston, "the most expensive and the most exclusive boys' preparatory school in the world." His mother packs his trunk, his father gives him money, and after a tearful goodbye, John T. Unger is off to attend school with boys from the country's wealthiest families.

In his second year at St. Midas, John meets Percy Washington. Well-dressed and reserved, Percy has little to say about his home or family, until he invites John to spend the summer at his family's home in Montana. On the train ride to Percy's home, Percy tells John that his father is "the richest man in the world" and that he has a diamond "bigger than the Ritz-Carlton Hotel."

The train stops in the dismal village of Fish, inhabited by twelve men who gape at the wealthy travelers. From here John and Percy take a buggy to another location, where an elaborate, luxurious car (which Percy dismisses as "an old junk") awaits them. At one point two black servants attach cables to the car, and it is hoisted over a rocky passage and set down on the other side. Percy tells John that his father has managed to prevent his land from ever being surveyed, and the only thing that could ever be used to find them is "aeroplanes"; fortunately, his father has anti-aircraft guns at the ready.

John is taken aback at this information until the sight of the Washingtons' impossibly lavish home sweeps all other concerns aside. As they walk through the halls, John discovers some are carpeted with fur, and some are made of crystal with tropical fish swimming beneath; at dinner, the family and their guest eat off plates made of solid diamond.

The next morning at breakfast, Percy tells John his family's history. Percy's grandfather, a direct descendant of George Washington, discovered the mountain-sized diamond when he went west to start his own ranch, just after the Civil War ended. He realized that if he tried to sell such a diamond, the bottom would fall out of the market. So after gathering a workforce of black slaves, whom he fooled into believing that the South won the Civil War, he set out to sell his diamonds in secret to assorted kings, princes, and other dignitaries. His son Braddock continued his work, and when he had amassed enough wealth to keep his family living in luxury for generations, he sealed up the mine.

After breakfast, John takes a walk on the property and runs into Kismine, Percy's younger sister, with whom he falls in love instantly. She tells him she likes him, as well. They walk back to the house together.

Later Percy and his father show John around the property. Mr. Washington shows him the slaves' quarters, housing descendants of his grandfather's original slaves. The current slaves still do not know that slavery has been abolished. He also points out the golf course, which is entirely a green, "no fairway, no rough, no hazards." Finally, they come to a deep pit, covered with an iron grating. Down in the pit, two dozen men are imprisoned. Mr. Washington tells John their crime: they are aviators who accidentally discovered the diamond mine and now must be prevented, at all costs, from revealing the Washingtons' secret.

As the end of summer nears, John and Kismine decide that they will elope the following June, since her father will never allow her to marry someone from John's lowly social and financial status. Kismine casually mentions some visitors she and her sister had. When John inquires further about these visitors, Kismine admits that her father had them murdered at the end of their visits, so they could not reveal the Washingtons' secret; she also admits that the same fate awaits John. Outraged, John tells Kismine they are not in love anymore and announces his intention to escape over the mountains before Mr. Washington can have him killed. Kismine tells him she wants to go with him, and John softens, realizing she must really love him. They plan to escape the next night.

Later that same evening, however, John is awakened by a noise, and thinking it is someone sent to kill him, he gets up and goes into the hall. He hears Mr. Washington urgently summoning his servants and realizes some crisis has occurred. He goes to Kismine's room; she tells him that there are at least a dozen airplanes over the property and that her father is going to open fire on them with his anti-aircraft guns. John and Kismine waken Jasmine, Kismine's older sister, and the three of them flee to a wooded area where they watch the battle.

By four in the morning, the planes have destroyed much of the Washingtons' property. John, watching from a distance, hears footsteps. Curious, he follows the sound and sees Braddock Washington on the mountain with two of his slaves, who are carrying an enormous diamond. Washington begins speaking, and John realizes he is talking to God—offering him the diamond as a bribe. He will give God the diamond if God will restore his life and property to its former glory.

The bribe does not work; the planes descend, and Washington and his wife flee underground, beneath the diamond mountain. When John tells Kismine and Jasmine this, the sisters scream. "The mountain is wired!" Kismine sobs. A few moments later, the mountain glows a brilliant yellow, and the Washingtons' lavish home explodes. Both the Washingtons and their riches are gone.

After fleeing to a distance safely remote from the scene of the battle, John asks Kismine to show him what jewels she has brought with her, to support them in the luxury to which she has become accustomed. After showing him the jewelry she brought with her, Kismine realizes she accidentally brought rhinestones she received from one of their ill-fated visitors. John gloomily tells her they will have to live in

Hades. Thinking of their poor future, they go to sleep under the stars.

CHARACTERS

The Prisoners
Underneath his all-green golf course, Braddock Washington has imprisoned two dozen aviators who had the misfortune to discover his property. They are a spirited bunch, shouting curses and defiant insults at Washington when he stops by for a visit but also trying to talk him into releasing them. When they hear that one of their number managed to escape, they dance and sing in celebration.

John T. Unger
John T. Unger is a young man from the town of Hades, "a small town on the Mississippi River." His family is affluent, but not as fabulously wealthy as the other families whose sons attend the exclusive St. Midas School.

He is more sentimental than the ultra-narcissistic Washingtons (when he parts with his father to leave for school, there are "tears streaming from his eyes,") but his blind adoration of wealth and the wealthy reveal him to be almost as shallow. The few early misgivings he has about the Washingtons are quickly swept away by his hedonistic enjoyment of their riches.

He tells Percy, "The richer a fella is, the better I like him." He repeatedly brings up the Schnlitzer-Murphys, a very wealthy family he visited one Easter, describing their jewels and quoting Mr. Schnlitzer-Murphy. When John falls in love with Kismine, their relationship has all the maturity of two ten-year-olds at play. John's love for Kismine is based on her physical perfection: "He was critical about women. A single defect—a thick ankle, a hoarse voice, a glass eye—was enough to make him utterly indifferent."

Even after seeing the men Braddock Washington has imprisoned, John does not seem overly concerned. It is not until he learns that he himself will be murdered to prevent his revealing the Washingtons' secrets that John becomes outraged.

Braddock Washington
The patriarch of the Washington family and the most extreme example of its arrogance and

self-importance, Braddock Washington is a cold, unfeeling man who is "utterly uninterested in any ideas or opinions except his own." He views people as either assets or liabilities, calculating what use can be made of them or what obstacle they might present. The most extreme example of this is his continued use of slave labor. Kismine echoes her father's attitude when the attacking aircraft destroy the slaves' quarters: "There go fifty thousand dollars' worth of slaves . . . at pre-war prices."

The pinnacle of Braddock Washington's arrogance comes near the end of the story when, with his home under attack, he climbs up the mountain along with two slaves carrying an enormous diamond, and offers the diamond to God as a bribe. In return, he requests that his life be restored to its former state. Even when speaking to God, Braddock is not humble; instead, he speaks with "a quality of monstrous condescension." Washington's idea of how life for himself and his family should progress is summed up in the design of his own golf course: "It's all a green, you see—no fairway, no rough, no hazards."

Jasmine Washington

Unlike Percy and Kismine, Jasmine shows small signs of being interested in people and events beyond herself. She had hoped to become "a canteen expert" during World War I, and near the end of the story, when it becomes clear that she, her sister, and John will all be poor, she volunteers to work as a washerwoman and support them all. However, the fact that she continues to invite guests to the Washington home, knowing their ultimate fate, and her great disappointment that the war ended before she could fulfill her "canteen expert" dream, indicate that Jasmine has not fully grasped the concept of compassion.

Kismine Washington

Percy's sister Kismine, who is about sixteen, is a curious combination of childlike innocence and callow self-absorption. Fitzgerald notes that both she and her brother "seemed to have inherited the arrogant attitude in all its harsh magnificence from their father. A chaste and consistent selfishness ran like a pattern through their every idea." While Kismine expresses sincere regret over the fate of visitors to the Washington home, her empathy is limited; she tells John she had not wanted to tell him about his impending

TOPICS FOR FURTHER STUDY

- In telling the Washington family history, Fitzgerald refers to several actual historical figures. Research the following names and write a short paragraph for each one, indicating the relevance of the historic figure to the story: George Washington, Lord Baltimore, and General Forrest. In addition, Mr. Washington's first and middle names, Braddock Tarleton, have historic significance; include these names in your research.

- Research the size of the world's largest diamonds. How do they compare to the size of the Washington's diamond? Make a chart comparing the size of the top three diamonds to each other and to the fictional diamond in Fitzgerald's story. Given the monetary value of the world's largest diamonds, estimate how much a diamond as large as this fictional diamond would be worth.

- Using the description of the Washingtons' chateau as a guide, draw or paint your own representation of the outside of the chateau, the interior, or one of the rooms described (John T. Unger's room and bath, for example).

- Fitzgerald uses exaggeration to make the Washingtons' home and lifestyle as outrageously lavish as possible. Try the opposite: Use exaggeration to describe, in a few paragraphs, the smallest and most simple living quarters you can imagine.

- John T. Unger tells Kismine that it is impossible to be both free and poor. Do you agree with him? Write a short essay explaining your position.

assassination, because she knew it would make things "sort of depressing" for him.

Kismine's lack of empathy is somewhat understandable, however, given her complete ignorance of the world beyond her own home. She is clearly unfamiliar with the concepts of poverty and suffering; when John tells her they must flee her home to get away from the attacking airplanes, she cries, "We'll be poor, won't we? Like people in books... Free and poor! What fun!"

Percy Washington

Percy, John's friend from school, is much like the rest of the Washingtons: shallow, boastful, and arrogant. The first words he speaks in the story are: "My father... is by far the richest man in the world." He is fawned upon by his mother, who has little interest in her two daughters.

THEMES

Immorality of the Wealthy

A common theme in Fitzgerald's work is that extreme wealth often leads to immoral behavior. In the case of the Washingtons, this effect is compounded by their near complete isolation from the rest of the world. Percy, Kismine, and Jasmine were brought up to believe they are better than all others by virtue of their fortune, and they were sheltered from anyone who might challenge this notion.

Imprisoning or killing visitors who might divulge their secrets has become a routine business tactic for Braddock Washington. Kismine finds this mildly upsetting, but her own distorted moral views are revealed when John asks her when her father has summer visitors murdered: "In August usually—or early in September. It's only natural for us to get all the pleasure out of them that we can first." Braddock Washington shares this belief that others are intended to be enjoyed or used by his family. Percy tells John that to design the Washingtons' chateau and grounds, his father simply kidnapped a number of design professionals and put them to work.

Does the acquisition of wealth lead to immoral behavior or is it that the people who pursue great wealth are already morally bankrupt? While Fitzgerald does not answer this question, he does illustrate how selfishness and delusions of self-importance are passed on from one generation to the next.

Freedom and Imprisonment

While most people equate greater wealth with greater freedom, this is not the case in "The Diamond as Big as the Ritz." Braddock Washington's prison is a luxurious one, to be sure, but it still isolates him from the rest of the world. He has no friends or colleagues, only slaves. He views others with suspicion. His children's visitors must be killed when their visit is over—certainly an impediment to their forming lasting friendships outside the family. His entire family is imprisoned by the diamond mountain they must protect at all costs.

There are numerous examples of imprisonment in the story. The most literal example is that of the aviators trapped under the Washingtons' golf course. Why does Braddock Washington imprison rather than kill the aviators? He seems to enjoy verbally sparring with them. Perhaps Washington, at some level, is so desperate for some peers of his own, some basic human connection, that he keeps them alive to fulfill that need.

Another example is the black slaves whom the Washingtons have tricked into believing that slavery was never abolished and that the South won the Civil War. Ironically, Washington's behavior towards the slaves, other than his obvious racism, is not much different than his behavior towards outsiders; since he views all people as commodities, it is not surprising he finds slave labor a sensible option.

When John and Kismine plan their escape from the Washingtons' property, Kismine is delighted at the prospect of being "free and poor." John tells her, "It's impossible to be both together." While there may be truth in this statement, it is also true that great wealth, for the Washingtons, has not resulted in complete freedom. The conclusion is that freedom is not a function of wealth or poverty at all, but rather a state of mind, a state of mind which, with their dependence on wealth and status, none of these characters has achieved.

American Idolatry of Wealth

John T. Unger personifies the fascination that the American middle class has with wealth and the wealthy. John quotes statistics about the number of millionaires in the United States, prattles on about the jewels owned by the Schnlitzer-Murphys, and sets aside his few reservations about the morals of the Washingtons when he sees their opulent home. According to Fitzgerald, John has been trained to feel this awe for wealth by his family and his hometown: "The simple piety prevalent in Hades has the earnest worship and respect for riches as the first article of its creed—had John felt otherwise than radiantly humble before them, his parents would have turned away in horror at the blasphemy." In the early 2000s, one can see the same fascination with the rich evinced by the success of tabloids that doggedly pursue rich celebrities, seeking to expose intimate details of their lives. One can imagine that John T. Unger would have been a big fan of the television show *Lifestyles of the Rich and Famous*.

STYLE

Point of View

"The Diamond as Big as the Ritz" is told from the third person point of view, from the perspective of John T. Unger. Through Unger's perspective, Fitzgerald condemns not just the Washingtons' amoral lifestyle, but also the middle-class attitude towards wealth that makes their lifestyle possible. The reader waits in vain for Unger to speak out, to express some outrage or horror at the Washingtons' way of life, but until his own life is threatened, Unger seems willing to overlook almost anything to continue enjoying the luxuries and pleasures of their home. Because Unger is not as wealthy as his classmates at St. Midas, he is even more easily seduced by their lifestyle, and his astonishment at the home's extravagance is more in line with what the average reader might feel.

Mythical Allusions

Many references to myths and fables make the story seem more like a fable itself. On the first page, when the reader learns that John is from Hades—the underworld of the dead in Greek myth—the story veers from the path of realism into the realm of fantasy. Characters in the story repeatedly make reference to how hot it is in Hades ("Is it hot enough for you down there?"), and when John leaves to go to St. Midas— another reference to a fable—his father assures him that "we'll keep the home fires burning."

Other references to historical and mythical figures abound. When Percy and John near the Washingtons' property, John muses, "What desperate transaction lay hidden here? What a moral expedient of a bizarre Croesus?" Croesus was a Greek king known for his great riches. More than once, the Washingtons' property is

referred to as "El Dorado," the name of a mythical South American kingdom fabled to be rich with gold. Finally, when Braddock Washington is offering his diamond bribe to God, Fitzgerald writes, "Prometheus Enriched was calling to witness forgotten sacrifices, forgotten rituals, prayers obsolete before the birth of Christ." This is a reference to *Prometheus Bound*, a drama based on myth by the Greek writer Aeschylus. Prometheus was a mythological character who defended men from the Greek god Zeus; Zeus punished him by chaining him to a rock and having an eagle endlessly eat his liver.

All these references to legend and myth cause the reader to think of the story as a symbolic fable, rather than a realistic story. Moreover, they suggest that the themes in this story are universal and ageless.

Hyperbole

Fitzgerald's use of hyperbole, or extreme exaggeration, increases the feeling of fantasy, and his descriptions of the Washingtons' home have a surreal quality. By making the chateau impossibly luxurious, Fitzgerald lets the reader know, once again, that this is not a literal or realistic story:

> There was a room where the solid, soft gold of the walls yielded to the pressure of his hand, and a room that was like a platonic conception of the ultimate prison—ceiling, floor, and all, it was lined with an unbroken mass of diamonds, diamonds of every size and shape, until, lit with tall violet lamps in the corners, it dazzled the eyes with a whiteness that could be compared only with itself, beyond human wish or dream.

A diamond as big as an entire mountain, a clear crystal bathtub with tropical fish swimming beneath the glass, hallways lined with fur, dinner plates of solid diamond, a car interior upholstered in tapestries, gold and precious gems— all these extravagant, surreal elements add to the otherworldly character of the Washingtons' property. Furthermore, they seemed to suggest a sense that too much is indeed too much. The overkill is distasteful, even grotesque.

Religious Imagery

Fitzgerald uses religious images throughout the story to illustrate, among other things, the absolute corruption of the Washingtons, and to a lesser extent, the corruption of John Unger. From his hometown of Hades (Hell), John's parents send him to St. Midas School. It is easy to guess the priorities of a school that would

COMPARE
&
CONTRAST

- **1920s:** Though more women are joining the workforce (21 percent of women aged sixteen and over—though most of them hold clerical, domestic, or factory jobs), women are still generally discouraged from working, especially if they are mothers. Therefore, most women's standard of living depends solely on the income of their husbands, and fathers (such as Braddock Washington) are reluctant to allow their daughters to marry men with unimpressive incomes. The average age for a woman to marry is twenty. (Zelda Sayre first refuses Fitzgerald and agrees to marry him only after he achieves some success with his writing.)

  Today: Over 60 percent of women aged sixteen and over are part of the U.S. workforce, and in over half of the country's married couples with children, both parents work outside the home. The average age for a woman to marry is about twenty-five.

- **1920s:** Following World War I, the United States retreats into isolationism. Congress votes against joining the League of Nations, paranoia about communism is rampant, and immigration is restricted.

  Today: Advances in communication technologies and global business trade make a policy of isolationism virtually impossible. In the latter half of the twentieth century and in the early 2000s, U.S. intervention in the affairs of other countries is common (though not always popular). One recent example of such intervention is the U.S. invasion of Iraq in 2003.

- **1920s:** In 1920, the yearly tuition at Phillips Exeter Academy in New Hampshire, one of the country's most exclusive prep schools, is two hundred and fifty dollars. In the story, John T. Unger attends St. Midas School, "the most expensive and the most exclusive boys' preparatory school in the world."

  Today: The yearly tuition for day students at Phillips Exeter Academy is over twenty-five thousand dollars a year; boarding students pay nearly thirty-five thousand dollars a year.

---

elevate the mythical King Midas to sainthood and the priorities of the parents whose sons attend it. From there John goes on to the Washingtons' home, stopping on his way at the village of Fish, inhabited only by twelve men. The fish, of course, is a symbol of Christianity, and the twelve men recall Jesus' apostles. The twelve men of Fish, however, are "beyond all religion." They all turn out to watch the train come in and the wealthy passengers disembark. In this context, even the apostles are spellbound by wealth.

The Washingtons' chateau and property are described as a paradise rivaled only by Heaven itself:

> The many towers, the slender tracery of the sloping parapets, the chiseled wonder of a thousand yellow windows with their oblongs and hexagons and triangles of golden light, the shattered softness of the intersecting planes of star-shine and blue shade, all trembled on John's spirit like a chord of music.

And, as with Heaven, John discovers that once he has arrived there, he cannot return to the mortal world, thanks to Braddock Washington, reigning god of this Eden. The climactic scene, in which Washington offers his bribe to God, illustrates that Braddock sees himself as God's equal, or even superior: "He, Braddock Washington, Emperor of Diamonds, king and priest of the age of gold, arbiter of splendor and luxury, would offer up a treasure such as princes before him had never dreamed of, offer it up not in suppliance, but in pride." When he finishes his proposal, he lifts his head up to the heavens "like a prophet of old." This perversion may be an allusion to Moses who in devotion goes up onto the mountain to receive the Ten Commandments.

These distorted, corrupted images of religion—apostles with no religion, a Heaven one can enter living but must die to leave, praying without supplication but with arrogance—are symbolic of the way the Washingtons' morals and values have become twisted by their own greed and materialism.

HISTORICAL CONTEXT

Isolationism and Prohibition

Before World War II (1939–1945), the United States had a tendency towards isolationism; Woodrow Wilson won reelection in 1916 running on the slogan, "He Kept Us Out of War." However, the next year the United States entered World War I, after German submarines sank the *Lusitania*, killing nearly twelve hundred people, among whom were over one hundred children and one hundred and twenty Americans.

By the time "The Diamond as Big as the Ritz" was published, the war had been over for almost four years, and the United States had retreated even further into isolationism. The Emergency Quota Act of 1921 became the first legislation to restrict immigration into the country, greatly reducing the number of immigrants allowed into the United States each year (immigration was even further restricted by the Immigration Act of 1924).

In addition to this retreat from the world community, Prohibition was in effect at this time. Ratified in 1919 and put into effect in 1920, the Eighteenth Amendment prohibited consumption of all alcoholic beverages. Also, the Sedition Act of 1918, which prohibited citizens from making public remarks critical of the government and its policies during war, had just recently been repealed in 1921. The combination of national isolation and restrictions of personal freedom caused many artists of the time to leave the country and spend time in Europe, most notably in Paris, where Fitzgerald himself lived while writing *The Great Gatsby*.

Postwar Economic Boom

The decade following World War I (1914–1918) was a prosperous time for the United States. More efficient methods of production had developed during the war to compensate for the reduced workforce. Now this increased productivity meant higher wages for workers and also shorter work hours, giving Americans both the means and the leisure to buy more goods. A new age of consumerism was born.

This was good news for Fitzgerald, whose stories often featured the antics of the extremely wealthy and frivolous. The popularity of his work declined considerably during the depression, in part because people struggling to make ends meet found these types of stories less entertaining and less relevant to their own lives.

New Freedoms for Women

Women won the right to vote in 1920, and they joined the workforce in greater numbers during this decade. These new freedoms, coupled with the prosperity of the times, gave birth to flappers, a term that refers to certain irreverent young women who challenged traditional mores with their shocking manner of dress, cropped hairstyles, and risqué attitudes towards men and romance. Fitzgerald first rose to fame with his stories about flappers, and stories such as "Bernice Bobs Her Hair," "The Offshore Pirate," and "The Jelly-Bean" are still reader favorites.

CRITICAL OVERVIEW

"The Diamond as Big as the Ritz" appeared in Fitzgerald's second volume of short stories, titled *Tales of the Jazz Age* (1922). Reviews of this collection were mixed, though many reviewers found it a definite improvement over his first collection, *Flappers and Philosophers*. In a review in the St. Paul *Daily News*, Woodward Boyd calls the collection "a better assemblage, on the whole, than *Flappers and Philosophers*." Hildegarde Hawthorne of the *New York Times Book Review*, writes that "There is plenty of variety in the new collection, more than in the *Flappers and Philosophers*."

However, many critics found the collection to be somewhat haphazard, featuring many lesser stories thrown in with a few of higher quality. A reviewer from the *Times Literary Supplement* notes, "none of the diverse elements in his book—fantastic, serious, or farcical—has been really mastered or drawn together." In agreement is a reviewer in the Baltimore *Evening Sun*, as quoted by Jackson Bryer in *The Critical Reputation of F. Scott Fitzgerald*, who writes that the stories "give the impression of being tossed off in rather debonair manner to show how easy it all is."

"The Diamond as Big as the Ritz" fared poorly with many critics. In her 1989 book,

The mountains of Montana provide the setting where Percy's family has built and horded their wealth attained from diamonds © *William Manning/Corbis*

Fitzgerald's Craft of Short Fiction: The Collected Stories 1920–1935, Alice Hall Petry writes: "So excoriating were the reactions to "Diamond" that one feels only relief that Fitzgerald did not use it as the title of the collection as he had briefly wished." Some of the critics were less harsh, however. As quoted in *F. Scott Fitzgerald in His Own Time: A Miscellany*, a 1922 article in the Minneapolis *Journal*, entitled "The Future of Fitzgerald," states, "'The Diamond as Big as the Ritz' is not perfect, but it is remarkable" and goes on to assert that Fitzgerald's strength lies in these imaginative types of stories, rather than in realism.

In hindsight, the story seems to occupy a more favorable light. First of all, attacking materialism, the American way of life, was unlikely to draw favorable reactions just a few short years after World War I. In addition, when seen in the context of Fitzgerald's entire career, "The Diamond as Big as the Ritz" stands out as a turning point in the development of a more mature style. James Miller, in his book *F. Scott*

Fitzgerald: His Art and his Technique, explains: "'May Day' and 'The Diamond as Big as the Ritz' mark important steps in the development of Fitzgerald's fictional technique ... he was using experimental techniques, and these experiments ... were to prove valuable to him in his longer works."

Whatever the critics' reactions in 1922, the story remained a favorite of readers in the years following, and it was anthologized in numerous collections of Fitzgerald's work.

CRITICISM

Laura Pryor

Pryor has a Bachelor of Arts degree from the University of Michigan and over twenty years experience in professional and creative writing with special interest in fiction. In the following essay, she demonstrates how "The Diamond as Big as the Ritz" can be interpreted as an allegory for political events in Fitzgerald's time.

WHAT DO I READ NEXT?

- Many of the same wealth-related themes presented in "The Diamond as Big as the Ritz" are explored in greater depth in Fitzgerald's most famous novel, *The Great Gatsby* (1925). Though the novel is more realistic, the main characters behave in a thoughtless, egocentric, and deadly manner, in some ways reminiscent of the Washingtons in "The Diamond as Big as the Ritz."

- "The Diamond as Big as the Ritz" was originally included in the short story collection *Tales of the Jazz Age*. It is also featured in *The Best Early Stories of F. Scott Fitzgerald* (2005), which includes selected stories from each of Fitzgerald's collections, explanatory notes, articles by Fitzgerald and his wife, and a short biography.

- Fitzgerald's life and troubles are told through his correspondence to friends and family in *Life in Letters: A New Collection*, edited and annotated by Matthew J. Bruccoli (1995). The letters are arranged in chronological order and discuss both his work and his difficult private life.

- While Fitzgerald was living in France, he became friends with fellow author Ernest Hemingway. The relationship was a complicated one, however, and in his book *A Moveable Feast* (1964), Hemingway paints a decidedly unflattering portrait of Fitzgerald and of his wife Zelda, whom Hemingway despised. The book is essentially a memoir of Hemingway's time in Paris and his friendships with luminaries such as Gertrude Stein, James Joyce, and, of course, Fitzgerald.

- Zelda Sayre Fitzgerald was also a writer, and while recovering from periods of schizophrenia in a mental hospital, she wrote a novel entitled *Save Me the Waltz*. Available from Vintage (2001), it is a thinly disguised account of her own life with F. Scott Fitzgerald.

> READ IN THE LIGHT OF THESE HISTORICAL EVENTS, 'THE DIAMOND AS BIG AS THE RITZ' CAN BE INTERPRETED AS A POLITICAL ALLEGORY IN WHICH THE THEME OF IMPRISONMENT BECOMES MORE IMPORTANT THAN THE INDICTMENT OF MATERIALISM AND GREED. "

Because F. Scott Fitzgerald's "The Diamond as Big as the Ritz" is written so like a fable, it is natural for the reader to try and ferret out a moral, a lesson to be learned. Is it a cautionary tale against greed and materialism? An indictment of the entire capitalist system? Or an allegory for something else entirely?

The time period in which this story was written (the early 1920s) was an eventful one in U.S. history. If Americans had materialistic tendencies, as the story would suggest, then the postwar boom of the time would have made these tendencies more obvious than ever. The end of World War I in 1918 helped boost the economy, women had just been given the right to vote (in 1920), and average wages increased, putting the country in the mood to celebrate. This made the restrictions of Prohibition (the Eighteenth Amendment, which made the consumption of alcoholic beverages illegal beginning in 1920) even more chafing to those who, like Fitzgerald, enjoyed high living.

While the economy was booming, the political climate was one of isolationism and suspicion. In 1917 in Russia, communist revolutionaries called Bolsheviks overthrew the Russian government, and in 1918, they executed Czar Nicholas II and his family. In the United States, this action generated a so-called Red Scare, paranoia over communism that led to even more restrictions on Americans' freedom of expression. In addition, immigration restrictions drastically reduced the number of immigrants allowed into the United States. The country had become a moral dichotomy: On the one hand, there were the irreverent flappers, speakeasies, and wild behavior associated with the Jazz Age, but on the other hand, a puritanical segment sought to impose a rigid moral code on the country through Prohibition and other restrictions.

Read in the light of these historical events, "The Diamond as Big as the Ritz" can be interpreted as a political allegory in which the theme of imprisonment becomes more important than the indictment of materialism and greed. In such an interpretation, Braddock Washington's hidden Montana empire represents the United States and capitalism. Washington himself seems to consider his land a country unto itself; when they reach the property, Percy tells John, "This is where the United States ends, father says." Logically, John asks if they have reached Canada, but Percy tells him they are in the Montana Rockies, on "the only five square miles of land in the country that's never been surveyed." Washington's country has its own anti-aircraft defense system, political prisoners (the aviators), even the capability to start war. (When Jasmine is disappointed that World War I ends before she can become a "canteen expert," Washington takes steps "to promote a new war in the Balkans" for her benefit.) This country even has its own languages; the Washingtons' slaves, so long isolated from the rest of the world, have developed their own extreme version of their original southern dialect, which only they can understand.

Like the United States, Washington's country has beautiful vistas, great natural resources, and wealthy citizens. This fictional country has taken isolationism to its most extreme: anyone who dares enter must be killed or imprisoned. Obviously, the United States had not gone to such literal extremes in the 1920s, but this could be a symbolic representation of the increasingly restrictive immigration quota acts of the decade. Different nationalities and races are represented in the story: Mrs. Washington is Spanish, the teacher who escapes and brings on the Washingtons' downfall is Italian, and one of the imprisoned aviators offers to teach Washington's daughters Chinese. As in the United States, however, the power lies in the hands of the Anglo-Saxon majority. A proponent of the Immigration Act of 1924, Senator Ellison D. Smith of South Carolina, said, "Thank God we have in America perhaps the largest percentage of any country in the world of the pure, unadulterated Anglo-Saxon stock; certainly the greatest of any nation in the Nordic breed.... let us shut the door and assimilate what we have, and let us breed pure American citizens and develop our own American resources." Braddock Washington offers up his own blatant racism when he explains to John that he

discontinued private baths for his slaves because "Water is not good for certain races—except as a beverage."

The exaggerated narcissism of the Washingtons could represent the U.S. refusal to become involved with the rest of the world, as when it declined to join the League of Nations or ratify the Treaty of Versailles. The country further isolated itself by placing tariffs on foreign goods, which greatly restricted foreign trade. The Washingtons are isolated not only geographically, but also by their wealth. Kismine shows how completely out of touch she is with the rest of the world when she says, "Think of the millions and millions of people in the world, laborers and all, who get along with only two maids."

Visitors to the Washington property must be killed, because they might talk; in the United States, the right of free speech had been seriously compromised during World War I by the Sedition Act of 1918 (which remained in effect until 1921).

Even as a political allegory, the story is still a cautionary tale against materialism and the idolization of wealth. As is often the case in his work, Fitzgerald seems to be cautioning against the very vices to which he had fallen victim. Fitzgerald and his wife were notorious for living well beyond their means, fraternizing with the types of people he negatively portrayed in his work, people like the Washingtons. Like John T. Unger, Fitzgerald was aware of the flaws in these people and their way of life but could not resist the magnetism of wealth. Ironically, this attraction is what led many immigrants to the United States in the first place, and it was a desire to retain that wealth, in part, that motivated the immigration restrictions. While Senator Ellison D. Smith spoke of preserving "Anglo-Saxon stock," he also expressed the fear that the waves of new immigrants entering the country would deplete U.S. resources, leaving less property for the current population. In other words, the more people, the less wealth to go around. The idea that a more diversified population would also give the country greater intellectual and creative resources was not considered by Smith, though even Braddock Washington acknowledges the necessity of new ideas, by kidnapping "a landscape gardener, an architect, a designer of state settings, and a French decadent poet," to help him design his chateau and grounds.

Fitzgerald usually took great pains to write stories that would be commercially viable, because with his way of life, he was frequently in debt. The irony of his writing "The Diamond as Big as the Ritz" (which was one of his personal favorites) was that because it so harshly criticized the capitalist system, Fitzgerald was unable to make much money from it; it was rejected by the conservative *Saturday Evening Post*, which had bought many of his stories, and instead Fitzgerald had to settle for three hundred dollars from *The Smart Set*, a lesser magazine.

Whether interpreted as political allegory or cautionary fable, the story clearly reflects a discontent with the American philosophy of life that was shared by many artists during this time; many left the country to live in Europe. High living and materialism was to be short lived, however, as in a few years the stock market would crash and plunge the United States into the Great Depression.

Source: Laura Pryor, Critical Essay on "The Diamond as Big as the Ritz," in *Short Stories for Students*, Thomson Gale, 2007.

William E. Rand

In the following essay, Rand compares F. Scott Fitzgerald's "The Diamond as Big as the Ritz" and Richard Wright's "The Man Who Lived Underground" and discusses the concept of being an outsider that permeates the stories.

Discussions of expatriate United States writers of the early twentieth century generally include both Richard Wright and F. Scott Fitzgerald. However, the literary works of Wright and Fitzgerald are rarely compared directly. Fitzgerald is compared to Ernest Hemingway; Wright is discussed in terms of Langston Hughes or Dostoevsky. In referring to Richard Wright's story "The Man Who Lived Underground," for instance, Abraham Chapman sees an "obvious allusion in the title to the Dostoyevskyan Underground." Nevertheless, as writers, Fitzgerald and Wright have much in common.

Although their perspectives may have differed, both Fitzgerald and Wright saw themselves as cultural and political outsiders. Fitzgerald's attitude toward the wealthy, for example, was noted by Malcolm Cowley, who says of Fitzgerald:

> ALTHOUGH THEIR PERSPECTIVES MAY HAVE DIFFERED, BOTH FITZGERALD AND WRIGHT SAW THEMSELVES AS CULTURAL AND POLITICAL OUTSIDERS."

His mixture of feelings toward the very rich, which included curiosity and admiration as well as distrust, is revealed in his treatment of a basic situation that reappears in many of his stories: ... a rising young man of the middle class in love with the daughter of a very rich family.

Considered through the concept of the insider/outsider, Wright may be closer to Fitzgerald than to Dostoevsky, as Michel Fabre observes concerning Wright's story "The Man Who Lived Underground":

As for the situation of the man underground symbolizing that of the Negro in American society ... [Wright] has painted it in a perspective which is exactly opposed to Dostoevsky's: rather than brooding over past humiliations, he sees his exclusion more as an opportunity to scrutinize his culture from the outside. Therefore, the underground rather clearly represents the marginal character of the black man's existence and his ambiguous rapport with American civilization.

Culture and race are typically seen to have produced Wright's feelings of alienation whereas social and economic class and culture are thought to have motivated Fitzgerald's views. Yet, political affiliations affected them both in ways that brought their fiction closer in structure and message. In the case of Wright, Katherine Fishburn asserts that there are several forces affecting the character Cross Damon in Wright's novel *The Outsider*:

Cross Damon is the double helix of American innocence and European nihilism. He is more alienated than his American predecessors and more influenced by his environment than his European contemporaries. Like Bigger Thomas [*Native Son*] before him, he is the result of a complicated battle among the forces of naturalism, Marxism, Freudianism, and existentialism.

Wright was a known Communist—for a time—but, interestingly, the word *Marxism* has also been associated with Fitzgerald.

Living in France, Fitzgerald could hardly have escaped some exposure to Marxist theories; however, Ronald Gervais asserts that Fitzgerald "developed in his work an attitude toward Marxism that was neither embrace nor rejection." Such an ambivalent perspective, combined with Fitzgerald's desire to be a part of the wealthy elite produced fiction with political and social statements similar to those in the later works of Wright. Gervais says the following of Fitzgerald's politics:

> Fitzgerald uses Marxism as an outlet for his ideals and frustrations; his qualified sympathy for it represents his most extreme protest against the excesses and failings of the *haute bourgeois* class which he describes so charmingly and judges so scathingly, and to which he felt his loyalty pledged—even if it seemed to him that the class was historically doomed.

Although Fitzgerald's birth and initial success predates Wright's by about a decade, they are essentially of the same generation, and at least two of their short stories manifest their varied feelings of isolation in similar literary themes and structures. "The Diamond As Big As the Ritz," published by Fitzgerald in 1922, and "The Man Who Lived Underground," first published by Wright in 1942, show similarities in form, imagery, and theme, all related to the same concept of the outsider.

Both stories present protagonists who enter worlds different from their own. In both cases, the protagonist is a naive outsider who must learn some moral truth that has, as its basis, the politics of wealth. Fitzgerald's story opens with John T. Unger, who "came from a family that had been well known in Hades—a small town on the Mississippi River—for several generations." The syntactic structure of the sentence, with its hyphenated appositive, initially suggests at least two things. First is that Unger's family enjoys a certain amount of social status in the town of Hades. The second suggestion undermines the first, however, in the naming of Hades as a small Mississippi town. The effect is to make the Unger family seem like big fish in a little pond, an effect confirmed in the last sentence of the first paragraph: "Nothing would suit [John's parents] but that he should go to St. Midas' School near Boston—Hades was too small to hold their darling and gifted son." John Unger then begins his journey.

Events of the next two pages, including the "asbestos pocket-book stuffed with money,"

suggest that the Unger family, while comfortable financially, is definitely not part of the power and money elite. In the preparatory school, therefore, John becomes the outsider who aspires to become a member of the group. He responds naively to his friend Percy Washington upon learning details of his family's fabulous wealth: "'He must be very rich,' said John simply. 'I'm glad. I like very rich people.'" What Unger must learn through the story is that Percy Washington's father is "a rampant capitalist who illustrates the ugliness of placing money and luxury above what Fitzgerald called 'the old values': moral integrity, self-discipline, love for one's family, and regard for one's fellow human beings." John Unger must learn to see the corruption beneath the facade.

Similarly, in Wright's story, Fred Daniels leaves one world for another of which he is unfamiliar. The narrative hook, "I've got to hide, he told himself," introduces a conflict between the protagonist and his society, stronger but not unlike the conflict in Fitzgerald's story. Both stories introduce a character who, for one reason or another, no longer belongs in his society and seeks another. John Unger seeks social and economic advancement; Fred Daniels seeks physical safety and escape as indicated by Wright's lines: "Either he had to find a place to hide, or he had to surrender." Unger leaves the comfort of his small town, ironically named Hades, for the disguised corrupted world of the wealthy, and Daniels leaves the dangerous, corrupt world above ground for the security of the sewer, "Wright's metaphor for the black ghetto," according to Susan Mayberry.

Both protagonists are, therefore, outsiders who must learn, but Wright's story differs in that his protagonist must, as an outsider, look back and become aware of the corruption in the society he has left. For both protagonists, however, little of their world is as it seems. Mayberry says that in Wright's story, "[t]he sewer water is described as warm, pulsing, womblike. Entering it, Man regresses to a world that offers both security and ignorance out of which he must finally climb." Daniels must climb out of his ignorance of the corrupted underbelly of society as must Unger. A superficial reading may suggest different sources of corruption in the stories: money in Fitzgerald's and racism in Wright's. Although the two concepts intertwine in both stories, the source of corruption in each case is wealth with its attendant power. Fred Daniel's fate, according to Patricia D. Watkins, is not primarily the result of his race:

> Racial identity does not directly determine what happens to Fred Daniels. Rather, environment—specifically, economic and social forces—seems to be a more important determinant of Daniels' fortunes. Before his arrest Daniels worked at the home of Mrs. Wooten, presumably as a servant. Hence, Daniels is at the lower end of the economic and social scale, like the white night watchman who shares his fate.

It is interesting that Fitzgerald also sets Unger at the lower end of the social and economic scale at the St. Midas Preparatory School. This position seems typical—albeit not exclusive—for the position of outsider in the works of both authors. Such is the position of Nick Carraway in *The Great Gatsby* and Bigger Thomas in *Native Son.*

In "The Diamond As Big As the Ritz" and "The Man Who Lived Underground," wealth not only initiates corruption, but it also provides the means of concealing it, leading to similar ironic juxtapositions by both Wright and Fitzgerald. Connotations associated with rising and descending, as well as those associated with light and darkness, are reversed. This technique is illustrated most strongly in Wright's oxymoron: "dark sunshine", Fitzgerald's ironic use of "Hades" for the name of Unger's home town and "Washington" for the name of the most corrupt and immoral—and richest—man in the world. In religious terms, one rises to Heaven and descends to hell or Hades. Yet in Fitzgerald's story, the bright god-like figure above Washington is evil. In Wright's story, the bright light from above means danger.

Other religious symbols appear in both stories, usually but not always in an ironic sense. Typically, for instance, the corrupt underworld is dark, and the pure world above displays a bright light. Yet in Wright's story, the light shining from above ironically represents the corrupt, violent society from which Daniels escapes, and in Fitzgerald's story Unger rises in an almost religious sense to the murderously corrupt Washington retreat:

> At a resounding "Hey-yah!" John felt the car being lifted slowly from the ground—up and up—clear of the tallest rocks on both sides—then higher, until he could see a wavy, moonlit valley stretched out before him in sharp contrast to the quagmire of rocks that they had just left.

Unger and Percy Washington arrive at the estate to more images of rising, light and darkness: "Full in the light of the stars, an exquisite château rose from the borders of the lake, climbed in marble radiance half the height of an adjoining mountain, then melted in grace, in perfect symmetry..." The twelve men of Fish who Percy and Unger encounter on their way to the estate present another religious image. They are, however, described by Marius Bewley as something other than ironic:

> The Christian implications of the fish symbol are certainly intended by Fitzgerald, and these are enforced by the twelve solitary men who are apostles "beyond all religion." These grotesque and distorted Christian connotations are strengthened by their dream-like relation to Hades on the Mississippi where John was born. What we are given in these paragraphs is a queerly restless and troubled sense of a religion that is sick and expressing itself in disjointed images and associations, as if it were delirious.

A similar disjointed, delirious religious image appears in Fred Daniels' dream in the Wright story. In the dream, Daniels walks on water to rescue a drowning woman's baby. The dream is a realistic representation of his concern for the dead baby in the sewer and his feelings of helplessness in helping it, but the dream also reflects Watkins' observation: "As he sheds his aboveground identity, Fred Daniels acquires a godlike identity."

The Fred Daniels god-like image does, in certain contexts, resemble the Braddock Washington god-like image in Fitzgerald's story. Both men create their own world and seek to make changes in it. Both reject values and morals of the society they left. Daniels no longer values the exchange function of money and jewels; Washington no longer values human life and freedom. The two authors present their god-like characters in different ways, however.

Fitzgerald uses narrative techniques to show Washington as a god-like figure. His character is rarely seen, but his control is always felt. When seen, he dominates absolutely. Representative is the scene with the captured aviators. They argue with and appeal to Braddock Washington, high above, as if to a powerful Roman god. Washington responds in kind:

> "I've offered to have all or any of you painlessly executed if you wish. I've offered to have your wives, sweethearts, children, and mothers kidnapped and brought out here. I'll enlarge your place down there and feed and clothe you the rest of your lives."

Later Washington appears like an all-knowing god along the path where John Unger and Kismine are talking: "Footsteps were coming along the path in their direction, and a moment later the rose bushes were parted displaying Braddock Washington, whose intelligent eyes... were peering in at them."

Wright, on the other hand, chooses both narration and symbols to show Daniels' god-like qualities. It is through Wright's narration of Daniels' god-like change that Daniels becomes the outsider: "Near the end of his second day underground, Daniels takes the first step toward creating himself and his world and hence becoming his own god: He begins rejecting his aboveground values and identity." The values he rejects are money and time, possibly the two things most valued by a capitalistic society.

Much has been made of Wright's affiliation with the Communist Party and his departure from the United States to live in Paris. For instance, Abraham Chapman notes: "His first writing was published in the Communist press, and for a while he was Harlem correspondent of *The Daily Worker*." Wright later left the Communist Party; nevertheless, that experience may have inspired the focus on money in "The Man Who Lived Underground" and Daniels' significant rejection of it in the story. Daniels comes to treat money and other forms of wealth with contempt from the dime payment he casts aside in the grocery store to the hundred dollar bills he casually uses as wallpaper in his cave. Patricia Watkins says, "His rejection of the valuation of money above ground is a liberating act." Watkins also notes that he rejects time in like fashion: "Daniels' enslavement to time ends when he prepares to nail valuable watches onto the same dirt wall on which he has just pasted the hundred dollar bills." These acts free Daniels from the entrapments of wealth. They also show him as god-like in his ability to remake his world and as such make him an outsider to the world aboveground.

As interesting, however, is the similarity that the message of his rejection has to Fitzgerald's story "The Diamond As Big As the Ritz." Fitzgerald creates two outsiders, John Unger and Braddock Washington, made such by the corrupting influence of excessive wealth. Unger, of course, is the admiring outsider to the wealthy elite. Washington is the self-imposed outsider to society who—in a god-like way

similar to Daniels—has created his own world. Unlike Daniels, however, he has embraced wealth to an insane degree. While Fitzgerald is not telling a story that condemns wealth and power per se, he does, in his examination of their excesses, show the corrupting effects in a way similar to Wright. Bewley notes that "[t]he major part of [Fitzgerald's] story is concerned with giving us a series of glimpses of life in this American dream—a fantasy on the theme of material possibilities run wild." Daniels' rejection of corrupt, aboveground values and Washington's rejection of the moral values of society make both characters appear god-like in a similar way and deliver the same moral message to the reader.

In addition to narrative structures, Wright employs symbols heavily to make Daniels appear god-like. The first occurs after the movie theater scene when Daniels "went back to the basement and stood in the red darkness." The scene leads to a symbolic rendering of the washing of the hands by the priest at mass and the changing of the water and wine to Christ's blood. The ceremony is a re-creation of Christ's actions at the last supper, with Daniels' experience a corrupted version of the same:

> He went to the sink and turned the faucet and
> the water flowed in a smooth silent stream that
> looked like a spout of blood. He brushed the
> mad image from his mind and began to wash
> his hands leisurely, looking about for the usual
> bar of soap.

The symbolism is carried further with the previously discussed dream in which Daniels walks on water. Both symbols occur immediately following events that further alienate Daniels from the world above, pushing him more into the role of outsider. The movie theater scene, in which Daniels experiences a renewed awakening to the world's corruption and in which he encounters the usher, leads into the washing of the hands. The walking on water dream is preceded by Daniels' eating the stolen sandwiches, his first meal and so the first sign of his self-sufficiency underground.

After Daniels hangs the watches and scatters the diamonds, signs of his rejection of aboveground values, he turns the radio on and subsequently has a god-like illusion:

> A melancholy piece of music rose. Brooding
> over the diamonds on the floor was like looking
> up into a sky full of restless stars; then the
> illusion turned into its opposite: he was high

up in the air looking down at the twinkling lights of a sprawling city. The music ended and a man recited news events. In the same attitude in which he had contemplated the city, so now ... he looked down upon land and sea as men fought, as cities were razed, as planes scattered death upon open towns, as long lines of trenches wavered and broke.

The juxtaposition of high and low continues with the comparison of the diamonds to stars as well as Daniels' imagined and god-like position high above mankind. The symbolism parallels Fitzgerald's depiction of the boys ascending above the town of Fish and being lifted over the rock barricade before entering the valley of the estate. Also similar is Washington's stance above the imprisoned aviators.

Such god-like representation in both stories favors the outsider interpretation of the characters. The true nature of an outsider may not be known to the group. According to the Bible, Christ's true nature on Earth went unseen or disbelieved by many; the job of the Apostles was to open peoples' eyes. The analogy becomes clear in close comparison between Fitzgerald and Ernest Hemingway. For example, the truth of Jake Barnes' true bitterness goes unseen to his fellow expatriates—most notably, Brett—who see him as a happy friend to everyone in Hemingway's *The Sun Also Rises*. Likewise, in Fitzgerald's *The Great Gatsby*, many of Jay Gatsby's freeloading guests know little about him, and he allows them to create their own myths. Nick Carraway takes on the role of apostle, trying to open the eyes of the reader.

In "The Diamond As Big As the Ritz," Percy relates the almost biblical tale of his father's lineage to John Unger, yet neither Percy nor his sisters see the evil behind the god-like figure of Braddock Washington for what it truly is. Braddock Washington is a god-like outsider to a nation that does not know that his world exists. John Unger is an outsider to the wealth and power elite as well as to the truth of his intended fate. Fred Daniels is an outsider not only to his fate but also to most of the people of the aboveground society.

In Wright's story, the theater usher gives Daniels his first experience as an outsider from the aboveground perspective. By the time he enters the theater, Daniels has begun to awaken to the corruption that exists beneath society's facade, but the usher, who acknowledges Daniels' presence, is blind to his true nature. Wright symbolizes the usher's blindness through his innocuous question and directions: "'Looking for the men's room, sir?' the man asked, and, without waiting for an answer, he turned and pointed. 'This way, sir. The first door to your right.'" The usher treats Daniels like any other movie theater patron, unable to see—or smell—the obvious signs of Daniels' time in the sewer, including "his shoes, wet with sewer slime." The usher is unable to note the condition of Daniels' clothing because the sewer foulness on his clothes symbolizes the corruption of his society, which he, like the rest of society, cannot see. That symbolic blindness then represents such a strong difference in perspective as to make Daniels a complete outsider. At this point, however, Daniels has not yet achieved his full awakening or, as Watkins describes it, his "godlike identity." Daniels simply dismisses the usher with the comment, "What a funny fellow!"

Daniels' realization really begins in the meat market. There the circumstance repeats when the white couple mistake him for a cashier, again failing to note the distinctive trappings of the sewer displayed by Daniels. Not surprisingly, money forms the catalyst for Daniels' irrevocable rejection of the world above and the formation of his new identity. In the story, the woman pays for the grapes with a dime, and, after some civilities, the couple leaves Daniels standing in the doorway: "When they were out of sight, he burst out laughing and crying. A trolley car rolled noisily past and he controlled himself quickly. He flung the dime to the pavement with a gesture of contempt and stepped into the warm night air."

However, Daniels' laughter signals a less-than-total awakening, Mayberry notes that this laughter recurs and reveals a growing awakening:

> This laughter occurs throughout the story at every significant event or lesson in Man's process of enlightenment. It marks his growing awareness of the vulnerable human condition and the universal human culpability that renders human life and love highest absolutes. Thus it becomes the ultimate signifier of the distance between these real values and the symbols substituted for them by members of society.

These symbols are, of course, the same as those used by Fitzgerald: money, jewels, and other blatant signs of wealth, all of which Daniels rejects in his awakening, and the characters in Fitzgerald's story lose.

Not only does Daniels laugh at certain painfully partial points of awakening, but others laugh as well. Wright uses laughter, joy and song ironically in the story to show ignorance or a gradual sense of awakening. The first instance occurs early in the story when Daniels comes upon the people happily singing at the church service. His first impulse on seeing them through the wall is to laugh, but guilt stops him. He is in the earliest stages of awakening and realizes only that something is wrong:

> They oughtn't to do that, he thought. But he could think of no reason *why* they should not do it. Just singing with the air of the sewer blowing in on them.... He felt that he was gazing upon something abysmally obscene, yet he could not bring himself to leave.

The laughter of the theater patrons has a similar effect on Daniels, and his own laughter is uneasy, guilty. At that point, Daniels has not yet come to terms with his new, developing identity, and, as Mayberry suggests, a feeling of superiority accompanies the laughter.

Fitzgerald uses the same technique, albeit not as often and with a bit more subtlety. The reason probably rests in the nature of the story. John Unger acquires his realization not by degrees like Daniels, but abruptly through Kismine's slip of information. His reaction is, therefore, different: "'And so,' cried John accusingly, 'and so you were letting me make love to you and pretending to return it, and talking about marriage, all the time knowing perfectly well that I'd never get out of here alive.'" Also in Fitzgerald's story, in addition to more abrupt awakenings, characters typically undergo relatively less of a personality change.

The first significant instance of expressed joy or laughter parallels the church service scene in Wright's story. During Percy's narrative of the family history, the elder Fitz-Norman Washington deceives his slaves into believing that the Southern armies have won the war: "The negroes believed him implicitly. They passed a vote declaring it a good thing and held revival services immediately." Fitzgerald's tone and direction suggest an intuition sufficient to intend an implication similar to Daniels' response to the church singing he witnesses: "Pain throbbed in his legs and a deeper pain, induced by the sight of those black people groveling and begging for something they could never get, churned in him." The second instance in the story, also regarding the slaves, suggests the conclusion to

the first. It occurs when Braddock and Percy Washington show John Unger the slave quarters. Braddock Washington makes a racist statement to which John Unger reacts:

> "I discontinued the baths for quite another reason. Several of [the slaves] caught cold and died. Water is not good for certain races—except as a beverage."
>
> John laughed, and then decided to nod his head in sober agreement. Braddock Washington made him uncomfortable.

Unger's mixed reaction reflects the higher moral, and less racist, character of his family clashing with his desire as an outsider to fit in with the Washingtons.

The next instance occurs when Washington tells the trapped aviators of the man who escaped. This instance signifies an important turning point in the story. Up to this point, the chaos in the characters' lives in both Fitzgerald's and Wright's stories has been shown in large measure by ironic reversals of the signifiers of symbols: up leads to corruption and down leads to enlightenment; light is corrupt and evil, and darkness is soothing and safe; laughter reflects pain and ignorance. Washington, intending to manipulate and deceive, tells his captives that one of their number has escaped. They react as expected: "A wild yell of jubilation went up suddenly from two dozen throats and a pandemonium of joy ensued. The prisoners clog-danced and cheered and yodled and wrestled with one another in a sudden uprush of animal spirits." In Washington's mind, the prisoners laugh in ignorance; however, subsequent events show their rejoicing to be genuine, for the Italian really had escaped.

Both Fitzgerald and Wright employ this double reversal, a strange kind of return to normalcy, to signal the story's turning point. Another turning point occurs with the coming of the air attack; once again, that which is high above is seen as good. When things look bad for the survival of his hidden empire, Braddock Washington prays, offering the ridiculous bribe to God. He is no longer god-like; he has reverted to the human appealing to God above. Finally, the evil Washington and his family go below into the mountain in a symbolic descent into hell. At the turning point of Wright's story, "the world above ground acquires the quality of darkness, and the world underground acquires the quality of light." This happens when Daniels rigs the electric lighting in the cave. That signifies his moment of psychological illumination. These respective literary turning points then lead to an inevitable confrontation of an outsider with society, bringing Braddock Washington and Fred Daniels to the same end as Jay Gatsby and Bigger Thomas.

Their endings seem quite different, with Wright's heavy message in the form of Lawson and Fitzgerald's almost lighthearted and certainly happy ending with Kismine grabbing the wrong jewels. Fitzgerald may be seen as reflecting the modernism of the Jazz Age, whereas Wright's anti-hero Daniels may be seen to nudge his story into post-modernism. Nevertheless, the awakening of Daniels and John Unger to the truth of their societies is similar. It seems, therefore, that the structure and techniques of the two writers are close enough to suggest the possibility that Fitzgerald could have influenced Wright's work in a positive way.

Wright began to write seriously in 1925, the same year that Fitzgerald published *The Great Gatsby*. Wright was a self-educated man, widely read, and it is improbable that he did not read Fitzgerald's work. He difinitely read Dreiser, Sherwood Anderson, and Edgar Allan Poe. Also, as already mentioned, the lives of Wright and Fitzgerald took certain parallel tracks. It is therefore not unreasonable to conclude that Wright saw a model in Fitzgerald as did both Fitzgerald and Hemingway in Gertrude Stein, Sherwood Anderson, and Jack London. Then, as with the other writers, Wright incorporated Fitzgerald's influence into his own maturing style and voice.

Source: William E. Rand, "The Structure of the Outsider in the Short Fiction of Richard Wright and F. Scott Fitzgerald," in *CLA Journal*, Vol. 40, No. 2, December 1996, pp. 230–45.

Ruth Prigozy

In the following essay, Prigozy gives a critical analysis of F. Scott Fitzgerald's work.

Although for the general reader F. Scott Fitzgerald's fame rests primarily on one novel, *The Great Gatsby* (1925), his creative life, from youth to early death, found full expression in some 160 short stories. These works not only provided the income that sustained Fitzgerald when writing his novels, but they also enhanced the legend that grew up around Scott and Zelda Fitzgerald after his first novel, *This Side of Paradise* (1920), appeared at the beginning of the Jazz Age. For ten years thereafter the pages of the *Saturday Evening Post, Redbook, Woman's*

> READERS LIKED THE COLLECTION MORE THAN THE CRITICS DID; MOST OF THEM REGARDED THE STORIES AS DIVERSIONS AND FAILED TO RECOGNIZE THE MERIT OF 'MAY DAY' OR 'THE DIAMOND AS BIG AS THE RITZ.'"

Home Companion, and other mass-circulation magazines were filled with romantic tales of young lovers, of dreamers and doers, of madcap heroines and sad young men, many of whom seemed to reflect aspects of the lives of their creator and his wife.

Fitzgerald is one of the most widely recognized names in American literature, yet the legend he so carefully cultivated has, paradoxically, tended to obscure the writer as well as his work. Fitzgerald was a major novelist, but at least a dozen of his stories rank among the very best short fiction written in the twentieth century. Fitzgerald'swhole life was bound up with his short stories; indeed, the story of his life cannot be told without them. Only through an acquaintance with his career as a short-fiction writer can the complex man who now occupies a major position in the literary and mythic life of the nation be understood.

Perhaps no other American writer has felt himself as inextricably tied to the history of his country as F. Scott Fitzgerald . Born in 1896, at the end of an era of unprecedented national growth, he lived to see the traditions that had guided his parents' generation and his own childhood cast aside; indeed, he was said by his contemporaries to have precipitated the upheaval in manners and morals that accompanied the end of World War I. Never as "lost" as the members of his generation described in Paris by Gertrude Stein, Fitzgerald nevertheless experienced and even personified the "boom" of the 1920s and the "bust" of the 1930s. America had sloughed off its past and headed for, as Fitzgerald said, the "greatest, gaudiest spree in history"; when it was over, he realized that the nation had been living on borrowed time, "a short and precious time— for when the mist rises . . . one finds that the very best is over."

The elegiac note that characterizes his reminiscences of the 1920s is typical of Fitzgerald's writing; its origins were in his early childhood and struggling adolescence. He felt himself always to be an outsider—from the elite society of the St. Paul, Minnesota, of his boyhood, from the spectacular achievements of the athletes of his school days, from the glittering social world of his young manhood, from the wealth and power of the American aristocracy, and even, at the end, from the literary life of his nation.

Fitzgerald's sense of estrangement was rooted in his family background. He never forgot that he was related, however distantly, to Francis Scott Key, a name that conjured up images of America's heroic past. He listened attentively to the tales his father, Edward Fitzgerald, told of the family's Confederate past. He noted the connection between his father's family and, through marriage, Mary Surratt, hanged as a conspirator in Lincoln's assassination. And on the side of his mother, Molly McQuillan, although the ancestry was not as patrician as his father's, he could point to the vitality of his grandfather, an Irishman who epitomized the self-made American merchants in the decades immediately following the Civil War. Fitzgerald admitted in 1933 in a letter to John O'Hara, "I am half black Irish and half old American stock with the usual exaggerated ancestral pretensions. The black Irish half of the family had the money and looked down upon the Maryland side of the family who had, and really had, that . . . series of reticences and obligations that go under the poor old shattered word 'breeding.'" When his own father experienced serious business failures during Fitzgerald's childhood, the boy was distraught. He experienced such severe anxieties that he expected the family to be taken to the poorhouse, and his later financial insecurity reinforced these childhood traumas. His life suggests that perhaps unconsciously he *had* to live on a financial brink.

The Fitzgerald family became increasingly dependent on the mother's relatives in St. Paul after moves to Buffalo, Syracuse, and back to Buffalo, with several different residences in each city. They moved several times in St. Paul, too, but always lived in rented houses or apartments in the Summit Avenue neighborhood where railroad tycoon James J. Hill kept his residence. The years of Fitzgerald's childhood and early youth were marked in his memory indelibly: he was the outsider, the poor relation, dependent on his grandmother and his aunt, admitted to but never really part of the social center of St. Paul life. That sense of estrangement so characteristic of his formative years marks much of his fiction, from the first short stories, written when he was about thirteen, to his last efforts in Hollywood. Similarly, despite his father's weaknesses and failures Fitzgerald was never to relinquish his loyalty to him and to the traditions he represented.

Fitzgerald was admitted to the St. Paul Academy, a private high school, in 1908, where he remained for three years. It was there, from 1909 to 1911, that he published his first short stories, in the school literary magazine *Now and Then*. In the late 1920s he re-created these years in the Basil Duke Lee stories, which depict the painful rejections Fitzgerald experienced at St. Paul Academy where he was disliked and socially unsuccessful. He attempted to use sports as a path to acceptance, but he did not have the physique for football stardom. His most cherished memories of the St. Paul experience were those connected with the stage. Fitzgerald always loved drama, and his earliest writing efforts were either in the form of short plays or stories with strong theatrical elements. When his poor grades at St. Paul Academy necessitated his changing schools, he was enrolled at the Newman School in Hackensack, New Jersey, where he could indulge his taste for the theater with a few thrilling trips to New York City, less than an hour away. Here he felt the glamour and excitement he had dreamed about in St. Paul. For the rest of his life New York City would hold a special magic for Fitzgerald: success, vitality, and enchantment.

His popularity improved slowly at Newman, but his opportunities to escape from an unpleasant reality were greater than they had ever been. And it was perhaps the color and excitement of the Broadway theater, particularly the musicals, that so captured Fitzgerald's imagination that he aspired throughout his life to achieve fame as a playwright or librettist. He continued to write short stories at Newman, where the school magazine, the *Newman News*, published three of his efforts. His Newman career was not the failure that the St. Paul Academy had been. At the beginning of his second year he met the person who would become the most influential figure in his early life, both creatively and personally, Father Sigourney Fay, who would become director of the school. Father Fay was a sophisticated, lively esthete, a friend of many well-known figures in arts and letters, including writer Shane Leslie. Fay revealed to Fitzgerald a far more attractive Catholicism than he had ever known and opened a world to him that suggested the beauty and richness of experience he would always try to capture in his writing.

Fitzgerald entered Princeton University in 1913, and although he never graduated, his years there were the most important to his development as a writer. He never lost his interest in sports, but knowing that he could not succeed as a participant, he sought other roads to success and the popularity he would always crave. His major activities at Princeton were in the Triangle Club, the *Tiger*, and the *Nassau Literary Magazine*.

In the first of the two periods he spent at Princeton (he left in his junior year as a result of poor grades and illness, returning the following year only to enlist in the army after the United States entered World War I) he contributed the plot and lyrics to a Triangle show and the lyrics to another, and he wrote a one-act play and a short story, "The Ordeal" (*Nassau Literary Magazine*, June 1915). In 1917, when he returned to Princeton, he wrote five stories and one short play as well as one Triangle show. The stories from this period reveal a growing maturity in the author. Three were later revised for publication in H. L. Mencken's *Smart Set*, two were incorporated into Fitzgerald's first novel, *This Side of Paradise*, and one, "Tarquin of Cheapside" (*Nassau Literary Magazine*, April 1917), later appeared in his second collection of stories, *Tales of the Jazz Age* (1922). Clearly these years were of major importance to his development as a writer.

At Princeton he expanded his literary horizons considerably, largely through his friendships with John Peale Bishop, who introduced him to poetry, particularly that of John Keats, and with Edmund Wilson, who would become the "intellectual conscience" of his life. He admired Christian Gauss, the teacher who recognized the unique quality of Fitzgerald's prose. In the richest intellectual environment he had ever experienced he read Oscar Wilde, Ernest Dowson, Algernon Charles Swinburne, and Compton Mackenzie, whose *Sinister Street*

(1913–1914) made a marked impression on him. Later at Princeton he read Bernard Shaw, Rupert Brooke, and H. G. Wells and dabbled in socialist theory. His social life broadened, too. He was elected to the Cottage, one of the most elite Princeton clubs, largely because his standing among his classmates was enhanced by his successes with the Triangle productions.

And it was while at Princeton that Fitzgerald met the girl who would become the prototype for so many of the beautiful but elusive women who appear in his stories and novels, Ginevra King. His meeting with Ginevra was so important that he used it, and his memories of her, in the Basil and Josephine stories over a decade later.

After receiving his army commission, Fitzgerald was stationed in Montgomery, Alabama, where he met the girl who was to become the single most important person in his life, Zelda Sayre. Like Ginevra, Zelda appears throughout Fitzgerald's fictional world. She is Sally Carrol in "The Ice Palace" (*Saturday Evening Post*, 22 May 1920; collected in *Flappers and Philosophers,'* 1920), the heroine of "The Last of the Belles" (*Saturday Evening Post*, 2 March 1929; collected in *Taps at Reveille*, 1935), and Jonquil in "The Sensible Thing" (*Liberty*, 5 July 1924; collected in *All the Sad Young Men*, 1926); she is the model for most of the women in his stories and novels until the late 1930s. Zelda was the most popular, daring, and vital girl in Montgomery. For Fitzgerald she represented the glamour of the unattainable, and he fell deeply in love with her. In the ledger that he kept until 1937 (published as *F. Scott Fitzgerald's Ledger*, 1973) Fitzgerald reported that his twenty-second year was "The most important year of life. Every emotion and my life work decided. Miserable and ecstatic but a great success." In the entry for September of that year he notes, "Fell in love on the 7th." Fitzgerald also wrote the first version of *This Side of Paradise* while in the army.

Much has been written about the relationship between Scott and Zelda Fitzgerald. It was stormy, passionate, fierce, often ugly. Despite their quarrels and mutual self-destructiveness, the bond between them was so strong that long after her mental illness had kept them apart he could not divorce her, even when he fell in love with Sheilah Graham during his last years in Hollywood. Zelda lacked any principle of order; she threw herself into the heady celebrations that marked her husband's early success. She competed with him; she goaded him; she joined him in showing the world how an attractive and successful young American couple could defy convention and live for the thrill of the moment.

Zelda wrote many poignant letters after her illness, and, indeed, she has emerged as a pitiable figure. particularly in recent years when she has come to be regarded as a casualty of the American system of marriage—a woman who needed artistic fulfillment of her own, struggling against the domination of a male-oriented society. That kind of conclusion is simplistic; the truth of the relationship cannot really be known. Zelda Fitzgerald, whatever anguish she experienced and caused in those around her, is inseparable from her husband's career. His initial struggle for literary success in 1920 was caused by Zelda's refusal to marry him because he did not have enough money to support them. Subsequently, he kept on writing the short stories that would provide the money for them to maintain the style of life they desired, to maintain her throughout years of medical care and hospitalization, and to pay for their daughter, Scottie's, care and education.

Fitzgerald wrote nineteen short stories in the spring of 1919, all of them rejected by magazines. In June *Smart Set* bought "Babes in the Woods," first published in the *Nassau Literary Magazine* in May 1917, for thirty dollars. (It appeared in the September 1919 *Smart Set* and was later incorporated into *This Side of Paradise*.) Fitzgerald was living in New York, working in advertising, and struggling to finish his novel.

In the summer of 1919 Fitzgerald left New York City for St. Paul, where he finished *This Side of Paradise* and resubmitted it to Scribners, who had previously rejected it but now accepted it for publication in the spring of 1920. While waiting, he sold six stories to the *Smart Set* for $215 in October and two more in November for $300. His big break came when his new agent, Harold Ober, sold "Head and Shoulders" to the *Saturday Evening Post*, where it appeared in the 21 February 1920 issue, for $400. Ober later sold the film rights to the story for $2,500. In the early months of 1920, soon after the publication of *This Side of Paradise*, Fitzgerald wrote one of his best stories, "May Day," which was rejected by the *Post* but admired by Mencken, who

included it in the July 1920 *Smart Set*. On 3 April 1920 Scott and Zelda were married in New York.

Scribners followed publication of the novel with Fitzgerald's first collection of short stories, *Flappers and Philosophers*. Although only three of the stories may be considered among his best ("The Ice Palace," "The Offshore Pirate" [*Saturday Evening Post*, 29 May 1920], and "Bernice Bobs Her Hair" [*Saturday Evening Post*, 1 May 1920]), the volume appealed to the audience that had embraced his novel. The collection sold 15,325 copies by 1922, with six printings. The reviews were not as enthusiastic as those for *This Side of Paradise*; indeed, Mencken made note of the two-sidedness of Fitzgerald's creative life—the serious writer and the popular entertainer. This view of Fitzgerald was to characterize critical judgments of his fiction, particularly in relation to the short stories, from the 1920s to the present day. From this point in his life short stories would provide Fitzgerald's major income. He never made much money from his novels, including *This Side of Paradise* which, despite its success, never achieved the sales of a best-seller. During the next twelve years the *Saturday Evening Post* was Fitzgerald's main outlet for short stories, his fees increasing to $4,000 per story for the years 1929 through 1932.

There is a popular conception about Fitzgerald's work for the *Post*—that his stories were written to slick-magazine specifications, and therefore they represent the commercial side of his talent. It is a common belief that Fitzgerald bartered his gifts by writing short stories acceptable to the *Post*, which was edited from 1899 to 1936 by George H. Lorimer. Lorimer demanded an unusually high standard from his *Post* writers, allowing them wide latitude in choice of subject and form. There were certainly standards of commercial acceptability to which he subscribed, but they depended on professional smoothness, readability, and verve. The *Post* encouraged, but did not demand, strong plots, leisurely narrative, a good mixture of dialogue and action, and vivid characters. These requirements, while not stimulating radical departures from convention, also did not necessarily constrict or hamper creative instincts. And they were characteristics of Fitzgerald's fiction long before the *Post* ever accepted one of his stories. Happy endings were not prescribed, as proved by the publication in the *Post* of "Babylon Revisited" (21 February 1931; collected in *Taps at Reveille*), "The Rough Crossing" (8 June 1929), "Two Wrongs" (18 January 1930; collected in *Taps at Reveille*), and "One Trip Abroad" (11 October 1930).

Fitzgerald's letters underscore his independence as well as his dedication to his work. Although commercial writing is, he admitted in a 1940 letter to Zelda, a "definite trick," he felt he brought to it the "intelligence and good writing" to which a sensitive editor like Lorimer might respond. In Wesley W. Stout, Lorimer's successor, "an up and coming young Republican who gives not a damn about literature," he placed the blame for the plethora of "escape stories about the brave frontiersmen . . . or fishing, or football captains, nothing that would even faintly shock or disturb the reactionary bourgeois." He conceded that he had tried but could not write such stories. "As soon as I feel I am writing to a cheap specification my pen freezes and my talent vanishes over the hill. . . ." To Harold Ober he confessed that he was unable to "rush things. Even in years like '24, '28, '29, '30, all devoted to short stories, I could not turn out more than 8-9 top-price stories a year. It simply is impossible—all my stories are conceived like novels, require a special emotion, a special experience—so that my readers . . . know that each time it'll be something new, not in form but in substance."

After their marriage the Fitzgeralds rarely remained in one place more than six months to a year. After a whirlwind descent on New York City, they retreated to Westport, Connecticut, and then to Europe. Back in America, they lived briefly in St. Paul where Fitzgerald revised his novel *The Beautiful and Damned* (1922) and put together *Tales of the Jazz Age*, in which only two pieces, "The Diamond as Big as the Ritz" (*Smart Set*, June 1922) and "Two for a Cent" (*Metropolitan Magazine*, April 1922), had been written after 1920.

The collection contained eleven stories, divided into three sections: "My Last Flappers," "Fantasies," and "Unclassified Masterpieces." The John Held cartoon cover and Fitzgerald's annotated table of contents made it an attractive volume. Sales were good: eight thousand copies sold in the first printing, followed by two more printings in the same year. Readers liked the collection more than the critics did; most of them regarded the stories as diversions and failed to recognize the merit of "May Day" or "The Diamond as Big as the Ritz."

During the next few years the Fitzgeralds moved frequently: from Great Neck to France, to Italy, to Delaware, and even to Hollywood, where Fitzgerald was invited to try his hand at screenwriting. He was, at the same time, writing the major novels for which he received critical acclaim, *The Great Gatsby* and *Tender Is the Night* (1934). During these years Fitzgerald was at the top of his form as a short-story writer not only in the quantity but also in the quality of the fiction he produced. Because he needed money to finance the writing of *The Great Gatsby*, he produced eleven short stories in just four months.

He was able to put together another collection in 1926, and this one, *All the Sad Young Men*, contained some of his finest work: "The Rich Boy" (*Redbook*, January, February 1926), "Winter Dreams" (*Metropolitan Magazine*, December 1922), "Absolution" (*American Mercury*, June 1924), and "The Sensible Thing." As was his practice, he meticulously edited the magazine versions, careful to remove passages that he had "stripped" from them for use in *The Great Gatsby*. It was characteristic of Fitzgerald to mine his stories for particularly felicitous passages which could be used in the novels.) This volume, too, was relatively successful, considering that short-story collections rarely sold well. It went into three printings, totaling 16,170 copies in 1926. The critics were decidedly more impressed with this collection than either of the two that had appeared earlier, yet in retrospect it is clear that few recognized its level of artistry.

Just as his months in Europe had provided Fitzgerald with new friendships and influences— Ernest Hemingway, Gertrude Stein, Gerald and Sara Murphy—his two-month sojourn in Hollywood in early 1927 introduced him to a world to which he would return in fiction and in reality many times before his death. In "Jacob's Ladder" (*Saturday Evening Post*, 20 August 1927) the young heroine is clearly patterned after actress Lois Moran, whom Fitzgerald met in Hollywood. As he would continue to do for the rest of his life, Fitzgerald used his own personal experience, particularly his marriage, as subject matter for his stories and novels. Zelda Fitzgerald's mental breakdown did not allow Fitzgerald to suspend his short-story writing to take care of her. Instead, he combined visits to her in various sanatoriums with bouts of writing that would provide the funds necessary for her care and treatment.

During the worst years of economic and emotional crisis Fitzgerald wrote some of his most eloquent stories. As Zelda moved in and out of clinics and he struggled to meet his responsibilities to her and to his daughter, he wrote the Basil Duke Lee stories (1928–1929), the Josephine Perry stories (1930–1931), and the story which is today regarded as an unqualified masterpiece, "Babylon Revisited." The stories from this period are retrospective, meditative, elegiac, certainly sadder than those he had written for the *Post* during the previous ten years, and the *Post* editors did not like them.

By the early 1930s Fitzgerald had lost his taste for writing the stories of young love which had brought him to the top of the magazine pay scale by 1929. Of the forty-two stories written in the six years from 1929 to 1935, eight (the Basil and Josephine stories) draw on autobiographical events and cultural attitudes that reflect the years from World War I through the 1920s. Five of the remaining stories are so trivial as to demand only wonder that they managed to find their way into print. ("The Passionate Eskimo" [*Liberty*, June 1935] and "Zone of Accident," [*Saturday Evening Post*, 13 July 1935] are among them.) But the other twenty-nine provide important insight into Fitzgerald's artistic crisis, when his subjects were as serious as his and the nation's trials demanded, but his plots were outworn, stale, mechanical—unintentional parodies of the exuberant accounts of young love and romantic longing that so captivated audiences during the boom years. These stories show Fitzgerald groping with painful subjects and achieving only intermittent success but on at least two occasions, with "Babylon Revisited" and "Crazy Sunday" (*American Mercury*, October 1932), producing masterpieces that incorporate the matter, if not the manner, of his more commercial contemporary work. In these two stories and in those that began to appear in *Esquire* in the mid 1930s, Fitzgerald was able to resolve his problems with plot and style, and to find a form suitable to the serious subjects that now interested him.

By 1934 Fitzgerald was writing one story a month and drinking excessively, until finally he collapsed. At this low point (he had been disappointed by the poor sales, despite critical praise, of *Tender Is the Night*, which had been published in April) he suggested to his editor at Scribners, Maxwell Perkins, a new collection of short stories, *Taps at Reveille*. The volume contained eighteen stories, including such Basil Duke Lee stories as "The Freshest Boy" (*Saturday Evening Post*, 28 July 1928) and "He Thinks He's Wonderful"(*Saturday Evening Post*, 29 September 1928), the Josephine Perry stories "First Blood" (*Saturday Evening Post*, 5 April 1930) and "A Woman with a Past" (*Saturday Evening Post*, 6 September 1930), and other first-rate examples of his art: "Crazy Sunday," "The Last of the Belles," and "Babylon Revisited." The first printing was 5,100 copies, and the reviews were generally good, but short-story collections at any time were luxuries, and in the Depression, with a $2.50 cover price, the volume did not attract a wide readership. Fitzgerald's *Post* price had dropped to $3,000 per story, and of the nine he wrote in 1935, the magazine accepted only three. His primary outlet in the late 1930s was *Esquire*, whose editor, Arnold Gingrich, encouraged Fitzgerald, agreeing to accept anything he wrote. The stringent space limitations of the magazine coincided with Fitzgerald's search for a new form and a new style, but its low fees ($250 per story) were insufficient to support him. In 1936 he wrote nine stories, semi-fictional sketches, and articles for *Esquire*, including "Afternoon of an Author" (August 1936) and "Author's House" (July 1936), but they brought him only $2,250. These were Fitzgerald's most anguished years: Zelda was hopelessly ill; his own health had deteriorated badly; his income had shrunk to $10,000 by 1937; and he suffered a serious breakdown, physically and emotionally.

In 1937 Ober secured a contract for Fitzgerald as a screenwriter for M-G-M studios. Although he worked on many films and screenplays, only *Three Comrades* (1937) gives him screen credit (as cowriter). Nevertheless, these last years were among Fitzgerald's most artistically creative and personally satisfying. Despite his family problems and his poor health, he found personal happiness in his relationship with Hollywood gossip columnist Sheilah Graham. In addition to the uncompleted novel *The Last Tycoon* (1941), Fitzgerald wrote a series of stories for *Esquire* about a Hollywood hack writer, Pat Hobby. Fitzgerald had a heart attack in November 1940 and died on 21 December after suffering a second attack. In his hand was the *Princeton Alumni Weekly*. At his death he was almost forgotten as a writer; his royalty statement for the summer of 1940 was $13.13. Since the 1950s his reputation has grown steadily, and today he is ranked among the most important writers of the century. And the short stories, long neglected or undervalued, are at last receiving the kind of serious attention they have always deserved. But Fitzgerald always knew their value: "I have asked a lot of my emotions—one hundred and twenty stories. The price was high, right up with Kipling, because there was one little drop of something—not blood, not a tear, not my seed, but me more intimately than these, in every story, it was the extra I had."

Fitzgerald did not have a notably idiosyncratic linguistic style, as did Hemingway or William Faulkner, but a Fitzgerald story is recognizable by its romantic rhetoric, characters, settings, and social concerns. Fitzgerald experimented frequently with plots, subjects, and characters. The late stories are markedly different from the early group; both in style and substance they are innovative and experimental. For example, from Hollywood and his experience as a scriptwriter, Fitzgerald borrowed techniques, such as fade-outs and the camera angle as point of view.

The stories reveal a pattern of development and fall into three groups: the early tales about golden flappers and idealistic philosophers; the middle, embarrassingly sentimental, often mawkish stories; and finally, the late works, marked by new techniques—ellipsis, compression, suggestion—curiously enervated, yet deeply moving. Similar to these, yet distinctly separate, stand the Pat Hobby stories, where the old vitality had become corrosive bitterness in a literature of humiliation.

Most of his stories employ standard fictional techniques used in the novels: central complication, descriptive passages, dramatic climaxes and confrontations, reversals of fortune. And like the novels, the stories rarely turn on one action; more often, even in the shortest, slightest story, there are several actions of equal weight. His major problem is with plot; Fitzgerald will often begin with a good idea, create dramatic scenes, and then let the story limply peter out, or resolve the complications mechanically. An ending technique he used often was to blanket the resolution in lyrical prose, thus concealing the weakness of the story's resolution. Another weakness in the stories is related to point of view and distance, particularly in relation to the protagonists. Fitzgerald is most successful when his central character is both a participant and an observer of the action, weakest when the protagonist is simply a member of the upper class or an outsider.

Fitzgerald's gifts as a writer were primarily lyric and poetic; lapses in plot and characterization did not concern him nearly as much as using the wrong word. His revisions show that he edited primarily for phrase or rhythm in a sentence. Thus, his stories, whatever their plots, are almost always notable for the grace and lyricism of his rhetoric. His descriptive gifts are strikingly apparent; with a few selected details, usually in atmosphere or decor, he creates a mood against which the dramatic situation stands out in relief. In "News of Paris," a late sketch (probably written in 1940, published posthumously in *Furioso* in 1947), merely two lines, "It was quiet in the room. The peacocks in the draperies stirred in the April wind," provide the background for a brief but haunting retrospective account of dissolution, apathy, and tired sexuality in the pre-Depression boom.

Through language Fitzgerald created another world in his stories, a fairy-tale world replete with its own conventions and milieus, free of the tensions in his own all-too-depressingly familiar environment; he projected his imagination through the rhetoric of nostalgia into the past, creating a never-never land of beauty, stupefying luxury, and fulfillment. Fitzgerald's other world is a refuge from fear and anxiety, satiety and void; it is his answer to death and deterioration. Through a profusion of words, images—especially the sights, sounds, smells of luxury—perhaps existence itself might take on new meaning and possibility. The words themselves, for Fitzgerald, may have provided refuge from the storms of his own life. His infusions of charged rhetoric throughout the stories offer unshakable evidence of his belief in and commitment to that other world beyond his own, a world of possibility, hope, and beauty. Through imagery, through sensory appeals, through the evocative re-creation of an idealized past and a fabulous future, Fitzgerald's stories as a whole have the effect of lifting and transporting the reader past the restrictions of his own world. Fitzgerald was not simply playing on the facile sensibilities of his readers. The stories testify to his abiding faith in the possibility, somewhere, of living a graceful life. That this life might be made up of questionable values—of riches, of Hollywood-like romance, of tinselly fairgrounds and gilded mansions—is less important than that Fitzgerald asks his readers to share, perhaps ingenuously, his dedication to a dream.

His prose is filled with imagery, sensory in the Keatsian manner. He describes bridges, "like dancers holding hands in a row, with heads as tall as cities, and skirts of cable strand" ("The Sensible Thing"); trees, "like tall languid ladies with feather fans coquetting airily with the ugly roof of the monastery... delicate lace on the hems of many yellow fields" ("Benediction," *Smart Set*, February 1920; collected in *Flappers and Philosophers*); and moonlight, "That stream of silver that waved like a wide strand of curly hair toward the moon" ("Love in the Night," *Saturday Evening Post*, 14 March 1925). And his stories are filled with colors, bright blue and gold, white and silver, occasionally coalescing in a symbol that evokes a range of meanings beyond the purely decorative. In "May Day" the "great plate-glass front had turned to a deep creamy blue, the color of a Maxfield Parrish moonlight—a blue that seemed to press close upon the pane as if to crowd its way into the restaurant. Dawn had come up in Columbus Circle, magical, breathless dawn, silhouetting the great statue of the immortal Christopher, and mingling in a curious and uncanny manner with the fading yellow electric light inside."

The world of Fitzgerald's stories is most frequently the world of the very rich. The milieus and manners constitute the backdrop against which a rags-to-riches story may unfold, a struggling young man is rescued by a benevolent tycoon, or a beautiful Cinderella meets her handsome, wealthy prince. Even in the more somber stories, manners and milieu are as important as the plot or the characters.

Although most of the stories can be classified as stories of manners, there are several that fall into the category of fantasy, using supernatural devices, suspense and mystery, and fabulous, fabricated milieus as critical elements of plot. In "The Adjuster" (*Redbook*, September 1925; collected in *All the Sad Young Men*) Fitzgerald combines a realistic surface, homiletic intention, and supernatural agent in a unique, yet not entirely successful, mixture. Dr. Moon, the supernatural figure, is introduced purely as a deus ex machina in a story which is concerned with the growth of maturity and responsibility in a selfish young married woman. Dr. Moon is a strange amalgam, half-psychiatrist, half fortune-teller. He appears at regular intervals when the plot begins to falter, reordering the events. Thus he prevents the woman, Luella, from deserting her sick husband; he compels her to take up the irksome, neglected role of wife, mother, and housekeeper; and he rewards her at the end by confessing that he has never really existed: she has merely grown up, and he symbolizes her growth. He is on hand, also, to deliver to her a final homily on performing one's duties unselfishly. In a portentous declamation at the end he reveals, "Who am I? I am five years."

Similarly, in another morality tale, "One Trip Abroad," the supernatural element again enters the plot, but here it is worked more closely into the fabric of the story. In this Dorian Gray-like situation a young couple, Nicole and Nelson Kelly, on the path of dissolution and degeneration, see themselves at crucial moments in the process of their decay in the guise of another young couple. The dissipation of which they are unaware in themselves they notice in their doubles. The most vivid scene occurs at the end, where in one horrifying moment the Kellys recognize themselves in the other couple. What adds to the impressiveness of this story is the suggestion of supernatural elements functioning in the background. All nature seems to reflect the tumult and disorder of the Kellys' lives, suggests, in fact, a primordial force surrounding and eventually engulfing them. It follows them through the pleasure haunts of Europe, where nature is majestic and threatening; and in a powerful storm the two supernatural elements, the other couple and the malign forces which seem to have been released into the universe, meet—and in their meeting, the Kellys realize at last that they have lost not only "peace and love and health" but their souls as well.

Whatever the form of the story, Fitzgerald's range of subjects is wide and varied. Within the larger themes of life, love, death, and the American myth of success there are incalculable shades and variations. Many of his later subjects are adumbrated in his juvenilia, collected as *The Apprentice Fiction of F. Scott Fitzgerald, 1909–1917* (1965). "A Debt of Honor" (*Now and Then*, March 1910) is a young boy's exploration of the meaning of heroism as embodied in conventional notions of self-sacrifice and military glory. "Reade, Substitute Right-Half" (*Now and Then*, February 1910) is a classic wish-fulfillment sketch of an underdog who makes good on the football field, whose speed and dexterity outclass his teammates' greater brawn. "Sentiment—and the Use of Rouge" (*Nassau Literary Magazine*, June 1917) contrasts the new, relaxed wartime morality with older, tested values. It touches on the breakdown of sexual codes, on personal morality, on religion and belief, and on the boredom and ritualistic emptiness of upper-class life. In "Shadow Laurels" (*Nassau Literary Magazine*, April 1915) Fitzgerald mourns the unlived life and celebrates the power of the romantic imagination; in "The Spire and the Gargoyle" (*Nassau Literary Magazine*, February 1917) he regrets wasted opportunity and unfulfilled potential. "The Ordeal" (later revised and published as "Benediction") presents a spiritual conflict in the soul of a novitiate between the call of "the world . . . gloriously apparent" and "the monastery vaguely impotent." "The Debutante" (*Nassau Literary Magazine*, January 1917) and "Babes in the Woods" treat class distinctions, young love, manners, morals, and the generation gap. In "The Pierian Springs and the Last Straw" (*Nassau Literary Magazine*, October 1917) the themes are the artist's source of inspiration and the cruelty and hatred that can accompany love.

Most of the stories are brief; the themes are suggested or superficially explored. In "Sentiment—and the Use of Rouge," however, Fitzgerald develops his theme with fictional sophistication. "Sentiment" is about Clay Harrington Syneforth, a soldier in World War I who returns to his home in England for a two-day leave. What he encounters on his visit forms the core of the story. The central theme is change: between the England Clay knew, was raised in, and loved and the new world to which he returns, its looser morals, neglect of conventions, and disillusion with the old ideals of heroism and love, a world totally committed to the present moment and dedicated to pleasure and momentary satisfactions. The war has created a new sexual license; the women who cannot be the wives of the soldiers must discard

conventional morality and be as much as they can to the soldiers in the little time they have.

But Clay does not understand. In the last section of the story, on the battlefield, Flaherty, an Irish-Catholic soldier, brings up the question of faith. Flaherty excoriates the English talent for prettying up reality. "Blood on an Englishman always calls rouge to me mind." The English, he says, see death as a game, but "the Irish take death damn serious." Fitzgerald is saying at the end that Clay's devotion to outward forms and conventions prevents him from perceiving what is really important in life. Because he lives and worships the surface symbols of a bygone era, he is incapable of recognizing that underneath the rouge, people have been genuinely and profoundly moved by the events behind the big, important words. Thus he dies uncomprehending, bewildered, frightened—of sex and sexual license, of the new morality, of the unexpected depths of feeling in his contemporaries—more afraid of life than of the death which awaits him on the battlefield.

There are many flaws in the story, particularly its schoolboy seriousness and its consciously "arty" narrative. But it is a very early example of Fitzgerald's concern with a major theme—social change and the accompanying dislocation of values—which he treats memorably years later in "Babylon Revisited."

The major subjects of Fitzgerald's short stories are the sadness of the unfulfilled life and the unrecapturable moment of bliss, the romantic imagination and its power to transform reality, love, courtship and marriage, problems in marriage, the plight of the poor outsider seeking to enter the world of the very rich, the cruelty of beautiful and rich young women, the generation gap, the moral life, manners and mores of class society, heroism in ordinary life, emotional bankruptcy and the drift to death, the South and its legendary past, and the meaning of America in the lives of individuals and in modern history. To these subjects which intrigued him from adolescence, he added Hollywood, where the American dream seemed to so many of his generation to have reached its apotheosis.

Many of Fitzgerald's finest stories date from the early 1920s. "Bernice Bobs Her Hair" is an early story, slight in intent but animated by an authentic and minute representation of manners and social milieu in which newly emancipated young American women live. It was the kind of story that Fitzgerald came to be associated with, for it typified the changes overtaking the new postwar generation. The central action is the transformation of a socially inept, unpopular girl, Bernice, into a much-sought-after, socially sophisticated "flapper." In the course of Bernice's education, Fitzgerald reveals the intricate system of manners on which social success depends. The plot hinges on Bernice's daring threat to bob her hair and invite her whole crowd to witness the momentous event. In the relationship between Bernice and her cousin Marjorie, Fitzgerald exposes the cruelty underlying the social conventions of young people, the competition for popularity which impels Marjorie to jibe at and cruelly taunt Bernice until she must carry out the threat Marjorie knows she had initially made as a joke. But Marjorie herself is an example of the newly emancipated woman who desires only to shake free from the limitations imposed upon her by society and to face life courageously, unhampered and unfettered. In a short, fervent speech she confesses to Bernice her abhorrence of society's hypocritical expectations of women and exhorts her cousin to relinquish the morals of a defunct generation. In this spirited story Fitzgerald sums up more accurately than any sociological analysis the rebelliousness and determination of the new generation and, particularly, of the new heroine.

Ardita Farnham, the heroine of "The Offshore Pirate," is the prize wealthy young Toby Moreland seeks because she possesses courage and independence, the most valuable attributes of Fitzgerald's flappers and philosophers. The story traces Toby's disguise as a jazz bandleader, Curtis Carlyle, who pirates the Farnham yacht with Ardita on board. A bored, spoiled debutante, she longs for someone with "imagination and the courage of his convictions." She refuses to meet anyone her family proposes and intends to run off with an older playboy. Toby's ruse works; he and Ardita fall in love on the ship, moored in a cavernous alcove, while "Curtis's" band plays music that enchances the romantic possibilities of the tropical paradise. The story seems bathed in the blue, silver, and gold of the sky and sun, and hero and heroine's paeans to courage, conviction, and the possibilities of the romantic imagination seem appropriate to the mood and milieu established by the opening lines:

> This unlikely story begins on a sea that was a blue dream, as colorful as blue-silk stockings, and beneath a sky as blue as the irises of children's eyes. From the western half of the sky the sun was shying little golden disks at the sea—if you gazed intently enough you could see them skip from wave tip to wave tip until they joined a broad collar of golden coin that was collecting half a mile out and would eventually be a dazzling sunset.

Fitzgerald sustains both rhetoric and idea—the power of the romantic imagination—throughout in a story that is among the best of his early works. Curtis Carlyle's tale of lost illusions parallels Fitzgerald's exploration of the meaning of natural aristocracy. The conflict within Fitzgerald between rival claims—aristocracy of the spirit versus aristocracy of wealth—is omnipresent throughout the stories. In his disillusionment he seeks to replace the values common to his society with a completely personal ethical standard; he ultimately exchanges moribund social values for a personal brand of heroism—in itself an aristocracy of the spirit.

Among the early stories, "The Diamond as Big as the Ritz" is notable not only because of the fine writing and historical resonances but because Fitzgerald's gift for fantasy is at its best. John Ungar, a middle-class boy, is invited by his classmate, Percy Washington, to spend his vacation at the latter's home "in the West." En route, Percy reveals that his father has a diamond "bigger than the Ritz-Carlton Hotel." John falls in love with Percy's sister, discovers the secret of the Washington wealth, and is almost killed before he can escape from a lavish and terrifying world. In this story Fitzgerald does not contain his subject and theme within a realistic setting. Here is an American West bigger and more extravagant than in the wildest Western tall story it subtly parodies. As the reader willingly suspends disbelief, the world of Fitzgerald's imagination takes on the colorations of the Oriental kingdom belonging to "some Tartar Khan." The Washington chateau is very like the pleasure dome of Kubla Khan, and the sights, smells, and sounds of luxury assault and ultimately deaden the senses until the lavish phantasmagoria moves as in a waking dream.

Remarkably, Fitzgerald sustains this geographic flight from the opening in Hades, "a small town on the Mississippi River," to St. Midas School near Boston, to the twelve wizened old men in the wasteland town of Fish, Montana, to the diamond mountain retreat of Braddock Washington. Yet the action, which departs wildly from probability, is so rooted in the familiar, recognizable patterns of human behavior that after the initial shock has receded and the reader has accepted the fanciful premise, he is forced to make invidious comparisons between the rise of American big business in the nineteenth and twentieth centuries and the growth of Braddock Washington's fortune.

Just as Fitzgerald used the American West in "The Diamond as Big as the Ritz" to explore American values in the context of American history, Fitzgerald used the American South to express the need for tradition, as embodied in his own father's values and manners. "The Ice Palace" is about the differences between the South—which stands for warmth, carelessness and generosity, feeling, tradition, and life—and the North—cold, hard materialism, selfishness, and death. The action involves heroine Sally Carrol Happer's desire for something more than the swimming, dancing, and playing that fill up her languid, somnolent, lazy summer days.

The opening of the story establishes the mood of the South, and at the end of part two, as Sally Carrol walks with her northern suitor, Harry Bellamy, through a Confederate graveyard, she defines the tradition she treasures:

> I've tried in a way to live up to those past standards of noblesse oblige—there's just the last remnants of it, you know, like the roses of an old garden dying all round us—streaks of strange courtliness and chivalry in some of these boys an'stories I used to hear from a Confederate soldier who lived next door.... Oh, Harry, there was something, there was something!

The tempo of the story quickens with the introduction of the northern element, Harry Bellamy, "tall, broad, and brisk." The warm summer is over; it is November and time for the serious business of life. Sally Carrol becomes engaged to Harry, and they plan to go North to meet his family. From the first line in part three—"All night in the Pullman it was very cold"—and for all the scenes laid in the North, it is penetratingly cold. There is no relief for Sally Carrol who cannot, for as long as she remains in the alien environment of Harry's home, get warm. The icy weather symbolizes a way of life: no sense of play, no social badinage, no graciousness, no heritage of manners and style, only a chilling obedience to the forms of life. Even the people are gray and desiccated.

Harry's "cold lips" kissing her reinforce the pervasive, unrelenting chill.

In the next part the relationship between Sally Carrol and Harry hardens after a quarrel at dinner when Harry refers to southerners as "lazy and shiftless," and later when the vaudeville orchestra plays "Dixie," she is painfully reminded of what she has left behind. Part five again takes up the motif of iciness, and the action builds to an apocalyptic climax as Sally Carrol loses her way in the glittering cavernous maze of the "ice palace, like a damp vault connecting empty tombs." Here, ice, snow, and palace are symbolically linked as death. As she falls down in the palace, she dreams of rejoining the dead Margery Lee, at whose grave she had sat and pondered the southern past back in Tarleton, her home town. The ice palace itself functions brilliantly as a symbol of the imminent death of the spirit, the inevitable accompaniment to life in a new, raw, mercantile northern city.

The last section returns to the original scene; it is April in Sally Carrol's southern town, and "the wealth of golden sunlight poured a quite enervating yet oddly comforting heat over the house where day long it faced the dusty stretch of road." Sally Carrol has experienced a purgatory in ice; chastened, contented, even indolent, she takes up her old life. There is much in the texture of the story that adds to its effectiveness: the decor, like the new but charmless library in Harry's house; dialogue, at the dinner-party where Sally Carrol first experiences disappointment and disillusionment with Harry; characters, the men—hard, brisk, athletic, and the women—faded, dull, apathetic; social position, shades and nuances of class distinction and throughout, wealth of goods going hand in hand with poverty of spirit, death and snow versus life and lilacs.

One of Fitzgerald's most effective and popular stories in which the primary emphasis is on social criticism is "May Day," yet he never wrote another story quite like it. Although the main character's story is characteristically Fitzgerald, the social / political criticism, developed in a subplot, is more overt than in most of his stories. He did salvage several structural and technical devices from the story—contrasting and parallel episodes, kaleidoscopic impressions, shifting rhetorical patterns—for use in other short stories but turned to the more expansive novel form to develop the multilevel plot.

Fitzgerald often opens a story with a philosophical passage that sets the tone and adumbrates the theme. In "May Day" the opening lines are heavily ironic, measured, musical, and solemn, with unmistakably biblical overtones.

> There had been a war fought and won and the great city of the conquering people was crossed with triumphal arches.... Never had there been such splendor in the great city, for the victorious war had brought plenty in its pain, and the merchants had flocked thither from the South and West with their households to taste of all the luscious feasts and witness the lavish entertainments prepared—and to buy for their women furs against the next winter and bags of golden mesh and varicolored slippers of silk and silver and rose satins and cloth of gold.

The passage serves to unify under a common subject the diverse episodes which follow. And, by offering moral commentary which is supported by the ensuing action, it raises that action to a level beyond its immediate significance.

The opening scenes of this story establish the setting and introduce the characters and major action—Gordon Sterrett's drift to death. The action is constructed around a series of contrasts between Gordon and a former Yale classmate, Philip Dean. Dean's social world, to which Gordon tries frantically to cling, is epitomized in expensive clothes and bodily well-being, the "trinkets and slippers," the "splendor" and "wine of excitement" of the invocation. Gordon asks Dean for a three-hundred-dollar loan that will enable him to extricate himself from the demands of a lower-class young woman with whom he has become involved. Dean, paying careful attention to his body and his wardrobe, listens to Gordon and refuses the loan. Gordon, like so many other poor young men whose dreams have been betrayed by a fiercely competitive system, is unprepared for the cold New York City which tosses people like him to their deaths.

His plight, made more poignant by beautiful Edith Braden's initial interest and subsequent rejection, is contrasted with that of two war veterans, unintentionally caught up in a socialist protest rally in the crowded streets. One of the soldiers, Carrol Key, whose name suggests that "in his veins, however thinly diluted by generations of degeneration, ran blood of some potentiality," is accidentally killed when he is swept up in the embattled crowd determined to put the Bolsheviks to rout. The last part of the story turns into a kind of social parable. The action moves from the Biltmore Hotel to Child's 59th

Street restaurant, and to the Biltmore elevator, where the ascent of Mr. In and Mr. Out serves as an ironic counterpoint to the descent of Gordon Sterrett and Carrol Key—and possibly to the struggle upward for success in America.

"Winter Dreams" was written three years before *The Great Gatsby*, "The Rich Boy" immediately after. Both stories are among Fitzgerald's best, and both plots turn on conflicts between the very rich and a representative of the middle class—a contrast explored in the minutiae of social gestures, moods, conventions, and customs. In the former, Dexter Green is the protagonist of the story. In the latter, Anson Hunter is "the rich boy," the subject of the story, which is narrated by an observer-participant in the action, a friend of Anson's who all his life has lived among the rich.

In "Winter Dreams" Dexter Green is a golf caddy at the luxurious club patronized by the wealthy inhabitants of Sherry Island. He meets Judy Jones, from one of the club's leading families, and she and her summer world become the focus of his winter dreams. Judy Jones epitomizes the very rich. She is beautiful, cold, imperious, and maddening. Dexter pursues her, but she eludes him; the struggle to attain Judy Jones becomes for him the struggle to realize his dream of entering the glittering world of those enchanted summers. But the world of Judy Jones—who comes to symbolize both the beauty and the meretriciousness of Dexter's dreams—is clearly revealed as cruelly, coldly destructive. Dexter, listening to the music wafting over the lake at Sherry Island, felt "magnificently attuned to life." His winter dream, simply, was to recapture the ecstasy of that golden moment: the sensation that "everything about him was radiating a brightness and a glamour he might never know again."

The story is richly evocative, containing some of Fitzgerald's best writing. The change of seasons throughout the story reflects and coincides with Dexter's moods; like other Fitzgerald characters, he is extraordinarily sensitive to the natural world, and it is in terms of its effects upon people's lives that nature fascinates Fitzgerald. Dexter's spirits soar with the "gorgeous" Minnesota autumn; October "filled him with hope which November raised to a sort of ecstatic triumph." That ecstasy, linked with the image of Judy Jones, is finally Dexter's vision of immortality, just as Daisy Buchanan was Gatsby's. If he could have had Judy he could have preserved his youth and the beauty of a world that seemed to "withstand all time." When the beauty of Judy Jones fades, his hopes fade with it, and that sense of wonder he cherished over the years is lost "in the country of illusion ... where his winter dreams had flourished."

"The Rich Boy" is the story of Anson Hunter, who lives in a world of "high finance, high extravagance, divorce and dissipation, of snobbery and privilege." The narrator immediately establishes his relationship to Anson. Brought together by chance as officers in the war, their backgrounds are totally dissimilar. Anson is the easterner, raised without "idealism or illusion," who accepts without reservation the world into which he was born. The narrator is from the West and thoroughly middle class, but he has lived among the "brothers" of the rich. He is thus capable of observing the nuances of upper-class manners and morals. His famous introduction, "Let me tell you about the very rich," clearly distinguishes the narrator from Anson and from the reader, thus effecting the necessary separation between subject and point of view which characterizes Fitzgerald's best stories. As though determined to prove for once that "the country of the rich" need not be "as unreal as fairyland," the narrator traces with clinical care the events and implications of Anson's life to their inevitable end.

Following a series of incidents chronicling Anson's courtship with Paula Legendre, the narrator returns to fill in the events and analyze the changes the last years have wrought in his friend. He is with Anson after the latter had learned of Paula's death in childbirth, and Anson, "for the first time in their friendship," says nothing of how he feels, shows no sign of emotion. The narrator wonders why Anson is never happy unless someone is in love with him, promising him something, perhaps "that there would always be women in the world who would spend their brightest, freshest, rarest hours to nurse and protect that superiority he cherished in his heart."

"Absolution" is one of the very few Fitzgerald stories that focuses directly on religion. Eleven-year-old Rudolph Miller is forced by his parents to go to confession, where the "half-crazed priest," Father Schwarz, listens to the boy's story. It is a tale of a young boy's fears and passions in an environment of rugged austerity and grim religiosity, ending with a lie in the confessional booth. When the confession is over,

the priest's complete breakdown reinforces the significance of the boy's story. The pressure of Rudolph's environment has driven him onto the "lonely secret road of adolescence." Father Schwarz had once followed that lonely road to the end years ago, suppressing along the way the natural passions aroused by the rustle of Swedish girls along the path by his window and in Romberg's Drug Store "when ... he had found the scent of cheap toilet soap desperately sweet upon the air."

Flashback adds dramatic intensity to the encounter by supplying the details leading up to Rudolph's spiritual crisis and connecting Rudolph's background with Father Schwarz's. It also points up the resemblances among apparently dissimilar characters by tying the quality in which Rudolph's father is deficient, the romantic imagination, to Rudolph's conviction that "there was something ineffably gorgeous somewhere that had nothing to do with God," and to Father Schwarz's dream of an amusement park where "things go glimmering." But Rudolph's life is just beginning, and his imagination restores him by providing an outlet for his buried life. He becomes Blatchford Sarnemington, a figure who exists outside of Father Schwarz's world, far from the confessional. Fitzgerald suggests that in Rudolph's perception of Father Schwarz's insanity and in Rudolph's commitment to his own dreams lie freedom and the possibility of romantic fulfillment.

In 1934 Fitzgerald told a critic that "Absolution" "was intended to be a picture of [Gatsby's] early life, but that I cut it because I preferred to preserve the sense of mystery." Fitzgerald told Maxwell Perkins that the story was salvaged from an earlier, discarded version of *Gatsby*; the 1923 start of the novel included a section on Gatsby's childhood, so it is likely that Rudolph is a preliminary version of a character who would become Jay Gatsby.

One of the most moving stories of the early 1920s, "The Sensible Thing" draws upon Fitzgerald's courtship of Zelda Sayre, as he describes George O'Kelly's rejection by Jonquil Cary because of his poverty and her subsequent acceptance after a year during which he has achieved the success that will now make their marriage possible. Again for Fitzgerald, the glow that first love imparts cannot be recaptured. In her acceptance of conventional advice by her parents, and, indeed, following her own convictions, Jonquil turned away George because he was not financially ready for her at the moment when they realized how much they were in love. Two months later, she tells him, "now I can't because it doesn't seem to be the sensible thing."

Although George does win her after a year in which a series of lucky breaks reward him with the success he had found so elusive previously, he learns that something rare and precious has been lost. "The sensible thing—they had done the sensible thing. He had traded his first youth for strength and carved success out of despair. But with his youth, life had carried away the freshness of his love." Thus, his lament at the end for that loss, "never again an intangible whisper in the dusk, or on the breeze of night....," conveys Fitzgerald's deepest conviction that the golden moment in one's life comes only once, and that subsequent fulfillment in love or in work can only be second best. Thus he ends the story on a note of both regret and acceptance: "Well, let it pass. . . . April is over, April is over. There are all kinds of love in the world, but never the same love twice."

From 1928 through 1931 Fitzgerald wrote fourteen stories in two series, the first, about Basil Duke Lee (1928–1929), comprising nine stories, one posthumously published, and the second featuring Josephine Perry (1930–1931). The Basil stories, for which Fitzgerald plumbed his own adolescence, take the character from his early school days, age eleven, through his entrance into college. From the beginning, Basil is never wholly accepted by the other youngsters. Because of his sensitivity, intensity, and competitiveness, he differs from them; they know it and resent it. He is frequently the butt of their jokes and recipient of their insults. Fitzgerald handles Basil's anguish and humiliation by bringing to bear the perspective of the adult on the loneliness and misery of an adolescent. Basil not only endures but even learns from each of his painful experiences: upstaging by Hubert Blair, that paragon of youthful charm and virtuosity; rejection by Imogene Bissel, a juvenile femme fatale; and, more seriously, ostracism and debasement by his prep-school classmates.

Basil's fatal flaw is his loquacity; he cannot resist pointing out his own superiority and his fellows' deficiencies. It is a hard lesson, but he finally learns, after years of misery, the value of

discretion. He is, however, destined to remain the outsider, "one of the poorest boys in a rich boys' school." By adopting Basil's hyperbolic evaluation of the situation, the narrative forms an ironic but not unkind commentary on the young hero's driving ambition. Because Fitzgerald understands and takes seriously the problems of adolescence and because he remembers the pain of his own youth, he remains always the detached but totally sympathetic observer.

The central situation in each Basil story is a two-fold struggle, within Basil for mastery over himself and between Basil and society for social acceptance. In each situation, although rebuffed and humiliated by his own fatal penchant for self-advertising and an unwillingness to temper his romantic illusions about others, Basil grows in awareness and perceptivity, particularly of his own character and motives. In "The Freshest Boy" he concludes that "he had erred at the outset—he had boasted, he had been considered yellow at football, he had pointed out people's mistakes to them, he had shown off his rather extraordinary fund of general information in class." The Basil Duke Lee stories treat the pain of adolescence without the sentimentality so characteristic of the popular Booth Tarkington stories.

Josephine Perry is an embodiment of the alluring yet cruel flapper, and Fitzgerald manages to convey the tragedy inherent in a totally self-absorbed life. Women like Josephine are doomed, he implies; momentary perception of their tragic destinies impels them to strike out at their world, and particularly at the young men who idolize them.

In "First Blood" Josephine is introduced during an argument with her family. Supremely self-confident in her budding beauty, Josephine sets her sights beyond the limits suggested by age and inexperience. She pursues and captures the most eligible "older" man in her set, only to reject his slavish devotion when it is finally proffered. The object of her desires, once attained, loses its fascination. Josephine must go on to ever more thrilling and elusive conquests.

In the first stories Fitzgerald's tone is unvaryingly indulgent toward the young woman and her romantic forays. But as the stories continue, Josephine's successes invariably prove empty. Perpetually seeking new thrills, she longs for the ideal man who she thinks might satisfy once and for all her craving for romance and novelty. In each story, however, the young man disappoints her. She gradually grows numb with satiety (in Fitzgerald's day promiscuity usually meant only kissing), until a kiss fails to arouse her.

The youthful flirtations of "A Nice Quiet Place" (*Saturday Evening Post*, 31 May 1930; collected in *Taps at Reveille*) deepen in "A Woman with a Past" into a frantic search for fulfillment in love, but each conquest brings Josephine only boredom and ennui. In "Emotional Bankruptcy" (*Saturday Evening Post*, 15 August 1931), the saddest and most serious story of the group, by the time Josephine finally meets the perfect man, a war hero, it is too late for her. She no longer has the capacity to feel anything for anyone. She is emotionally bankrupt, no longer appealingly flirtatious and amusing either to the author or the reader, but empty, frozen, slightly repellent. Fitzgerald drops his ironic detachment at the end and moralizes on the human waste which might be tragic were it associated with someone less trivial and self-centered than Josephine Perry.

From the time Fitzgerald made his first trip to Hollywood in the late 1920s, he was fascinated by what he described as "a tragic city of beautiful girls." By 1940 he reported that there is "no group, however small, interesting.... Everywhere there is ... either corruption or indifference." Hollywood was to provide Fitzgerald with the subject of some of his important fiction, notably the short story "Crazy Sunday," based upon his own experience at actress Norma Shearer's party, and partly inspired by her husband, M-G-M chief Irving Thalberg.

"Crazy Sunday" is a story about Hollywood and about one extraordinary man, Miles Calman, as observed by Joel Coles, a young writer. From the outset Hollywood, a "damn wilderness," vies with Joel and Miles for center stage. Hollywood transcends, compels, structures the plot. The rhythm of the story is the rhythm of Hollywood life, from crazy Sunday, "not a day, but rather a gap between two other days," to the other six days of frantic irrelevancy in a plastic wasteland.

The action begins and ends in Miles Calman's house where the ambience promotes the wildly exhibitionist performance which wins Joel instant notoriety. When Joel regards the assemblage, he is driven in a moment of semi-drunken, lavish goodwill to entertain them, and the tensions within him, suggested earlier,

become insistent and are released in his outrageous performance. The focus of the story, however, is the intricate relationship between Miles and Stella Calman which ensnares Joel. The Calmans fight with one another but remain, to the end, self-sufficient, tightly insulated by mutual desire and mutual dependency. Joel can never really matter to them.

The story culminates, after Miles's death, in the circuslike parade Joel observes at the theater as he waits for Stella. Everything seems tinselly, tawdry, as artificial as a Hollywood B-picture. At the end Joel leaves the Calman house and bitterly takes up his life made empty and futile after the death of "the only American-born director with both an interesting temperament and an artistic conscience." "Crazy Sunday" is a haunting vignette of Hollywood, and it is measure of Fitzgerald's artistry that he succeeds despite the flaw of conflicting centers of interest, Miles and Joel. Joel is able both to evaluate and at the same time participate in events, and Fitzgerald's narration is often indistinct from Joel's observations. Yet the fascination lies, for Joel and for the reader, in Miles Calman, an early version of Monroe Stohr, the subject of Fitzgerald's last, incomplete novel, *The Last Tycoon*.

Many critics and scholars regard "Babylon Revisited" as the best of Fitzgerald's short stories. Written in 1930, at a particularly low point in his own life, it reflects the meditative sadness of a man looking back, in the Depression, on the waste and dissipation of the boom. More than perhaps any of his stories, it blends personal and historical elements to form a commentary on an era. It is about Charlie Wales, who, through indiscretions resulting in the death of his wife, made himself an outsider to the "good" people, represented by his sister-in-law and her husband, Marion and Lincoln Peters. In order to win back his child, Honoria, from the Peterses, who have been caring for her, he must establish for them his new stability and adherence to their values. The difficulty of his task is compounded by Marion Peters's dislike and distrust of him. Fitzgerald constructs the plot around a series of contrasts: between Charlie and the Peterses, past and present, illusion and reality, dissipation and steadiness, gaiety and grimness, Paris and America, adults and children. The author's tone, detached, critical, and ironic, merges with Charlie's self-critical but not self-pitying awareness, heightening the contrasts and adding meaning to even the briefest observation. "I spoiled this city for myself. I didn't realize it, but the days come along one after another, and then two years were gone, and everything was gone, and I was gone."

Charlie Wales of the Depression is no longer the same young man who coasted along on the joyride of the boom years. The story is about his exploration of the problems of character and responsibility, particularly the power of one's past to shape and determine his future. Against a background of change and dislocation wrought by social upheaval, the story of Charlie Wales is a search for latent values residing within the individual, values that provide the courage and resiliency to remake a squandered life. And it is all based on character, the "eternally valuable element." Charlie is left to examine the ruin of the past, to discover what, if anything, is worth the survival. He admits, "I lost everything I wanted in the boom," and his one hope for the future is continuity of character, as if by passing on to his daughter some lesson from his past, he will thus preserve part of himself in her.

"Babylon Revisited" is not a simple morality tale. Charlie is acutely sensitive to himself and to the Peterses, and he is eager to assume responsibility for Honoria's life and for his own. But "character" does not insure happiness for Charlie Wales. In this story, perhaps his most moving statement on the subject, Fitzgerald indicates that it is strictly a mode of individual survival, that not only may character not bring Charlie happiness along with his newly discovered values, but it may even intensify his despair and corrode his hopes.

In his late works, dating from 1936 to his death in 1940, Fitzgerald's style was markedly different from the early lyrical prose. The tone becomes flat, almost essayistic; narrative is unemotional and economical, yet strangely haunting in its dry precision. These are brief, autobiographical sketches, semifictional attempts to reinterpret his life and his art. In "Afternoon of an Author" the protagonist prepares to go outside for a walk, the first one in many days. His thoughts are of mental and physical fatigue—his own and others. On the bus ride, in the barber shop, he ruminates over what he is now, what he once was, what he might have become, his struggles and especially his weariness and inertia. There are no highs and lows, only a quiet drift toward death. The faint note of self-pity stems from physical debility rather than emotional outrage.

The author in "Author's House" surveys his youth, his illness, his mistakes and failures, and waits for death. All he has left is despair, knowing he can never dwell again in the turret of his symbolic house, knowing that success has ultimately eluded him.

In "An Author's Mother" (*Esquire*, October 1936) the title character, with her "high-crowned hat," incipient cataracts, and air of hopeless bewilderment, is a touching relic of another era. The modern world is obviously too much for her. She is proud of but cannot understand her son's success, for she associates "authors" only with Mrs. Humphry Ward, Henry Wadsworth Longfellow, Edna Ferber, and especially the sentimental poetesses Alice and Phoebe Cary. Uncomplaining and uncomprehending, she, too, retreats from life through the back door of her memories. For her there is nothing left but death.

Fitzgerald's vitality did burst forth again in his last years with a series of stories about Pat Hobby, a has-been screenwriter. Pat Hobby is among Fitzgerald's most intriguing characters, perhaps because the author was exorcizing the dark, defeated side of his own nature. Pat is an incompetent, an alcoholic, a petty blackmailer, a dreamer, a would-be lecher, a leech, a whiner, a conniver, a thief, a scab, a coward, an informer, an eternal outsider. He is lazy, ubiquitous, and dishonest. Although he is rigidly excluded from the Hollywood power center, his perverted sense of justice leads him to identify with the producers rather than their hireling writers like himself and the exploited or discarded actors and directors. He aspires to every flashy Hollywood-American success symbol—Filipino servants, swimming pools, liquor, girls, and meals at the Brown Derby. Pat is a firm ally of the status quo, or more properly, the past, into which he seeks to escape the sordid present.

Fitzgerald's technique in the Pat Hobby stories is to devise situations in which Pat, faced with alternatives, consistently selects the action most likely to degrade him further. In one story after another, Pat sinks to lower and lower levels of activity; trickery and connivance are his tools. But for all his duplicity, Pat is pathetically unsuccessful in his attempts to "put one over on them." Each situation ends in debacle, humiliation, and further degradation. And yet, for all his faults, he is a strangely moving figure in these stories of the absurd: the eternal fall guy who admits honestly in a moment of painful clarity, "I've been cracked down on plenty." The language of these stories is racy and colloquial, and the tone consistently ironic and detached. The stories were published in *Esquire* during the last year of Fitzgerald's life and in 1941, after his death. He worked on them as carefully as he could, often sending Arnold Gingrich telegrams requesting minor revisions even after a story had been set in print. At the same time Fitzgerald was working on his other Hollywood story, *The Last Tycoon*. It is probable that the Pat Hobby stories served as a release for his black vision of Hollywood and of his own career, allowing a final blossoming of his artistry.

F. Scott Fitzgerald's reputation as a short-story writer has risen considerably since his death, and at least a dozen of his stories rank with the most notable in American literature. And though his reputation as a major American writer rests primarily on his novels, especially *The Great Gatsby*, in variety, in range, and in stylistic excellence, his short stories are an intrinsic part of his fictional world.

Source: Ruth Prigozy, "F. Scott Fitzgerald," in *Dictionary of Literary Biography*, Vol. 86, *American Short-Story Writers, 1910–1945, First Series*, edited by Bobby Ellen Kimbel, Gale Research, 1989, pp. 99–123.

SOURCES

"American Short Stories," in *Times Literary Supplement*, April 19, 1923, p. 264.

Boyd, Woodward, "*Tales of the Jazz Age*: The Fitzgerald Legend," in *F. Scott Fitzgerald in His Own Time: A Miscellany*, edited by Matthew J. Bruccoli and Jackson R. Bryer, Kent State University Press, 1971, p. 340, originally published as "The Fitzgerald Legend," in *Daily News* (St. Paul), December 10, 1922.

Bryer, Jackson, *The Critical Reputation of F. Scott Fitzgerald: A Bibliographical Study*, Archon Books, 1967, p. 41.

Fitzgerald, F. Scott, "The Diamond as Big as the Ritz," in *The Best Early Stories of F. Scott Fitzgerald*, edited by Bryant Mangum, Modern Library, 2005, pp. 191–229.

"The Future of Fitzgerald," in *F. Scott Fitzgerald in His Own Time: A Miscellany*, edited by Matthew J. Bruccoli and Jackson R. Bryer, Kent State University Press, 1971, p. 413, originally published in *Journal* (Minneapolis), December 31, 1922.

Hawthorne, Hildegarde, Review of *Tales of the Jazz Age*, in *New York Times Book Review*, October 29, 1922, p. 12.

Miller, James E., Jr., "Transition," in *F. Scott Fitzgerald: His Art and His Technique*, New York University Press, 1964, p. 59.

Petry, Alice Hall, "Tales of the Jazz Age," in *Fitzgerald's Craft of Short Fiction: The Collected Stories 1920–1935*, UMI Research Press, 1989, p. 61.

Smith, Ellison D., "'Shut the Door': A Senator Speaks for Immigration Restriction," in *Congressional Record*, Vol. 65, pp. 5961–62, www.historymatters.gmu.edu/d/5080 (accessed October 29, 2006).

FURTHER READING

Bruccoli, Matthew J., *Fitzgerald and Hemingway: A Dangerous Friendship*, Manly, 1994.

Bruccoli, considered one of the foremost experts on Fitzgerald's life and work, uses the correspondence between these two authors to analyze their friendship. He documents the progress of the relationship from its amiable early days in Paris in 1925 to its more contentious times in the 1930s, when Hemingway became increasingly critical of Fitzgerald.

Bruccoli, Matthew J., and Scottie Fitzgerald Smith, *Some Sort of Epic Grandeur: The Life of F. Scott Fitzgerald*, University of South Carolina Press, 1981.

This book is considered by many to be the definitive biography of F. Scott Fitzgerald, written by Fitzgerald expert Bruccoli and Fitzgerald's own daughter. An unsentimental and thorough examination of Fitzgerald's life, including his alcoholism and his wife's mental deterioration, the book includes examples of Fitzgerald's correspondence to friends and relatives.

Fitzgerald, F. Scott, *The Crack-Up*, edited by Edmund Wilson, New Directions Publishing, 1945.

This collection of confessional essays, letters, and journal entries describes Fitzgerald's gradual decline, both emotionally and professionally. The title essay was first published in Esquire magazine in 1936. The collection was edited by Edmund Wilson, a longtime friend of Fitzgerald.

Mangum, Bryant, *A Fortune Yet: Money in the Art of F. Scott Fitzgerald's Short Stories*, Garland, 1991.

In this book, Bryant Mangum, a professor of English at Virginia Commonwealth University, explores Fitzgerald's depiction of wealth and the wealthy in his short fiction, and the writer's simultaneous fascination with, and disdain for, the very rich.

A Girl like Phyl

PATRICIA HIGHSMITH

1980

Several reviewers cite Patricia Highsmith's "A Girl like Phyl" as one of the best stories in her collection, *Nothing That Meets the Eye: The Uncollected Stories of Patricia Highsmith* (2002). They applaud its taut construction and fascinating portrait of the troubled main character, forty-year-old engineer Jeff Cormack. Highsmith's documented interest in existentialism becomes apparent in this story of a man who struggles to find a clear sense of himself and a purpose for his life when confronted by the meaninglessness of the modern world. The story contains some of Highsmith's trademarks: the shock of the extraordinary in a seemingly ordinary world and the violence that lurks just beneath a calm surface. Here Highsmith explores the devastating consequences of shattered dreams and recognition of painful realities.

AUTHOR BIOGRAPHY

Patricia Highsmith was born Mary Patricia Plangman in Fort Worth, Texas, on January 19, 1921. Her parents, both commercial artists, separated before she was born, and she did not meet her father until she was twelve. She later took her stepfather's surname. Highsmith was raised by her maternal grandmother for several years until her mother remarried. Her relationship with her mother, who admitted to trying to abort her by swallowing turpentine, remained

Patricia Highsmith © *Sophie Bassouls/Corbis Sygma*

troubled, and she ended her relationship with her father after he tried to seduce her during their first meeting. The tensions she experienced in her family during her childhood were recreated in many of her stories and novels. Highsmith's grandmother taught her to read when she was two, and by the age of eight, Highsmith was interested in Karl Menninger's *The Human Mind*, especially the parts that focused on mental disorders, such as pyromania and schizophrenia. In her teenaged years, she began writing short stories and showed a talent for painting and sculpture.

After she graduated from Columbia in 1942, Highsmith settled in New York City and began writing text for comic books, which included profiles of Einstein, Galileo, Oliver Cromwell, and Sir Isaac Newton, and the script for the Captain America character, among others. Her first novel, *Strangers on a Train*, published in 1950, focuses on two men who meet on a train and plan to swap murders. While the novel did not gain much attention, a year later Alfred Hitchcock directed a film version, which became a commercial and critical success and sparked interest in Highsmith's works.

Highsmith had a long, successful literary career, authoring several volumes of short stories in the fantasy, horror, and comedy genres, including *Nothing That Meets the Eye: The Uncollected Stories of Patricia Highsmith*, published posthumously in 2002, which includes "A Girl like Phyl." She also wrote several novels, the most famous of which center on her series character, Tom Ripley, who has inspired several films, most notably Anthony Minghella's version of *The Talented Mr. Ripley* in 1999.

Highsmith's personal life, however, was not as successful. She struggled with alcoholism during most of her life and never was able to establish lasting relationships. She had several lesbian relationships and formed short-term relationships with the novelist Marc Brandel in 1949 and in 1959 with Marijane Meaker, who wrote under the pseudonym M. E. Kerr. Many acquaintances considered Highsmith to be misanthropic and often cruel although others insisted that her shyness made her appear withdrawn. Highsmith did admit, however, that she preferred the company of animals to humans and spent most of her life as a recluse. In 1963, she moved to Europe, living in England, France, and Switzerland where she died of leukemia on February 4, 1995.

Her awards include the O. Henry Award for best first story for "The Heroine" in *Harper's Bazaar* in 1946; the Edgar Allan Poe Award for best novel in 1951 for *Strangers on a Train* and in 1956 for *The Talented Mr. Ripley*, which also won the French Grand Prix de Litterature Policiere in 1957; the British Crime Writers Association Award in 1964; and the Grand Master Award by the Swedish Academy of Detection in 1979.

PLOT SUMMARY

As "A Girl like Phyl" opens, Jeff Cormack, a forty-year-old American engineer, is waiting to board a plane at Kennedy Airport to take him to Paris. The fog has caused several delays. As he waits at the gate, he sees a woman who makes him "stop and stay motionless for a few seconds." He thinks it is Phyl, but then he immediately insists that it could not be her since the woman looks so young. He notes though that the resemblance to the woman he knows as Phyl is remarkable. When he finally looks away, his hands tremble and he feels "shattered." He tells himself that he cannot look at her again or try to find her if she is on the same flight. As he walks to the airport bar, he thinks about how late he will be arriving in Paris and that he will still try to reach Semyon Kyrogin that night to work on a deal with Jeff's oil rig company, Ander-Mack. Jeff is not sure, however, where the man will be staying.

The young woman's face takes him back twenty years to the time he had met Phyl, whom he has thought of repeatedly. For a few years after they broke up, Jeff thought about her constantly, a time he called the "Awful Years." After that, he pushed her out of his mind by working hard at his career and soon met and married Betty and had a son, Bernard, now a teenager.

Seeing a woman who looks so much like Phyl dazes him to the point that he does not realize that he has ordered coffee. As he looks around the bar, Jeff spots the young woman sitting at one of the tables. He realizes that she might be Phyl's daughter, remembering "with painful accuracy" that Phyl had gotten married nineteen years ago. He acknowledges that he is still in love with her, a fact he has had to live with for all these years and hopes he will not be seated next to the young woman on the plane.

Once the plane takes off, Jeff tries to relax and think about the upcoming meeting with Kyrogin. He wonders if there is anyone from a rival company on the flight preparing to meet with the man. Just as he is about to doze off, however, he hears Phyl's voice saying, "*You haven't any time for me anymore.*" He thinks about how he lost her, that he was so consumed with making money and becoming successful that he did not spend enough time with her and so she drifted away from him.

After the plane lands, Jeff stands in the passport line and watches the young woman, who is just ahead of him, drop a stuffed panda. When Jeff hands it to her, he notices that she has Phyl's teeth. When he gets to his hotel, he tries to phone Kyrogin but has no luck. Later, he runs into the young woman downstairs at the bar. A mistake in her reservation has left her without a room, and she complains to Jeff that she has nowhere to stay for the night.

After Jeff confirms with the desk clerk that there are no more rooms, he suggests that the woman share his suite. While she freshens up in the bathroom, Jeff tries unsuccessfully to get hold of Kyrogin and imagines that some competitor got to him first. The woman tells him that her name is Eileen, and he offers her some scotch. The two chat about his business proposition to Kyrogin. When she tells him that he is "a very serious man," he notes that her voice is like Phyl's.

Eileen tells Jeff that she is in Paris to get married and that her mother will arrive the next day. In a few days, after her fiancé arrives, they will all go to Venice where the ceremony will be held. She admits though that she is not sure that her mother will come with them, insisting that "she's funny." Eileen then tells Jeff that she is not sure that she wants to get married since she is only eighteen and does not want to get tied down.

As she takes a shower, Jeff decides that Eileen's wanting to stop the marriage is a result of her need for rebellion, the same urge that caused Phyl to leave her fiancé for Jeff and then return to him a year later. The idea that she came to him only because of her need to rebel is "a horrible thought for him." Then he laughs when he notes that the only thing on his mind is breakfast, not the attractive young woman in his shower.

When Eileen comes out of the bathroom, she tells Jeff that her father, as well as her mother, Phyl, wants her to get married. The confirmation that Phyl is her mother stuns Jeff. Noticing his pale color, Eileen tries to comfort him, praising him for being "a man of the world." When she puts her arms around him, he holds her for a minute and then steps back. Eileen tells him that she wants to go to bed with him, insisting that she would not tell anyone. For a moment, Jeff considers her proposition, imagining what Phyl would think if she found out, but he decides that he does not feel vindictive.

He also decides that while he desires her, he does not want to lose his memory of Phyl as she had been when they were together, and Eileen would interfere with that memory. Jeff then becomes angry at Eileen, thinking that if she had the opportunity, she would cause him to fall in love with her and lead him "into misery" as Phyl had done.

A call from Kyrogin breaks the tension. Jeff makes arrangements to call him later that morning at ten a.m. When Eileen looks at him with admiration after his productive phone call, Jeff remembers how Phyl had encouraged him and helped him become successful. For a moment, he looks at Eileen with desire, but the feeling passes, and he decides to get some sleep after gaining a promise from her that she would not mention him to her mother.

After a few hours sleep, Jeff says goodbye to Eileen, wishing her luck, and leaves for his meeting with Kyrogin. Jeff seals the deal with him in less than half an hour and thinks again of Phyl and of how he would come home to her after clinching a similarly important deal.

When Jeff returns to the hotel to pick up his suitcase, he sees Eileen and Phyl in the lobby. As he watches Phyl scold Eileen, Jeff watches her, noting the face that had gotten fatter and her oddly colored hair. What upsets him, however, is her "ugliness of spirit" as she yells at Eileen, he assumes, for spending a night with a man in his hotel room. He sees her conventionality and her hypocrisy, railing against her daughter for doing the same thing she had done with him years ago. He also concludes that if he had married Phyl, she may have betrayed him just as she had her fiancé.

The recognition of Phyl's true character devastates Jeff as he picks up his suitcase and walks out of the hotel, feeling as if he has "been living on a dream" of Phyl and of his relationship with her. He reminds himself of his success with Kyrogin but then realizes that the deal does not matter to him, that nothing matters, not his business or his family or his life. At that moment, he looks up and, realizing that he is at a busy crossroads, he throws himself in front of a speeding truck.

CHARACTERS

Jeff Cormack

Jeff is a forty-year-old engineer who seems to have made a successful life for himself and his family. He is part owner in an oil rig company and clinches an important deal during his trip to Paris. His confident exterior, however, hides his obsessive, tenuous vision of Phyl and their relationship. This vision has enabled him up to this point to have a clear sense of himself as a man of determination and purpose. He appears tireless in his pursuit of the deal that brings him to Paris, staying up most of the night in order to track Kyrogin down and get the man to agree to an early morning meeting. Jeff calls Kyrogin's hotel

TOPICS FOR FURTHER STUDY

- Read Sartre's *Nausea* and write a compare and contrast essay on the hero of the Sartre novel and Jeff. Analyze each character's behavior and motivations and how each displays existential angst.

- Imagine what would happen if Jeff had survived the accident. What would it take for him to find the courage to live? What kind of life do you think he would have ten years after the story ends? Add a few pages to the end of the story, describing Jeff ten years later.

- Patricia Highsmith had a very troubled life, as documented in the biography, *Beautiful Shadow: A Life of Patricia Highsmith*. Read the biography and present a PowerPoint demonstration that traces the influences that her life had on her work.

- Investigate the causes of suicide and the treatment of suicidal tendencies and be ready to lead a class discussion on these topics.

every fifteen minutes hoping to catch him as he arrives from the airport but before he goes up to his room. His tenacity with Kyrogin ensures that he will be the first to pitch a deal to the man and so get a jump on any competitors.

Jeff's ambition appears to have been triggered by Phyl who gave him enough confidence to strike out on his own in the business world. When his vision of her is shattered, his identity fades to the point where nothing has any meaning for him. Lacking the strength to face this emotional abyss, he kills himself.

Eileen

Eileen is Phyl's eighteen-year-old daughter who has come to Paris to get married. She is sexually confident, which she proves by her repeated attempts to seduce Jeff. Jeff suggests that these attempts reveal her rebelliousness. They could also suggest her shallowness. She is easily impressed by Jeff's initial attempts to complete his business deal, which suggests her lack of worldliness. She is also too trusting of a man she has just met, agreeing to spend the night in his hotel room. She does appear to show some strength of character when she stands her ground as her mother verbally attacks her in public.

Phyl
When Jeff sees Phyl in the hotel lobby, she is middle-aged and coldly berating her daughter. He accuses her of being a hypocrite and prudish, but these qualities cannot be proven since he can only assume what she is saying. Readers never get a chance to observe any other actions or hear her speak. She is present in the story as part of Jeff's comforting vision until the end when she represents his sense of betrayal and meaninglessness.

THEMES

The Ordinary and the Extraordinary
Highsmith is known for her ability to juxtapose the ordinary with the extraordinary as she chronicles the uneventful lives of her seemingly average characters. Often the extraordinary elements that suddenly appear in those lives suggest a shocking unpredictability as well as a darkness and the danger of violence just beneath the surface. On the surface Jeff appears to be an ordinary business man arriving in Paris to complete a deal for his company. That morning he had said goodbye to his wife and teenaged son, assuming that he would return to them in three days. An extraordinary event occurs, however, that shakes up his seemingly normal world.

Only after he meets Elaine are readers given his vision of Phyl, her mother, who has been a consuming obsession for Jeff and will eventually destroy him when it is shattered. Jeff realizes that "if he only hadn't seen her this morning," he would have been able to continue living his ordinary life, secure in believing the sense of himself that his relationship with her had provided him. When he is forced to realize Phyl's true character, however, when he sees her berate her daughter in the hotel lobby, he self-destructs. Unable to face his loss of purpose and therefore his sense of self, he commits suicide. It is this collision of the ordinary and the extraordinary in Jeff's life that makes the story so suspenseful and

disturbing to readers who are forced to realize that the world can be more dangerous than they have suspected.

Betrayal
One of the triggers for the destruction of Jeff's vision of Phyl and his relationship with her is his sense of betrayal. He slowly comes to realize Phyl's true character as he spends the evening with Eileen, who exhibits striking similarities to her mother. Initially, he feels flattered that Eileen wants to have sex with him, but then he realizes that she is betraying her fiancé in the same way that Phyl had betrayed Guy when she left him for Jeff. He recognizes that if he and Phyl had married, she might have eventually treated him the same way. This sense of her capacity for betrayal, coupled with the coldness, conventionality, and hypocrisy he sees in her behavior toward Eileen, destroys his vision of her and his concept of the world.

STYLE

Selective Omniscience
Selective omniscience is a type of third-person narration. Stories told from this point of view come from a nonparticipant in the action who focuses on the thoughts of one of the characters. Highsmith employs this device in "A Girl like Phyl" to help provide insight into Jeff's troubled psyche. The narrator does not need to spend time digging into Eileen's or Phyl's thoughts since the focus of the story is on the fictive world that Jeff has created and the devastating consequences when that world is shattered. This point of view also encourages readers to sympathize and identify with Jeff, which adds to the tension of the story.

Title
The title of the story works on two levels: first, it relates to the main story line that involves Jeff meeting and spending time with Phyl's daughter who looks remarkably like her mother and reminds him in her actions and voice of her mother at that age; and second, it suggests the illusory nature of Jeff's vision of Phyl. Jeff has constructed his own version of Phyl, based on his memories of her as she was twenty years before. When he finally sees her again, she is an older woman and not much like the girl he remembers.

COMPARE
&
CONTRAST

- **Late 1970s and Early 1980s:** The phrase, Me Generation, comes to represent this period, an age when self-interests are encouraged above all else.

  Today: The phrase, family values, has become the popular buzzword in an age when many Americans try to promote traditional social mores.

- **Late 1970s and Early 1980s:** The dominant economic philosophy proposes that tax breaks for the wealthy eventually strengthen the economy.

Today: President Bush provides tax breaks and cuts for the wealthiest in the United States. While the stock market hits record highs in 2006, middle-class Americans do not see significant increases in their wages.

- **Late 1970s and Early 1980s:** Political analysts conclude that democrat Jimmy Carter is elected president in 1977 because of a backlash against Republicans after the Watergate fiasco.

  Today: Democrats regain control of Congress in 2006 because of public disapproval of President Bush's Iraq policies as well as incidents of Republican corruption.

The change in her leads to his grappling with a sudden revision of the world as he understands it, and this sudden change destroys him.

HISTORICAL CONTEXT

The Me Decade

By the end of the 1970s, Americans had become pessimistic. The disastrous losses and outcome of the Vietnam War and the criminal activities during the Watergate scandal had shaken their confidence in the U.S. government, and a distrust of human nature had grown after the assassinations of John F. Kennedy, Robert Kennedy, and Martin Luther King Jr. Many Americans tried to relieve their pessimism through the acquisition of material goods.

In the 1980s, the government's political and economic agenda, with its championing of U.S. capitalism, triggered a surge in self-interest to such a degree that the age has been tagged, the "Me Decade." This period, which actually began in the late 1970s, was sanctioned and promoted by the election of Ronald Reagan as president. The presidential inauguration in 1981 cost eleven million dollars. Soon after, the First Lady continued the spending spree with expensive renovations at the White House, which

included a new set of china that cost over two hundred thousand dollars. Initially, the Reagans' lavish spending was criticized, but soon, the entire country became caught up in the attraction of wealth.

The philosophy behind Reaganomics was that the encouragement of the free-market system, which depends on the individual pursuit of wealth, would strengthen the economy. This vision included the theory of trickle-down economics: As businesses were freed from governmental regulation, their profits would eventually trickle down through the creation of jobs and raises to ordinary middle-class Americans. Americans would then be able to spend more money, which would further strengthen the economy.

Republicans argued that the welfare programs implemented in the 1960s had turned many citizens into government dependents and that only the reality of poverty would inspire lower-class Americans to develop an independent spirit for free enterprise. This championing of the free market system focused the country's attention on the amassing of wealth and material possessions, fostering a dramatic escalation in consumerism and a new zeitgeist for the age.

As the gap between rich and poor Americans widened, those who did not enjoy the luxuries that wealth affords felt especially discontented. Unable to cash in on the promise of trickle-down economics, blue-collar workers resented their inability to attain the American dream, and as a result, they became increasingly frustrated with their lot.

Consumerism

In the late 1970s and through the 1980s, American goods were more plentiful than ever, and Americans began to feel that they had the right to acquire them. This age of self-interest was promoted by the media through periodicals such as *Money* magazine that taught Americans how to dramatically increase their earnings and through the glorification of entrepreneurs such as Steven Jobs, the founder of Apple Computers, and real-estate tycoon, Donald Trump. One of the most popular television shows of the time was *Lifestyles of the Rich and Famous*, which brought viewers into the lavish homes of the super-rich.

Shopping became Americans' favorite pastime during this period. The time spent in malls was surpassed only by time spent at work, school, and home. Consumers could also satisfy their shopping urges by accessing the mall from home. With the advent of the shopping television network, QVC, and catalogues and telemarketing from a wide range of mail-order companies, such as L. L. Bean and Lands End, consumers could purchase a variety of goods over the phone.

WHAT DO I READ NEXT?

- *The Stranger* (1942), by Albert Camus, presents the author's absurdist view of the nature of existence as it focuses on Meursault, an amoral young man who is tried for murder. The existentialist theme of the novel suggests that one must find personal dignity in an indifferent world.

- In *The Talented Mr. Ripley* (1955), Highsmith draws her readers into the world of seemingly ordinary Tom Ripley, who turns out to be a charming sociopath. The novel was made into a hit film in 1999.

- *Strangers on a Train*, Highsmith's 1950 thriller, focuses on another sociopath who passes as an ordinary man. This one tries to convince another man to exchange murders with him.

- *Nausea* (1938), by Jean-Paul Sartre, is an important existentialist text. The story chronicles the experience of Antoine Roquentin, a French writer who catalogues in his diary his responses to his world and his struggle to comprehend and exist within it.

CRITICAL OVERVIEW

Most of the reviews for *Nothing That Meets the Eye* praise Highsmith's characterizations and originality of plot. A reviewer for the *Virginia Quarterly Review* insists that "the psychological complexity of these stories will satisfy Highsmith fans, as well as those discovering her for the first time," while Charlotte Innes in the *Los Angeles Times* describes them as "classic Highsmith fare." James Lasdun, in his review for *The Washington Post*, finds that "one of the exhilarating effects of reading Highsmith's stories . . . is the greatly enlarged sense of her range and energy as a writer" as she creates an "astounding" variety of characters. He argues, "Equally prodigious is her capacity for coming up with the

wildly inventive plots that set these creatures in motion."

Some reviewers, however, found fault with Highsmith's plot construction in the collection. The *Virginia Quarterly Review* claims that "although these stories brilliantly dissect the darkest side of human nature, they are not as meticulously and masterfully crafted" as her other works, "and thus [are] less compelling from the point of view of plot." Also commenting on plot, Lasdun concludes that the stories' "machinery can clunk at times . . . especially as they accelerate toward their sometimes strained dramatic climaxes, but they are seldom less than entertaining, and often wonderful." He adds that "they lack perhaps the singularity of tone and atmosphere that her best novels possess, but in their surehandedness, their amazing breadth and abundance, as well as the dark delight they convey in their own making, they compel attention, and they add significantly to her already formidable presence."

Innes claims that "not all of [the stories] succeed. Some of the narrative tricks are too obviously manipulative, and there are just too many stories that end abruptly and unconvincingly in suicide." She determines, however, that "whatever their flaws, they all have the Highsmith magical narrative pull" and often contain "a nugget of bitter truth." Innes concludes, "there's no doubt that this new collection, however uneven, reminds us that Highsmith was a literary artist who was so accomplished she could seduce the reader even with work that was less than her best."

Several reviewers cite "A Girl like Phyl" as one of the collection's best stories. Innes praises its characterizations while a reviewer for *Kirkus Reviews* concludes that the story crams "a life's worth of devastation into a few pages." James Campbell, in the *New York Times Book Review*, insists that its "nuances of desire and repulsion are expertly controlled." He adds that "almost every piece . . . contains touches that reveal what a subtle writer Highsmith was."

CRITICISM

Wendy Perkins

Perkins is a professor of American and British literature and film. In the following essay, she examines existential themes in the story.

Scholars have noted Patricia Highsmith's appreciation of John-Paul Sartre and Albert Camus, especially their exploration of existentialism, a philosophical movement that had its beginnings in the writings of nineteenth-century, Danish theologian Søren Kierkegaard. In the twentieth century, existentialism evolved into an influential movement through the work of Sartre (*Nausea*, 1938) and Camus (*The Stranger*, 1942). Existentialist philosophy, according to *Oxford Concise Dictionary of Literary Terms*, defines human freedom "in terms of individual responsibility and authenticity." This dictionary explains the philosophy's main premise as the belief that "human beings have no given essence or nature but must forge [their] own values and meanings in an inherently meaningless or absurd world of existence." Russell Harrison notes in his biography of

> WHEN HIS NEW LIFE DID NOT GIVE HIM A SENSE OF PURPOSE OR MEANING, HE RETURNED TO HIS OBSESSION WITH PHYL, CREATING A VISION OF HER THAT SUSTAINED HIM."

Highsmith (1997) that much of Highsmith's fiction contains existential elements. This observation is proved in her short story "A Girl like Phyl" in its exploration of the devastating consequences that result from one man's struggle to create inauthentic values in order to survive in a meaningless world.

Jeff Cormack, a forty-year-old engineer, found himself living an absurd existence twenty years earlier when Phyl, the woman he loves, left him. The years following the breakup were "Awful Years" for him as he struggled to find a sense of identity without her. He notes that Phyl had brought him luck; she had "launched him like a rocket . . . and had given him all the confidence in the world and all the happiness." She had given him the courage to quit his job and start a new company. He wanted to be a success, "to prove himself, in the way he thought would count with Phyl, by making money, solid, big money." Yet ironically, this prevented him from spending enough time with her and so she left.

After the breakup, he struggled to fill the emptiness in his life by working harder and by marrying and having a son. During this three to four year break, he had not thought of her with the same intensity. Yet his new life provided only the "outer trappings" of happiness, "solid, tangible . . . as a bullet that might penetrate his forehead and kill him." Jeff insists, though, that "a man didn't commit suicide, didn't ruin his career, just because he was in love with a girl he couldn't have." When his new life did not give him a sense of purpose or meaning, he returned to his obsession with Phyl, creating a vision of her that sustained him. He admits that he has learned to live with his love for her by being with her "in bed, out of bed, just existing with her" in his mind.

Unable to confront the anguish of living without Phyl, he returns to the same patterns he followed while he was with her. He puts all of his energy into becoming a financial success, staying up through the night in Paris so that he can seal an important deal for his company. His relives with Eileen, Phyl's daughter, the sense of accomplishment he felt when he gained similar successes when he was with Phyl. Since Eileen looks so much like her mother, he is able to perpetuate and intensify his vision of Phyl. He responds to "the girl's zest and pleasure in his success . . . as he had felt Phyl's in the old days," and so he feels toward Eileen the same stirrings of desire. Eileen strokes his ego as Phyl had done, telling him how much she admires him for "being a man of the world," for "doing something important." When he seals the deal with Kyrogin, Jeff understands that the time he has spent with Eileen has brought Phyl even closer to him, "Phyl with the twinkle in her eyes, her pride in his victory that was like a whole football stadium cheering." Jeff, however, cannot allow himself to be seduced by Eileen because "he didn't want to lose his memory of Phyl, Phyl as she had been with him."

During his night with Eileen in his hotel room, reality begins to encroach on the world that he has constructed in order to establish a sense of meaning and purpose. When Eileen tells him that she is not sure that she wants to get married, he understands that she is rebelling against convention and realizes for the first time that Phyl had acted in the same way when she left her fiancé for him. The thought that Phyl rebelled just for the sake of rebelling is "horrible" to Jeff because it interferes with his vision of their perfect time together. Later, when Eileen redoubles her efforts to seduce him, Jeff becomes angry, determining that she "would lead him on . . . exactly as Phyl had . . . into misery."

When he sees Phyl confronting Eileen in the lobby of the hotel, his dream crumbles. As he watches her scolding Eileen, most likely for spending the night with a strange man in his hotel room, the "prudishness, the conventionality, the phoniness . . . the hypocrisy" that he sees in her tirade against her daughter stuns him as he wonders, "Was *this* what he'd been in love with all this time?" He recognizes that "there was nothing lasting for girls like Phyl" who had a "certain coldness at the heart." This understanding of Phyl's true character shatters his vision of her

and along with it the only thing that has sustained him, and so Jeff feels "about to die." Although he appears in a daze, he knows "that somehow nothing mattered any longer, where he went, what he did, where he was, even who he was." When Jeff thinks now of his future, of returning to his office where he will finish the deal with Kyrogin and to his family with its "phony outward appearance of a decent marriage," he realizes that his life no longer means anything to him. Not being able to think anymore, Jeff acts, by stepping in front of a speeding truck.

Twice Jeff has faced with a fading sense of identity in a world that has become meaningless to him. The first time, after Phyl left him, he coped with the angst he felt by creating an inauthentic vision of her and their time together in order to sustain him and provide him with purpose. However, when reality destroys his vision of her and along with it his sense of worth, he cannot find the strength to forge a new direction for himself. In her compelling portrait of Jeff in "A Girl like Phyl," Highsmith explores the existential emptiness of modern life and the difficulties inherent in the struggle to find meaning.

Source: Wendy Perkins, Critical Essay on "A Girl like Phyl," in *Short Stories for Students*, Thomson Gale, 2007.

David Kelly

Kelly is an instructor of creative writing and English literature. In the following essay, he looks at Highsmith's limitations as a writer and finds that she uses her shortcomings to her advantage.

Throughout her long writing career, Patricia Highsmith garnered a legion of fans, a base that continued to grow after her death in 1995. Those who appreciate her work, however, frequently find themselves embittered about how limited her literary reputation is; many feel that Highsmith has been unfairly dismissed as a minor talent, dismissed as a mere genre writer. Some explain this slight with the belief that she was a victim of the prejudices of an unenlightened society, an audience that could not deal with the fact that Highsmith, a woman, wrote so often about the seamier aspects of modern life. Her supporters point to other writers who crossed over from the small category of mystery writer and gained a wider audience, from Georges Simenon to Raymond Chandler to Elmore Leonard, and note the absence of females on the list, which they attribute to narrow-minded assumptions about what was and was not

> IN WHAT AMOUNTS TO AN ALMOST COMICAL REVERSAL OF THE TRADITIONAL MYSTERY, THE PROTAGONIST IS *NOT* VICTIMIZED BY A MYSTERIOUS, MALICIOUS FORCE: HE IS NOT EVEN A VICTIM OF THE OPPRESSIVE WEIGHT OF EVERYDAY LIFE."

considered proper subjects for female authors. Another common theory for Highsmith's long critical neglect is based on her sexual orientation, as fans presume that only a strong heterosexual bias on the part of the literary establishment could explain why her books and stories were relegated to the ghetto of genre fiction for so long.

There is something to each of these theories, of course: Highsmith was a woman, and she was gay, and each of these facts may have had some effect on the critics who read her. But there is a much easier explanation. Highsmith was in truth a genre writer with limited scope. Her characters are mostly two-dimensional, seldom motivated by anything more subtle than the extremes of anger, shame, or lust. The situations in which they find themselves often dramatize the programmatic dilemma of kill or be killed: such dramas are not instructive about coping with daily existence. Highsmith's characters inhabit their own world, which has its own set of rules. Readers who understand and accept those limits are her likely audience, but a wider audience may be less able to meet her on her own terms.

In itself, calling her work generic should not rankle Highsmith's fans, since it makes no claim about her overall effectiveness. Her novels and short stories are indeed highly effective, for the very reason that they are chiseled from a reality that only slightly resembles common life. More often than not, she keeps readers well aware of the differences between her world and theirs, and she is astute enough to use that awareness to make her point.

Take, for example, the story "A Girl like Phyl," a story based on stereotypes and propped up by the insinuation of a case of international espionage, with a surprise twist in the last line that seems to derive only from the paragraph

that comes before it. Judging by its basic components, the story should be not only a failure, but a failure of the most miserable kind: one that makes implicit promises to its reader that are not fulfilled. But "A Girl like Phyl" is a success because Highsmith works within her limitations and makes the most of what she knows to be her audience's expectations.

The main character of "A Girl like Phyl" is Jeff Cormack, a man who is as average as his name. He is a middle-aged Caucasian, an executive with an oil company who, as the story begins, is embarking on a business trip. He does not want adventure; he does not want romance. He simply wants business to go well—to be victorious, in a modestly aggressive business sense—so that he can return home to his wife, Betty, and his fifteen-year-old son, Bernard. Highsmith gives few details about the family. Readers are told that Bernard is going to Groton and that he does not know what he wants to do yet, and the very fact that the boy's indecision passes through Jeff's mind indicates that he disapproves of uncertainty. Nothing substantial is said about Betty. Jeff Cormack presumably is a standard corporation man of the postwar period, a functionary who knows and cares much about his business while being only marginally aware of the quality of his own life. He is a standard, familiar character, common in the literature, both high and low, of the late twentieth century.

But Highsmith adorns Jeff's story with two exciting, though unlikely, possibilities that serve to keep her audience's attention. For one thing, the business meeting is steeped in exoticism and the potential for international intrigue. He is flying to Paris to hunt down a Russian, Kyrogin, who is described as "an important man but not a Communist deputy." At the time, the Communist Party of the Soviet Union operated under such a blanket of secrecy that it would have been impossible to fully understand its involvement or intent. Readers can expect the unexpected under such circumstances, where there is serious money to be made or lost by trusting an operative from a foreign government. This is not a circumstance that most businessmen would encounter when traveling to a meeting, and Highsmith uses the situation's unfamiliarity and the uncertainty of the motives of all parties to raise the story's tension. Each unanswered telephone call hints that Kyrogin has abandoned Jeff or plans an even worse treachery. Fans of international intrigue read this story with their senses alert to the possibility that Jeff's trip could go terribly awry, sending his physical or financial health plummeting without a moment's notice.

But that is only one device. The other, more central to the story's plot, is Jeff's involvement with Eileen—the "girl like Phyl" of the story's title. It starts when he notices her at the airport in the story's third paragraph and is thunderstruck by how much she resembles Phyl, his lover of twenty years earlier. She is more than just a reminder of the most romantic episode of his life, however. As the story progresses, it turns out that she is staying at Jeff's hotel. Or, rather, she is supposed to, but her reservation is lost, which gives him the opportunity to come to her aid and offer her his room, where she can freshen up and have a drink. Coincidentally, this girl who triggers his memories and is with him from Kennedy Airport to the lobby of his hotel actually *is* the daughter of Phyl. The odds against such a thing happening in the real world are considerable.

As with Jeff's urgent, middle-of-the-night business with the Russian, the relationship with Eileen is implicitly fraught with danger. The fact that such things simply do not happen in the real world is used, in this sleepless night of Jeff Cormack's life, to indicate that there is some unseen hand pulling the strings. Readers have to wonder what is really behind these events that Jeff naively accepts as coincidence. A coincidence would be if the girl he noticed in New York ended up at his hotel, or if the girl he talked to at Orly Airport was stranded without a room when he went to the hotel bar or even, by some stretch of the imagination, if the girl who reminded him of Phyl actually turned out to be the daughter of Phyl. As presented, this situation implies that someone is keeping something back. If one of the characters asks readers to believe that these events happen this way, then they know that there is certainly a sinister plot against Jeff. The other option, though, is that Highsmith wants readers to believe in the possibility of such unlikely events.

A true mystery story would unravel the hidden elements of the plot. The mysterious Russian might show up offering the hand of friendship, but he would do so only to string Jeff along, to swindle him, to turn the tables. Or Eileen might turn out to have arranged their

meeting from the start. A compact story would bring the two strands of the plot together, showing a relationship between Kyrogin and Eileen that Jeff was too distracted by greed and nostalgia to notice. Such a story would reach its climax with Jeff realizing that each thing that seemed to fall into place for him was actually arranged to give him a false sense of security.

But Highsmith drives this story in a different direction. In what amounts to an almost comical reversal of the traditional mystery, the protagonist is *not* victimized by a mysterious, malicious force: he is not even a victim of the oppressive weight of everyday life. Jeff Cormack, faced with potential disasters throughout the story, waltzes easily through them and comes out triumphant.

How he eventually finds Kyrogin and consummates the deal is handled by Highsmith in a way that defies any expectation of impending danger. The Russian turns out to have no ulterior motive; his chummy offer of a cigar and vodka is not a ruse to make Jeff lower his guard. It is even Kyrogin's idea for Jeff to phone New York and share the good news with his partner, a suggestion that, in a story about betrayal, would be used as a distraction. The deal that Jeff comes to Paris to pursue is resolved with unexpected good will.

Similarly, the relationship with Eileen, which could have turned sour at any point along the way, never does. She accepts Jeff's offer to come to his room and freshen up and then turns out to be sexually attracted to him, but she is willing to accept his rebuff with no hard feelings. Phyl does show up but never finds out that Jeff is in Paris or that he and her daughter came close to intimacy. In all, a situation that seemed to be ripe for turning terrible at each step actually turns out to be ideal for Jeff, as he has been given another chance with his lost love through her closest surrogate, her daughter, and has been able to walk away from it, this time on his own terms.

It is not until the end of the story, in its final paragraphs, that Highsmith reveals what this story has really been about all along. Jeff sees that his swoon for Phyl's image and the sense of impending danger in the high-stakes business deal only mask the terrible reality that there is no romance or danger in his life. His ultimate response to life's lack of drama is to throw himself in front of a truck, which is perhaps the most unnecessarily dramatic thing he could do. The reader is left in the end with a sense that his existential revelation must have been a powerful one to drive Jeff to such an extreme, but also with the feeling that his behavior in his moment of truth is, fittingly, the kind of decisive action that the story has promised all along.

It is an effective ending, but it would not be so if Highsmith were any more complex or subtle in her handling of her characters. The inherent drama of the situations in this story creates a sense that something harsh and unexpected is going to happen; then the situations all resolve themselves to Jeff Cormack's benefit. With his final realization that his mind has been driven throughout his adult life by a memory that has grown into a delusion, Jeff creates the powerful moment for himself. It is the sort of ending for his life that readers familiar with the twists of the mystery story expect the author to throw at him. This story would not work if the reader's appetite for the destruction of this oil company executive had not been whetted by the promise of startling revelations, or if Highsmith did not have the confidence to ignore those promises. Readers expect things of a genre story, and they recognize this to be a genre story, and so they expect the end to present a surprise. But the surprise they expect is in Jeff's circumstances: they do not anticipate the collapse of his world view.

It is no insult to Patricia Highsmith to say that she was a writer of limitations. It would, of course, be bad for her if she had lofty ambitions that she was too limited to reach, but a story such as "A Girl like Phyl" proves that she knew how to arrange her characters for maximum effect. Jeff Cormack is not an insightful person, and his revelation, at the end, that his life has been a meaningless sham does not make him any more insightful. Even so, Highsmith makes his experience a moving one by having him go through the situations of a mystery plot and come out of them unscathed. The events of this story might make Jeff realize that his life has been a delusion, but readers who have see the falseness of Jeff's character all along share his realization that life is made interesting by the anticipation of the double-cross, the unexpected romance, or the revelation of buried news. It takes a mystery writer like Patricia Highsmith to bring that truth to light.

Source: David Kelly, Critical Essay on "A Girl Like Phyl," in *Short Stories for Students*, Thomson Gale, 2007.

> NOT ONLY IS THE AMERICAN READING PUBLIC TAKING NOTE OF THIS SEMINAL WRITER WHO HAD PREVIOUSLY BEEN RELEGATED TO MARGINALITY, BUT ALSO THE ACADEMY IS FOLLOWING SUIT."

Karl L. Stenger

In the following essay, Stenger gives a critical analysis of Patricia Highsmith's work.

In his foreword to the 1972 edition of *Eleven* (1970), Patricia Highsmith's first collection of short stories, English novelist Graham Greene dubs her "the poet of apprehension rather than fear" and characterizes her achievement:

> She is a writer who has created a world of her own—a world claustrophobic and irrational which we enter each time with a sense of personal danger, with the head half turned over the shoulder, even with a certain reluctance, for these are cruel pleasures we are going to experience, until . . . the frontier is closed behind us, we cannot retreat, we are doomed to live till the story's end with another of her long series of wanted men.

Highsmith has been acclaimed as a great writer by authors such as Brigid Brophy, Julian Symons, and Peter Handke and has long been widely read in England, France, Spain, Germany, Switzerland, and Austria. European movie directors, including René Clément, Claude Miller, Claude Chabrol, Wim Wenders, and Hans W. Geissendorfer, have adapted Highsmith's books to the screen.

Having enjoyed a brief burst of fame in the United States when Alfred Hitchcock made a movie of her first novel, *Strangers on a Train* (1950), in 1951, Highsmith during her life was largely ignored by the American reading public. Many of her books quickly fell out of print in the United States, and her popularity and reputation declined. Several reasons have been cited for the lengthy neglect Highsmith and her work suffered. One of them is the relentlessly negative depiction of the American middle class and of American politics in her works. Another reason mentioned is the fact that Highsmith was labeled a "suspense writer" at the outset of her career and that this label prevented serious consideration of her books. An additional reason given for the reluctance of the American public to embrace the writer is Highsmith's reclusive and prickly personality.

After Highsmith settled in Europe permanently in 1963, she only grudgingly promoted her books and avoided book signing tours and readings as much as possible. Even though she granted interviews, she ferociously protected her privacy and deliberately shocked her interviewers with such outrageous statements as her 1976 assertion to Peter Ruedi (collected in *Patricia Highsmith: Leben und Werk* [1996], edited by Franz Cavigelli, Fritz Senn, and Anna von Planta): "If I saw a kitten and a little human baby starving in the street, I would feed the kitten provided no one saw me." Otto Penzler, one of Highsmith's American publishers, attested to her abrasive personality in *Entertainment Weekly* on 14 January 2000: "She was a mean, cruel, hard, unlovable, unloving human being. I could never penetrate how any human being could be that relentlessly ugly. . . . But her books? Brilliant." Gary Fisketjon, who published her late novels, added: "She was very rough, very difficult. But she was also plainspoken, dryly funny, and great fun to be around." It is difficult to assess to what extent Highsmith's misanthropy was genuine and to what extent it was a pose to safeguard her privacy. Since Highsmith's death in 1995 her reputation has risen in the United States. Her five novels featuring Tom Ripley have been republished, gaining the author an increasing readership. Anthony Minghella's 1999 movie version of *The Talented Mr. Ripley* (1955) helped to solidify her growing popularity in the United States. In 2003 Liliana Cavani chose *Ripley's Game* (1974) as the starring vehicle for John Malkovich, whose assumption of the title role was described as "quintessential" by *The New Yorker* and "definitive" by London's *New Statesman*. Additional movies based on her novels are in development, and her out-of-print books are being republished. Interest in the author is further attested to by the 2003 publications of Marijane Meaker's memoir *Highsmith: A Romance of the 1950's* and Andrew Wilson's *Beautiful Shadow: A Life of Patricia Highsmith*. As Mark Harris stated in *Entertainment Weekly* (24–31 August 2001), "Highsmith is in the final lap of a posthumous victory mile that should cement her standing as a no-longer-neglected master of character-driven suspense fiction."

Highsmith was born Mary Patricia Plangman in Fort Worth, Texas, on 19 January 1921, the only child of Jay Bernard Plangman, a graphic artist of German extraction, and Mary Coates Plangman, an illustrator and fashion designer. Patricia's parents were divorced five months before her birth, and she was raised together with her cousin Dan Coates, who was like a brother to her, by her maternal grandparents in Fort Worth until she was six years old. She did not meet her father until she was twelve years old, and even though she found him likable, they had nothing to say to each other. In 1925 Patricia's mother married Stanley Highsmith, an advertising illustrator, and the family moved to New York City two years later. Patricia Highsmith recalled in a 1979 interview with Noelle Loriot (published in *Patricia Highsmith: Leben und Werk*) the trauma she suffered because of the move: "Something went to pieces in me when I left my grandmother. I completely withdrew into myself." Stanley Highsmith did not officially adopt his stepdaughter, but her mother registered her as Patricia Highsmith when she enrolled her in elementary school. Patricia later decided to keep the name as a tribute to this extremely patient and upright man.

While she liked her stepfather, Highsmith did not love her mother and, as she revealed to Loriot, blamed the failure of her second marriage on her quarrelsomeness and selfishness: "Why don't I love my mother? First, because she turned my childhood into a little hell. Second, because she herself never loved anyone, neither my father, my stepfather, nor me." Her feeling that she was unloved and unwanted was confirmed when her mother confessed that, while she was pregnant with Highsmith, she had unsuccessfully tried to induce abortion by drinking turpentine.

In an attempt to escape the frequent quarrels that she was forced to witness in the cramped two-room apartment in Greenwich Village, Highsmith immersed herself in the works of Fyodor Dostoevsky, Charles Dickens, Henry James, Edgar Allan Poe, Robert Louis Stevenson, Hugh Walpole, and T. S. Eliot. She was also fascinated by Karl Menninger's *The Human Mind* (1930), a book including case studies of kleptomaniacs, pyromaniacs, and serial killers, because she realized that the man, woman, or child next door could be strange even while appearing normal and that anybody one meets in the street could be a kleptomaniac, a sadist, or even a murderer.

Highsmith discovered the power of language when her composition about her trip to the Endless Caverns in Virginia, which had been discovered by two boys chasing a rabbit through a crevice, left her classmates spellbound. Her first short stories and poems appeared in *The Bluebird*, the Julia Richmond High School magazine, and the story "Mighty Nice Man" won first prize, which consisted of copies of Marcel Proust's *Du côté de chez Swann* (1913) and Virginia Woolf's *Mrs. Dalloway* (1925). Having graduated from high school in 1938, Highsmith enrolled in Barnard College at Columbia University and studied English, Latin, and Greek. She published short stories in the *Barnard Quarterly* on a regular basis, eventually serving as editor of the periodical. "The Heroine," a story she wrote in 1941 about a governess who sets the house of her employers on fire so that she can save the children, was rejected by *Barnard Quarterly* but eventually published in 1944 by *Harper's Bazaar* and included in *O. Henry's Best Short Stories of 1946*.

Upon graduating from college in 1942, Highsmith moved into a room of her own on Sixtieth Street in Manhattan and eked out a living by composing text for comic strips such as *Superman* and *Batman*. She continued writing short stories and immersed herself in the bohemian life of Greenwich Village, meeting Truman Capote, Paul and Jane Bowles, and Carson McCullers. In 1943 she spent five months in Taxco, Mexico, where she worked on the unfinished novel titled "The Click of the Shutting" and considered becoming a professional painter. The novel revolves around the relationship between two New York boys, prefiguring the pattern Highsmith later followed in many of her works, namely "the meeting, the close friendship of two people who are unlike one another," as she stated in a 1987 speech quoted by Wilson.

Having moved to a cold-water flat on East Fifty-sixth Street in 1944, Highsmith began work on *Strangers on a Train*. After the first chapters of the novel had been rejected by six publishers, she was admitted to Yaddo, the artists' colony in Saratoga Springs, New York, based on recommendations by Capote, the composer David Diamond, and Mary Louise Aswell, the chief editor of *Harper's Bazaar*. Freed from external pressures and provided with an ideal working environment, Highsmith was able to rewrite the novel from scratch. While at Yaddo she also got engaged to Marc Brandel, a fellow writer, only to break off the engagement shortly before the wedding ostensibly because of her fear of being a mother: "I would not have had the patience to raise children," Highsmith admitted to Loriot.

Soon after its completion *Strangers on a Train* was acquired by Harper and Sons and published in 1950. Hitchcock purchased the movie and stage rights for $6,800 and put Raymond Chandler in charge of writing the screenplay. The collaboration between the opinionated men, however, was strained, and Chandler was eventually replaced by Czenzi Ormonde, an associate of Ben Hecht's. When the movie was released in 1951, it was a great success, and Highsmith became famous overnight.

Strangers on a Train established a pattern that recurs, with variations, in many of Highsmith's works. In her book *Plotting and Writing Suspense Fiction* (1966), which offers a fascinating glimpse into the writer's work, Highsmith describes this motif: "The theme I have used over and over again in my novels is the relationship between two men, usually quite different in make-up, sometimes an obvious contrast in good and evil, sometimes merely ill-matched friends." In *Strangers on a Train* the two men are Guy Daniel Haines, a twenty-nine-year-old aspiring architect, who is traveling by rail to Texas in order to pressure his estranged wife into agreeing to a divorce so that he can marry his new girlfriend, and Charles Anthony Bruno, a young ne'er-do-well who lives off his rich parents. The aimless Bruno immediately latches on to the initially reserved and aloof Guy, being attracted by his apparent seriousness of purpose. Guy is repelled by Bruno's appearance, effete mannerisms, and "the desperate boredom of the wealthy"; yet, he is also fascinated by Bruno's bold suggestion to commit perfect murders by exchanging victims: "We murder for each other, see? I kill your wife and you kill my father! We meet on the train, see, and nobody knows we know each other! Perfect alibis!"

Even though Guy himself had once thought of murdering his wife's lover, he rejects Bruno's assertion that any person is capable of murder: "I'm not that kind of person." In spite of Guy's clear rejection of the murderous plan, Bruno travels to Texas several weeks later and strangles Guy's wife in an amusement park. He then pressures and eventually blackmails an initially resisting Guy into killing Bruno's hated father. The plan to commit perfect murders, however, gradually unravels when Guy is racked by guilt and pestered by Bruno, who has developed a homoerotic attachment to his involuntary fellow conspirator. Bruno subsequently invites himself to Guy's wedding as well as to a housewarming party and showers Guy with gifts, which causes Guy to reflect: "He might have been Bruno's lover ... to whom Bruno had brought a present, a peace offering." Because of Bruno's obsessive behavior a detective is able to establish a connection between the two murderers, and they eventually receive their just deserts. At the end of the novel Guy accepts the inevitable punishment. His last words to the detective are "Take me."

When one compares Highsmith's novel and Hitchock's movie, the differences in focus and plot are readily apparent, as MaryKay Mahoney has shown in her essay "A Train Running on Two Sets of Tracks: Highsmith's and Hitchcock's *Strangers on a Train*" (1994). Whereas Hitchcock clearly contrasts Bruno, the psychopath, with Guy, the innocent hero who "will eventually emerge uncorrupted from the world of darkness into which Bruno has temporarily plunged him," Highsmith focuses on the two men as "inextricably linked doubles." Guy becomes the author's mouthpiece when he declares, having murdered Bruno's father, that "love and hate, . . . good and evil, lived side by side in the human heart, and not merely in differing proportions in one man and the next, but all good and all evil. One had merely to look for a little of either to find it all, one had merely to scratch the surface."

Highsmith's second published novel, *The Price of Salt* (1952), was a considerable departure from her first. In the afterword to the 1993 edition of the novel, which she originally published pseudonymously as Claire Morgan, Highsmith writes of how, to her surprise, she became a "suspense writer" overnight when *Strangers on a Train* was published as "A Harper Novel of Suspense," even though the novel was not categorized in her mind as such. For her it was "simply a novel with an interesting story." Highsmith's publisher and agent urged her to write another book of the same type in order to strengthen her reputation as a suspense writer. Highsmith, having just completed a novel about a lesbian relationship, decided to publish her new work under a pseudonym partly to escape the label of "lesbian-book writer": "I like to avoid labels. It is American publishers who love them."

Highsmith goes on in her afterword to detail the genesis of *The Price of Salt*. Before *Strangers on a Train* was published, Highsmith had taken a temporary job in the toy department of Bloomingdale's in Manhattan during the 1948 Christmas rush. There she was fascinated one day by a blonde woman in a mink coat who "seemed to give off light." The woman bought a doll from Highsmith, providing her name and address because the doll was to be delivered out of state. While the encounter was a routine transaction, Highsmith "felt odd and swimmy in the head, near to fainting, yet at the same time uplifted, as if I had seen a vision." Even though the odd feeling revealed itself the next day as the beginning of a chicken pox infection, the germ for the novel was born. Highsmith immediately wrote down the entire story line of the novel in less than two hours: "It flowed from my pen as if from nowhere—beginning, middle and end." Because of Highsmith's predilection for letting ideas simmer for a while, the novel was not completed until 1951.

The Price of Salt tells the story of Therese Belivet, a nineteen-year-old stage designer who has taken temporary work as a salesgirl at Frankenberg's department store. Her inability to find a permanent position in her chosen field is aggravated by the confusion she is experiencing in her personal life. Her boyfriend of ten months, a painter with whom she has been intimate on several occasions, has proposed marriage to her, but she has rejected his proposal because her feeling toward him bears no resemblance to what she had read about love: "Love was supposed to be a kind of blissful insanity." Therese suddenly and unexpectedly experiences such a passion when she meets customer Carol Aird, a married woman and a mother. Carol eventually relinquishes all rights to her daughter in order to be with Therese, and Therese in turn realizes after an unsuccessful attempt to be with a lesbian actress that "it was Carol she loved and would always love."

As Highsmith acknowledges in her afterword, *The Price of Salt* was most likely the first novel about homosexuals that ended on a happy note. When the book was published in hardcover in 1952 and as a paperback in nearly a million copies a year later, Highsmith received many fan letters addressed to Claire Morgan from women as well as men thanking her for her positive portrayal of a loving relationship among well-adjusted lesbians. After Highsmith had acknowledged her authorship of the novel in 1991, she admitted in an interview with Janet Watts, collected in *Patricia Highsmith: Leben und Werk*, that she had fallen in love with the woman—identified by Wilson as Kathleen Senn—who had served as the prototype for Therese, though she stopped short of declaring her lesbianism.

The financial success of her first two novels enabled Highsmith—who had visited England, France, and Italy briefly in 1949—to begin a European sojourn in 1952 that lasted more than two years. She traveled in the footsteps of her literary idol, James, from London to Paris, Munich, Salzburg, Trieste, and Florence. In the southern Italian town of Positano she rented a house and, watching a young, possibly American man walk along the deserted beach one morning lost in thought, she was inspired to invent a story about a young American vagabond who is sent to Europe with the mission to convince another American to return to the States. Having returned to the United States at the beginning of 1954, Highsmith moved into a cottage near Lenox, Massachusetts, where she began writing the first in a series of five adventures featuring her best-known creation, Tom Ripley.

Before Ripley made his appearance, however, Highsmith published another novel, *The Blunderer* (1954), that involves another perfect murder as well as a pair of murderers, one an ice-cold psychopath, the other a bumbling blunderer. Melchior Kimmel, a pornographic book dealer, has murdered his wife by assaulting her at a rest stop on a bus trip, having arranged a secure alibi. Although police assume that Kimmel's wife was killed by a stranger, Walter Stackhouse, a lawyer who is locked in a miserable marriage with "a pint-size Medusa," is able to piece together the true circumstances of the murder based on newspaper reports and his empathy with the murderer. When Stackhouse's wife commits suicide before Stackhouse can emulate Kimmel's crime, the lawyer's feeling of guilt at having planned her murder causes him to act suspiciously. Because of his obsessive urge to seek out Kimmel, he unwittingly directs suspicion toward the source of his inspiration. Stackhouse eventually does turn into a murderer, and Kimmel is arrested after a policeman witnesses him stab Stackhouse, his "enemy number one," to death, calling him "murderer, idiot, blunderer, until the meaning of the words

became a solid fact like a mountain sitting on top of him, and he no longer had the will to fight against it."

James Sandoe, reviewer for the *New York Herald Tribune Book Review*, accorded Highsmith underhanded praise when he stated that she "manages so well with the understandable if mussy Stackhouse that she can trample plausibility and drag us along in spite of it. Her fancy is at once extravagant and acute." He preferred *The Blunderer* to Highsmith's first novel: "She has written a remarkable tale and a far more telling one (for me, at least) than its celebrated predecessor, *Strangers on a Train*." Symons, in *The New York Times Book Review*, proclaimed *The Blunderer* one of the one hundred best detective novels of all time.

In Highsmith's best-known and arguably most accomplished novel, *The Talented Mr. Ripley*, the "criminal-hero," as she calls him in *Plotting and Writing Suspense Fiction*, receives no punishment for his misdeeds and escapes scot-free. Tom Phelps Ripley, a twenty-five-year-old unsettled and unemployed aspiring actor who has an amazing gift for mimicry, is asked by Herbert Greenleaf, the well-to-do owner of a small shipbuilding company, to convince his son, Dickie, who has been living in Southern Italy for two years dabbling in painting, to return to the States and to take over the family firm. Tom, whose life is based on the philosophy that "something always turned up," accepts the mission because it provides him with a clean slate: "He was starting a new life. Goodbye to all the second-rate people he had hung around and had let hang around him in the past three years in New York. He felt as he imagined immigrants felt when they left everything behind them in some foreign country, left their friends and relations and their past mistakes, and sailed for America."

When Tom meets Dickie and his girlfriend, writer Marge Sherwood, in Mongibello, he is immediately fascinated by their carefree and luxurious way of life, their independence, and their air of sophistication. Tom insinuates himself into Dickie's life: he confesses the true reason for his trip and switches sides by supporting Dickie's plan to remain in Italy. Their friendship, which includes an ever-increasing element of homoeroticism, grows until Dickie witnesses Tom impersonating him in front of a mirror and pretending that he is strangling Marge. Tom eventually kills Dickie and assumes his identity. He later kills Dickie's friend Freddie Miles to protect his secret. Whereas Tom regrets having murdered Dickie, he feels no qualms about Freddie's murder: "He hadn't wanted to murder, it had been a necessity." When he seems about to be caught, Tom slips back into his old identity and eventually manages to convince Dickie's father that his son committed suicide. Dickie's will, which has been forged by Tom to his advantage, is accepted as authentic, and Tom is assured the life of luxury he had yearned for.

The positive ending of the novel has drawn comparisons with André Gide's *Les Caves du Vatican* (1914; translated as *The Vatican Swindle*, 1925) in which, according to Anthony Channell Hilfer in *The Crime Novel: A Deviant Genre* (1990), "by a chain of extraordinary coincidence Lafcadio escapes the consequences of the gratuitous murder he has committed." Consequently, Highsmith, like Gide, was accused by some of promoting an amoral and even immoral worldview. *The New Yorker* (7 January 1956), for example, called the novel "remarkably immoral" and its protagonist "one of the most repellent and fascinating characters," and Craig Brown stated in *The Times Literary Supplement (TLS):* "it is a rare villain or psychopath whom the reader does not find himself willing toward freedom, a rare investigator or victim (sometimes the one becomes the other) whom the reader is unhappy to see dead." The following 1942 entry from Highsmith's notebook, quoted by Wilson, shows that her accusers were not far off the mark:

> The abnormal point of view is always the best for depicting twentieth-century life, not only because so many of us are abnormal, realizing it or not, but because twentieth-century life is established and maintained through abnormality. I should love to do a novel with all the literary virtues of *Red Badge of Courage* about one abnormal character seeing present day life, very ordinary life, yet arresting through it, abnormality, until at the end, the reader sees, and with little reluctance, that he is not abnormal at all, and that the main character might well be himself.

German critic Michael Dunker has shown that Highsmith masterfully employs the literary device of the third-person narrator who provides the reader with an insight into the criminal-hero's state of mind and his motivations, subtly manipulating the reader's sympathies toward the protagonists in all her novels.

Highsmith publicly responded to the accusations of promoting amorality in *Plotting and Writing Suspense Fiction* with characteristic bluntness. She stressed that "art essentially has nothing to do with morality, convention or moralizing" and threw back a charge of hypocrisy: "I find the public passion for justice quite boring and artificial, for neither life nor nature care if justice is ever done or not. The public wants to see the law triumph, or at least the general public does, though at the same time the public likes brutality." Tellingly, in Clément's movie adaptation of *The Talented Mr. Ripley*, *Plein Soleil* (1959), the ending of the novel is changed and Ripley is caught. Even in Anthony Minghella's 1999 version, Tom does not entirely escape punishment. Although he is not caught by the police, he suffers a retribution of his own making: he is forced to kill the man he really loves in order to safeguard his future. Highsmith's first Ripley novel was given a special award by the Mystery Writers of America in 1956 and the Grand Prix de Litterature Policiere and the Edgar Allan Poe Scroll of the Mystery Writers of America the following year.

Highsmith followed up her masterful Ripley novel with another masterpiece. *Deep Water* (1957), the exploration of a hellish marriage and its deadly consequences, is considered by Russell Harrison, author of *Patricia Highsmith* (1997), as one of the writer's most accomplished novels and characterized by Anthony Boucher in the 6 October 1957 issue of *The New York Times Book Review* as a "full-fleshed novel of pity and irony." Victor Van Allen, the independently rich publisher of limited luxury books, is chained to a "wild horse" of a wife who, as a sign of her "constitutional rebelliousness," has many extramarital affairs while refusing to agree to a divorce. Victor does not object to Melinda's affairs per se but rather to the fact that she picks "idiotic, spineless characters" and that she is not discreet, flaunting her affairs in their small, conservative Berkshire town. During a pool party Victor manages to drown one of his wife's lovers without being observed and without experiencing any guilt. Melinda suspects that her husband is guilty of the murder but is unable to prove it. When Melinda later threatens to leave Victor to marry a building contractor, Victor throws the new lover down a cliff and submerges the body in a deserted quarry. When he is drawn back to the scene of the crime to check on the status of the corpse, he is discovered by Don Wilson, a hack writer who has suspected him of murder for some time. In an explosion of violence Victor strangles the woman who has made his life a living hell: "Medea. Mangler of children and castrator of husbands. Fate had overtaken her at last." He accepts his punishment defiantly:

> . . . it was not bad at all to be leaving them. The ugly birds without wings. The mediocre who perpetuated mediocrity, who really fought and died for it. He smiled at Wilson's grim, resentful, the-world-owes-me-a-living face, which was the reflection of the small, dull mind behind it, and Vic cursed it and all it stood for. Silently, and with a smile, and with all that was left of him, he cursed it.

Boucher called the novel Highsmith's "coming of age as a novelist; less startling than *Strangers*, it is incomparably stronger in subtlety and depth of characterization."

After collaborating with Doris Sanders on a children's book, *Miranda the Panda Is on the Veranda* (1958), Highsmith published *A Game for the Living* (1958), a novel that even after four rewrites she considered her "one really dull book." In *Plotting and Writing Suspense Fiction* she blames its failure on her own weakness in constructing a whodunit: "I had tried to do something different from what I had been doing, but this caused me to leave out certain elements that are vital for me: surprise, speed of action, the stretching of the reader's credulity, and above all that intimacy with the murderer himself. I am not an inventor of puzzles, nor do I like secrets."

Despite its shortcomings, the novel is of interest because of its exotic location and the portrayal of the relationship of two mismatched friends. Theodore Schiebelhut, a rich German painter who has adopted Mexican citizenship, and his friend Ramon Otero, a professor and devout Catholic, are suspected of brutally raping, murdering, and mutilating Lelia, a woman who had an intimate relationship with both. While the two men initially suspect each other, they gradually learn to appreciate each other's similarities and differences. As Noel Dorman Mawer shows in her 1991 essay "From Villain to Vigilante," Highsmith is no longer confining herself "to the mutually destructive effects of complementary pathologies, but rather is portraying the mutual misunderstandings of two essentially rational, humane people who have contrasting cultural backgrounds." Because the novel focuses on the

relationship between the friends, the solution of the murder mystery—a marginal figure is revealed as the perpetrator—seems tacked on and unsatisfactory.

Highsmith moved to a house in the Catskills near Palisades, New York, in 1958, and two years later she shared an old farmhouse outside New Hope, Pennsylvania, with the lesbian author Meaker. Highsmith's next two novels, *This Sweet Sickness* (1960) and *The Cry of the Owl* (1962), complete what Harrison calls her "exurban trilogy," which she had begun with *Deep Water*. Both books are set in claustrophobic and narrow-minded small-town America, and both describe a character's obsessive fixation on an inappropriate object of desire and the clash between fantasy and reality.

In *This Sweet Sickness*, David Kelsey, the chief engineer of a fabrics manufacturing plant, is not able to adjust to the fact that Annabelle, a former girlfriend of his, has married another man. He creates a fantasy world in which Annabelle and his alter ego, "William Neumeister," can live happily together. While residing in a dingy boardinghouse during the week, he spends the weekends in a house that he has furnished in preparation for his reunion with Annabelle. Even though she keeps rejecting his persistent overtures, David blames "the Situation" on the fact that Annabelle is not herself and that she is not able to see anything in perspective: "she was immersed, drowned now in what she considered reality."

David himself is being romantically pursued by Effie Brennan, a secretary who lives in the same boardinghouse. When Annabelle's husband, Gerald, pays a surprise visit to David in his dream house one Sunday in order to warn him off, David kills him accidentally during a scuffle. He takes the body to the police and, in the guise of William Neumeister, reports the accident. Since David's fantasy world has been breached, he sells the house, gives up his job, and moves to another city. The tables are turned on him when an obsessed Effie pursues him to his new residence and sullies the bed that was meant solely for Annabelle: "He was through with the house. Effie had ruined it. There was nothing in it that he wanted any longer. . . . he would never come back. Never." Having killed Effie accidentally while dragging her from the bed and throwing her to the floor, David flees to New York City and, being pursued by the police, throws himself off an apartment building. In his last moments he desperately clings to his fantasy: "Thinking no more about it, he stepped off into that cool space, the fast descent to her, with nothing in his mind but a memory of a curve of her shoulder, naked, as he had never seen it."

Highsmith explored the theme of obsession with an unresponsive love object again two years later in *The Cry of the Owl*. Robert Forester, a lonely and depressed aeronautics engineer whose marriage has collapsed, starts spying on Jenny Thierolf, a young woman who lives alone in a secluded house. Robert's peeping serves as a palliative to the fiasco of his marriage and allows him to create, in Harrison's phrase, a "fantasy of perfect domesticity."

When Robert is discovered by Jenny and invited into the house, reality does not match up with the fantasy he has created. Although he enters into a nonsexual relationship with Jenny, he does so without much enthusiasm. Greg Wyncoop, Jenny's former fiancé, eventually provokes a fight with Robert, who saves Greg from drowning when he falls into a river. Greg and Robert's vindictive former wife, Nickie, hatch an involved plot to frame Robert for Greg's faked death, which in the end results in Jenny committing suicide and Greg being arrested for attempted murder. While out on bail Greg stabs Nickie to death when she tries to break up a fight he is having with Robert. The wary Robert makes sure that he is not implicated in the stabbing: "The knife was at his feet, not a bloodstain on it that he could see. He bent to pick it up, then stopped. Don't touch it, he thought, don't touch it." Hitchcock purchased the rights to the novel in 1961 and used it as the basis for an hour-long segment of his television series, *Alfred Hitchcock Presents*, titling it "Annabelle."

In both novels Highsmith portrays the protagonists' community as a vengeful and unreasonable mob. A suicidal David Kelsey is urged on by a heckling crowd to jump off the building, and Robert Forester is immediately suspected by his community of a murder that may or may not have taken place. Harrison makes a convincing case that by portraying the community "as a collection of prejudiced, irrational, witch-hunting individuals … Highsmith has constructed something like an allegorical tale of the witch-hunt, of the blacklist, in short, of McCarthyism." The writer, whose political sympathies rested with

the Left, alluded to political developments in the United States increasingly in subsequent novels. The political and cultural changes the country experienced in the early 1960s may have been one of the reasons why Highsmith moved to Europe permanently. After a third extended trip to Rome and Positano in 1961-1962 she settled in the south of England in 1963 to be with her lover, Barbara, the wife of a London businessman.

The first novel to be published after Highsmith's permanent move to Europe was *The Two Faces of January* (1964). Like several of her works the novel features an exotic locale—in this case Greece—and two men chained to each other in a love-hate relationship. Rydal Keener, a young American with an air of melancholy, has a chance encounter in an Athens hotel with Chester MacFarland, a crook who has fled the United States, where he has committed stock fraud, and his wife, Colette. Rydal is attracted to Chester, because he strongly resembles his recently deceased father, and to Colette, who reminds him of his first love, Agnes. Rydal is soon caught up in Chester's criminal activities and becomes a suspect when Chester kills a police official. When Rydal's attraction to Colette intensifies, Chester attempts to murder his rival but kills his own wife by mistake. Faced with exposure, the two men close ranks against the police and protect each other. Chester's false deathbed confession absolves Rydal from any guilt. Whereas Rydal had deliberately missed his own father's funeral, his decision to attend Chester's signals his reconciliation with the past. Highsmith was highly gratified when the novel, which had been rejected twice by Harper and Row, was awarded the Silver Dagger for best foreign novel by the Crime Writers Association of Great Britain.

Highsmith also had difficulty finding a publisher for *The Glass Cell* (1964). In *Plotting and Writing Suspense Fiction* she describes the genesis of the novel in great detail, including its rejections and revisions. The book is based on the theory of "the deleterious effect of exposure to brutality in prison, and how this can lead to anti-social behavior after release." Philip Carter, an engineer, is made the fall guy for his employer's illegal scheme to overcharge customers for inferior building materials. In prison he is exposed to constant brutality, injustice, and degradation. When Max, a forger who has befriended Philip, is brutally killed during a prison riot, Philip avenges the murder by killing the likely perpetrator. Eventually his ten-year sentence is reduced by three years for good conduct, and Philip is released into a hostile world. Unable to find suitable employment because of his prison record, he gradually discovers that his wife, Hazel, is having an affair with his lawyer, David Sullivan. Philip kills David, "the lily-livered swine," in a fit of uncontrollable rage and subsequently a blackmailer who has knowledge of the murder. Having been punished for a crime he did not commit, a hardened Philip escapes punishment for the murders he has committed. Highsmith explains, "because Carter has been through so much in prison, I wanted to have him cleared of his post-prison murder. A double miscarriage of justice, if you like. I wanted him by some quirk to go free."

Highsmith followed up the grim depiction of prison life and its effects with *A Suspension of Mercy* (1965), a novel of black humor in which she examines the theme of fantasy versus reality through another portrayal of an unhappy marriage. Sydney Smith Bartleby, the American protagonist, is the creator of a British television adventure show titled *The Whip*, about a charming criminal who is never caught. Bartleby loathes his wife, Alicia, and frequently thinks of killing her. Instead of realizing his fantasies, however, he writes them down in his notebook with the plan to use them in his fiction. When she disappears, the notebook leads the police to suspect Sydney of murder. His elderly neighbor is convinced of his guilt because "Americans are violent. Everyone knows that." After Sydney discovers that Alicia has assumed a new identity to protect her affair with Edward Tilbury, a London lawyer, she commits suicide, and Sydney exacts revenge on Alicia's lover by forcing him to swallow an overdose of sleeping pills. When the police accept the lawyer's death as a suicide, Sydney feels invincible: "As he touched the notebook, Sydney thought that he would write a description of the Tilbury murder in it, while his recollection was still very clear, because the notebook was now, after all, the safest place in which to write it."

Bored with England and mourning the demise of her four-year relationship with Barbara, Highsmith moved to France in 1967 and purchased a house in Samois-sur-Seine, where she lived with her close friend Elizabeth Lyne. In her next two novels she featured some of the exotic

and picturesque locales she had visited during her frequent trips. *Those Who Walk Away* (1967) is set in Venice and describes yet another cat-and-mouse game between two men. The American painter Ed Coleman blames his son-in-law, Ray, for the death of his daughter, who has committed suicide during her honeymoon. He pursues Ray through the canals and piazzas of Venice and makes several attempts on his life. Ray, like Greg in *The Cry of the Owl*, hides after one attack, and Coleman is suspected of his murder. Coleman eventually ceases the assaults, and Ray begins to understand his father-in-law's grief: "he wasn't on the defensive or angry with Coleman any longer, and he could afford to feel sorry for him, even sympathize."

The Tremor of Forgery (1969), set in Tunisia, was Highsmith's (as well as Greene's) favorite of her novels and, in Harrison's view, marks a watershed in her career because it and subsequent works are less concerned with crime and more focused on political and social issues. Howard Ingham, an American writer, is sent to Tunis, where he is supposed to write the script for a movie to be directed by his friend John Castlewood. While waiting for the director to arrive, Ingham is bewildered by the strange country and its customs and befriends Anders Jensen, a homosexual Danish painter who feels comfortable in the alien land. When Ina Pallant, Ingham's fiancée and script supervisor for the movie, arrives, Ingham learns that Castlewood has committed suicide because Ina, with whom he has had an affair, was unwilling to leave Ingham. One night Ingham surprises a burglar trying to break into his bungalow, and he throws his heavy typewriter at the intruder, wounding him. Hotel employees remove the burglar's body as well as any signs of the attack; thus, the only act of violence in the novel is one of self-defense, and Highsmith leaves open the question of whether it has serious consequences.

Initially Ingham feels guilty about the incident and considers informing the police, but eventually he adopts the fatalistic attitude of the natives. He decides to stay on in Tunisia in spite of the fact that the movie has been canceled, and he immerses himself in the local customs, with Jensen as his expert guide. One sign of Ingham's learning process is his changing attitude toward homosexuality. Early in the novel he is propositioned by Jensen and refuses the offer. Throughout the novel the two men get closer and Ingham's reluctance to have sex with a man is less pronounced:

> . . . Ingham recalled one night when he'd gone along to the coffee-house called Les Arcades, and had come near to taking home a young Arab. The Arab had sat at the table with him, and Ingham had stood him a couple of beers. Ingham had been both sexually excited and lonely that evening, and the only thing that had deterred him, he thought, was that he hadn't been sure what to do in bed with a boy, and he hadn't wanted to feel silly. Hardly a moral reason for chastity.

Harrison points out in *Patricia Highsmith* that the gradual loosening of sexual barriers and the break with Western conventions is reminiscent of Gide's novel *L'Immoraliste* (1902; translated as *The Immoralist*, 1930). The novel also shows the influence of Albert Camus's *L'Etranger* (1942; translated as *The Stranger*, 1946). Harrison argues that "the treatment of the political issues . . . reflects Highsmith's position as a representative of a formally noncolonialist power suffering internal divisions over its neoimperialist project in Vietnam."

From 1970 to 1991 Highsmith published not only eight novels, including four featuring Tom Ripley, but also seven collections of short stories. These stories attest to the wide range of the author's interests and talent and include a variety of genres, such as horror, science fiction, fantasy, and fairy tale. Only a few of the stories deal primarily with crime. The first collection, *Eleven*, gathers some of her best stories, including "The Heroine," the short story that had been published in *O. Henry's Best Short Stories of 1946*, and Greene's favorite story, "When the Fleet Was in at Mobile," the portrait of a young woman who unwittingly exchanges a life of prostitution for an abusive marriage. "The Cries of Love" details the disturbing relationship between two elderly women who torture each other by destroying each other's favorite possessions. In "The Snail Watcher" and "The Quest for Blank Claveringi," animals take revenge on humans, and in the memorable story "The Terrapin" a young boy avenges the cruel killing and dismemberment of a soup turtle by subjecting his mother to a similar treatment.

At the beginning of *Ripley under Ground* (1970) the criminal-hero has settled down in Villeperce-sur-Seine near Paris, where he and his wife, Heloise, a rich, cultured, and amoral Frenchwoman, enjoy a life of luxury in their villa, called "Belle Ombre." Ripley collects paintings by such artists as Vincent Van Gogh, René Magritte, and Chaim Soutine; enjoys good food and drink, classical music, and traveling; tends his garden; and commits occasional crimes in order to supplement his income. He has devised a scheme with friends in London to sell fake paintings, pretending they are the work of Derwatt, a famous painter who is supposedly leading the life of a recluse in Mexico but who actually committed suicide in Greece three years before.

When Thomas Murchison, a rich and knowledgeable American art collector, suspects the fraud, Ripley impersonates the dead painter in an attempt to allay Murchison's suspicions. Failing to do so, he kills the collector in his wine cellar with a bottle of his best Margaux while feeling no remorse: "Tom didn't feel that it was a crime." Although Ripley is able to deflect the suspicions of the police, the situation becomes precarious when Bernard Tufts, the young painter who produces the fake Derwatt paintings, threatens to expose the scheme. After Tufts attacks Ripley and leaves him for dead, Ripley is able to haunt the painter like a ghost, causing his suicide. The police are suspicious of Ripley but are unable to connect him to either of the deaths. He has gotten away with murder once more.

In 1971 Highsmith moved to Montmachoux and later to Moncourt, both situated near Fontainebleau. In his article "The Woman Who Was Ripley" (*The Independent on Sunday Magazine*, 13 January 2000), Wilson suggests a possible explanation for the writer's restlessness: "her romantic attachments were far from settled—she lived with a handful of women, none for longer than a couple of years at a time, often moving countries in a bid to escape the emotional fall-out that accompanied the breakdown of a relationship." Frequent trips to the United States provided Highsmith with the inspiration for four non-Ripley novels that include unflattering portrayals of her former homeland.

A Dog's Ransom (1972) depicts New York City as a dangerous urban jungle, torn apart by class and ethnic hatred, in which muggings, burglaries, kidnappings, and blackmail are the order of the day. Kenneth Rowajinski, a former construction worker of Polish extraction who is living on disability, kills a dog belonging to Ed and Greta Reynolds and extorts a ransom from the couple, pretending that the dog has been kidnapped. The Reynoldses, who lost their daughter in a drug-related shooting, are devastated by the loss of their beloved pet: "A dog, a daughter—there should be a great difference, yet the feeling was much the same." Clarence Duhamell, a young policeman who has been assigned to the case, quickly becomes obsessed with tracking down the dognapper in order to win the couple's approbation and gratitude. When the policeman discovers the perpetrator, a deadly game of cat and mouse ensues. Rowajinski, "the Pole," taunts Duhamell and harasses his girlfriend, Marilyn. When the policeman finds Rowajinski lurking around Marilyn's apartment, he beats him to death with his revolver. Having taken the law into his own hands, Duhamell is shot by one of his colleagues. The novel was savaged by *TLS* on 12 May 1972: "Patricia Highsmith's new novel belongs in what is becoming a depressingly substantial sector of her total output—it is a mechanical exercise in self-pastiche, employing all her familiar devices and rehearsing most of her familiar obsessions, but with none of the vigor, inventiveness or intensity which in her best work makes those devices and obsessions seem so riveting." In contrast, Harrison has shown that *A Dog's Ransom* "reveals social and economic conflict more clearly than any of the author's other novels. But at the same time, the author's inability to resolve successfully any of these conflicts makes *A Dog's Ransom* both an authentic expression of its times and an unusually moving, if flawed, novel."

Ripley's Game, which takes place six months after *Ripley under Ground*, is the darkest of all the Ripley novels. When Ripley is commissioned to assassinate two mafiosi who threaten illegal gambling activities in Hamburg, Germany, he rejects the offer because the Derwatt episode has not blown over yet and because he "detested murder unless it was absolutely necessary." He hatches, however, a fiendish plan in order to punish Jonathan Trevanny, an Englishman who owns a small picture-framing shop, for "sneering" at him once at a party. Ripley, knowing that Trevanny suffers from leukemia, spreads the false rumor that Trevanny is dying and manages to falsify medical reports to that effect. He hopes to make Trevanny receptive to the murder scheme in order to provide for his family, a challenge made especially attractive by the fact that Trevanny "looks the picture of

decency and innocence." Trevanny initially rejects the plan but, believing that he is about to die, eventually agrees to it and travels to Hamburg, where he shoots one of the mafiosi. When Ripley realizes that his experiment to corrupt an innocent has succeeded, he helps Trevanny murder the second mafioso. Several mafiosi track the assassins to France, and Ripley has to join forces with Trevanny in order to eliminate them. Trevanny is killed in a shootout, and his wife, Simone, who hates Ripley for having corrupted her husband, cannot resist the lure of the blood money: "Simone was just a trifle ashamed of herself, Tom thought. In that, she joined much of the rest of the world. Tom felt, in fact, that her conscience would be more at rest than that of her husband, if he were still alive."

Highsmith, a fervent animal lover who was surrounded by cats and snails throughout her life, allows such diverse animals as elephants, camels, dogs, cats, pigs, horses, chickens, hamsters, and ferrets to avenge the cruel treatment they have been subjected to by humans in the appropriately titled collection *The Animal-Lover's Book of Beastly Murder* (1975). In the same year Highsmith, who had frequently been accused of promoting misogyny in her novels, deliberately poured gasoline on the fire when she published *Kleine Geschichten für Weiberfeinde*, translated two years later as *Little Tales of Misogyny*. The stories, with such telling titles as "The Coquette," "The Fully-Licensed Whore, or, The Wife," "The Breeder," "The Mobile Bed-Object," and "The Perfect Little Lady," are clearly written tongue in cheek, and Highsmith was obviously thumbing her nose at the critics while trying to *épater le bourgeois* (to shock the middle classes). She was no doubt highly gratified when she and Roland Topor, illustrator for the book, received the French Grand Prix de l'Humour Noir in 1977.

Edith's Diary (1977), another novel in Highsmith's American cycle, is one of her most accomplished novels. Since the writer did not acknowledge authorship of her lesbian novel *The Price of Salt* until 1991, *Edith's Diary* was the first Highsmith book to provide the readers with a positive depiction of a strong female protagonist. The fact that Highsmith's novel revolves around an intelligent, educated, and accomplished woman who is destroyed by an oppressive patriarchal society helped to allay somewhat the charge that her novels promoted misogyny. Edith Howland, a freelance writer and housewife, tries "to organize and analyze her life-in-progress" by keeping a diary. Slowly but inextricably her life becomes a living nightmare when her husband, Brett, unexpectedly demands a divorce so that he can marry a younger woman. He leaves Edith caring for his bedridden and sickly Uncle George, who refuses to move to a nursing home even though he requires constant care. Edith is also left in charge of their son, Cliffie, a good-for-nothing who drops out of school, moves from one part-time job to the next, gets hooked on alcohol and drugs, injures a man in a drunken driving accident, and eventually kills Uncle George by administering an overdose of codeine. Edith's diary increasingly serves as her means to escape an unbearable reality. She invents an imaginary son who, having graduated from Princeton University, works as a successful and well-paid engineer in Kuwait. While the real Cliffie is reduced to masturbating into socks at night, Edith's imaginary Cliffie has married a beautiful wife and fathered two adorable children. Edith is aware of the fictional and therapeutic character of her diary entries, but those around her start questioning her sanity. When two doctors, hired by her former husband, insist on having her examined by a psychiatrist, Edith accidentally slips on the stairs and falls to her death. In her final moments the fantasy of a beautiful son is replaced by Edith's "personal sense of injustice."

Highsmith's collection *Slowly, Slowly in the Wind* (1979) includes two of her strongest stories, "The Network" and "Broken Glass." Both stories reflect, according to Harrison, "socioeconomic changes as they affect that free-floating urban middle class ... with remarkably unsettling results for the reader." In "The Network" middle-class New Yorkers, who feel that they have been disfranchised in favor of minorities, bond together in the attempt to deal with an increasingly threatening environment. In "Broken Glass" Andrew Cooperman, an eighty-one-year-old retired newspaper typesetter who is living on a meager pension, is mugged by a young black man. Cooperman refuses to become a prisoner in his own apartment—as have many of his elderly neighbors—and fights the same mugger the next time he encounters him, stabbing him in the stomach with a pane of glass. His action, however, leads to his death when he is attacked by the injured mugger's friends.

Ripley the corrupter undergoes a dramatic metamorphosis in *The Boy Who Followed Ripley* (1980), as he turns into the compassionate protector of a young man. When Frank Pierson, a sixteen-year-old American who has pushed his wealthy, wheelchair-bound father off a cliff and who has been on the run since the murder, shows up on Ripley's doorstep, Ripley offers him shelter. Frank is racked with guilt and hopes to gain absolution by confessing his deed: "Frank felt guilt, which was why he had looked up Tom Ripley, and curiously Tom had never felt such guilt, never let it seriously trouble him." Ripley and Frank quickly develop an intense friendship with a strong homoerotic undercurrent. While spending a weekend in Berlin they find themselves accidentally in a gay bar called "Glad Ass," where Ripley enjoys the attention he and his friend attract: "Tom himself was an object of envy for having a nice looking boy of sixteen in his company. Tom could in fact see that now, and it made him smile." When Frank is kidnapped, Ripley delivers the ransom money and frees the boy. He eventually convinces Frank to return to the United States and to face his family. Although he prevents Frank from jumping off a cliff at one point, he is ultimately unable to prevent the young man's redemptive suicide.

Highsmith presents a blackly humorous view of old age in "Old Folks at Home," one of the best stories in her collection *The Black House* (1981). When Lois and Herbert McIntyre, a couple of young, successful professionals, decide to "adopt" an elderly couple from an old-age home, their good deed turns into a nightmare. The elderly couple turns out to be argumentative, demanding, and incontinent. An attempt to return the adoptees to the old-age home fails, and the young couple has to rent offices outside their own home in order to be able to work. When their house catches on fire, the McIntyres save their books and papers but leave the old folks to their fate.

In the last ten years of Highsmith's life her literary output dwindled considerably, and the writer isolated herself more and more. In 1982 she moved from France to Switzerland, first settling in Aurigeno and then in Tegna, where she withdrew into a house that she had built according to her own designs. The home resembled a bunker: situated at the foot of the Alps, it kept the world at bay.

In *People Who Knock on the Door* (1983), a "mordant indictment of contemporary middle America" according to Holly Eley in *TLS* (4 February 1983), Highsmith savagely attacks fundamentalist religion, moral hypocrisy, and the right-wing government of Ronald Reagan. Richard Alderman, an insurance salesman in a small Indiana town, embraces fundamentalist Christianity when Robbie, his younger son who has become seriously ill, is seemingly saved through the power of prayer. Richard is transformed into a rigid and uncompromising moralist overnight, and he turns his eldest son, Arthur, out of the house when he discovers that Arthur has helped his pregnant girlfriend to obtain an abortion. Richard, however, does not practice what he preaches and is caught having an extramarital affair with Irene, a former prostitute whom he has taken under his wing. When Robbie, who has become a reborn Christian as well, discovers that his father is responsible for Irene's baby, he shoots him in a fit of righteous indignation, claiming "Dad deserved it!"

Highsmith's last two collections of short stories, *Mermaids on the Golf Course* (1985) and *Tales of Natural and Unnatural Catastrophes* (1987), reveal the writer's growing fascination with an apparently decaying American society and her desire to explore current political and social concerns. Such a desire is also evident in her last novel set in her homeland, *Found in the Street* (1986). Like *People Who Knock on the Door*, it also features an obsessed moralist who believes it is his mission to protect the innocent in what he considers the debauched cesspool of New York City. Ralph Linderman, an eccentric security guard who has named his dog "God," latches on to naive and innocent Elsie Tyler, who has just moved to New York. He tries to protect her from such seemingly predatory men as Jack Sutherland, a book illustrator who has befriended the woman. Linderman harasses and badgers Sutherland and blames him for Elsie's death when she is murdered. In fact, he is so blinded by his moral outrage that he does not realize that Elsie is a lesbian and that she has been murdered by the jealous partner of one of her former girlfriends. While Highsmith in most respects paints a positive picture of the gay world in the novel, Harrison suggests that her use of a highly unrealistic gay-on-gay murder points to some ambivalence on her part: "This misrepresentation of reality would seem to suggest a mild antipathy or unease toward the milieu that Highsmith has—at least ostensibly—been painting in such 'normal,' even flattering colors."

In 1990 Highsmith was honored by the French government when she was named Officier dans l'Ordre des Arts et des Lettres (Officer of the Order of Arts and Letters), and in 1991 she was nominated for the Nobel Prize in literature. The same year she published *Ripley under Water* (1991), the last novel of the cycle, in which Ripley is the victim of a meddlesome American couple, David and Janice Pritchard, who have moved into the French village to torture him with their knowledge of some of his youthful offenses. First they call Ripley, pretending to be Dickie Greenleaf; then they follow him and his wife to Tangier, Morocco. They eventually succeed in recovering the remains of Thomas Murchison, the art collector Ripley killed in *Ripley under Ground*, which they leave on Ripley's doorstep. Ripley's response to the constant harassment is unusually restrained. Even though he considers killing Pritchard on several occasions, he does not give in to this urge. The Pritchards get their just deserts, though, when they drown in their own pond while trying to recover Murchison's remains after Ripley has deposited the "bag of bones" there. Ripley disposes of the last incriminating object, one of Murchison's rings, in the nearby river, ensuring his unencumbered future. Some critics have considered the later Ripley books less successful than the first ones; Symons, for example, in the third edition of *Bloody Murder* (1993), blames the fact that Highsmith "has been self-indulgent" in relation to her favorite character for the preposterousness of Ripley's later exploits. Tellingly, the Ripley omnibus published by Knopf as part of the Everyman's Library in 1999 only includes the first three novels of the series.

Highsmith died in a Locarno hospital on 4 February 1995 of cancer, and her ashes were interred in Tegna on 11 March. She bequeathed her $3,000,000 estate to Yaddo, the Upstate New York artists' colony that had been instrumental in launching her career. Shortly after her death her last novel, *Small g: A Summer Idyll* (1995), was published in London. This book hearkens back to *The Price of Salt* and features a large cast of gay, bisexual, and heterosexual characters whose goal is to live peacefully side by side. They mingle in a Zurich saloon called Jakobs Bierstube, the clientele of which is predominantly straight during the week. On weekends the bar is known as "Small g," a reference to its mixed clientele of gays and straights. The tranquil atmosphere is threatened when Renate Hagenauer, a prudish and homophobic fashion designer, incites violence in an attempt to break up relationships. Renate eventually dies in an accident, and the balance is restored. While the lovers in *The Price of Salt* form a monogamous relationship that mirrors a heterosexual marriage, the protagonists in *Small g* have to be satisfied with nonexclusive relationships: Rickie Markwalder is content sharing his boyfriend, Fredy Schimmelmann, a married policeman, with his wife; and bisexual Luisa Zimmermann forms a ménage à trois with the lesbian Dorrie Wyss and the heterosexual Teddie Stevenson.

Whereas *Small g* rapidly sold almost forty-six thousand copies in French translation, the novel was not published in the United States until almost 10 years later. Its fate is indicative of the reception of most of Patricia Highsmith's books, as is noted by Harrison in his study: "for the American author who expatriated herself to Europe for most of her adult life, whose novels often dealt in evasions of various sorts, this last European success and American failure seem a not altogether unfitting conclusion." A boom in interest in Highsmith's life and art in the United States, however, may be righting this imbalance. Her out-of-print books are being republished by Norton; *The Selected Stories of Patricia Highsmith* (2001), which includes all her previously published short-story collections except for *Eleven*, became a best-seller; and *Nothing That Meets the Eye: The Uncollected Stories of Patricia Highsmith* was published in 2002. Even *The New Yorker*, the magazine in which Highsmith had most fervently hoped to be published during her lifetime, helped renew interest in her work by printing her short story "The Trouble with Mrs. Blynn" in 2002. Not only is the American reading public taking note of this seminal writer who had previously been relegated to marginality, but also the academy is following suit. In his essay "Reality Catches Up to Highsmith's Hard-Boiled Fiction" from the *Chronicle of Higher Education* (20 February 2004), Leonard Cassuto expains why the author, who was once belittled as a "dime-store Dostoyevsky," is more popular than ever in the United States, and why she is being canonized as a major American artist:

Never at home in her own context, she fits perfectly into ours. ... it's clear that the politics—sexual and otherwise—of her dangerously unstable fictional world are a lot like our own. Homosexuals are out, but still the center of political and cultural (to say nothing of religious) debate. And life in today's age of terrorism creates the kind of anxious foreboding that Highsmith evoked again and again. People never know whether something (or someone) might explode next to them. We also live in an era where surveillance is everywhere, and where people live at risk of being turned in and taken away. These times are the closest we've ever come to the '50s, when anxiety boiled beneath the surface of the prosperous facade of American living. We've moved to the creepy neighborhood where Patricia Highsmith lived all her life.

Ed Siegel, writing in the *Boston Globe* (27 January 2002), also believes that changes in American society have contributed to the reassessment of Highsmith's importance: "In the wake of September 11, Highsmith's world is not only more like ours, where crime and punishment or cause and effect don't necessarily go hand in hand, she seems a more important writer than ever."

Source: Karl L. Stenger, "Patricia Highsmith," in *Dictionary of Literary Biography*, Vol. 306, *American Mystery and Detective Writers*, edited by George Parker Anderson, Thomson Gale, 2005, pp. 144–61.

Thomson Gale

In the following essay, the critic gives an overview of Patricia Highsmith's work.

As the author of numerous short story collections and novels, including the well-known *Strangers on a Train*, American-born Patricia Highsmith enjoyed greater critical and commercial success in England, France, and Germany than in her native country. As Jeff Weinstein speculated in the *Village Voice Literary Supplement*, the reason for this is that Highsmith's books have been "misplaced"— relegated to the mystery and suspense shelves instead of being allowed to take their rightful place in the literature section. As far as her ardent admirers in the United States and abroad are concerned, Highsmith was more than just a superb crime novelist. In fact, declared Brigid Brophy in *Don't Never Forget: Collected Views and Reviews*, "Highsmith and Simenon are alone in writing books which transcend the limits of the genre while staying strictly inside its rules:

> "HIGHSMITH'S PROTAGONISTS ARE NEVER
> HEROIC,' WROTE DAVENPORT-HINES IN ASSESSING *THE*
> *SELECTED SHORT STORIES,* BECAUSE 'HEROES HAVE
> FREE WILL AND EXERCISE BRAVE CHOICES;
> HIGHSMITH'S CHARACTERS ACT ON IMPULSE AND
> CANNOT CONTROL WHAT THEY DO.'"

they alone have taken the crucial step from playing games to creating art."

The art in Highsmith's work springs from her skillful fusion of plot, characterization, and style, with the crime story serving primarily "as a means of revealing and examining her own deepest interests and obsessions," according to a *Times Literary Supplement* reviewer. Among her most common themes are the nature of guilt and the often symbiotic relationship that develops between two people (almost always men) who are at the same time fascinated and repelled by each other. Highsmith's works therefore "dig down very deeply into the roots of personality," wrote Julian Symons in the *London Magazine,* exposing the dark side of people regarded by society as normal and good. Or, as Thomas Sutcliffe explained in the *Times Literary Supplement,* Highsmith wrote "not about what it feels like to be mad, but what it feels like to remain sane while committing the actions of a madman."

Also in the *Times Literary Supplement,* James Campbell stated that "the conflict of good and evil—or rather, simple decency and ordinary badness—is at the heart of all Highsmith's novels, dramatized in the encounters between two characters, often in an exotic locale, where it is easier to lose one's moral bearings. Usually, we see events from the point of view of the innocent, the blind, as they stumble towards doom."

Highsmith's preoccupations with guilt and contrasting personalities surfaced as early as her very first novel. *Strangers on a Train* chronicles the relationship between Guy Haines, a successful young architect, and Charles Bruno, a charming but unstable man slightly younger than Haines. The two men first meet on a train journey when Bruno repeatedly tries to engage his traveling companion in conversation. He eventually persuades Haines to open up and talk about feelings he usually keeps to himself, including the feelings of resentment he harbors toward his wife. Bruno, who has long fantasized about killing his much-hated father, then suggests to Haines that they rid themselves of the "problems" once and for all: Bruno will kill Haines's wife for him, and Haines in turn will kill Bruno's father. Since there is no connection between the victims and their killers, Bruno theorizes, the police will be at a loss to solve the murders. With more than a hint of reluctance, Haines rejects the plan, but to no avail; Bruno remains intrigued by it and proceeds to carry out his part.

As Paul Binding observed in a *Books and Bookmen* article, "the relation of abnormal Bruno to normal [Haines] is an exceedingly complex one which is to reverberate throughout Patricia Highsmith's output. On the one hand Bruno is a *doppelgänger* figure; he embodies in repulsive flesh and blood form what [Haines's] subconscious has long been whispering to him. . . . On the other hand Bruno exists in his own perverse right, and [Haines] can have no control over him. . . . As a result of [Bruno's] existence, and of its coincidence with [Haines's] own, the rational, moral [Haines] becomes entangled in a mesh which threatens to destroy his entire security of identity. . . . [Haines is a man] tormented by guilt—guilt originally inspired by interior elements. Yet [he becomes], in society's eyes, guilty for exterior reasons." With the exception of the Ripley books—*The Talented Mr. Ripley, Ripley under Ground, Ripley's Game, The Boy Who Followed Ripley,* and *Ripley under Water*—which focus on the activities of the opportunistic and amoral Tom Ripley, a man incapable of feeling guilt, these themes are at the heart of Highsmith's fiction.

According to Symons, Highsmith typically launched her stories with the kind of "trickily ingenious plot devices often used by very inferior writers." He hastened to add, however, that these serve only as starting points for the "profound and subtle studies of character that follow." As Burt Supree observed in the *Village Voice Literary Supplement,* most of Highsmith's characters, none of whom are "heroes" in the conventional sense, are likely to be "obsessive, unquestioning, humdrum men with no self-knowledge, no curiosity, and Byzantine fantasy-lives—respectable or criminal middle-class, middle-brow people of incredible shallowness. Nowhere else will you find so many characters you'd want to smack." Supree added, "Like lab animals, [they] come under careful scrutiny, but [Highsmith] doesn't care to analyze them or beg sympathy for them. They go their independent ways with the illusion of freedom. Contact seems only to sharpen their edges, to irk and enrage." Yet as Craig Brown pointed out in the *Times Literary Supplement*, "it is a rare villain or psychopath [in Highsmith's fiction] whom the reader does not find himself willing toward freedom, a rare investigator whom the reader is unhappy to see dead. Those she terms her 'murderer-heroes' or 'heropsychopaths' are usually people whose protective shells are not thick enough to deaden the pain as the world hammers at their emotions. . . . Some live, some die, some kill, some crack up."

Sutcliffe echoed this assessment of Highsmith's characters as basically sane people who commit apparently insane acts, usually while under considerable strain. "What she observes so truthfully is not the collapse of reason but its persistence in what it suits us to think of as inappropriate conditions," Sutcliffe assessed. He continued: "Even Ripley, the least scrupulous and likeable of her central characters, has motives for his actions, and though they are venal and vicious they are not irrational. Her suburban killers remain calculatingly evasive until the end. . . . They don't hear voices and they don't have fun. Indeed in the act of killing their attitude is one of dispassionate detachment, of a sustained attempt to rationalize the intolerable. . . . In all the books death is contingent and unsought, almost never meticulously planned and very rarely the focus for our moral indignation."

In the eyes of most critics, it is Highsmith's skill at depicting a character's slide into derangement or death that distinguishes her "in a field where imitative hacks and dull formula-mongers abound," remarked a *Times Literary Supplement* reviewer. Symons declared, "The quality that takes her books beyond the run of intelligent fiction is not [the] professional ability to order a plot and create a significant environment, but rather the intensity of feeling that she brings to the problems of her central figures. . . . From original ideas that are sometimes far-fetched or even trivial she proceeds with an imaginative power that makes the whole thing terrifyingly real." The world she creates for her characters has a "relentless, compulsive, mutedly ominous

quality," asserted Hermione Lee in the *Observer*, one that leaves the reader "in a perpetual state of anxiety and wariness."

The prose Highsmith uses to communicate a sense of chilling dread and almost claustrophobic desperation is flat and plain, devoid of jargon, cliché, and padding. Some find it reminiscent of a psychological case history, a detailed and dispassionate account of a life moving out of control. According to Reg Gadney in *London Magazine*, "It is a characteristic skill of Miss Highsmith to convey unease and apprehension with an understated narrative style and painstaking description of domestic practicalities. Her characters often seem to counterbalance their expectation of fear by entrenching themselves in domestic routines. . . . [Their] tenacious efforts . . . to keep hold of everyday reality and logic serve to heighten the menace and chaos." *New Statesman* reviewer Blake Morrison, in fact, believed Highsmith is "at her most macabre when most mundane."

In Brown's opinion, "her style, on the surface so smooth and calm, underneath so powerful and merciless," is precisely what "entices the reader in and then sends him, alongside the 'psychopath-hero,' tumbling against the rocks." Weinstein agreed that "the reader has no choice but to follow the work, nothing could go another way. You are trapped in the very ease of the reading. The result is like suffocation, losing breath or will." Orhan Pamuk, reviewing the "Ripley" books in the *Village Voice*, described the fascination: "To know that people really will be hurt bonds the reader, with an almost self-destructive joy, to Highsmith's novels. For the reader has already discovered that the banality and pettiness, which spread like an epidemic in every one of her books, are those of his own life. He might as well begin to loathe himself. We rediscover, in each novel, the vulnerability of our existence."

Symons identified several qualities in Highsmith's work that make her, in his words, "such an interesting and unusual novelist." He had particular praise for "the power with which her male characters are realized," as well as for her ability to portray "what would seem to most people abnormal states of minds and ways of behavior." Symons continued: "The way in which all this is presented can be masterly in its choice of tone and phrase. [Highsmith's] opening sentences make a statement that is symbolically meaningful in relation to the whole book.... The setting is also chosen with great care.... [She seems to be making the point that] in surroundings that are sufficiently strange, men become uncertain of their personalities and question the reason for their own conduct in society." In short, remarked Symons, Highsmith's work is "as serious in its implications and as subtle in its approach as anything being done in the novel today."

Curiously, Highsmith's final novel before her death in 1995 departed from her successful formula of suspense. *Small g: A Summer Idyll* features almost no mystery, death, or intrigue. Set in Zurich, Switzerland, the novel revolves around a group of characters who frequent Jacob's Bierstube-Restaurant, known in gay travel-book parlance as a "small g": a place frequented by both straight and gay patrons. Rickie is a middle-aged gay man who is mourning his dead lover and coping with recent news that he is HIV-positive. He becomes friends with Luisa, a young woman stuck in the unpleasant employ of Renate, a crippled fashion designer who controls Luisa's life and actions. Eventually, Luisa inherits a fortune and gets away from Renate, while Rickie finds out that he is not HIV-positive after all. Many critics expressed disappointment with the novel, noting that Highsmith's trademark strengths were simply missing in this work. *New Statesman & Society* reviewer Julie Wheelwright, for instance, noted that "the plot moves along pleasantly enough; but for a writer so skilled in creating suspense and insightful portraits, these qualities seem distinctly lacking in *Small g*. One wishes that, for her final novel, Highsmith had left a more lasting work than this light 'summer idyll.'" While praising the author's "limpid prose" and "deft characterization," *Times Literary Supplement* contributor James Campbell remarked that "if [*Small g*] can be read as a final utterance, Patricia Highsmith died having made peace with her demons. Good triumphed over bad. Too bad for her readers."

Homosexuality had been one of Highsmith's themes since the beginning of her career. Her second novel, *The Price of Salt*, was published under the pseudonym of Claire Morgan in 1952 because of its overt and unapologetic lesbianism. Despite the conservatism of the times, and the fact that the book had a relatively happy ending—not the usual conversion to heterosexuality or death of the gay character—the novel sold almost a million copies. In 1991 *The Price of Salt* was reissued under Highsmith's real name, and some critics began to see similarities between the lesbian relationship of Carol and Therese and that of Tom Ripley and Dickie Greenleaf which the author explored a few years later in *The Talented Mr. Ripley*.

Sixty-four of Highsmith's stories appear in *The Selected Stories of Patricia Highsmith*, published posthumously in 2001. The book, along with the 1999 film version of *The Talented Mr. Ripley* and the announcement of two new biographies in the works, prompted a new appreciation for Highsmith's oeuvre among American critics, who have taken to eulogizing her as one of the literary world's more astute observers of human psychology. *The Selected Stories* is the first of fifteen books that publisher W. W. Norton will issue in order to bring many of her novels back into print after a long absence. Many of the stories feature animals or other non-human forms of life that often exact retribution on cruel and unthinking people. Neil Gordon of the *Nation* explained how the animals' actions are perfectly suited to Highsmith's fiction: They "are the perfect murderers, killing with neither malice nor, really, violence, in that their use of their physicality is instinctual and they are, after all, only protecting themselves." And Richard Davenport-Hines commented in the *New York Times Book Review*, "Human beings are inconvenient in many Highsmith stories," adding, "there is relief when they disappear or fall into delusions that leave them utterly isolated." In "The Stuff of Madness," a woman keeps the stuffed bodies of her dead pets in her garden, and in "Hamsters vs. Websters," a maniacal hamster bites the neck of a salesman and kills him.

"Highsmith's protagonists are never heroic," wrote Davenport-Hines in assessing *The Selected Short Stories*, because "heroes have free will and exercise brave choices; Highsmith's characters act on impulse and cannot control what they do." Many of the stories take place in a seemingly soothing middle-class world, where the lives of average people are disrupted catastrophically by murder or suicide. Some critics noted an uneven quality in the writing; Mark Harris of *Entertainment Weekly* surmised that this is because Highsmith's genius depends on a "gradualness" of suspense developed over the course of a novel, and the stories are too short to impart the same quality. Nevertheless, "the best of these pieces have a startling quality that may be likened to getting a shove near the edge of a train platform," wrote Penelope Mesic in *Book*, "even if we emerge physically unscathed, the daily routine can never seem so harmless again."

Highsmith's reputation as a top-notch suspense writer remains secure. A *Times Literary Supplement* reviewer reflected on the dilemma facing those who attempt to evaluate Highsmith's work, explaining that, in essence, "it is difficult to find ways of praising [her] that do not at the same time do something to diminish her. . . . With each new book, she is ritually congratulated for outstripping the limitations of her genre, for being as much concerned with people and ideas as with manipulated incident, for attempting a more than superficial exploration of the psychopathology of her unpleasant heroes—for, in short, exhibiting some of the gifts and preoccupations which are elementarily demanded of competent straight novelists." According to the same reviewer, Highsmith can best be described in the following terms: "She is the crime writer who comes closest to giving crime writing a good name." And J. M. Edelstein in a *New Republic* article summed up: "Low-key is the word for Patricia Highsmith. . . . Low-key, subtle, and profound. It is amazing to me that she is not better known for she is superb and is a master of the suspense novel. . . . [The body of her work] should be among the classics of the genre."

Source: Thomson Gale, "(Mary) Patricia Highsmith," in *Contemporary Authors Online*, Thomson Gale, 2004.

Charlotte Innes

In the following review, Innes comments on Highsmith's use of noir themes, which explore humanity's desires and disappointments.

A sculptor is sick of his wife's being the perfect wife and mother. She's given up her art for him. She cooks. She takes care of their baby. She's happy. Despite his urging, she won't even have an affair. So he kills her. For being too nice. And then he kills himself. By bashing his head against his jail cell wall.

This melodramatic reversal of the usual man-threatened-by-wife's-career theme is as contrived as it sounds. And yet, somewhere in the midst of the contrivance, one gets a little chill. One starts to think about love and all its delusions, about marriage and how hard it can be, about the way love can die slowly, almost imperceptibly, and how life is filled with losses—until one is just about ready to do oneself in.

"HER HEROINES IN THE SHORT STORIES ARE BITTER, UNHAPPY WOMEN, INCLUDING THE NAGGING MOTHER IN 'A GIRL LIKE PHYL.'..."

That's the Patricia Highsmith effect, as demonstrated in "Things Had Gone Badly," one of 26 stories in *Nothing That Meets the Eye*, a posthumous collection of Highsmith's short stories. Not previously collected (or in some cases never before published) and spanning 1938 to 1982 (she died in 1995), these stories are classic Highsmith fare.

Not all of them succeed. Some of the narrative tricks are too obviously manipulative, and there are just too many stories that end abruptly and unconvincingly in suicide. Perhaps that's why Highsmith held some of them back from publication. Nevertheless, whatever their flaws, they all have the Highsmith magical narrative pull. One wants to keep reading, even when the payoff isn't as strong as it could be, because, however artificial the plot, there is usually a nugget of bitter truth at its heart. Highsmith understood the psychology of people's darker urges.

It's startling to realize that some of these stories were written while she was still at Barnard College at New York and, though they may lack the fluency and the light sardonic humor of some of her later work, they are nevertheless extraordinarily accomplished. All the noir themes that characterize her great novels, such as *The Talented Mr. Ripley* and *Strangers on a Train*, are here. There are stories about bad marriages, loneliness, madness, murder, the emptiness of modern life, told with typical Highsmith wit or, occasionally, with a kind of spare, unsentimental lyricism, proving yet again the long-standing critical mantra that Highsmith is Not Just A Genre Writer.

One reason for the critical acclaim is that Highsmith doesn't write typical murder mystery stories. Her heroes often get away with their dastardly deeds and manage to be simultaneously appalling and likable (Mr. Ripley being the most famous and perhaps most convincing example). In contrast to the feel-good narratives of lesser literary thrillers in which good triumphs over evil, Highsmith's novels are vehicles to explore the dark side of the human psyche—the urge to do violence that most people occasionally think about but never pursue. And the murders in her books are the logical outcome of the kind of contorted thinking that hampers everyone from time to time, prompting people to make odd choices that in saner moments they might reject.

There are similar psychologically truthful murder stories in *Nothing That Meets the Eye*, even though, along with most of her previously published short stories, they lack the complexity of her novels. Usually, the stories' originality comes in the form of a clever twist. In "It's a Deal," a man kills his wife, who's already been beaten nearly to death by her lover. The husband just finishes her off, then frames the lover. In "The Second Cigarette," a man's subconscious self materializes to taunt him. When the man tries to throw the annoying shadow off a balcony, the shadow throws him off instead, suggesting that, in fact, the man wants to kill himself.

These murder stories are tinged with the kind of irony that is Highsmith's trademark in story collections such as "The Animal-Lover's Book of Beastly Murder," in which animals get their revenge on humans. In "Music to Die By," a story in this new collection, a post office employee fantasizes about murdering his colleagues. When he confesses to the bombing of a post office where he used to work, he is imprisoned (even though he didn't do it) because people believe he is crazy enough to have committed the crime.

What's different about *Nothing That Meets the Eye*, however, is that the majority of the stories do not involve a murder. Suicide and accidental death, yes, but not murder. In the book's afterword, German critic Paul Ingendaay suggests that Highsmith may not have attempted to publish some of her earlier work because it didn't have the commercial allure of a suspense story. And it's true that these stories focus more on ordinary yearnings and disappointments, such as the loneliness of a working woman in New York City in "Where the Door Is Always Open and the Welcome Mat Is Out" or a woman's depression and alienation when she marries a Mexican hotel manager in "The Car." (Though Highsmith was an American who lived most of her life in England and Switzerland, she took many trips to Mexico. A sense of displacement is a common theme in her work.) Many of these stories also feature female protagonists, which is unusual for Highsmith.

In interviews, she said she preferred writing about men because they were more active and therefore more interesting than women. And she has been criticized for her negative portrayals of women in, for example, her collection of short stories, *Little Tales of Misogyny*, in which each heroine represents a female stereotype—although, as some critics have pointed out, these stories may also be seen as satire. Highsmith also was a product of the conservative 1940s and '50s. But she didn't always fall in with traditional views. The one early book with sympathetic heroines and a happy ending was "The Price of Salt," about a lesbian relationship, which she published in 1952 under the pseudonym Claire Morgan. Highsmith was a lesbian who didn't want to be typecast as a lesbian writer. But in 1991, the novel was reprinted in England under her own name with the title "Carol."

In contrast to the women in "The Price of Salt," career women who found love and happiness, most of the women in *Nothing That Meets the Eye* are victims, reflecting Highsmith's belief that women are "pushed by people and circumstances instead of pushing," as she put it in her nonfiction work *Plotting and Writing Suspense Fiction* (1966). Her heroines in the short stories are bitter, unhappy women, including the nagging mother in "A Girl Like Phyl" or the childlike hypochondriac Agnes in "The Pianos of the Steinachs" whose only happiness comes from a fantasy that a visiting music student is in love with her.

At best, the women in these stories are bored housewives cheating on their husbands. The overtly good women are locked into classic sacrificial female gestures. Dying Mrs. Palmer in "The Trouble With Mrs. Blynn, the Trouble With the World" selflessly decides to give her treasured amethyst pin to the mean-spirited nurse who covets it, in protest against life's "flaw," the "long, mistaken shutting of the heart." Or they are given the traditional reward for stereotypical female virtues. The working woman in "Doorbell for Louisa" stays home from work to take care of some sick neighbors and is subsequently asked out on a date by her boss, who misses her presence at work.

To be fair, the men in *Nothing That Meets the Eye* don't hold up too well either. Many also suffer loneliness and disappointment. Many cheat and lie. And there's at least one child molester, possibly two, if one reads between the lines. But when men are rewarded in these stories, they, unlike the women, undergo an affirmation of self. In "Man's Best Friend," a man who idolizes a woman who's not quite the goddess he thought learns that he can live happily alone with his dog. And men's kindnesses are not quite so saintly as the women's. In "A Bird in Hand," a man makes his living off reward money for returning missing birds to their owners—not the actual birds but similar-looking ones he has bought at a pet store. Yet he is seen by his victims as a sort of Santa Claus, spreading kindness throughout the world, even though they are on to his game.

Whatever one makes of Highsmith's biases—and I confess I have a built-in antipathy for writers who see the world in such a lopsided, cynical fashion, as a dark place where meanness and manipulation are the dominant emotions—there's no doubt that this new collection, however uneven, reminds us that Highsmith was a literary artist who was so accomplished she could seduce the reader even with work that was less than her best.

Source: Charlotte Innes, "When the Milk of Human Kindness Sours: *Nothing That Meets the Eye*," in *Los Angeles Times*, December 1, 2002, p. R4.

James Lasdun

In the following review, Lasdun comments on the broad range of styles and techniques, the "astounding" variety of characters and the dark themes Highsmith employs in her short stories.

Most readers know Patricia Highsmith primarily as the creator of the affable sociopath Tom Ripley. But one of the exhilarating effects of reading Highsmith's stories—the 700-page *Selected Stories* that came out last year and now another 400-plus pages of "uncollected" ones in *Nothing That Meets the Eye*—is the greatly enlarged sense of her range and energy as a writer that they impart. The sheer variety of beings (human and otherwise) whose skin she slips in and out of from story to story is astounding—a Mexican street hustler one moment, a pair of quarrelsome pigeons the

next, with a compendious assortment of white-collar, blue-collar, American, English, German, canine, sane and insane individuals in between.

Equally prodigious is her capacity for coming up with the wildly inventive plots that set these creatures in motion. Like the plots in Maupassant's stories, which she particularly admired, Highsmith's tend to turn more on action and external circumstance than on interior states, offering the pleasures of vivid detail and brilliant contrivance over those of emotional nuance and poetic intensity. Their machinery can clunk at times—as Maupassant's also could—especially as they accelerate toward their sometimes strained dramatic climaxes, but they are seldom less than entertaining, and often wonderful.

"Short stories are absolutely essential to me," Highsmith said in an interview. Under the cool perfection of her novels was a broad and antic imagination that clearly needed other, quicker, perhaps less exacting vehicles for the overflow of its productivity. The stories also exhibit a greater freedom—risking silliness, implausibility, even an otherwise most uncharacteristic sentimentality, for the sake of whatever ingenious notion caught her fancy. Highsmith generally manages to make something charming or droll or briefly chilling of even the slightest of them—e.g., a man who collects parakeets of every color in order to be able to claim rewards when pet birds go missing, by "returning" a matching bird of his own ("A Bird in Hand"). She tries out all sorts of different styles and techniques: turn-of-the-century high polish in "The Pianos of the Steinachs" ("Languid fingers of the weeping willow, their chartreuse just beginning to turn with autumn"); a folktale-like simplicity in "Uncertain Treasure," in which two low-lifes squabble over a mysterious abandoned bag; the hilarious knockabout comedy of "Two Disagreeable Pigeons"; gritty urban plainspokenness (her vignettes of '40s New York with its grime and hustle and noisy isolation, are superb); and Gothic melodrama. She also, occasionally, employs a delicate psychological realism without any overt artifice at all, as in "The Returnees," which beautifully and painfully chronicles the breakdown of a marriage when a refugee couple return to post-war Germany.

Loneliness, stoical melancholy, a sense of emotional or physical inadequacy, frustration that turns either outward to murder or inward to self-destruction characterize most of the individuals in these pages. Fraudulence also figures prominently, as it does in the novels. "The Great Cardhouse" features a collector of forgeries ("bona fide masterpieces were too natural, too easy, too boring") who, in one gloriously macabre scene, reveals his own body to be almost entirely fake, dismantling himself—toupee, artificial hand, glass eye—before a startled acquaintance. A crazed postal worker in "Music to Die By" keeps a diary in which he records murders he hasn't actually committed. And in "A Dangerous Hobby," a vacuum salesman, impotent and misogynistic, impersonates researchers in order to set up meetings with women so that he can indulge his hobby of robbing them of small possessions.

Over these figures you feel the presence of Tom Ripley, deadliest of all impostors, hovering like a ghostly amalgam: In their respective traits of boredom, playful whimsy, inchoate rage and sexual confusion, you sense something of the multitude of different psychological sources that must have fed into that inspired creation. The stories gathered here cover a long period, from 1938 to 1982. Highsmith never collected them in her lifetime, but neither did she destroy them as she did other writings. One or two of the earlier pieces are lame or else rather blandly diagrammatic. Some repeat ideas she may have felt she handled better elsewhere. Quite a few conclude with a disconcertingly abrupt suicide, and as the fifth or sixth protagonist plunges over a balcony or leaps in front of a truck, you might start to wonder if this is really a satisfactory way to end an otherwise absorbing narrative, and whether Highsmith herself might not have been wondering that too, as she put the piece on ice.

Would the stories by themselves have secured Highsmith a lasting reputation? They lack perhaps the singularity of tone and atmosphere that her best novels possess, but in their surehandedness, their amazing breadth and abundance, as well as the dark delight they convey in their own making, they compel attention, and they add significantly to her already formidable presence.

Source: James Lasdun, "Little Terrors," in *Washington Post*, October 13, 2002, p. T13.

SOURCES

Baldick, Chris, *The Concise Oxford Dictionary of Literary Terms*, Oxford University Press, 2004, p. 89.

Campbell, James, "Murder, She (Usually) Wrote," in *New York Times Book Review*, October 27, 2002, p. 30.

Highsmith, Patricia, "A Girl like Phyl," in *Nothing That Meets the Eye: The Uncollected Stories of Patricia Highsmith*, Norton, 2002, pp. 359–80.

Innes, Charlotte, "When the Milk of Human Kindness Sours; *Nothing That Meets the Eye: The Uncollected Stories of Patricia Highsmith*, in *Los Angeles Times*, December 1, 2002, p. R4.

Lasdun, James, "Little Terrors," in *Washington Post*, October 13, 2002, p. T13.

Review of *Nothing That Meets the Eye: The Uncollected Stories of Patricia Highsmith*, in *Kirkus Reviews*, Vol. 70, No. 17, September 1, 2002, http://web.ebscohost.com.ez proxy.umuc.edu/ehost/delivery?vid = 36&hid = 120&sid = 51ad4 (accessed September 12, 2006).

Review of *Nothing That Meets the Eye: The Uncollected Stories of Patricia Highsmith*, in *Virginia Quarterly Review*, Vol. 79, No. 3, Summer 2003, p. 92.

FURTHER READING

Durkheim, Emile, and John Al Spaulding, *Suicide*, Free Press, 1997.

> The authors present the subject from a sociological perspective, offering a statistical analysis of the types of people who commit suicide.

Jamison, Kay Redfield, *Night Falls: Understanding Suicide*, Vintage, 2000.

> Redfield, a Johns Hopkins psychiatry professor, focuses on the reasons for and the methods used in committing suicide and the treatment of suicidal tendencies.

Marino, Gordon, ed., *Basic Writings of Existentialism*, Modern Library, 2004.

> Marino collected instructive essays on the subject from the most important philosophers, including Kierkegaard, Nietzsche, Dostoevsky, Sartre, and Camus.

Wilson, Andrew, *Beautiful Shadow: A Life of Patricia Highsmith*, Bloomsbury, 2003.

> Wilson draws from Highsmith's journals and letters as well as interviews with those who knew her in his account of her complex personality and her life.

The Girls

JOY WILLIAMS

2004

"The Girls," by Joy Williams, was first published in the *Idaho Review VI* in 2004 and later reprinted in *The Best American Short Stories 2005*, edited by Michael Chabon. Williams, who began publishing fiction in the 1960s, is often compared to Flannery O'Connor, an American writer known for her Southern gothic stories. Although Williams is not a southern writer, she does use the gothic and grotesque to great effect in her work. Williams has also been compared to American writer Raymond Carver. Devoted to the short story form, Carver is known as a minimalist—a style reflected in Williams's own stories, which critics have sometimes described as cool and terse. Her style is a unique blend of the weird and the grim. Williams does not flinch from the harsh realities of life or bury her characters in fantasy, but her fiction always has a flavor of the fantastical or hyper-realistic.

"The Girls" is a story about cruelty and family dysfunction, featuring two sisters who are closer than twins and behave as if they are evil incarnate. The girls occupy themselves with tormenting their parents' houseguests—until one guest turns the tables on them. This story, as with many of Williams's other works of fiction, selects death as an available escape from life's travails.

AUTHOR BIOGRAPHY

Williams was born February 11, 1944, in Chelmsford, Massachusetts, to William Lloyd,

a minister, and Elisabeth (Thomas) Williams. She graduated magna cum laude with a Bachelor of Arts degree from Marietta College in Ohio in 1963. Williams received her Master of Fine Arts degree in creative writing from the University of Iowa in 1965.

After college, Williams worked as a data analyst for the U.S. Navy for three years before turning to fiction writing full-time. Her first novel, *State of Grace* (1973), garnered Williams a lot of attention from readers and critics. *Taking Care* (1982), her first collection of short stories, exhibited Williams's ability with short fiction. As of 2006, she had written nine books of fiction and non-fiction. "The Girls" was originally published in the *Idaho Review VI* in 2004 and then anthologized by Michael Chabon in the 2005 edition of *The Best American Short Stories*.

Williams is known for her terse, direct prose and an imagination that makes free use of grotesque elements. Her stories and novels are unwavering in their handling of difficult subjects and emotions. Death and dysfunctional marriages appear frequently but always with a fresh flair. She frequently publishes her stories and essays in literary magazines, such as *Granta* and the *New Yorker*. Williams's work has also been widely anthologized over the course of her more than forty-year-long career. She received a National Endowment for the Arts grant in 1973 and a Guggenheim Fellowship in 1974, among other honors. She was a finalist for the 2001 Pulitzer Prize in Fiction for her novel, *The Quick and the Dead*. She has taught at many universities, including the University of Houston, the University of Florida, the University of Iowa, Ithaca College, and the University of Texas in Austin.

Williams married writer and editor Rust Hills, and they have a daughter together. As of 2006, Williams lived in Florida and Texas.

PLOT SUMMARY

"The Girls" opens with two sisters going through the personal belongings of their parents' houseguest, Arleen, while she is in the shower. They are looking for her journal. They find the book, but Arleen finishes her shower before they can read anything so they flee downstairs. Arleen appears later and asks if the cat litter pan can be taken out of the bathroom because it smells.

The girls are shocked at this request because they believe their cats can do no wrong. They dislike Arleen and wish she would leave so they ask her about her home. Arleen tells them it has very steep stairs which sometimes discourages her from going out because then she has to climb the stairs to return home. They also ask her how her birthday was, but their question is sneering because they feel that "The Birthday was more or less an idiotic American institution." A few days earlier, on the evening of Arleen's birthday, Arleen and Father Snow gave their house gift to the girls' parents. It was a cocktail shaker, and the girls embarrassed everyone by showing off the other ten cocktail shakers their parents have already received as gifts.

Arleen leaves the girls to join Father Snow in the garden. The girls think about Father Snow, whom they feel is too indulgent in his grief. Holding their two cats, the sisters watch Arleen and Father Snow from a window and are convinced that she is in love with the sad man. The girls retire to the enclosed porch where they work on collages using found and stolen objects. The girls love the old house they live in with their parents but resent the fact that their parents have houseguests coming and going all summer long. The girls have never been interested in any of the houseguests except for one young woman who was an artist. None of the guests ever returns for a second stay—except for Father Snow, who is on his third visit. When Arleen first arrived, they did not think much of her, but now they dislike her.

Mommy calls her daughters to her and tells them Arleen saw their cats maim a mockingbird in the garden. The girls tell Mommy that their cats would never do that because they are nice house cats, even though they know the cats have already killed a dozen songbirds so far this summer. The sisters then leave for the beach where they lay in the sun, nude and admired, talking about their parents. They are worried that their parents are aging badly. When they return home, the house is quiet. Mommy has left a note telling them they are napping, and Father Snow and Arleen have gone out for ice cream. The girls immediately go upstairs to investigate their guests' rooms. In Father Snow's room, they find two smooth black stones which they think might represent him and his dead lover Donny. In Arleen's room, they find her journal. Arleen appears just as they are about to start reading, and she tells them what she has written. It is about their mother. The girls find this very odd, and when Arleen mentions Mommy's dreams, they do not believe her. Arleen takes her journal and leaves.

The girls go to their third-floor room to bathe before dinner. They come downstairs for cocktails and overhear Daddy telling Father Snow about a previous houseguest who had out-of-body experiences. The sisters do not think they can bear another night of their parents mingling with Father Snow and Arleen. Father Snow stirs the martinis and offers a prayer and then a toast for "those not with us tonight." Father Snow, still profoundly unhappy, confesses that he is thinking of resigning. The girls repeatedly say awkward or insulting things about Donny, but Father Snow does not seem to hear them. Bored, the sisters change the topic of the conversation, asking Mommy to tell everyone about how Daddy proposed to her. Mommy tells them about his sentimental proposal, but the girls want to hear the whole story so they tell it themselves.

It was winter and Daddy was in a hurry to meet Mommy for their date. He hit a man on the side of the road and did not stop because he did not want this new life which lay before him to be disrupted. Father Snow is deeply disturbed by this account. Mommy and Daddy are ashamed that their secret has been let out. Mommy tries to smooth it over with Father Snow, who is profoundly uncomfortable. The girls, meanwhile, are happy because they like this grotesque little tale about the beginning of their family. Mommy says she wants to do something about this accident after all these years, and Father Snow preaches about the meaning of the word repent and how inadequate it is. Daddy makes no apologies, stating, "We've had a good life … Full. Can't take that away from us."

The cats enter the room and jump on Arleen's lap. She pets them, pulling a bloodsucker off of each, which the girls think is disgusting and falsified. They do not believe their cats would carry around such nasty little creatures and accuse her of being a magician. Arleen tells them she is a companion and adviser, and Father Snow praises her ability to listen and make decisions. Arleen suddenly turns to Mommy and tells her to get rid of her daughters. "High time for them to be gone." She tells the girls that they are killing their mother. The girls are astonished, and no one knows what to say. Mommy tries to pass out more crackers and cheese, but the girls tell her to sit down. She does so, but her face goes strange, and she slides to the floor, taking a lamp with her and hitting her head on the fireplace lintel. Arleen and Father Snow get down to tend to her, but she is dead. Father Snow shakes off his depression and returns to his professional demeanor as he prepares to aid the newly dead.

CHARACTERS

Arleen

Arleen is Father Snow's companion and advisor. She joins him while he is a guest at Mommy and Daddy's big nineteenth-century house. She and Father Snow do not have a romantic relationship; she seems to be helping him work through his problems, probably in relation to his grief over the death of his lover Donny. Arleen is the only American character in this story, which is set in Great Britain. The girls describe her as plain and shy with long, beautiful auburn hair. They often belittle her clothing, demeanor, and mannerisms. Arleen catches the girls with her diary and recites for them what she has written in it about their mother. It does not make sense to the girls, who refuse to believe that their mother would be so intimate with this woman. This journal contains Arleen's notes because she is also examining Mommy to see what is making her ill. At the end of the story, Arleen reveals her diagnosis by recommending that Mommy kick her daughters out of the house because the girls are slowly killing her. If this wild declaration were not odd enough, Mommy suddenly has a stroke and drops dead.

Clarissa

See Mommy

Daddy

Daddy is a nearly invisible character. The girls worry that he is unhappy because he is drinking and smoking more than he used to and is sometimes harsh with them. In the final scene of the story, the girls reveal that Daddy hit and probably killed a man on the side of the road while driving to meet Mommy for a date and to ask her to marry him. The evening and the life ahead of him, he felt, were too important to muddle up with an accident so he drove on. This heartless and morally reprehensible act is reminiscent of how his daughters behave.

TOPICS FOR FURTHER STUDY

- Residents of England and the United States both primarily speak English but have very different cultures. These differences are evident in vocabulary, which holidays are celebrated and how they are celebrated, dress, humor, food, sports, and more. One example of this cultural divide is that many English prefer tea whereas Americans generally prefer coffee. Do you know of any other cultural differences between England and the United States? Make a list of at least ten differences, researching them if need be. Share your list with your class to build a master list. Have hot tea with milk and sugar and shortbread cookies for full effect.

- Some people prefer cats, some prefer dogs, and others prefer neither. In "The Girls," the sister are definitely cat people, and their cats seem to be reflections of their own personalities: aloof, lazy, and predatory. Research the history, biology, and culture of cats. A good reference for the culture of cats is Elizabeth Marshall Thomas's *Tribe of Tiger*. Write a brief report that summarizes the most interesting things that you learned about the history, biology, and culture of cats. How does this expand your understanding of Williams's story?

- Siblings are people born of the same parents or people who are raised together. Sometimes siblings are close friends, and sometimes they fight endlessly. Do you have any siblings? If so, do you fight a lot or are you very close or somewhere in between? If you do not have siblings, who do you spend a lot of time with outside of school? Maybe it is a cousin, a friend, or a neighbor. Do you get along or do you fight a lot? Write an essay about your sibling or friend, describing what you love and what you do not like about that person.

- Bullies pick on other people to hide their own insecurities, much like the girls in Williams's story. Bullies use abusive language, physical force, and sometimes more subversive methods like exclusion. Write a short story about a bully from the bully's point of view.

The Girls

The girls are sisters, thirty-one and thirty-three years of age. Their names are not given. They are the point of view characters and their personalities are indistinguishable. They do not have the closeness of twins, who do exhibit distinct personalities despite outward similarities. These sisters think and act as a single entity. They are British, beautiful, and obsessed with the idea of their own importance and attractiveness. They declare that they have never been in love and do not plan to marry because it would mean some level of separation from each other. They go to clubs but talk only to each other. The girls like to make collages with found items. They own two cats, on which they dote. They have a more than hearty enjoyment of the grotesque, from their cats' killing songbirds in the garden to their father's striking down a man on the side of the road and leaving him there to die while Daddy hurried on to propose to his girlfriend. The girls are aware that their parents are unwell but refuse to believe that it has anything to do with them. They are narcissistic and believe themselves to be above reproach.

Mommy

Mommy is the mother of the two girls. She and Daddy have been married thirty-five years. Their daughters still live them in their nineteenth-century, three-storey house. Mommy is a very accommodating woman. Mommy and Daddy entertain houseguests all summer long, every summer, which irritates the daughters. The girls note that Mommy's "enchantment with life seemed to be waning," and they are concerned for her health. As revealed in Arleen's journal, Mommy has been consulting with Arleen about her health. Arleen reveals to the family at the end of the story that the girls are killing their mother and must move out. Caught between Arleen and her daughters, Mommy does not know what to do. She tries to pretend everything is normal, but she seizes up, possibly from a stroke or heart attack. Mommy falls to the floor, hitting her head on the lintel of the fireplace, and dies.

Father Snow

Father Snow is pastor at the city's Episcopal Church. He is a houseguest at Mommy and Daddy's house and is the only repeat house-guest, possibly because he is oblivious to the girls' torments. The girls call him Father Ice behind his back, a nickname they see as ironic since he is anything but ice-like, being very emotional. In this story, Father Snow is deeply depressed about the death of his lover, Donny. He likes to drink martinis, which he mixes for the family during cocktail hour. Father Snow snaps out of his depression at the very end of the story when Mommy drops dead, and he must use his training as a minister to tend to her departing soul.

THEMES

Arrested Development

Arrested development is a term that refers to a maturation process which has ceased to progress. In "The Girls," the title characters are in their early thirties but still live with their parents as if they were teenagers or younger. They do not hold down jobs, they do not have friends or boyfriends, and they are not attending college or in any way pursuing a life beyond the circle of their immediate family. This arrested development is a detriment to the girls themselves and the quality of life they lead, and in this case, it is also makes the girls a nuisance and occasional terror to their parents' summer houseguests. The direst result of the girls' arrested development is the drain on their mother. Because the girls have never broken away from their parents, they are in some mysterious way still drawing on their life force, particularly their mother's. Arleen points this out to the entire family in the climax

of the story, warning Mommy that she must make them leave, or they will literally be the death of her.

Arrested development is also reflected in Father Snow's ceaseless mourning for his now deceased lover, Donny; however, his condition is temporary. In the midst of the story and from the mocking point-of-view of the girls, it seems that Father Snow will never stop weeping over Donny, but when Mommy falls and dies at the end of the story, he immediately leaves behind his grief to resume his professional role as a minister. Father Snow merely required a catalyst to launch him out of his depression. By contrast, the girls do not seem to be changeable in the least.

Narcissism

Narcissism is self-love. In the field of psychology, narcissism is considered a personality disorder that is diagnosed from a list of traits, of which at least five traits must be applicable. These traits include: a sense of self-importance; fantasizing about ideal love and unlimited success in life; belief that one is special and can only associate with certain other people; a belief that one must be admired; a sense of superior entitlement; a tendency to take advantage of others; an inability to empathize with other people; envy of other people or beliefs that others are envious of oneself; and arrogance. The girls exhibit many of these traits. Like narcissists, the girls also react badly to anyone who criticizes them because they take such criticism as an unwarranted, prejudicial indictment. Arleen refuses to see the girls as they want to be seen, and so they despise her. They also dislike Father Snow and think he is slow-witted because he cannot be affected by their tormenting.

Psychologists argue that narcissism, while its source is genetic, is exacerbated by poor parenting. In light of this view, the girls' father can be seen to have actually done greater damage to his family when he chose not to turn back and help the man he hit on the side of the road and instead chose to hurry on to his date with his soon-to-be fiancée. This self-involved and morally reprehensible behavior has been distilled in his daughters.

Sadism

Sadism is taking pleasure in inflicting emotional or physical pain on another living creature. It is a pervasive theme in "The Girls," in which the sisters commit cruel acts. They delight in tormenting their parents' houseguests, whom, as a rule, they despise. Their most recent victims are Father Snow and his American companion, Arleen; however, Father Snow is deaf to their incendiary comments. Thus, he is the only repeat houseguest the girls' parents have had. The girls focus their cruelty on Arleen, snickering about her clothing, her whale-shaped purse, her shyness, how she celebrates her birthday, and what they imagine her relationship with Father Snow must be. They search her room for her journal, even going so far as to read it in front of her. The cats, as a reflection of their owners—the girls—hunt songbirds in the garden; their killing the birds delights the girls.

STYLE

Climax and Denouement

The climax of a story occurs when the plot reaches its crisis. It is often the most exciting part, when secrets are revealed. "The Girls" arrives at its climax when Arleen tells Mommy to get rid her daughters because the girls are killing her. This extraordinary announcement is surprising because it comes from quiet and differential Arleen and because of *what* Arleen is saying. The girls are shocked and, of course, deny her statement, but the reader, having seen into the mean, cold hearts of these sisters, knows what Arleen says is true. Arleen's courageous statement about how toxic the girls are creates the climax of the story by bringing the truth out in the open.

Denouement derives from a French word meaning, to untie. It occurs after the climax and is the point in the story when the secrets and questions put forth in a story are resolved. In Williams's short story, the denouement comes very quickly after the climax. Mommy tries to act as if everything is normal, offering her company more hors d'oeuvres. Her strange facial expression probably indicates a stroke. She falls off her chair and hits her head on the lintel of the fireplace, dying.

Protagonist and Antagonist

The protagonist is the main character of a story and often times the point-of-view character as well. The protagonists of "The Girls" are the girls themselves. Unlike many protagonists, though, these daughters are not sympathetic characters. They are needlessly cruel to others, spoiled, manipulative, and self-absorbed.

An antagonist is the character who opposes the protagonist. Although the antagonist is often a villain of some sort, in Williams's story the antagonist is Arleen—the most realistic and sympathetic character in the story. Arleen reveals herself as the antagonist when she tells Mommy at the end of the story to get rid of the girls. The girls have thought that she was a silly woman and are shocked to discover that she is their most serious adversary.

HISTORICAL CONTEXT

Terrorism

Terrorism is an act of indiscriminate violence against civilians carried out by people of some political or religious affiliation with the intention of subverting the dominant power. Worldwide numbers of people who have died as a result of terror are usually much fewer than one thousand per year, as reported by the U.S. Department of the State, which has collected statistics on terrorism since 1968. The numbers of people killed or injured in terrorist attacks worldwide was especially high in 2001 at more than 3,500. Terrorist attacks have been a means of exerting pressure around the world for much of human history but were prominent in the minds of Americans in the early 2000s because of attacks such as the one against the *U.S.S. Cole* off the coast of Yemen on October 12, 2000 (17 dead and 40 wounded) and the one against the World Trade Center and Pentagon on September 11, 2001 (2,997 dead and an unknown number injured). Prominent terrorist attacks from the early 2000s outside the United States include the bombing of the Indian Parliament on December 13, 2001 (15 dead); the Passover Massacre in Israel on March 27, 2002 (30 dead and 140 wounded); the Bali bombing on October 12, 2002 (202 dead and 209 wounded); the Moscow Theater siege from October 23 until October 26, 2002 (171 dead and over 1,000 injured in the subsequent rescue-raid); and the Istanbul truck bombings of November 15 and November 20, 2003 (57 dead and 700 wounded). These attacks only represent a small number of the many terrorist actions that happened around the world in the early 2000s, especially in Israel and Iraq. Williams's story is concerned with a kind of terrorism closer to home: the girls are indiscriminate about torturing their parents' guests, so long as they keep their parents isolated from other people and thus have them all to themselves.

Anglo-American Relations

The United States and the United Kingdom have a close diplomatic relationship. They are each other's dearest political allies. In the early 2000s, U.S. president George W. Bush and U.K. prime minister Tony Blair joined forces in the so-called war on terror. The United Kingdom, among other European nations, assisted the U.S. invasion of Afghanistan that began in October 2001; however, the United Kingdom stood alone among major European nations in supporting the U.S. war in Iraq, beginning in March 2003. President Bush maintained an approval rating of more than 50 percent for the first term of his presidency. His ratings fell below and stayed below 50 percent starting in spring of 2004. Prime Minister Blair likewise came under heavy criticism for supporting the United States in the Iraq invasion, especially after the revelation that there existed no weapons of mass destruction in Iraq—the reason given by the Bush administration for invading the country in the first place.

The United States and the United Kingdom also have a strong trade relationship, investing heavily in each other's economies. Both countries have large Christian populations although diversity in ethnicity and religion is supported by law. The modern U.S. government was founded by English colonists escaping religious persecution in England which ties both nations together historically and culturally. Nevertheless, over two hundred years of separation between the two countries has led to significant cultural differences such as are seen in slang, popular foods, sports, and senses of humor. In Williams's story, the girls pick on Arlene about celebrating her birthday, declaring it to be a silly American custom. Although this is not an opinion shared with a majority of British citizens, the girls' general attitude also underlines the fact that the United States and the United Kingdom even differ in their approaches to common holidays and celebrations. For example, Halloween (October 31) is very popular in the United States whereas in the United Kingdom, Halloween is only briefly acknowledged as people prepare to celebrate Guy Fawkes Day on November 5 with bonfires, fireworks, and parties.

CRITICAL OVERVIEW

Williams began her writing career with strength on her side: her first novel, *State of Grace* received a glowing review from *New York Times* critic Gail Godwin. Godwin hails Williams as a "first-rate new novelist." Alice Adams, in the *New York Times Book Review*, praises Williams as "talented" and "skillful," but her review of *The Changeling* is thoroughly negative. Adams is completely turned off by Williams's wild tale of animals as people and vice versa. Anatole Broyard's June 3, 1978, review of the novel for the *New York Times* is similarly proportioned: he is a fan of Williams's work in general but despises this book in particular. Both critics acknowledge that Williams took risks with her novel, pushing the boundaries of character and delving into the avantgarde.

Williams's first collection of short stories, *Taking Care*, received modest but positive attention. Her third novel, *Breaking and Entering*, was the subject of another good review in the *New York Times*. Reviewer Bret Easton Ellis, not a fan of Williams's first novel, found this book to be a better representation of her potential: "She's a stronger writer when she's less of a poet." Rand Richards Cooper, in reviewing Williams's third short story collection, *Escapes*, for the *New York Times Book Review* calls her landscapes, "both quirky and ominous," a description echoed by other critics, such as Michiko Kakutani.

Williams's fourth novel, *The Quick and the Dead*, was a finalist for the 2001 Pulitzer Prize. An anonymous reviewer of that novel for *Publishers Weekly* describes Williams as "an artist attentive to real people's psyches." A critic for the *Economist* gives the novel a mixed review, claiming that its edginess can make the reader weary, but overall celebrating the author as "original, energetic, and viscously funny." Williams's foray into nonfiction, *Ill Nature*, a book about environmental degradation, was a cautious success. Stephanie Flack, writing in *Antioch Review* in the Fall 2002 issue, was impressed with her effort and scholarship but a little taken aback by the tone.

The family in this story lives in a nineteenth-century house, perhaps like the one depicted here © *Philippa Lewis; Edifice/Corbis*

Williams's third collection of short stories, *Honored Guests*, was received coolly by the anonymous reviewer for *Kirkus Reviews*, who found the stories "seldom involving." A reviewer for *Publishers Weekly* was more impressed, describing the collection as "rich, darkly humorous and provocative." Benjamin Schwarz, reviewing for the *Atlantic Monthly* also praises Williams's collection of quirky tales and points to a legacy many critics observe: "Williams is ... the heir to Flannery O'Connor—but she's also among the most original fiction writers at work today." David Gates, for *Newsweek International*, is charmed by restraint that "seems almost classical" and compares Williams, as others have, to writer Raymond Carver. But Stephen Metcalf, writing for the *New York Times Book Review*, gives a cool review. He is underwhelmed by her "terse, dread-filled writing style." *Books & Culture* critic Sara Miller also ends on a chilly note, observing that the stories "stop shy of redemption."

"The Girls" has not been collected in a book by Williams but was honored by Michael Chabon by inclusion in *The Best American Short Stories 2005*. Reviews of this collection make note of Williams's short story as one of the stronger ones in the collection. Kakutani's words from a review of *Escapes* also serve as a good summation of Williams's writing career:

> At her best ... Ms. Williams demonstrates an intuitive ability to delineate the complexities of an individual character in a few brief pages, a gift for finding those significant moments that reveal the somber verities lurking beneath the flash and clamor of daily life.

CRITICISM

Carol Ullmann

Ullmann is a freelance writer and editor. In the following essay, she explores the theme of evil in Williams's short story.

"The Girls," by Joy Williams, is a story in which evil reigns, front and center. The protagonists—the main characters—are cruel and

WHAT DO I READ NEXT?

- *Will You Please Be Quiet, Please?* (1976) is Raymond Carver's first collection of short stories. He was dedicated to short forms of writing, leading some to declare that he revived the short story in North America. Williams and Carver were contemporaries (Carver died in 1988), and Williams's style is sometimes compared to his.

- *A Good Man Is Hard to Find and Other Stories* (1955), by Flannery O'Connor, is a collection of short fiction by the famed but unfortunately short-lived southern American author. Williams is often considered by critics to be using styles and themes that are reminiscent of O'Connor's work, especially in both authors' use of the gothic and grotesque.

- *State of Grace* (1973) is Williams's first novel. It tells the tale of Kate Jackson's flight from her minister father's heavy-handed upbringing—and her eventual, inevitable return home.

- *Ill Nature: Rants and Reflections on Humanity and Other Animals* (2001) is Williams's book-length foray into non-fiction. She writes primarily about environmental degradation and no less urgently about human responsibility.

- *Summerland* (2002), by Michael Chabon, is a young adult novel about children who save the world by playing baseball. Chabon is the editor who chose Williams's "The Girls" for inclusion in *The Best American Short Stories 2005*. He often incorporates fantastical elements into his work, but it is far from gothic in nature.

- *Stranger Things Happen* (2001), by Kelly Link, is a collection of fantastical short stories. These stories lack the grimness of Williams's fiction but are equally wild in imaginative elements. Link appears alongside Williams in *The Best American Short Stories 2005*.

> THE REALITY, AS REVEALED BY ARLEEN AND THE DEATH OF MOMMY, IS THAT THE GIRLS ARE PREDATORS, JUST LIKE THEIR CATS, AND ARE UNABLE TO DENY THEIR PETS' TEMPERAMENT...."

unsympathetic. Their antagonist, Arleen, is the one with whom the reader sympathizes because she is so credibly normal and appears to be vulnerable to the girls' attacks for much of the story. The evil within the girls seems outwardly expressed by their cats that kill songbirds in the garden, lounge around the house, and are generally aloof. Arleen's picking bloodsuckers off the cats at the end of the story is symbolic of her exorcising them of evil. The sudden death of the girls' mother following Arleen's pronouncement that the girls are killing her appears to validate what Arleen has said: her daughters are actually toxic.

The girls are born of the evil act generated by their father, who struck a man on the side of the road on a snowy night and kept driving, too eager to pursue his own plans to take care of another person. Grotesquely, the girls delight in this story, as if they were part of some fantastical movie rather than privy to a horrible breach of moral responsibility in their parents' lives. Daddy's lack of conscience makes him in essence as evil as his daughters. Although the ways and reasons are never made explicit, Mommy and Daddy have clearly spoiled their daughters and encouraged their dependence. Their emotional development has been stunted, and they behave as if they were half their actual age—sneaky, naughty teenagers, completely absorbed in their own physical beauty and concerned only with what is of interest to them—themselves, their cats, and their parents. Completely narcissistic, the girls believe they are special, important, and do not tolerate their opinions being challenged. They manipulate their parents and try to manipulate the houseguests. They declare that they have never fallen in love and do not intend to marry. Disturbingly, the girls turn their self-absorption toward each other in a kind of twisted self-love. They are inseparable to the extent that they have no individual identity. Williams does not distinguish them (or their cats) with names. They move together, behaving in unison.

Their childish, narcissistic behavior has led them to treat most people around them with cruelty. They insinuate that Arleen should leave by asking her about her home as well as by asking Arleen if she had a nice birthday after telling everyone that they think birthdays are an "idiotic American institution." The sisters delight in embarrassing Father Snow and Arleen over their house gift of a cocktail shaker. They go searching repeatedly for Arleen's journal and when they find it, they intend to read it even when Arleen comes upon them. The sisters ask Father Snow about his relationship with Donny, trying to drive him to anger or depression. When that fails, they comment on Donny's poor teeth and revel in the awkward silence. In an act of ultimate cruelty, the girls reveal their parents' awful secret about how their father hit a pedestrian with his car the night he proposed to Mommy. Their malice in embarrassing their parents before Father Snow and Arleen with this tale is surpassed in evilness only by their pure delight in the sordid story.

Father Snow represents goodness, although he is blind to evil. His name, Snow, implies purity, and his profession of Episcopal priest also speaks to his righteousness. Strangely, he is not the one who faces off with evil; indeed, he seems unable to recognize it. Although the girls make snide comments directly to Father Snow, he never replies or acknowledges in any way that he has heard these things. He seems to be particularly friendly with Mommy, holding her hand when she is distressed after her daughters tell everyone the terrible family secret of the man Daddy killed over thirty years ago. Father Snow is also the only person to call Mommy by her name, Clarissa. While he is impervious to their evil, he also cannot stop the daughters from hurting others. Father Snow's immunity to the girls' cruelty means that he is the only one of Mommy and Daddy's houseguests who has been able to make a return visit.

Arleen is Father Snow's companion and advisor as he works through his grief. She is able to follow through where Father Snow cannot. She recognizes the damage the girls are doing to the family and confronts the problem at the end of the story, telling Mommy to get rid of her daughters because they are killing her. While Arleen is unable to save Mommy, Mommy's sudden death provides Father Snow with the professional distraction he needs to move past his own grief over Donny and care for the newly dead.

Arleen is an antidote to the evil of the girls. The girls do not like Arleen, constantly making fun of her dress and behavior behind her back: "She had very much the manner of someone waiting to be dismissed. The girls loved it." But Arleen does nothing offensive to them. They are simply too self-absorbed to feel anything except adversarial toward other people. The girls also do not like the thought that their parents are friends with Father Snow and Arleen. But Arleen is helping Mommy as well as Father Snow, diagnosing Mommy's fading vigor. Although the girls do not recognize what the contents are about, Arleen's journal describes Mommy's ailments. The girls have already realized that something is wrong with their parents: Daddy "was sometimes gruff with them as though they were not everything to him! And Mommy's enchantment with life seemed to be waning." The reality, as revealed by Arleen and the death of Mommy, is that the girls are predators, just like their cats, and are unable to deny their pets' temperament: "they were efficient and ruthless and ... the way in which they so naturally expressed their essential nature was something the girls admired very much." Given the evidence against the girls, it is perhaps not surprising to the reader that Mommy and Daddy fill their house with guests as often as they can, as a buffer against the poison of their daughters.

When Arleen pulls bloodsuckers off the girls' cats at the end of the story, she is in effect exorcising them of evil influence. The girls do not believe anything so disgusting could be found on their cats and that Arleen must be making it up. The betrayal of their cats is the kind of variance that the girls cannot tolerate because of their narcissistic certainty that they are more important to their cats than anyone else—that they are, in fact, the center of the universe. In the ancient Egyptian mythos, cats were sacred to the gods and sometimes enacted their vengeance. In the Middle Ages, cats were believed to be companions to witches. In "The Girls," the cats share a little in both these personas. From the perspective of the girls, the cats are indeed precious and admirable. From Arleen's perspective, the cats are familiars to the wicked girls. Her plucking of bloodsuckers from their coats is her way of freeing them from the girls.

Mommy was not freed soon enough, however. Her health, especially her heart, is strained by the effort of supporting her narcissistic girls and her manslaughtering husband. "Daddy said that when you look death in the eye, you want to do it as calmly as a stroller looks into a shop window." This calm—attributable to a lack of conscience, perhaps—pervades Daddy and the girls as well, leaving Mommy to feel everything and to go into death gracelessly.

The irony of Mommy's death is that although the girls cause it, they probably do not want her dead because she takes care of them. The girls have so much control over their lives, their bodies, their pets, and their parents that they are completely astonished when Mommy falls and dies right at their feet. Neither the girls nor Daddy stands and rushes to Mommy's side which makes the three of them seem cold by contrast to Arleen and Father Snow (who is not cold and impersonal as his name might imply). Arleen and Father Snow rush to Mommy's side to hold her head and say the necessary prayers. It is also ironic that just before dying, Mommy is trying to repent for a decades-old sin which was the fault of her husband. She fails to complete her repentance before she collapses.

Evil is a balance for good. Some would even go so far as to describe the relationship between the two as interdependent, assuming *without evil, there is no good.* Williams provides interest in her short story by making the evil, unsympathetic characters, the girls, the protagonists and the heroine, Arleen, the antagonist. "The Girls," therefore, is a not-so-classic story about the never-ending struggle between the forces of good and evil. The ending, in terms of this struggle, is ambiguous. Neither good nor evil wins this time. Arleen, fighting for good, still loses Mommy, who is broken down by her daughters' stronger willpower. The daughters, in siding with evil, have still lost their mother and perhaps gained some skeptics.

Source: Carol Ullmann, Critical Essay on "The Girls," in *Short Stories for Students*, Thomson Gale, 2007.

> IN THE END, WILLIAMS'S STORY SUGGESTS THAT THE MATERIAL BENEFITS OF THE DREAM LIFE, HOWEVER IMPRESSIVE THEY MIGHT APPEAR ON THE SURFACE, ARE SPIRITUAL HANDICAPS, PRODUCING A VACUOUS WASTELAND WITHIN WHICH THE ONCE REALIZED DREAM PROVES TO BE MUCH MORE A DIVERSION THAN A CLEARLY DEFINED PATH TO THE FUTURE."

Klay Dyer

Dyer holds a Ph.D. in English literature and has published extensively on fiction, poetry, film, and television. He is also a freelance university teacher, writer, and educational consultant. In the following essay, he discusses "The Girls" as a story of dislocation and almost pathological insularity, showing its similarity to earlier stories by Poe and Faulkner.

The short story as a compressed narrative is a form particularly well suited to explore small worlds to explore the lives of individuals and communities that are closed off from the larger world. The catalogue of famous stories that deal with these small worlds includes Edgar Allan Poe's "The Fall of the House of Usher" (1839), William Faulkner's "A Rose for Emily" (1930), and Shirley Jackson's "The Lottery" (1948). Each of these antecedents is a story about a dangerous stasis, an unwillingness or inability to change or to evolve in response to changing times. These are stories, too, that focus on characters who resist such changes, hiding themselves in houses or behind insular mindsets that are inevitably used to resist new ideas or visions about what the world is and might become.

At times, as in Jackson's small town, the results of such a closing off are horrific. At other times, the implications are grotesque, as in the moment when Faulkner's townspeople realize the necrophilic behavior of Emily Grier. The sisters in Joy Williams's "The Girls" are the next generation of such closed off people. Reinforced by faith in the American dream, which promises to bring a regenerative prosperity and an organic goodness to the modern world, the sisters hide behind an almost pathological insularity. In tracing the sisters' movement toward what Father Snow calls the transformative illuminations of *meta-noia* (a profound change of mind), Williams underscores the temporary joys and the inevitable dangers of living a life with eyes half closed.

As Arthur Miller's classic play *Death of a Salesman* (1949) underscores dramatically, the American dream of shared prosperity and a good life does not automatically come true. Paradoxically, as Miller shows, the achievement of a higher standard of living in the postwar United States did not necessarily translate into the better life. As the dream lost its energy, the spiritual and cultural life waned, exemplified in Williams's story in Father Snow's crisis in faith and in the superficiality of the girls' lives. The post-dream world becomes a metaphoric desert in which the detritus of past generations is constantly recycled into imitative trends rather than producing rich sediment that can serve as the foundation for a balanced and invigorating vision of the future. It is a world, as Father Snow comes to recognize, of the "old dead" rather than of "the quickening new."

As Williams underscores, the residents of this world cannot see themselves as spiritually vacuous or particularly superficial. For instance, the sisters cannot see the ethical implications of their search of Arleen's room, an incident that is the culmination of "the girls many clandestine visits to her room to find anything of interest." More telling is the family's reaction to the girls' favorite story about how "Daddy ran over that man that winter night" and "didn't stop even though he knew he'd very likely killed him because [he was] going to a concert." Clearly, this is not a family that cares much about forging spiritual and personal connections but defines itself instead through a smug resistance to such connections. They are more concerned with getting on with selfish pursuits than with considering such troubling ideas as "guilt" or even *poenitare*, "which merely means to feel sorry, suggesting a change in the heart rather than in the mind."

The disruptive presence of Father Snow and Arleen in the family's daily routine underscores the woefully myopic condition of the culture that the girls define. The guests are a potentially transformative energy in the house, outsiders who have loved and lost and who bring to the jaded residence a willingness to recognize the beauty of the rain-drenched moors. They also recognize without hesitation the problems festering in the family like the bloodsuckers hiding in the fur of the family's cats.

Like most truth speakers or visionaries, Arleen is seen by the sisters as little more than an old maid, a pathetic "*troll*" whose love life is described as "safe," whose stories are "so droll, so retarded," and whose willingness to tend to the cats' wellbeing is marked as "disgusting." Her views on life and on politics are devalued in a world that privileges insularity, pithy commentary, and an unfounded sense of moral and intellectual superiority. The girls scoff at Arleen, believing that she has lost sight of the dream-like prosperity around her. Seeing Arleen as an adversary instead of guest, a delusional antagonist rather than a seer, the girls delegitimize her potentially transformative interpretation. In turning away from the potentially redemptive powers in her observations, the girls turn away, too, from an enlightening moment and from an epiphany that might connect them for the first time to the world beyond the garden walls.

Closed to both the musings of both Arleen and Father Snow, including his discussion of repentance, the girls emphasize their obsessive attachment to the two remaining house cats and ignore the deeper truths circulating around them. The girls are drawn almost hypnotically to their pets. When confronted with Arleen's observation that the cats have injured a mockingbird earlier in the day, the sisters resist: "'Those weren't our cats,'" they rejoined almost in unison, "'our cats are sweet cats, old stay-at-home cats." Moreover, they assert with passion, "'such dreadful things don't happen in our garden.'" The sisters state these beliefs as truth despite their firsthand knowledge that "even this early in the summer the cats had slaughtered no less than a dozen songbirds by visible count."

To soothe themselves, the girls believe many self-deluding fictions, from the innocence of their beloved cats to the belief that to have "never been in love" marked them as somehow morally superior to Arleen and Father Snow. Even when Arleen catches the sisters in the act of reading her private journal, the sisters remain firm in their moral righteousness. Their reaction is not one of guilt or even embarrassment but "a perturbed silence" and forced imitation of "extreme wonder."

But even their insularity has its limits. Forced to serve as captive audience to the real life trials and struggles that their two guests bring to the household, the sisters hear about failed and unrequited love affairs, a profound crisis of faith, and a range of intense, real world emotions that are almost beyond their imagining. Considered individually and as a couple, the guests are seen by the girls as antithetical to a household culture defined by stasis and homogeneity.

The girls are willing prisoners within their own home and eccentrics or oddities outside of it. Living "fearful of crime" and of any real engagement with the world, they are emotionally and intellectually bankrupt, a fact that leads Arleen to challenge them openly about their lies, their beloved cats, and, most provocatively, about the pressures they bring upon an aging mother whose health is in decline. Totally reliant on their parents, and totally cut off from the adult world in which they cannot function, the girls are seemingly oblivious to the fact that "Mommy and Daddy [are] changing" and that a powerful force is "hastening" toward their parents, "slowly ... cloaked in the minutes and the months." Hiding away in their "three-storied nineteenth-century house with fish shingles," the sisters withdraw from the outside world into a place that is "tasteful, cold, and peculiar."

The danger behind this peculiar, insular world is revealed when Arleen pulls the fat bloodsuckers from the beloved cats Challenging the girls' vision of the world and speaking volumes to the oppressiveness of their spiritual void, Arleen's actions symbolize the parasitic, which the sisters represent. Dismissing the truth that lies squirming before their eyes as "disgusting," the girls push deeper still into their denial to accuse Arleen of producing the bloodsuckers "fraudulently" or through an "unchristian" magic.

Shock soon turns to grief, though, when Arleen speaks the taboo truth. Turning to Mommy, she says bluntly, that it is "high time for [the girls] to be gone" from the house that has shielded them from reality and moral responsibility. Unlike the other visitors who have passed through the home for decades, Arleen understands fully the erosion of the social and moral framework that grips the family, and she declares what all who have come before have also known to be true. As Father Snow acknowledges, Arleen is a woman who "can listen to anything and come

> IN HER NOVELS AND SHORT STORIES, WILLIAMS WRITES WITH A SURREALISTIC INTENSITY OF HOW ORDINARY LIVES ARE VULNERABLE TO HORROR AND HOPELESSNESS."

to a swift decision" about what action needs to be taken. What she sees is a family that has been dying for years, Arleen is determined to burn away the "old dead" and move forward into a world energized by "the quickening new."

Tragically, the truth brings death into an insular world that seems destined to change only in unhealthy ways. Sequestering themselves in their home and encountering the world with assumed superiority, the girls dislocate themselves, disconnecting from the ability to dream of a better place of intimate connections and organic humanity. In the end, Williams's story suggests that the material benefits of the dream life, however impressive they might appear on the surface, are spiritual handicaps, producing a vacuous wasteland within which the once realized dream proves to be much more a diversion than a clearly defined path to the future.

Source: Klay Dyer, Critical Essay on "The Girls," in *Short Stories for Students*, Thomson Gale, 2007.

Thomson Gale

In the following essay, the critic gives an overview of Joy Williams's work.

"I think Joy Williams may be the most 'relevant' woman writing at this time," remarked Anatole Broyard in his *New York Times* review of Williams's first novel, *State of Grace.* "I can't tell which moves me more: her historical inevitability or her talent." In her novels and short stories, Williams writes with a surrealistic intensity of how ordinary lives are vulnerable to horror and hopelessness. Although critics have responded somewhat unevenly to her fiction, they nonetheless recognize her unique talent and skill. Gail Godwin observed in the Chicago *Tribune Books:* "Joy Williams 'writes like' nobody but Joy Williams, and that is distinctively sufficient. ... She has her own sound. Her writing style is laconic, austere, yet numinously suggestive."

Williams first attracted popular and critical attention with *State of Grace*, an impressionistic novel in which "shards of experiences slowly assemble into a powerful portrayal of ... a heroine cursed by total recall," said an *Antioch Review* contributor. The novel follows the heroine "from her pregnancy to the birth of her child," wrote David Bromwich in *Commentary*, "with generous flashbacks to her religious childhood and her early free-living and free-loving adulthood." Godwin cautioned in the *New York Times Book Review* that while the "fated heroine of this bleak but beautifully-crafted first novel may well be the final perfected archetype of all the 'sad ladies' ... [she] is no simple 'slice-of-despair' character; her sad story becomes, through the author's skill and intention, transubstantiated into significant myth." Although the *Antioch Review* contributor believed the book's nonlinear structure causes problems with unity, the critic found a "totally involving immediacy" in the novel and concluded: "All Joy Williams needs is the ability to better organize and control the visions of her extraordinary imagination. She is almost certain to write a novel that will be even finer than this one."

The Changeling, Williams's impressionistic and not easily categorized second novel, did not quite fulfill the expectations several critics held for it. Broyard, for example, acknowledged in the *New York Times* that *State of Grace* is a "startlingly good novel, but it pains me to have to say that *The Changeling* is a startlingly bad one.... Harsh as it may sound, I find that nothing works." Broyard called the story line "an arbitrary muddle about a young woman who is more or less kidnapped by a man who marries her and takes her to live on an island." Strange occurrences on this island prompted a *New Yorker* contributor to wonder whether this is a "horror story or something more serious? The steady decay of [the heroine's] mental powers, skillfully rendered by Joy Williams, may persuade the reader that the title is a metaphor for a schizophrenic." In the *Hudson Review*, Patricia Meyer Spacks assessed the novel as an "increasingly surrealistic account ..., which retreats altogether from the public realm into a self-indulgent phantasmagoria of privacy"; Spacks also suspected that the corresponding stylistic shift from "outer to inner events ... reflects unsure novelistic purpose." Similarly, Godwin found the stream-of-consciousness ending disappointing and seemingly evasive because of its

unanswered questions. However, Godwin concluded in the Chicago *Tribune Books* that Williams may be luring the reader to his or her "own solutions—and to await with anticipation her future fictions."

Discussing *The Changeling* in the *New York Times Book Review*, Alice Adams appreciated the inherent difficulty in writing about the "borderland between psychosis and reality, the land of private mythology of the 'grotesque.'" And while she believed Williams is a "talented, skillful writer ... [who] evokes the feel and smell of certain moments with an eerie precision," Adams found the novel "unconvincing and ultimately unsatisfactory ..., instead of the very good one that I believe Joy Williams could write." Nevertheless, D. Keith Mano wrote favorably in the *National Review* of the multifarious elements in *The Changeling*, crediting Williams with a willingness "to stretch and reconnoiter her talent" on what he deemed "a book of risks: primeval myth, enchantment, animal metamorphosis, strange island, symbolism, insanity: more Gothic architecture than Chartres has. Only a daredevil novelist would try to renovate this tenement genre."

Taking Care, Williams's first collection of short stories, has generated much favorable response from critics, many of whom have considered the stories both individually and collectively successful. The "finely made and perfectly matched stories ... hold love up to us like a dark, fractured bauble that we should see, reflected and to our astonishment, what moments in our familiar lives it dominates," wrote Richard Ford in the Chicago *Tribune Books*. David Quammen of the *New York Times Book Review* suggested that "social disfunction and the discontinuity of relationships" permeate the collection, and he added that most of the stories are "focused on the imperfect efforts of husbands and wives trying marriage for the second or third time, and on the children surviving (in various degrees of disability) from earlier attempts." Ford found that "most often and touchingly, Williams' characters live without love, and grow melancholy for wanting it"; he maintained that "Williams writes about such yearnings and their attendant pretensions with a rare, transforming intelligence." Joyce Kornblatt, who detected a similarity in spirit between these stories and those of Flannery O'Connor and Joyce Carol Oates, observed in the *Washington*

Post Book World that "madness, murder, the surrender of hope become commonplace rather than extreme behaviors, and even those characters who sustain the ability to love seem perplexed, even encumbered, by their triumph."

Caroline Thompson wrote in the *Los Angeles Times* that "gathered together, the stories project a cumulative impression that couldn't be communicated by any single of them." Brina Caplan commended Williams for the subtle yet devastating effect of her collection, and wrote in the *Nation:* " *Taking Care*, story by story and incident by incident, withdraws meaning from the lives it represents. In each case, what remains is a gem of despair, worked into the shape of finality by skillful slights of hand." Kornblatt suggested, "Transcending religious and political systems of belief, Williams speaks to us from a plane of pure feeling." She continued, "Like fine music, these stories circumvent the intellect. Williams seems to make the works themselves transparent and we gaze directly into the souls of her characters." Williams wrote the 1988 novel *Breaking and Entering* before returning to the short-story genre with *Escapes* two years later. Her skill in short fiction, evidenced by the 1982 and 1990 collections, earned her prestigious Rea Award in the category in 1999.

Williams once worked for the U.S. Navy as a researcher and data analyst at its Mate Marine Laboratory in Siesta Key, Florida. The experience impacted her life and her fiction in a number of ways: she made the Florida Keys her permanent home and developed a strong interest in environmental and ecological issues, which would become a recurring theme in her later work. In 1997, she wrote a long piece for *Harper's* magazine about the radical animal-rights movement. Her 2000 novel, *The Quick and the Dead*, touches upon some of these themes through Williams's characterization of the prickly, opinionated heroine, Alice. *The Quick and the Dead* was selected for the cover of the *New York Times Book Review* that October, with an illustration of a grimacing blond teenager wearing a "THANK YOU FOR NOT BREEDING" T-shirt.

The Arizona teenager is a caricatured symbol of the radical environmentalist and pro-animal fringe. Alice is politically astute, a vegetarian, and well informed on population control, conservancy issues, and the planet's beautifully balanced ecosystem. Alice has difficulty endearing herself to other humans, however. She has a bad

experience as a babysitter for two children, whom she disliked: "They cried frequently, indulged themselves in boring, interminable narratives, were sentimental and cruel, and when frustrated would bite," reads one passage of *The Quick and the Dead*. Alice tries to teach them how to marvel at nature and urges them to question their teacher, but their hairdresser mother accuses her of satanism and refuses to pay her. At the end of the first chapter, the woman leaves Alice stranded in a state park.

Alice returns home, where she lives with her grandparents, and as *The Quick and the Dead* unfolds, readers learn that she and two of her close friends are all motherless. Corvus lost her parents in a bizarre drowning death, while Annabel's spirited mother was struck by a car. All deal with their loss through different means: Corvus is deeply heartbroken—as is her dog— while Annabel seems unfazed. Alice vents her anger on the larger world. A series of events follow to mark the girls' passage into adulthood. Corvus's beloved dog runs afoul of a neighbor who dislikes it; the man kills it, and the girls, at Alice's urging, extract a terrible retribution. The lives of other characters entwine with theirs, but the animal world seems to keep intruding.

Alice moves toward increasing radicalism in the environmental movement, but realizes that this, too, is a form of the conformity and consumerism she so despises. "Like Alice, *The Quick and the Dead* is odd, intelligent, unsettling and sometimes spectacularly uningratiating," noted *New York Times Book Review* writer Jennifer Schuessler. But the critic also termed it "beautifully written, and often very funny." Schuessler felt that the author's fourth novel had some structural flaws. "Williams' language runs with virtuosity across a wide range, from dead-on vernacular to the gorgeously, unabashed oracular," opined Schuessler. "But even her perfect pitch can't keep this scattered, jumpy book from falling to pieces at times." Other reviewers commented more favorably on the "episodic, meandering structure," as a *Publishers Weekly* critic termed it, and the somewhat inconclusive ending. "But these are deliberate choices, made by an artist attentive to real people's psyches," the reviewer concluded. A *U.S. News and World Report* contributor termed *The Quick and the Dead* an "unsparingly bleak (yet often beautiful) novel," and even Schuessler concluded that Williams's gifts were evident in the book's flaws. "Sometimes the animals barge in awkwardly on the human stories Williams is telling, trying the reader's sympathies," Schuessler noted. "But the need to disrupt the easy flow of sympathy—to call into question the self-serving sentimentality that tends to get filed under 'affirmations of the human spirit'—is one of the book's themes, and part of its strange fascination."

Williams's 2000 book of environmental essays was hailed as "sharp, sarcastic and uncompromising" by a *Publishers Weekly* reviewer. Her collection of nineteen essays, including "Safariland," "The Case against Babies," and "Save the Whales, Screw the Shrimp," deals with animal rights and the abuse and overuse of the natural world by the human population. "As a whole the work is effective and will likely leave the reader angry, frustrated, distressed, or depressed, which is, after all, her intent," wrote Maureen J. Delaney-Lehman in *Library Journal*. *Booklist* reviewer Donna Seaman concluded, "These howls, protests and pleas for sanity are lacerating, brilliant, and necessary."

Source: Thomson Gale, "Joy Williams," in *Contemporary Authors Online*, Thomson Gale, 2005.

SOURCES

Adams, Alice, "Someone Else's Dream," in *New York Times Book Review*, July 2, 1978, p. 6.

Cooper, Rand Richards, "The Dark at the End of the Tunnel," in *New York Times Book Review*, January 21, 1990, p. 9.

Ellis, Bret Easton, "The Things They Babbled to Willie," in *New York Times*, June 5, 1988, p. A1.

Gates, David, Review of *Honored Guest*, in *Newsweek International*, January 10, 2005, p. 49.

Godwin, Gail, Review of *State of Grace*, in *New York Times*, April 22, 1973, p. 276.

"Joy Williams's Teenage Misfits," in *Economist*, No. 358, January 13, 2001, p. 7.

Kakutani, Michiko, "Taking to the Highway, Fleeing the Inescapable," in *New York Times*, January 5, 1990, p. C28.

Metcalf, Stephen, "The Small Chill," in *New York Times Book Review*, December 19, 2004, p. 14.

Miller, Sara, "Holy Animals," in *Books & Culture*, Vol. 11, No. 3, May–June 2005, p. 14.

Review of *Honored Guest*, in *Kirkus Reviews*, Vol. 76, No. 16, August 15, 2004, p. 776.

Review of *Honored Guest*, in *Publishers Weekly*, Vol. 251, No. 35, August 30, 2004, p. 30.

Review of *The Quick and the Dead*, in *Publishers Weekly*, Vol. 247, No. 38, September 18, 2000, p. 88.

Schwarz, Benjamin, Review of *Honored Guest*, in *Atlantic Monthly*, Vol. 294, No. 5, December 2004, p. 124.

Williams, Joy, "The Girls," in *The Best American Short Stories 2005*, edited by Michael Chabon, Houghton Mifflin, 2005, pp. 212–22.

FURTHER READING

Christopher, David, *British Culture*, Routledge, 2006.
Christopher's book is an introduction to the major movements within British culture, covering politics, language, literature, media, architecture, and more.

Hogle, Jerrold E., *The Cambridge Companion to Gothic Fiction*, Cambridge University Press, 2002.
This book collects fourteen essays which examine gothic literature in the eighteenth, nineteenth, and twentieth centuries, drawing out connections to politics, racism, theater, film, human identity, and more.

Hotchkiss, Sandy, *Why Is It Always about You?: Saving Yourself from the Narcissists in Your Life*, Free Press, 2002.
This book about clinical narcissism was written for the popular market. It has chapters for different relationships, including parent, spouse, child, and coworker, and tips on how to live with a narcissist.

Oates, Joyce Carol, ed., *American Gothic Tales*, Plume, 1996.
This collection of forty short stories spans two hundred years of American gothic fiction and includes favorite American writers such as Washington Irving, Edgar Allen Poe, Stephen King, and Anne Rice.

Here's Your Hat What's Your Hurry

ELIZABETH McCRACKEN

1993

In the short story, "Here's Your Hat What's Your Hurry," Elizabeth McCracken introduces a larger-than-life character, Aunt Helen Beck, a woman in her eighties who has traveled the country for most of her life, showing up at the homes of distant relatives who have only vaguely heard of her, if they have at all. She arrives at an island in Seattle's Puget Sound to stay with a great nephew and his wife. In the course of her visit, they learn to put up with the trials of having their lives invaded by an outspoken aged relative. At the same time, their suspicions grow that she is actually not who she says she is. Each character is rendered imaginatively as a familiar type, but also as a unique individual. McCracken tells the story with an unerring eye for details and a subtle sense of humor that recognizes the underlying strangeness of ordinary modern life.

"Here's Your Hat What's Your Hurry" was published in McCracken's 1993 short story collection of the same name. This was her first story collection, published when the author was just a few years out of college, and it helped to establish McCracken as one of the most gifted young writers of her generation.

AUTHOR BIOGRAPHY

Elizabeth McCracken was born in 1966. Her father, Samuel McCracken, was a writer and editor and an assistant to the provost of Boston University, where

her mother, Natalie, also worked. McCracken attended Boston University, where she graduated cum laude with a Bachelor of Arts and a Master of Arts in English, both in 1988. She then attended the University of Iowa Writers' Workshop, taking an M.F.A. in 1990. She earned a Master of Science degree in library and information science from Drexel University in 1993. After graduation she was the circulation desk chief at the Somerville Public Library, in Somerville, Massachusetts, where she lived from 1993 to 1997. She was the community arts director for the Somerville Arts Council in 1995 and 1996.

McCracken's first book was the short story collection, *Here's Your Hat What's Your Hurry*, a compilation of nine stories that was published in 1993. The book earned her critical and popular attention, and it was listed as a Notable Book of the Year by the National Library Association. Following its publication, McCracken taught writing at the Somerville Arts Council, the Iowa Writers' Workshop, and at Western Michigan University. She published her first novel, *The Giant's House* in 1996, again to strong critical praise. It was followed in 2001 by the novel *Niagara Falls All Over Again*. Her short stories and essays have appeared in leading magazines.

McCracken has been the recipient of several important awards. Her works were included in *Best American Short Stories* in 1991 and 1992 and in *Best American Essays* in 1994. The American Academy of Arts and Letters awarded her the Harold Vursell Award in 1997. She won the *Salon* Award and was included among the Best Young American Novelists, both in 1996, for *The Giant's House*. In 1998, she won a prestigious Guggenheim Foundation Fellowship.

PLOT SUMMARY

"Here's Your Hat What's Your Hurry" starts by introducing Aunt Helen Beck, a legendary older woman who stays in the houses of relatives so frequently that the children in houses where she stayed lived to tell stories about her to their own children, some of whom eventually meet her themselves when she comes to stay. Among her eccentricities is her dictation of letters for the children to write to people she has known who are dead; another is that she carries a small change purse with two pennies in it, though she will not show the pennies to anyone.

Aunt Helen Beck arrives at Orcas Island in Puget Sound to stay with Ford and his wife, Chris, after having stayed with Ford's sister Abbie a few years previously. When they meet her at the ferry, Ford asks how long she intends to stay, and Aunt Helen Beck (who is always referred to by all three names) becomes defensive and asks if he is trying to chase her away already, using the colloquial expression for being pushed out the door that gives the story its title. She gives Ford a small framed photo of a man who she says is his great-grandfather, Patrick Corrrigan, explaining that she always brings gifts for the people with whom she stays.

When they drive her back to their house, they are met by Mercury, a boy who lives in a nearby trailer. Aunt Helen Beck chides him about his long hair, which he says he likes. During the discussion while dinner is being prepared, Aunt Helen Beck says that she came up from Vallejo, California, where she stayed for a while with a niece. She lists some of the people at whose homes she has been a guest over the years.

When dinner is over, she tells them about the change purse she carries with the two pennies, explaining that it was made for her by her brother George, who was a child preacher but died young.

About a week into her stay, Aunt Helen Beck allows Chris to overhear her making a phone call to someone, suggesting that she might come to visit and clearly giving a negative response. Chris, feeling that she does not feel welcome to stay, tells her that she should plan on staying with them for as long as she likes.

Mercury becomes very attached to Aunt Helen Beck, following her around the house. When she hears about how his mother treats her children, Aunt Helen Beck disapproves. She recites morbid poetry to Mercury and tells him stories about her life. She feeds him molasses, an old health cure, and is surprised to find that Mercury is one of the few children she has met who actually enjoys it. She has him write letters for her to departed relatives, a practice that she has followed in other relatives' houses.

The day after she shows him her change purse, though, it disappears. Aunt Helen Beck is deeply distressed by the loss of the talisman she has carried with her for more than sixty years.

After the house is searched, Mercury is confronted, and he denies taking it, but his denial is unconvincing. He continues to deny it, and the loss of her one reminder of Georgie Beck, her brother who died when he was a child, changes Aunt Helen Beck's view of the world, throwing her into despair.

Details in Aunt Helen Beck's biography start raising suspicions. She says that her mother raised twenty-one children and that her family was Jewish, though Ford knows nothing about any Jewish relatives. She senses Ford and Chris's suspicions and feels uneasy about her stay.

One day Mercury shows up at the house and politely asks Aunt Helen Beck to cut his hair. His mother, he explains, likes it long and would not cut it if he asked. She obliges. Mercury is pleased with the job that she does, though Ford worries about what the boy's mother will say.

Chris and Ford confront Aunt Helen Beck about whether she is actually related to Ford. She refuses to answer, even when Ford offers to accept her if she is only a close family friend. She explains that she came to be connected with the family after Ford's sister donated some magazines to the public library, finding her address on the mailing labels. There was a real Georgie Beck, she tells them: he was a child preacher who she went to see when she was sixteen; she nursed him when he was ill, taking his name and the change purse after he died. Ford starts to say that she does not have to leave, but Chris interrupts him to say that she should.

In the night, Aunt Helen Beck steals a candlestick to give as a gift to whoever is to be her next hosts. She leaves the house as the sun is rising and is stopped by Mercury, whose mother, angry about his haircut, has thrown him out of the house. As they walk away from the house together, she puts a hand on him and asks if he likes to travel.

CHARACTERS

Aunt Helen Beck

Aunt Helen Beck is an elderly woman who has never owned a home. Throughout her long life—at the time of this story, she is in her eighties—she has traveled the country, staying with people to whom she says she is related. Generations of people have grown up believing that she is their aunt.

None of these presumed relatives has ever called her anything other than "Aunt Helen Beck."

In truth, she has no known relatives. When she was sixteen and homeless, she went to visit a child preacher who had once toured through her town, named Georgie Beck. She established a bond with him and nursed him when he was ill. When Georgie died, she kept his last name and began the practice of presenting herself at the homes of strangers, claiming to be a distant relative.

She stays with people who are amused by her eccentric ways. They compare stories about the things they have observed her doing, such as having children write the letters that she dictates to people she has known, who are now dead, or reciting the works of obscure poets with three names. Often, when she has stayed with someone, she will eventually end up at the door of that person's relatives. Wherever she goes, she arrives with a small gift for her hosts, claiming that it is a family heirloom, even if it is just something that she bought or stole from strangers.

In this story she arrives at Orcas Island to stay with a young couple, Ford and Chris, claiming to be related to Ford's great-grandfather, Patrick Corrigan. Several years earlier, she had stayed with Ford's sister, Abbie. She is outspoken with Ford and Chris about things that she does and does not like and is defensive about anything they say that might indicate that they would like her stay to be brief. She does, however, try to be as little trouble to them as a houseguest can be. She buys them meager little gifts when they go to town.

Aunt Helen Beck forms a bond with the boy who lives in a nearby trailer, Mercury. When the change purse that she has carried for more than sixty years disappears, she is distressed: "What will become of me without it?" she asks no one in particular. It was made by Georgie Beck. She becomes lonesome after Mercury, denying anything to do with the purse's disappearance, stops coming to visit. He later shows up and asks her to cut his long hair, which she dislikes, as an unspoken act of contrition.

After she slips up and tells conflicting stories about her father, Ford becomes suspicious and, doing some research, discovers that she is no relation at all, and Aunt Helen Beck agrees to leave the house. Before she goes, though, she steals a candlestick as a present for the next people she will visit. At the story's end, she appears ready to invite Mercury to join her in her travels.

Chris

Chris is married to Ford and, therefore, has never been led to believe that Aunt Helen Beck is a relative of hers. For this reason, Chris has less sentimental attachment to the old woman and is less likely to find charm in her manipulative ways. She works carefully, meticulously, at stringing beads to make necklaces, which she sells in local shops. Aunt Helen Beck characterizes Chris as "quiet and perennially embarrassed," which she approves of, even though this means that Chris's personality is the opposite of her own. As she lives with them, Aunt Helen Beck becomes more accustomed to Chris, getting over her initial hesitation about Chris's friendly hugs. When it is discovered that Aunt Helen Beck is not really related to Ford, it is Chris who takes personal offense, calling the older woman a liar and a fraud and insisting, when Ford starts to weaken, that she really must leave their house.

Ford

Ford lives with his wife, Chris, on Orcas Island, in Puget Sound, Washington. They are vegetarians, and Ford does the cooking at least part of the time. When Aunt Helen Beck shows up, she explains that she is related to Ford's great-grandfather, who was an uncle of hers, though not a blood relation. She gives him a picture of the man she says is their distant relative, though it later turns out that the person in the picture is an actor wearing a costume moustache.

Because he is a gentle person, Ford tries to calm any situation. When Aunt Helen Beck seems to take offense that he is thinking of keeping her visit short, Ford tries to make it sound as if it would be a favor to them if she would stay. When her change purse disappears, he recognizes it for its psychosocial significance, calling it her "talisman": he rationally suggests that she replace it with another object that could have just as much emotional significance to her. After becoming convinced that Aunt Helen Beck is a fraud and not related to him at all, he confronts her only reluctantly, not nearly as willing as Chris is to insist that she leave. Ford is spiritual; he writes poems addressed to "The Earth" and "The Goddess" and leaves them around the house. He is an intellectual and plainly longs to discuss theories of sociology and religion with an older relative: recognizing this leads Aunt Helen Beck to understand that

"he was the type of man who wanted to be invited to join every club there was. Even hers."

Gaia

Gaia does not appear in the story, but she is talked about. She is a single mother, raising four children in a trailer down the hill from Ford and Chris's house. Her children are all named after planets: Mercury, Jupiter, Venus, and Saturn. She works part time at the Healing Arts Center, doing a form of massage therapy.

Although Gaia has a casual attitude toward having children and raising them, she also has a strict side, a harsh temper, and can be abusive. Angry that Mercury has let Aunt Helen Beck cut his hair, she locks the boy outside all night to teach him a lesson.

Mercury

Mercury is a young boy who lives near Ford and Chris's house. He is brash and undisciplined: when he first appears in the story, for instance, he sees Ford, Chris, and Aunt Helen Beck in a car and says to Chris, "You're ridin' in back like a *dog*." He has long hair because his mother, Gaia, does not believe in cutting her children's hair.

Mercury and Aunt Helen Beck form an unlikely alliance. When she gives him molasses, for instance, he does not reject her, as other children might: to her surprise, he likes the taste. He follows her around as she does her household chores and agrees to write a letter for her, even though he knows only a few words and the letter she is dictating is to an old acquaintance who is now dead.

Mercury commits a serious offense against Aunt Helen Beck when he steals her change purse: she says that it was given to her more than sixty-five years earlier by Georgie Beck, who she claims was her brother, and is the one constant in her vagabond lifestyle. Mercury denies taking it and is banished from the house. Later, he gets back into Aunt Helen Beck's good graces by coming to her and asking her to cut his hair.

Cutting his hair makes Mercury's mother angry at him, and his punishment is that he is locked out of the family trailer all night. As with all other signs that he is a neglected child, Mercury is passively disinterested in this fate. In the morning, when he runs into Aunt Helen Beck as she is leaving, she shows an interest in taking him along on her uncharted travels.

TOPICS FOR FURTHER STUDY

- Find a picture of a person from a hundred years ago or more. Write a short story that explains this person as a distant relative of yours, including details about real relatives that would make your story sound factual to people who know you.

- Contact a social services provider and interview the people there about what they would do with an unattached homeless woman like Aunt Helen Beck. Record your specific questions and the answers you receive, and then write your recommendation about how Aunt Helen Beck should be convinced to apply for social help.

- In the story, Ford makes quinoa, which he refers to as "the grain of the ancient Aztecs." Research the diets of the Aztecs, and find out how important quinoa was to their balanced nutrition. Then prepare an Aztec meal.

- Aunt Helen Beck writes letters to old acquaintances who are dead: research two methods that people have used to communicate with the dead, and write a story that incorporates one of these methods.

- This story ends with Aunt Helen Beck and Mercury leaving for unnamed places. Compare this conclusion to the ending of Mark Twain's novel *Huckleberry Finn*, which many consider to be the great American novel. In what ways do the two endings imply the same things? In which ways do they symbolize different destinies for their characters?

THEMES

Mourning

Throughout "Here's Your Hat What's Your Hurry" one of the most telling clues of Aunt Helen Beck's elusive personality remains hidden: readers are not made aware of the depth of her true relationship with Georgie Beck until the story's end. When she first explains him to Ford and Chris, Aunt Helen Beck says that he was her younger brother, a child preacher who toured the South proselytizing. Before his untimely death, she says, he made the change purse for her as a gift, and she has carried it with her for most of her life. After she is exposed as not a real member of Ford's family, she admits that she was not really related to Georgie either. As a sixteen-year-old with nowhere to live, she was attracted to him because she once saw him preach, and she stayed with him through his final illness, stealing the change purse he had made for his real brother.

Although Aunt Helen Beck is untruthful about much in her life, her emotional attachment to the boy who died more than sixty years earlier is sincere. She is genuinely distraught when the change purse disappears because it is, as she explains, the only remaining thing on earth that Georgie Beck would have touched. When she is found out as a fraud and reflects on her true relationship with Georgie, she dwells on the fact that he once told her that he loved her, putting more emphasis on that fact than on his subsequent statement that God loves her, too. She held onto the change purse over the decades as a tangible symbol of his love, and when it disappears she becomes uncertain of her own identity. Her relationship to the memory of Georgie Beck has an emotional truth that means more to Aunt Helen Beck than any of the details about reality, which she has learned to manipulate over the years.

Journey

Aunt Helen Beck's life is one long journey. She never stays in one place very long, always making preparations for her next stopping place. It is not a quest, because she is not looking for any one particular thing that will fulfill her inner needs. Still, she would be willing to stop her travels immediately, if the situation allowed it: while staying with Ford and Chris, she reflects that "all it would take would be one person saying, Aunt Helen Beck, here's where you belong, and she'd stay in a minute."

At the end of the story, she is clearly on the verge of inviting Mercury to be her traveling companion. Although she has been angry at Mercury, she realizes that he is a neglected child being raised in an instable home and that he would be better with a life like hers, on the road, with no ties. For people like Aunt Helen Beck and Mercury, life is a journey.

Family

One family presented in this story is Gaia's. Gaia has several children by different fathers and is likely to have several more, and she leaves the children to roam the neighborhood unsupervised. Her situation is described to Aunt Helen Beck by Ford and Chris, who excuse it as harmless. At the end of the story, however, it turns out that Gaia is not just a nontraditional parent, but a dangerous one: offended that Mercury has had his hair cut, she locks the young boy out of his home, leaving him exposed the elements all night.

When she arrives at their house, Aunt Helen Beck falls naturally into the role of a parent figure for Ford and Chris. To Ford, she is someone with whom he can discuss moral and religious issues for which he wants answers, and she compares his own spirituality with that of Georgie Beck. She is even more of a companion for Chris, whom she admires for her patience as she works at home beading necklaces. They both ask her about family and history, the way a child would do of a parent.

The strongest familial bond in this story is the one that develops between Aunt Helen Beck and Mercury. Despite her natural distrust of children, particularly male children, he attaches himself to her. Mercury actually likes the molasses that other children on whom she has foisted it have rejected, and he is willing to write the letters she dictates, even though he is embarrassed about his weak writing skills. After being alienated from her because of the missing change purse, he atones by allowing her to cut his hair. Together, Aunt Helen Beck, Ford and Chris, and Mercury temporarily create an artificial family of grandmother, parents, and child, even though the group is not actually related that way.

STYLE

Legend

The first section of "Here's Your Hat What's Your Hurry" establishes Aunt Helen Beck as a legendary figure. Her advanced age is not specifically stated but is instead suggested through the impressions of people who experienced her strange visits when they were children and then,

when they were old enough to have their own children, saw her again. Her personality quirks, such as her belief in molasses as a medical cure or her interest in certain poets, help to make her memorable to readers, but they also help readers see her as someone who would be talked about by friends and relatives, to such a degree that people who never met her would recognize her from stories that they had heard. McCracken capitalizes the expression, Aunt Helen Beck Stories, to let readers know that the legends told about her have a life of their own, independent of the woman herself.

With this background established, the story uses Aunt Helen Beck's activities on Orcas Island as a way of contrasting her life there with her larger-than-life legend. When she gives Mercury molasses, for instance, or when she dictates a letter to him, readers recognize actions that have been identified as the ones that are discussed about her. When she takes an interest in Ford and Chris's lives, though, the details of her life make her appear more ordinary than the Aunt Helen Beck who stars in the family tales. Her time with Ford and Chris might eventually serve to expand her legend, but for the time covered in the story this legendary figure is presented as an ordinary human being.

HISTORICAL CONTEXT

Homelessness

In this story, Aunt Helen Beck travels around the country, moving from the home of one family of strangers to another. She has been doing this since the Great Depression. She has never had a home of her own. Because of her considerable survival skills, readers may be inclined to admire her for her freedom, but in fact she is an unusual example of homelessness, a serious and pervasive problem in the United States.

According to estimates made in the 1996 *National Survey of Homeless Assistance Providers and Clients*, conducted by the U.S. Census Bureau, at any given time, there are about 800,000 people in the United States without a home, including about 200,000 children who are members of homeless families. There are many causes of homelessness. While some people, like Aunt Helen Beck, may chose a nomadic lifestyle for personal reasons, many people find homelessness a most unwanted situation. Some lose their homes due to natural disasters, such as the devastation that Hurricane Katrina caused to tens of thousands of people in Louisiana and Mississippi in 2005. Some become homeless when an unexpected personal catastrophe, such as an illness, wipes out their savings and makes them unable to pay for their living quarters. Other factors can include an inability to assimilate, due to language or cultural barriers, after immigrating to a new country, and an inability to reenter society after a prison sentence or military commitment has been completed.

Estimates provided by the Coalition for the Homeless Mentally Ill reported in an fact sheet available at http://www.barkson.com/chmi/causes.htm (accessed September 11, 2006) that the homeless who have serious mental illness run as high as 33 percent. Added to that is how much addiction to alcohol and other drugs determines the number of homeless people who are unable to maintain steady housing; though not definitively measurable, some researchers estimate 38 percent of the homeless population are affected by substance abuse problems. There is no clear consensus about whether substance abuse causes homelessness or vice versa, but it is clear that there is a disproportionately high co-occurrence of substance abuse and homelessness.

In the last decades of the twentieth century, homelessness was a serious yet increasingly hidden problem in the United States. This trend began in the 1970s, a result of the Community Mental Health Act passed by Congress in 1963. The act was intended to integrate mental health patients into regular society, but underfunding led to turning thousands of people out on the streets without the social support they would need to fend for themselves. At the same time, many urban areas were eliminating the very least expensive available housing, the Single Room Occupancy hotels (SROs). Between 1970 and the mid-1980s, the United States lost a million inexpensive rooms that were available to the poor, as sections of cities that had been considered skid rows were transformed into desirable urban areas. The homeless were also removed from view by a wave of anti-loitering laws passed in large cities in the 1980s that were designed to make downtown areas less threatening and more appealing to suburbanites with discretionary money to spend. The result moved homeless people from the streets to less public areas, such as parks and subways, but it did nothing to address their problems.

By the 1990, around the time when this story was written, there was a renewed interest in the plight of the homeless. Celebrities did public service announcements to make the issue more visible, and it was used as a subject for television dramas. Still, the fact that laws in larger cities were purposely aimed at keeping this problem out of the public eye led the majority of people to miss the fact that, even with the booming economy in the 1990s, the homeless population continued to grow.

CRITICAL OVERVIEW

From the very start of her career, Elizabeth McCracken has been recognized as a major literary talent. "Here's Your Hat What's Your Hurry" comes from her first published book, a short story collection of the same name. Some of these stories were written when McCracken was still in college. Stories from the book were included in the *Best American Stories* collections for 1991 and 1992, and the book was listed as an American Library Association Notable Book of 1993. Reviews of the collection were generally favorable. Many mentioned the title story as a good example of McCracken's skill in handling eccentric characters that are, despite their eye-catching flair, viewed with compassion and humanity. As Janet Ingraham puts it in a review entitled "Word of Mouth," in *Library Journal*: "These nine stories reveal the oddness of ordinary life by inverting the theme of skeletons in the closet: the characters appear unusual but live familiar lives of quiet hardship and comedy." Eight years later, after the publication of McCracken's novel *The Giant's House*, *Library Journal* came back to *Here's Your Hat What's Your Hurry* in an overview of books that readers may have missed the first time around, with reviewer Nancy Pearl concluding that "McCracken's vision is at once both eccentric and wise, an unbeatable combination that makes for great reading."

The Giant's House, McCracken's first novel, was almost universally praised by critics. Her second book, *Niagara Falls All Over Again*, was met though with mixed praise: many critics proclaimed it another triumph of her voice, but Daniel Mendelsohn, writing in *New York*

The family in this story watches the sun set over the Puget Sound in Washington © *Matt Brown/Corbis*

magazine, found it to be overambitious, attributing its weakness to a common conceptual problem that writers fall into with second novels. The main character is simply "not a character you're necessarily very interested in," Mendelsohn writes. "Nor, more to the point, does McCracken seem to be—though she tries mightily to liven up the proceedings . . . What's wrong with this overeventful but oddly inconsequential book (though let's be clear—there's plenty that's right) is what's typically wrong with sophomore novels: Overstuffed, overambitious, it tries too hard for too much. But that overabundance in itself suggests that there's much more to come." Even this unenthusiastic review, however, falls in line with most of McCracken's critics by acknowledging in the end that "McCracken's act is one that every lover of serious fiction should follow."

CRITICISM

David Kelly

Kelly is an instructor of creative writing and English literature. In the following essay, he examines the techniques that McCracken uses to elevate the character of Aunt Helen Beck to legendary status.

In "Here's Your Hat What's Your Hurry," Elizabeth McCracken introduces Aunt Helen Beck, an unforgettable character so clearly

realized that most readers, like the characters whose lives she invades in the story, will find themselves feeling a vague sense of familiarity with her. She seems like a family member or an echo of a character from another work of literature. This is not to say that there is anything at all unoriginal about Aunt Helen Beck: on the contrary, the sense of familiarity that clings to her is precisely because McCracken has created her with such specific details that she seems strikingly authentic. She speaks her mind even at the risk of upsetting her hosts, taking advantage of the fact that the small, residual respect for elders that still exists in modern society will make them go easy on her. She laughs and loses her patience sometimes, and at others she is touched by the simplicity of the lives lived by her purported nephew Ford and his wife Chris, a couple at least two generations removed from her own. It is true that McCracken knows how to form a well-rounded and amusing character and that any of the story's other three characters could be the basis for a good story, but Aunt Helen Beck stands alone. In a story that is wonderfully evocative of reality, Aunt Helen Beck is something more important than it all: she is legendary.

Just how McCracken goes about making a legend out of her character is no secret. In the story's opening paragraphs, she gives generalizations about the woman, speaking about her the same way others have spoken about her at

WHAT DO I READ NEXT?

- Critics praised Elizabeth McCracken's first novel, *The Giant's House*, which was published in 1997. The plot concerns interesting characters in circumstances as innovative as they are in this story: a lonely librarian in a small town falls in love with a boy fourteen years younger than she and stays true to him as he grows to nearly nine feet tall.

- The loose border between reality and fantasy that McCracken flirts with in this story is pushed further in Michael Paterniti's *Driving Mr. Albert: A Trip across America with Einstein's Brain* (2000). Paterniti's book chronicles an actual journey across the country in a Buick Skylark, with the brain of Albert Einstein, which was removed from Einstein's body upon his death in 1955, and the aged pathologist who removed it.

- McCracken's style and literary sensibilities have often been compared to those of Ron Carlson. Carlson's collection of stories *Plan B for the Middle Class* includes a varied selection of tales about ordinary people reaching middle age and wondering about their lives. Published in 1992, about the same year that McCracken's *Here's Your Hat What's Your Hurry*, this collection is available in a reprint edition from Penguin Press.

- Elizabeth McCracken has clearly drawn inspiration for part of this story from another writer who was just as inventive and just as strongly associated with the Iowa Writers' Workshop: Flannery O'Connor. Her 1949 novel *Wise Blood* includes a young street-corner preacher trying to outrun his guilt and the conniving world of would-be religious figures surrounding him.

- Mary Karr, a college professor, poet, and critic, published a memoir in 1995 about her childhood in east Texas called *The Liar's Club*. The events of her life are scarcely believable, loaded with alcoholism, abuse, gunplay, and reckless spending; despite the serious nature of the events, though, Karr writes with an unfailing sense of humor and appreciation of humanity that matches McCracken's own.

- Readers of this story may gain a better appreciation of Aunt Helen Beck by reading the works of one of the poets whom she identifies as being morbid and three-named. James Whitcomb Riley is seldom remembered anymore, but in the early decades of the twentieth century most schoolchildren in the country were familiar with at least a few of his poems. They are collected in Indiana Press's 1993 volume *The Complete Poetical Works of James Whitcomb Riley*.

---

different times and places. Readers are told, for instance, that the following circumstances prevailed at many different homes—that she slept on sofas that were too short for her and subsequently kicked over lamps; that she dictated to children letters to deceased acquaintances; that she spoke about dead, morbid, three-named poets; that she talked about the purse that she had carried for sixty-five years and claimed that it had two pennies inside. As if it were not enough to paint a portrait of the woman with these details, McCracken also uses these early paragraphs to illustrate her situation: she is obviously a woman who has the time and patience to spend with children, which is not something that one would consider obvious when she later becomes a somewhat stern confidante of Mercury, the boy who lives in the nearby trailer. Also, she has been traveling around for so long that the children of people who knew her as

> UNDERSTANDING READERS' ASSUMPTIONS MIGHT JUST BE McCRACKEN'S GREATEST GIFT AS A WRITER, WHICH, GIVEN HER CONTROL OF LANGUAGE, HER SKILL AT INNOVATION, AND HER UNDERSTANDING OF ECCENTRIC PERSONALITIES, IS CERTAINLY SAYING A LOT."

children can become acquainted with her anew. This longevity and her association with children, the most imaginative members of society, are the perfect ingredients for achieving legendary status.

But there is one other element to her elevation from well-written character to legend, and that is the fact that McCracken continually affirms some of the details that have been told about her, while leaving other details to speculation. In doing this, she allows readers the thrill of discovery, of connecting those facts dictated in the early part of the story with details played out in front of their eyes as Aunt Helen Beck goes about her daily life. This interplay between things gossiped about her and things that are verifiably true gives the story life. It also broadens the story with each specific detail: seeing the things that are true about her and knowing that there are other details that are left undemonstrated, readers are seduced into believing that just about anything about her can be true.

For example, she dictates letters to the dead. On the second page of the story, McCracken describes a scene that has presumably been played out repeatedly, with young children who feel mixed emotions (they are "terrified of the enormous old lady on the sofa," but they love scribbling her words) about interacting with this woman whose reason for being in their house is, in itself, a mystery. It is only one sentence, but it is a memorable one, and McCracken even starts it with "After a while," to make readers aware of the overarching scope of this development. After a while, when she is settled into the house, Aunt Helen Beck dictates one of these letters to Mercury, the child of the particular household

where she is staying. Readers have a chance to see the story's early narration confirmed. McCracken's gift is that she does not dwell on this structural device: readers hardly have time to think about how Mercury is becoming a member of something, a society of dozens of children who have had the benefit of Aunt Helen Beck's company over the decades. Readers are more focused on the immediate details of the scene, such as "Mac" identity, the trouble arose between Mac and Aunt Helen Beck, and of course Mercury's limited, if enthusiastic, literacy.

Only some of the rituals that Aunt Helen Beck is said to observe actually show up during her stay with Ford and Chris and Mercury. She does, as the narrator explains in that opening passage, have a change purse that she has carried with her for years, and she does give molasses to children, because she believes it is good for them. There are other details that do not materialize throughout the course of the story, though. There is no incident in which she knocks over any lamp by sleeping on a short sofa. She never directly talks about any three-named, morbid poets—the poem about goblins that she relates to Mercury could well be James Whitcomb Riley's "Nine Little Goblins," but that is never stated.

For the sake of building her legend, the details that are left to the imagination are just as important as the ones that are dramatized in the immediate story. The life of Aunt Helen Beck is so amazing, so varied, that it would be too much to ask for a reader to want each one of these claims to manifest itself in this stay. It would be too formulaic: instead of appreciating Aunt Helen Beck and the others for their interesting, flexible personalities, the story would turn into a seek-and-find puzzle. As it is, the reference to Riley's goblin poem might already be too specific: so much is made of him in the introduction, with the flowers that young Helen Beck presented to him and his drunkenness, that bringing him up later would, unlike the molasses and the letters to the dead, confer upon him an importance that he does not really have in the story. McCracken avoids this mistake by leaving his name out of it. Readers can guess, at the mention of Aunt Helen Beck's reciting a poem, that it is probably by someone morbid who has three names, but the story does not say so, leaving it to be assumed without forcing the issue.

Understanding readers' assumptions might just be McCracken's greatest gift as a writer, which, given her control of language, her skill at innovation, and her understanding of eccentric personalities, is certainly saying a lot. In creating a legendary character such as Aunt Helen Beck, the author has to know which parts of her life to leave a mystery and which parts readers will feel the need to know. It is common for writers to get the balance wrong: to tell too much or to withhold too much. For instance, readers are eventually told why Georgie Beck was so important to this woman that she would spin her whole long life off her fabricated relationship to him: he is the one person in her life who she felt truly loved her. Readers can, therefore, see why the change purse, which he made and is a symbol of him, would be so very important to her. But why does it have two cents? Readers really do not need to know the answer to that question to understand this story, and McCracken understands that sometimes it is better to leave loose ends loose.

If all of the fascinating details about Aunt Helen Beck's life were explained by the end of this story, she would not be a legendary character, just a well-rendered one who behaves according to the currents of her past life. That would not do. This woman has lived a life of mystery, showing up on people's doorsteps and passing as a relative when she is in fact a stranger: it is a life that can only be followed by leaving some questions unanswered and, even more importantly, by making readers forget that they even have questions. Aunt Helen Beck has a talent for casting a spell over her hosts so that they enjoy the richness of her personality and then enjoy even more the things that they do not know about her. Elizabeth McCracken has the same skill, making her something of a legend herself.

Source: David Kelly, Critical Essay on "Here's Your Hat What's Your Hurry," in *Short Stories for Students*, Thomson Gale, 2007.

Thomson Gale

In the following essay, the critic gives an overview of Elizabeth McCracken's work.

Elizabeth McCracken is a novelist and short story writer whose work has been cited for deep and endearing characters and plots built on the vicissitudes of loving human relationships. Writing for *World and I*, Jill E. Rendelstei

> IN THE *LOS ANGELES TIMES BOOK REVIEW*, FRANCINE PROSE WROTE, 'MCCRACKEN'S ATTENTION TO DETAIL AND TO THE TRUTHS OF THE HUMAN HEART, HER EAR FOR THE RHYTHMS OF SPEECH, HER WRY, STRAIGHTFORWARD AND COMMONSENSICAL LITERARY VOICE GROUND EVEN THE MOST FANTASTIC TALES IN SOLID . . . REALITY.'"

claimed that McCracken "is a storyteller to the core, always giving us complete access to her realm of fantasy. But it is the vivid life within McCracken, her intensity as a person, and her love that show through in her writing, making it so distinctive and alive." *New York* reviewer Daniel Mendelsohn observed in McCracken's writing "a unity of potent elements: beauty of expression; a rather shy, almost offhand way with painful emotional insights; a truly wacky sense of humor; and a kind of disarming, old-fashioned charm." In the *New York Times Book Review*, Francine Prose praised McCracken for her "sense of play, a nervy willingness to imagine a wide range of characters and situations, estimable powers of empathy and the enjoyment of watching a talented writer beginning to come into her own."

McCracken's first published book was a collection of nine short stories titled *Here's Your Hat What's Your Hurry*, which was praised by reviewers both for its eccentric characters and its elegant writing style. In the *Los Angeles Times Book Review*, Francine Prose wrote, "McCracken's attention to detail and to the truths of the human heart, her ear for the rhythms of speech, her wry, straightforward and commonsensical literary voice ground even the most fantastic tales in solid . . . reality."

Uniting many of the stories in *Here's Your Hat What's Your Hurry* are the sometimes bizarre efforts characters make to insinuate themselves into the fabric of life. The opening tale of the collection, for example, tells the story of a young woman who turns her body into a "love letter" for Tiny, her husband who works as a tattoo artist. The collection's title story features "Aunt Helen," who arrives at the home of a Washington family for an extended visit—until it is discovered that she is an imposter who spends her time visiting one "relative" after another. In "What We Know about the Lost Aztec Children," an armless woman who lives in a suburb of Cleveland brings home an old friend from the time she spent as a sideshow performer in the circus. And in "Mercedes Kane," an Iowa woman gives a home to an eccentric woman in the belief that the woman is a famous 1940s child prodigy. Other stories feature a man who has finished serving a prison term for murdering his wife; two children whose father takes in drunks and deadbeats; and two men who become friends because each has a relative in a treatment facility for head-injury patients. Taken together, the stories, with their oddball characters and unconventional relationships, form a kind of lesson in the meaning of family, love, and connectedness, according to Prose in the *Los Angeles Times Book Review*.

McCracken followed *Here's Your Hat What's Your Hurry* with her first novel, *The Giant's House*. Written in a low-key style and lightened with touches of humor, *The Giant's House* is a modern fairy tale featuring Peggy Cort, an old-maid librarian living in a Cape Cod town in the 1950s. Peggy's world is a lonely, emotionless one, punctuated only by her dry wit ("In reference works, as in sin, omission is as bad as willful misbehavior") until the day she meets eleven-year-old James Sweatt, a gentle, six-foot two-inch schoolboy afflicted with gigantism. James, too, is lonely, and soon he and Peggy fill some of the emotional voids in one another's lives. His loving but eccentric family adopts Peggy, giving her contact with a life larger and more interesting than her own. James grows to more than eight feet tall and weighs over four hundred pounds, but in time his health declines and he finally succumbs to the disorder. Events take a surprising turn when Peggy becomes pregnant by James's long-lost father, and after she gives birth, she sees the child as the offspring of James himself.

Writing in the *New Yorker* about *The Giant's House*, Daphne Merkin asked rhetorically, "Who would have thought it—that you could take one overaged virgin and one oversized boy and end up with a story that captures

the feel of passion, its consuming hold?" Merkin answered her own question by pointing out the "incantatory power" that makes this unlikely romance between unlikely characters seem real and thoroughly grounded both in their characters and in the details of their lives. A *Publishers Weekly* reviewer commented, "McCracken shows herself a wise and compassionate reader of the human heart." Likewise, *BookPage* correspondent Laura Reynolds Adler concluded: "In the hands of McCracken, this unusual, unconsummated love story about a librarian who finds the courage to love is not scandalous, but sweet and inevitable."

Spanning the better part of a century, *Niagara Falls All Over Again* is the fictitious chronicle of a two-man comedy team, narrated by the straight man, Mose Sharp. Through recollections of episodes in his life, from a childhood in Des Moines, Iowa, to an adulthood making movies and money in Hollywood, Sharp reveals the central relationship that informs his life, his working partnership with fat funny-man Rocky Carter. Like its predecessor, the novel garnered good reviews. In her *BookPage* commentary, Jenn McKee called it "flat-out fun—a heartbreaking and exhilarating ride." Mendelsohn felt that the book "offers many of the pleasures familiar from [McCracken's] earlier work," adding: "McCracken's act is one that every lover of serious fiction should follow." In her *New York Times Book Review* piece, Francine Prose commended the novel for its ambitious scope. The critic observed: "McCracken manages to consider an impressive number of substantial ideas, to ruminate on subjects like the comic impulse, the eroticism of partnership, the congruences and differences between the theatrical and the authentic, the compulsions that might lead someone to become an entertainer, the payoffs and drawbacks of sacrificing one's personal life for art." *New York Times* columnist Janet Maslin praised the work for its "peculiarly sweet, gravity-defying bounce," suggesting further that "there is a tender quality to Ms. McCracken's descriptive powers." Maslin concluded of *Niagara Falls All Over Again:* "The best of [the] book brims with fondness for these game, playful characters and the lost wonders of the vaudeville world."

Source: Thomson Gale, "Elizabeth McCracken," in *Contemporary Authors Online*, Gale, 2002.

Sybil Steinberg

In the following review, Steinberg discusses McCracken's career and the use of eccentric characters in unusual relationships in her work.

Forget Marian the Librarian. Elizabeth McCracken pursued the profession for a decade, but she'll never fit the stereotype of a stern or sedate guardian of bibliophilic decorum. An engagingly forthright young woman who takes her comic turn of mind seriously, McCracken writes books about idiosyncratic characters who find themselves in unlikely situations. Her second novel, *Niagara Falls All Over Again* (Forecasts, May 28), out this month from Dial Press, is the exuberant and poignant saga of a two-man comedy team whose physical appearances and personalities (the fall guy: fat and dopey; the straight man: thin and sporting a mortarboard) are only the outward manifestations of an inspired and loving companionship ultimately riven by a fundamental difference in their views of life.

Eccentric characters joined in unconventional relationships are a hallmark of McCracken's fiction. In general, they're aware of their place on the outposts of society, accustomed to loss, searching for connection and love. The tall woman married to a tiny tattoo artist who maps his wife's entire body with his art in the short story collection *Here's Your Hat What's Your Hurry* is one such example, as is the armless wife and mother in another tale, whose gift to her children is to make herself seem normal. McCracken's first novel, *The Giant's House*, is narrated by a lonely librarian in her mid-20s who befriends and then falls in love with a young boy afflicted with gigantism, despite the 15-year difference in their ages. McCracken presents all her characters with a mixture of dry wit and bemused tolerance. A characteristic tone of plangent nostalgia is leavened by snappy, tart dialogue, quirky but surprisingly apt similes (one character is "as chinless and gloomy as a clarinet," another's eyebrows are "so plucked that they looked like two columns of marching ants") and aperçus that resonate with earthy wisdom.

Beginning in the 1920s, *Niagara Falls All Over Again* chronicles the life of Mose Sharp, scion of a Jewish family from Valley Junction, Iowa, a suburb of Des Moines. The only boy among six sisters, Mose decides early on that he'll be stifled if he takes over his father's haberdashery. Mose and his older sister Hattie plan to

IN CONTRASTING HER CHARACTERS' HOPEFUL BEGINNINGS AND THE VICISSITUDES OF THEIR TROUBLED LIVES, SHE MAINTAINS A SYMPATHETIC UNDERSTANDING OF THE RESILIENCE OF THE HUMAN SPIRIT."

run away and become stars in vaudeville, but after a stunning tragedy, Mose goes on the road alone. When pudgy comedian Rocky Carter anoints Mose as his straight man, a nerdy know-it-all called the Professor, the team of Carter and Sharp savor the heady rush of fame, first on the vaudeville circuit, then in Hollywood. The lifelong partnership is both enriching and all-consuming. It's only after he marries and has children that Mose realizes the downside of the relationship, the way Rocky's self-destructive personality threatens to rob Mose's own life of warmth and tenderness. A constant thread throughout the narrative is Mose's wonder at the miracle that a Jewish boy from Iowa (Mose's father was born Jakov Sharansky in Lithuania) could gain celebrity and wealth.

McCracken says she did not intend that Mose would be the protagonist of her narrative. She had begun a novel about the Jewish population of Des Moines, based loosely on the experiences of her mother's family. "Everyone in my family loves to tell stories," she says, recalling her delight as a child when her mother talked about her own early years. An elderly cousin was another repository of family anecdotes; it was she who showed McCracken two photos that haunted her imagination. Both were of the real Mose, a great uncle. One showed him as a young man, "in a very theatrical pose, looking beautiful, with thick black hair," McCracken remembers. The other picture captured him in his 50s, "looking broken. He's wearing an undershirt, he's bald, and he has a cigarette dangling from his mouth. He became a shopkeeper. And my cousin said to me: 'It's a shame he wasn't born into another family. He should have gone into vaudeville. He was so funny.'"

In typical fashion, McCracken acknowledges her unromantic Midwestern setting in the novel's first sentence: "This story—like most of the stories in the history of the world—begins far away from Des Moines, Iowa." Yet to McCracken, who was born in Boston and raised there and in Portland, Ore., annual visits to Des Moines made it "the constant in my childhood." Her grandmother Ruth Jacobson, a lawyer and a tireless civic activist, was a magnetic figure. Grandma spun endless reminiscences about her own grandfather, Des Moines's first ordained rabbi; his son (her father), the owner of a furniture store; and her 10 siblings, all of whom earned professional degrees. During McCracken's two years of postgraduate study at the Iowa Writers Workshop, she visited her grandmother often; *Here's Your Hat* is dedicated to her. Ruth Jacobson died three months after the book was published, but not before she'd had a chance to take McCracken around town and introduce her as "the youngest person ever to publish a novel." "The only thing true in that sentence is that I'm a person," McCracken says with a smile. "It was not a novel, and I wasn't even close to being the youngest. But she wanted to make sure her enthusiasm was commensurate with her pride in me."

McCracken herself relates family stories with gusto. She has a mobile and expressive face, with earnest brown eyes and heavy brows that furrow when she carefully considers a response to *PW*'s questions. Dark brown hair curls haphazardly over her shoulders. Her full lips seem designed for pouting until they break into a grin that awakens the trace of a dimple. When she meets *PW* in a cafe in Manhattan, she's wearing a demure black blouse turned camp by a necklace with luridly colored medallions of old-time cartoon characters (Blondie, Skeezix, Smilin' Jack), a chic white skirt and black net stockings that would be comfortable doing the can-can. She's in town from her home in a Boston suburb to hear her agent, Henry Dunow, read from his new memoir, *A Way Home*. It's given her a chance to eat an Abbott and Costello sandwich at Lindy's and to buy her older brother, Harry, a nest of Russian dolls that portray a riot of Fleisher comic-book characters in diminishing sizes.

It was her brother's interest in old comic strips, radio shows and movies that awakened McCracken's self-styled "obsession with the past." The siblings watched "hundreds of films

with every comedy team there was," she says. Now a computer journalist, Harry still shares her frame of reference. They're both members of a "tent" or chapter, of the international Laurel and Hardy society called Sons of the Desert. McCracken was watching a tape of the last Laurel and Hardy movie, *Atoll K*, when she heard Hardy utter a line that she later used for *Niagara Falls*'s epigraph. "Haven't I always taken care of you? You're the first one I think of." The quote encapsulates Carter and Sharp's symbiotic bond. One of McCracken's last research forays for the book was a sentimental journey with her brother to L.A., where they attended a 90th birthday party for one of Harry's friends, the legendary animation designer Maurice Noble. Noble's clear memory of filmland in the 1930s and '40s provided McCracken with authentic background material. He died soon afterward.

The dedication to *Niagara Falls* offers a clue to McCracken's wisecracking fictional voice: "To Samuel and Natalie Jacobson McCracken/ My favorite comedy team." In explanation, McCracken says, "I come from a family of tremendously eccentric people." According to McCracken, her parents are deadpan comics of memorable wit, albeit temperamentally unmatched. Her father is quiet and reserved, with an encyclopedic memory; her mother is social and outgoing. Physically, too, they are a startling contrast. Samuel McCracken, a Chaucer scholar who for three decades has been Provost John Silber's assistant at Boston University, is "6′2″ or 6′3″—a really big guy." Natalie McCracken is 4′11″, and she walks with two canes, the result of a birth injury. She holds a Ph.D. in theater, and is head of publications at BU. "They're a distinctive couple," McCracken says, "sort of a team of their own. You can recognize their silhouettes from blocks away."

Her parents' tolerance of their mixed-religion marriage undoubtedly influenced McCracken's eclectic view of human nature. When they visited Des Moines, McCracken's family worshiped both at the Cottage Grove Presbyterian Church and her grandmother's temple. Her ecumenical grandmother Jacobson believed to the end of her life that Easter was a secular holiday. Grandfather McCracken was a professor of classics at Drake and the editor and publisher of *American Genealogy* magazine. From both sides of the family, McCracken stresses, she received a strict sense

of right and wrong, and a feeling of civic obligation. "A combination of guilt and moral imperatives never hurt anybody," she deadpans.

McCracken's own career path has followed
parallel channels. She took a part-time job at the
Newton, Mass., local library when she was 15,
and stayed there seven years, through high
school and college. Early on, she determined
that being a librarian would be her "money
job," and she earned a library science degree
in 1993. Meanwhile, she devoted herself to writing fiction. Her books carry acknowledgments
and thank-yous to Sue Miller, who taught
McCracken creative writing at BU, and Allan
Gurganus, who was her teacher at Iowa. During
her first session at the Fine Arts Work Center in
Provincetown, in 1990, she met Ann Patchett,
who was working on *The Patron Saint of Liars*.
She and Patchett became fast friends and first
readers of each other's works. "We understand
how much to say to each other," McCracken
observes. "We have very similar views of fiction
writing, but extremely different methods. She's
very plot oriented, and I'm not so handy with
plot. She writes much tighter first drafts than I
do. My first drafts are horrific and inefficient; I
write pages and pages that don't get into the
book. She's very good at seeing the book within
the book."

A tight circle of other writer friends (she
thanks Karen Bender, Bruce Holbert and Max
Phillips, among others) also offer advice. It was
Phillips who recommended McCracken to agent
Henry Dunow, during McCracken's second year
at Iowa. Dunow read several of her stories over a
weekend, and called her up on the following
Monday. Since McCracken says she never
thought ahead to possible publication, she's
grateful for the benevolence of fate. "I'm appalling about the future," she says. "It's not that I
lack ambition; it's that I lack forethought."

Even *Here's Your Hat* being the last book
with the Turtle Bay imprint turned out to be
lucky for McCracken. Susan Kamil went to
Dial Press, where she edited *The Giant's House*,
which was an NBA finalist in 1996 and earned
McCracken a place on Granta's Best Young
American Novelists list that same year, and the
current novel. "She's a great editor," says
McCracken of Kamil, "one of the best. She
rarely says she doesn't like something in my
work. She asks leading questions about my
intentions, and sometimes she tells me I haven't

got there yet," McCracken says. "I really need
everything slapped out of my hands. I'm an
endless reviser." That same focus on the present,
and the past that formed it, determines the voices
in her work. All are first-person narratives,
whose protagonists' distinctive voices come to
her easily. "I end up thinking like the character
I'm writing about," she says, confessing an
instinctive empathy for people on the fringes.
"I think that people are more eccentric as a whole
than popular culture would have you believe,"
she observes with the air of one who dares you to
disagree. "The moment that someone reveals
some strange quirk, I begin to like them a lot."
McCracken's favorite book is *A Confederacy of
Dunces*; she says that her own work is "never as
funny as I want it to be." Her interest in the past
also determines the structure of her fiction,
because "the only way I know how to give my
books resonance is by going to the backstory."
In contrasting her characters' hopeful beginnings and the vicissitudes of their troubled
lives, she maintains a sympathetic understanding
of the resilience of the human spirit.

McCracken gave up her library job to write
The Giant's House, but she went back to work
there two days a week for a while after that book
was published. Now she sometimes misses her
former career. "As a writer, you're essentially
alone, and you're necessarily the most important
person in the world. That's not psychologically
healthy. If you've got a family to balance it out,
maybe you're not so self-absorbed. For a librarian, though, there's a fuller spectrum. People
come in and say: 'I need this, or I need that' ...
I love the sheer randomness of it."

Appropriately, the sheer randomness of life
acquires enchanting resonance in McCracken's
fiction.

Source: Sybil Steinberg, "A Priest & a Rabbi Walk into a
Bar...," in *Publishers Weekly*, Vol. 248, No. 32, August
6, 2001, pp. 56–57.

Brendan Dowling

*In the following interview, McCracken discusses
her career as a librarian, her writing style, and
what and who helps shape her stories and
characters.*

Elizabeth McCracken first came to the
attention of the literary world in 1993 with her
debut collection of short stories, *Here's Your
Hat, What's Your Hurry*, an ALA notable
book. These stories, populated by heavily

tattooed librarians, faded child prodigies, and retired circus freaks, were widely praised by critics. Shortly thereafter, *Granta Magazine* named her one of the Best Young American Novelists. Her 1996 novel *The Giant's House*, which revolves around the idiosyncratic relationship between a librarian and her eight-foot-tall patron, was met with critical acclaim and listed as one of the National Book Award finalists. McCracken, a former public librarian, currently resides just outside of Boston where she is finishing her second novel, *Niagara Falls All Over Again*, to be published in 2001.

[*Brendan Dowling*:] *I'm interested in what drew you to library school. By the time you began your MLS work, you had already sold your first book of short stories and earned an MFA from the Iowa Writer's Conference at the University of Iowa. What made you decide to become a librarian at that point?*

[Elizabeth McCracken:] I'd already decided some years before that. On my fifteenth birthday, I walked into the Newton (Mass.) Free Library and got a job shelving fiction A–SM (it was a wonderfully strange old building, and fiction SM–Z was in another room). I stayed there for seven years, eventually working behind the circulation desk, and I loved every minute of it—a lot of that had to do with my boss, Cathy Garoian, who was one of the great circulation librarians of all time. (Circulation is still my favorite department.) I left to go to grad school, but I always knew I'd come back to library work one way or the other.

An MFA is not a professional degree. I really wasn't fit for employment once I had one, especially because I didn't want to teach five sections of composition a semester, which was the kind of job I would've gotten had I been very lucky. Some writers have no trouble working jobs they hate and then coming home to write. Not me. I wanted my "money" job to be something as gratifying as writing. 1 didn't want to have to scramble for work. And, besides that, I really loved being a civil servant. I miss library work. I miss having colleagues and regular patrons.

A lot of your work focuses on marginalized members of society, and you have been praised for your ability to humanize eccentric characters (like the suburban mother who used to be a circus freak in "What We Know About the Lost Aztec Children," *and James in* The Giant's House). *What draws you to these characters?*

The general population is much more eccentric than much pop culture would have you believe. That's what I think. People are idiosyncratic; the "average" American is much less interesting than any individual "real" American. I think that I'm drawn to people who are physically anomalous because I believe they really are as ordinary as anyone, and because I'm interested in how who we are physically both defines us and doesn't define us.

You've talked in past interviews about borrowing events from your mother's life to put in stories, and your family has made cameos in your work (e.g., your Aunt Blanche in A Giant's House). *How else has your family affected your writing?*

Oh, in every way. First of all, I come from a family of writers (my parents and my brother are also professional writers, though not of fiction); both my parents came from families filled with professional and amateur artists. Nobody ever thought that becoming a writer was an odd thing to do. Nobody suggested that I should go to law school. (There are also a lot of librarians in my mother's family.)

Now, I don't know whether my family really *is* more eccentric than other people's, or whether they're just less inhibited about their eccentricities. I grew up hearing stories about family members on both sides, and some of those characters—my great-great-aunt Mary George, my great-great-uncle Mose, my great-aunt Edna—had died long before I was born but were nevertheless as vivid to me as if they'd been living. Maybe more vivid. There's a kind of resonance that happens when you hear story after story about relatives you don't know, and that resonance is what turns a collection of anecdotes into a novel. It matters that Aunt Mary George's first husband was a butcher who killed himself; if you've heard enough Aunt Mary George stories, you think: Of course he was a butcher! Of course he killed himself!

I also have a great resource in my father, whose memory is—and I don't use this word lightly in a library publication—encyclopedic. This week, I had to call him up with questions about train service in the Midwest in the 1930s. Just being a train buff does not explain his ability to immediately tell me how someone would get from Des Moines, Iowa, to Los Angeles, California, in December of 1939, and what the dining car would look like, and whether the train was all-Pullman or not. He knows everything. I think my tendency to want to cram as much information into a novel or short story as I can—for me, revision is often a matter of weeding extraneous information out—comes from listening to my father talk about his various passions, a sort of did-you-know-the-following-fascinating-fact approach to writing.

You have a very unique writing style. Daphne Merkin likened you to a lot of Southern authors, but your editor, Susan Kamil, talks about how you subvert the Southern Gothic style with an almost New England-like pragmatism. Would you agree with these assessments? What writers, past and present, do you look up to?

I do love Southern Gothic writers, especially Carson McCullers. *The Heart is a Lonely Hunter* is one of my favorite books of all time. I've recently been rereading the work of another Gothic writer, Nathanael West, though he's sort of hardboiled Californian Gothic. Like most novelists I know, I worship *Lolita*. I love Dickens and Browning and Ralph Ellison and Tennessee Williams. Among living writers: Rose Tremain, Grace Paley, Calvin Trillin, Studs Terkel, Jonathan Ames, Barbara Gowdy, Edwige Danticat, Frank Bidart—I'm limiting my choices to people I don't know personally, because I know too many writers whose work I love and I don't want to leave anyone out.

The older I get, the more direct inspiration I get from poetry. Some of that might have to do with knowing more poets.

Talk a little bit about the library programs that you and fellow author Ann Patchett have presented. What has it been like returning to libraries in a different role?

As writers, we have similar world views but entirely different approaches. We love and deeply respect each other's work—there's nobody I can imagine trusting with my work the way I trust Ann. I can send her something in a very tender stage, and she's somehow able to see what it will eventually become. So we talk about our friendship and our work relationship, and we talk about how different we are as writers. We both love fielding questions, and I love hearing her answer. Once we appeared at a private girls' school together. Ann talked nostalgically about her own school days, and how she loved her uniform (she went to Catholic school; the girls at this academy wore kilts). I said, "I never had to wear a uniform," and the woman who was showing us around said, "We know. We can tell by your writing."

I don't think that explains the difference in our work, but it certainly explains the difference in our personalities, and maybe the difference in our work habits. Ann is much more disciplined. She once said that she would kill herself if she wrote as inefficiently as me—I write pages and pages and pages that never see the light of day. Her work is gorgeous and complicated and terrifically moving; at the same time, there's a real rigor when it comes to the plot and the goings-on of the physical world in her work that I could strive for and continually miss. I think maybe it all boils down to her having worn a kilt for twelve years of her childhood.

This is all to say: when we speak together, audiences get two pretty different kinds of writers, who nonetheless believe in each other's work.

I've given readings at libraries and talks at a few regional library conferences (in Texas, New Hampshire, New Jersey, and Massachusetts), and I always have a great time. Librarians and library users—they're my people. At a Texas Library Association meeting last year, I read a section from *The Giant's House* about library buildings (largely inspired by the Newton Free Library building) that talks about how all librarians, deep down, hate their buildings, and it was a little like preaching in church—librarians in the audience began to voice their agreement. If I had said, "Can I get an Amen?" I would have gotten several.

Whenever I read in a library, I want to ask if I can staff the circulation desk for half an hour. I've never done it, though.

What are you currently reading?

I am reading, in manuscript, a collection of wonderful essays called *Famous Builder* by Paul Lisicky (whose first novel, *Lawnboy*, won an ALA Gay and Lesbian Roundtable Award—I think I got the name of that right). Patchett's next novel, *Bel Canto*, will be published by HarperCollins next year and is absolutely extraordinary. Just recently, I read *The Dream Songs* by John Berryman, and have been dipping into Elizabeth Bishop's poetry.

What are you currently working on?

I'm just finishing a novel called *Niagara Falls All Over Again*. It's about a comedy team, two guys who work in vaudeville and eventually hit it big in movies. It just might kill me. Right now I'm typing the whole thing over, which is something I've never done before. I think it's a useful experience, but it's also pretty tedious.

What advice would you give to young writers?

The usual: read a lot, write a lot. One of my favorite pieces of writing wisdom is that in order to write well, you need to be willing to write badly. Some days I'm appalled by how true that is for me, though usually I find it inspiring: if there's a day that I hate everything I write, I can believe that I'm on my way to something better.

You need to be unafraid of making tremendous blunders. Tremendous, giant, ugly, heart-rending blunders—not just because good fiction takes risks, but because mistakes are the heart of good fiction. Anyone can take a class or read a book and follow a list of rules designed to keep students from making mistakes; you can teach yourself to write quite an unobjectionable story that way. And what, I ask you, is worse than an unobjectionable story?

When you're writing, save all your ambition for the page. Being too career ambitious will make you more fearful in your work.

Be willing to break your own heart.

Source: Brendan Dowling, "Be Willing to Break Your Own Heart: An Interview with Elizabeth McCracken," in *Public Libraries*, Vol. 40, No. 2, March/April 2001, pp. 91–92.

SOURCES

Ingraham, Janet, "Word of Mouth," in *Library Journal*, Vol. 118, No. 19, 1993, p. 128.

McCracken, Elizabeth, "Here's Your Hat What's Your Hurry," in *Here's Your Hat What's Your Hurry: Stories*, Turtle Bay Books, 1993, pp. 55–82.

Mendelsohn, Daniel, "Sophomore Shlump?" in *New York*, August 13, 2001, p. 56.

Pearl, Nancy, "The Reader's Shelf," in *Library Journal*, March 1, 2001, p. 164.

FURTHER READING

Felder, Leonard, *When Difficult Relatives Happen to Good People: Surviving Your Family and Keeping Your Sanity*, Rodale Press, 2005.

Felder's analysis of family dynamics, especially in relationship to extended families that span several generations, apply aptly to the interactions that take place between Aunt Helen Beck, Ford and Chris, and Mercury.

Ford, Charles V., *Lies! Lies!! Lies!!! The Psychology of Deceit*, American Psychiatric Publishing, 1999.

Despite its overexcited title, this is actually a very scholarly work on what makes people like Aunt Helen Beck live their lives deliberately trying to mislead others. Even so, it is written with a tinge of humor that renders its lessons in a way that anyone can appreciate and understand.

Gaines, Stephen, *Marjoe: The Life and Times of Marjoe Gortner*, Harper & Rowe, 1973.

This is the biography of a man who became an ordained Pentecostal preacher at the age of four, lived an early life of a con man, and became a movie star as an adult. His life story gives insight into the type of life that Georgie Beck may have lived and the type of man he may have become if he had survived his childhood illness.

Thompson, Tim, and Eric Scigliano, *Puget Sound: Sea between the Mountains*, Graphic Arts Center Publishing Company, 2000.

This book combines artistic photos and lyric prose to give readers a sense of the natural and cultural ambience of the area where this story takes place.

Last Night

JAMES SALTER

2002

James Salter's "Last Night" was first published in the *New Yorker* magazine in November 2002; it was reprinted in 2005 as the final story in a collection of the same name. Salter has been widely recognized for his treatment of the physical and spiritual conditions of people living in a culture that is increasingly adrift of traditional standards of faith, personal integrity, and civil behavior. Within the condensed recounting of the presumed last night of one woman's life, Salter manages to explore a number of volatile social issues, including the legalities and ethics of assisted suicide, the disintegration of a marriage under the pressures of an extramarital affair, and the general malaise of a certain kind of culture. Walter Such is a representative of masculinity and integrity for the new world of the late twentieth century, a man notable for his frayed moral fiber and for the double betrayal of the one woman he claims to have loved.

AUTHOR BIOGRAPHY

James Salter was born James Horowitz on June 10, 1925, in Passaic, New Jersey, but he was raised in New York City. Educated at the U.S. Military Academy at West Point (B.S., 1945) and later at Georgetown University (M.A., international affairs, 1950), Salter was a member of the U.S. Air Force (1945–1957), attaining the rank of lieutenant colonel during the Korean War. Given that he flew more than one hundred combat missions, it

James Salter Photograph by Ed Betz. AP Images

MEDIA ADAPTATIONS

- The story "Last Night" was adapted as a short film by Sean Mewshaw in 2002, starring Frances McDormand (Marit Such), Jamey Sheridan (Walter Such), and Sheeri Rappaport (Susanna). Although difficult to find in standard retail outlets, many public and school libraries as of 2007 had access to copies through lending networks.

seems natural that Salter's first two novels would draw on his air force years, specifically on his adventures as a fighter pilot. Both the much-acclaimed *The Hunters* (1957; revised as *Counterpoint* in 1999) and the forgettable *The Arm of Flesh* (1961; revised as *Cassada* in 2001) explore the coded politics and personal pains that define modern war experiences. *The Hunters* was adapted for film in 1958, with Robert Mitchum starring as fighter pilot Major Cleve Saville.

After leaving the air force, Salter expanded his writing repertoire to include screenplays for film and television. His short documentary film about college football, entitled *Team, Team, Team,* won a first prize at the 1962 Venice Film Festival. Salter followed this early success with more than a dozen television documentaries (including a ten-part series on circus life) as well as a handful of film screenplays, most notably *Downhill Racer* (1969), which starred Robert Redford and won Salter a Writers' Guild of America nomination for best screenplay; *Three* (1969), an adaptation of an Irwin Shaw story that Salter also directed; and the sci-fi drama, *Threshold* (1981). In an interesting twist on the traditional relationship between film and literature,

Salter converted one of his rejected screenplays (for a movie about mountain climbing) into his 1979 novel, *Solo Faces*, which acquired cult status worldwide among climbers.

While his television and film work flourished, so too did Salter's literary career. His early novels revealed his eye for detail and nuance and his ongoing interest in the frustrations and struggles of lives defined by marriage and career breakdowns, debilitating addictions, and failed dreams. Salter's characters are trapped in a kind of earthly purgatory and weakened spiritually. In his 1975 novel, *Light Years*, for instance, he traces the decay and dissolution of a suburban marriage.

In 1997, Salter published *Burning the Days: Recollections*, a book ten years in the writing and noted for its intimate portrayal of the pilot's life and its reflections on the writer's life. His 1988 collection, *Dusk and Other Stories*, was awarded the PEN/Faulkner Award, and Salter was a finalist for the same award in 2006 for *Last Night*. Salter was honored as New York State Author from 1998 to 2000. As of 2006, Salter was married to the playwright Kay Eldredge. He continued to write as both a vocation and an inspiration to explore the world.

PLOT SUMMARY

"Last Night" is a compact story that focuses on the presumed last night of Marit Such, who is dying from metastasized uterine cancer. Rather than suffer a slow and debilitating death, Marit solicits the assistance of her husband, Walter, in taking her life by an overdose of her prescription painkiller. As Marit arranges herself and her affairs in preparation for her last night, she invites a young and beautiful family friend, Susanna, to join the couple for Marit's "farewell dinner" and to support Walter as he struggles to deal with the repercussions of the events of the evening.

As Marit organizes her personal possessions, she thinks often about the changes in her body and about how she must look to others as the cancer strips away her physical vitality and her forceful spirit. She laments quietly to her husband that having "no energy" is "the most terrible part" of her condition. "It's gone," she explains. "It doesn't come back," and she is no longer able "to get up and walk around." In these moments, too, she drifts gently into memories of being a girl, of the home that she has built with Walter, and of the time before the cancer.

Knowing that she has a syringe and vial of morphine sitting securely in the refrigerator, Marit turns her attention to dinner and conversation with the twenty-nine-year-old Susanna. Interrupted only momentarily when they change rooms in the hotel restaurant in order to avoid a "talkative couple" whom Walter and Marit know, the dinner is a quiet affair highlighted by two bottles of very expensive wine. Softening the emotions of the evening, the wine brings to Marit's spirit a gentle melancholy, a mood that continues to hold her during the car ride home.

Upon the group's return from dinner, Walter becomes increasingly nervous as he considers again his role in the plan that is drawing ominously nearer. With a translator's eye for subtleties and minutiae, he imagines, though "trie[s] not to dwell on," the details of the arrangement: how the refrigerator light will come on when the door is opened, the angle of the stainless-steel point of the syringe, and the vein into which he will insert the point. Breaking Walter's momentary reverie, Marit recalls her own mother's final stories about the various sexual affairs that had shocked the previous generation. Almost abruptly, her storytelling ends, and she declares herself ready to go upstairs, taking the steps to prepare herself for the final stages of the last night. Left alone with Susanna, Walter pleads with the younger woman to stay in the house, to be in the lighted room when he

comes downstairs after administering the injection to his wife. Susanna's hesitation to become more deeply involved in the evening is obvious, and their conversation is stilted before collapsing into silence.

In the kitchen, Walter nervously prepares the syringe of morphine, lingering momentarily in the memories of past summers when he and Marit had made strawberry preserves in the old-fashioned kitchen. With the final arrangements made, Walter feels less and less attached to the reality of the moment, becoming in his own mind as "light as a sheet of paper, devoid of strength." In the bedroom upstairs, Marit has taken great care in preparing herself, making up her eyes and selecting "an ivory satin nightgown, low in back" as the "gown she would be wearing in the next world." As weariness settles into Marit's body, so too does a deep nervousness, which, despite the wine of the evening, seems to also be taking a toll on Walter, who rushes back downstairs to pour and quickly drink a glass of vodka that he hopes will steel his nerves.

Returning to the bedroom, Walter and Marit declare their love for each other and reminisce briefly about when they first met and began dating. As he injects his wife with the lethal dosage of morphine, Walter is overwhelmed by the silence of the house and by the ambiguous balance of "enormous relief and sadness."

Returning slowly downstairs, Walter seeks out Susanna, who has been waiting in her car, unable to leave but also unable to stay in the house. Re-entering the house, the two continue to drink and talk, revealing that their friendship has been, in fact, much more intimate than they had been letting on. Susanna wonders aloud if Marit might have known of their supposedly clandestine affair before inviting her to dinner, but Walter reassures her that his wife had no idea and no ulterior motive to her invitation. Their conversation gives way inevitably to a passionate night of lovemaking; having put the body of his wife to rest, Walter finds comfort and pleasure in the body of the younger lover whom he has been hiding, or so he believes, from his wife.

As the morning breaks, Walter thinks about the calls that need to be made following Marit's death and the memories of his first sight of Susanna. Surprised from his daydream by a sound behind him, he turns to see Marit descending the stairs from the upstairs bedroom, still alive due to Walter's ineptitude with the syringe. Her remark is direct and tragic in its appeal: "I thought you were going to help me." Walter's final words of apology echo pathetically, as he pleads with her before running out of words totally: "'I'm sorry,' he said. 'I'm so sorry.' He could think of nothing more to say.'" At Marit's re-entry into his world, Walter is speechless, unable to respond to her questions about what went wrong and unable to console her in her most intense suffering, as she realizes the double betrayal of her husband. The story ends hauntingly though anticlimactically, with no direct reference to Marit's fate and a brief reference to the inevitable end of the relationship between Walter and Susanna.

CHARACTERS

Marit Such

Marit Such, wife of Walter, is a once-beautiful woman who is dying from metastasized uterine cancer. Her skin, once luminescent, is now "pallid," and seems to "emanate a darkness," a corporeal reminder that she has become a physical and emotional shadow of the young woman she once was. Still a woman of strong resolve, however, she has decided to end her life with an overdose of her prescription morphine, assisted by her husband, after an evening of fine food and even finer wine. As the preparations for her last night continue, Marit comes to recognize both the joys and the difficulties that have accumulated over her lifetime. It is a realization that leaves her frightened, searching for a certainty from which she might gain strength for what lay ahead. Reflecting upon what she remembers as happy days, for instance, she allows "a frightening smile" to cross her face, one that "seemed to mean just the opposite" of what it appears to signal. During dinner, she comments, for instance, that she never had a child and that her friendships, though plentiful, have never reached a depth of intimacy that has sustained her fully or completely. She is a woman of surfaces and of an inner peace that is more illusion than reality.

On the eve of her own death, Marit orchestrates a dinner that includes a mutual friend, the young and beautiful Susanna, whom she intuits is having an affair with her husband. Their conversation is stilted and elliptical, hinting at issues of mutual concern but never addressing directly

the implications of their decisions and indecisions. As the evening progresses, Marit drinks to numb the physical and emotional pain yet she holds onto a belief in the beauty of the world and the inevitability of her own role in it. Following an elaborate and almost ritualized preparation, the lethal dose of morphine is injected, and Marit finds a momentary peacefulness in the belief that "she would live again, be young again as she once had been." When the assisted suicide goes wrong, however, and Marit lives to see another morning, she awakens into the same old world and a new understanding of the meaninglessness of her own life, of her husband's very visible weaknesses, and of the illusions that had sustained her marriage.

Walter Such

Walter Such is a translator, primarily of Russian and German, and is a "sometimes prickly man," susceptible to an overblown sense of his own intellectual prowess, moral and emotional strength, and the broad-mindedness of his attitudes towards such issues as sex, marriage, and art. "In good health," with a "roundish scholarly stomach" and "hands and nails well cared for," he has remained detached from the passions of life, living through the words and ideas of others rather than bringing a creative spirit to the world himself.

Having agreed to assist his wife in her suicide, he finds himself hesitant and unsure as the preparations progress, gradually coming to recognize his weak resolve and his fear at the thought of being alone in the world. Bracing himself with alcohol, he finds himself overwhelmed in the moments after the supposedly fatal injection by a telling blend of "enormous relief and sadness."

It is a depth of feeling, however, that lasts only briefly, as the narcissistic Walter gives in to his sexual desire for Susanna, with whom he has been having an affair as his wife struggled with cancer. In the end, he proves himself a man who understands the world as a reflection of his own needs and desires. When he awakens into a morning that is defined in his own mind by the presence of a new lover rather than by the absence of his late wife, Walter is peaceful, calm, and at ease. It is only when forced to confront the fact that he has botched the injection that Walter faces the a new world in which neither wife nor lover has faith in him. All he can manage to say, in the end, is "I am sorry . . . I am so sorry."

TOPICS FOR FURTHER STUDY

- Research the history of the concept of beauty, from its classical origins through to modern implications in the fashion and cosmetic industry. Make a timeline that traces the major shifts in the understanding of the term, with a visual representation of how the ideal of beauty might have looked across the centuries.

- Research the debate over euthanasia or assisted suicide. Write a summary of the key points of the arguments on both sides, including legal protections being put in place that might protect individuals who wish to end their own lives. Be balanced in your research, as though you are preparing for a debate that might position you on either side of the issue.

- Study the subject of memory. How do memories form and where do researchers believe that they are stored? What triggers recall of remembered events, and how accurate are these memories? Write an essay describing how memory works, making reference to the

flashbacks that both Marit and Walter experience in Salter's story.

- Imagine that you have been asked to select a song (from any era and any genre) that you feel captures most effectively the main theme, idea, or tone of "Last Night." Write an essay in which you discuss the song that you have selected, giving the main reasons why you selected it. Be sure to avoid general and vague comments. Instead, focus on specific elements of the song (specific lines or words in the lyrics, for instance) and explain in detail how these specific elements of your song correspond to specific moments, words, or images in the story.

- Research the Russian symbolist movement and the style of Alexander Blok's poetry, both of which explored the mysteries of common events and everyday things. Write a poem in the symbolist style that celebrates a room in your home, a meal that you have enjoyed, or an aspect of your daily routine.

Susanna

Susanna is twenty-nine years old, unmarried by choice, and exuding a blend of physical beauty and liberal attitudes. With a casual seductiveness and an appearance that reminds those who see her of "the daughter of a professor or banker, slightly errant," Susanna is both a healthy, youthful counterpoint to Marit and a physical reminder of the illusions of depth and harmony that have been erected around the marriage. Fueled by the wine she consumes over the course of the evening as well as by her sense that she is a source of salvation for the older man, she gives in to Walter's ill-timed and shockingly disrespectful sexual advances, only to find herself positioned as witness to Marit's unplanned survival. Following the debacle of the last night, Susanna returns to the sexual relationship

with Walter a few more times, before walking away without any lingering sense of responsibility or guilt. Susanna is the embodiment of a moral and spiritual decay that, like Marit's cancer, cannot be excised from the world.

THEMES

The Illusions of a Good Death

"Last Night" explores the morality and ethics of euthanasia, a word derived from the Greek terms for *eu* (good) and *thanatos* (death). Marit wants to die with dignity. Exhausted by advanced cancer, she moves in her final arrangements towards a deeper engagement with the world. As she prepares herself for the evening, she recalls with fondness the gentle moments and quiet beauty in the everyday world in which she has lived. She remembers, for instance, the wonders of watching "the swirling storms of long-ago winters" and of "the lamplight in which her mother was holding out a wrist, trying to fasten a bracelet." As her last night unfolds, Marit begins, too, to recognize similar small wonders in a world that she has until now taken for granted; she comes to appreciate deeply, for instance, the taste of the fine red wine and the beauty of the night sky and the "brilliant blue clouds, shining as if in daylight." In planning and scheduling her own good death, Marit comes to see clearly the small things that gather, over the course of a lifetime, to make a "beautiful life."

At the same time, however, "Last Night" works to undercut the apparent dignity of Marit's decision, revealing a culture that is driven more by vanity and self-centeredness than by compassion. Marit's world-weariness is symptomatic of a chronic malaise in the world of the story that makes a good death unlikely. Marit lives in a world of idle chatter, seemingly casual affairs, and spirits weakened by alcohol and years of intellectual stagnation. In short, her world is lacking in the strength of spirit and conviction that such a dramatic and morally conflicted act as euthanasia demands.

Nowhere is this subversion of the good death more evident than in the actions and attitudes of Walter, who has agreed to assist his wife during the course of her last night. Weak in mind and body, he botches the injection and then has sex with his mistress shortly after injecting his wife. Walter shows himself to be wholly "devoid of strength" and unable to assist in any way in the realization of his wife's good death. Rather than reinforcing the connection between husband and wife, and more generally between human beings, Marit's decision to arrange her own death leaves all the people involved in the evening feeling more isolated, more distanced from their own humanity, and more detached from the wonders of life and its passing. As the narrator observes in one of the final sentences of the story, the failure of the last night leaves all involved knowing that "whatever holds people together was gone."

Life in an Age of Disbelief

"Last Night" presents a bleak picture of people whose lives have lost moral focus. Caught up in a culture of accumulation, the characters fill their days with interests that appear intellectually and spiritually stimulating but over time prove empty of stabilizing certainties. Surrounded by literature, art, natural beauty, fine foods and wine, these men and women are unable or unwilling to engage these offerings in meaningful ways. A professional translator, Walter, for instance, approaches the great literature of the German poet Rainer Maria Rilke (1875–1926) with the passion and sensitivity of "a mechanical device." Always willing to point out the beauty of Rilke's poetry by way of proving his intellectual superiority, he remains unable to recognize the resonances of the poetry in his own life and how the lines speak volumes about his own emotional, intellectual, and spiritual withdrawal from the world and from his marriage. Similarly, Marit, a woman of apparently fine taste, allows her appreciation of the finer things to settle quietly into an accumulation of "jewelry, bracelets and necklaces, and a lacquer box" full of rings. Living in a house full of "books on Surrealism, landscape design, or country houses," Marit is left, at the end of her life, to admit that her collection remains unread and unappreciated. As the narrator observes of Marit's final perusal of the bookshelves and the beautiful furniture that she has collected: "She looked at it all as if she were somehow noting it, when in fact it all meant nothing."

For Walter and Marit, the dulling effects of alcohol, and to a lesser degree sex, have overwhelmed the poetry and art that surrounds them. They drink rather than read or talk or engage with the world in a thoughtful way. They drink as a means of escaping the emptiness of their cluttered lives, which, however full of books and talkative friends it might appear, is proven on the last night to be void of any deep and lasting connections. Their lives, both individually and collectively, are defined by surfaces and veneers of caring and compassion rather than the dignity that Marit seems determined to embody with her final act.

STYLE

Point of View

The story is told in the third person by a narrator who remains independent of the actions that are taking place during Marit's last night but who at the same time has a subtly articulated opinion about the people, the decisions, and the general condition of the depicted culture. When Marit tries to remember her past as a happy time, for instance, the narrator recognizes in her "frightened smile" a flash of emotion that "seemed to mean just the opposite." The implications of this observation are clear: despite her best attempts to present to herself and to others an image of her life as happy and full, she is painfully aware of the illusion in surface harmonies and the inevitability of decay.

Chronology

Another important element in the construction of the story is the use of flashbacks, a strategy by which a character recollects, and often comments on, events or actions that occurred before the beginning of the story or in the historical past of the story. The flashbacks pull the story of Marit and Walter in two directions within the story. On those occasions when Walter or Marit remember earlier moments in their lives or their marriage, Salter imbues the story with a gentle nostalgia and with the sense of a couple that shares a quiet history of caring and respectful love. But when Walter later remembers his first vision of Susanna, "shapely and tall," readers are shown another side of this marriage, a darker, less respectful side that has remained hidden for years. It is this underside of the marriage that makes its appearance dramatically at the close of the story, when Marit walks in on Walter, thinking not of her absence from his world but of "mornings to come" with his lover Susanna.

Foreshadowing

Salter uses subtle foreshadowing in "Last Night," introducing episodes or images that allow for a fuller understanding of events that unfold later. When Marit recalls the "things" that her own mother wanted to tell her before she died, the story she recounts is of Rae Mahin and Anne Herring, two married women who had slept with the unmarried advertising man Teddy Hudner. Marit's story foreshadows the reader's later recognition that Marit possibly knew that her husband had begun an affair with Susanna, despite Walter's belief that "she didn't know a thing."

Irony

As the title of "Last Night" underscores, this is a story thick with irony, a term that comes from the Greek word *eironeia*, which originally referred to a strategy of dissimulation through understatement. The title of the story is proven ironic with Marit's appearance in the kitchen the morning after what was supposed to be her last night alive. The last night shows itself to be an evening of failure at so many levels, from the failed imagining of a good and dignified death and the inability of the intoxicated Walter to inject the morphine effectively to the failure of Walter to put his own appetites aside even temporarily.

Moreover, the arrogance of the characters in the story, and their seemingly blatant disregard for conventional morals, is proven to be a shadow of what Marit, Walter, and Susanna believe to be true about themselves. In this sense, Salter's story is a satire of the pretentiousness of an entire generation as it plods aimlessly forward, lacking the guidance of tradition and the appreciation of beauty in its moral as well as aesthetic form. As Marit descends the stairs, the image of Walter's self-proclaimed commitment to his wife and to their relationship is revealed for what it is, a thin covering over a hollowness of spirit and intellect. The sad irony of the story becomes the inability of these three people to see beyond their own grand illusions and their pseudo-liberal pretensions of superiority and open-mindedness.

HISTORICAL CONTEXT

Legalization of Euthanasia in the United States

With the development of medical science in the latter half of the nineteenth century, human experiences of pain and death were gradually disconnected from the spiritual meanings given to them in previous generations. The moment of death, once considered the transition from the corporeal to the spiritual realm of what Marit Such refers to as "an afterworld," became reconceptualized within the English-speaking world as a moment of loss, a literal and metaphoric stripping away of defining human characteristics. As early as 1887, such physicians as William Munk (*Euthanasia, or Medical Treatment in Aid of an Easy Death*, 1887) were writing in support of the value in assisted death in the cases of some terminally ill patients.

It was during this period, too, that the first proposals to legalize euthanasia in the United States appeared. Of particular concern to these early advocates was the means by which they might integrate a new openness toward even the idea of assisted suicide into a medical tradition that had long held at its philosophic and ethical core the first rule to do no harm. Often uttered in the same breath were concerns about the potential for abuse by both the medical community and the patient's family. These concerns remained at the forefront of the euthanasia debate as it evolved through the twentieth century, moving in and out of the public consciousness and intersecting regularly with related but distinct debates over such issues as eugenics and biomedical technologies.

A galvanizing moment in the history of this debate came in 1994 when the state of Oregon held a referendum that eventually introduced into law the first fully realized legalization of euthanasia in the United States. After various legal efforts had been made to reverse the decision, a second referendum was held in 1997, during which state voters strongly endorsed their initial decision. What has come to be known as the Death with Dignity Act took effect on October 27, 1997, making provisions by which terminally ill patients whose conditions will lead to death within six months can request and receive a prescription for a lethal dosage of medication. These patients can then administer the medications to themselves if and when they choose. (The Oregon law does not permit a physician or any other person to administer the lethal dose.) The formal screening process also guaranteed that the patient must be recognized as capable of making and communicating decisions about his or her health care, and the patient must make one written and two oral requests. There are also substantive safeguards in place to address such potentially contentious questions as the confirmation of the diagnosis and prognosis, the determination that the patient's judgment is not impaired by depression or other disorders, and the assurance that the patient has been fully informed of alternatives.

Despite predictions of widespread use, only a small number of people have actually taken the necessary steps to receive prescriptions for lethal doses of medication. Statistical reports in the *New England Journal of Medicine* indicate that from 1998 through 2001, for instance, only one hundred and forty patients received such prescriptions, and of those only ninety-one actually ingested the medications. Tellingly, most of the patients who have

chosen to end their lives under the terms and conditions of the Death with Dignity Act have, like Marit Such, suffered from metastatic cancer. Still, the debate over euthanasia continues in both public and private forums around the world, making Salter's imagined case relevant.

Family Values and Shifting Attitudes

Given that it is possible to date Salter's story as post-1990 (the wine that Walter orders with dinner is marked clearly as a 1989 vintage), "Last Night" can be read as commentary on shifting attitudes toward a wide range of family issues, most notably those associated with questions surrounding individual autonomy within marriage, pre- or extramarital sex, the politics of remaining single, and choosing to remain childless.

Shifts in attitudes toward family and personal relationships were particularly dramatic in the second half of the twentieth century. Women's employment in the public sphere increased dramatically and expanded to include mothers of young children. The marriage and baby booms that erupted after World War II were followed by steady and substantial declines, which makes Marit and Walter Such's childless marriage not as unusual as it would have been two or three generations earlier. Divorce rates accelerated in the post-1960 era, as did premarital sexual activity (fueled, in part, by the availability of the birth control pill), non-marital cohabitation, and out-of-wedlock childbirth. Put simply, the traditional institutions of family and marriage were being reconsidered and redefined within North American culture.

Although it might be expected that such shifting attitudes toward sex and marriage would be accompanied by greater tolerance toward extramarital affairs of the nature detailed in Salter's story, the inverse is, in fact, the case. If anything, the 1980s and 1990s saw an increased disapproval of extramarital affairs among both men and women. A *National Survey of Americans on Values*, undertaken by the Kaiser Family Foundation in 1998, for instance, reinforced a gathering body of statistical evidence that suggested by the late 1990s almost 90 percent of American men and women said that they believed extramarital sex was almost always wrong. Nearly 75 percent of the respondents also reported feeling that an affair while married was not only unacceptable but should not be tolerated by the other partner within the marriage.

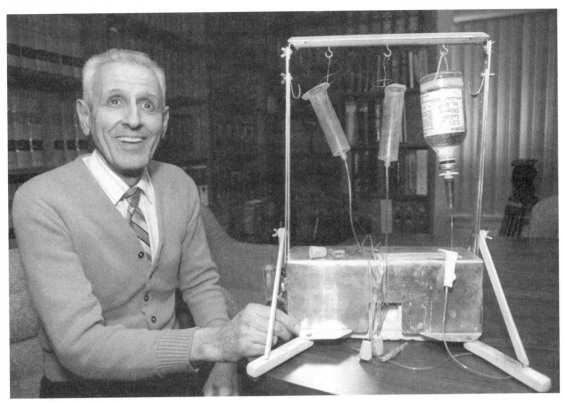

Dr. Jack Kevorkian, with his "suicide machine," brought the issue of assisted suicide to the forefront of national and state politics during the 1990s AP Images

CRITICAL OVERVIEW

Salter's collection *Last Night: Stories* was well-received by reviewers and served to reinforce his already-impressive reputation as a writer's writer with an uncanny eye for the undertones and subtleties of the world of manners and cultured people. Dinitia Smith writes of Salter's fiction generally in the *New York Times* (1997):

> In the universe of James Salter's novels, men are men and women don't have jobs. The characters drink Chateau Margaux and Kirs and Calvados. The women give the men long, narrow looks and say wry things, and when they make love, the earth does not just move. It quakes.

Such observations apply well to the stories collected in *Last Night: Stories*, as does the assessment of another *New York Times* writer, Adam Begley, who describes Salter's fictions as "a dazzling display of polished surfaces."

Reviewing the collection for *Booklist*, Brad Hooper wonders if "perhaps this collection of Salter's artful yet definitely embraceable short stories will shake him free of the impositions of

his reputation as a writer's writer." Celebrating Salter's prose as "subtle but not abstruse," Hooper marks Salter's keen eye in dealing with human relationships and his ability to find "corners of peculiarity to illuminate, even though outward appearances may seem so ordinary." Hooper's most singular praise is reserved for the title story of the collection, calling it "a tour de force about assisted suicide gone wrong—for several reasons. Salter's genius," he continues, "is most apparent in the effectiveness of this short and direct dialogue, which he uses not only to reflect real people talking but also to distill character to sheer essence."

Focusing on similar qualities, the reviewer for *Publishers Weekly* praises the "reserved, elegiac nature of Salter's prose" as the foundation of "stirring stories" that reveal themselves as "worthy additions to an admirable body of work." The same reviewer marks the title story as "especially impressive" in its movement toward "the haunting conclusion" that illuminates Walter's betrayal of his wife. As this reviewer notes, this is a powerful collection of

WHAT DO I READ NEXT?

- For another view of Salter's world, *There and Then: The Travel Writing of James Salter* (2006) offers a collection of two dozen essays recounting the global travels and observations of this peripatetic writer.

- The stories of John Cheever, like those of Salter, explore the spiritual and emotional emptiness of middle-class, suburban life. *The Stories of John Cheever* won the Pulitzer Prize for Fiction in 1979.

- Another frequent contributor to the *New Yorker* magazine, Canadian story writer Alice Munro writes in a much more elaborate style than Salter but focuses, as he does, on the ambiguities of life and on its open secrets and profound ironies. *No Love Lost* (2003) is an excellent sampler of Munro's work, bringing together ten of the best stories from her previously published books, with commentary by noted Canadian novelist Jane Urquhart.

- Readers who appreciate Salter's analysis of people who find their dreams overwhelmed by the pressures and disappointments of everyday life might also enjoy any of the following collections from Raymond Carver,

one of the most influential American story writers of the twentieth century: *Will You Please Be Quiet, Please* (1976), *What We Talk About When We Talk About Love* (1981), or *Cathedral* (1983).

- A minimalist in the tradition of Carver, Amy Hempel turns in her collection *The Dog of Marriage* (2005) to often dark, angular explorations of love (in its many forms) and the disintegrations of marriage. It was published the same year as Salter's *Last Night: Stories.*

- For a novel-length exploration of the spiritual and emotional malaise that weighs heavily on the life energies of suburban America, Jeffrey Eugenides's 1993 novel *The Virgin Suicides* is a provocative read. Set in the 1970s, the novel recounts the stories of the suicides of the five Lisbon sisters and the impact their decisions have on a seemingly happy community forced to make sense of their seemingly senseless deaths. Director Sofia Coppola adapted this novel into a critically acclaimed movie of the same title in 1999.

"compact, unsettling stories" of "teetering marriages, collapsing relationships and other calamites of the heart."

CRITICISM

Klay Dyer

Dyer holds a Ph.D. in English literature and has published extensively on fiction, poetry, film, and television. He is also a freelance university teacher, writer, and educational consultant. In the following essay, he explores the failure of Walter and Marit Such to engage in a meaningful

way the attitudes and philosophies of a Lost Generation that they so clearly resemble.

When Ernest Hemingway (1899–1961) drew upon one of poet Gertrude Stein's (1874–1946) apocryphal sayings as the basis for his now-famous epigraph for his novel *The Sun Also Rises* (1926), it is doubtful that he was aware that the statement "You are all a lost generation" would come to define a whole generation and would continue to resonate with near-mythic power in American culture for decades to come. Referring to the generation that came of age in the United States during and following World War I, Hemingway's Lost Generation was a population of artists and intellectuals that looked to European ideas as an antidote to what they perceived as the stagnant middle-class morality of American culture. However broadly ranging and even contradictory these quests for a new way of seeing the world might have been, the Lost Generation very quickly established itself as an identifiable subset of American culture. This varied collection of writers and artists recognized an opportunity to reinvigorate their home country with their ideas, their passion for art and literature, and their intellectual disdain for what they saw as the oppressive values of their elders. In France, they were called the *Génération au Feu* (Generation of Fire), but on this side of the Atlantic their names became synonymous with a complex set of attitudes and behaviors. Disillusioned with social standards, they fueled their lives with an almost ritualized reverence for alcohol (often to the point of abuse), a proclivity for sexual (mis)adventures (often extramarital), and for a persistent struggle to nurture their creative energies.

James Salter's short story "Last Night" is a haunting evocation of the darker side of the disillusionment and aimlessness of the Lost Generation. Married but childless, Walter and Marit Such live in a world that appears to be defined by poetry, art, and beauty. As Salter marks in the opening lines of the story, for instance, Walter has a keen ear for languages and a public appreciation for poetry. Earning his living as a translator, he finds pleasure in "recit[ing] lines of Blok in Russian and then giv[ing] Rilke's translation of them in German, pointing out their beauty."

Salter's reference to the work of the Russian lyric poet Alexander Blok (1880–1921) suggests Walter's sense of himself as a man celebrating beauty in the world and the words that define his life. The unofficial leader of what came to be known as the Russian symbolist movement, Blok wrote poetry which is remarkable for its rich rhymes and celebration of the beauty he saw in the most common surroundings. His poetry serves as a kind of intellectual debate between the classical ideals of beauty (as an appreciation of goodness, harmony, and a meaningfulness to life) and the inability of the common man to nurture beauty in the world of the everyday. Blok's understanding is grounded in a Platonic ideal that extends the concept of beauty beyond the appreciation of shapes, color, and sounds to the appreciation of beautiful thoughts, actions,

IN A WORLD DEFINED BY EMPTY RELATIONSHIPS AND A BETRAYAL OF BEAUTY, EVEN THE ART OF DEATH IS DENIED THE DIGNITY IT DESERVES."

and customs. Beauty and goodness are, at one level at least, synonymous within the Platonic ideal that Blok celebrates.

Tellingly, Walter consciously engages the beauty of Blok's poems through the filter of an intermediary; able to read Russian, he chooses instead to celebrate the poems in their *translated* form rather than allowing the original words to speak authentically for themselves. Moreover, in foregrounding the words of Rainer Maria Rilke (1875–1926), Walter repositions Blok's poetry in a dark world of anxiety, solitude, and struggle within an ethos of disbelief and disconnection. As understood by Rilke, as it is by Walter, beauty is intimately related to a sense of terror. It is a cracking open of the certainties of a harmonious, good-spirited world into a chaos of infinite darkness, unending space, and spiritual emptiness. As Salter establishes early in "Last Night," Walter's appreciation of the beauty of the world is not what it first appears to be. His vision is tainted by his own lost sense of wonder at the world of emotion and art engaged most fully in its untranslated form.

While Walter marks his ambivalent relationship with beauty through the words of poetry, Marit opts to celebrate the more sensual aspects of a life lived beautifully. Even as the metastasized uterine cancer strips her once vibrant body of its vitality, Marit finds comfort in the beautiful things that have been a part of her life for so many years. Dressing for dinner on her last night, she selects an elegant "red silk dress in which she had always been seductive" as well as a number of rings from "a lacquer box" nestled amongst her elegant "bracelets and necklaces." Before leaving for dinner, she spends a moment reflecting upon the room in which she felt most comfortable, an especially artfull space defined by "photographs with their silver frames," fine lamps, and "large books on

Surrealism, landscape design, or country homes." Even the rug comforts her, "with its beautiful faded color."

For Marit, beauty provides a kind of solace, a respite from her pain and from the harsh reality of the assisted suicide that she plans. Following a dinner that includes overindulgence in an expensive but "fabulously good" red wine, she takes particular note of the night sky with its "brilliant blue clouds, shining as if in daylight." A brief exchange of words with her husband underscores powerfully the common ground upon which Marit and Walter have built their lives and, however tenuous it might be, their relationship: "'It's very beautiful tonight, isn't it?' Marit said. 'I'm struck by that. Am I mistaken?' 'No.' Walter cleared his throat. 'It is beautiful.'" Still later in the evening, as she awaits the lethal injection that her husband has agreed to administer, Marit takes pride in her preparations for passage into the afterworld, selecting for herself "an ivory satin nightgown, low in back" and taking care to make up her eyes and put on a fine "silver necklace."

If, like the Lost Generation before them, Walter and Marit are comforted by their appreciation for the finer things in life (including poetry, clothing, and wine), they echo, too, their cultural predecessors' frustration with the Victorian morality that had carried over into American culture from the late nineteenth century. Childless in marriage and expansive in their appetites for alcohol, they are representative counterpoints to the normative morality shaping American culture of the day, which has long been based on an ethic of self-discipline, especially in sexual matters. Like both the Lost Generation and the generation of his own parents, who came to accept extramarital affairs as commonplace, Walter has chosen to opt out of normative pressures. Instead he chooses what he perceives as the more cosmopolitan openness to excessive drinking and sexual relationships outside the marriage. Imagining himself to be part intellectual and part cultural iconoclast, Walter scripts himself into his life as a kind of Hemingwayesque figure, the hard-living rogue with the eye of the artist and the soul of the poet. The episode of his lovemaking with Susanna in the hours following Marit's injection is punctuated by words that underscore the intensity that Walter believes he brings to his life. His kisses are passionate, his sexual prowess

is devouring, and his post-coital sleep is described as "profound."

What Salter illuminates in "Last Night" is not the couple's successful regeneration of the near-mythic ideals of their Lost ancestors, but the ultimate betrayals (of each other and of the ideals of beauty) that come to define their lives. The world of Walter and Marit proves to be little more than a thin veneer covering a set of beliefs that are, as Walter notes of himself as he fills a syringe, as "light as a sheet of paper, devoid of strength." Hiding behind their poetry and walls of unread books, the couple comes to be defined by their limitations rather than their horizons and by their weaknesses rather than their strengths. Just as Walter finds the beauty in Rilke's translation of Blok, the couple inhabits a translated world in which the goodness and the beauty that surrounds them are never realized directly but are filtered through a series of self-limiting assumptions.

In contrast to the generation that came before them, Walter and Marit have lost the passion of engagement necessary to create new ideas and progressive horizons. They simply mimic those earlier ideas. Whereas the excesses of the Lost Generation contributed to the creation of art, literature, and music, the excesses that accumulate during Marit's last night lead only to a botched assisted suicide and a drunken sexual encounter. The image of Marit descending the stairs the morning after the last night embodies perfectly the total collapse of the Suchs' illusions. Moreover, her descent also signals the failure of their attempt to orchestrate an act of euthanasia, a term derived, not coincidentally, from the Greek terms for *eu* (good) and *thanatos* (death): "Marit came unsteadily down the stairs. The makeup on her face was stale, and her dark lipstick showed fissures." Pale, cancer-ridden, and stripped of her once beautiful surface, Marit descends into a world of disbelief and betrayal. In other words, she reenters a world that, like the unread books that fill the shelves, means nothing at all when seen in the cold light of morning. In a world defined by empty relationships and a betrayal of beauty, even the art of death is denied the dignity it deserves.

In the Paris of the 1920s, the Lost Generation found a sense of community that its members believed could bring to them a new commitment to create and, more importantly, to create intelligently. Being lost, in this sense, was a liberating experience, a kind of spiritual rebirth and intellectual response to the feelings of displacement for a group of artists who should have felt most at home in a culture, but did not. By the late 1990s, however, the condition of being lost was, like Marit's smile, a condition that "seemed to mean just the opposite" of what it could mean. Awakening into a world of betrayal and emptiness, Marit and Walter wander unsteadily and without the beauty of their youth into a world that has truly lost its way.

Source: Klay Dyer, Critical Essay on "Last Night," in *Short Stories for Students*, Thomson Gale, 2007.

David Kelly

Kelly is an instructor of creative writing and English literature. In the following essay, he argues that Salter has built "Last Night" out of four distinct shorter stories.

James Salter has long been considered a master storyteller, a writer's writer. Salter is widely respected for his gift of compression: he is able to convey a whole character, a whole scene, or a whole life in just a few words or in one sentence. This talent enables a writer to keep readers engrossed and likely to find new meaning each time they reread the story. Of course, such a gift of compression may be a mixed blessing. Most short stories, even the short shorts of one page or so, need to immerse readers in something that feels like a setting. If Salter or someone like him really could give the whole story in just a sentence or two, then what would be the point in their writing anything more than the equivalent of a small poem?

Salter might be able to put all of a story's impact into one line, but it is unlikely that one line could evoke the feel of life. A focused short story writer needs a narrative of some length to carry the more potent lines, so that the reader can find a context in which to appreciate what those concentrated lines have to offer.

One way to do this is to have a story that is mostly set-up, leading to a moment of shocking honesty. This is often the effect that one feels after reading a great short story, one which saves all of its impact for one culminating revelation. But there is another way, the path that Salter follows in his story "Last Night": instead of just leading to one grand moment, Salter takes readers through what amounts to a series of four short stories, each reaching its own climax and each with its own emotional implications. A story developed

> THIS SECTION IS SUCH AN INDEPENDENT STORY THAT IT NEVER DOES REVEAL WHETHER MARIT WENT ON TO COMMIT SUICIDE SUCCESSFULLY, OR DIED NATURALLY OF CANCER, OR LIVED ON, WITH OR WITHOUT WALTER."

this way can, as "Last Night" does, follow the same sequence of events within a continuous period of time, while changing emphasis. Done right, it spares the author the necessity of limiting himself to just one narrative line. Done wrong, however, it can lead to a collection of barely related stories that feel stuck together for superficial or insufficient reasons.

For most of the time—that is, for roughly ten of its pages—"Last Night" is the story of one woman's last night. Marit Such is dying of cancer. She is still well enough to walk and eat, but she is certain enough that her illness will eventually defeat her that she has decided to beat it to the punch by taking her own life. The story is not told from her perspective, however, but from the perspective of her husband, Walter, who is to administer a lethal injection to Marit at the end of the evening, after one superb dinner, her last meal, a quiet little celebration with a chosen family friend.

There are a few elements that make this a compelling story. Death, of course, captures the readers' attention, all the more so when one has awareness of a planned impending death, and when it cannot be avoided. Such a story leading to its inevitable end is so inherently tense that readers can practically hear a clock tick minute-by-minute as they read. More compelling than what is known about Marit's situation, however, are those parts that are not known. For one thing, the story never says why she is so certain that she has to die. Medical treatment for cancer in the twenty-first century can be successful: Marit is ambulatory and lucid, and it is clear that, though weakened, she is far from devastated by the disease. It takes something like a reverse leap of faith for someone in her condition to be absolutely certain that nothing more can be done: Marit has made that decision, but she made it before the story begins, so readers can only look for signs of her absolute lack of hope in the ways she looks backward at life as she thinks about the night sky, her childlessness, and memories of her mother's death.

Interestingly, the main story is not really the story of the dying woman at all. The narrative stays with Walter Such, who is introduced in the first paragraph as an emotionless person who is moved more by habit than by feeling, writing with the same kind of old-fashioned pen and then "raising it in the air slightly after each sentence, almost as if his hand were a mechanical device." He is not the sort of person to look to for an understanding of the emotional implications, but Salter implies that it is Walter who occupies more of the drama in this base story.

By making Walter the focus, Salter indicates that there is really not that much to say about the story of someone who is facing a prearranged suicide because the situation is so potent that it will speak for itself. The real story lies with the close observer, the conspirator who has to watch and help but cannot make the decisions. Marit's story is one of heartache about imminent death, but come morning, Walter will be the one left to face the ethical question of whether he did the right thing.

Their story ends with the fatal injection, with Walter wavering "with despair" for a moment when asked if he loves her, then replying "Yes," and then confirming it with an exclamatory "Yes!" He gives Marit the drug that is supposed to take her out of the world as he and she know it, and thus in the act, he believes he "slip[s] her, as in a burial at sea, beneath the flow of time." Throughout the first nine pages, there has been the underlying question of whether one or the other would back out of this final act, and in the end, neither does. Marit dies muttering how lucky she was the night she met him, and Walter, having given her the shot, walks downstairs to find Susanna, the family friend that accompanied them to dinner. At this point, Salter begins what could be considered another story, which will color the reader's understanding of all that has come before.

This story is shorter, of course: with the situation well established in the preceding pages, there is little that needs to be set up. Readers know Walter Such to be a finicky man, uncomfortable with emotions; he struggles to understand that what he and Marit shared was indeed love and that he nevertheless has to

be the agent of her death. When he begs Susanna to stay in the house until after the mercy killing is accomplished, it might just be read as his need for the comfort of company. But in this second segment, when Susanna asks if Marit really wanted her there on the night of her death, readers are left for a moment with a mystery. Having had the selection of Susanna explained as another element of the Such couple's emotional coolness—they did not want anyone *too* close when Marit died, presumably to avoid the messiness of grief—they now have to wonder why Susanna would be there, or why, in fact, anything would be part of that night's arrangements if Marit did not want it. Salter answers this question with Walter's next line, one of those lauded cases where the author is able to cut to the essence of a situation in just one sentence: "Darling," Walter says, revealing the nature of his relationship to Susanna, "*she* suggested it." Walter goes on to assure her that Marit knew nothing about their affair.

If the Walter of the first part of the story was a poor soul torn between loss and duty, the Walter of this segment—the same man, of course, just minutes later—is a heartless conniver, an aggressor who has little concern for Susanna's feelings, who only lusts for her body, a man capable of assisting his wife in her suicide and in the next moment able to relate sexually to his mistress. Although there is good reason to believe that Marit died having no idea that her husband and her friend were lovers, there is also evidence that she might well have suspected what was going on. It might just be a coincidence that her final discussion with Susanna was about her own mother spending her last moments obsessing with who was sleeping with whom, but it could also have been a clue that she was actively trying to block out such thoughts on her own last night. Asking about Walter's love for her, in the past tense no less, is another reason to believe that Marit might suspect his disloyalty to her. If Walter were being honest with Susanna, he might at least admit a little uncertainty about what Marit knew.

He is not honest, though: he is desperate. He calms Susanna's guilt with unfounded certainty, plies her with drink, and takes her sexually, putting a hand on her mouth when she tries to speak and "devouring" her. All of this with his wife, dead from his own hand, in another room of the house. Salter has imbued Walter's character with enough humanity to let readers believe that he is not necessarily acting out of complete disregard for both Marit and Susanna but that he might just be channeling his grief into sexuality. Still, the fact that he and Susanna had already betrayed Marit before that night is clear, and that is certainly not something that one expected of the Walter of the story's first part. He is so ruthless in this second section that there is even reason to question whether he might be a murderer, having pushed Marit into an unnecessary suicide in order to clear the way for his new life with his lover.

The third part of the story is shorter still, just more than a page in length. It concerns the unexpected turn of events of the next morning when Marit, having been unsuccessfully injected, comes downstairs to find Susanna and Walter together at the kitchen table. This is, obviously, the high point of the overall sequence of events in "Last Night." In a flash, Walter, the story's protagonist, realizes that he has been a failure to both women. He has left Susanna in a position to be discovered, even though he had promised her that Marit would die without knowing about their affair, and he has botched the job of giving Marit a peaceful death. Walter of the first part is a man conflicted, Walter of the second part is a man driven to frenzy with lust, guilt, or some combination of the two, but this third Walter is a man sentenced to know that he is neither a great husband nor a great lover.

In the previous sections, Walter is an obscure figure to the reader because he identifies himself in terms of the women: in this segment, he severs his ties to them both, leaving him to face his empty self. Ironically, this scene ends up having nothing, really, to do with the infidelity being uncovered: Marit mentions Susanna's presence at the breakfast table casually, but her real horror is focused on having to commit suicide all over again, which is the same thing that horrifies Walter. Readers might focus on the discovery of the affair, but, for that moment at least, the Suchs are still of one mind, focused on greater issues of how Marit can face death twice.

It is not until the story's final paragraph that Salter takes an honest look at the affair between Walter and Susanna. It is over by then: they "came to part, upon being discovered by his wife," a phrasing that suggests nothing about the high drama of Marit's suicide attempt. This section is such an independent story that it never

does reveal whether Marit went on to commit suicide successfully, or died naturally of cancer, or lived on, with or without Walter. To make matters more complex, it may even hint that Marit staged the assisted suicide with a placebo drug perhaps, just to catch her husband and friend and rid her husband of both his marital and extramarital relationships. This section certainly concerns Walter's grief over a situation that is never explained in the story. When the focus is on Walter and particularly on Marit, Susanna only plays a functional part, as the woman he turns to for solace and practically molests. In five sentences, Salter is able to fill Walter with the complexity of a basically emotionless man who has loved then lost, alluding to a situation—"Whatever holds people together"—that has played no real part in the story up to this point. Readers who are looking for the author's famed skill at rendering a lifetime in just a few words need look no further than here, a perfect example of his understanding of just how little needs to be said.

"Last Night" is not really a collection of different stories, but one story, told by carefully tracking the changes that come over a man on this most important of nights. Over the course of these pages, readers' understanding of Walter Such evolves. For most of the story, a quiet, musical, melancholy span, he is a devoted husband, trying to do the best he can for his sick wife of many years; that ends, though, and readers quickly see him as a desperate aggressor; immediately after, his pretenses at being either dutiful or lustful are punctured, as he is revealed in one quick moment to be nothing but a failure; and finally, readers find that Walter, who has seemed so mechanical throughout the previous pages, has actually had an emotional attachment to Susanne. The "last night" of the title, presumed to be about Marit's life, is actually about something as small and tawdry as an affair with her friend. Of course, none of the second, third, or fourth stories would make sense without the background information provided in the first, but they each seem to take on an independent existence as Walter appears to be a different type of person in each one. The various Walters are just the kinds of personalities that James Salter can deliver quickly with just a few spare lines, but it is their relationship to each other that makes the writing work.

Source: David Kelly, Critical Essay on "Last Night," in *Short Stories for Students*, Thomson Gale, 2007.

Jennifer Bussey

Bussey holds a master's degree in Interdisciplinary Studies and a bachelor's degree in English Literature. She is an independent writer specializing in literature. In the following essay, she explores the theme of translation in James Salter's "Last Night."

"Walter Such was a translator." This opening line of James Salter's "Last Night" establishes that translation is going to be an undercurrent in this winding and emotional story. It is the story of a man whose wife, Marit, is terminally ill with cancer. The couple and another woman, a friend, go for one last dinner before Walter assists in his wife's suicide. As soon as he has injected her with the necessary poison and she drops to her pillow, the reader learns that the other woman, a twenty-nine-year-old named Susanna, is actually Walter's mistress. In a strange act of betrayal, vulnerability, and grief, he beds Susanna that very night. When Marit makes her way down the stairs the next morning and finds them together having coffee, Walter's life is thrown for an unexpected loop. It seems the poison was not adequate or it was given wrong: Marit survived. But Walter's relationship with Susanna does not survive because, in the words of the narrator, "Whatever holds people together was gone."

Throughout this story, Salter subtly weaves the theme of translation. Walter is a translator by profession. He is so settled into his role as a translator that he has particular ways he likes to work. He has a green fountain pen, and he raises it in the air after every sentence. He can also recite lines from a work in a foreign language, followed by the work of another translator, followed by commentary on the craftsmanship of the translation. Walter's habits and mannerisms, along with his expansive knowledge of—and passion for—translation demonstrate how much translation is part of his identity. It is much more than a job he performs simply because he has to make a living; translating is part of the fiber of his being, and he is comfortable with it.

To appreciate fully Salter's use of translation as a theme, it is important to examine what is significant about the process of translating one thing into another. Walter's job is essentially to take passages in one language and make them meaningful in another. Translators must also stay as true to the original text as possible, so

> AGAIN, WALTER SHOWS HIMSELF TO BE SKILLED AT TRANSLATING PASSAGES OF TEXT INTO MEANINGFUL LANGUAGE, BUT AN UTTER FAILURE AT TRANSLATING REALITY INTO MEANINGFUL TRUTH."

the job requires a deep understanding of the original text as well as familiarity with every tool of language. In "Last Night," truth, intention, and appearance are not always in line, despite the effort to make them seem so.

Salter introduces irony in the story as a pointed reminder of how the way appearance diverges from reality is often itself revealing. It is, in essence, a break in translation. Sometimes the break is intentional, and sometimes it is not. In "Last Night," it is the narrator who reveals irony to the reader, betraying the characters' efforts to fool the outside world. When the reader first sees Marit, she is dressed to go to dinner in a "red silk dress in which she had always been seductive." This description is ironic because she is not gaunt from the cancer, and her husband has given his lustful affections to another woman. A half-page later, Marit has a drink and offers a toast that is obviously ironic, even to Susanna and Walter. Salter writes: "'Well, happy days,' she said. Then, as if suddenly remembering [that they were gathered for her assisted suicide], she smiled at them. A frightening smile. It seemed to mean just the opposite." After dinner, Marit goes upstairs to wait for Walter to come with the syringe that will relieve her of her suffering. Salter writes at the beginning of a paragraph, "Marit had prepared herself," then proceeds to describe what she has done with her appearance as if that is how a woman prepares herself to die. The irony of this statement is clear in the last sentence of the same paragraph: "The wine had had an effect, but she was not calm." Although the reader is told that Marit has prepared herself, she is not fully prepared and relaxed as she faces what is about to happen.

After Walter injects Marit and believes she is dead, he retrieves Susanna. When she says she feels funny, he pretends to be worried that she is sick and insists that she lie down for a little while. This is ironic because his intention is not at all what it seems. He seems to be concerned about his mistress, but in fact he is steering her toward a bedroom so that he can be with her. The self-ishness of his intention is clear in the brief description of their lovemaking, which is very intense and all about him. In the morning, the reader is treated to another ironic description, this time of the house. Salter remarks that the house stands out from the others in the neigh-borhood because it is "more pure and serene." Of course, that this house appears pure is a mere illusion, considering that in the house is, presum-ably, a man, his dead wife, and his half-dressed mistress. That the house is serene is about to become ironic because within the next half-page, the "dead" wife will make her way down the stairs to discover her husband with another woman. By integrating irony into the story, Salter keeps the reader sensitive to the tension between reality and appearance. This sensitivity shows the reader what happens when translation is distorted.

Walter intentionally sets out to present a façade as reality. As a translator, presentation is the ends and translation is the means. If he can manipulate the ends, then perhaps he can over-look the fact that he has falsely translated truth. Although there are hints along the way, the reader is not sure that Susanna is more than a "family friend" (as she is described at the begin-ning of the story) until Walter has injected his wife with the poison and believes she is dead. Until that point, he has managed to take the truth (that he has a young mistress) and twist it so that he appears to be a loving and devoted husband to the end. Susanna even worries that maybe Marit somehow knew, and Walter assures her that Marit never suspected there was anything illicit going on between them. In his mind, his presentation of reality is flawless. It seems odd that a translator, whose job it is to maintain the integrity of the original to the most detailed level possible, would be so cavalier about the integrity of his own life. Still, he does what many people in affairs do: he brings all of his resources to bear on covering it up.

In the end, however, Walter's façade crum-bles. Reality refuses to be mistranslated, and he is discovered. After leaving his wife upstairs, he makes an error when he assumes that his wife is dead. He accepts her death at his hands as a fact, but this time, reality has turned on him. His assumption is basically a mistranslation. Marit is not dead; the injection did not work, and she comes down the stairs to find her husband hav-ing morning coffee with a partially dressed "fam-ily friend." Because of his error, his entire reality collapses. Although the narrator does not tell us what becomes of Marit, he does tell us that Susanna leaves Walter shortly after Marit's failed assisted suicide. The reader is left with an image of Walter all alone.

There is another subject of Walter's mis-translation, and that is Susanna. He has under-stood her to be in love with him, available to him, and his future. He feels so close to her and opens his life up to her so much that he allows her to be part of the night he is to help his wife commit suicide. This should have been such an intimate and emotionally charged evening, yet he agrees to have Susanna join them for dinner. He is obviously secure enough in the secrecy of their relationship that he feels comfortable invit-ing her into the darkest and strangest hour of his life, yet their bond is breakable. After they are discovered by Marit, they meet a few more times "at his insistence," but the magic is gone for Susanna. She leaves him, telling him "she could not help it," and that is the end of the relation-ship. Susanna is not the woman Walter has thought she was. Again, Walter shows himself to be skilled at translating passages of text into meaningful language, but an utter failure at translating reality into meaningful truth.

Looking at the story broadly, the narrator is ultimately the story's translator. While Walter might be the professional text translator, the narrator provides the reader with the informa-tion and the perspective to understand what it really going in within these characters. The nar-rator in essence takes the text of the characters' lives and translates it into the meaningful lan-guage of the story presented in "Last Night." The narrator first presents the story as Walter's experience saying good-bye to his wife, but in the end the narrator presents the story as Susanna's story of saying good-bye to Walter.

Source: Jennifer Bussey, Critical Essay on "Last Night," in *Short Stories for Students*, Thomson Gale, 2007.

Thomson Gale

In the following essay, the critic gives an overview of James Salter's work.

Author and screenwriter James Salter wrote his first two novels, *The Hunters* and *The Arm of Flesh*, based on his years in the Air Force and his service as a fighter pilot. He revised both, and they were each reprinted approximately forty years later. *Times Literary Supplement* contributor Mark Greif reviewed the new version of *The Hunters*, which was originally published one year before Salter left the Air Force, and wrote, "more than four decades after its publication, this newly revised edition of James Salter's *The Hunters* speaks more eloquently to the universal pains of competition, longing, envy, and betrayal than it could have when the events of America's Korean War were still fresh. It is a brisk, controlled novel, written on titanic lines. As other books of its era have fallen away, this one turns out to be a classic."

After Salter left the Air Force in 1957 he made a short documentary film, *Team, Team, Team*, which won first prize at the 1962 Venice Film Festival. After that critical recognition, he wrote a number of documentaries, including a ten-part series about the circus for public television. Four of his scripts were filmed, the most successful being *Downhill Racer*, starring Robert Redford. His relationship with movies has been ambivalent although he wrote and directed a film starring Sam Waterston and Charlotte Rampling, titled *Three*.

Salter's second book is set in occupied Europe during World War II. In reviewing *Cassada*, the newer version of *The Arm of Flesh*, a *Publishers Weekly* writer said that "Salter's feeling for weather and for the dark mysteries of solitary flight is exemplary." Salter considers his first good book to be *A Sport and a Pastime*, a novel that has been reprinted many times and is both a cult and writers' icon. It is the story of a Yale dropout in Paris and his love affair with an eighteen-year-old shop girl. Adam Begley wrote in the *New York Times Magazine* that Salter's details, "unobtrusive in themselves, conspire to create an atmosphere so real that the love affair—agonizing, inevitable—seems to break out from the comforting confines of the imaginary." Reynolds Price, a critic for the *New York Times Book Review*, said "of living novelists, none has produced a book I admire more than *A Sport and a Pastime*.... In its peculiar compound of lucid surface and dark interior, it's as nearly perfect as any American fiction I know."

> KAKUTANI CALLED SALTER'S CHARACTERS 'SOMEWHAT PASSIVE CREATURES, EAGER FOR REDEMPTION BUT THWARTED IN THEIR FEEBLE ATTEMPTS TO OVERCOME THE DIFFICULTIES OF THE PAST, BE IT DIVORCE, ALCOHOLISM, OR A FAILED CAREER....'"

Light Years is about a suburban New York family, "the record," wrote Begley, "of a marriage and a way of life that seems, at first blush, whole and perfect, the bright flower of a peculiar American hybrid, bohemian bourgeoisie; later, the illusion of harmony, like the marriage, decays. The things remembered in this deeply sad life are often just that—things; and so the narrative reads at times like a lush mail-order catalogue, a dazzling display of polished surfaces."

In 1977 actor Robert Redford asked Salter to write a screenplay about mountain climbing. An amateur athlete, Salter, at age fifty-two, took up the sport and climbed for several years in the United States and France, intent on knowing his subject. Redford rejected the script, but a friend, Robert Ginna, editor-in-chief at Little, Brown, asked Salter if he would rewrite it as a novel, and *Solo Faces* was published. Begley wrote that the novel "is perhaps too dark, its hero too tongue-tied and solitary to appeal to a popular audience. Rock climbers, however, revel in the meticulously observed depiction of their sport; admirers of exact prose are similarly impressed."

Michiko Kakutani reviewed Salter's *Dusk and Other Stories* in the *New York Times Book Review*. Kakutani said that "like the stories of John Cheever, James Salter's tales shine with light—morning light, summer light, the paralyzing light of noon, and the sad, dusty light of early evening." The stories, peopled by the upper middle class, are set in New York City, on Long Island, and in Europe. Kakutani called Salter's characters "somewhat passive creatures, eager for redemption but thwarted in their feeble attempts to overcome the difficulties of the past, be it divorce, alcoholism, or a failed career.

The best stories in *Dusk* point up the author's gift for condensation. Mr. Salter can delineate a character in a line or two, giving us, in addition to his melancholy heroes, bright, hard cameos of the people they encounter." *People Weekly* contributor Ralph Novak called the mood "consistent, reflecting a pervasive sense of resignation and disconnection."

Playwright A. R. Gurney wrote in the *New York Times Book Review* that *Dusk and Other Stories* "is no idle title. It is a central image and an underlying concept. Dusk, of course, is that time of day when the light changes, when we suddenly see things differently, when we are made aware of the inevitable approach of chaos and dark night. Mr. Salter writes about the 'dusk' that suddenly arrives in a relationship, in a life, and—most grimly—in a culture or civilization." Gurney said that "this is fine writing, these are first-rate stories, and James Salter is an author worth more attention than he has received so far."

Salon.com reviewer Dwight Garner called Salter's memoir, *Burning the Days: Recollection,* "a remarkable book... a lovely and expertly crafted elegy for Paris, for youth, for flight, for food, for women, for life itself." Salter writes of his childhood, his years at West Point, his military experiences, and his friendships with men like Redford, Roman Polanski, Irwin Shaw, and John Huston. Garner said that "it's impossible to read *Burning the Days* without feeling the glow of a life vigorously lived. Salter's days weren't burned while he wasn't looking. He lit them himself."

Richard Bernstein wrote in the *New York Times Book Review* of *Burning the Days,* "on balance, it is the dazzle, the power of the lens that this underrated writer's writer applies to his uncommon journey that stays in the mind, along with the feeling that Mr. Salter deserves to be better known and more celebrated than he has been."

Samuel Hynes, also writing in the *New York Times Book Review,* felt that the memoir could be read for the intimate portraits Salter paints, to understand the places, particularly France, or for the descriptions of what it is like to be a pilot. Hynes then said that "to me there is another reason for reading Salter's book: for its eloquent witness to the writer's faith in the craft he practices. Not in style, but in the power of the human imagination to recreate in language the feeling of being, with all its elations and despairs. That belief compels high standards, and Salter

has always had them." *Library Journal* reviewer Charles C. Nash noted the book's "unwavering tone of humility, candor, and authenticity." "Salter writes about tragedy and regret with irresistible eloquence," wrote a *Publishers Weekly* contributor.

Salter told *CA:* "The writer's life exists for only a small number. It can be glorious, especially after death. There are provincial, national and world writers—one should compete in one's class, despise riches, as Whitman says, and take off your hat to no one." He also once wrote, in *Burning the Days,* "It is only in books that one finds perfection, only in books that it cannot be spoiled."

In a long essay summarizing American fiction over the final twenty-five years of the twentieth century, Michael Dirda in the *Washington Post Book World* wrote, "Salter is the contemporary writer most admired and envied by other writers... (he) displays perfect control and understated grace; he can, when he wants, break your heart with a sentence.... *Light Years,* his ambitious, somewhat neglected account of a marriage winding down, may be his masterpiece.'

Source: Thomson Gale, "James Salter," in *Contemporary Authors Online,* Thomson Gale, 2006.

William Dowie

In the following essay, Dowie gives a critical analysis of James Salter's life and work.

James Salter is an artist, living or dying by his style, which is original, spare, and soulful. His work is admired more by his peers than by the public. Saul Bellow, Graham Greene, Mavis Gallant, John Irving, and Reynolds Price, among others, have all praised his work convincingly. Four of his stories are in O. Henry prize collections; one ("Foreign Shores") appears in the 1984 *Best American Stories* anthology; and one story, "Akhnilo," is anthologized in *American Short Story Masterpieces* (1989), edited by Raymond Carver. Salter received the 1989 P.E.N./ Faulkner Award for fiction in recognition of his collection *Dusk and Other Stories* (1988).

Reviewers and critics agree that Salter is important; it has become almost a critical cliché to speak of him as an underrated writer, even "the most underrated underrated writer," as James Wolcott dubbed him in *Vanity Fair* (June 1985). His admirers, devout in their loyalty, pass his name along to the uninitiated with the trust of a personal secret.

ONE OF SALTER'S FAVORITE AUTHORS, BABEL,
SAID HE DID NOT WRITE, HE COMPOSED. ONE COULD
SAY THE SAME ABOUT JAMES SALTER. HE IS A
COMPOSER: HIS THREE BEST NOVELS ARE LIKE
SONATAS, AND HIS FINEST SHORT STORIES ARE LIKE
ARIAS."

What they say about his writing is that it is lyrical and canny and that his best work—passages from *A Sport and a Pastime* (1967), *Light Years* (1975), *Solo Faces* (1979), and *Dusk*—will take the reader's breath away because of sudden glimpses deep into the pool of life. Indeed it is hard to read a Salter story or novel without being ambushed by recognitions, things one knew instinctively but never thought about or acted on. Salter believes in the power of language to move readers, and he stakes much of his fictional gamble on brief, piercing passages. In the novel *Light Years* he writes about a book a character is reading: "The power to change one's life comes from a paragraph, a lone remark. The lines that penetrate us are slender, like the flukes that live in river water and enter the bodies of swimmers." This declaration could stand as Salter's credo. He constantly strives for such illuminations, usually the effect of a final sentence that crystallizes what has gone before.

James Salter was born James Horowitz in New Jersey on 10 June 1925. His father was an engineer. Salter grew up in New York City only a few blocks from the Metropolitan Museum of Art. As a boy he painted, drew, and wrote. While attending the Horace Mann School in Riverdale (1938–1942), he worked on the literary magazine, won mention in a national poetry contest, and had poems published in *Poetry* magazine. Accepted at Stanford University, Salter was set to go west when his father, who had graduated first in his class at West Point, arranged a second alternate's appointment for his son. Salter took the entrance exam as a filial favor, never expecting both the principal and first alternate to fail. As he recalls in his 1992 essay "You Must," "Seventeen, vain, and spoiled by poems, I prepared to enter a

remote West Point." After initially rebelling against the rigidity of a place he compares, with its dark passages and Gothic facades, to James Joyce's Conglowes Wood College, Salter accepted the discipline as an arrow pointing toward the ongoing struggle of World War II. He graduated in 1945 and immediately entered the air force, too late for the war he describes as "the great forge of my time. It was the reality of the grown-up world when I entered it (that world) and its indelible imprint has never gone."

Salter's career as an air-force pilot lasted twelve years, during which time he kept his literary interests to himself since any sign of intellectual ability usually put one at risk of being assigned a desk job. In fact air-force regulations at the time forbade publication of anything that had not been previously approved by headquarters. Because of the necessity of keeping his two lives separate, he adopted the pen name James Salter when he first tried his hand at a novel while stationed in Honolulu in 1946. It was finished in 1949 and turned down by publishers, though Harper and Brothers expressed interest and wanted to see his next. In 1950, still in the air force, he completed an M.A. in international affairs at Georgetown University. The year was also memorable because it marked his first visit to Paris, signaling the end of his formal education and the beginning of another kind, as he says in the essay "Europe" (1990): "not the lessons of school but something more elevated, a view of how to endure: how to have leisure, love, food, and conversation, how to look at nakedness, architecture, streets.... In Europe the shadow of history falls upon you and, knowing none of it, you realize suddenly how small you are." Part of the enlargement Salter experienced was literary, as he read more by European writers, eventually counting among his exemplars André Gide, Louis-Ferdinand Céline, Henry de Montherlant, Jean Genet, and, especially, Isaac Babel. Europe thereafter would become a permanent recourse, Salter returning whenever possible throughout his life, usually to rent houses in provincial towns.

In 1951 Salter served for six months in Korea, where he flew one hundred combat missions. Later that same year he returned to Fort Meyer, Virginia, to marry a Washington, D.C., woman, Ann Altemus. His air-force career progressed through assignments to fighter squadrons in the United States (1951–1953) and Germany (1954–1957), while he used his spare time on weekends and at night to write. When his first novel, *The Hunters*, was published in 1956, it was the signal he needed to switch careers. He resigned from the air force in 1957 (with a wife and two small children); returned to the United States to live in the Hudson Valley, first in Grandview, then in 1958 in New York City; and became committed to pursuing a life of writing.

The Hunters, based upon Salter's aerial combat in Korea, conveys with an assured voice the experience of being a fighter pilot under fire. Neither this book, however, nor its less accomplished successor, *The Arm of Flesh* (1961), which draws on his flying career as well, amounts to more than an apprenticeship in writing. Able to look at his own work with a cold eye, Salter has refused the offer of North Point Press, which has published handsome new editions of his other novels, to reprint the early books.

In 1962 twins were born into the Salter family. Seeking ways to supplement his writing income, Salter met Lane Slate, a television writer, and the two collaborated on a documentary film about collegiate football, *Team, Team, Team*, which was awarded first prize at the Venice Film Festival. Other documentaries followed, including a ten-part series on the circus for public television and a film for CBS about contemporary American painters, an abiding interest of Salter since his youth. In the mid 1960s offers came to write for Hollywood. Four of Salter's filmscripts were made into movies, the best known of which is *Downhill Racer* (1969).

Not until the publication of *A Sport and a Pastime*, a novel Reynolds Price (*New York Times Book Review*, 2 June 1984) judged "as nearly perfect as any American fiction I know," did Salter's writing career pass from possibility to actuality. It is a classic tale of youth and desire, as well as a hymn to provincial France and a young woman that belongs to it so thoroughly that she embodies its abiding beauty, narrowness, and glory.

Salter's first short story, "Am Strand von Tanger" (*Paris Review*, Fall 1968; collected in *Dusk*), did not appear until over a decade after his initial novel. The story, like *A Sport and a Pastime*, tells of an American youth abroad; in the story he is an aspiring artist living in Barcelona. The image of the developing artist dominates Salter's early short fiction, appearing in three other stories published in the *Paris*

Review: "The Cinema" (Summer 1970), "The Destruction of the Goetheanum" (Winter 1971), and "Via Negativa" (Fall 1972)—all in *Dusk*. Together his *Paris Review* stories constitute Salter's "Portrait of the Artist as a Young Man," although clearly their themes are not exclusively about art. The young male protagonist in each of the stories has a desire for greatness and a need to have the image of his own greatness confirmed by someone else, a woman. Aside from this, each version of the artist differs.

Of the early stories "Dirt" (in *Dusk*; originally titled "Cowboys" in *Carolina Quarterly*, Spring 1971) is unique for its southwestern setting, flat tone, and blue-collar characters. There are no artists as such, although the grizzled American day laborer, Harry Mies, mixes concrete and pours foundations with the care of one. Readers glimpse Harry's life as it nears its end; the integrity of his work; the loyalty of his young helper; and the joy of the stories the old man likes to tell of California and days gone by. Lives, the tale implies, have a way of touching, each person's story impinging on others. Harry will one day be a legend like those in his stories. After he dies and his helper, Billy, heads to Mexico with a local girl, "they told each other stories of their life." The title, "Dirt," reflects both the earth on which Billy is crawling at the outset and the earth in which Harry is laid to rest. Life whisks by, and only tales and memories remain.

Divorced in 1975, Salter began living with writer Kay Eldredge in 1976, and the two have been together since, wintering in Aspen, Colorado, where Salter has been going since 1962, and summering on Long Island. As often as possible, usually at least once a year, they go abroad, spending weeks, sometimes longer, in France, Italy, or England. One such visit in 1985 to Paris was timed to coincide with the birth of their son.

The genre of the novel consumed most of Salter's creative energy in the 1970s, but the short story drew his attention in the 1980s. Six stories were published in magazines, and in 1988 *Dusk* was published.

Three of Salter's 1980s stories deal with men's lives, three with women's. "Akhnilo" (1981) and "Lost Sons" (1983) focus on men confronting their pasts. In the case of Dartmouth graduate Eddie Fenn in "Akhnilo," the past means failure to follow his dreams and to make money. One evening he awakens to what he imagines to be the distant sounds of those dreams, but it is too late. Ed Reemstma in "Lost Sons" returns to a reunion of his college class, hoping to revise somehow his outcast standing, only to find that the past is irreversible and that he still lives in its long shadow.

The male characters in "American Express" (1988), Salter's own favorite among his stories, are anything but failures or outcasts. Frank and Alan are lawyers and sons of lawyers, who have come down the fast track of success and are on holiday in Europe, eventually picking up an Italian schoolgirl. Salter says (in an unpublished interview) that the story "evolved from long days spent in the trash heap of things heard, known, imagined." Although it is his longest story, it is a masterpiece of compression, as if Tom Wolfe's *Bonfire of the Vanities* (1987) had been distilled into twenty-two pages. "American Express" is a story of vanity; New York life; eastern wealth; the American dream of success, which is always to some extent a wet dream; and finally of time passing. Salter's tone is imbued with sympathy, nostalgia, and respect for each character's weakness. In all his stories, his attitude can be described by what one of the lawyers says in "American Express": "No defendant was too guilty, no case too clear-cut." Each character, even minor ones, is drawn so carefully that whole lives are discerned in an instant.

"Dusk," first published as "The Fields at Dusk" in *Esquire* (August 1984), is among Salter's best stories, with all his characteristic strengths of compression, detail, juxtaposition, and telling metaphor combining in a portrait of a forty-six-year-old woman who has survived losses and defeats only to be faced with one more. Her husband gone and her son dead, Mrs. Chandler maintains herself as she maintains her beautiful Hamptons house—with dignity. This dignity remains intact even after Bill, a man of whom she has grown fond, announces that his wife has come back and that he will not be seeing Mrs. Chandler anymore. The story closes with a dazzling, inspired connection by Salter, as he describes Mrs. Chandler first looking at a mirror realizing "she would never be younger," then turning her thoughts to geese being hunted in the surrounding fields at dusk, imagining one particular bird lying bleeding in the grass: "She went around and turned on lights. The rain was coming down, the sea was crashing, a comrade lay dead in the whirling darkness."

Both "Foreign Shores" (1983) and "Twenty Minutes" (1988) are about women of a class comparable to Mrs. Chandler. The settings are different—one in the Hamptons, the other out west, probably in Colorado—but the women are alike in that they are no longer married (both former husbands are in California) and they are young, knowledgeable, and affluent enough to live well. Salter's empathy with these women is remarkable. In "Foreign Shores" readers meet Gloria and see her shock at the explicit letters her Dutch au pair has been receiving; the ending reveals a surprising jolt of jealousy. In "Twenty Minutes" Jane Vare, crushed by her horse falling on her, lies alone in the fields and knows she will die before long. She remembers the highs and lows of her life. The tale is a tour de force, taking about twenty minutes to read but made resonant by the poignancy of her memories and the tapestry they create.

In the fall semesters of 1987 and 1989 Salter taught at the Iowa Writers' Workshop, and in spring 1991 at the University of Houston; he had been a writer in residence at Vassar in 1986. He continues to spend his winters in Colorado and summers on Long Island, after 1985 in the new house he had built amid fields in Bridgehampton. He is friendly with other writers and artistic and literary people who live on this northeast corner of the island. About his place—his significance in this community and in the larger one of writers present and past—he is hopeful, perhaps even expectant, of confirmation by a wider reading public. He has all the confidence, but none of the arrogance, of genius, and he takes the long view of history because he knows the scroll of writers whose fame came only after death.

One of Salter's favorite authors, Babel, said he did not write, he composed. One could say the same about James Salter. He is a composer: his three best novels are like sonatas, and his finest short stories are like arias.

Source: William Dowie, "James Salter," in *Dictionary of Literary Biography*, Vol. 130, *American Short-Story Writers Since World War II*, edited by Patrick Meanor, Gale Research, 1993, pp. 282–87.

SOURCES

Begley, Adam, "A Few Well-Chosen Words," in *New York Times Book Review*, October 28, 1990, p. 40.

Hooper, Brad, Review of *Last Night: Stories*, in *Booklist*, March 1, 2005, p. 1142.

Review of *Last Night: Stories*, in *Publishers Weekly*, Vol. 252, No. 7, February 14, 2005, p. 51.

Salter, James, "Last Night," in *Last Night: Stories*, Alfred A. Knopf, 2005, pp. 120–132.

Smith, Dinitia, "Fighter Pilot who Aimed for Fiction but Lived on Film," in *New York Times*, August 30, 1997, p. 13.

FURTHER READING

Dowie, William, *James Salter*, Twayne, 1998.
  The first book-length study of Salter's early works, this readable and well-organized guide provides a blend of biographical details and critical evaluations of his writing, from his early journalistic endeavors through his screenwriting successes and early novels.

Gorsuch, Neil M., *The Future of Assisted Suicide and Euthanasia*, Princeton University Press, 2006.
  Gorsuch, who holds a doctorate in legal philosophy from Oxford University and a law degree from Harvard University, is widely published on the legal and ethical questions surrounding assisted suicide. An accessible discussion of the various philosophic arguments supporting both sides of the euthanasia debate, as well as the seminal case histories in the United States and abroad, this book ultimately builds a clear but subtle argument against further legalization of assisted suicide.

At the same time, however, it establishes a substantive argument for the rights of patients to autonomy when faced with such issues as unwanted medical care and intervention.

Lewis, Milton James, *Medicine and Care of the Dying: A Modern History*, Oxford University Press, 2006.
  This sometimes dense but nonetheless enlightening study describes the historical and cultural contexts that have shaped the shifting understanding of health, care, and death within Western culture. Lewis traces the source of contemporary conflicts and concerns through the twinned, though not always harmonious, rise of scientific medicine and the coincidental decline in religious influences within the English-speaking world. The philosophic terrain of conflict is clearly established: between the increasingly strident belief in the need to avoid death at all costs and the longstanding understanding of death as a natural and inevitable part of life.

Vernon, Alex, *Soldiers Once and Still: Ernest Hemingway, James Salter, and Tim O'Brien*, University of Iowa Press, 2004.
  This study is an analysis of how three American writers explore issues of identity and community through their stories of war and war-time experience. Focusing on three writers of radically different literary voices and styles, Vernon also extends his study across three generations of American wars and three levels of authorial engagement: World War I with the noncombatant Hemingway; World War II and Korea with the fighter pilot Salter; and the Vietnam conflict with army infantryman O'Brien.

A Nurse's Story

PETER BAIDA

1998

Peter Baida's "A Nurse's Story" was published in the *Gettysburg Review* in 1998. The story met with critical acclaim, was awarded first place in the O. Henry Short Story Award competition in 1999, and was reprinted as part of the anthology affiliated with the award. It was reprinted again in 2001 as the title story of the posthumous collection *A Nurse's Story and Others*. Within the complicated but delicately managed episodic structure of "A Nurse's Story," Baida tells the story of Mary McDonald, who is dying of cancer. Interwoven with Mary's story is the story of the town, Booth's Landing, in which collective histories and personal memories intermingle. There is the story of nurses and of the nursing profession, which is fraught with political and ethical frustrations. Finally, the story hints at the feminist movement of the 1960s, during which women came together to initiate social and professional changes. In telling "A Nurse's Story," Baida brings to the surface a series of philosophical questions, which resist easy answers or familiar platitudes, demanding instead that readers think about the world in which they live and the lives that they nurture.

AUTHOR BIOGRAPHY

Peter Baida was born on July 26, 1950, in Baltimore, Maryland. After receiving degrees from Harvard College (B.A., magna cum laude, 1972) and Boston University (M.A., 1973), he completed an

M.B.A. at the University of Pennsylvania in 1979. Upon graduation he began a lifelong affiliation with the Memorial Sloan-Kettering Cancer Center in New York City, where he took on diverse responsibilities, culminating with an extended and successful tenure as the center's director of direct mail fundraising from 1984 through 1999.

Since Baida established himself within the financial and business communities of New York, it is perhaps not surprising that his first book-length project was on business. His *Poor Richard's Legacy: American Business Values from Benjamin Franklin to Donald Trump*, published in 1990, was immediately well received as an entertaining social history that explored the personalities and business acumen of entrepreneurs and also showed the spirit of the country as it was captured in self-help books of the day as well as in the critical writings of such critics as Henry David Thoreau (1817–1862), Sinclair Lewis (1885–1951), and Canadian-born economist John Kenneth Galbraith (1908–2006).

Complementing Baida's success in the business world and in writing about the affairs and personalities associated with the wealth of the nation were the short stories that he submitted to a number of prominent U.S. literary magazines. In 1998, the *Gettysburg Review* published "A Nurse's Story," a story that blends the worlds of business and of illness, both of which were familiar to Baida, given his work experience and that fact that he was a hemophiliac. The story was a critical success and garnered a first prize in the 1999 O. Henry Short Story Awards. It was reprinted as part of the annual O. Henry Prize anthology and again in 2001 as the title story of Baida's first and only collection of short fiction.

Baida died of liver failure and post-surgical complications on December 10, 1999, within months of receiving his O. Henry Award.

PLOT SUMMARY

"A Nurse's Story" begins with the pain that sixty-nine-year-old Mary McDonald feels in her bones. A nurse for forty years, she is dying slowly from a cancer that first appeared in her colon and now has spread to her liver and bones. Confined to her room on the third floor of the Booth-Tiessler Geriatric Center, she is still very much in control of her faculties, which allows her to recognize where her pain "comes from and what it means." Acutely aware of the pressures of nursing, she is determined to raise the issues of wages and working conditions with a new nurse at the center, Eunice Barnacle, whose reaction is to walk away from any conversation that even touches upon the question of her worth to the institution in which she works.

Sitting in her room, Mary reflects upon a patient from forty years earlier, Ida Peterson, who was admitted to Mary's ward "with a tumor in her neck near the carotid artery." When Mary was called into Ida's room following a rupture of the artery that left the patient and the room covered in blood, she was forced to confront both the physical shock of the scene and the philosophic implications of Ida's desire for a "good death," which in Ida's case meant a death that did not involve medical intervention and allowed her to die in the presence of her husband. In this single moment, Mary's view of health, death, and the dignity of the individual all changed dramatically. This remembered episode also reveals that Mary respected Ida's wish for a "good death," allowing her to die as she wanted.

Now, Mary and Eunice continue their conversation about Mary's past work in the Booth-Tiessler Community Hospital. Specifically, the younger nurse is interested in Mary's role in bringing a nurses' union into the hospital in the mid-1960s, and whether Mary feels that the struggles for certification helped the cause of the nurses.

Next, the narrator gives a brief history of the "unpretentious" and historically rich community of Booth's Landing. Located "on the east side of the Hudson River, fifty miles north of New York City," the town was shaped, both economically and politically, by the energies of its two most prominent families: the Booths and the Tiesslers. Paragraph after paragraph in this section of the story details the presence of these two families in the town, beginning with the recognition that "for as long as anyone can remember, one member of the Booth family has run the town's bank, and one member of the Tiessler family has run the silverware factory." In tracing civic and philanthropic endeavors of the two families, the narrator connects their presence in the town with the history of Mary, who not only lives in a geriatric care center that bears both their names but whose professional life as a nurse began when she "fulfilled the requirements for her nursing degree" at Booth-Tiessler Community College.

Moving back and forth in time the episodic story continues with Mary remembering one of her first conversations with Clarice Hunter, a colleague at the Booth-Tiessler Community Hospital who in 1965 had solicited Mary's help in the movement to form a nurses' union. Frustrated with both Mary's narrow range of vision and what she calls Mary's Catholic "programming" to be compliant, Clarice challenged Mary's beliefs about life, work, and her sense of her own value as an employee of the hospital and as a person living in a modern society.

Next, Mary remembers her first meeting with her future husband George McDonald, who at the time was a twenty-seven-year-old military veteran of the Battle of the Coral Sea and the Battle of Midway. Thinking of the movies they saw and the meals they ate on their earliest dates, Mary remembers their shared history with fondness, commenting on the integrity of their thirty-nine-year marriage, on the three children that they raised, and on the lessons that they learned together. Filled with tenderness towards his gentle, unambitious spirit, she recalls specifically one conversation that they had on their second date, a picnic at Dabney Park. George stated his indifference to making a lot of money and she agreed, saying, "There's more to life than money."

Back in the present, Mary meets with Dr. Tom Seybold, who is treating her for the colon cancer that is, in Mary's words, "chewing up [her] liver." Gentle and humane, Dr. Seybold is another reminder of Mary's connections to the town and to the people who live and die in it. In a brief but telling episode-within-an episode, Mary remembers her own time spent with Tom's mother, Laura, following two miscarriages, and again after she had tried to commit suicide in the aftermath of losing her babies.

A brief episode follows, dominated by quick bursts of dialogue in which Mary and a group of residents at the Booth-Tiessler Geriatric Center complain about the food and about the money they spend for what they consider to be second-rate care. The episode that follows opens with Mary remembering her grandmother, who died of colon cancer in the mid-1950s. The memories of her grandmother's fate and Mary's own interweave as this episode begins, connecting the generations of women by the stories they share and the cancers they battle. Mary remembers, too, the powerful relationship that had formed between her own grandmother and her colleague, Clarice Hunter, during the final days of the older woman's life. Seeing Clarice as a treasure of humanity for the care she gave and the comfort she provided, Mary's grandmother was ferocious in one of her final demands: that Clarice be summoned to her bedside in order to witness her passing and tend to the her body following her death.

A brief episode follows again on the nurse-patient relationship, as Eunice gives Mary a needle and asks her an important question: "What was it made you want a union?" The answer comes by way of a flashback, or looking back in time, to 1965 when an exhausted Clarice and an equally drained Mary complained to each other bitterly about the expectations and workload placed upon them by the hospital administration. The implications are clear from their conversation: Mary's support for the union movement was born in her frustration as she watched her friend and coworker breakdown to tears over the workload.

Set just three days after the conversation between Clarice and Mary in 1965, the next episode recounts the weeks leading up to the nurses' vote on unionization. Mary, who was initially against unions, swung her vote in favor of certification. The ripple effect of Mary's declaration of support speaks to Mary's reputation and influence with the other nurses. As the narrator observes: "if you talked to other nurses, you found out that Mary's opinion made a difference." The episode ends with a summary of the outcome: "The vote drew near. Arguments are made, pro and con. Tempers flare. In September, 1965, the nurses voted in favor of a union."

Returning to the present, the next episode is a conversation between Eunice Barnacle and Pam Ryder, a colleague at the hospital. Talking casually about Mary's past involvement with the union movement, Eunice dismisses the value of Mary's struggle for recognition: "'That union can't help her now,' Eunice says." Next is an extended episode in which Mary remembers her sixty-ninth birthday party, held two months previous, when all her children gathered with her for what might be the last time: Brad, the youngest, who came from Seattle, where he has spent a decade making his own mark in the world of computer technology; George Jr., the one-time star athlete who has matured gracefully into a "quiet-voiced" attorney; and Bostonian Jane, a nurse like her mother, but with a troubled past and ongoing struggles to maintain sobriety.

The memory of the family gathering is juxtaposed suddenly with an episode in which Eunice, giving Mary a back rub, recounts the history of her own mother, who is currently serving a life sentence for the shotgun murder of her abusive boyfriend, Jethro. An obvious counterpoint to Mary's family history, this episode underscores the strengths of family ties, as the narrator implies that one of the reasons that Eunice moved to Booth's Landing was to be close enough to make the thirty-minute drive to visit her mother every Sunday.

The next episode focuses on the month of September 1967, a time of two important events in Mary's memory. The first was a forty-yard pass from her son, George Jr., to Warren Booth Jr. that won the county championship for the local high-school football team. The second event was the nurses' strike, which saw Mary on a picket line for the first time. With Clarice Hunter as the head of their strike committee, the nurses wanted more money and better job security, though the management of the hospital claimed in the press that the main issue was staffing levels. The spokesperson for the hospital, Sister Rosa, is a no-nonsense administrator who believes firmly that the role of management is to manage for the betterment of the institution as a whole, even if that might mean overlooking the needs of the employees.

Mary and the other nurses carried picket signs for six months, and the strike took its toll on the tightly knit town as people took sides, some supporting the nurses and others the hospital, which had hired "a company that specialized in fighting strikes." The strike was covered by newspaper reporter, Richard Dill, who Mary now knows as someone who lives on the same floor of the geriatric center as she does.

Their histories are, like so many in the town, casually connected: Richard's son Roger, a reporter for the local newspaper, once attended a camp at which Mary's daughter was a counselor. Richard's wife, Jennifer, was a patient of Mary's after a surgery that left her needing a colostomy bag. But as Mary remembers, many of the threads weaving through town life were frayed during the strike. Even her son George Jr. complained to her that the strike was potentially damaging his relationship with his football teammate and star receiver, who also happened

to be the son of Warren Booth, chairman of the board of the hospital. However much Mary loved football (she is a committed fan of the New York Giants), she was unbending in her determination to continue to walk the picket line in support of the nurses.

As Mary and Eunice talk about the 1967 strike at the beginning of the next episode, Mary explains that the Booth-Tiessler General Hospital is part of a chain of Catholic facilities, an affiliation that Mary claims was the reason that the nurses eventually had the strike turn in their favor. Standing in front of television cameras on a bitterly cold winter day, Mary had read the Sisters of Mercy mission statement aloud, noting that they were, on paper at least, committed "to act in solidarity with the poor, the weak, the outcast, the elderly, and the infirm."

Mary's reading, coupled with an extended fast by Beverly Wellstone, turned the tide of public opinion in the nurses' favor. The strike ended following a visit to Sister Rosa by an "emissary of the cardinal" that shifted the tone and spirit of the negotiations. In the end, the nurses received half of the salary increase they had asked for as well as more staff in the hospital. As Mary says to Eunice: "For the next three years, after we signed the contract, we had the staff to give the kind of care we wanted to give."

Mary returned to the hospital in which she had worked three days before her death on December 16, a date that Roger Dill notes in the obituary that he writes for the Booth's Landing *Gazette*. Mary's death sends ripples through Booth's Landing. Warren Booth Jr., the town's leading banker, reacts as his father might have at the news, with a businessman's blend of condolence masking a deeper indignation at the trouble the nurse had brought to his family's business and legacy. To Eunice Barnacle, Mary's death proves an impetus to begin her own agitation for fair wages and better working conditions and to begin talking with her generation of working women about the benefits of bringing a union to the Booth-Tiessler Geriatric Center. Nick Santino, the proprietor of Santino's Funeral Home, balances his embalming of Mary's body with stories about the care Mary gave his dying mother many years earlier. He recalls how Mary had attended his mother "like she was taking care of her own mother."

In the story's final episode, Mary falls into a dream-like state as she nears death. Sister Rosa comes to her in a vision, reassuring the dying nurse of what is to come and settling, finally, their still-unresolved debate over workers' rights and management's responsibilities. In a turn-about that surprises Mary, her one-time nemesis acknowledges that she was glad that the nurses had fought for their beliefs; "the whole system depends" on workers fighting for fair treatment, Sister Rosa concludes. With her children gathered around her, Mary closes her eyes and dies. When she opens her eyes, she finds herself reunited with her husband in the afterworld.

CHARACTERS

Eunice Barnacle

Born in Richmond, Virginia, into a deeply troubled family, Eunice Barnacle is "a lean, sharp-featured black woman in her middle twenties, with a straight nose, small teeth, wary eyes, and a straightforward manner." A recent addition to the staff at the Booth-Tiessler Geriatric Center, she is responsible for the daily care of Mary McDonald, whom she questions intermittently about the history of the nurses' union that Mary helped establish in the mid-1960s. One reason Eunice moved to New York, with her three-year-old daughter Coretta in tow, is to be nearer her mother, who is serving a life term for murder in Sing Sing Prison, located in nearby Ossining, New York.

Warren Booth

Chairman of the board of the Booth-Tiessler Community Hospital during the 1967 nurses' strike, Warren Booth stands for the complexities of the politics and the civic spirit of Booth's Landing. Generously philanthropic, he is, at the same time, unyielding in his business ethic.

Warren Booth Jr.

Son of the chairman of the board of the Booth-Tiessler Community Hospital during the 1967 nurses' strike and recipient of a pass from George McDonald Jr. that had won the high school football team the county championship in the year of the strike, Warren Booth Jr. is the town's leading banker. He is resentful still about the impact that the 1967 strike had on his family and his own teenage life. He remains a symbol, even in the 1990s, of the conservative base upon which small towns like Booth's Landing are often built.

Richard Dill

Richard Dill is a reporter on the Booth's Landing *Gazette* who covered the 1967 nurses' strike and who now lives on the same floor as Mary McDonald at the Booth-Tiessler Geriatric Center. His son, Roger, has followed in his father's footsteps and works for the local newspaper.

Roger Dill

Son of Richard Dill, Roger Dill follows in his father's journalistic footsteps and becomes a reporter for the Booth's Landing *Gazette*. Unlike his father, though, Roger is neither excited nor inspired by the events of the small town and remains emotionally and imaginatively disengaged from its workings. He is responsible for writing Mary McDonald's obituary.

Eunice's mother

Sixteen years old when she gave birth to Eunice Barnacle in Richmond, Virginia, Eunice's mother is serving a life term in Sing Sing Prison for killing an abusive boyfriend, Jethro. As Eunice tells the story, her mother bailed Jethro out of jail in order to kill him. At the time of the story, Eunice's mother is thirty-nine years old.

Clarice Hunter

Ten years older than Mary McDonald, Clarice is a colleague who solicited Mary's help in 1965 in taking the first steps toward forming a nurses' union at the local hospital. She is also the first person to challenge Mary on her beliefs about life, work, and her sense of her own value as a person, a woman, and a hospital employee. Clarice Hunter was the head of the nurses' strike committee in 1967.

Clarice is also more intimately connected to Mary McDonald's past than union-building suggests. A lifelong friend, she was the nurse who cared for Mary's grandmother in the final days of her terminal battle with colon cancer. Mary's grandmother, who asked little from life or those around her, saw in Clarice "a jewel" of humanity. Even when surrounded by family as she lay dying, Mary's grandmother demanded with "a look so fierce that Mary still remembered it" that Clarice be at her bedside when she died.

Jane

Mary and George McDonald's only daughter, Jane, is a nurse. She has a troubled history and is always on the edge of alcoholic relapse. Living in Boston, she has two young daughters.

Sister Margaret

Sister Rosa's successor in the role of executive director of the Booth-Tiessler Community Hospital, Sister Margaret became head of the institution in 1984. Her expertise in materials management "dazzled everyone who worked with her." She is also the director of the hospital when Mary McDonald is transferred there for the final days of her life.

Brad McDonald

The youngest child of Mary and George McDonald, Brad has moved to Seattle where he is making his own mark with the corporate giant Microsoft.

George McDonald

George McDonald is Mary's husband, whom she first met in 1948 while she was working in the emergency ward of the local hospital. He was twenty-seven when they met, "a big man, six foot three, with hair the color of fresh corn and a big boyish smile" that in many ways belied the fact that he had already fought in two significant battles of the World War II: the Battle of the Coral Sea and the Battle of Midway. Not ambitious, he taught music at the local high school and was happy being what he was in Booth's Landing. Married to Mary for thirty-nine years, he was a devoted husband and proud father of three children, "all of them grown now and moved away." He died of kidney failure in 1988, and Mary remembers him as "A man who rarely lost his temper, a father who taught his sons how to scramble eggs and his daughter how to throw a baseball, a small-town music teacher who loved the clarinet." As Mary dies, she awakens into a bright new world in which she is reunited with a young, healthy George.

George McDonald Jr.

Mary and George McDonald's oldest son is George Jr., a "gangling, loose-jointed, long-armed boy" who has grown up to be an "earnest, quiet-voiced" Chicago attorney dressed in rumpled suits." He is remembered by the townspeople for a touchdown pass that he threw to Warren Booth Jr. that won the local high school team the county championship in 1967, the same year as the now infamous nurses' strike.

Mary McDonald

A working nurse for forty years, sixty-nine-year-old Mary McDonald is dying slowly from a cancer that appeared first in her colon but has spread to her liver and bones. Confined to her room on the third floor of the Booth-Tiessler Geriatric Center, she is known as a political activist who advocates on behalf of patients' rights but, more importantly, on behalf of nurses and their struggle for fair pay and improved working conditions. She was, as Eunice Barnacle notes, one of the driving forces in bringing unionization of nurses to the local hospital and thus a symbol of the power of women to initiate a revolution both locally and nationally.

But as the story unfolds, Mary emerges as a much more rounded character, one who remembers fondly the courtship with her late husband George in the late 1940s, the raising of her children (George Jr., Brad, and Jane), her passion for beer (especially Guinness) and football (especially as it is played by the New York Giants), and her struggle with her faith when it comes in conflict with political necessity. Moreover, the story of her life soon becomes the story of the town and of the births, deaths, and tragedies that continue to be its daily business. At once individual, representative of a town and of a profession, Mary becomes, too, a symbol of an entire generation of revolutionary women.

Mary's Grandmother

A strong woman, Mary's grandmother died of colon cancer in the mid-1950s. "A plain-looking, plain-talking woman, with only an eighth-grade education," Mary's grandmother "expected nothing from life and generally got what she expected." A genealogical connection with Mary McDonald that expresses itself in the stories that they share and in the disease that kills them, Mary's grandmother is also a narrative thread that links the two women to Clarice Hunter, a union-raising colleague of Mary's and the nurse who tended her grandmother in her final days.

Ida Peterson

A minor character in the sense that she was a patient of Mary McDonald's more than forty years earlier, Ida Peterson is important because she brought to Mary's world a new understanding of the human need "to die a peaceful, dignified death," which in Ida's case meant a "natural death" (without medical intervention) in the presence of her husband. Although Mary had dealt with hundreds of patients since Ida, the memory of their brief interaction changed the way Mary thought about life, death, and the dignity of the individual.

Sister Rosa

The executive director of the Booth-Tiessler Community Hospital during the 1967 nurses' strike, Sister Rosa had worked with Mary McDonald in 1962 on a plan to improve the patient scheduling in the radiation department. A "short, no-nonsense woman," Sister Rosa worked by the very simple mandate that "management must *manage*" for the best interest of the institution, which might at times come into direct conflict with the best interests of the employees. Sister Rosa comes to Mary McDonald as she slips into a dream-like state in the final moments of her life, talking with her one-time nemesis and reassuring her about what lay ahead and discussing, for one last time, the 1967 strike.

Nick Santino

Proprietor of Santino's Funeral Home, Nick Santino embalms Mary McDonald's body, while remembering how she took care of his own mother while she was dying. As he handles Mary's body with the latest embalming equipment, he remembers with tenderness how Mary treated his mother with humanity and deep respect, how she washed his mother's feet.

Laura Seybold

Mentioned briefly during one of Mary McDonald's memory episodes, Laura Seybold is the mother of Dr. Tom Seybold. Mary had cared for Laura during both of the miscarriages that had taken "the life out of her eyes" as well as later "during the three days [Laura] spent in the hospital after the Saturday night when she swallowed every pill in the house."

Dr. Tom Seybold

Mary McDonald's doctor, Tom Seybold, is "a large man with a friendly face, pink skin, and paprika-colored hair. His breath smells like peppermint." With strong hands and gentle humor, he is a representative of the many connections that Mary McDonald feels to the town, to the stories

TOPICS FOR FURTHER STUDY

- Write two or three more episodes that might be included in Baida's story, focusing in your original writing on the perspectives of characters other than Mary McDonald. You might consider, for instance, writing from the point of view of Eunice Barnacle or Dr. Tom Seybold. Alternatively, you might look to other members of the town who come in contact with Mary during the course of her life, such as Nick Santino or Laura Seybold.

- Recalling Mary's story of the picket lines and the slogans that appeared on the signs that the nurses carried, do some research into the history of slogans of this sort. Think of possible situations in which such sayings might prove useful: marking support for a football team or a political candidate, for instance, or during a labor dispute of some sort. Build a catalogue of possible slogans, noting as well the context in which you think each would be most effective.

- Research the history of the debate over unions within the Catholic hospital system. Prepare a series of newspaper editorials based on these facts. Be sure that some of your opinion pieces support the union effort and that others support the rights of the hospitals to function without unions as part of their business plans.

- Draw a tourist map of Booth's Landing as you might imagine it to look from the details of the story. Be sure to include brief descriptions and histories of the most important landmarks, as well as a couple of paragraphs recounting the history of settlement.

of the people who live in it, and through both of these lines of continuity, to her own history.

Ruth Sullivan

Ruth Sullivan is a nurse who worked with Mary McDonald and Clarice Hunter in the 1960s and during the tumultuous years leading up to the nurses' union vote.

Beverly Wellstone

"A nurse who had once been a nun," Beverly Wellstone fasted for thirty-three days in support of the striking nurses. Her decision marked the turning point in the strike.

THEMES

The Struggle for Wage Equity

Prior to the 1960s, women working outside the home confronted a longstanding and substantial wage gap both in respect to the wages paid male workers in the same industry and to wages for so-called women's jobs, including nursing and care-giving. Fueled in part by the advances initiated by the burgeoning civil rights movement, women saw the sixties as an era in which barriers to employment equity and educational achievement would be challenged aggressively.

As Baida's "A Nurse's Story" reveals, this new political awareness was unprecedented in its influence. In taking the initial steps towards unionizing the nurses in the Booth-Tiessler Community Hospital, Mary McDonald and Clarice Hunter initiated a challenge that cut across age barriers (Clarice was ten years Mary's senior), issues of faith (a Catholic, Mary pickets a hospital run by the Church), and racial differences, as Eunice Barnacle's growing interest in the benefits of unionization underscores. Regardless of their differences or the historical period in which they find themselves working for a living, the women of the story are united by one question, repeated often by Mary and picked up at the end of the story by Eunice: "You think you're paid what you're worth?" In this sense, Baida's story captures the beginning of a revolution that shifted forever the way a country thought about sex, race, and wealth.

It was a revolution, too, that changed in equally important ways the intimate social fabric of communities across the nation, from the largest city, in which women in factories and offices united, and, as in "A Nurse's Story," to the smaller towns, founded upon a densely coded fusion of history, civic pride, and capitalist spirit. In a town like Booth's Landing, in which two prominent families are so influential and in which every story is interwoven with numerous

other stories, the strike changed the way people looked at each other and talked to each other. As the narrator observes, the strike caused townspeople to take sides and begin to target individuals such as Mary McDonald as the source of the tension in the town. "In an interview on TV," for instance, "Cheryl Hughes, a woman whom Mary had always liked, whose husband prepared Mary and George's tax returns, said, 'If you ask me, it's an outrage. Let's just hope nobody dies. Those women ought to be ashamed.'"

Such tensions ripple through the town, captured in Warren Booth's scowl and in the struggle of Mary's own son George Jr. to reconcile his mother's battle for equity and respect with his own loyalty to the local football team and to his star receiver, who also happens to be the son of the hospital's chairman of the board. As Mary tries to explain to her son, the world is evolving and old certainties, like new contracts, are open to renegotiation: "Out in the world," Mary observes, "where I work—well, let's just say that Warren's dad isn't my teammate." As Mary's one-time and now-dead nemesis, Sister Rosa, confirms when she speaks to Mary in the last moment of the nurse's life, the fight was, in the end, necessary and progressive. "Workers have to fight," Sister Rosa states succinctly. "The whole system depends on it."

The Power of Memories

Memory provides a holistic view of Mary's life, taking into account not only the political activism that so many people in town define her by, but expanding outwards to give readers a sense of her other passions (her family and the New York Giants football team), her faith, and her politics both before and after the strike. Memory, in this sense, never allows Mary (or the reader) to find a single angle from which to view her life and the decisions that shaped it. At any point in the story, a once-stable memory can be frayed by another version of the same story within a different episode. When the proud mother recollects her son's finest moment on the football field, for instance, she is creating, briefly, a fond memory that is put slightly askew later in the same episode by her remembering that the year of the catch was also the year of the strike. Her original memory is twisted in another direction a bit later in the story when her son steps forward to educate his mother about how her activism is affecting his preparations for a coming game. With memory, in other words, comes diverse perspectives within Mary's own reflections on her life, which is, as her memory underscores again and again, a work in perpetual progress.

STYLE

Point of View

The omniscient third-person narrator of "A Nurse's Story" is free to take on the perspective of any character, regardless of the time or place in which that character lives. The narrator is god-like in his ability to look into the mind of every character and to communicate to readers private motivations, desires, and thoughts. Readers discover, for instance, that Warren Booth Jr. still harbors deep resentment because of the strike's negative impact on his family and on his own preparation for an important football game. Moreover, the narrator is free to articulate and, even comment on, the limitations of Warren's own understanding of past events and of himself, as when the narrator notes that "[t]he fact that [Warren] himself has never managed any great enterprise did not occur to him" or later when he debates with himself whether to attend Mary McDonald's funeral. His decision, never spoken but accessible to the narrator (and through him to the reader), speaks volumes about the humanity of one of the town's leading men: "Forget the funeral. Send a card."

Episodic Structure and Lack of Chronology

"A Nurse's Story" is structured as a series of episodes that move fluidly across the history of Mary McDonald's life. Although each episode can stand alone as a component of the story, it is more important to see them as interdependent units, with each memory shaping the one that came before and after. Characters appear and reappear in new contexts, as connections between the various aspects of Mary's life reveal themselves, allowing patterns to form and reform as the story unfolds. Reading Baida's story is like living a life, an exercise that involves both a rethinking of each experience gained over the years and a rereading of the entire story with the maturity that comes over time.

HISTORICAL CONTEXT

Women's Rights and Political Change

The 1960s and 1970s were decades of remarkable political and cultural unrest in the United States, as young adults questioned vigorously their government's foreign policies and indifference to deeply rooted inequalities at home. As had been the case in the late nineteenth century, when female suffrage was in the forefront of political debates, women mobilized dramatically in support of civil rights, antiwar and antipoverty issues, and labor movements. Many of the younger women of the era subscribed to a new feminism that focused on gender discriminations in employment, education, sexual conduct (culminating in the Supreme Court's *Roe v. Wade* abortion ruling of 1973), and family-based issues. Older and more moderate women were behind the formation of the National Organization of Women (NOW) in 1966. Under the leadership of noted feminist and activist Betty Friedan (1921–2006), the organization focused on a number of gender-related issues and the process known as consciousness raising in which individuals discuss inequities to become more aware of what has been tacit and covert.

With regards to the types and degrees of employment equity issues explored in Baida's "A Nurse's Story," the first big challenges to sex discrimination in the early sixties came from wage-earning women who had continued to secure factory work after the gender-breaking boom that accompanied World War II. After the war, women stayed in the workforce during marriage and even after the birth of their children.

Linking their own concerns with those being raised by civil rights activists, advocates from the labor movements scored a major coup in 1965 when the Equal Employment Opportunities Commission (EEOC) began to deal officially with complaints concerning inequities in wages, sex-biased recruitment policies and promotion, and substandard working conditions. (The first chairperson of the commission was Franklin D. Roosevelt Jr.) In the first year alone, more than two thousand complaints were filed with the commission from working women from all classes, races, and ethnic backgrounds. Such efforts were brought to public awareness by media that covered discriminatory employment practices and women's struggles to raise consciousness regarding them.

WHAT DO I READ NEXT?

- Margaret Edson's play, *Wit*, portrays a professor of metaphysical poetry, especially the work of John Donne, who struggles to accept the inevitability of her own death after being diagnosed with ovarian cancer. A scathing commentary on the ethos of medical intervention driven by the imperatives of research rather than care, the play traces, too, the friendship between the dying scholar and her attending nurse. *Wit* won the Pulitzer Prize for Drama in 1999 and was adapted into a 2001 television movie, starring Emma Thompson.

- Another strong-willed woman is portrayed by Margaret Laurence in her novel *The Stone Angel* (1964). Ninety-year-old Hagar Shipley remembers her life on the Canadian frontier and the disintegration of her marriage, and nearing the end of her life, she faces failing physical and mental health.

- Clara Bingham and Laura Leady Gansler's *Class Action: The Story of Lois Jenson and the Landmark Case that Changed Sexual Harassment* (2002) is an account of an important case in the evolution of sexual harassment laws in the United States. The book tells the true story of the injustices and personal humiliation faced by a small group of women who went to work the iron mines of northern Minnesota. This book was the inspiration for the 2005 movie, *North Country*, directed by Niki Caro and starring Charlize Theron.

- Football as both literary device and metaphor for small-town culture is captured in Buzz Bissinger's 1990 novel, *Friday Night Lights: A Town, a Team, and a Dream.* Tracing the trials and successes of a high school football team in the small, economically depressed town of Odessa, Texas, the novel underscores both the advantages and disadvantages of a culture in which sports teams and athletes are seen as saviors and superstars. The novel was adapted into the 2004 movie *Friday Night Lights*, directed by Peter Berg and starring Billy Bob Thornton.

Health Care and the Catholic Church

Historically, the Catholic Church has been a significant influence in both the business and the philosophy of health care in the United States, especially in the care that is delivered in hospitals. The mandate of such hospitals has remained clearly focused: to offer substantive health care in accord with the example set out in the life and actions of Christ. This commitment is expressed in practical terms, as Baida's story highlights, in a dedication to providing care for those who are impoverished and most in need.

Extending the definition of health care to include the social terms and conditions of an individual's wellbeing, Catholic hospitals are equally committed to changing the conditions that lead to a decline in health. They are dedicated to the common good. Accordingly, these organizations examine the causes not just the symptoms of poverty and raise questions about the accessibility of health services and discrimination in health care delivery. Although Catholic hospitals have been configured under their own direction as a private, not-for-profit enterprise, they have been forced by the Church and by others to rethink their mandate in the modern world, which includes the need to review their philosophy on such issues as contraception, reproductive technologies, and labor practices. In 2006, the debate over unionization of Catholic hospitals continued in the pages of such widely read publications as the *National Catholic Reporter* and *U.S. Catholic*.

CRITICAL OVERVIEW

Although not widely reviewed in the year of its release, Peter Baida's collection *A Nurse's Story*

and Others was very well received by those critics
who did review it. As Aoibheann Sweeney notes in
the *New York Times*: "Baida . . . is not a sucker for
happy endings. The nine stories in his posthumous
collection are about the kinds of characters—
nurses, patients, old unionists and old friends—
who make mistakes they cannot fix and confront
questions they cannot resolve." Jeff Zaleski of
Publishers Weekly concurs with this suggestion
that Baida's stories are open-ended. Zaleski
concludes that Baida's "stories offer no grand
epiphanies, no tidy resolutions—but they
address complicated issues of loyalty, class,
race, ethics and family in a spare, direct style
that is insightful and moving."

Although critics tended toward plot summary of the stories rather than extensive praise
for any single one, their comments are consistently directed at celebrating Baida's humanity.
In the end, as Sweeney concludes, Baida's only
collection does what the most carefully crafted
fiction should do: it "leaves us not with a more
comfortable sense of the world's injustices but
with a keener one." Though assessments of
Baida's work are few, the collection was highly
recommended as part of Ellie Barta-Moran's
listing of adult fiction in *Booklist*.

CRITICISM

Klay Dyer

*Dyer holds a Ph.D. in English literature and has
published extensively on fiction, poetry, film, and
television. He is also a freelance university
teacher, writer, and educational consultant. In
the following essay, he explores the dynamics
and politics of Mary McDonald's retrospective
reading of the town of Booth's Landing.*

Peter Baida's "A Nurse's Story" is written in
an episodic style that accentuates the links
between the remembered episodes that constitute Mary McDonald's fragmented life review.
At the same time, the story illuminates the layers
of stories that come from the history of a small
town. Openings and closings accumulate slowly
in the story, turning "A Nurse's Story" into a
kind of archaeological site within which layers of
memory blend together, making reading the
story a process of sifting through and reordering
events. In Mary's story, connections are made
retrospectively through an awareness of what is

> HERS IS A DYING LIVED IN RETROSPECT, A
> JOURNEY AWAY FROM THE KNOWN AND THE
> KNOWABLE TO THE ILLUMINATING EDGES OF OPEN
> SECRETS AND WHISPERED PASTS."

to come and which aspects will assume significance and which others will not.

With its nonlinear style of storytelling, "A
Nurse's Story" generates a form that is ideally
suited for exploring the external and internal
forces that have gathered over time to crisscross
the spiritual and emotional foundations of
Booth's Landing. Never really challenged by
the threat of an advancing urban sprawl or by
economic downturns or factory collapses, town
is split instead by tensions between its history
and its present, two threads that come together
in the life and the story of Mary McDonald.

The story of Mary's transformation from passive Catholic nurse to confident political activist is
also the story of one woman's struggle to establish
connections, a word that Baida never actually uses
in his story but which resonates through each episode Mary remembers. In large part, this search
consists of Mary's movement toward understanding how experiences link people's lives. Like life
itself, Mary's journey is uncertain, but she comes
to appreciate and even celebrate the ambiguities in
what she has long considered the knowable, ordinary events of the town.

At the beginning of her career, for instance,
Mary was forced to deal with Clarice Hunter, a
woman who is, in many ways, a mirror-image of
Mary herself. World-weary, physically and emotionally exhausted, on the one hand, Clarice is, on
the other, "a jewel" and "a blessing" of a nurse
whose genuine humanity connects her to her
patients. Clarice is especially connected to Mary's
grandmother, who called for her nurse not her
family to comfort her in her dying moments:

> Mary called Clarice, who came to the hospital
> at two in the morning. At three, Mary's grand-
> mother fell asleep with her mouth wide open.
> At six, with a terrifying snort, she woke and
> died. Clarice helped the night nurse wash the
> body. Then she worked the day shift.

Through her early contact with Clarice, who badgers her about her Catholic passivity and political neutrality, Mary began to sense that there are worlds and realities lying alongside the one she knows. At times, these are troubling worlds in which unanswerable questions about value and worth are asked regularly and with passion. These worlds often offer themselves as enlightening complements to the reality of Mary's life at the hospital. The world of Ida Peterson, for instance, gave Mary her first real experience with blood and with the strength of a woman determined to die with dignity. The aging Mary vividly remembers Ida's death: "She still remembers the splash of blood on her face when she stepped into Mrs. Petersen's room. She still remembers how long it took Mrs. Petersen to die."

Still other of these worlds appear to Mary (and to the reader) like objects viewed in a fun-house mirror, generally recognizable but marked by a darkened, almost surreal difference. The briefly recounted story of Laura Seybold, for instance, lingers in Mary's mind with its central image of a young woman, "the life . . . out of her eyes," wandering "through town with a bleak, dazed, shell-shocked look on her face" as she heads home one Saturday night to swallow "every pill in the house." Or, later, the story of Eunice Barnacle's mother, who bails her abusive boyfriend out of jail so that she can murder him with a shotgun, an act that gains her both a life sentence at Sing Sing Prison and a place in town's expanding lore.

As she moves from episode to episode, Mary gradually comes to see for the first time the fissures in the peacefulness of Booth's Landing. At one extreme lies the world of the masculine and the powerful, symbolized by the omnipresence of the town's most prominent families, the Booths and Tiesslers, whose connections reach back to the Revolutionary War period. "In every generation," as Mary acknowledges, "for as long as anyone can remember, the Booths and the Tiesslers have been the town's leading families" as well as the foundations of its economic fortunes. Seen from this angle, Booth's Landing is a world of banks and factories, of civic pride and philanthropic gesture, and of football heroics that figure in local mythologies.

At the other extreme is an ever-expanding community of disenfranchised women that begins to arrange itself around the local hospital and that eventually fractures the town with its push for union certification. "For six months, the nurses carried picket signs outside the hospital," Mary recalls. "Twenty nurses, on the picket line, every day and into the night." She recalls how local residents were divided about the strike, how many of them scorned the nurses and how hard it was to persist.

Yet beneath the surface of this apparently split world, as beneath the surface of all the worlds Mary touches, circulates a rich diversity of opinions and attitudes toward love and sex, faith and religion, wisdom and knowledge. In this sense, "A Nurse's Story" is arranged as a series of questions that Mary faces: questions of love, sexuality, power, mortality, and spirituality, all of which culminate in her experience with political activism.

What Mary gradually understands is that no experience or person exists in isolation. She comes to sense the insufficiency of any of these other worlds to synthesize fully the complexities she recognizes as essential to her own sense of truth. For her, each world is incomplete and rigidly exclusive rather than cumulative and inclusive. With each new experience and story, Mary also gains understanding of the different strategies others use to organize their reality, to piece together their own memories.

The story ends with Mary sensing, but not understanding fully, the meaning in the visit of the ghostly Sister Rosa and of Mary's long-dead husband's sudden youthfulness, as he re-enters her story with "hair . . . the color of fresh corn" and his clarinet held between "fingers . . . as thick as cigars." She finally understands that each story she set out to tell inevitably spirals outward to include other stories told by other people. These other stories appear in various forms and stages of completion. They are allusive, metaphoric, or nostalgic. Moreover, these other stories are often contradictory, equally believable visions and revisions of a single event; the layering of stories produces what Mary herself recognizes as a system of stories circulating within and around her. Hers is a dying lived in retrospect, a journey away from the known and the knowable to the illuminating edges of open secrets and whispered pasts.

In this sense, "A Nurse's Story" is a richly patterned fiction about the need to structure subjective experiences through the complex act of fiction making. Mary's maturing corresponds with her accumulation and transcendence of storytelling. It is a story, too, in which the reader is implicated, made aware of the assumptions (cultural, historical, and ideological) that limit the way Mary reads the people and worlds around her. How the aging nurse reads the various "texts" of her existence comes to reflect on how readers approach the story of Mary's life, a reminder of people's need for clarity and order and for the meaning that comes through reading.

Source: Klay Dyer, Critical Essay on "A Nurse's Story," in *Short Stories for Students*, Thomson Gale, 2007.

Carol Ullmann

Ullmann is a freelance writer and editor. In the following essay, she explores the meaning of a "good death" in the context of a life well-lived and how people are remembered after they die in "A Nurse's Story."

"A Nurse's Story," by Peter Baida, reflects upon the life and death of nurse Mary McDonald, who is dying from colon cancer. Mary is content with her life and calm in the face of death; indeed she knows too much about her condition because of her training as a nurse to be mistaken about the deterioration of her body. Mary knows that everybody wants a "good death," but she is unsure what that really means. For Ida Peterson, a good death meant a "natural death," which Mrs. Peterson believed meant she would die peacefully with her husband nearby. This is not the death that Mrs. Peterson got because she actually died from a ruptured artery. Frightened, Mrs. Peterson died covered in her own blood, clutching Mary's hand, a nurse she barely knew. In the face of her own imminent death, Mary chooses instead to focus on her life, a life that was well-lived and fulfilling in its own quiet way.

Mary lived her entire life in Booth's Landing, a small town on the Hudson River in New York State. "You can do worse than to live and die in a place like Booth's Landing," and Mary indeed refuses to go with her son George to Chicago or anywhere else in her last months because she wants to die in Booth's Landing. Mary married George, a gentle man who loved to play clarinet and taught music at the local high school. They were married thirty-nine years and had three children together before George died. On their second date, Mary assured George that "there's more to life than money" after he told her that he would like to

> "... MARY LIVED AS WELL AS THE GOOD DEATH SHE IS GRANTED, REUNITED WITH HER LOVING HUSBAND AND ALL REGRETS IN LIFE SETTLED."

live in Booth's Landing for the rest of his life and teach clarinet. He said, "I don't think I'll ever make much money.... I've never cared much about it." At the time in which "A Nurse's Story" takes place, George has been dead eight years but is never far from Mary's thoughts. She misses him deeply and remembers with affection how he was a good father to their children and passionate about playing his clarinet. Their love, like their lives, was quiet and thorough.

Mary had no hobbies. After her love for her family, the New York Giants, and dark beer, she poured all of her passion into nursing. Nursing is part technical know-how (managing medicines, operating hospital machinery, and following procedure) and part personal touch (soothing people through pain and fear, being strong for others when they are weak, and having compassion). Mary touched the lives of many people in Booth's Landing, often seeing people at their lowest moments. For example, the doctor caring for her, Dr. Tom Seybold, is the son of Laura Seybold, a patient Mary nursed after a suicide attempt following her second miscarriage, before she and her husband conceived Tom. Mary was considered by her colleagues and neighbors to be a good nurse; people called her for medical advise before they called their physician. "She knew things that only nurses know." But Mary was not the only good nurse in Booth's Landing. When Mary's grandmother was dying from colon cancer, Mary's friend Clarice Hunter was the nurse on duty. Mary's grandmother was so touched by Clarice's careful ministrations that she insisted on having Clarice at her bedside in the last hours of her life, just as if Clarice were another member of her family. "This woman is a jewel. ... This woman is a blessing," Mary's grandmother explained. Mary's grandmother, one could argue, also had a good death, eased by the care of an excellent nurse. Mary recognizes the ephemeral qualities of a good nurse in Eunice

Barnacle, her attending nurse at Booth-Tiessler Geriatric Center.

Mary's life was, by her choice, relatively uneventful. Her participation in the 1967 nurses' union strike was her one deviation from everything the world expected of her. Mary's participation in the formation of the union in 1965 and the subsequent strike was important to the other nurses who held her opinion in high regard—"if you talked to other nurses, you found out that Mary's opinion made a difference." Baida never explains why this is, but the reader is left with the sense that Mary's steady sensibilities and skill as a nurse earned her the respect of her peers. The strike overall was a dramatic event in the history of the town: nurse Beverly Wellstone on a hunger strike lasting thirty-three days; Warren Booth Jr. and George Jr. stressed about the strife between their parents during an important high school championship football game; Sister Rosa bringing in scab nurses to cross the picket lines; striking nurses praying outside the hospital in the dead of winter; and Mary standing proudly with her coworkers despite the comments made by her neighbors. Mary, after all, had dedicated her life to caring for other people's health, and this union put her social and professional life on the line. It was a gamble, but the rewards were an investment in the well-being of the nurses and, by extension, the patients. The irony is that some people, like Carl Usher or Cheryl Hughes, were affronted at the idea of the nurses striking because they felt that patients were being neglected. Cheryl said: "Let's just hope nobody dies. Those women ought to be ashamed." These people never looked more closely at the issue and understood that the nurses were picketing, in part, to improve patient care.

What Mary and others remember about the strike is that it lasted over three months and took a stranger coming into their small town—an emissary from the cardinal—to bring the strike to conclusion. With the union officially recognized, Mary and her colleagues were able to earn a fairer wage and better staffing. In the long term, the union would also give the hospital's nurses an avenue by which they could get any other needed changes.

Mary did not regret her participation in the union, and it did not alter her conservative political and economic convictions. Eunice sees that the union is not doing much for Mary now that she is sick and dying, but Mary knows the union

is important for other reasons because she urges Eunice to unionize the nurses at the Booth-Tiessler Geriatric Center. Just as Mary and Clarice once did, Eunice and her coworkers debate the possibility of a union for the Geriatric Center nurses. Just as Mary was reluctant to become a "troublemaker," so do some of Eunice's coworkers refuse to get involved. Trouble is sometimes what is needed to oust complacency. One of the defining points the nurses then and now come around on is the question of whether they are being paid what they are worth. Nurses are highly skilled and often work in intense environments, caring for multiple patients and working long shifts to ensure continuity of care. Eunice knows, as Mary long ago determined, that self-respect is worth fighting for.

Baida is illustrating how some aspects of human nature and patterns in history are continual, but they are perhaps rarely observed in their entirety by individuals caught in the midst of events. A minor era is passing with Mary's death, but the seeds of the next generation of nurses—Eunice and her burgeoning union at the Geriatric Center and Mary's daughter Jane who is an exhausted nurse and mother of two wrestling with alcoholism. Mary's son George Jr. is a reflection of his father—large, quiet, and earnest. Brad is Mary and George's wild card, the prodigy with a successful job far away from Booth's Landing. All of Mary's children come home to be with their mother when her health takes a permanent turn for the worse, and it is clear that there is real affection between her and her children. Mary is succumbing to colon cancer just like her grandmother did almost forty years earlier. She has had her entire life to prepare for the possibility of this inherited disease; the cancer is, again, inoperable and unavoidable. With the bulk of her happy life behind her, Mary takes on her impending death tranquilly.

Mary's memories of her life and the author's description of the ongoing activity in the town after her death demonstrate Baida's sense that life in a small town is like a "tightly spun" web. Everyone is connected, sometimes indirectly or invisibly. Richard Dill, former town reporter and Mary's neighbor at the Geriatric Center, watches her fade away and remembers how she cared for his wife Jennifer after surgery. After Mary dies, Warren Booth Jr. remembers her in the context of the nurses' strike which disrupted his family and his football season. He selfishly assigns blame to Mary for making him unhappy almost thirty years earlier, but his own lack of compassion is a strong contrast with Mary's personality and reflects poorly upon him. He thinks to himself, "What great enterprise had they ever managed?" The irony, of course, is that nurses deal with life and death every day whereas Warren Booth Jr. grew up in a privileged family and inherited his job from his father. "The fact that he had never managed any great enterprise did not occur to him." Roger Dill, son of Richard, who reported on the nurses' strike, doesn't remember Mary's effect on his life. He is bored and indifferent as he writes up a standard obituary for Mary, oblivious of the knowledge that Mary was the nurse who cared for his mother twenty years ago. Nick Santino, the undertaker, lovingly prepares Mary's body, cognizant of how carefully, tenderly Mary cared for his own mother when she was dying. He is sad to see that Mary has died. Sister Margaret, the current hospital administrator, remembers Mary as a "*damned* good nurse"—a strong compliment coming from a nun and also significant considering that Sister Margaret and Mary, as employer and employee, had their "differences."

Mary's one lingering regret as she lay dying is that she disappointed the formidable Sister Rosa, who was hospital administrator during the union strike. Mary laments: "Oh, Sister Rosa, how I admired you! How I hated doing anything that might displease you. How I wanted you to *like* me." Sister Rosa was strict and held everyone to a high standard. She was also extremely stubborn and held out (along with the chairman of the board Warren Booth) against the striking nurses until the cardinal intervened. In her last days Mary is visited by the deceased Sister Rosa in a vision. Sister Rosa assures Mary that she did not take the strike personally and is actually glad that it happened. Sister Rosa says: "Workers have to fight. . . . The whole system depends on it." Reassured, Mary wakes and talks to her children one last time before slipping into unconsciousness where she is greeted by her late husband George. She has missed him so much, and the sight of him gladdens her heart. "The smile on his face made Mary want to get up and throw her arms around his neck." "A Nurse's Story" illustrates the good life that Mary lived as well as the good death she

is granted, reunited with her loving husband and all regrets in life settled.

"A good death. That's what everyone wants." A good death is defined by the life that was lived, the impact he or she had, and by what people remember of that person. A good death cannot be simply defined by how or why a person is dying. Baida leaves his readers with the sense that Mary's death was a good one—despite the fact that she has suffered from colon cancer—because she has lived a happy life, has had the respect of her peers and the unconditional love of her family. In the embrace of her community, Mary does not fear death. Her compassionate care as a nurse has touched many of her neighbors, some of whom are not aware of how Mary impacted their lives, but Mary did not give of herself because she expected anything in return. Like Clarice Hunter said when caring for Mary's grandmother, "Just doing my job." Most of the people who do remember Mary's gentle strength remember her with pride, respect, and perhaps a little awe.

Source: Carol Ullmann, Critical Essay on "A Nurse's Story," in *Short Stories for Students*, Thomson Gale, 2007.

Jennifer Bussey

Bussey holds a master's degree in Interdisciplinary Studies and a bachelor's degree in English Literature. She is an independent writer specializing in literature. In the following essay, she considers how Peter Baida reveals the nurses' strike as the defining moment in Mary McDonald's life in "A Nurse's Story."

Peter Baida's O. Henry award-winning "A Nurse's Story" is the story of a dying nurse, Mary McDonald. Baida takes the reader on a journey through Mary's past and present. During her last three days of life, Mary is in a room in a geriatric hospital. She passes the time reflecting on the past, talking to her nurse about starting a union, and preparing herself for the death she knows is imminent. As Baida guides the reader through numerous episodes of Mary's life, the reader comes to know her—and her community—well. It soon becomes apparent that the defining moment in Mary's life was a nurses' strike in 1967, an event that forced Mary to take a stand despite creating division in her close-knit community.

Baida's narrative style is unique and effective. The short story is essentially divided into

> BAIDA MAKES IT CLEAR THAT HER PAST
> INVOLVEMENT IN A UNION AND A SUBSEQUENT STRIKE
> WAS PIVOTAL IN MARY'S LIFE. SEVENTEEN OF THE MINI-
> CHAPTERS IN THE STORY RELATE DIRECTLY OR
> INDIRECTLY TO MARY'S UNION INVOLVEMENT."

thirty-one mini-chapters, about half of which relate to Mary's past. The overall effect is realistic; Mary is fully aware she is in the last days of her life, and her mind wanders naturally from the past to the present. Her interactions with the people around her are calm and devoid of the panic or terror other patients might feel at the prospect of dying soon. Perhaps because she has been a nurse her whole adult life, Mary made her peace with death long ago. Her love for her husband is deep and abiding, and she is comforted in the knowledge that she will see him soon. But she is not one to waste away her last days of influence. She encourages her son to lose weight and take better care of himself, and she tries to convince her nurse, Eunice, to pursue a union for herself and the other geriatric nurses.

The issue of the union dominates Mary's thoughts and words during her time in the hospital. Baida makes it clear that her past involvement in a union and a subsequent strike was pivotal in Mary's life. Seventeen of the mini-chapters in the story relate directly or indirectly to Mary's union involvement. The reader gets the first taste of this when Mary is talking to Eunice about how hard nurses' work is and how little they are paid. Eunice is resistant to the idea of a union, but then, so was Mary at first. As the story unfolds, the reader understands that Mary had always been against unions until her own professional life seemed hopeless. In 1965, she and the other nurses felt overworked, underpaid, and unheard. To the surprise of her coworkers, she ultimately decided to vote for the union. Now, Eunice is the one who is reluctant to pursue a union, and Mary knows how she feels. Toward the end of the story, Eunice remembers Mary commenting that unions had their good sides and their bad sides. Unfortunately, Mary dies before Eunice

has the chance to ask her about it again. Eunice thinks to herself that now, she will never know what Mary would have said. But the reader and Eunice know that Mary would have given both sides, only to conclude that unions are good for nurses. Her insistence that Eunice consider it is evidence of that. Eunice may not get the details from Mary, but her position is made clear. There is a scene in which Eunice is talking to a friend about the possibility of pursuing a union. It is reminiscent of Mary's past, when she turned from reluctance to endorsement. Eunice was opposed to the idea of a union when Mary first talked to her about it, but in this scene, she tries to convince another woman that it might be a good idea after all. Both Mary and Eunice love nursing and want to give their patients the best, which requires better working conditions.

Mary (when she was younger) and Eunice have something else in common—they need to make as much money as they can to support their families. Mary's husband was a music teacher who knew he would never make much money; Eunice is a single parent of a three-year-old. They both have practical needs to meet in their jobs, as well as personal ones. Baida tells the reader enough about Mary's past and personality that her love for nursing and nurses is undeniable. Apparently Mary had no hobbies or social groups. She loved football, beer, and nursing. In fact, she passed her love of nursing to her only daughter, who also enters the profession. This insight into Mary's heart is important because it gives significance to the way she talks to Eunice about unions and being the best nurse she can be.

When people are dying, the most significant people and events return to their thoughts. In many cases, people are plagued with guilt and regret. But in Mary's case, she lingers on her relationship to the nurses' union back in the 1960s. Why? As Baida slowly reveals, joining a union is initially contrary to Mary's nature, and her coworkers know it. Mary is also influential among her peers at the hospital, so the other nurses are interested in where she will land on the issue. When she changes her mind and decides to support the union, it is not just a hot topic among her peers, it marks a turning point for Mary. Rather than adhere to her existing views and beliefs, she takes into account how the issue particularly relates to her and her fellow nurses' work situation. She opens her mind and ultimately changes it. That the other nurses knew enough about her politics to know she would likely oppose a union demonstrates that Mary was outspoken about her views. This makes her willingness to change her mind a particularly strong indicator about the nature of her character.

Once the union was formed, it was not easy. Only two years later, the union decided to go on strike, complete with picketing and media attention. Her participation in the strike cemented Mary's commitment to the union. As a striker, she faced the disapproval and rejection of friends and other people she respected. She even had to strike the hospital owner's home, despite the fact that her son George and the owner's son were teammates on the football team. The whole union experience, then, represented a time in her life when Mary took a public stand for which she could *not* be universally popular in her community. It is little wonder she would reflect on this time in her final days. The memories are vivid, and they are both empowering and defeating. But her commitment to the union was really a commitment to herself and the other nurses at the hospital. Now, on her deathbed, she is in a hospital being cared for by a nurse she likes and respects. Her heart returns to that time of camaraderie, and she wants Eunice to have the ability to be the best nurse—and mother— she can be.

Mary's involvement in the strike continues to affect her life through the attitudes of other people in the community. Even now when she is sixty-nine, her association with that strike defines the way some people in the community think of her. As he reads her obituary, Warren Booth remembers little else about her than her holding a picket sign in front of his house all those years ago. Warren had been George's teammate, and when she picketed his father's house, it affected him as a teenager. He feels no sadness at her death and no real feelings of sadness for George, either. He toys with the idea of going to the funeral with a "why not?" attitude, but ultimately decides that he will just send a card to George. His lingering hostility is based solely on Mary's involvement in the strike decades ago. Similarly, Sister Margaret (who took over for Sister Rosa as the hospital's executive director) is sad to hear that Mary has died, although she hastens to add that she and Mary had their differences. Sister Margaret was not

even the executive director at the time of the strike, yet her compassion for Mary is accompanied by a twinge of resentment over her union activities.

To other members of the community, however, Mary's identity as a union member is secondary to her identity as a caring and skilled nurse. At the funeral home, Mary's body is prepared by two men, one of whom is Nick Santino. Nick tells the other man that he is sad to see Mary go because he remembers how she took care of his mother in the hospital. He does not just remember that she attended to his mother's basic needs; he remembers how she washed her feet, even using a toothbrush to clean her toes. What Nick does not know is that Mary wanted to provide that level of detailed care to all her patients and that only through the met demands of the union for more staff could she provide it. Readers may recall a previous passage in which Mary and another nurse are physically and emotionally drained by having as many as twenty patients. It is fair to infer that Nick's mother was admitted to the hospital after the strike and after more staff were hired.

The ripples of the strike go out to people who do not even realize that their lives are affected by it. For some, like Warren and Sister Margaret, the effects are negative, but for countless others, like Nick, they are positive and unforgettable. If Mary had been alive to hear Nick's story, it would have only affirmed her difficult decision to commit to the nurses' union. That turning point in her life made possible the legacy she wanted as a nurse who cared for her patients in a way that mattered.

Source: Jennifer Bussey, Critical Essay on "A Nurse's Story," in *Short Stories for Students*, Thomson Gale, 2007.

Thomson Gale

In the following essay, the critic gives an overview of Peter Baida's work.

After earning a master's degree in business administration from the University of Pennsylvania, Peter Baida began twenty years of employment at Memorial Sloan-Kettering Cancer Center in New York City. At the time of his death in 1999, he led the center's fundraising operations. The business executive wrote *Poor Richard's Legacy: American Business Values from Benjamin Franklin to Donald Trump*, an "ingeniously conceived and brightly executed social history" according to Genevieve Stutta-ford in *Publishers Weekly*. The 1990 publication includes figures from as early as the seventeenth century as well as more recent figures such as Cornelius Vanderbilt, John D. Rockefeller, Andrew Carnegie, and Henry Ford. When high-lighting key business personalities, Baida avoids life histories, instead giving readers "the patterns of behavior insofar as they affect business val-ues. ... the person's philosophy," recognized *Business History Review* contributor Joseph F. Rishel. Baida also examines "the literature of success in the nineteenth and twentieth centu-ries." In the book, Baida recounts "the trend in which business values have changed from colo-nial times to the present in astonishing and self-destructive ways. ... TAs a consequence of mass production of consumer goods, salesmanship (that is, style, wit, charm) replaced character," informed Rishel. "Baida is careful not to preach; he doesn't need to," stated Stuttaford. Baida's survey of business ethics across time "fills an academic vacuum and fills it abundantly," remarked Rishel, forecasting that "the book. . . . should be well-received."

"The style [of *Poor Richard's Legacy*] is read-able and often entertaining," described Rishel. In *Washington Monthly*, John Schwartz prefaced complaints of "silly writing" and errors due to "Baida's reliance on books and clippings instead of his own digging, "with the comment "any book that tries to do so much in so little space is going to have failings." Schwartz was extremely compli-mentary, calling *Poor Richard's Legacy* "a damn useful book, a kind of Cliffs Notes of business history and thinking." Schwartz recommended *Poor Richard's Legacy* to "anyone who reads the business pages."

Baida also wrote "A Nurse's Story," a prize-winning short story based on a nurses' strike. Its complete story collection was published in 2001. Peter Baida's widow, Diane Cole, wrote in the book's afterword: "No publication is as poign-ant as that of a posthumous first volume of fiction. With Peter Baida's "A Nurse's Story and Others," this sense is further compounded by the fact that the author died within months of the title story winning first prize in the O. Henry Short Story Awards.

"Rather than allow life's heavy-handed irony to overshadow Peter's work, however, I prefer to let it serve, instead, as a lens that helps illuminate Peter's literary achievement. On the most obvious

level, given Peter's own history of illness, it is no accident that many of his stories are set against a medical backdrop. More subtly, these stories reveal that what Peter learned from his travels in the world of illness was a compassion for the vulnerable. And it is this understanding, one that goes beyon empathy, that suffuses his work.

"As the title of the collection's concluding story so aptly puts it, there is always a "reckon-ing," and its impact endures for generations. And now, with Peter's death, comes the sum-ming up of his life, and his work. He lived the way he wrote, with a straightforward grace, pre-cision, and insight—and yes, a dark, inescapable irony—that everyone who knew and loved him will miss. But Peter's voice, in all its fullness, is here, in his stories, to be read, and cherished. The writer's legacy he would have wished."

Source: Thomson Gale, "Peter Baida," in *Contemporary Authors Online*, Gale, 2004.

SOURCES

Baida, Peter, "A Nurse's Story," in *A Nurse's Story and Others*, University Press of Mississippi, 2001, pp. 3–35.

Barta-Moran, Ellie, "Adult Books: Fiction," in *Booklist*, Vol. 97, No. 13, March 2001, p. 1224.

Sweeny, Aoibheann, Review of *A Nurse's Story and Others*, in *New York Times Book Review*, April 15, 2001, http://query.nytimes.com/gst/fullpage.html?res= 9F0DE7D8143EF936A25757C0A9679C8B63 (accessed September 9, 2006).

Zaleski, Jeff, Review of *A Nurse's Story and Others*, in *Publishers Weekly*, Vol. 248, No. 3, March 26, 2001, p. 61.

FURTHER READING

Goodman-Draper, Jacqueline, *Health Care's Forgotten Majority: Nurses and their Frayed White Collars*, Greenwood Publishing Group, 1995.

> Speaking to the dynamics of a healthcare debate that has historically overlooked the political and fiscal well-being of patients and front-line workers as part of its implicit strat-egy, this book deals with one important group that is most often overlooked: nurses. Although addressed to a professional audience, this study does foreground many of the same issues raised by Baida in "A Nurse's Story" while at the same time exploring the nursing population as a more complex and politically

dynamic community than it might appear to the casual observer.

Kelly, David F., *Medical Care at the End of Life: A Catholic Perspective*, Georgetown University Press, 2006.
Having worked with healthcare professionals for more than three decades, Kelly has confronted many difficult, often painful issues that concern medical treatment at the end of life. Here, he outlines succinctly many major issues regarding end-of-life care as understood within the traditions of Catholic medical ethics.

Nelson, Siobhan, and Suzanne Gordan, *The Complexities of Care: Nursing Reconsidered*, Cornell University Press, 2006.
Written for a general audience, this collection of essays provokes a rethinking of many assumptions that continue to inform both popular and political thinking about nurses and the nursing profession. Many of the essays included here warn of the dangers of oversimplified images of nursing.

Rosen, Ruth, *The World Split Open: How the Modern Women's Movement Changed America*, Penguin, 2001.
Popular historian Ruth Rosen chronicles the trajectory of the American women's movement from its beginnings in the 1960s to the late twentieth century. Interweaving personal stories with political analysis, she remembers the events and the people who defined this social revolution. Working with resources from archives, traditional research, and personal interviews, Rosen invites readers to appreciate the impact of the women's movement and to agree with her argument that the need for attention to these issues is far from over.

Perfection

MARK HELPRIN

2004

"Perfection," by Mark Helprin, was published in the 2004 collection *The Pacific and Other Stories*. The protagonist, a Hasidic Jewish boy called Roger Reveshze, lives in post–World War II Brooklyn and becomes the unlikely ally of the New York Yankees baseball team in helping them out of a string of defeats. Roger is physically puny and knows nothing about baseball but draws his power from a divine source (angels help him hit the ball out of the stadium). This agency is available to him because of his extraordinary piety and devotion to perfection in his own life. In the greater scheme of things, his unusual abilities are portrayed as a God-given compensation for the Holocaust, in which he lost his parents in horrific circumstances. Rejecting the cynicism of much twentieth- and twenty-first-century literature, Helprin invokes such traditional themes as the perfection of God's ordering of creation, the inspirational quality of the life lived with honor and integrity, and the limitations of materialism.

AUTHOR BIOGRAPHY

Mark Helprin was born on June 28, 1947, in New York City, the son of Morris, a motion picture executive, and Eleanor Helprin. He was raised in New York City, the Hudson River Valley, and the British West Indies. He received his undergraduate degree from Harvard College

Mark Helprin Photograph by Sara D. Davis. AP Images

in 1969. While he was an undergraduate, at the age of twenty-one, he sold his first story to the *New Yorker*. He received a master's degree in Middle Eastern studies from Harvard's Graduate School of Arts and Sciences in 1972 and then did postgraduate work at Oxford University in England and at Princeton and Columbia in the United States. He has served in the British Merchant Navy, and from 1972 to 1973, he served in the Israeli infantry and the Israeli Air Force. On June 28, 1980, he married Lisa Kennedy, a tax lawyer and a vice president of Chase Manhattan Bank. As of 2006, they were still married.

Helprin believes that his work speaks for itself and seldom talks about it or about himself. However, he has described himself as Jewish by birth and by faith, though not in the orthodox tradition, and depicts his books as religious. Politically, he labels himself a Republican. He has also spoken about his pursuit of exceptional experiences; he is a skilled mountain climber.

Three quotations from Helprin collected in John Affleck's dissertation, "Birds of a Feather: The Ancient Mariner Archetype in Mark

Helprin's 'A Dove of the East' and *A Soldier of the Great War*," shed light on Helprin's motivation in writing and on his choice of themes. Affleck cites Helprin as writing that he loves literature "not only because it is so pleasingly beautiful, but because it is so deeply consequential." Affleck adds that in an epigram to *A Dove of the East and Other Stories*, Helprin quotes Dante in Italian: "*amor mi mosse, che mi fa parlare*," (love moved me, and makes me speak). Finally, Affleck cites Helprin's remark to a *Paris Review* interviewer:

> I write in service of illumination and memory. I write to each into "the blind world where no one can help." I write because it is a way of glimpsing truth. And I write to create something of beauty.

From 1985 to 2000, Helprin wrote political opinion pieces for the *Wall Street Journal*; he was appointed a contributing editor to the *Journal* in 1991. He has also published stories and essays on politics and aesthetics in the *Atlantic Monthly, New Criterion, Commentary*, the *New York Times*, the *National Review, American Heritage*, and *Forbes ASAP*. During the 1996 U.S. presidential election campaign, it was revealed that Helprin had written the nomination acceptance speech of Republican Party candidate Bob Dole. As of 2006, he was a senior fellow at the Hudson Institute, a conservative think tank.

Helprin's books include *A Dove of the East and Other Stories* (1975), the novel *Refiner's Fire: The Life and Adventures of Marshall Pearl, a Foundling* (1977), the critically acclaimed *Ellis Island and Other Stories* (1981), the novel *Winter's Tale* (1983), the children's book *Swan Lake* (1989), and the highly praised *A Soldier of the Great War* (1991). Thereafter followed two children's books, both with illustrations by Chris Van Allsburg, *A City in Winter: The Queen's Tale* (1996) and *The Veil of Snows* (1997). *The Pacific and Other Stories*, which contains the story "Perfection," was published in 2004, and *Freddy and Fredericka* in 2005.

Helprin's work has garnered many awards. He received a PEN/Faulkner Award, the National Jewish Book Award, and an American Book Award nomination in 1982, all for *Ellis Island and Other Stories*. In the same year, he was awarded the American Academy and Institute of Arts and Letters Prix de Rome. In 1984, he was awarded a Guggenheim Fellowship. His novel for young adults, *A City in Winter: The Queen's Tale*, won a World Fantasy Award for

MEDIA ADAPTATIONS

- *The Pacific and Other Stories* was released in an unabridged version as an audio CD by Sound Library in 2004. It is narrated by William Dufris. As of 2006, it was available from amazon.com.

Best Novella, World Fantasy Convention in 1997. In 2001, the Center for Security Policy gave Helprin a Mightier Pen Award.

PLOT SUMMARY

"Perfection" opens in the Hasidic Jewish community in Brooklyn in June 1956 but immediately flashes back a year to March 1955, to the incident that sets off the events of the story, when "the Saromsker Rebbe opened the wrong drawer." (Rebbe is the Hasidic Jewish word for rabbi, which means spiritual teacher or master while Saromsker refers to the Hasidic dynasty or family group from which the rebbe descends.) The Saromsker Rebbe's family had taken in many children who survived the Holocaust though their parents had not.

The events leading up to the drawer incident are described. The Saromsker Rebbe wishes to telephone another rabbi to discuss a theological point. But snow has snapped some telephone lines, so the Saromsker Rebbe puts his points in a letter and asks one of his students which student may be trusted to take the message to the other rabbi. The student recommends Roger Reveshze, a fourteen-year-old boy who escaped the Majdanek Nazi extermination camp in Poland and spends much time praying for his parents. The student says Roger is suitable for the errand as he is extraordinarily fast and has unusual spiritual purity. The Saromsker Rebbe summons Roger and asks him what he sees when he closes his eyes. Roger describes a scene in

Eastern Europe with an old man (probably his father) with snow settling on his hat.

Looking for sealing wax for his letter, the Saromsker Rebbe opens a drawer of his desk. It is the wrong drawer, and when he sees what is in it, he rapidly slams it shut, though not before Roger catches sight of it. It is a box marked with the brand name "Lindt," a kind of Swiss chocolate which is non-kosher.

Roger reflects that the Saromsker Rebbe has eaten non-kosher food over time, lied, and concealed his sin from his followers. Roger concludes the rebbe is imperfect. Roger hates lying because it weakens a person against worse evils. He knows what happened to his parents and others in the Holocaust, and he is determined to bear witness to this truth until he dies. He aims for perfection in this aspect of his life, in the conviction that his persistence and love will lead to reunion with his parents in the afterlife. The Saromsker Rebbe's lie tells Roger that the rebbe cannot be trusted to study current affairs honestly and sense when there may be another impending holocaust. Roger decides that he himself must listen to the radio. His classmate Luba, who works for the butcher, Schnaiper, tells him that in the butcher's shop there is a radio that cannot be turned off. Roger arranges to do Luba's job in order to listen to the radio.

Roger hears an entrancing narrative on the radio. Schnaiper tells him that it is a baseball game taking place in "the House That Ruth Built." This is a popular nickname for Yankee Stadium in the Bronx, after the famous baseball player for the Yankees, Babe Ruth, the nickname of George Herman Ruth Jr. (1895–1948). Roger, in his ignorance of U.S. culture, believes that it is a reference to Ruth, the supposed author of the book of Ruth in the Old Testament. Ruth is celebrated by Jews as a convert to Judaism as well as for being the great-grandmother to King David of Israel (c. 1011 B.C.E.–971 B.C.E.), from whose lineage Jews believe that the Messiah will come.

Roger is excited that there is a place in the Bronx with a direct link to the Israelites. He asks Luba about it, and Luba solemnly describes his fantasy as if it were reality. He envisions a huge sacred construction, lit by divine light and filled with beautiful women who are descended from Ruth. There are rabbis reading sacred Jewish texts, Jewish bands playing music for dancing, and endless supplies of Jewish food. Luba says that no one can go there except if they die, when they are taken there on a sled, or the women are in danger and need a champion to save them. In his Western mind, Roger knows that what Luba says is impossible, but in his Eastern mind, he knows that rabbis and mystics could defy gravity and fly.

From his time spent in Schnaiper's shop listening to baseball games on the radio, Roger emerges with the garbled message that the Yenkiss (the Yankees) are suffering a string of defeats, and even with the great Mickey Mental (the real-life player Mickey Mantle, 1931–1994) on their team, the Kansas City team could easily "kill" them.

After much prayer, Roger knows the answer. He has to save the Yankees. Dressed in his Hasidic black robes and fur hat on a hot June day, he packs a suitcase and sets off on the subway for the House of Ruth, where he is convinced that "a miracle will come." Roger arrives at the stadium and, though he has no money to buy a ticket, gets in by helping a peanut delivery man carrying in supplies. He goes to the stands and watches as Mantle and Berra (the real-life player Lawrence "Yogi" Berra, born 1925) are engaged in a practice session. Roger repeatedly calls out, "Mickey Mental!" Mantle thinks he is being mocked. He walks over to Roger and asks what he wants. Roger says that God has sent him "To lift you from the darkness of defeat," adding that he has received no specific instructions as to how. He asks Mantle where the ideal place to direct the ball is, and Mantle replies that it is over the clock and out of the stadium. Roger offers to show him how to do this. Mantle discusses the idea with Berra. Berra thinks that Roger is a "hayseed" (a mispronunciation of the word Hasid) and that Mantle is also a "hayseed" (a nickname for a person with a farming background). Based on this logic, he thinks that Roger should be allowed to try.

Berra brings out the rest of the team. Roger holds the bat aloft like a sword, and as he dances and twirls with it, the sun shines on it, and it glows. He feels love in his heart. The Yankees do not know that Roger is here to test God's justice, according to the verse from the book of Ruth, "May the Lord deal kindly with you, as you have dealt with the dead." One of the coaches, Wylie, who does not believe in Roger, challenges him to hit the ball so that it knocks off the minute hand of the clock. The pitcher throws the ball, and Roger hits it so hard that it shatters into tiny

particles. Roger apologizes and tries again. This time, the ball, trailing orange flame, hits the minute hand of the clock, which drops to the ground. Roger rises to each challenge the players set him, including putting a hole in the clock. Stengel (Casey Stengel, the real-life manager of the Yankees, 1890–1975) emerges and promises that if Roger can consistently hit the ball out of the stadium, he will double each player's salary and hire Roger for a million dollars a year. But if Roger fails, Stengel will not hire him, and each player will have his salary halved. Roger protests that he is not interested in money; he only wants to teach the team "to hit these objects, these . . . *balls*, with perfection."

The Yankees look on awestruck as Roger hits one ball after another out of the stadium. Roger also shows that he can make brilliant catches. Stengel bribes the witnesses to Roger's performance to keep silent, so as to maintain his team's tactical advantage. He is worried that Roger will not be able to play in the World Series because it takes place close to Rosh Hashana, the Jewish New Year, a time of reflection and penitence that Roger is determined to observe.

Over the following weeks, the sporting and Jewish communities are surprised by the changes that take place regarding the Yankees. The hot dogs sold at the stadium are now all kosher, the stands echo with Hebrew prayers, Hasidic rabbis stand behind the umpires, the team refuses to play on Saturdays, the Jewish sabbath, and some of the players have adopted the Jewish head-covering.

The Yankees now lose by lesser margins, and the players perform better as they strive to match Roger. No one realizes that Roger closes his eyes after the pitch, feels an angel's arms take hold of the bat, and levitates slightly with joy. Hitting the ball is a mystical experience. Even with eyes closed he sees it coming, and it seems to grow and stop in front of him, asking to be hit. The angel hits the ball with great power, and it flies out of the stadium, slowly enough to be seen by an ecstatic crowd.

On the occasion of Roger's first game, his astonishing performance brings the Yankees a win over Kansas City. In the locker room after the game, the team picks Roger up and carries him about in triumph, chanting his name. He insists that they stop, because he is not responsible; God is. He also stops them from worshipping his bat. The press bursts into the locker room demanding to see Roger, but Mantle hides Roger in a laundry cart and Berra says that Roger has gone to his hometown, Milledgeville. A media storm of speculation follows about who he is and where he comes from. Roger is oblivious to the fame as his entire being is taken up with the experience of being within the embrace of an angel.

Roger's second game brings the Yankees a dramatic win over the White Sox. Stengel asks Roger to hold a clinic to teach the rest of the team how to play like he does. Roger warns him that he knows nothing about baseball but offers to teach them what he does know. The seminar takes place at the Yankees' secret practice ground. Roger tells the team that locks—both locks in doors and locks in canals—illustrate the mechanism of creation. God is perfect, and his creation is perfect, so that all fear and suffering in the world are ultimately counterbalanced, just as to allow a door lock to turn, each pin in the lock mechanism must be raised sufficiently to allow the lock to turn. Some pins are raised more, and some less. Though people live very different lives, with different levels of suffering, all are raised by God in various and invisible ways, so that the perfection of creation will not be broken. Similarly, a canal lock is a mechanism to lift or lower a boat that gets its power from the urge of all water to find its own level. People's reception of God's compensation, which is called holiness, is more real than the world itself. Roger says his strength and skill on the baseball field are supplied by God in compensation, resulting in perfection. The Yankees can tap into this, but not if their object is only to win games, which is a diminishment of God's infinite universe. Mantle asks Roger what his object is. Roger replies, "Because of the imperfection I have seen, I live for the hope of restoration."

Roger tells his story. Born in Majdanek, he saw so much killing that he thought it was natural. He was sustained by his parents' love. Just before the camp was liberated by the Allies, when he was three, he and his parents were marched out to the edge of a pit. Everyone was shot except for Roger, who escaped the bullets because of his small size. A soldier threw him into the pit on top of the bodies. Gasoline was thrown onto the bodies, which were set alight, but Roger escaped. Now, all he wishes for is a sign that somewhere forward in time or beyond time there is a justice in the world that will lift up those he loves from the grave they were given.

The Yankees return from the seminar with the ruthlessness of an efficient army bent on vengeance. For two weeks, they win every game they play. They no longer care about their salaries or their standing in the league. They care only about perfection.

Roger's last game takes place. Roger is cheered by people in the streets as well as in the stadium, which is filled to double capacity. Roger hits one ball after another out of the stadium. Everyone looks on in wonder and delight and feels as if "the world were ablaze with the light of perfection."

Roger is happy to return to his humble home in Brooklyn and does not miss the luxury hotel in which he has been staying. He knows that the value of the Hasidic rituals and manner of dress is that they put the things of the world in their place. As the subway train twists and turns on its journey towards his home, Roger closes his eyes and sees his mother and father. He opens his eyes and reflects that what happened in the House That Ruth Built is like a song that he has been brought up to sing, in protest of mortality and for the love of God.

CHARACTERS

Berra

Berra is a fictionalized version of Lawrence "Yogi" Berra, the real-life catcher who played for the Yankees baseball team at the time in which the story is set. The real-life Berra was famous for his malapropisms and his idiosyncratic use of the English language. Helprin exploits this reputation by having his character Berra utter cryptic remarks such as, "The start of the middle is the end of the road for the beginning" and mixing up the terms "Hasid" and "hayseed." Berra has a spiritual streak that makes him instinctively supportive of Roger from the moment when he first appears at Yankee Stadium.

Rabbi Eisvogel

Rabbi Eisvogel is a member of the Hasidic Jewish community in which Roger lives at the story's opening. He is a wise man who allows Roger to listen to the radio in Schnaiper's shop for long periods, even if it means missing his studies, because he knows it is important to Roger's spiritual quest.

Luba

Luba is Roger's classmate in the Hasidic Jewish community. He has a job in Schnaiper's shop until Roger bribes him to let him take it over so that he can listen to the radio. After Roger hears the baseball game "from the House That Ruth Built" on the radio, he asks Luba about the House of Ruth. Luba is one of those Jews for whom "dreams are real" because they have lost everything. He has a vivid imagination and launches into a fantasy that describes Yankee Stadium as a kind of theme park dedicated to the Biblical character Ruth.

Mickey Mantle

Mickey Mantle, or Mickey Mental, as Roger calls him with his Yiddish accent, is a fictionalized version of the real-life baseball player for the Yankees. Roger begins his quest to rescue the Yankees by standing at the rail during a practice session and shouting repeatedly, "Mickey Mental!" Mantle is irritated but walks over to question Roger about why he is there. Against his better judgment, Mantle believes what Roger tells him about being sent by God to save him "from the darkness of defeat."

Mel

Mel is a radio sports commentator (one half of the commentating duo, Red and Mel). Though they work together, both are from Alabama, and both are described as prima donnas, Red and Mel clearly dislike one another. Their on-air bickering is temporarily interrupted by their astonishment at Roger's performance. Mel is stocky, with blue-black hair, and is portrayed as "what you might call a garage guy."

Mickey Mental

See Mickey Mantle

Red

Red is a radio sports commentator (one half of the commentating duo, Red and Mel). Red is red-haired and thin, high strung, and aristocratic.

Roger Reeves

See Roger Reveshze

Roger Reveshze

Roger, the protagonist, is a fourteen-year-old Hasidic Jew who, at the story's opening in 1955, lives in a Hasidic community in Brooklyn. He is described as a strange-looking boy with "wild eyes, big ears, and big teeth." He is physically undersized, even puny, and what certain children might call a "spastic." Nevertheless, he is deemed remarkable by his classmates and the elders of his community because of his extraordinary speed and his great spiritual purity. His piety and devotion to God have given him access to ecstatic spiritual states. When he prays, his body defies gravity and he spins head-over-heels and sees light.

Roger has a horrific past, having been born in and narrowly escaped from a Nazi extermination camp where he witnessed his parents and everyone he knew being murdered by the Nazis. Since then, Roger has devoted his life to praying for his parents' souls, seeking some compensation for their terrible deaths. He is devout yet intellectually independent, so he is ready to question the authority of the Saromsker Rebbe when he discovers that he has been eating non-kosher chocolate and soon sets out to remedy the imperfection that has crept into his life as a result of the rebbe's lie. Roger is a seeker after perfection, both in his own life and in the universe as a whole. Like many Jews who have lost everything (according to the story), he is susceptible to glorious dreams and is inspired to go to help the Yankees out of their run of defeats because he believes that they inhabit the divinely sanctioned "House That Ruth Built."

Roger has another motive for helping the Yankees. In the Hasidic tradition of spiritual mischief, he wants to challenge God. God, he feels, must compensate him for the deaths of his parents. Though people can be cast down by suffering, he believes, the perfection of creation demands that God raise them up by a sufficient degree to compensate for the suffering. God does not disappoint Roger. While Roger knows nothing about baseball, by drawing upon the infinite skill and power of angels, he is able to hit ball after ball out of the stadium. In the short time that he plays for the Yankees, he inspires the team to pursue perfection over and above all material considerations and brings a glimpse of perfection to thousands of awed spectators.

Roger's unimpressive physique, his ignorance of baseball, and even the Hasidic dress in which he introduces himself to the Yankees and which is completely unsuited to sports activity, are set against his extraordinary performance on the baseball field. The gap between the two is both a source of the story's comedy and emblematic of the nature of divine grace, which, the story suggests, ignores rational and logical considerations and works according to its own immutable laws.

During his time playing for the Yankees, he is given the more Anglo-Saxon-sounding name, Roger Reeves.

Saromsker Rebbe

The Saromsker Rebbe is a member of the Hasidic Jewish community in which Roger lives at the story's opening. His family has rescued numerous Holocaust survivors. A man of considerable spiritual insight, he questions Roger and is quick to see his spiritual purity. However, he has neglected his own religious duties by eating non-kosher chocolate and lying about it. He has allowed imperfection to enter his life. His character is not examined further, his role in the story being to provide the catalyst for Roger's quest for perfection.

Schnaiper

Schnaiper is a butcher who serves the Hasidic Jewish community in which Roger lives. Schnaiper in unique in the community in that he has a radio, and Roger takes a job in his shop so that he can listen to it. The radio is always tuned to a baseball game, which Schnaiper tries to explain to Roger.

Stengel

Stengel is a fictionalized version of Casey Stengel, the real-life manager of the Yankees baseball team at the time in which the story is set. He is a cynical businessman who thinks in financial and material terms. When he first sees Roger, he promises that if Roger can consistently hit the ball out of the stadium, he will double each player's salary and hire Roger for a million dollars a year. But if Roger fails, Stengel will not hire him, and each player will have his salary halved. Stengel finds it hard to understand that Roger is not motivated by money and even harder to understand that Roger will not play in the World Series because God told him not to play during Rosh Hashana, a Jewish time of penitence.

Wylie

Wylie is one of the Yankees' coaches. "Mean and small of soul," he is the most cynical character in the story. He claims that Roger is using tricks to

TOPICS FOR FURTHER STUDY

- Research the Holocaust that took place during World War II. Write and give a presentation on the conditions leading up to it, what happened, and the aftereffects. Include in your presentation some ideas on how such an event might be prevented from happening again.

- Either (1) interview some survivors of the Holocaust, and/or members of a family whose parents or grandparents survived the Holocaust, about their experiences, and create a report, film, or CD based on your findings; or (2) read some firsthand accounts of survivors of the Holocaust and create a report, film or CD based on your findings.

- Read about Hasidic Judaism—its beliefs, customs, and adherents—and write an essay on the subject. If you wish, you may include quotes from, or information about, literature written by or about Hasidic Jews.

- Research areas where Hasidic Jews have set up communities. Tell the story of one such community—who set it up and why, where the community came from, and what kinds of lives its members forged in their adopted area. Information can be gathered from any source you wish, including interviews.

- Research the subject of peak experiences, which may be defined as sudden feelings of intense happiness and well-being, and an awareness of ultimate truth and the unity of all things. Based on your findings, give a presentation or write a poem or short story about this subject.

- Helprin is known as an author who deals in grand themes, such as love, truth, and honor. Write a story, poem, short story, or short play around one such grand theme, showing how it transforms a life or lives.

fool people into thinking that he is striking the minute hand off the clock or hitting balls out of the stadium.

THEMES

The Importance of Truth

The events of the story are set in motion by Roger's discovery of the Saromsker Rebbe's imperfection—his deception about eating non-kosher chocolate. Roger has witnessed an extreme "imperfection," the Holocaust in which his parents were murdered. He knows that he can no longer trust the Saromsker Rebbe to bear witness to the truth with the absolute integrity needed to avoid another Holocaust. He himself intends to bear witness to the truth of the Holocaust until the day he dies. In order to know the truth of the current political situation, he listens to the radio, but what he learns leads him to another task: saving the Yankees from a string of defeats. In a broader sense, Roger lives his life in accordance with the truth, in that he is incapable of lying. He knows that a lie is the beginning of the breakdown of integrity, "the outrider of malevolent forces, which come first with a lie so that they might not have to fight to subdue you."

In this story, there are different types of truth. Rational truth is shown to be extremely limited, in that something can be spiritually true but rationally ludicrous. An example is Roger's belief, reinforced by Luba's fantasy, that Yankee Stadium is "the House That Ruth Built" in the biblical sense. While this is not true, it inspires Roger to become a champion of perfection for the Yankees.

The Perfection of God's Creation

Roger is prompted to set out on his quest to save the Yankees by the Saromsker Rebbe's imperfection. Roger believes that "The balances of the universe are precise and delicate.... One uncourageous lie destroys the core of the imagination." The balance of the universe demands that someone—in this case, Roger—must express the perfection that is truth. Despite knowing nothing about baseball and being physically frail, Roger is able to help the Yankees because he devotes his life to perfection, which involves a commitment to truth and to God. The image to which he clings in this quest is the resurrection of those who are gone, including his parents, somewhere in future time or beyond time: "All was grace and perfection there, all just and redeemed, all prayer answered, ratios exact, rhythms

perfect, law obeyed." The spiritual lifting up of those who have met with a terrible death, and of himself, is seen by Roger as divine compensation for the horror of the Holocaust and an affirmation of God's perfect ordering of creation. When he arrives at Yankee Stadium, he is testing God's justice, challenging him to provide such compensation, and God does not let him down. Drawing upon the power of angels, Roger accomplishes marvelous feats on the baseball pitch that enable the Yankees to win and also teaches them, and the audiences in the stadium, the importance of commitment to perfection.

Closely related to the theme of the perfection of God's creation is the theme of the glory and beauty of creation. It is the Hasidic belief that God is immanent in, but also transcendent beyond, every part of creation. An example of such awareness occurs when Roger looks out from his hotel room on a glorious sunset and feels no personal pride in his accomplishments, only a reminder of the "kind of high glory that rides from place to place and time to time on a shower of sparks."

The Power of Holiness and the Limitations of Materialism

The unlikely premise of "Perfection" is that a physically weak, bookish, and unworldly Hasidic boy can single-handedly save the Yankees baseball team from a losing streak by his extraordinary performance on the field. The paradox is reinforced by the stereotypical image that prevails about Jewish boys: that while they may excel at intellectual and artistic pursuits, they are less likely to excel at sports. The narrator underscores this message in the following passage: "Jews couldn't hit, never could. Their job in the mystery of things was to take on the kidney a baseball thrown by a tall Irishman or a giant Pole." In other words, their role in creation up to now (until Roger's epiphany) has been to miss hitting balls thrown at them and be bashed on the kidney by the ball. The prevailing stereotype is also that the guy who is good at jock-type activities is likely to be a big Irishman or a Pole. The effect of this improbable plot is to displace reason and logic (which define the material world) and to announce to the reader that another law applies. This law, the story suggests, is the infinite grace of God and, by extension, the infinite possibilities open to a person who perfectly aligns his or her life and will with God.

How People Deal with Loss

Roger lost his parents and everyone he knew in the extermination camp at Majdanek. He copes with this loss by focusing on the image of his parents restored to glory in some future time or some place beyond time. He tells the Yankees: "Because of the imperfection I have seen, I live for the hope of restoration. That's all I live for, even if it be a sin." Hoping is one way of dealing with loss; another way is dreaming. The author suggests that for Jews, many of whom at certain times in history have lost everything, dreams are a vital part of real life: "for those who have nothing, dreams are real." Luba's dream-like fantasy about the House That Ruth Built in the Bronx inspires Luba and causes Roger to respond to its elevated tone by spiritually rising to the occasion and saving the Yankees.

STYLE

Magical Realism

This story has little in common with those works of twentieth- and twenty-first-century fiction which tend to emphasize realism, moral ambiguity, doubt, and cynicism. But it has strong elements of the genre known as magical realism, in which magical or supernatural elements (such as Roger's divinely assisted feats in baseball) appear in an otherwise realistic setting and in which all elements are treated as real.

Symbolism

Symbolism occurs in literature when something is used to represent something else, often when a material object represents both itself and something immaterial. Throughout "Perfection," Roger is surrounded by images of light and elevation, which symbolize his spiritual illumination and exaltation. With regard to light, a student tells the Saromsker Rebbe of Roger, "When he prays, white light bathes the walls." When Roger, with the help of an angel, hits balls out of the Yankee Stadium, they trail orange flame.

With regard to elevation, both in Brooklyn and while he stays in a luxury hotel, Roger inhabits the upper floors of tall buildings. In addition, Roger is frequently connected with birds in the story, which are creatures that inhabit the heavens and, like the angels that help him play baseball, have wings.

Metaphor

A metaphor is a similarity drawn between one thing and another to which it is not literally applicable. In this story, Roger uses metaphors of locks (both on doors and in canals) to describe the perfection of the mechanisms of God's creation. Military metaphors are used to suggest the war between good and evil that is played out in the events of the story.

The assumptions underlying Roger's lock metaphors are that God is perfect and that his creation is perfect, so all fear and suffering in the world are ultimately counterbalanced. Injustices are corrected, but sometimes this happens far away from people in space and time, so that they cannot see the mechanism in its entirety. All souls are equal in the eyes of God, and everyone finally comes to the same reward. To allow a door lock to turn, each pin in the lock mechanism must be raised sufficiently to allow the lock to turn. Some pins are raised more, and some less. Though a beggar lives a different life from a king, both "are lifted by God variously and invisibly, but equally, even in this world, so that the perfection will not be broken." Similarly, a canal lock is a mechanism to lift or lower a boat that gets its power from the urge of all water to find its own level. In life, those who suffer know, too, the level of compensation they acquire. The reception of this compensation, which is called holiness, is more real than the world itself. Roger's extraordinary feats on the baseball field, accomplished with the help of angels, are a divine compensation for the horrors he has suffered in the Holocaust.

Military metaphors are apt for a story that takes place against the historical background of the Holocaust of World War II. Roger and his allies are seen as warriors against evil and materialism. Luba talks of the rescuer of the inhabitants of the House That Ruth Built—the role that Roger takes on—as a "champion." This champion, says Luba, "must have great virtue, for he will carry in his hand the very staff of the Lord." This language connotes both scenes from the Old Testament and the Western European tradition of a chivalrous knight, called a champion, who fights for God, virtue, and truth. Helprin's invocation of the tradition of chivalry also has the effect of distancing his story from the cynical, materialistic outlook of much twentieth- and twenty-first-century literature. It hearkens back to an age which, it is suggested, valued truth, honor, and spiritual purity.

Military metaphors are also used to describe the Yankees after their transformative seminar with Roger. They seem no longer mere baseball players, but "soldiers," and they are referred to by the press as "The Invincible Engine," like some lethal military killing machine. Galvanized by Roger's account of his response to the Holocaust, they are "bent on a certain kind of vengeance"; they want "only to play to perfection" and "to speak directly to God, and to face like men the fact of evil and sorrow in the world." The suggestion is that they have, in some sense, become warriors for good against evil.

Humor

The story contains much comedy, most notably in the unexpected image of an undersized Hasidic boy in traditional dress showing the Yankees how to hit a ball out of the stadium. The bizarre juxtaposition helps to break the boundaries of reason and to open the reader's awareness to a reality beyond reason. But sometimes, the humor has a darker hue. When Roger plays for the Yankees against Kansas City, the Orthodox Jewish contingent in the stands fears lest "he would be the reason for the defeat of this otherwise invincible gentile team . . . and that this might result in a pogrom." As the Yankees win, while the gentiles "shook the pillars of the world with their shouts . . . the Jews prayed silently, thankful to have been spared." This is a joke, of course, because it is unlikely that another Holocaust could result from a Jewish boy's letting down the Yankees in a baseball game. But the humor has a serious point. During a baseball game or any sporting event, a crowd can be whipped up into a highly emotional and irrational state, overwhelmed with suddenly felt hostilities. It is just such emotion that Hitler succeeded in manipulating to gain support for his anti-Semitic policies, of which the Holocaust was the extreme example (it is no coincidence that Hitler often used large sports stadiums similar to Yankee Stadium for his rallies). Many Jewish people are sensitive to such

irrational winds of change, as they fear they could be forerunners of a new Holocaust.

HISTORICAL CONTEXT

The Holocaust

The Holocaust is the name given to the genocide of the Jews and other minority groups and so-called undesirables carried out by Nazi Germany and its allies during World War II (1939–1945). It is estimated that around six million Jews were killed in the Holocaust in what the Nazis called the final solution of the Jewish question or the cleaning. The Nazis promoted the belief that the Jews were a physically and morally inferior group that should be exterminated. Hundreds of thousands of Jews perished in the extermination camps set up in Germany and collaborating countries by the Nazis. Early on in the war, as happened to Roger's parents, many were marched to the edge of a pit, where they were shot, a method later found to be too costly a use of ammunition. The pit was then filled in by bulldozers. Later when the Nazis wanted to speed up the killing and use a cheaper method, death camp prisoners were gassed in custom-made chambers with a common delousing poison, zyklon B.

Minority groups murdered by the Nazis in extermination camps included Roma (gypsies), Poles, Serbs, homosexuals, mentally and physically disabled people, communists, dissidents and intellectuals, black people, resistant Catholic and Protestant clergy, and various criminals. Taking these groups into account brings most estimates of those killed in the Holocaust to an estimated eleven million.

The Nazi extermination camp at Majdanek, where Roger was born and where he witnessed his parents being murdered, was two miles from the Polish city Lublin. It was one of two camps where zyklon B was used in the gas chambers, though carbon monoxide was also used. According to data from the Majdanek State Museum, about 300,000 inmates passed through the camp, of whom over 40 percent were Jews. It is estimated that around 100,000 Jews lost their lives there, half dying from disease, exhaustion, and harsh conditions, and half being executed or gassed.

COMPARE
&
CONTRAST

- **1940s:** The Nazis murder approximately six million Jews, in a genocide that comes to be known as the Holocaust, in extermination camps in Germany and its allied countries.

  1950s: In the United States and other countries to which Jews immigrate after World War II, the Holocaust is not much discussed either within or outside Jewish circles. Jews who survive the Holocaust and immigrate to the United States are discouraged by customs officials from talking about their experiences, on the presumption that Americans are not interested.

  Today: The Holocaust is the subject of documentaries, films, and books and is commemorated in museums and monuments. Holocaust denial is illegal in many countries.

- **1940s:** The Holocaust destroys all Hasidic groups in Eastern Europe.

  1950s: Survivors of the Holocaust immigrate to various countries, including the United States and Israel, and establish new centers of Hasidic Judaism modeled on their original communities. In the United States, the largest communities are in Brooklyn, New York.

  Today: Hasidic Judaism thrives, especially in U.S. cities, with approximately 165,000 Hasidic Jews living in the New York City area. Hasidic Jews preserve the Yiddish language and many of the religious traditions of pre-Holocaust Eastern European Judaism. The American Hasidic Jewish reggae artist Matisyahu is popular. His music is primarily aimed at non-religious Jews to bring them closer to Judaism.

- **1940s:** Palestine is partitioned into Arab and Jewish regions, and the Jewish state of Israel is set up in 1948, largely to provide a homeland for the Jewish people where they can avoid the possibility of another Holocaust.

  1950s: From 1951 to 1956, hundreds of attacks on Israel are carried out by Arab resistance groups called fedayeen, operating from the Arab countries of Egypt, Jordan, and Syria. In 1956, Egyptian president Nasser's nationalization of the Suez Canal, an international waterway through which Israeli ships passed, threatens British and French oil and trade interests in the region. In the hope of ending the fedayeen attacks, Israel joins with France and Britain in attacking Egypt, though this war ends in the same year.

  Today: Hostilities between Israel and neighboring Arab countries continue. Israel builds a West Bank barrier purportedly to defend the country against attacks by Palestinian groups, though opponents claim the barrier is a way for Israel to appropriate land.

Holocaust Denial

Some people do not believe that the Jews were killed in an event of genocide during World War II. People who do not believe the Holocaust occurred are commonly called Holocaust deniers, but they themselves generally favor the term Holocaust revisionists. Key beliefs of Holocaust deniers include rejecting the fact that the Nazi government had a deliberate policy of targeting Jews for extermination; that around six million Jews were killed in the Holocaust; and that mass extermination of Jews occurred in camps designed for that purpose. Some Holocaust deniers claim that the gas chambers found in the camps after the end of the war were for delousing inmates and that the camps were for prisoners of labor and not for extermination. In the last decade of the twentieth century, some commentators claimed that Jews invented or exaggerated the Holocaust for financial or political gain. They coined the term, Holocaust industry, to describe this notion. In "Perfection," the character of Roger is placed in opposition to Holocaust deniers, in that he is determined to "bear witness" to the truth of the death of his parents and so many others, "even as others might forget, ridicule, dismiss, or demean it."

In many countries, Holocaust denial is illegal. In 2005, British historian David Irving was sentenced to three years imprisonment in Austria based on books he had written and speeches he had given claiming the scale of the extermination of Jews in World War II was exaggerated, that Hitler knew nothing of the Holocaust, and that there had been no gas chambers at the Auschwitz camp. In 1998, Irving launched an unsuccessful libel suit against U.S. academic Deborah Lipstadt and her publisher. The presiding judge, Charles Gray (as reported in the *Guardian Unlimited* article, "The Ruling against David Irving: Excerpts from High Court Judge Charles Gray's Ruling in the David Irving Libel Suit"), ruled that characterizations that Irving is a "Holocaust denier," that he is "anti-Semitic," and that he has "for his own ideological reasons persistently and deliberately misrepresented and manipulated historical evidence" were "substantially true." The case also demanded that the judge rule on the truth or otherwise of the events of the Holocaust itself. After hearing evidence from both sides, the judge concluded, "It is my conclusion that no objective, fair-minded historian would have serious cause to doubt that there were gas chambers at Auschwitz and that they were operated on a substantial scale to kill hundreds of thousands of Jews."

Hasidic Judaism

Hasidic Judaism, of which Roger is an adherent, is a form of Haredi Judaism, which in turn is sometimes known as Ultra-Orthodox Judaism. The word, Hasidic (Chasidic is an alternative spelling) derives from the Hebrew word for "piety." Hasidic Judaism was founded by Rabbi Yisroel ben Eliezer (1698–1760), a mystic who is commonly referred to by Hasidic Jews as the Baal Shem Tov (generally translated as Master of the Good Name), or as Besht for short. Hasidic Judaism stresses joy, faith, and ecstatic prayer, accompanied by song and dance, and places religious exaltation above intellectual knowledge. One of its central beliefs is that the entire universe is a manifestation of God but that God also transcends the universe. This belief tends to give rise to optimism about the human condition, as it teaches that everyone and everything possesses a divine spark in which God is manifested.

Hasidic beliefs and practices are expressed in "Perfection" in Roger's love for, and wonder at, the marvels of creation; in his sensitivity to visions of "the House That Ruth Built" as being filled with music and dance; in his easy familiarity with ecstatic states; and in his assumption that he and, ultimately, the Yankees can reflect divine perfection in the relatively mundane act of playing baseball.

Hasidic dress is distinctive. Hasidic men usually wear a black hat and black clothes with a white shirt, and on the sabbath they wear a black satin or silk robe with a prayer belt. In common with other Jews, Hasidic Jews follow dietary laws, and food produced in line with these laws is called kosher. In "Perfection," under Roger's influence, some Jewish rules of dress are adopted by the Yankees baseball team, and some of the dietary rules are followed within the stadium, shocking the media and the public.

CRITICAL OVERVIEW

Helprin published *The Pacific and Other Stories*, the collection in which "Perfection" appears, in 2004, after a seven-year absence from fiction publishing. The critical reception was mostly positive, although Helprin's embrace of such old-fashioned themes as beauty, truth, and honor, and his affirmation of moral absolutes, was not universally admired.

In his mostly enthusiastic review for *Newsday* entitled "Glimpses of Lives Honed on Honor," Dan Cryer remarks that Helprin is an "unabashed cultural conservative" who writes about "great qualities" without irony or "the wink of postmodernist qualification." While he calls the collection "uneven," Cryer notes that it has a coherent theme, "the grace imparted by a life honed on honor." He singles out "Perfection" as an "exuberant story" and "one of the oddest, and funniest, of baseball stories," combining magical realism with an "unabashed moral focus." Overall though, Cryer's main

Hasidic Jewish boys (and men) have a distinctive way of dressing that would have made the main character in this story stand out on a baseball field Hulton Archive/Getty Images

criticism of the collection is that sometimes the stories fall into "heavy-handed didacticism."

Michiko Kakutani, in his review for the *International Herald Tribune*, was less impressed. Kakutani comments that "Helprin's focus on moral absolutes seems to have hardened, if not calcified," resulting in "heavy-handed, stage-managed fictions," which display a "growing sanctimony."

In her review for the *San Francisco Chronicle*, "Fuzzy Lives in Perfect Detail: Characters Act Precisely as They Seek Redemption," Jennie Yabroff highlights a feature of the stories that is simultaneously a strength and a weakness. "God," she writes, "is in Helprin's details." She praises Helprin's precise and lucid descriptions of how things work (examples might include Roger's explanation of how canal locks and door locks work and the narrator's detailed description of a baseball game) but feels that the characters lack emotional depth. Pointing out that "Most of his male characters are uncommonly brave," she comments: "Helprin becomes a generalist when writing about how people operate. His stories read more like fables than observations of actual human behavior."

No such reservations are recorded by the *Los Angeles Times* critic, Nick Owchar, in his review, "Appreciating Life's Moments of Perfection." Owchar calls the collection "splendid" and notes that it has "plenty of magic" of the "earthly, human" kind. Owchar identifies a consistent theme in the collection that also applies to "Perfection": "attaining holiness and practicing charity in an age obsessed with science and reason. . . . Helprin presents us with people confronting life's ugliness with small acts of perfection." He praises "Perfection" as "exquisite," noting that the abundant comedy in the story is "underscored by a tragic sense of cosmic balance."

WHAT DO I READ NEXT?

- "Perfection" is one of the short stories collected in Helprin's *The Pacific and Other Stories* (2004). The other stories focus on honorable characters who, in the interests of honing their lives in the direction of perfection, perform extraordinarily unselfish acts.

- Helprin's acclaimed novel *A Soldier of the Great War* (2005) tells the story of a young Italian man from a privileged family who finds the direction of his life changed forever by World War I. Along the way, he loses and rediscovers love and has to find a way of reconciling his love of beauty and religious faith with the horror of war.

- *The Collected Stories of Isaac Bashevis Singer* (1983) provides an exuberant exploration of Jewish life, traditions, religion, and folklore from modern New York City to the Eastern European villages of Singer's ancestors. A central theme is the power of benevolence.

- The Nobel Peace Prize winner Elie Wiesel wrote a moving memoir *Night* (1982) about his teenage experience at Auschwitz with his father. The work tries to reconcile his former fervent religious belief with the horror of the Holocaust that killed his parents.

- Martin Buber's classic work *Tales of the Hasidim* (first published in German as *Die chassidischen Buecher: Gesamtausgabe* in 1928, translation by Olga Marx and published as *Tales of the Hasidim*, 1948, reprinted by Schocken, 1991) is an entertaining, thought-provoking, and inspiring collection of stories and anecdotes about the lives of the Hasidic masters.

CRITICISM

Claire Robinson

Robinson has an M.A. in English. She is a writer, editor, and former teacher of English literature and creative writing. In the following essay,

> ROGER'S PIETY AND DEVOTION TO PERFECTION IN HIS LIFE CREATE A MOMENT IN WHICH THE WITNESSES TO HIS PERFORMANCE ARE LIFTED INTO A PERCEPTION OF DIVINE ORDER."

Robinson explores the significance of the theme of perfection in Mark Helprin's "Perfection."

The opening incident of "Perfection" sets up the moral and spiritual framework for the entire story. A chain of events is set off when the Saromsker Rebbe opens the wrong drawer, allowing Roger to see that he has been eating non-kosher chocolate and lying about it. In the framework of Helprin's story, this imperfection creates an imbalance in the universe that has to be compensated for by a manifestation of perfection. This is less a matter of morals than it is a law of physics. The fact that the Saromsker Rebbe's offenses may have been morally forgivable is not the point. "The balances of the universe are precise and delicate. ... One uncourageous lie destroys the core of the imagination." Roger knows that a lie is "the outrider of malevolent forces, which come first with a lie so that they might not have to fight to subdue you."

Roger follows this line of reasoning to its conclusion and decides that he can no longer trust the rebbe to listen to and report current affairs with truth. The rebbe could miss the signs of a future Holocaust. Roger, who saw his parents murdered in the Holocaust in horrific circumstances, has devoted his life to bearing witness to the truth of that event. Roger feels he must take over the job that the rebbe, in his imperfect life, may have done less than perfectly, and he must listen to the radio himself. In this way, he is introduced to the plight of the Yankees, whom he decides to save from a run of defeats. This resolve leads to his challenge to God on the baseball pitch, the essence of which can be summed up as follows: God's creation is a perfect mechanism comparable to a well-functioning lock, in which pins are raised and lowered just enough to allow the lock to turn. Thus God must raise up Roger in compensation for the horrors he has known in the Holocaust.

God does not fail Roger, who, in spite of knowing nothing about baseball and being physically puny, achieves inspired feats on the baseball pitch by drawing upon the power and skill of angels. No one realizes that after the pitch, Roger always closes his eyes, and "It was then that he felt the arms, fluttering and feathered, golden and shiny, reach from behind him and slowly, viscously, take hold of his hands on the bat." But onlookers do see the results in the shape of the ball flying out of the stadium, never to fall to earth. This process of divine grace not only confirms Roger's hopes of redemption, but inspires the Yankees to pursue perfection in their play. It also displays a glimpse of divine perfection to all the spectators, who experience an ecstatic joy as they watch Roger hit balls out of the stadium which fly off into the infinite heavens—and are never seen to come down again. As for the reader, who has been told that Roger has neither the physique nor the talent for excelling at baseball, there is only one way to look for the source of his power, and that is in the direction of the divine. As Roger tells the Yankees' manager, Stengel:

> I weigh thirteen and three-quarter *shvoigles.* I'm two *yumps* tall. How do you think I hit the ball out of the house? Do you think I could do such a thing alone? Who do you think is in charge here? You? Me?

It can be seen from the trajectory of these happenings that seemingly small and trivial events, such as the Saromsker Rebbe's opening the wrong drawer, can have great effects in the scheme of things, as Helprin portrays it. Thus, Helprin suggests, the ways in which a person chooses to live his life is of vital importance. It is significant that the Saromsker Rebbe, at the same time as he is neglecting truth in his life, is much occupied in pondering theological disputes. The implication is that such intellectual quibbles are as nothing compared with spiritual purity. Roger's observance of the pieties of his religion, such as not playing baseball during Rosh Hashana, the time of penitence, is part of his philosophy of not compromising and of pursuing perfection. Only such perfection will ensure an atmosphere of truth and clarity that will reveal the first approach of such dangers as another Holocaust. Catastrophes such as the Holocaust, the story suggests, can unfold from an apparently tiny lie. The historical evidence, indeed, supports such a theory, in that many commentators have remarked that the Holocaust was enabled by many small acts of deception, negligence, and denial on the part of ordinary individuals.

Versions of the notion that great consequences can spring from a person's acts and choices can be found both in physics and religion. The New Testament teaches, "whatsoever a man soweth, that shall he also reap" (Galatians 6:7). Hinduism teaches the law of karma, that what a person gives out comes back to the person. This is reflected in Newton's third law of physics, that forces occur in pairs, and so for every action there is an equal and opposite reaction. Chaos theory in physics and mathematics is an extension of this idea. The theory tries to explain the phenomenon whereby small occurrences significantly affect the outcomes of seemingly unrelated events, leading to results which are apparently random but are in fact determined by tiny variations in the initial state. This high dependence on initial conditions is called the butterfly effect, which refers to the idea that a butterfly flapping its wings might create tiny changes in the atmosphere that ultimately cause a tornado or prevent it.

The equivalent in "Perfection" to the butterfly's flapping its wings is the Saromsker Rebbe opening the wrong drawer. Helprin creates a universe in which everything is minutely interconnected with everything else, giving a sense of the intelligence and unity underlying creation. However, while the term, chaos theory, tends to be associated in the layperson's mind with increasing disorder in a system (though to scientists, the theory simply explains apparently random results that are really determined and therefore not random), the theory that governs the world of "Perfection" is the opposite. Roger's piety and devotion to perfection in his life create a moment in which the witnesses to his performance are lifted into a perception of divine order. The narrator explains, "For the moment, at least, they felt as if the deepest circles within them had been squared, their ragged doubts knit smooth, and the world were ablaze with the light of perfection." In the intricate system of balances that makes up the universe, Roger's actions, motivated by altruism and love for God and humanity, have served as an antidote to the chaos set off by the Saromsker Rebbe's deception.

Helprin uses symbolism to support his portrayal of Roger as a spiritually pure human

A childhood interaction with Mickey Mantle, seen here batting for the New York Yankees, provided Helprin with the inspiration for this story © Bettmann/Corbis

being. Roger is surrounded by images of light, suggestive of spiritual illumination. A student tells the Saromsker Rebbe of Roger, "When he prays, white light bathes the walls." Under questioning from the Saromsker Rebbe, Roger reveals that when he prays, he is blinded by light and spins head over heels. The Saromsker Rebbe notes that at such moments, Roger's spiritual purity makes him pass beyond the law of gravity, in the manner of the levitating mystics of historical tradition that are mentioned in the story. When Roger, with the help of an angel, hits balls out of Yankee Stadium, they trail orange flame, a sign to onlookers that something beyond the mundane is occurring.

Another symbolic thread emphasizing Roger's spiritual status is images of elevation. On his journey to Yankee Stadium, Roger sleeps on the roof of an elevated subway station; when the Yankees accommodate him in a luxury hotel, he inhabits a room with windows "as high above the earth as an airplane." At home in Brooklyn, Roger lives on the top floors of his building. He spends hours in prayer there and gains the knowledge that he must go to "the House of Ruth, where a miracle will come," whereupon he comes "down from his perch."

As well as suggesting spiritual elevation, the image of the perch connotes birds, creatures whose element is the sky. Roger is frequently connected with the imagery of birds. To persuade the Yankees out of their rationalism, Roger points out that "God shifts an untold number of birds twice a year from the top of the earth to the middle, and from the middle back to the top." When Roger shows the Yankees his batting skills, following his miraculous hit of the minute hand of the clock, a seagull examines the broken clock, then "rose like a rocket and disappeared into the clouds." This image foreshadows Roger's hitting the ball so far and high that it disappears up into the heavens and is not seen to return to earth. Roger's questioning of Berra about what lies beyond the stadium, where the balls travel (the Bronx, then Long Island Sound, then Long Island, then the ocean) has the effect of extending the reader's boundaries towards infinity. Such images of elevation also relate to the theme of the perfection of God's creation, whereby God raises up people in different ways to compensate for their suffering.

While such compensation may not come immediately or even within the limits of time, the story suggests the perfection of creation demands that it must eventually arrive. Indeed, if it were possible to see the entire picture at any one time, then it would be clear that the "counterweight for which we long—to right wrongs and correct injustices" is always present, though it may be far away in space or time. In Roger's words, as his experience in the baseball stadium shows, "forward in time, or where time does not exist, there is a justice and a beauty that will leap back to lift the ones I love from the kind of grave they were given."

Source: Claire Robinson, Critical Essay on "Perfection," in *Short Stories for Students*, Thomson Gale, 2007.

Thomson Gale

In the following essay, the critic gives an overview of Mark Helprin's work.

Mark Helprin is a writer whose fiction is marked by language "more classical than conversational," observed Michiko Kakutani in the *New York Times*, and one who shapes his short stories and novels "less to show my place in the world than to praise the world around me." Explaining his artistic distance from the sparse, clean prose of writers such as American author Ernest Hemingway, Helprin told Jon D. Markman of the *Los Angeles Times*, "My models are the *Divine Comedy*, and the *Bible* and Shakespeare—where they use language to the fullest." Helprin's political concerns—he pursued Middle Eastern studies in graduate school and later served in the Israeli Infantry and Air Force—figure in his newspaper and magazine articles; his books, he has often said with little elaboration, are religious.

Majoring in English as an undergraduate at Harvard, Helprin wrote short stories and sent them to the *New Yorker* with no luck until 1969, when the magazine accepted two at the same time. These became part of his first book, *A Dove of the East and Other Stories*, in which critics have noted the author's grand depictions of nature as a source of strength and healing and his concern with characters who survive loss, particularly that of loved ones.

> "... IN *ELLIS ISLAND AND OTHER STORIES* HELPRIN 'REVEALS RANGE AND INSIGHT WHETHER HE IS WRITING OF CHILDREN OR ADULTS, OF SCHOLARS, TAILORS, AND LOVERS. HIS EYE IS PRECISE AND HIS SPIRIT IS COMPASSIONATE, AND WHEN WE FINISH THE STORIES WE HAVE BEEN REWARDED, ONCE MORE, WITH THAT ASTONISHING CATALYST OF ART.' "

Some critics were impressed with the wide range of settings and the graceful prose exhibited in *A Dove of the East*. In the *Saturday Review* Dorothy Rabinowitz described Helprin's stories as "immensely readable," some "quite superb," writing that his "old-fashioned regard shines through all his characters' speeches, and his endorsement gives them eloquent tongues. Now and again the stories lapse into archness, and at times, too, their willed drama bears down too heavily. But these are small flaws in works so estimably full of talent and ... of character." Amanda Heller, however, complained in the *Atlantic Monthly* that, as a result of Helprin's "dreamy, antique style," the stories' "sameness of tone" becomes monotonous. "It appears that Helprin is striving for loveliness above all else," Heller commented, "a tasteful but hardly compelling goal for a teller of tales."

Duncan Fallowell allowed in the *Spectator* that some selections from *A Dove of the East and Other Stories* are "unbeatably vague," but praised Helprin for "recognising the intrinsic majesty" of seemingly meaningless events, because, as Fallowell wrote, "he is also a seeker after truth. Bits of it are squittering out all over the place, sufficiently to fuse into a magnetic centre and make one recognise that the book is not written by a fool." Dan Wakefield, even more appreciative of Helprin's work, observed: "The quality that pervades these stories is love—love of men and women, love of landscapes and physical beauty, love of interior courage as well as the more easily obtainable outward strength. The author never treats his subjects with sentimentality but always with gentleness of a kind that is all too rare in our fiction and our lives."

Helprin's first novel, *Refiner's Fire: The Life and Adventures of Marshall Pearl, a Foundling*, further interested critics. A *New Yorker* reviewer found that Helprin describes the protagonist's boyhood "lyrically and gracefully" and proves himself to be "a writer of great depth and subtle humor." For Joyce Carol Oates the problem is "where to begin" in admiring a novel she described as a "daring, even reckless, sprawling and expansive and endlessly inventive 'picaresque' tale." She added: "At once we know we are in the presence of a storyteller of seemingly effortless and artless charm; and if the exuberant, extravagant plotting of the novel ever becomes tangled in its own fabulous inventions, and its prodigy of a hero ever comes to seem more allegorical than humanly 'real,' that storytelling command, that lovely voice is never lost."

With *Ellis Island and Other Stories* Helprin secured his place among contemporary writers, winning for this work a PEN/Faulkner Award, a National Jewish Book Award, and an American Book Award nomination—a rare feat for a collection of short stories. Though some critics, such as Anne Duchene in the *Times Literary Supplement*, found that Helprin's language sometimes overwhelms his intent, the greater critical response was laudatory. In the *Washington Post Book World*, Allen Wier called the collection "beautifully written and carefully structured.... His rich textures alone would be enough to delight a reader, but there is more: wonderful *stories*, richly plotted, inventive, moving without being sentimental, humorous without being cute." Harry Mark Petrakis stated in the *Chicago Tribune* that in *Ellis Island and Other Stories* Helprin "reveals range and insight whether he is writing of children or adults, of scholars, tailors, and lovers. His eye is precise and his spirit is compassionate, and when we finish the stories we have been rewarded, once more, with that astonishing catalyst of art." Reynolds Price, writing for the *New York Times Book Review*, cited as particularly memorable "The Schreuderspitze," in which a photographer who has lost his wife and son in a car accident risks his life to climb a mountain in an effort to regain his spirit; the first half of the title novella, and "North Light," which Price called "a brief and frankly autobiographical recollection of battle nerves among Israeli soldiers, a lean arc of voltage conveyed through tangible human conductors to instant effect."

Winter's Tale, Helprin's second novel, held a place on the *New York Times* bestseller list for four months despite mixed critical opinion. Seymour Krim, writing for *Washington Post Book World*, described the allegorical novel as "the most ambitious work [Helprin] ... has yet attempted, a huge cyclorama" with a theme "no less than the resurrection of New York from a city of the damned to a place of universal justice and hope." In Krim's view, however, the novel reveals itself to be "a self-willed fairy tale that even on its own terms refuses to convince." In the *Chicago Tribune Book World* Jonathan Brent called the book "a pastiche of cliches thinly disguised as fiction, a maddening welter of earnest platitudes excruciatingly dressed up as a search for the miraculous." In the opinion of *Newsweek*'s Peter S. Prescott, "Helprin fell into the fundamental error of assuming that fantasy can be vaguer than realistic fiction."

In the view of Benjamin de Mott of the *New York Times Book Review*, however, neither through the unique and compelling characters nor "merely by studying the touchstone passages in which description and narrative soar highest" can the reader "possess the work": "No, the heart of this book resides unquestionably in its moral energy, in the thousand original gestures, ruminations, ... writing feats that summon its audience beyond the narrow limits of conventional vision, commanding us to see our time and place afresh." *Detroit News* reviewer Beaufort Cranford found that the book "fairly glows with poetry. Helprin's forte is a deft touch with description, and he has as distinct and spectacular a gift for words an anyone writing today." Further, Cranford noted, "Helprin's fearlessly understated humor shows his comfort with a narrative that in a less adroit grasp might seem too much like a fairy tale."

Openers contributor Ann Cunniff, who also caught the humor in *Winter's Tale*, praised "the beautiful, dreamlike quality" of some passages and Helprin's "frequent references to dreams." "All my life," Helprin explained to Cunniff, "I've allowed what I dream to influence me. My dreams are usually very intense and extremely detailed and always in the most beautiful colors.... Frequently, I will dream, and simply retrace that dream the day after when I write. It's just like planning ahead, only I do it when I'm unconscious."

In 1989 Helprin collaborated with illustrator Chris Van Allsburg on *Swan Lake*. Michael Dirda wrote in the *Washington Post Book World*, "The book is so attractive—in its story, illustrations and general design—that by comparison the original ballet almost looks too ethereal." In the *Chicago Tribune*, Michael Dorris raved, "This is one of those rare juvenile classics that will keep you awake to its conclusion . . . [and] will become, I predict, among those precious artifacts your grownup children will someday request for their own children." Helprin and Van Allsburg also combined their talents in 1996's *A City in Winter: The Queen's Tale* and 1997's *The Veil of Snows*.

In *A Soldier of the Great War*, which Shashi Tharoor described in the *Washington Post Book World* as "marvelously old-fashioned" and "a mammoth, elegiac, moving exegesis on love, beauty, the meaning of life and the meaninglessness of war," Helprin seemed to have transcended the criticism leveled at his earlier work. According to John Skow in *Time*, in this tale of the old Italian soldier Alessandro, Helprin has "simplified his language, though he still works up a good head of steam, and he has moderated his enthusiasm for phantasmagoric set pieces. He has also picked themes—war and loss, youth and age—that suit a large, elaborate style." Ted Solotaroff commented in the *Nation* that in *A Soldier of the Great War* Helprin takes "his penchant for life's heightened possibilities and transcendent meanings down into the vile trenches and nightmarish forests and jammed military prisons of the Italian sector of the war." Tharoor concluded: "Clearly a writer of great sensitivity, remarkable skill and capacious intellect, Helprin relishes telling stories in the grand manner, supplying details so complete as to leave the reader in no doubt about the texture of each place and the feelings of each character in it."

Helprin produced yet another expansive, picaresque novel with the mysteriously titled *Memoir from Antproof Case*, which was published in 1995. The story is the memoir of an elderly narrator who relates his fantastic and vivid life in a document he keeps locked inside an ant-proof case. While packing a pistol and hiding from his enemies in Brazil, the narrator describes his early life near New York City, his stay in a Swiss insane asylum, his involvement in World War II, his marriage to a wealthy heiress, and his employment with—and scheme to steal from—a powerful investment brokerage. While telling his life's story, the narrator divulges an odd obsession: the hatred of coffee, including the substance itself as well as the people who drink it. *Los Angeles Times Book Review* contributor Adam Begley described the novel thusly: "More odd mysteries than the anti-coffee mania await unraveling; lyrical passages brim with high-toned literary prose; broad comic riffs announce themselves with take-my-wife subtlety; and tall tales sprout magically at every turn, fed by a steady stream of flamboyant exaggeration."

Critics were positive in their appraisal of *Memoir from Antproof Case*, commending the author's trademark high-wire prose styling and his creation of another unusual, colorful, and rambling narrative. Terry Teachout, writing in the *Washington Post Book World*, called the novel "long, extravagant, daring, occasionally tedious but more often impressively compelling." Similarly, *New York Times Book Review* contributor Sven Birkerts remarked that the story "is rendered with great anecdotal charm and is embroidered throughout with vivid descriptions and delightful reflections." Not all reviewers' comments were positive; Begley, for instance, noted a "lurching Ping-Pong pattern" in the novel in which "suspense alternates with silliness," and Teachout declared that certain elements of *Memoir from Antproof Case* are "exasperating in the extreme." However, Teachout concluded, while "Helprin is a bit of a blowhard, . . . he is also one of the most ambitious novelists of our day."

In addition to his nine fictional works, Helprin wrote articles for the *Wall Street Journal* from 1985 to 2000. "Many people would probably be surprised to know that the same man who writes political commentary for the *Wall Street Journal* cites as his motto a line from Dante's *Inferno* that translates 'Love moved me, and makes me speak,'" remarked *American Enterprise* reviewer, John Meroney. Helprin also came to the political forefront in 1996, when word leaked out that he was the author of presidential candidate Bob Dole's strong resignation speech from the U.S. Senate. Meroney quoted from the speech: "I will run for President as a private citizen, a Kansan, an American, just a man." Dole's speech was "an unusually lyrical oration by the Kansas solon's dry standards," commented *Salon.com* contributor Mark Schapiro, who continued by noting

" AND HIS PURPOSE WAS ACTUALLY TO SEE IF
THERE COULD BE PERFECTION IN THE UNIVERSE, IF
AFTER THE HOLOCAUST, IT WAS POSSIBLE TO HAVE A
MOMENT OF PERFECTION."

that "Helprin's soaring words were widely credited with at least temporarily recharging Dole's languishing presidential campaign."

In 2001 Helprin was awarded the Mightier Pen Award by the Century for Security Policy. The Center's president and chief executive officer, Frank Gaffney, Jr., stated that Helprin is "one of the most important writers at work today." "Helprin's creative flair is tempered by intelligence, wisdom, and experience," noted John Elvin in *Insight on the News* in reference to Helprin's receipt of the Mightier Pen award.

Source: Thomson Gale, "Mark Helprin," in *Contemporary Authors Online*, Thomson Gale, 2005.

Scott Simon

In the following interview, Helprin discusses the stories in his collection The Pacific and Other Stories.

[*Scott Simon:*] *The characters in Mark Helprin's new book,* The Pacific and Other Stories, *range around the world and the whole range of life from blood to opera to baseball: a wounded British paratrooper in Germany, reaching for his daughter's hand; a hungry laundress in Venice who becomes a diva; a September 11th widow; a lonely Israeli army reservist; and a putz of a 14-year-old religious student who becomes the savior of the New York Yankees. Mark Helprin is among that short list of writers acclaimed as the finest fiction writer of our times.* The Pacific and other Stories *is his new collection of short stories. Several have previously appeared in* The New Yorker *and* The Atlantic.

Mr. Helprin, who's won a PEN/Faulkner Award and others for previous books that include Ellis Island and Other Stories, Winter's Tale, Soldier of the Great War, *now joins us from Charlottesville, Virginia.*

Mr. Helprin, thanks very much for being with us.

[Mr. Mark Helprin:] Delighted.

Is there a theme to this collection? I apologize for such an obvious one.

It's about many things, but there is no single agendum. It's about art. It's about making amends. It's about memory, childhood, marriage, sacrifice, honor, perseverance, courage, war, putting materialism in its place, infatuation, resolution, the Holocaust, baseball, God, redemption, loyalty, show business, dictatorship, love for one's family, New York in 1869, the loss of a child, Herman Melville, adultery, World War I, the mountains, the Schtedle(ph), idolatry, technology, ocean racing, dying, the nature of love, the Middle East, the Second World War, California and redemption denied. And that's a partial list.

That's an awfully good answer, Mr. Helprin. I have to ask about your story of perfection. Fourteen-year-old Hasidic Jew who feels called on to become the savior of the New York Yankees.

The story arose in 1954, actually when I, as a child, was taken to Yankee Stadium to the only baseball game that I ever saw in my life. And I was brought there by Allen Funt. Remember "Candid Camera"?

Of course.

And we got there early, and we went to the left field fence. And he stood at the fence, bellowing, 'Hey, Mickey! Hey, Mickey! Hey, Mi'—because Mickey Mantle was at the plate. Yogi Berra was catching, and Billy Martin was pitching. There was nobody in the stadium—I mean, a few people, but virtually no one. And Allen Funt just yelled this for half an hour until finally the three of them walked over. It looked like they were going to hit us with a baseball bat, you know. They were really irritated. And they came over to us, and we then spent about 10 or 15 minutes talking to them, because Allen Funt had filmed a Wheaties commercial with Mickey Mantle, so he knew him. And Mickey Mantle didn't realize that when Allen was yelling at him.

But, anyway, in the story, Mickey Mantle thinks that H-A-S-I-D, Hasid, as in Hasidic Jew, is pronounced Hasid (pronounced HAY-seed). And the confusion of language is such that they tell him that he is a hayseed, which he thinks is a Hasid, and he doesn't quite understand it.

I mean, this is a real boy's fantasy in a sense, the teen-ager who becomes the savior of the New

York Yankees. And yet, in a sense, that aspect of the story is lost on this young man, because—if I might put it in parlance—he might say, 'Well, you know, what does he know from baseball?'

Oh, he knows nothing about baseball. He never heard of baseball.

Yeah.

He never heard of the Yankees or Yankee Stadium or anything. He mistook it for the House of Ruth. He thought that the House of Ruth was in the Bronx and that they were in trouble, so he went up to find them. And his purpose was actually to see if there could be perfection in the universe, if after the Holocaust, it was possible to have a moment of perfection, because if there were, then that was the beginning of the answer to the question, 'If there is a God, how could he have have allowed'—not just the Holocaust, but everything that the Holocaust may symbolize as well, you know, the suffering of anybody anywhere in the dreadful ways that they do.

You have a story principally set in Venice, a man who becomes an impresario. You refer to it somewhat as, in a sense, a man paying penance for making dreams come true. This is a man who had discovered a laundress and facilitated the ability of the rest of the world to share her gift.

She's the leading soprano in the world, and he is her agent. And it's a matter of great regret, because she was actually happy before he plucked her out of it. She was a laundress hanging up sheets, and she had a man that she loved. He couldn't handle her fame, and he committed suicide.

But it didn't end there, because what happens is the impresario is ordered by this diva to go to Venice to, as she says, 'check out the Bellini,' the paintings that have been restored in the Academia. And when he goes to Venice, he's in the Academia, looking at a painting which reminds him of his daughter, and he hears a beautiful song coming from outside on the street. And he knows immediately this is the best singer in the world, who's singing on the street for contributions in a hat. And he rushes out to find her. She is an Estonian. And she has her boyfriend, who is a guitarist.

And the story then proceeds with the relations between the impresario and these two people whom he finds on the street. And the imbalance between the guitarist and the singer is just as immense as it was between the diva and the soldier, because the guitarist cannot make it, and the impresario knows that. So he hesitates to offer the singer all the things that he knows will come in train with his representation. And in the end, he gives them money, and he advises them to go back to Estonia to think about it and etc., etc. And this is his way of making amends. So what happens is that he finds a way to restore the color of his life by making these amends very late.

It's interesting to me, being a little bit familiar with your background—you were educated at Harvard, Princeton and Oxford, went into the Israeli armed forces and the British Merchant Navy—it seems to me you write a good deal more about soldiers than you do about academics, and entertainers for that matter.

Yes, I do. It's—you know, I once had an argument with a friend of mine that lasted about eight hours. He said that a poet living in a garret is more of a hero than a soldier who gives his life. And I said, 'Now wait a minute. You know, if you die, that's it. You don't have another chance. You can't look forward to much else.' And we had this long argument. What I'm—the reason I brought that up is that when you're talking about war or anything in which physical death is at risk, it has a tremendous reverberation for everyone, because people know about war, and they dread it, and they fear it, and they have suffered because of it.

Daughters appear a lot in your stories.

I have two.

Well, there's your answer.

Yeah. My . . .

And my pronunciation is going to be bad. "Charlotte of the Utrecht . . ."

Utrechtsaveg(ph). It means the road to Utrecht.

It's so beautiful and so sad. This is a British paratrooper, and—well, I almost can't bring myself to utter it—his thoughts as he is involved in an enterprise that is both, he firmly believes, protecting his daughter and yet is the one thing that will prevent them from seeing each other again.

This is a major in the battle—in Operation Market Garden, the battle of Arnhem in World War II, when we overextended our forces and dropped a lot of paratroopers where, as it turns out, we couldn't support them. And it's a very simple story. It just tells how he left England and saw his daughter for the last time. His daughter was manning an anti-aircraft gun in Chelsea. And she was more or less the daughter of the regiment. Everyone's heart went out to her, because she was very clumsy, and she tripped, and she dropped her books, and she wore big, thick glasses. She was very beautiful, even though she had the glasses. And every man in the regiment, even the coarsest man, felt protective of her. And then he gets in a glider, and they come in on the field, and I describe the combat, and he goes down. And as he's dying—and it takes him a while to die—he envisions his daughter.

You're left with the impression that she, his daughter, is put on this Earth precisely to get him to reach out.

That's true. It's just a—what the final moment is is an imagination of a man's last and how, in the final moment, he can close off his life in a way that will somehow balance it out and make something of beauty and something that's worthwhile, something ineffable and very, very powerful.

Mr. Helprin, thanks very much.

Thank you so much.

Source: Scott Simon, "Interview with Mark Helprin," in *NPR: Weekend Edition*, November 6, 2004, pp. 1–3.

Michiko Kakutani

In the following review, Kakutani is unsettled by Helprin's penchant for "moral absolutes."

There is water, water everywhere in Mark Helprin's soggy new collection of stories. Whether it takes the form of the Atlantic or the Pacific, a Venetian canal or a Canadian snowfield, water plays a symbolic role in virtually every one of these tales, an emblem of the obliviousness of the physical world, and the possibility of renewal and redemption. It is a metaphor for Nature, for Eternity, for Life and for Death; a reminder that Helprin is interested not in the minutiae of daily life but in the Big Picture and big questions about truth and goodness and mortality.

In the past, this outlook, together with a prodigious imagination, has resulted in some potent fiction: the fierce, faintly surreal improvisations of *Ellis Island and Other Stories* (1981) and the haunting, picaresque reminiscences of a war veteran in *A Soldier of the Great War* (1991). But this time, Helprin's focus on moral absolutes seems to have hardened, if not calcified, and most

of his philosophical excursions into fable-land result in heavy-handed, stage-managed fictions.

The lugubrious tale "Jacob Bayer and the Telephone," for instance, pits a modest, truth-seeking teacher against a bunch of philistines who worship the telephone; it bludgeons home the author's point that tradition is admirable, while blind belief in progress and technology is stupid. "Reconstruction" similarly juxtaposes a bunch of spoiled, acquisitive yuppies with a man's memories of his father, a World War II veteran.

Helprin, who, in addition to writing fiction, has written speeches for former Senator Bob Dole and political columns for *The Wall Street Journal*, tends to view things, in these stories, in black-and-white, all-or-nothing terms. As a result, his heroes often emerge as cardboard exemplars of virtue. Many are preoccupied with lofty matters like how to die with honor, how to serve God, how to remain true to their ideals.

In "Perfection," a 14-year-old Holocaust survivor who becomes obsessed with the Yankees because they dwell in "the house of Ruth" helps the Bronx Bombers to a series of stunning wins with his divinely inspired baseball skills; in doing so, he makes his teammates play not for the sake of winning but for the sake of perfection, as a means of speaking "directly to God."

In "Monday," a saintly New York City contractor, who is "faultlessly honest" and always "gave reasonable estimates, did the highest-quality work, finished on time," decides to spend his own money to renovate an apartment for a woman who lost her husband in the terrorist attacks of 9/11. Self-conscious, even self-congratulatory about his good deed, he feels that the project imbues him and his men with a sense of holiness. Predictably enough, their "sacrificial labor" results in a masterpiece.

As readers of the author's earlier fiction well know, Helprin is highly skilled at creating dramatic sequences that are prickly with suspense, and this volume is no exception.

"Mar Nueva" recounts a chilling showdown between an autocratic tyrant and an outspoken and idealistic young woman who dares to stand up to him. While "A Brilliant Idea and His Own" provides a harrowing account of a British parachutist's efforts to cope with the injuries he received during a bad jump behind enemy lines and his heroic attempts to radio back intelligence to his comrades in arms. But these stories, by far the strongest in this volume, feel more like bravura set pieces than full-fledged, emotionally satisfying fictions.

As for the remaining tales, they tend to be a cloying, synthetic lot. Some pivot heavily around a terrible irony: a Jewish music hall performer decides to travel to Poland on the eve of Hitler's march through Europe. Others feature contrived. Henry-esque twist-endings: a man who is obsessed with his luxurious, perfect house loses it to a fire; years after discovering a great opera star, an impresario stumbles across another amazing young talent but instead of instantly signing her decides to warn her about the perils of fame.

At once predictable and unbelievable, these stories not only fail to provide a durable showcase for Helprin's instinctive gifts as a storyteller, but they also point up a growing sanctimony and schematism to his writing.

Source: Michiko Kakutani, Review of *The Pacific and Other Stories*, in *International Herald Tribune*, November 4, 2004, p. 14.

SOURCES

Affleck, John, "Birds of a Feather: The Ancient Mariner Archetype in Mark Helprin's "A Dove of the East" and *A Soldier of the Great War*, http://www.lib.ncsu.edu/staff/kamorgan/affleck.html (accessed October 27, 2006).

Bible (King James Version), Galatians 6:7.

"Concentration Camp," in State Museum at Majdanek website, http://majdanek.pl/en/oboz.htm (accessed October 27, 2006).

Cryer, Dan, "Glimpses of Lives Honed on Honor," in *Newsday*, November 11, 2004, p. B04.

Helprin, Mark, "Perfection," in *The Pacific and Other Stories*, Penguin, 2004, pp. 125–95.

Kakutani, Michiko, Review of *The Pacific and Other Stories*, in *International Herald Tribune*, November 4, 2004, p. 14.

Owchar, Nick, "Appreciating Life's Moments of Perfection," in *Los Angeles Times*, October 25, 2004, p. E7.

"The Ruling against David Irving: Excerpts from High Court Judge Charles Gray's Ruling in the David Irving Libel Suit," in *Guardian Unlimited*, April 11, 2000, http://www.guardian.co.uk/print/0, ,3984993–103501,00.html (accessed October 27, 2006).

Yabroff, Jennie, "Fuzzy Lives in Perfect Detail: Characters Act Precisely as They Seek Redemption," in *San Francisco Chronicle*, November 7, 2004, p. M2.

FURTHER READING

Buber, Martin, *The Way of Man: According to the Teaching of Hasidism*, Routledge, 2002.

This popular book (first published in German in 1948 as *Der Weg des Menschen: Nach der chassidischen Lehre*, first English translation by Maurice Friedman published in 1950 as *The Way of Man According to the Teachings of Hasidism*) presents the essential teachings of Hasidic Judaism through a collection of imaginative stories.

Dorfman, H. A., and Karl Kuehl, *The Mental Game of Baseball: A Guide to Peak Performance*, Diamond Communications, 2002.

This book, which has been highly praised in sporting circles, is aimed at players at all levels. It teaches the mental skills necessary to achieve peak performance in baseball, but the work has gained the reputation of helping people to function better in all areas of life.

Douillard, John, *Body, Mind, and Sport: The Mind-Body Guide to Lifelong Health, Fitness, and Your Personal Best*, Three Rivers Press, 2001.

Many athletes experience periods when they can do no wrong, when every hit is brilliant, when the body feels weightless, and action is effortless. This state has become known as being "in the zone" and has been likened to ecstatic spiritual experiences. In this practical guide, Douillard shows that there is nothing accidental about such experiences—they can be cultivated and are available to everyone, whatever their beginning level of fitness.

Gilbert, Martin, *The Holocaust: A History of the Jews of Europe during the Second World War*, Owl Books, 1987.

Gilbert provides a comprehensive introduction to the history of anti-Semitism in Europe and how it culminated in the Holocaust. He describes the systematic destruction of European Jewry and the widespread disbelief that such an event could be happening.

Plato, *Plato's Ion and Meno*, Agora Publications, 1998.

These are two of the most accessible and entertaining of Plato's dialogs and complement Helprin's story of Roger's unexpected abilities on the baseball field in Helprin's "Perfection." In *Ion*, Socrates probes the nature and source of human creativity, concluding that it is divine and owes nothing to the personality, intellect, or moral stature of the artist. In *Meno*, Socrates investigates the source of goodness and considers the hypothesis that all knowledge is recollection of something that the soul knew before birth.

The Price of Eggs in China

DON LEE

2000

Don Lee's story "The Price of Eggs in China" is concerned with art and love. The main character, Dean Kaneshiro, is a furniture builder who creates chairs so beautifully formed to the human body that, though he is only in his thirties, his works are on display in several important museums. He is dating Caroline Yip, who has had one successful book of poetry published, years earlier. At the time of its publication, Caroline came to be known in the press as "Oriental Hair Poet No. 1," because another young woman with long hair, Marcella Ahn, traveled in the same social circles and published a book of poetry at the same time. When Dean is hired to make a custom chair for Marcella, old rivalries rise up, and his loyalty to his craft and to the woman he loves is challenged.

Dean Kaneshiro takes a decidedly Japanese approach toward woodworking, with care for understanding the flow of each piece of wood he is cutting, attuning his tools to its nature. For Marcella and Caroline, who are, respectively, Korean and Chinese, race is most significant in the way that they are interchangeable in the public imagination, even though they write in strikingly different styles. Still, even though all three main characters in the story are of Asian descent, their setting has more to do with who they are than their ethnicity: they are residents of a sleepy coastal California town, spending time at the small diner and talking with the local police officer.

Don Lee Don Lee. Reproduced by permission

AUTHOR BIOGRAPHY

Don Lee was born in 1959 in Tokyo, Japan, to parents that were second-generation Korean Americans. His father was a career diplomat for the U.S. State Department. Lee spent most of his childhood in Tokyo and Seoul. He originally majored in engineering at the University of California at Los Angeles but found it boring; an English teacher encouraged him to take a creative writing class, and doing so determined his career path. He graduated from UCLA with a bachelor's degree in English literature then went to Emerson College in Boston for a Master of Fine Arts in creative writing and literature.

After graduation, Lee taught a creative writing workshop at Emerson for three years and then took over as managing editor and assistant

Don Lee is best known in literary circles as the long-time editor of *Ploughshares*, one of the most respected literary journals in the United States. This story, which was originally published in the *Gettysburg Review* in 2000, won the Pushcart Prize for that year. It is included in Lee's 2001 collection, *Yellow*.

MEDIA ADAPTATIONS

- Lee maintains a personal website, http://www.don-lee.com/index.htm, with links to publications, appearances, and other matters of interest to fans.

fiction editor of *Ploughshares*, a famous and highly respected literary magazine. He became the editor of *Ploughshares* in 1988. He also occasionally served as a writer-in-residence in Emerson's M.F.A. writing program.

Yellow, the short story collection in which "The Price of Eggs in China" was published, was written over a long period of time, due to Lee's slow writing process. Sometimes he completed only two stories a year. The book won the Sue Kaufman Prize for First Fiction and the Asian American Writers' Workshop Members' Choice Award. Lee's next work was a novel, *Country of Origin*, about a graduate student from Berkeley who goes to Japan to do research for her dissertation, ends up working in a nightclub and disappears into the seamy underworld of Tokyo nightlife: as in many of Lee's stories, questions of mixed racial identity and mixed national background are brought into play.

Lee's second novel, *Wrack and Ruin*, set in the fictional town of Rosarita Bay, which also serves as the setting for the stories of *Yellow*, was anticipated to appear in print in late 2007 or early 2008.

PLOT SUMMARY

"The Price of Eggs in China" begins with Dean Kaneshiro arriving at the house of "Oriental Hair Poet No. 2." This poet, Marcella Ahn, called Dean two years earlier to hire him to make a chair for her. A master furniture builder and much in demand, Dean could not give her an earlier date to measure her. As the time of their appointed fitting has neared, Dean has sought out Marcella, only to find that by now she has moved to Rosarita Bay. There is already an Asian poet with beautiful long hair living in the town: Dean's girlfriend, Caroline Yip.

Dean measures Marcella and asks her questions about her work then observes her as she sits at her chair and writes for twenty minutes, in order to understand her working habits. When she asks if she can come to his studio to watch him work, he adamantly refuses.

When he tells his girlfriend about having measured Marcella for a chair, Caroline is outraged and recounts her history with the other woman. They both lived in Cambridge, Massachusetts, when they were in their early twenties and were best friends. Their first books of poetry were published at about the same time, which earned them the collective nickname "The Oriental Hair Poets," although their styles were completely different: Marcella Ahn's poetry was quiet and thoughtful, while Caroline Yip's was written in "a slangy, contemporary voice, full of topical, pop culture allusions." After the books were published, Marcella attracted all of the critical attention, earning the coveted teaching jobs and having her picture on the covers of the best magazines. Caroline was left to linger in the shadow of Marcella's career. Then a man who had been dating Caroline for seven years broke up with her, explaining that it was because of a remark Marcella had made, and Caroline moved away from the literary scene to live in isolation in California, where she met Dean.

Caroline assumes that Marcella moved to Rosarita Bay specifically to torment her, that she might need to torment Caroline for artistic inspiration. She tells Dean that, since he has no contract, he has no obligation to make the chair for her, but he says that he must.

Caroline begins receiving vague, mysteriously sinister gifts: candy and flowers, stuffed animals, lingerie and more. Afraid that she is being stalked, she moves in with Dean. Behind his house is a shed where he keeps the wood that he uses for furniture making: the wood is from rare Japanese zelkova trees that are a thousand to two thousand years old, and it must be stored in a controlled climate. Because it is so rare and will someday soon be unobtainable, Dean has stockpiled thousands of dollars of raw wood.

One day Marcella comes to Dean's workshop, even though he has given explicit instructions against being interrupting. Despite Caroline's insinuations, Marcella insists that

moving to Rosarita Bay was just a coincidence. She also mentions that the only place she has seen a Dean Kaneshiro chair is in the Museum of Modern Art in New York. When she leaves, Caroline is furious: she had not known that Dean's works were so famous that they were in museums or that he had received a grant that gave him fifty thousand dollars a year for five years. Feeling humbled, she moves out of his house and back to her apartment.

Dean tries to win her back, going repeatedly to the diner where she works, though she refuses to talk with him. One day, he receives a summons to go to the police station, where he is questioned about harassing Marcella: leaving gifts at her door and leaving angry, threatening messages on her answering machine. The calls have been traced to pay phones, and the voice is not identifiable because the caller used a voice changing machine. Dean starts to believe that Marcella Ahn might be as fixated with Caroline as Caroline says she is.

Despite warnings to stay away from her, Dean goes to find Caroline. She has chopped her own hair off in a fit of manic worry. Dean devises a plan to implicate Marcella as a stalker. He finds out her routine then buys a voice changer and a lock picking kit. After phoning his own answering machine to make a threatening call with his voice disguised, he calls the police, who still are not convinced. He breaks into Marcella's house and takes a pair of her boots, some of her hair from a brush, and the ingredients for a firebomb. He then goes back to his house and starts a fire in his shed of rare, irreplaceable wood.

The fire causes more damage than he planned, since the sprinkler system does not go off. The evidence that he planted against Marcella is not noticed by the small town police force, but she agrees to leave town. Caroline submits her second book of poetry, and it is published to great reviews, and it wins awards.

Just before Marcella leaves town, Dean delivers her chair to him. He asks her to read Caroline's new poems and tell him if they are good. She tells him, during their conversation, that it was Caroline who prepared all of the phony evidence of being stalked, in order to frame Marcella. He refuses to believe her, and when she says that she does not think the poems are very good, he does not believe her about that either, insisting that he could see in her face as she read that she liked them. In the end, Dean and Caroline and their daughter, Anna, live happily together.

CHARACTERS

Marcella Ahn

Marcella is introduced into the story as "Oriental Hair Poet No. 2," a designation that identifies her in relation to Caroline Yip. The two women have a long history together. They were inseparable friends in their twenties, when they were both young writers. When they had books of poetry published at the same time, Marcella's was the one that was favored by the critics. Her book, *Speak to Desire*, was considered to be filled with serious poems of quiet observations. She was offered teaching jobs, awards, and residencies, taking all of the honors that Caroline applied for and was refused.

Marcella comes from a wealthy family: her father was a shipping tycoon, and she lives off the millions of dollars in her trust fund. She is Korean, wears heavy makeup, exercises regularly, and wears clothes that resemble lingerie.

Although Marcella is paying thousands of dollars for a desk chair to use when she writes, after the events of the story she never writes another collection of poetry.

Anna

At the end of the story, when the trouble with Marcella is over, Dean and Caroline have a baby named Anna, who cements their previously shaky relationship with each other.

Gene Becklund

Gene Becklund is a sergeant at the Rosarita Bay police department. He questions Dean about the threatening messages that have been left on Caroline's answering machine. He feels that, since the couple has been broken up, Dean is a prime suspect, even though Caroline herself thinks it is Marcella Ahn who is stalking her. When Dean's shed has been burned, he calls on Sergeant Becklund to investigate, intending Becklund to find the evidence he has planted against Marcella: Sergeant Becklund does a cursory examination of the scene and pronounces it arson but does nothing to find out who did it.

Dean Kaneshiro

Thirty-eight-year-old Dean Kaneshiro is a carpenter of Japanese descent. He is an exacting artisan. In order to make custom chairs, he measures the buyers in detail; if possible, he watches how they sit at their desk; if not, he gets the measurements from their tailor and watches a video of them at work if the buyers live far away. He is so good at what he does that his chairs are included in museum collections and are compared to works by famous architect Frank Lloyd Wright. He is modest about his fame, though. He lives in a little house in a small town on the California coast, where even his girlfriend, Caroline Yip, is not aware of the fact that the Kaneshiro chair is so highly regarded in the art world.

Dean is devoted to Caroline, even though she is his opposite in many ways: sloppy where he is neat, loud where he is quiet, vulgar while he is polite, and insecure while he is confident. When she breaks up with him after finding out that he is not just a simple carpenter but is an internationally celebrated artist, he pursues her passively, going to the diner where she works until she eventually talks to him. Though he does not initially believe her assertion that Marcella Ahn is in Rosarita Bay to do her harm, his fear for her convinces him. His plan against Marcella includes breaking into her house to steal items that he can plant as evidence against her and starting a fire in his supply of zelkova wood, even though it is extremely expensive and increasingly rare.

Although he blames Marcella Ahn for threatening Caroline, he does finish her chair and deliver it to her, as a matter of honor. When Marcella tells him that Caroline made up the stalking incidents, his faith in Caroline is only shaken for a second. For the rest of his life, he suppresses his suspicion that Caroline fabricated the entire problem with Marcella Ahn, staying true to his woman despite his creeping doubts.

Hayashi Kota

Hayashi Kota is one of only three traditional master woodcutters in Japan who can cut the zelkova tree to Dean's specifications. His eye for choosing the right trees and cutting along the right part of the grain with the correct saw is irreplaceable, but he is sixty-nine and will soon not be reliable as a supplier.

Evan Paviromo

Evan Paviromo, the editor of a literary journal, dated Caroline Yip for seven years. She expected to marry him eventually and have children with him. He broke it off with her one day, offering no explanation until she pressured him: he then told

TOPICS FOR FURTHER STUDY

- Go to a museum or a museum website and examine chair designs by Frank Lloyd Wright and other modern artists. From these designs, along with Lee's description in the story, draw what you visualize as a Dean Kaneshiro chair.

- Write a poem in the style of Caroline Yip and a poem in the style of Marcella Ahn.

- Dean has a problem in this story because there are only a few master woodcutters left who can work properly with zelkova wood. Find out how zelkova is harvested. Report on the process commonly used, and how it differs from how other types of wood are gathered. Do a report on the wood in which you take a position on using nonrenewable natural resources.

- Buy or make a voice changer. Try it out in your class, giving classmates a chance to guess whose voice they are hearing when blindfolded.

her that Marcella had told him that he was generous for staying with someone whose work he did not respect, which made him realize that he is not really that generous at all, and his disrespect for Caroline's work would eventually become an issue between them.

Caroline Yip

Caroline is known in the literary world as "Oriental Hair Poet No. 1" because she has long hair and published her first book of poetry at the same time as her friend, Marcella Ahn. Caroline's poetry is much more earthy and vulgar than Marcella's is, and possibly as a result of that, it received less critical praise upon its publication. At about the same time that she watched her friend's poetry lauded, Caroline's seven-year relationship with her boyfriend, Evan Paviromo, ended because of a remark that Marcella made to him. Caroline dropped out of literary society, moved to Rosarita Bay, and became a waitress.

Caroline dresses plainly and talks crudely. She is distant to her boyfriend, Dean Kaneshiro, at first refusing to admit that she loves him and then breaking up with him when she finds out that his work is internationally famous and displayed in museums: she accuses him of having more in common with Marcella than with her.

When Caroline reports to the police that someone has been leaving anonymous gifts on her doorstep and calling her answering machine and leaving threats with a disguised voice, the police assume that it is Dean, with whom she has broken up. After Caroline cuts off her long hair and almost faints in his arms in the street, Dean is overcome with worry about her, and he becomes convinced that he has to do something against Marcella, who is a threat to Caroline's physical and mental health. Later, Marcella tells Dean that it is obvious that Caroline planted all of that evidence herself, which is a suspicion that he must struggle to suppress.

At the end of the story, Caroline is successful. She and Dean have a baby, Anna, together, and she publishes her second book of poetry to great critical acclaim, while her rival, Marcella, never publishes again.

THEMES

True Love

The relationship between Dean Kaneshiro and Caroline Yip does not seem to have the ingredients of true, lasting love. Dean and Caroline are opposites in many ways: she is outspoken and he is quiet; she is messy and he is fastidious; she is hot tempered and he is unemotional. Still, at the end of the story, they are together, committed to one another and to their child, despite any suspicions each holds about the secrets the other might be hiding.

To some extent, their opposite personalities help them have a well-rounded relationship because they compliment one another. Caroline is clearly the decision maker in the relationship, holding back her declaration of love until weeks after Dean has left himself exposed by announcing that he loves her. She mocks and challenges him for his timidity and his lack of verbal skills. The equilibrium they have established is upset when she realizes that Dean is not simply a local carpenter who is impressed by her skill as a poet but is actually a renowned artist. At that point, with her dominant position threatened, she leaves him. They come back together after he humbles himself by coming to her place of work day after day with no encouragement from her. When he burns the rare wood that he needs for his chairs, he shows that Caroline is more precious to him than his art.

The story raises the question of whether the relationship between Caroline and Dean is one of true love or is just a case of psychological codependence between a needy person and a person who needs to be needed. In the end, Don Lee implies that true love is not really different than codependence.

Sacrifice

Dean Kaneshiro lives for his art. The story's first scene, in which he measures Marcella Ahn for a chair, shows the seriousness with which he takes his work: he follows strict rules, obeying his self-imposed standards, barely allowing conversation with his subject. When he won hundreds of thousands of dollars from an important grant, he used the money to buy more zelkova wood because it is the right wood for the kind of carving he does. He drives a ten-year-old truck and lives in a little house with cheap furniture. He does not pay attention to the circumstances of his life, engrossed in his work as he is.

Still, when he feels that Caroline is being threatened by Marcella, he is willing to sacrifice his irreplaceable zelkova wood to protect her. His scheme of burning the wood to implicate Marcella in a crime falls flat—the small-town police are not talented enough to find the evidence that he left against her, and a failed sprinkler system means more of the wood is burned than he anticipated. Dean is willing to sacrifice the art that he holds so dear for Caroline's safety, which places her above everything else in his life.

Reputation

Caroline is portrayed as very competitive, but Lee explains that she was not always that way. When they were young students, she and Marcella were best friends. Caroline's insecurities arose after her first poetry collection received much less critical and scholarly praise than Marcella's collection. In response to being considered a less talented writer, Caroline dropped out of the literary world, hiding herself away from the very idea of building an artistic reputation by becoming a waitress in a small, remote town.

Over time, Caroline has become comfortable with her lack of reputation. In the course of this story, however, two things happen to shake her complacency. The first is the reappearance of her old rival, Marcella, who garnered the reputation that Caroline felt she deserved. The second is finding out that Dean, who she thought was an inarticulate carpenter, far from the world of art, is in fact the recipient of major awards, grants, and museum retrospectives. The anxiety caused by having her own weak artistic reputation brought up makes her lash out at Dean and makes her probably try to frame Marcella as a stalker.

The story ends with the balance of power restored to Caroline and Dean's relationship when she publishes a book of poetry that earns her the recognition that she has felt she deserved. Her literary reputation is made even more secure when Marcella Ahn disappears from the literary world without ever writing again, and the public forgets her.

STYLE

Point of View

By telling "The Price of Eggs in China" from a limited third-person point of view, Don Lee is able to control the information that readers are given. It is considered limited because most of the story is told from one character's perspective, that of Dean Kaneshiro. Readers are not told of any occurrences that Dean does not know about.

Given this point of view, readers remain involved with Dean; the story unfolds on the page in the same order that it does in his life. But it also keeps readers from directly knowing what is going on in Dean's head: some of his thoughts are conveyed, but his thought process is not revealed totally. For example, the narrative can be specific enough to tell readers that Dean wants to do all that he can to protect Caroline, but it can also be vague enough not to say exactly what Dean is planning when he breaks into Marcella's home. Dean is a quiet person, not much given to saying what he is thinking or planning, and the author's choice of point of view takes advantage of that to keep his behavior mysterious. Then too the limited third person restricts information about other characters' motives. The mysterious phone caller and the gifts are not explained, though clearly someone in the story knows about them. Withholding this information adds to the suspense of the story by leaving Dean in the dark about what really happens between Marcella and Caroline.

HISTORICAL CONTEXT

Asians in California
Traditionally, U.S. history books have discounted the history of Asians in the United States and have focused instead on the path that European settlers followed, first to the New England colonies and then across the continent to the Pacific. In fact, there is evidence that Chinese admiral Zheng He reached North America seventy-two years before Christopher Columbus arrived in 1492. It is well documented that Filipinos working on Spanish galleons traveled to North America in 1587, fifty years before the British settled Jamestown. Since the Philippines were colonized by Spain, there were Filipinos in all of the Spanish communities, including Mexico, the southern United States, and the area that became California. A Filipino colony, the first Asian community in North America, was established in the Louisiana bayous in 1781. Soon, more Chinese men moved to the continent. Prohibited from gaining citizenship, many associated with the criminal element, such as the over two hundred men of Chinese descent who were documented in the 1760s as living on Calle de los Negros, a notorious center for illicit dealings in what later became Los Angeles. Around this same time, travel from China to Hawaii became common, and sailors frequently continued on from the islands to locations along the Pacific Coast, a practice that continued well into the twentieth century.

In the nineteenth century, U.S. businesses imported hundreds of thousands of Asian workers, mostly from China. Although these workers were not slaves, they could not apply for citizenship either, and so they were made to work for wages that were about half the going rate for Europeans. Approximately 90 percent of the workers on the Transcontinental Railway, built between 1864 and 1869, were Chinese.

By the time that Portsmouth Square was established in 1847 in what became San Francisco, there was already a strong Chinese presence in the area. The discovery of gold two years later led to the California gold rush, which drew many people from all over the world, including tens of thousands from China.

Throughout the twentieth century, Asian immigration to the United States continued. Most Asian immigrants came from China, which should not be surprising given that the Chinese population has always been many times that of all of the rest of Asia put together. Starting in the 1950s, Chinese emigration was curtailed by strict rules imposed by the communist government. Around that time, wars with Japan (1941–1945) and North Korea (1950–1953) made the United States an inhospitable place for Asians, slowing immigration.

The Immigration Act passed by Congress in 1965 raised the limits on Asian immigrants but also added restrictions that favored the middle class over the poor, which shifted the demographic of immigrants to more developed countries.

In the early 2000s, nearly one third of citizens of Asian Pacific descent lived in California. The Asian population increased about 30 percent between 1985 and 2005. This rate of growth was expected to continue as international travel became increasingly easy and employment opportunities attracted new immigrants.

CRITICAL OVERVIEW

After it was initially published in the *Gettysburg Review*, "The Price of Eggs in China" was chosen as one of the winners of the Pushcart Prize, and was subsequently included in the anthology *The Pushcart Prize XXVI: Best of the Small Presses 2002. Yellow*, the collection by Lee that includes this story, won the 2002 Sue Kaufman Prize for First Fiction and was a Barnes and Noble Discover Great New Writers selection.

Because Lee's ethnic background is connected to the subject matter of the stories in *Yellow*, it is not surprising that the book received much attention from the Asian-American press. Andrew Sun, of the website *Asiaweek.com*, notes that "*Yellow* is mature and complex in its emotional dynamics. The tales are elegant, almost Chekhovian meditations on people trying to pick up the pieces of their lives." A review at the similarly named *AsianWeek.com* site focuses

A Japanese man planing wood in his workshop © *Horace Bristol/Corbis*

on "The Price of Eggs in China" in particular, and concludes that "Lee's stories are utterly contemporary, incredibly California, but grounded in the depth of beautiful prose and intriguing storylines."

Beyond the Asian-American press, however, *Yellow* received national attention, with favorable reviews in many major media sources. *Publishers Weekly* tagged it as one of the most important short story collections of 2001, advising potential buyers that "*This appealing collection shouldn't be relegated to Asian Studies shelves*" at libraries and bookstores. In the *New York Times Book Review*, writer Will Blythe observes that Lee "proves himself a worthy practitioner of realistic fiction in the vein of writers like Richard Yates and Andre Dubois. His narratives zip along, encapsulating whole lifetimes of intelligent men and women whose self-awareness is insufficient for the gauntlets they must run." Jan Alexander, in a review in the *Chicago Tribune*, singled out "The Price of Eggs in China" as "by far the most scurrilously funny story" in *Yellow*. She praises Lee's treatment of female characters but states that "his true talents emerge in his panoply of Asian-American men,"

WHAT DO I READ NEXT?

- Don Lee followed *Yellow*, the collection which contains this story, with his 2004 novel, *Country of Origin*. This critically acclaimed book centers on a mystery. A graduate student of Japanese-African-American descent goes to Tokyo to do research, ends up working in a men's club and disappears, leaving a Foreign Service junior officer and a jaded police detective to look for clues.

- Amy Tan's 1989 novel *The Joy Luck Club* takes place in San Francisco's Chinatown, and like *Yellow*, it tells the interconnected stories of a community. It is often credited with starting a national trend toward interest in the Asian-American experience. *The Joy Luck Club* was reissued in an edition by Penguin in 2006.

- Chang-Rae Lee is a much-lauded Korean-American writer. His novel *Aloft* (2004) was on the *New York Times* bestseller list: it is about a white middle-class patriarch of a family that is becoming diverse and divided.

- Marilyn Chin, an Asian-American poet who blends tradition with confrontational language, is the kind of outspoken writer that Lee might have had in mind when he described Caroline Yip's contemporary writing style. Her poems in the 2003 collection, *Rhapsody in Plain Yellow: Poems*, have been lauded for their innovation and daring.

noting that he renders them "with a flair for dialogue that crackles with implications beyond what the characters are capable of articulating."

Lee's follow-up publication, the 2004 novel *Country of Origin*, was just as widely praised by reviewers for its wit and insight. With a mystery plot at its heart, it drew a more crossover audience, beyond the literary readers who already knew him for his work on *Ploughshares*.

CRITICISM

David Kelly

Kelly is an instructor of creative writing and English literature. In the following essay, he looks at how this story, which seems to be about three people's bonds, is actually about how much easier it is to face loss when one has less to lose.

In his short story "The Price of Eggs in China," Don Lee presents a relationship triangle formed by Dean Kaneshiro, Caroline Yip, and Marcella Ahn, three artists who live in a fictional California coastal town and whose lives are connected, although the story never really makes clear if their connection is the result of fate or of cunning. They are undeniably bound to each other, though. Dean has been hired to build a chair for Marcella, and even though she hired him years earlier, a contract is an unbreakable vow to him. He goes to great trouble to locate her when it comes time to fulfill his contract, only to find that by then she has moved several times and has ended up in the same small town where he lives. At the same time, he is in love with Caroline, who, even though she is cool to him, seems to love him, too. Marcella and Caroline are linked by their friendship years earlier and, more annoyingly, by the literary critics, who have lumped them together as "Oriental Hair Poet No. 1" and Oriental Hair Poet No. 2."

With so much interdependence, this would appear to be a story about connections. To some extent, it is: the climax of the story occurs certainly when Dean and Caroline are able to get beyond the external forces that pull them apart and just bask in each other's love. But more than a story about love, this is a story about loss, and particularly about how much loss each of these guarded characters is able to endure.

If it is loss that hounds them, then it would seem that Caroline is in the most stable position of all of the characters. The story begins years after her one brush with fame, after the publication of a book of poetry right after college. Then, she was a rising star in the literary world: now, she is a waitress in a café. This change of circumstances would be fine if she were someone who found that fame was not for her and she preferred the quiet, simple life, but she clearly is not that person. She has not found peace, as her chronic insomnia indicates.

" BUT DEAN IS IN LOVE, AND HE HAS NO CONTROL

OVER THE ONE THING THAT IS MORE PRECIOUS TO

HIM THAN MONEY, FAME, OR TALENT. CAROLINE'S

INSTABILITY FRIGHTENS HIM AND FORCES HIM TO

TAKE STEPS THAT ARE NOT CONSISTENT WITH HIS

PROFESSIONAL DETACHMENT TOWARD LIFE."

To say that something is bothering Caroline is an understatement. She is desperate. As Lee puts it: "she had done everything possible short of psychology—which she didn't believe in—to alleviate her insomnia and insistent stress: acupuncture, herbs, yoga, homeopathy, tai chi." Dropping out of literary society has evidently not helped her. In addition, she has a casual attitude toward Dean's affection for her. She admits to not loving him when he declares his love for her, and she drives him away from her in anger when she finds out that he is more than just a talented local carpenter. It appears that Caroline has very little to lose, that her life is already too messy for her to sink much lower.

Yet, her violent negative reaction to Dean's artistic success is a clear indicator that she does still have a self-image to protect. Her fear and hatred of Marcella Ahn is another sign that Caroline feels she has something that can be threatened. She may be right, and Marcella may have planned to become involved with Dean as part of a grand scheme to humiliate Caroline, even though Marcella first contacted him years before Dean even met Caroline. More likely, the threat that she feels from Marcella is so intense that it drives Caroline into extreme fear. Chopping her own hair is an act that conveys Caroline's self-destructiveness and her fear of being compared with the other Oriental Hair Poet.

In contrast to Caroline, Marcella Ahn seems to have a great deal to lose, even though she seems to be in a position to handily absorb anything life offers to her. Money means nothing to her, as she has inherited millions and has had her pick of high-paying teaching jobs and grants. Prestige is at her fingertips and has been since she and Caroline published their first books of poetry. Physically,

Caroline is probably an attractive woman, although the story does not actually establish that. Lee describes her as muscular and tall, but he avoids making any particular judgment about whether she is good looking, taking instead the sort of detached and professional mien that Dean himself would take to her: even though the narrative lingers over the fact that she has "a good butt, a firm, StairMastered butt, a shapely, surprisingly protuberant butt," it is not done as a comment on her appeal so much as it is an indication of Dean's clinical approach to details concerning his customers' body types and how they will fit his chairs.

With all these advantages, Marcella Ahn could easily put herself above the personal drama that is played out in Rosarita Bay between Dean and Caroline. For most of the story, it seems as if she is in fact above it. She does flirt with Dean, but her flirting is not necessarily a jibe at her old rival Caroline: she might just be the kind of person to whom flirting comes naturally. She seems capable of accepting anything that comes to her with ease, until the story's end.

Dean asks Marcella's opinion of the poems that Caroline has written because he knows his own limitations. He works with his hands and is uncomfortable with words. Yet he reads beyond what Marcella says, interpreting her facial expression as suggesting that Marcella is impressed with Caroline's poetry. It would be easy to believe that Dean is simply seeing what he wants to see, in defense of the woman he loves. But when Marcella loses her composure over the issue, the story provides proof that she has an emotional involvement in believing Caroline to be untalented. At the height of the story, Marcella is desperate to have Dean believe that her composure is intact, and her desperation is proof that her self-esteem is shaky. Further proof lies in the fact that, after the events at Rosarita Bay, Marcella goes on to never publish poetry again. The story links her loss of writing to the trauma of finding Caroline to be a talented writer, and she tries to suppress that knowledge.

Like Marcella, Dean seems to have little to lose. He is respected for his artistry to a degree that is beyond the reach of most artists. Hundreds of thousands of dollars flow his way from grants and commissions; his work is displayed in museums; he is compared to the greatest artists who have worked in his field; and all of this recognition has occurred, as Caroline points out, while he is still a relatively young man. To make matters even better, Dean has won all of this acclaim without even trying for it, on the basis of his impressive talent alone: his phenomenal skill is second only to his artistic integrity. For many other artists, he is living the ideal life.

But Dean is in love, and he has no control over the one thing that is more precious to him than money, fame, or talent. Caroline's instability frightens him and forces him to take steps that are not consistent with his professional detachment toward life. First, he deludes himself, believing against all evidence that Marcella is behind the disguised-voice phone calls and mysterious packages that Caroline claims to have received. He then goes further in his desperation, to the point where he tries to frame Marcella for a crime. It is a foolish scheme, but he thinks it will protect Caroline.

Dean pays for his foolishness. He loses his rare zelkova wood, and by extension he forfeits a part of his artistic integrity—the substitute, English walnut, may be good, but it is a compromise nonetheless. Worse, by going about helping Caroline in the way he has—and it may well be the only way Caroline would let herself be helped—Dean has created a secret that he can never discuss with her, even if they live the rest of their lives together, as the story suggests they will. In the end, Dean and Caroline speculate about what secrets are held by the product of their union, the child Anna, who has inherited Caroline's uneasiness even as Caroline has learned to sleep comfortably.

Everybody pays a price in "The Price of Eggs in China." Marcella loses her ability to produce artistically, and Dean loses his artistic purity. Caroline, who has been pushing herself for years to deny her talent, faces her worst fears about herself: in the end, she is happy and well-adjusted, a better person for having paid the price.

Source: David Kelly, Critical Essay on "The Price of Eggs in China," in *Short Stories for Students*, Thomson Gale, 2007.

Klay Dyer

Dyer holds a Ph.D. in English literature and has published extensively on fiction, poetry, film, and television. He is also a freelance university teacher, writer, and educational consultant. In the following essay, he discusses "The Price of Eggs in China" as a quest story, in which an artist changes his vision and finds a new art style and life.

Any artist can attest that creative vision is not static. Rather, at any one point, vision and

> " ... DEAN ESTABLISHES HIMSELF AS A NEW MAN, AN ARTIST WHO WORKS WITH MORE AFFORDABLE AND MARKETABLE ENGLISH WALNUT, AND A NEW FATHER WITH THE BIRTH OF HIS DAUGHTER ANNA."

artwork are, like one of Dean Kaneshiro's chairs, a carefully crafted negotiation of numerous pieces "put together by joints, forty-four delicate, intricate joints." Over time, the vision and artwork change. For most artists, the work is a process of defining one's style in reference to tradition and also to current ideas or circumstances. An artist who aims to replicate one work of art, Dean learns in this story about how artistic vision and artwork can change with circumstances.

Some artists sustain one artistic vision, become "tenaciously, permanently locked" on it, as though their identity, their style, and their artwork are all fused. These artists combine their sense of tradition and ancestry with their sense of contemporary culture. These individuals are fitted into their artistic identity so neatly that it cannot "budge" or "squeak." Yet even for such artists, the defining vision can evolve through stages, change out of necessity or impulse; commitment to replication shifts or revises over time.

Dean is determined in his dedication to the "traditional method of Japanese joinery dating to the seventeenth century," and he uses this method to perfect the chair that carries his name. Successful with making this one object, Dean becomes increasingly committed to replicating the single product, his chair. He is increasingly focused on this one design idea, though over time that idea has changed a little. "He made only armchairs now, one chair over and over, the Kaneshiro Chair." Focused on the craft rather than the art, he admits, his ultimate goal is "to get to a point where he could make a Kaneshiro Chair blindfolded."

At the same time that he is set on producing the chairs, Dean practically hordes the raw materials he uses. The chairs are made of rare and exorbitantly expensive Japanese zelkova wood. He has stockpiled the wood, almost finding the wood itself more important than what he can make from it. In fact, he responds emotionally to the raw materials of his craft: "When he went into the shed to select a new board," he confesses, "he was always overcome by the beauty of the wood, the smell of it. He'd run his hand over the boards—hardly a check or crack on them—and would want to weep."

This hesitation to use the raw materials seems akin to Dean's apparent discomfort with commercial success and art world fame. His chairs are exhibited at the Museum of Modern Art and the American Craft Museum, and he is able to charge ten thousand dollars for a single chair, which takes him less than three weeks to build. Known in the art world and earning a lot of money, he could live among the elite. Yet he chooses to live where he is unknown, in "secluded and quiet" Rosarita Bay, a place that seems in some ways too small and too remote, "a no-man's-land, a sleepy, slightly seedy back-water . . . a place of exile." Here, Dean hides his urban reputation and recognition.

Moreover, Dean's productivity in this town is stymied by the presence of two poets who are themselves in conflict: Marcella Ahn and Caroline Yip. These women were once seemingly joined at the hip, close friends whom popular media labeled "'The Oriental Hair Poets,' 'The Braids of the East,' and 'The New Asian Poetresses.'" But in truth the women contrast with each other in their own poetic styles. Marcella, who has commissioned Dean to build her a chair, is a critically successful poet. She is "obsessive-compulsive neat," media savvy, and potentially "a vulture, a vampire." Marcella is dangerous to Dean's art, to his physical health, and to his relationship with Caroline. Marcella's poetry is "highly erudite, usually beginning with mundane observations about birds or plant life, then slipping into long abstract meditations." By contrast, Caroline Yip is a romantic at heart and a writer who carries the scars of being "skewered" for a poetry that has "a slangy, contemporary voice, full of topical, pop culture allusions." Hot-tempered Caroline is threatened when Marcella moves to town and she is upset to learn that Dean has measured her for one of his chairs. Dean gets caught between these competing women, and his involvement and responses affect his raw materials and in turn his artwork.

At once sustained and burdened by his early acclaim as an artist, Dean struggles to move forward in his art. He does not question himself about what his art might stand for, and he buffers himself against bigger questions. Is he comfortable, for instance, with the fees he charges for his chairs, and if so, why does he live like he poor? Has the medium of his art and his quest for perfection erased the creative energy that made possible his early success? Has he allowed this drive for perfection of a single idea to overtake the once powerful drive to create new forms and explore new ideas? Has he been corrupted by the commodity-driven American culture in which he works and, connected to that, has his artwork become commodity?

As Marcella's appearance in town threatens his relationship with Caroline, Dean is forced to find a new path between the opposite impulses or contrasts that press in upon him. As he contends with the interactions between Marcella and Caroline he undertakes a quest for a new inspiration and a new way of making his art. Dean is compelled by a series of events to re-create himself and his art. Accused of making obscene phone calls and forced to admit that Marcella might be stalking Caroline, Dean tries to clear his name, free Caroline from her competition with Marcella, and cut himself off from the elitist traditions that the zelkova represents. Setting fire to his own wood shed and destroying most of the stock, Dean hopes to frame Marcella for the crime, an act that contributes to her leaving Rosarita Bay. With Marcella gone, Dean establishes himself as a new man, an artist who works with more affordable and marketable English walnut, and a new father with the birth of his daughter Anna. In other words, Dean finds a way to live a more ordinary life, able to market his chairs more widely, able to settle into a family life.

With the fire, Dean brings about a new vision of himself and his work. By replacing the zelkova with a populist wood that is "pretty, durable, [and] available," Dean becomes a hybrid, one that combines the old joinery techniques and new wood. In this newly created form, he finds a truth that extends beyond tradition and beyond his obsessive search for the perfect chair. He finds a truth about himself that lies, ultimately, in the dreams of his infant daughter who, "still asleep, lolled her head, her lips pecking the air in steady rhythm—an infant soliloquy." In paying "the price of devotion" to both Caroline and his art, Dean sees in his daughter's dreams an inspiration that he never before imagined.

Source: Klay Dyer, Critical Essay on "The Price of Eggs in China," in *Short Stories for Students*, Thomson Gale, 2007.

Thomson Gale

In the following essay, the critic gives an overview of Don Lee's work.

Don Lee, a third-generation Korean American, began his education at the University of California Los Angeles as an engineering major during which time, he told Jessica Brilliant Keener of *Poets & Writers* he was "bored to tears." After encouragement from an English composition instructor to take some creative-writing courses, he was "hooked." Thus began his career in the writing field. His book of short stories, *Yellow*, won the Sue Kaufman Prize for First Fiction from the American Academy of Arts and Letters, and individual stories in the book won an O. Henry Award and a Pushcart Prize.

Yellow is a collection of six interwoven stories and a novella all with Asian-American protagonists and all set in a fictional coastal town in California. Janice Bees wrote in *Kliatt* that the stories are "compact, complicated, energetic, and sharply written." Reviewing the book for the *Los Angeles Times*, Tim Rutten commented: "Lee is unafraid of flirting with the perils of melodrama and even sentimentality—if it is the service of narrative. His prose is spare and free of literary allusions, and he is unafraid to take narrative chances, including what some might consider Hollywood action set pieces." Rutten called *Yellow* a "triumph of the artful over the didactic," and stated that the characters filling its pages "constitute a rich and unusually complete portrait of contemporary Asian America."

Lee's book was a long time in the making, with some stories dating back thirteen years before their publication. The author told Keener that, due to the long process, people might assume he was having difficulty selling the manuscript. Not so, he contended: "I just wasn't writing. I wrote one story every year or two and published in literary journals. I was a hobbyist." He noted that his job as editor of *Ploughshares* is demanding and his days are filled with programming computers, writing grant applications, organizing information for tax returns, and a myriad of other responsibilities. "The editing part is the easiest and most enjoyable part, but it's also the smallest percentage of an editor's time," he commented.

In order to write his novel *Country of Origin*, Lee declared to Keener, he first had to believe he could; this was his greatest challenge. He then negotiated with Emerson College, his employer, to take Fridays off from his editorial job at *Ploughshares* and he worked on his book Fridays, Saturdays, and Sundays, spending four months in research, one year on his draft, and six months in revision. The schedule he set himself was two chapters per month, with each chapter approximately twelve to fifteen pages long. "I followed through, and it was pretty miraculous," he told Keener.

The basis of *Country of Origin* is identity. Based in Tokyo in 1980, the story centers around a half-Korean, half-white foreign-service officer and a Japanese police officer who unite to search for a missing black American woman who may be half Japanese. Through the characters' interlocking stories, Lee explores issues of race, identity, social conventions, the Japanese sex trade, and the law.

In an interview with Terry Hong for *AsianWeek*, Lee explained why he is "so hung up on identity." The son of a U.S. state department officer, Lee was born in Tokyo and moved with his family to a U.S. Army base in Seoul, South Korea, when he was four years old. Japanese was the only language he knew; he had always thought of himself as a Japanese kid. Now, was he a Korean kid? And on an American army base? Then it was back to Tokyo where he spent his adolescence. "Given my background, I was fascinated by the milieu of foreign service officers and ex-patriots," Lee told Hong, and the breakthrough in finding a theme for his book came when a young English woman—a hostess in Tokyo—went missing. "So now I had my story," he said.

Lee wrote on his Web site that all the themes in *Country of Origin* about identity and race were explored "on a subconscious level," and only after many interviews did he consciously understand those themes. While several reviewers called the book subversive, Lee responded to Hong: "That's because everything in the book deals with artifice.... Everyone is trying to deny or preserve or find their origins, but the point, I think, is that identity is elusive. It can't be easily defined, it can't be appropriated or simulated, and maybe the search for it, at least on an external level, is futile."

Entertainment Weekly contributor Rebecca Ascher-Walsh called *Country of Origin* an "elegant and haunting debut." Frank Sennett, writing in *Booklist*, deemed it "as satisfying as it is unsettling," and a *Kirkus Reviews* critic explained that "Thriller conventions draw the reader, like the characters, into a gallery of human enigmas," adding that the novel's author "leaves no fingerprints: his cool, precise prose captures his characters without overexplaining them."

Source: Thomson Gale, "Don Lee," in *Contemporary Authors Online*, Thomson Gale, 2006.

Jessica Brilliant Keener

In the following review, Lee discusses balancing his career as an editor for Ploughshares *with the demands of being a writer.*

Perhaps best known as editor of *Ploughshares*, a post he's held for sixteen years, Don Lee published his first book, *Yellow* (Norton, 2001), at the age of 41. The story collection won the Sue Kaufman Prize for First Fiction from the American Academy of Arts and Letters; individual stories earned him an O'Henry Award and a Pushcart Prize.

Norton will publish Lee's first novel, *Country of Origin*, in July. Set in Tokyo in 1980, a half-Korean, half-white foreign service officer and a Japanese cop are assigned to find a missing young American woman. *Publishers Weekly* gave it a starred review, calling it "sharply observed, at turns trenchantly funny and heartbreakingly sad . . . could be a breakout book for Lee."

But Lee's future as a writer was not always certain. He started as an engineering major at UCLA, and was "bored to tears" until a composition teacher urged him to try a few creative writing courses. Once he did, Lee was hooked. Two years later he applied and was accepted to the MFA program at Emerson College in Boston. One of his teachers, Dewitt Henry, founder and editor of *Ploughshares*, asked him to read submissions for the journal. Lee eventually joined the staff as office manager/assistant fiction editor and was later promoted to editor. In the early 1990s, under Lee's editorship, *Ploughshares* received a Lila-Wallace Reader's Digest Grant of $125,000. The grant was a boon for the magazine, says Lee, but not for

his writing. "It required me to work 10 to 12 hour days for two years. I threw my life into it."

Poets & Writers Magazine asked Lee how he balanced the demands of writing a novel with his editorial duties at *Ploughshares*.

[Don Lee:] Well, you know what? My toughest challenge was believing I could do it. Haruki Murakami, in an interview about writing, said that it was all about concentration. That's true, but for me it was all about confidence. I was terrified throughout the entire process. I researched for about four months and then I wrote the first draft in a year and revised for 6 months.

[*Jessica Brilliant Keener:*] *That's pretty fast.*

Well, I negotiated with Emerson College and got Fridays off from my job, and wrote Friday, Saturday, and Sunday. During the summer I took time to go windsailing [laughs] so there were some days that I skipped. But essentially, I set a schedule for myself: two chapters a month, with each chapter 12 to 15 pages long. I followed through and it was pretty miraculous.

At the same time, do you think you had a great apprenticeship as an editor, reading so much fiction and being in the world of fiction?

I think that's a misconception about what editors at literary magazines do. Most of my job involves writing grant applications, fund raising, programming computers, getting together a tax return. It's all the nuts and bolts involved in running a magazine. The editing part is the easiest and most enjoyable part, but it's also the smallest percentage of the editor's time.

You know, I talk about focusing on editing and working at *Ploughshares*, but part of that is that I was afraid to put myself on the line. Some people might assume that I was struggling to sell the manuscript [of *Yellow*] and couldn't. That wasn't the case at all. I just wasn't writing. I wrote one story every year or two and published in literary journals. I was a hobbyist. The other thing people always assume is that it must have been hard for me to see my peers go on in their literary success. That's also not the case. How can you be jealous if you're not doing it yourself?

When I'm on these panels [at writers conferences] about how to get published, what I try to emphasize, but what often doesn't get through, is that it's the writing that counts. People are often trying to find some secret to getting published. They think there's some kind of trick or nepotism or magic procedure to getting that story published, but it's the work, and if you're not doing that work, then it's not going to happen.

As editor, you've seen writing trends come and go. Have any of these trends influenced your own style over the years?

I don't think so. You build your affinities for literary works very early. But I don't think I've been influenced by the work I've come across in my work as an editor. Because that would mean the work is derivative of other people's, and although you can argue that everything you write is somehow a reaction or possibly a replication of what you've read before, you need to make your own style.

You sound very centered.

No, I think it's bravado. I say these things with the greatest confidence, but really, underneath, most writers are quaking with self-doubt. That's certainly the case with me, as evidenced by my whole experience of writing this novel. I talk a good game but I'm just like everyone else. I don't know if what I'm doing is good and I don't know if I'll be able to produce something that's good in the future.

What do you find most satisfying in your dual roles as an editor and writer?

As an editor—other than the obvious, which is trying to get these issues out the door on time and trying to keep things afloat because you're always worried about money and whether things are going to fall apart—it's still that thing where you discover new writers. It comes out of nowhere. It's a terrific piece and you publish it. Then you're able to help that writer get a leg up. An agent calls. An editor calls. Or it makes getting the next publication easier simply by putting on the cover letter that *Ploughshares* has published the work, so another editor takes it more seriously. Really, when it comes down to it, that's our function.

As a writer, what I felt with this novel was a real sense of accomplishment, because I wasn't sure I was going to be able to do it. But it also worked on another level. You hope that the language is good. You hope that you're doing something more than filling up pages; that you're actually able to write something that's compelling and effective and has some impetus

in your larger themes. It sounds hokey but you really hope to change the way someone looks at the world after reading your work.

As an editor who is also writing, have you ever been in danger of self-editing to the point of inhibiting your creative writing?

As fastidious and compulsive as I was, the pleasure of writing is in the surprises. For instance, an entire character—the cop in *Country of Origin*—was unplanned. He was a big pleasure. I had no idea that he would arrive. That's the joy of writing, when these things pop up. On a smaller scale, it's the particular turn of phrase or simply a good line that you write and can take some pride in. But as far as the symbiosis between writer and editor, I think that, for me, being a writer helps being an editor more so than the other way around. It's very easy for me to line edit a story of other people's work. I understand that process as a writer. I also can be more sensitive to the process.

Earlier on, my editor [Alane Salierno Mason at Norton] told me, "You really have to change how you look at yourself. You're not an editor first and a writer second. You have to look at yourself as a writer first and an editor second." I'm still warming up to that. I'm looking at the longer view and trying to improve with each book, trying to expand my range.

Source: Jessica Brilliant Keener, "Don Lee on Building Confidence as a Writer and the Editor of *Ploughshares*," in *Poets & Writers Magazine*, May 26, 2004, pp. 1–3.

Robert Lee Brewer

In the following interview, Lee talks about the process of putting together a collection of short stories and getting published.

Don Lee, author of the story collection *Yellow*, did not exactly sweat over getting his first book published. As Lee relates, "I'm 41 now, but when I was 38, I started thinking about turning 40. That was looming over my head, and I thought to myself, 'You know, I would really like to have a book—something to show for all these years.' That's really what pressed me into putting together a collection."

Lee, who is also the editor of a well-known literary journal, has been publishing stories for years. However, he's the first to admit he doesn't work at the most prolific pace. "I pretty much relegated writing to a hobby and considered myself an editor, both as a career and vocation.

> " BUT WITH THIS PARTICULAR STORY, I DECIDED TO WRITE A FIRST DRAFT, PERIOD, ALL THE WAY THROUGH. I USED A YELLOW LEGAL PAD, WROTE IT ON MY COUCH, AND DID NOT GO BACK UNTIL I HAD FINISHED THE FIRST DRAFT. I WROTE IT IN SOMETHING LIKE SIX WEEKENDS."

Essentially, every year-and-a-half to two years, I would write and publish a story."

The result has been successful. *Yellow* has been compared to such big gun story collections as Sherwood Anderson's *Winesburg, Ohio* and James Joyce's *Dubliners*. All the stories revolve around a fictional town in California called Rosarita Bay and deal with the issues of being Asian American in a mostly white American society.

Here Lee talks about *Yellow*, as well as the business of getting a collection of stories published.

[*Robert Lee Brewer:*] *Was this book a premeditated collection or did it just sort of come together?*

[Don Lee:] A long time ago I was taking a train from San Francisco to Los Angeles. We were pretty far inland and riding along this back-water canal. There was a seaplane moored on this canal, and I thought, "Who owns this seaplane? What is it doing that far inland when there isn't any kind of river or lake for it to take off?" So that starting image inspired the story "Casual Water." I don't think I named the town at that time, but I started writing stories around the same kind of geographical locale and scenery. I thought this might eventually come together as a collection, but I was sure taking my sweet time.

As the editor of a literary journal, did you find inspiration through working with other writers and editors?

I think actually being an editor is detrimental to being a writer. It might be the worst job possible to have if you want to be a writer, because you're doing this all day long. You're part of the industry and just surrounded by it. I think it's hard to sustain that energy when you go home at night and on weekends, if it's the same sort of arena. I kind of decided to forsake my own career as a writer to be an editor first. I realized that if I was looking at the editing job as the sinecure for my writing but I wasn't making progress with my writing, I would start to beat myself up mentally. It would be harmful to my psyche. So I took the opposite route. But as I said, it lingered in the background there. And so, that whole thing about turning 40 and thinking I wanted to have some sort of tangible evidence of accomplishment as a writer—I think in the back of my mind I thought, I don't want to be one those would've, could've, should've's. You see a lot of people who have backgrounds in creative writing going into book publishing, and it's very difficult to sustain that desire and the work habits to keep going on as a writer yourself.

Did you learn things to do and not to do from examples set by other writers' submissions to you?

This is where my experience as an editor really comes into play. I did have all the advantages in the world, not only of seeing and knowing the pitfalls and the good things other writers do when they're submitting stuff, but I also understood the process and what to expect all the way through. There haven't been any real surprises for me. For instance, I know as a short-story collection that this is not going to be a bestseller or an Oprah pick. It will be nice if it gets good reviews and sells a few copies, but I don't sit there and hold hope that this is going to be a breakthrough book of any sort. But I can still take pride in it. As far as getting an agent, I sent a letter, asked them if they would be interested in reading this manuscript, listed my credits, and so forth. I approached four top agents and made actually one caveat. I said that I didn't have a novel and I didn't know if I would have one in the future. So what I wanted to know was whether it was possible to sell this as a one-book deal, instead of a two-book deal. All four of them said no, that the stories were finely written and everything, but they just didn't think they could sell it as a one-book. I think they also were indicating to me that maybe they could, but it wouldn't be worth their efforts. One of them told me a story about a writer who will remain nameless. But the agent ended up sending that person's short-story collection to 19 publishers in the first round, and they all said no. Then they went through a second and third round. It was just heartbreaking for the agent to see a work he thought was very good, but not being able to find a market for the collection. Of course, there are ebbs and flows of the market. Sometimes collections are more appealing to publishers than others. But it's always a tough sell in comparison to a novel. And so, I approached two more agents, and this time they both said they thought they could sell it as a one-book deal. I went with one of them, and it ended up that I had to sign a two-book deal with Norton.

What sort of relationship did you have with your agent?

It was actually fairly quick. We drew a list of ten names for the first round. Mainly, she asked me if I had any connections with these editors whom she thought might be interested in the book. It ended up to be very few editors I knew personally or had any contact with. Her function is to warm up those editors before she sends it out, to mention to them over lunch, a phone call, drink, or something, "Hey, I've got this interesting book I think you might like." And then, she follows up with phone calls, finds out if there's any interest, and tries to get them to make a decision. And it turned out that quite a number of those ten didn't even make a decision. One thing that went to our disadvantage was, this happened before the Christmas holidays. So people were backlogged and maybe didn't even have time to read the book. But it's interesting to me that after the sale and the contract is signed, you move to the next keeper of the house, which is the editor, and work intensively with the editor, while hardly at all with the agent. When it comes time for the book to come out, you move from the editor to the publicist. Now I don't have much contact with the editor or agent at all. It's the publicist I'm talking to all the time.

Do you think self-promotion should be a concern for a writer?

It's interesting, because most people become writers in that they're introspective and withdrawn in the first place. When they start publishing their work, they're expected to be an entirely different person, an extrovert, someone who can be charming and dynamic. But it is important. You have to be able to carry a conversation with a reporter and answer things you might not want to answer. You have to go to bookstores and have a decent reading voice to keep people awake. So in terms of self-promotion, I think

that's the extent of a writer's responsibility. I think there are other people who will go to great lengths to sell their books. They'll go to malls and hand sell to people in the halls. I'm not sure if that kind of hand selling is going to make a huge difference.

What do you think was your greatest task in putting this book together?

What turned it around for me was one particular story called "The Price of Eggs in China," which is the opening story to the collection. First of all, it was the easiest time I ever had writing a story. Ever since I heard about Japanese joinery, I was interested in writing a story about a Japanese chair-maker. I'd been collecting research for a long time about that and knew I wanted to write a story about it. But I didn't know what the story was going to be. Then that whole thing about the Oriental Hair Poets just came out of the blue. I was going to meet a friend and had about ten minutes before I had to leave, but in that ten minutes I wrote the first page and a half, which has not changed in that time. Before I'd always been a bleeder and not a gusher. I'd always eke one word at a time and did not go on before I was satisfied with what I'd written. That's a painful way to write. But with this particular story, I decided to write a first draft, period, all the way through. I used a yellow legal pad, wrote it on my couch, and did not go back until I had finished the first draft. I wrote it in something like six weekends. It was the first time I'd allowed myself to be a little looser in the process and the story itself. I think that made a big difference, because when I went back to revise the stories, I took out a lot of the earlier literary pretensions and symbolism and made them more readable.

What do you think other less experienced writers should know about trying to get a collection of stories published?

They should be prepared that it's going to be difficult to do. If they have an idea for a novel and a few stories and are trying to decide which to devote attention to, I would say that writing a novel would be the easiest route for publication. In terms of writing advice, I always tell people a couple of things: One is not to try too hard. What I see as an editor are writers trying too hard to impress in the first few pages instead of letting a natural narrative voice develop. The second thing is, you really have to be passionate about what you're writing and not let the market dictate what you're writing. In other words, you write what you want to first with all the heart and craft you can muster. Then you find a market for it, not the other way around.

Source: Robert Lee Brewer, "Don Lee: Writing for Himself First," in *WritersMarket.com*, April 2001, pp. 1–4.

SOURCES

Alexander, Jan, "Variations on Asian States of Mind," in *Chicago Tribune*, July 8, 2001, Section 14, p. 2.

Blythe, Will, "Both Sides of the Hyphen: Two Very Different Story Collections Explore Questions of Asian-American Identity," in *New York Times Book Review*, July 15, 2001, p. 6.

Review of *Yellow*, in *AsianWeek.com*, March 30-April 5, 2001, http://www.asianweek/com/2001_03_30/ae3_litpicks. html (accessed September 11, 2006).

Review of *Yellow*, in *Publishers Weekly*, April 2, 2001, p. 38.

Sun, Andrew, "Beyond Racial Melodramas," in *Asiaweek.com*, September 21, 2001, http://www.asiaweek. com/asiaweek/magazine/Life/0,8782,174693,00.html (accessed September 11, 2006).

FURTHER READING

Cranz, Galen, *The Chair: Rethinking Culture, Body, and Design*, Plume, 2004.
> This history of chair design, focusing on the more recent developments in ergonomics, is the kind of work that the story's Dean Kaneshiro might read.

Huang, Guiyou, *The Columbia Guide to Asian American Literature since 1945*, Columbia University Press, 2006.
> This book breaks down Asian-American writings since World War II into specific genres, showing those who paved the way for contemporary writers such as Lee.

Manning, Kathleen, and Jerry Crow, *Half Moon Bay (Images of America Series)*, Arcadia Publishing, 2005.
> This pictorial history of the town on which Lee based his fictional Rosarita Bay gives readers a sense of the places that he describes in this and other stories.

Novas, Himilce, and Lan Cao, *Everything You Need to Know about Asian American History*, Norton, 2000.
> Written in a more lighthearted style than most history texts, this book covers the lives of people from the Pacific Rim going back to before Columbus.

The Rememberer

AIMEE BENDER

1997

Aimee Bender's unusual short story, "The Rememberer," was first published in the *Missouri Review* in the fall of 1997. In 1998, Bender included the story in her debut collection, entitled *The Girl in the Flammable Skirt*. Most of the stories in the collection have a surreal, fairy-tale quality, and several feature bizarre physical transformations (in one story, for example, a woman gives birth to her own mother, and her husband wakes up to find a hole in his stomach "the size of a soccer ball").

"The Rememberer" tells the story of a woman whose lover, overnight, begins to evolve in reverse, from a man to an ape and then to a sea turtle. Though the situation is bizarre, it is placed in a realistic setting; the characters have an unremarkable relationship, ordinary jobs, and a normal home. This juxtaposition of the ordinary and the bizarre is a hallmark of magical realism, a modern literary genre used by authors such as Gabriel García Márquez and Angela Carter. Though the events are not based on reality, the themes explored are relevant to the real world; for those who care for frail elderly parents or spouses with Alzheimer's disease, the story of a woman watching a loved one regress into mindlessness strikes a familiar emotional chord. Bender also examines the idea that as people become more and more cerebral, they lose the ability to feel emotion and become detached from the actual experience of their lives.

The Girl in the Flammable Skirt was well-received by critics, who praised Bender for both

Aimee Bender © *Jerry Bauer. Reproduced by permission*

her wild imagination and insight into human emotions. Bender followed the collection with her first novel, *An Invisible Sign of My Own*.

AUTHOR BIOGRAPHY

Aimee Bender was born in Los Angeles, California, on June 28, 1969. The youngest of three girls, Bender idolized her older sisters and often tagged along after them. Bender's father, a psychiatrist, and her mother, a choreographer, were early influences; in an interview with *pif* magazine, Bender said, "My dad, through psychiatry, is dealing with the unconscious . . . and my mom is delving into her own unconscious to make up dances. . . . And I'm sort of the combo platter, in that psychiatry is so essentially verbal . . . and also I am like her in that it's all about creating from this inexplicable mysterious place." Another early influence was the book *Transformations* by Anne Sexton, a volume of rewritten fairy tales, which Bender read as a teenager. "Only later, in rereading it, did I see how hugely it had influenced my own stuff," she said in a 2006 interview with the *Yalobusha Review*.

Bender received her undergraduate degree from the University of California at San Diego, then went on to get her Master of Fine Arts from the University of California at Irvine. While at UCI she studied with Judith Grossman and Geoffrey Wolff. Soon Bender's stories were being published in literary reviews such as the *Threepenny Review*, *Granta*, and *Story*, and in 1998, her first collection of stories, titled *The Girl in the Flammable Skirt*, was published ("The Rememberer" is included in this collection). Her debut was very successful; the book was chosen as a *New York Times* Notable Book of 1998 and spent seven weeks on the *Los Angeles Times* bestseller list.

After this first collection, Bender took on a new challenge: her first novel. In 2000, Doubleday published *An Invisible Sign of My Own*, the story of a young second-grade math teacher dealing with anxiety and depression. Then in 2005, Bender returned to the short story with her second collection, *Willful Creatures*.

In addition to writing, Bender has taught writing at several universities. As of 2006, she was teaching full time at the University of Southern California in Los Angeles.

PLOT SUMMARY

As "The Rememberer" opens, the female narrator informs readers that her lover is "experiencing reverse evolution." A sentence later it becomes clear that she does not mean this in a figurative sense; her lover, Ben, turned first into an ape, and now, a month later, he is a sea turtle.

After this startling introduction, Annie, the narrator, explains that she has determined Ben is "shedding a million years a day." His office has called asking where he is, and Annie told them he was sick. She keeps Ben, the sea turtle, in a baking pan full of water; each day when she returns home, he has regressed into a more primitive form.

Annie describes the day he first began his backwards journey; Ben had been lamenting, in his sad way, that people think too much. "Our brains are getting bigger and bigger, and the world dries up and dies when there's too much thought and not enough heart." Annie and Ben made love, and to reassure him, Annie whispered in his ear, "See, we're not thinking." Afterwards, they went outside to the patio. Ben said he wanted to sleep outside, so Annie left him there and went to bed by herself. When she woke up the next morning, she looked outside and Ben the man was gone; in his place, a large ape lay on the patio.

At first Annie handled the situation calmly, thinking Ben would eventually return to normal. Now, however, she has realized this may not happen.

Now Annie returns home from work and Ben, in his baking pan, has become a small salamander. Seeing this, she realizes, "This is the limit of my limits...I cannot bear to look down into the water and not be able to find him at all." So she takes the pan, with Ben inside, to the beach, where she sets it afloat on the water and waves goodbye.

Now she waits, wondering if Ben will ever return as a man. She makes sure all her memories of him are still vivid, "because if he's not here, then it is my job to remember."

CHARACTERS

Annie

Annie is the female narrator of the story. Ben, her lover, laments that he and Annie "think far too much." There is ample evidence throughout the story that Annie, indeed, thinks too much. For example, when Annie describes the first time she and Ben had sex, she says that she "concentrated really hard on letting go," a sort of emotional oxymoron. Also, the fact that she consults a teacher at the community college to determine the rate of Ben's backward progress indicates her intellectual, rather than emotional orientation.

There is evidence too that Annie is aware of the way she overthinks life and is trying to change. At one point, Ben takes her outside, shows her the stars, and tells her, *"There is no space for anything but dreaming."* She goes back to bed but cannot sleep and ends up outside again, trying hard to dream, as Ben suggested, but she is not sure how.

Though she over intellectualizes, Annie is not a cold or unsympathetic character. Her love for Ben is real, and she expresses many tender sentiments about him. Even when Ben becomes an ape, Annie says, "I didn't miss human Ben right away; I wanted to meet the

TOPICS FOR FURTHER STUDY

- After Ben begins his reverse evolution, Annie asks a biology professor to make her an evolutionary timeline. The professor's timeline turns out to be wrong. Research theories of evolution, and using your research, create your own evolutionary timeline.

- Ben tells Annie, "We're all getting too smart. Our brains are just getting bigger and bigger." Do you agree? Write an essay explaining your position. Use factual evidence (IQ statistics, medical research, etc.) to support your opinion.

- Due to the aging of the baby boomer generation, soon more and more people will find themselves in the caretaker role that Annie assumes with Ben. Research the number of Americans over sixty years of age, and make a graph showing the increase in this age group by the year 2020, the year 2030, and the year 2040.

- "The Rememberer" begins *in medias res*, a Latin term meaning "in the middle of things." The term usually refers to a story that begins in mid-action; in this story, Ben has already regressed to the form of a sea turtle when the story begins. Write a short story that begins *in medias res*.

ape, too, to take care of my lover like a son, a pet; I wanted to know him every possible way."

Ben

Ben, Annie's lover, is "always sad about the world." This is probably because Ben, like Annie, thinks too much. In fact, rather than just being sad and experiencing that emotion, Annie says that she and Ben would "sit together and be sad and think about being sad and sometimes discuss sadness." After he becomes an ape, the bookstore calls to tell him that his "out-of-print special-ordered book on civilization" is ready to be picked up, indicating that even though Ben knew he and Annie were thinking too much, he was unable to stop. The night before he begins his regression, he tells Annie that he hates talking, and he wants to communicate with her just by looking into her eyes. Finally, it seems the only way Ben can stop thinking so much is to actually de-evolve, to stop being human.

Bender makes an interesting choice in naming this character: Ben becomes what has been before, what humans were before they were human.

THEMES

The Burden of Caregiving

The gradual regression of Ben from human to salamander is analogous to the progressive decline of an Alzheimer's patient. Caring for the frail elderly or any loved one with an injury or progressive disease that deteriorates cognitive ability places enormous stress on the caregiver. Like Annie, caregivers feel the need to become the rememberer, both in a sentimental sense (being sure to retain the patient's life memories and recall the person's original personality) and also in a practical sense (taking over the paying of bills, scheduling appointments, remembering when medication must be taken, etc.). The reader gets the feeling that, unlike someone suffering with dementia or Alzheimer's, Ben has made a conscious decision to give up thinking, thus burdening Annie with the responsibility of thinking for both of them. Near the beginning of the story, Annie asks Ben, the sea turtle, "Ben . . . can you understand me?" Close to the end (when Ben is a salamander), she asks again, "Ben . . . do you remember me? Do you remember?" Of course, she gets no answer, and once again the burden of decision-making is hers. The stress of the burden is evident in this passage: "Now I come home from work and look for his regular-size shape walking and worrying and realize, over and over, that he's gone. I pace the halls. I chew whole packs of gum in mere minutes." Finally, Annie reaches "the limit of [her] limits" and decides to let Ben go, releasing him into the ocean, just as many caregivers must make the final decision to cease life-prolonging procedures (such as intravenous feeding and other life-support mechanisms) and let nature take its

course. In Bender's scenario, the caregiver suffers more than the actual patient, and her final decision is born of her own desire to avoid more suffering: "I cannot bear to look down into the water," she says, "and not be able to find him at all." Ben, who is no longer burdened by thought, is now at peace; Annie is the afflicted one. Bender poignantly illustrates the emotional strain of being the rememberer.

The Dangers of Intellectualism

Ben tells Annie that they both think too much, "and the world dries up and dies when there's too much thought and not enough heart." This is an interesting choice of words by Bender, because as Ben devolves, he progresses from a land mammal (an ape) to an aquatic creature (a sea turtle and then a salamander). Apparently he has reversed the drying up process, by eliminating thought.

Later in the story readers learn that before becoming an ape, Ben had ordered a book on civilization from the bookstore. Perhaps Ben was interested in the evolution of civilization, in which the focus of society shifted gradually from religion and towards science, explaining away the mysteries of the stars and planets and other natural phenomena. The shift away from religion and towards science placed more emphasis on rational thought and less on superstition and intuition. While this is generally considered positive, many people (like Ben) feel that it has also insulated people from their own emotions. Ben is craving life on an intuitive, instinctive level, away from thought; he takes Annie outside under the stars and tells her, "*Look, Annie, look—there is no space for anything but dreaming.*"

The popularity of meditation, in which one attempts to gradually leave the busy thoughts of the mind behind and simply exist in the moment, indicates that Ben is not alone in his desire. Ben's difficulties raise an intriguing question: though people normally consider the increasing sophistication of the human brain as evolutionary progress, is there a point at which it becomes counterproductive? Has an increase of intellect led to similar emotional progress, or has emotional evolution lagged behind? Some might consider the continued proliferation of war and crime evidence that humans have evolved less on an emotional level than intellectually. Bender's story illustrates the struggle to find a balance between emotion and thought. Ben, in his desire to abandon thought, regresses in all areas, until he becomes a less complex form of life (a salamander) and is still continuing to regress. Most people would prefer a middle ground; one could say that humans must learn to be amphibious, able to exist both in the depths of their emotions and on the dry land of their intellect.

STYLE

Magical Realism

Bender's writing style is usually categorized as magical realism. The term is a suitable oxymoron, combining two contradictory ideas because that is what happens in this style. Magical realism refers to the practice of placing bizarre, surreal events in a realistic context, and treating the unrealistic events as real. Certainly the premise of a human undergoing reverse evolution from a man to a salamander is not realistic, but Bender places these events in the context of an ordinary life. Co-workers call and wonder where Ben is, a book he ordered at the bookstore goes unclaimed, Annie continues working and coming home each day to a smaller and more primitive Ben. When Ben turns into a sea turtle, she keeps him in an ordinary glass baking dish on her kitchen counter. These pedestrian details ground the story for readers, allowing them to imagine themselves in a situation far beyond the realm of reality.

The use of the present tense also makes the story more real and immediate. Annie relates the story as it is happening. Because it unfolds in the present tense, she cannot be imagining these events or embellishing on something that occurred in the distant past.

Point of View

Because "The Rememberer" is written in the first person, from the point of view of Annie, the reader has access to the thoughts and emotions brought on by Ben's bizarre regression, yet not to the possible explanations that Ben himself could provide. There are clues that this reverse evolution is something that Ben actually desired and wished for, but like Annie, readers cannot be sure, since by the time the story begins, Ben is no longer able to communicate verbally. Annie must decide, without Ben's help, how much of the Ben she knew is actually left. The first-person viewpoint allows readers to experience Annie's uncertainty and bewilderment in making this decision.

Humor

Bender skillfully uses humor throughout the story, enough to entertain, but not so much that the reader suspects the whole premise is a joke. After Ben becomes an ape, Annie sits with him on the patio, stroking his hand. When he reaches out to her, Annie's reaction is both realistic and funny: "I said No, loudly, and he seemed to understand and pulled back. I have limits here." As Annie fields calls from coworkers, "Ben, the baboon, sat in a corner by the window, wrapped up in drapery, chattering to himself." For the most part, the sheer absurdity of the story's premise provides its own humor. In the first paragraph, Annie explains, "One day he was my lover and the next he was some kind of ape. It's been a month and now he's a sea turtle." Though the overall tone of the story is bittersweet and melancholy—it is essentially a story of loss—Bender tells readers that few situations in life are without humor, even those that cause grief. Then, too, these scenes lend themselves to psychological readings. Readers might see parallels to a kind of relationship that deteriorates apace with one partner's quick changes in behavior or might see analogies to those situations in which one partner is on the phone trying to explain the other partner's silence or withdrawal to the partner's coworkers or boss.

Flashback

When the story begins, Annie's situation with Ben has already reached a crisis point (he is a sea turtle); Annie informs readers through a series of flashbacks, starting with more recent events, and eventually working her way back to the beginning of Ben's regression, and then further back to a brief history of their relationship. Once readers have the full story of her dilemma, Annie returns to the present, in the thick of her emotional debate: when should she give up and let Ben go? By the time Annie returns to the present tense, readers are fully vested in the story, and the decision she makes carries more emotional weight.

HISTORICAL CONTEXT

Aging of the United States Population

The generation known as baby boomers is usually defined as those individuals born between 1945 (the end of World War II) and 1964. In 1997, when "The Rememberer" was first published, older baby boomers had reached middle age, and many had become caregivers for their aging parents. Soon baby boomers got a second nickname: the sandwich generation. Caregivers—usually women—were sandwiched between caring for their own children and caring for their aging parents. The stress of this double burden was compounded by the grief of watching a parent deteriorate physically and often mentally. It is common for the care of the parent to fall to one family member while others, unwilling to witness their parent's decline, stay away. Though Annie is caring for her lover, not a parent, the stresses are essentially the same. In her character readers see both situations at once: she has the stress and anxiety of being the sole caregiver but also the desire to avoid witnessing Ben's regression. She realizes she cannot stand to watch him completely de-evolve into a "one-celled wonder, bloated and bordered, brainless, benign, heading clear and small like an eye-floater into nothingness." So for the sandwich generation, as adults watch their own children evolve into adults, they often face the hardship of witnessing their parents diminish into the aged equivalent of uncertain and frightened dependent toddlers.

Scientific Breakthroughs

It is no wonder Ben and Annie think too much; the late 1990s presented everyone with plenty to ponder. In February 1997, scientists in Edinburgh, Scotland, announced that they had successfully cloned a female sheep, which they named Dolly. This event immediately gave rise to heated debates over the ethical and moral issues involved in the eventual cloning of human beings. A year earlier, in 1996, analysis of a Mars meteorite found in Antarctica revealed some evidence of life on the planet, including fossil-like depressions and organic compounds usually created by bacteria. In July 1997, NASA's Mars Pathfinder actually landed on the surface of Mars and sent back hundreds of pictures of the red planet.

Bender makes references to science in the story; one of her first actions after Ben begins his backward journey is to contact a biology professor for an evolutionary timeline. She anticipates Ben's eventually becoming a "one-celled wonder" that she will need a microscope to find. Ben also laments that "our brains are getting bigger and bigger," and as the story ends, Annie feels her skull "to see if it's growing." These scientific breakthroughs, the ideas they suggest, and the questions they pose seem to stretch people's sense of what the individual is, how the individual is created, and what the limits of life might be beyond what was formerly believed.

CRITICAL OVERVIEW

Critical reception to Bender's first short story collection, *The Girl in the Flammable Skirt* (which includes "The Rememberer") was very positive: The *New York Times* selected it as a Notable Book of 1998, and the *Los Angeles Times* named it one of the best works of fiction for that year as well. A reviewer from *Publishers Weekly* calls the collection "a string of jewels," and Fiona Luis of the *Boston Globe* writes, "Each short story packs quite a hefty punch, and each should be savored." Several reviewers single out "The Rememberer" for praise, including Margot Mifflin of *Entertainment Weekly*, who writes that Bender's "account of a woman whose lover evolves backward [is] superbly imagined."

More than one reviewer praises Bender's ability to combine her bizarre and sometimes comic story lines with genuine, deeply felt emotion. This ability is evident in "The Rememberer"; Luis writes, "This bizarrely comic tale would be rib-splittingly funny save for the simple fact that Bender breaks your heart." Praising this same skill in the collection as a whole, the reviewer from *Publishers Weekly* writes: "While full of funny moments, these tales are neither slight nor glib. They recognize that to be human is to be immensely fragile, and their characters are always unmistakably human."

Some reviewers feel that while the debut is impressive, Bender's relative inexperience as a writer sometimes shows. Mifflin writes, "Some of Bender's forays into magical realism feel like collegiate exercises," and Lisa Zeidner of the *New York Times Book Review* agrees: "The weakest [stories] juxtapose multiple plot lines—a standard creative-writing workshop ploy—without much more point than to showcase the skill of the juggler." Both Mifflin's and Zeidner's overall reviews of the collection, however, are positive.

Many reviewers praise Bender's singular style; the reviewer from *Publishers Weekly* writes, "Bender's is a unique and compassionate voice," and Christina Schwarz, in an *Atlantic Monthly* review of Bender's later collection, *Willful Creatures*, says that Bender's prose is

The sea turtle, as seen here on a beach, was one of Ben's stops on his path of devolution © *Wolfgang Kaehler/Corbis*

"so animated it seems almost capable of writing itself," and is "just plain fun to read." Overall, the consensus seems to be that Bender's talent as a writer is evident in these stories and that she has the potential to become even more skilled in the future.

CRITICISM

Laura Pryor

Pryor has a Bachelor of Arts degree from the University of Michigan and over twenty years experience in professional and creative writing with special interest in fiction. In the following essay, she compares the transformation of Ben in "The Rememberer" to that of Gregor Samsa in Franz Kafka's "The Metamorphosis."

Aimee Bender's story "The Rememberer" centers on the transformation of the narrator's lover from a man to an assortment of animals, as he de-evolves. Arguably the most famous story of such a transformation is Franz Kafka's "The Metamorphosis," in which the main character,

Gregor Samsa, wakes up one morning to discover that he has become a huge insect. Though Bender's and Kafka's writing styles are drastically different, the two stories share thematic similarities beyond the metamorphosis of man to beast.

In "The Rememberer," Bender implies, through flashbacks to earlier conversations with Ben, that his transformation was not an entirely unwelcome event, but rather something desired. Though Gregor Samsa probably did not wish, specifically, to become an insect, the transformation brings him some obvious benefits, too. Gregor despises his job, so much so that his hatred of it supersedes even his horror at becoming a giant bug; even after making the discovery that he has transformed, his thoughts immediately turn back to his job: "Oh God . . . what a grueling job I've picked! Day in, day out—on the road." Once he becomes an insect, he can no longer continue his job as a traveling salesman. He has escaped.

Ben seeks to escape not his job, but the tyranny of his own intellect. He tells Annie, the narrator,

WHAT DO I READ NEXT?

- Gabriel García Márquez is the preeminent practitioner of magical realism, the genre with which Aimee Bender's work is often associated. Márquez's novel *One Hundred Years of Solitude* (1967) is considered to be one of his finest works.

- Angela Carter is another well-known magical realist. Bender cites "The Company of Wolves," a retelling of Little Red Riding Hood, as one of her favorite Carter stories. This story can be found in the collection, *The Bloody Chamber* (1979), which includes Carter's unique take on several other fairy tales.

- Bender cites *Transformations* (1971), by poet Anne Sexton, as an early influence. Sexton retells familiar fairy tales such as Snow White and Little Red Riding Hood; Sexton's versions are dark, twisted, and sometimes humorous.

- Bender's first novel, *An Invisible Sign of My Own* (2000), tells the story of twenty-year-old Mona Gray, who teaches second-grade math. Mona has gradually withdrawn from life since her father began to suffer from an unnamed illness; in helping one of her students cope with tragedy, Mona begins to recover herself.

- *Willful Creatures*, published in 2005, is Bender's second short story collection. The stories in this collection take a darker turn than those in *The Girl in the Flammable Skirt*, but the plots are just as surreal, including a couple with pumpkins for heads and a man who buys a miniature man at a pet shop and keeps him in a cage.

- Bender's older sister Karen is also an author. Her debut novel, *Like Normal People*, tells the story of Ella Rose, an elderly woman, and her daughter Lena, who is retarded and living in a group home.

> IN BOTH STORIES, THE METAMORPHOSIS PLACES A SIGNIFICANT AMOUNT OF STRESS ON THE TRANSFORMER'S LOVED ONES."

"We think far too much." Since Ben is a man of conscience, his thinking extends beyond himself to the woes of the world. Annie says, "He was always sad about the world." In his transformation, Ben seeks to escape the burden he has taken on, the troubles of the entire planet. Gregor Samsa's burdens are closer to home; he supports his parents and his teenage sister, and in addition, he is paying off a debt his parents owe his employer. He thinks to himself, "If I didn't hold back for my parents' sake, I would have quit long ago." He imagines leaving his job once he pays off the debt, but since "that will probably take another five or six years," Gregor's immediate future looks pretty bleak. Interestingly, after their transformations, both men are contacted first by their employers, demanding to know where they are. Gregor's manager barely allows him an hour's grace before he actually arrives at the Samsas' house, at 7:15 a.m., berating him. Annie fields calls from Ben's office: "Why wasn't he at work? Why did he miss his lunch date with those clients?" Once the employers find out the men cannot work (Gregor's boss actually sees him in his insect state, whereas Annie tells Ben's office that he is suffering from a "strange sickness"), they never contact them again. Implied is the idea that men, in contemporary society, are still valued mainly for their ability to be productive, to make a contribution; once they lose this ability, they are abandoned.

In both stories, the metamorphosis places a significant amount of stress on the transformer's loved ones. Annie feels the need to pick up thinking where Ben left off: "I review my memories and make sure they're still intact because if he's not here, then it's my job to remember." Gregor's family is not only horrified at his new form, they are also left without income, and his father, mother, and sister must all seek employment to compensate. Annie's reaction to Ben's situation is a deep sadness; she reviews poignant memories of their time together and searches for explanations. Gregor's family reacts at first with horror, then grief, but eventually they come to resent Gregor's abandonment of them and the burden he has thus placed upon them. In one scene, when Gregor leaves the confines of his room, his father pelts him with apples; one lodges in his flesh and remains there, festering, for over a month. Only his sister treats him with kindness, but she too eventually turns on him. This is ironic, since it is likely that Gregor's resentment of the burden his family placed upon him is what caused the transformation in the first place.

Because "The Metamorphosis" is written from the viewpoint of the character who transforms, the reader knows Gregor is still capable of intelligent thought and human emotion. Since "The Rememberer" is told from Annie's point of view, not Ben's, there is no way of knowing if Ben is still thinking in the human sense. The logical assumption is that he is not, since thought is exactly what Ben sought to escape. Still, Annie attempts communication with him, even when he is a lowly salamander, asking "Do you remember me?" No one in the Samsa family speaks to Gregor; they all assume that because he is an insect, he can no longer understand them. This assumption leads to increasing neglect. His sister stops cleaning his room, and though at first she takes pains to find out what foods he will enjoy, later in the story, she "hurriedly shoved any old food into Gregor's room with her foot."

Both men are eventually abandoned. Gregor's family does their best to ignore his existence, and his sister actually encourages Mr. and Mrs. Samsa to "try to get rid of it." This turns out to be unnecessary, because his sister's betrayal is the last straw for Gregor: He dies shortly afterwards. Annie's abandonment is less harsh: She simply releases Ben into the ocean. Still, as with the Samsas, the motive behind her action is not concern for Ben, but an unwillingness to endure more grief: "I cannot bear to look down into the water and not be able to find him at all, to search the tiny clear waves with a microscope lens and to locate my lover, the one-celled wonder."

In the end, Gregor's family undergoes a transformation as well. Unable to continue to use Gregor as a crutch, they all become more self-sufficient. Gregor notices that his once stooped and shuffling father "was holding himself very erect . . . his usually rumpled white hair was combed flat, with a scrupulously exact,

gleaming part." His sister blossoms into a woman and gets "livelier and livelier" after Gregor's death. Annie, by contrast, continues to wait for Ben's return: "I make sure my phone number is listed. I walk around the block at night in case he doesn't quite remember which house it is." Still, Annie is also changed. She has learned something about the limits of the intellect; at the end of the story, she says, "Sometimes before I put my one self to bed, I place my hands around my skull to see if it's growing, and wonder what, of any use, would fill it if it did."

Both stories can be interpreted as cautionary tales about seeking to escape the burdens of life. Both men wished to be free of the weight they carried—for Gregor, the weight of supporting his family, and for Ben, the weight of constant thought and worry. It is probably safe to assume, however, that neither wished for the specific form that their liberation took; Ben probably did not specifically wish to de-evolve into a salamander, and Gregor certainly did not yearn to be a giant insect. Their escape from their problems simply handed them a new, radically different set of hardships. In getting rid of their burdens, they also lost the people they loved. The price of freedom turned out to be far higher than Ben or Gregor could have known.

Source: Laura Pryor, Critical Essay on "The Rememberer," in *Short Stories for Students*, Thomson Gale, 2007.

Klay Dyer

Dyer holds a Ph.D. in English literature and has published extensively on fiction, poetry, film, and television. He is also a freelance university teacher, writer, and educational consultant. In the following essay, he discusses Bender's story as an example of metafiction, as a story that traces its own construction from the original moment of an idea through to a fully realized narrative complete with setting, plot, and characters.

Metafiction is a style of writing that draws attention to itself in order to pose questions about the relationship between fiction and reality, as well as delighting in the nature of its own storytelling. In Aimee Bender's "The Rememberer," metafiction is a reflexive exercise that, like a funhouse mirror, allows readers to experience a "reverse evolution." Aligned with such important antecedents as Miguel Cervantes's *Don Quijote* (1605) and Jane Austen's *Northanger Abbey* (1817), Bender's story does more than expose the

FEARFUL THAT SHE WILL QUEST PERPETUALLY FOR THE IRRETRIEVABLE STORY OF BEN, ANNIE RECOGNIZES THAT SHE NOW SEES THE WORLD WITH HER HEART AND CAN APPRECIATE ITS MYSTERY AND WONDER."

act of writing to new scrutiny. It also questions a world increasingly predisposed to ignore the mysteries shaping everyday occurrences in favor of the comforts of the known and the knowable.

Annie, the narrator of Bender's "The Rememberer," opens her own story with an amazing announcement: Her "lover," Ben, "is experiencing reverse evolution." This dramatic statement connects Annie's story to the great creation myths from Genesis through to Darwin's *Origin of Species* (1859). Ben is recreated through a series of clearly defined, but wholly fantastic, devolutionary stages. Originally a human, he soon is reimagined as an ape, a sea turtle, and finally a salamander. As Annie points out, following her exchange with "the old biology teacher at the community college," the creative revisioning of Ben moves across time in ways that defy understanding. "He is shedding a million years a day," she calculates, despite the fact that she openly admits she is "no scientist" and prefers to see his condition as "a strange sickness." To understand Ben's relocation along the evolutionary line as anything other than a freak show or sickness demands a leap into the world of the creative imagination, which Annie is not quite ready to take.

As Annie struggles to understand Ben's condition, his importance in her life gradually reveals itself to be much more than that of a casual lover. He was the source of her inspiration and the stimulus for her own stories. Through his reverse evolution, Ben provides a primer on how to live a creative life, a how-to-guide to remembering. On the last day that she sees Ben as a human, for instance, Annie talks with him about the sadness he feels and about his view of a world increasingly dominated by intellect. To Annie and to the attentive reader, Ben's realization is profound: "Our brains are just getting bigger and bigger," he concludes, and "we think

far too much." Reminding his lover of the need to see her world with her heart and imagination rather than allowing herself to be controlled by her mind, Ben essentially counsels her to turn off reason in order to feel: "The world dries up and dies," he warns her, "when there's too much thought and not enough heart."

At first, Annie admits that this new way of seeing is foreign to her. She finds it difficult not to concentrate "really hard on letting go" when she makes love with Ben, leaving their attempt at physical intimacy unconsummated in the sense of being left off "in the middle of everything." Their interrupted lovemaking is replaced by " an hour-long conversation about poetry."

Annie remembers their discussion of Walt Whitman's famous poem "When I Heard the Learn'd Astronomer" (1900). They go outside to contemplate dreaming under the night sky: "He woke me up in the middle of the night," she recalls, "lifted me off the pale blue sheets, led me outside to the stars and whispered: "Look, Annie, look—there is no space for anything but dreaming." In a moment that speaks volumes about the limitations that she has placed on her heart and imagination, Annie is forced to acknowledge that she does not yet know how "to dream up to the stars." She says, "I tried to find a star that no one in all of history had ever wished on before and wondered what would happen if I did."

But as the story unfolds, Ben becomes smaller and increasingly amphibian, and Annie's heart and imagination grow larger. She imagines a world that exists beyond words, a place past metaphor. She feels more and conveys emotions with a look rather than with words. In one of her final conversations with Ben, Annie opens herself to his desire to avoid language. He would rather, he explains, "look into [her] eyes and tell [her] things that way." Once she crosses this threshold of language and reason, Annie responds physically and connects emotionally with the quickly devolving Ben. When her lover looks into her eyes, she feels her "skin lift." The next morning, when human Ben has morphed into an ape, Annie reacts with understanding and curiosity instead of with panic or loathing. In other words, she reacts with her heart instead of her mind. The reverse evolution continues: Annie comes home one day to find Ben is "some kind of salamander now."

Salamanders have the ability to regenerate lost limbs: Annie can regenerate her own storytelling. Forcing herself to "review [her] memories and make sure they're intact," Annie becomes a storyteller who watches her own story of Ben. She is, in other words, a storyteller who experiences what she acknowledges is "the limit of [her] limits": she looks, metaphorically, into the microscopic origins of her own inspiration. Fearful that she will quest perpetually for the irretrievable story of Ben, Annie recognizes that she now sees the world with her heart and can appreciate its mystery and wonder. Searching for Ben as both a human and a story, Annie comes to imagine the stories that circulate within "the one-celled wonder, bloated and bordered, brainless, benign, heading clear and small like an eye-floater into nothingness."

Having returned Ben the salamander to the sea, Annie returns to her world a changed woman and a changed storyteller. Just as Ben has reverse evolved to the simpler form of the salamander, Annie's story of Ben returns to the point where all stories must begin: in a moment of insight and in a flash of imagination. As she releases Ben at the water's edge, Annie releases herself. Annie becomes a rememberer, someone who lives life fully aware of the past.

She knows that to engage life as a writer is to live, as she observes early in the story, in "a sea of me." With Ben gone, Annie is able to become, for the first time, the "one self" that she has always hoped to be rather than a writer who is defined by other people's dreams and visions. She is free to transcend the limitations of her previous existence and to become more than "a poor soul with all the ingredients but no container" in which to store them.

In this sense, Bender's story is testament to Annie's own evolution, to her rememberings of journeys away from an imagined life that had left her trapped in reason. Ben's release occurs as Annie turns her back on the shore and waves. She returns to her car ready to begin her journey into the new world. The story ends, too, with Annie hoping that Ben might one day "wash up on shore" and comes back to her. Bender's "The Rememberer" ends with a looping back, a return to the beginning: Annie returns to the world in order that she might tell the story of a lover who, as the opening sentence announces, "is experiencing reverse evolution."

Source: Klay Dyer, Critical Essay on "The Rememberer," in *Short Stories for Students*, Thomson Gale, 2007.

Thomson Gale

In the following essay, the critic gives an overview of Aimee Bender's work.

Aimee Bender is a writer and teacher of writing whose short stories have appeared in numerous publications. Bender's *The Girl in the Flammable Skirt: Stories* is her debut collection of sixteen modern adult fairy tales which feature unusual characters, many with physical deformities. *Library Journal* reviewer Joanna M. Burkhardt wrote that the events and people in the collection "somehow acquire the bizarre, the grotesque, and the darkly satirical." The title of Bender's collection is a reference to the cheap rayon skirts that combusted at the touch of a flame.

In "The Rememberer," a woman watches her lover go through reverse evolution—from ape to sea turtle to salamander—and then releases him to the ocean and says goodbye. "What You Left in the Ditch" tells of a woman's seduction of a teen grocery clerk after her soldier husband returns from war minus his lips. In "Quiet Please," a librarian has encounters with a succession of men in the library's back room, her way of dealing with grief after her father's death. A woman steals a ruby in "The Ring" and then finds that everything it touches turns red. In another story a woman gives birth to her own elderly mother, while at the same time a hole appears in her husband's body where his stomach had been.

A *Publishers Weekly* reviewer commented that "as Bender explores a spectrum of human relationships, her perfectly pitched, shapely writing blurs the lines between prose and poetry." Lisa Zeidner wrote in the *New York Times Book Review* that Bender's stories "are powered by voice—by the pleasure of the electric simile." Zeidner noted the "magic realism" of Bender's Los Angeles, calling it "Malibu Marquez." Zeidner categorized the stories she felt were most realistic as being about "Fatalistic Dating," while the "weakest ones juxtapose multiple plot lines." In *The Girl in the Flammable Skirt* Bender "aims to be sneakily incendiary and often succeeds," continued the critic: "Many of these stories are as catchy as [the book's] title, with a winning cheekiness."

Bender's next work was the novel *An Invisible Sign of My Own*. In this work, Bender tells the story of twenty-year-old Mona Gray, a second grade mathematics teacher in a small town. Leading an unhappy life full of anxiety and depression, Mona is also obsessed with numbers. Reviewing this work for *Booklist*, Michelle Kaske noted that *An Invisible Sign of My Own* is a "wonderful . . . treatment of anxiety, depression, and compulsion."

In her collection *Willful Creatures: Stories*, Bender offers fifteen stories that explore the unusual, and frequently cruel, interactions between people who love each other. The tales are "daringly original," and "bursting with heart and marvel," according to a *Publishers Weekly* writer. Some of the stories are somewhat realistic, others more surrealistic. Characters include a boy with key-shaped fingers, who wishes to unlock his father's secrets; a group of cruel teenaged girls; and a couple whose child is killed by the weight of his own huge head. With these tales, Bender shows that she is "intent on rewriting the grim fable of modern life," noted a *Kirkus Reviews* writer, who praised the author for writing "with bite and wit."

Bender's work has been described as having a mythical quality, something the author cultivates in her stories. As she told Dave Weich in an interview for *Powells.com:* "Saying 'the man' or 'the woman,' sometimes I like those words better than the words of names, even though it's true that once you name someone they're more specific and the reader can identify with them more. Maybe it's just an attraction to a kind of fairy-tale storytelling—it feels like names would be slightly too specific for the story. . . . It feels like a texture to me. The texture would go a little wrong if the character was named, if the story wants to be more mythic. As soon as someone is named, the story enters the world of reality a little more. As soon as a capital letter comes into play, it looks different and it feels different."

Source: Thomson Gale, "Aimee Bender," in *Contemporary Authors Online*, Thomson Gale, 2006.

Ryan Boudinot

In the following interview, Bender talks about the mental and physical aspects of her writing and the thematic unity in The Girl in the Flammable Skirt.

[*Ryan Boudinot:*] *Why did you divide your book into three different sections? Do you feel a sort of thematic unity to these stories?*

> I'M JUST INTERESTED IN MEN AND WOMEN AND SEEING AND GUESSING THEIR RELATIONSHIP WITH THEIR BODY—IT'S SO MYSTERIOUS, AND YET YOU CAN GLEAN THINGS FROM EACH PERSON."

[Aimee Bender:] The three parts—I must admit it was the editor's original idea but I liked it because three is such a good mythic number. I had them loosely titled *Loss, Rage and Magic* but it didn't totally work because the mermaid story isn't rageful at all and a lot of the stories have some of all three of those things in them, so making up the mini titles felt false. Hopefully, within the structure of three parts, there is a certain kind of flow to the order, in that some of the more intense stories peak in the middle, and there's a lifting up with some of the later ones.

Do I feel a thematic unity to the groupings or to the stories as a whole? Tell me which one before I go off and make a huge list for you and embarrass myself.

With the stories as a whole. Not within the sections.

Themes in the stories as a whole—here are some: desire for connection, isolation from others, burden of caretaking, the ways loss gets expressed, suppression of passion, acting out of desires in a painful way, self-mutilation, deformity as a way to show loss or change, the connectedness of everyone, sex as an expression of loss rage obliteration connection or freedom, hmmmm, man vs. man, man vs. nature, man vs. himself—ha.

Hmmm. Kind of a weighty list. Plus I know I'm missing tons of them. But there's a start.

You mentioned one of your parents is a psychiatrist. It felt to me there was a lot of subconscious material in your stories. What's the relationship between your subconscious and your writing like?

Hooray! It's my favorite question on earth. Really. First I will say I'm just going to use the word unconscious instead of subconscious though I'm not sure I know the difference. But that's the word I'm used to. I talk about this a lot, with myself and other people. So I am glad for the question and appreciate your interest. I realized about a year ago that my parents, in a way, had a similar job: my dad, through psychiatry, is dealing with the unconscious and forging his way through other people's unawareness and bringing them into the air to look at, and my mom is delving into her own unconscious to make up dances. She's a dance teacher and choreographer. And I'm sort of the combo platter, in that psychiatry is so essentially verbal and well, duh, of course so is writing, and also I am like her in that it's all about creating from this inexplicable mysterious place. I think the human brain is so thrilling when viewed from this angle—that I am writing images without necessarily analyzing them and later, I can look at a certain sentence and the meaning is suddenly laid bare. This, I find, is like a miracle. It's like outer space exploration and the Bible. It's just such an amazing capacity that human beings have. How does the brain do that? How does free-association lead the way to emotional revelation? And yet, it DOES. So, that is where I think they link up: the use of metaphor is so innate in human beings, it's like a sixth sense, the need to make a comparison to describe experience. But how weird when you think about it, that we can't just name our experiences as they come, we are always, constantly making metaphors. And I think psychiatry is also all about metaphors or what I find most beautiful about it is metaphorical.

When I was a kid, I remember being terrified of thunder and talking to my dad about it, and at some point having the fear released when I admitted I was angry at someone, and this was like magic—I'd thought I was really truly scared of thunder. When my dad suggested I might be a little mad I thought, at first, he was insane. A friend of mine recently suggested that learning this so young, that metaphors can work this way, was like learning piano young, it gave me some kind of easy access, and it has affected my fiction since then. Because I was mad, and my dad was right, and I hadn't planned on being scared of thunder, I just was, and I made that up on my own, without planning, without a thought to how beautiful and simple it was. So. I think, even then, at age nine or whatever, I thought: this is the coolest g——d—— thing. That is truly beautiful. And I'm sure on some level that is also what motivates my fiction for me. It seems the best work I do is when I am really allowing the unconscious to rule the page and then later I can go

back and hack around and make sense of things but the queen of the story is that part of my brain and the stories wouldn't work, wouldn't move me, wouldn't have any power, unless they had a strong connection to my unconscious. That's why the whole concept of planning fiction is so ridiculous. I just think the more you loosen the reins, the more resonant the work can be. It's so funny when people put down art as not essential to a society, because it's like pretending that people don't have dreams. As if dreams don't reveal an entire subterranean world happening that must be acknowledged. Even those people who say they don't dream still do, they just forget them. People are so so so much more than just eating sleeping working machines. I am in awe of brains that way. Each one is like a little beautiful religious thing.

That is way too long. I'm not even sure if I really answered your question. But I answered something.

How do you get all that unconscious material down on the page without second-guessing it?

Mainly it's just sitting there and trusting that the connections are being made and that I don't have to work so hard but then anxiety creeps in, like what if it's not true? Or what if this time it won't work? And that needs to STOP. So the more I get reassurance from the world through various artists, etc., about the whole creative process, the better I feel. I once asked my mom for something like that and she said, "Oh, I have total faith," and I said, "In me?" and she said, "Yeah, but I meant in the whole process of making something, I have faith in that." Which I thought was great. That it wasn't even really faith in me specifically was comforting because it was more mysterious than even that, it was about trusting the art made by people since people have been. So then I try to write using the good old "follow your nose" approach, which for me means to write each day just what I feel like and not feel obligated or forced to try to make connections or make a point or anything. Trusting that the point is ingrained, which is always a better point anyway. A more complex point.

I just put a new screen saver on my computer with fish and spent a few minutes this morning looking at the virtual fish. They were soothing. And feeling like: that's okay. Fish are good to look at. If I want to look at fish, that can be more useful this exact moment than trying to figure out why this particular goddamn character is being such a pain in the ass. I have about ten signs above my computer saying "faith" in various synonym forms. Also, I think the way to get the unconscious revved up is to make a little contract with time, i.e. I have to sit at the desk for this long every day, a set amount, and that's just the law. I believe in laws like that. Then the unconscious knows what's what, it's like a teenager, and it will follow those laws. Eventually it'll start putting out. Uh oh. Now the teenager metaphor switched on me. But you get my point.

If the specifics, the discipline, is in place, then the rest will work. Within structure things loosen up. And here, the structure is just plain time on the chair. And that's where I think the sole thing that'll kick you out of your chair at that point is a crisis of faith and that's why it's so crucial to have support on that subject and to remind yourself constantly and crucially that that is the whole POINT, that writing can't be thought out and known, that something happens between the brain and the fingers that is different than thought. It just is. It's a new path. That's why it works. I can't think a story. I can tell one out loud and write one but I can't think one. It gets stopped in the first paragraph and then I digress. I'd have to voice it out to make it work. Wild, that. Why is that? I don't know. But it just makes me believe that the pathway, the wiring is different, and to think we can think through that wiring just isn't true.

Is there a particular state you find yourself in when you write, and if so, do you use any particular means to get to it?

Well, I wear that leopard skin hat on my head and do yoga chants and then light candles and then do bicep stretching.

Ohm.

No. No state. Right when I wake up. Closest to dreams I can get. Sleepy and bugged. Also I want to get it out of my way so I can have the rest of the day without writing guilt.

I'll do my best Charlie Rose here and ask about the novel mentioned on the jacket of your book. If you're not at a place with it where'd you'd like to comment, that's fine. Otherwise, I'd be interested in knowing what kind of direction it's going.

I don't want to talk about it concretely because it feels so weird, like footsteps all over my brain, my response is so visceral, like "what the hell is another person doing in here? Get out!" but I love to talk abstractly about novel-writing. Which is: I keep just following my nose

on it and things are linking up but it's never like one day *boom* it is all clear where it's going. It's very slow, very little by little. I can see why people get discouraged so often writing novels, because they don't trust that the thing will evolve. I was not kidding about looking at the virtual fish—that is sometimes how I write my novel. Slow. I love it when it is not causing me total anxiety. I am trying my best to let it be what it is and also let myself write what I want and allow it to be what it is and also let myself write what I want and allow it to be different than the stories and also related, thematically or tonally or whatever, to them, too. There are a lot of numbers in it, bizarrely. And hardware and amputation. All that I will say.

You used the word visceral. I'd say that word could be applied to your whole book. The human body appears in your stories as something in a constant state of flux, something malleable and vaguely threatening, but also the source of a great deal of power. I'm wondering if this has arisen from your experience with dance? We've talked about the mental aspect of your work; let's talk about the physical. (Your mom side as opposed to your dad side)

I think I just like the human body so much as a whole landscape of everything—it seems like it's immediately resonant. So much happens. I am definitely fascinated by people's relationship to their bodies, what isn't their head. I could watch people dance for hours, like in college, just because it told me so much about them, how comfortable they were, how performative, all that. My mom's brother is a basketball coach and it's interesting that they both chose a path that is physically oriented. I'm not sure why, but my mom definitely uses her body when she talks, she acts like a dancer, and my uncle talks about basketball all the time, he is full of juicy details. I'm just interested in men and women and seeing and guessing their relationship with their body—it's so mysterious, and yet you can glean things from each person. It IS so powerful, that whole landscape—holds love, loss, pain, pleasure, self-destructiveness, kindness, some of that can be reflected pretty fast. I'm being vague. I can't think of a specific right now. It was interesting teaching elementary school—there's an interesting mix of female elementary school teachers—there were a LOT of sexy ones who were really into being overtly sexy which was interesting and then there were plenty of repressed ones who were really pretending like they were old ladies at age 25. Makes sense to me that you'd find both those types in extreme around kids ... Interesting also—the kids responded to both but I think were less likely to be super huggy with the repressed ones. Makes sense too.

One day in seventh grade my class had a substitute teacher who made us write on note cards what qualities we looked for in a teacher. My best friend Epi Sedano wrote on his, "Likes to have fun with underage boys."

Funny.

I'm sort of overloaded with lurid testimony at the moment. You keeping up on the Clinton investigation thing?

I know, this Clinton thing is intense. The heartbreaker is reading about Monica saying s—— like, "Why don't you ask me questions about myself?" Ugh. I think she really had hopes. But also, I don't want him to be impeached. It's just gross to see the weird power s—— that gets into the sex there.

A lot of your stories seem to veer off in unexpected directions. I'm interested in "Quiet Please" in particular [in which a librarian has sex in the library with every man in sight to deal with the death of her father]. What interested me wasn't necessarily the premise, but the place it found itself in the end. I know each story must come into the world in its own way, but do you find yourself starting with a particular scenario and taking off from there?

Yeah, I just was running with the premise of this librarian and her coping mechanism and the pain of that moment and then it veered quite organically on its own. Same with a story like "The Ring." It's like grabbing hold of a running horse. So much is about plain "feeling right"—I have a fair amount of false endings and the right one always feels good. . . .

Source: Ryan Boudinot, "Interview with Aimee Bender," in *www.PifMagazine.com/SID/498/*, November 1998, pp. 1–5.

SOURCES

Bender, Aimee, "Marzipan," in *The Girl in the Flammable Skirt*, Anchor Books, 1999, p. 39.

————, "The Rememberer," in *The Girl in the Flammable Skirt*, Anchor Books, 1999, pp. 3–7.

Boudinot, Ryan, "Interview with Aimee Bender," November 1998, http://www.pifmagazine.com/SID/498 (accessed November 12, 2006).

"An Interview with Aimee Bender," in *Yalobusha Review*, Vol. XI, 2006, http://www.olemiss.edu/yalobusha (accessed November 12, 2006).

Kafka, Franz, "The Metamorphosis," in *The Metamorphosis*, edited by Stanley Corngold, Norton, 1996, pp. 3–4, 28, 32, 37, 42.

Luis, Fiona, "Bender Evokes Laughter Subdued by Absurdity," in *Boston Globe*, August 11, 1998, p. E2.

Mifflin, Margot, Review of *The Girl in the Flammable Skirt*, in *Entertainment Weekly*, No. 440, July 10, 1998, p. 68.

Review of *The Girl in the Flammable Skirt*, in *Publishers Weekly*, Vol. 245, No. 21, May 25, 1998, p. 61.

Schwarz, Christina, "A Close Read: What Makes Good Writing Good," in *Atlantic Monthly*, October 2005, p. 124.

Zeidner, Lisa, "What We Talk About When We Talk About Lust," in *New York Times Book Review*, August 23, 1998, p. 10.

FURTHER READING

Burling, Robbins, *The Talking Ape: How Language Evolved*, Oxford University Press, 2005.
    This book explores how human language came to be and examines competing linguistic theories and controversies. Burling traces the development of language from gestures and early sounds to the language of modern times.

Grimm, Jacob, and Wilhelm Grimm, *The Annotated Brothers Grimm*, translated by Maria Tatar, Norton, 2004.
    Critics have described Bender's stories as modern fairy tales. This collection of the Grimm brothers' original fairy tales includes their most famous tales as well as a few that were left out of many books, once the brothers realized that parents were reading the stories to children. The book includes explanatory notes on the historical and cultural origins of the stories.

Parent, Marc, ed., *The Secret Society of Demolition Writers*, Random House, 2005.
    This collection of short stories by popular contemporary authors has a unique twist: the authors do not use their real names, leaving the reader to guess who wrote what. The book includes stories by Aimee Bender, Benjamin Cheever, Alice Sebold, Sebastian Junger, and many others.

Young, David, ed., *Magical Realist Fiction: An Anthology*, Oberlin College Press, 1984.
    This sizable anthology (over 500 pages) contains stories in the magical realism style from a wide variety of authors, including Tolstoy, Faulkner, Kafka, and García Márquez.

The Shell Collector

Anthony Doerr's "The Shell Collector" is the first story in his collection by this title, which appeared in 2002. The eight stories included depict unusual characters, often in exotic places. In "The Shell Collector," which is set near Lamu, Kenya, the blind protagonist, a man of sixty-three, gains international notoriety after two people dangerously sick with malaria are suddenly healed by being exposed to the poisonous venom of a certain snail in a cone shell. Doerr explores man's relationship to nature and the complications that arise when a reclusive person living a simple life in a remote place is suddenly bombarded by the news media and urban dwellers. Doerr is knowledgeable about nature and the environment, and his scientific interest informs his creative writing. Foreign and scientific terms occur frequently in this story; when they appear in this chapter, they are explained parenthetically.

AUTHOR BIOGRAPHY

Anthony Doerr, also known as Tony Doerr, was born October 27, 1973, in Cleveland, Ohio. In high school, he developed an interest in writing, and by the time he was in his mid-twenties, Doerr was submitting his work to magazines for publication. Although his mother was a high school science teacher who encouraged family interest in science, Doerr, who writes a lot about science and the environment, did not

ANTHONY DOERR

2002

Anthony Doerr Ulf Andersen/Getty Images

pursue formal education in science. He obtained a B.A. in history at Bowdoin College in 1995 and an M.F.A. in writing at Bowling Green State University in 1999. After that, he taught at various institutions, including the University of Wisconsin at Madison, Boise State University, and Princeton University.

Doerr's essays and short stories have appeared in various magazines and journals, including the *Paris Review*, the *Atlantic Monthly*, and *Zoetrope: All Story*. In addition, some of his stories have been anthologized: for example, "The Shell Collector" was included in *Best American Short Stories 2003*; "The Caretaker" appeared in *The Anchor Book of New American Short Stories* (2004); and "The Demilitarized Zone" was included in *The Best Underground Fiction, Volume One* (2006). His book reviews, often connected to science, appeared frequently in the *Boston Globe* during the early 2000s.

In 2004, Doerr's first novel, *About Grace*, appeared. This work tells the story of a man who is haunted by dreams that come true. When he dreams that he in unable to save his infant daughter, Grace, from drowning, he abandons his wife and daughter without offering an explanation. He harbors the hope that doing so will avert the

fulfillment of this apparent prophecy. Doerr's *Four Seasons in Rome: On Twins, Insomnia, and the Biggest Funeral in the History of the World* was expected to appear in 2007.

Doerr's short stories collection, *The Shell Collector: Stories*, won the Barnes & Noble Discover Prize, two O. Henry Prizes, the Ohioana Book Award, and the Rome Prize. *About Grace* won the 2005 Ohioana Book Award for Fiction, for the best book of the year. As of 2006, Doerr and his family lived in Boise, Idaho.

PLOT SUMMARY

"The Shell Collector" opens at the kibanda (beach house) of a blind shell collector, who is cleaning limpets (a marine mollusk that clings to rocks). A water taxi arrives, bringing two overweight journalists (both named Jim) from a New York tabloid, who offer the shell collector ten thousand dollars for his story. They ask him about his childhood experience hunting caribou, about his losing his eyesight, and about the recent cures, but they do not ask about his son's death. They ask about cone shells and the strength of their venom. They wonder how many visitors come to the shell collector's home.

The men stay overnight and are bothered in their sleeping bags by biting red ants called siafu. Next morning the shell collector goes out to the water, led by his German shepherd, Tumaini. The collector walks quickly and with confidence, while the heavy New Yorkers lumber well behind him.

The shell collector hears the muezzin (the English word for the Muslim official who calls the daily hours of prayer to the Islamic faithful) in the nearby town of Lamu and explains that it is Ramadan (the sacred ninth month of the Islamic year celebrated with fasting from dawn to dusk). He collects shells by wading out on a reef a kilometer or more from shore. He handles a number of different kinds of shells and snails, some of which are poisonous. For example, he finds nematocysts, which are poisonous even after they have died. Meanwhile, the journalists use snorkel masks to examine marine life.

The reclusive shell collector is something of a local celebrity now, in part because rumor has spread the news of his having cured a Seattle woman of malaria, who was accidentally stung by a cone shell in his kitchen. The narration turns at this point to the collector's life up to the time when the two New York journalists arrive.

At the age of nine, the protagonist had hunted sick caribou with his father. He had leaned out a helicopter and culled the herds. But shortly thereafter he developed choroideremia (progressive degeneration of tissue behind the retina in males) and degeneration of the retina; by the time he was twelve, he was blind. At that point, his father took him to Florida to an ophthalmologist, who instead of examining him removed the boy's shoes and socks and walked the child out the back of his office and onto the beach, introducing him to shell creatures. The introduction to the sea "changed" the boy. He saw the shells more clearly than anything else; feeling them gave him all the details he needed. Immediately, "his world became shells."

Back in Whitehorse, Canada, the boy learned Braille and read books on shells throughout the coming winter. When he was sixteen, he left home and worked as a crewmember on sailboats traveling in the tropics. He was obsessed with "the geometry of exoskeletons." He came back to Florida and completed a B.S. in biology and a Ph.D. in malacology (the study of mollusks). After that, he traveled around the equator; visited Fiji, Guam, and the Seychelles; discovered some types of bivalves and several other kinds of shell creatures.

After publishing on these subjects and after having "three Seeing Eye shepherds, and a son named Josh," the shell collector, then fifty-eight years old, went into retirement, settling near the Lamu Archipelago. He spent his days on the beach and wading out onto the reef, identifying and collecting shells, always fascinated by the "endless variations of design." He made his living by shipping these collections to a university where they were studied.

In the recent past, at the age of sixty-three, the collector found an incoherent American woman on the beach: Nancy was suffering from sunstroke and malaria. He took her into his kibanda and called Dr. Kabiru for help. When she recovered, Nancy talked about her life, her husband and children in Seattle, her travels to Cairo, and her meeting with a "neo-Buddhist." The collector and Nancy had a sexual relationship, but they did not understand each other.

Then one day a cone shell got in the kibanda and stung Nancy, causing a catatonic trance and slow heartbeat. Certain cones have tusks "like tiny translucent bayonets." The sting causes paralysis. The doctor came to attend her and assumed her condition was fatal. Ten hours later she recovered, claiming to be cured of the illness and suddenly feeling "*balanced*," almost euphoric. She even begged to be stung again. A week later, the doctor returned with the mwadhini (the Swahili word for muezzin) from the largest Lamu mosque and some of his brothers. The mwadhini asked the collector to give his dangerously ill daughter, Seema, the same treatment that saved Nancy. The Muslims insisted that the collector find a cone shell and take it to the sick child and deliberately sting her with its venom. He acquiesced with great reservations; he went to the city and put the cone into her hand, closing the fingers around it. To the collector's amazement, the child recovered quickly. This event was perceived to be a miracle by townspeople.

Word of the so-called miraculous cure spread "like a drifting cloud of coral eggs, spawning." A local paper ran an article, and a radio station gave a one-minute spot to the story. This news transformed the hermit's kibanda into "a kind of pilgrim's destination." Sick and mentally ill people lingered around his place. Others carried off his conches, limpets, and Flinder's vase shells. Some even followed him into the lagoon, many falling and injuring themselves. The collector had a feeling of dread that something really terrible would happen, so he stopped collecting. When reporters came, he advised them to write of the danger of cones and not of these recent miracles. But these people only focused on miracles.

The collector's thirty-year-old son, Josh, wrote, saying news of the miracles had reached the United States. He also said he had joined the Peace Corps and had taken an assignment located in Uganda but would visit his father first. When he arrived, Josh cleaned up inside the kibanda. He tried to help the people gathered around outside and invited them to dinner, saying his father "can afford it." The collector stopped collecting shells because he did not want people who followed him into the water to get hurt; instead, he began slipping away on the trails to walk with his dog in new areas inland. He was fearful of thickets, though, and often hurried back. One day on a path he found a cone shell half a kilometer from the sea, an inexplicable event. Increasingly, he found cones inland, on tree trunks, and in a mango cove. Then he began to doubt himself, wondering if he mistook a stone for a shell, a marine mollusk for a tree snail. The island became "sinister, viperous, paralyzing." Back at the kibanda, Josh gave away "everything—the rice, the toilet paper, the Vitamin B capsules." Josh was enthusiastic, altruistic, but naïve. He relished the idea of doing good, but he dismissed his father's warnings. While Josh busied himself with the little boys, his father sensed an impending disaster.

After three weeks, Josh told his father that U.S. scientists believed cone venom may have medicinal applications for stroke and paralysis victims and that what his father did may help "thousands." Josh read the collector's books in Braille and took three mentally ill boys searching for shells. The collector warned them, but they would not believe the shells were dangerous. Then Josh was stung on the hand and died within an hour. The mwadhini arrived to comfort the collector, telling him he would be left alone from now on. The mwadhini compared the collector to a shelled creature, blind, armored, and able to withdraw. One month later the reporters named Jim arrive.

The reporters want the story. They say Nancy has given them "exclusive rights to her story." The shell collector imagines how his experience will morph into tabloid text: "a dangerous African shell drug, a blind medicine guru with his wolfdog. There for all the world to peer at." At dusk on the second day, the collector takes the two Jims to Lamu, where the streets are crowded and vendors are selling food and other items. While they are eating kabobs, a teenager sells them some hashish, which they smoke with a water pipe. The teenager tells them: "Tonight Allah determines the course of the world for next year."

The three men return by taxi after midnight, getting out of the boat into "chest-deep water." Under the drug's influence, they try to make their way to shore, and as the Jims admire the phosphorescence of some sea creatures, they ask the collector what it feels like to be stung by a cone shell. The collector takes up a search for a cone shell, turning in circles, becoming disoriented, thinking he will find one and sting the Jims with it. He loses his bearings, indifferently lets his sunglasses slip away, and realizes he has

lost his sandals. He finds a cone shell and carries it, he thinks, toward the kibanda, thinking first of killing the Jims with it and then realizing he does not want to hurt them. He heaves the shell back into the sea: "Then, with a clarity . . . that washed over him like a wave, he knew he'd been bitten." He realizes he is lost in the lagoon and lost in other ways also as the venom pulses through his body: "The stars rolled up over him in their myriad shiverings."

In the morning, he is found by Seema, the daughter of the mwadhini whom he cured with the cone shell. He is a kilometer from his kibanda, and his shepherd is with him. Seema gets him into her boat and takes her to his beach house. There over the following weeks she cares for him, visiting daily, giving him chai, keeping him warm. Gradually, she engages him in conversation about shells and collecting; as he recovers, she takes him by the wrist and guides him into the shallows.

The final scene takes place a year after the collector is stung. He is wading on the reef, "feeling for shells with his toes." On a rock nearby, his shepherd sits, and near the dog, Seema sits, "her shoulders free of her wraparound," and her hair down. She is comforted by being with a person who cannot see and who does "not care anyway." The collector feels a bullia (a slender, spiraled shell creature) under his foot. It moves blindly along, "dragging the house of its shell."

CHARACTERS

Jims

Described and referred to collectively as "the Jims," the two New York journalists representing some U.S. tabloid publication are thrust into the natural world of coastal Kenya by their work assignment. Heavy-set, out-of-shape, they lumber clumsily through the environment, ignorant of its risks. They represent a world that exploits the strangeness of an exotic place, distorting it for profit but not seeking to understand it. That they ask only some questions while avoiding other ones suggests that they investigate only up to their set boundaries of preconceived conclusions.

Josh

At the outset of the story, Josh, the idealistic, thirty-year-old son of the shell collector, has died of a cone shell sting. Reared by his mother, Josh joined the Peace Corps and stopped in Kenya to see his father en route to Uganda where he planned to begin his assignment. Described as a "goody-goody," Josh was sincerely intent on helping and yet dangerously chose to dismiss his father's warnings about the risks in this environment. With the idealistic optimism of the young and untried, he made the fatal mistake of not heeding the advice of his father about cone shells.

Dr. Kabiru

Dr. Kabiru, the local physician from Lamu, comes by water taxi to the collector's kibanda when Nancy is sick and when the collector's son is bitten. In each case, Dr. Kabiru can do nothing to help. His delayed arrival attests to the local obstacles to traveling quickly and delivering immediate medical assistance in emergencies. After the miraculous cures, Dr. Kabiru claims to have conducted research on cone venom and to have anticipated the positive outcomes for both Nancy and Seema.

Muezzin

See Mwadhini

Mwadhini

The mwadhini is the official at the largest mosque in Lamu whose role it is five times each day to call the faithful to prayer. (The English word for his title is muezzin.) He is described as having "a strident, resonant voice," one that "bore an astonishing faith." When his daughter, Seema, falls dangerously ill with malaria and the congregation's prayers seem to no avail, the mwadhini enlists the help of the shell collector, coercing him to expose Seema to the cone shell venom.

Nancy

A Seattle-born wife and mother, Nancy happened upon the shore near the collector's kibanda, suffering from sunstroke and recurrent malaria. She told the collector that she had a sudden realization back in Seattle that "her life—two kids, a three-story Tudor, an Audi wagon—was not what she wanted." In Cairo, she met a "neo-Buddhist" who introduced her to the value of "inner peace and equilibrium," terms that seemed to focus her quest. Ironically, the venomous sting of a cone shell, that puts her in a catatonic trance, makes Nancy feel "*balanced*" for the first time, completely cured of her recurrent malaria, and even willing to return to Seattle.

TOPICS FOR FURTHER STUDY

- Find or purchase a seashell and write a poem or short story about it in which you characterize the creature that lived within it in terms of its shell.

- Do some research on various mollusks and then make a chart on which you describe their distinctive characteristics. Give a presentation to your class.

- Interview someone who has made a lifelong study of some particular subject, spent years at a particular hobby or at creating a collection, and then write a report about the person, in which you describe the activity, information gained from it, and any recommendations the interviewee has for others who are interested in making collections.

- Visit a nature center or natural museum, see the exhibits and pick up various brochures available that describe programs and activities offered by or sponsored by the center or museum. Bring these brochures and information to your class and enlist others who may be interested in attending a future event. Talk about what you learned during your visit.

Ophthalmologist

The ophthalmologist met the protagonist when he was twelve years old and already blind. Instead of wasting time examining the boy's eyes, the wise doctor removed the child's shoes and socks and led the boy by the hand to the beach. Thus, this doctor ushered the boy into the world of shells that became the protagonist's lifelong obsession.

Seema

The eight-year-old daughter of the mwadhini, Seema is dangerously ill with malignant malaria. Urged by her father as a last resort, the shell collector deliberately encloses a cone shell in her hand, stinging her. Seema recovers within the next twelve hours. As if returning that assistance, Seema discovers the collector on the morning after he is bitten, gets him back to his kibanda, and thereafter cares for him daily.

Shell Collector

The unnamed protagonist of the story was born in Canada and as a boy of nine shot sick caribou while leaning out of his father's helicopter. By the age of twelve, he was blind from a disease of the retina. Introduced to shells, he took on the study of conchology, learned Braille, and became "obsessed over the geometry of exoskeletons." He earned a B.S. in biology and a Ph.D. in malacology (a branch of zoology that studies mollusks). He married, had a son, was divorced, and succeeded in an academic career during which he published widely in his field. Yet he retired at fifty-seven and withdrew to the remote exotic coastal region of Kenya near the island of Lamu. There, by a sequence of accidental events, he observes both the surprising benefit of cone shell venom in treating malaria and the anticipated deadliness of the sting when it takes the life of his son.

THEMES

The Effects of Sea Creatures on Humans

"The Shell Collector" is mostly about the effects sea creatures can have on human beings. The blind protagonist is obsessed with marine shell life, a part of the natural world he can investigate through his sense of touch. But when some sea life comes into contact with humans, it can be hurtful, even fatal. The cone shell kills Josh and threatens the life of the collector himself. The people who fall against fire coral are badly cut and burned. It takes knowledge and care to avoid being injured, and the collector avoids being hurt until the night he is drugged with hashish. Nearby in Lamu, people believe the sting of the cone shell which cured Seema may be able to deliver them from various other afflictions: lepers and mentally ill people flock to the collector's kibanda and take away shells in hopes of a cure. Josh reports that American scientists believe the venom of the cone shell may have medicinal uses. Indeed, the collector makes his living by supplying university researchers with boxes of shells. The story seems to be a qualified recommendation of the cone shell as possibly a medical gift from the sea. The recommendation comes with a warning, though, that carelessness or uninformed handling of sea life may take its toll on unsuspecting humans.

Urban versus Indigenous Life

"The Shell Collector" contrasts urban life with the life lived in nature far removed from twenty-first century western technology and amenities. The protagonist is presumably a Canadian by birth, a highly educated and well-traveled man. But from the age of fifty-eight on, he lives more in the style of indigenous people, in contrast to his son, who grows up in the United States. The collector lives in harmony with nature, aware of its wonders and respectful of its dangers. He is remote even from the closest small town, Lamu, and finds the incursion of motor boats both stressful to him personally and destructive to the vulnerable reefs near his kibanda. The technically developed centers, such as the university to which he sends boxes of shells and the urban center where his son studies current shell research findings, are placed at the periphery of the story. In the foreground is the Lamu Archipelago, the heaving presence of nature, the abundant wildlife, the smallness of the individual human in the vastness of the natural environment. The collector lives in and with nature. He is surprised when Josh wipes up the counters and when Nancy talks loudly and fast about her life in Seattle. The modern world and people from it generate shockwaves in this pristine setting and against the eardrums of this blind man who has developed a simple lifestyle in harmony with nature. The health problems that plague people in such a remote area are acknowledged: if a doctor can be found he may well arrive too late, and poverty and scarcity of supplies leave many in need of medical treatment to suffer alone. But also acknowledged is the naivety and arrogance of urban people who presume uninvited upon such a setting, presumptuously imposing their values on it. It is a mixed problem with perhaps a mixed solution: Nature is often the resource for new medicines, but nature mishandled can take its toll on human wellbeing. Both urban and remote locations offer knowledge, but the people in them have different sets of assumptions, beliefs, and goals. When people from these different places meet, the clash can be less than productive. Certainly, Josh's fate suggests that negative effect: he arrives newly enlisted into the Peace Corps with altruistic intentions, but because of his inexperience and ignorance, he is snuffed out like a little flame.

The Role of Broadcast and Print Media

"The Shell Collector" dramatizes the way sensationalism affects the choice of subjects covered in the media. It also shows the limitations both of journalists in writing on subjects they do not really understand and of newscasters who can only devote brief attention to a given subject, no matter how complex it is. After both Nancy and Seema recover, rumors spread fast through Kenya of the miracle cures. At first not a big media story, the events are covered by the local radio and newspaper. However, as news spreads further, other journalists arrive. These reporters want to cover only the sensational angle. They ask the shell collector if he has "tried pressing cone shells to his eyes." The story is promoted in a U.S. magazine, *The Humanitarian*, yet humanitarianism had nothing to do with these events. What kind of reportage the Jims do after their visit to the kibanda is left to the reader's imagination; however, when the collector imagines it, he envisions a lurid text that distorts every aspect of what he believes is true. In all of these ways, the story seems to recommend a good dose of skepticism on the part of those who depend on the news media. By contrast, the story recommends the serious investigation and research that the collector engages in as a boy and in his university training. These serious ways of learning increase one's understanding and respect for nature and help prepare a person who wants to investigate natural creatures firsthand.

STYLE

Setting

"The Shell Collector" is set on the northern shore of Kenya, near the island of Lamu. This setting provides a perfect location for a reclusive shell collector. So remote from western lifestyle, this world offers natural riches to a man who has an endless enthusiasm for sea life and who has recoiled, for whatever reasons, from the academic and urban life he led during his middle years. Nature in this area is not compromised by modern technology, except for the motorboats that threaten the coral reefs, nor is the area much able to benefit from current medical research for people who contract malaria or are otherwise injured by contact with natural phenomena, such as fire coral. Such a place provides a plethora of marine life, shows how people live with nature and are subject to it, and offers a setting in which there is a high likeliness of contracting malaria. The presence of media representatives from Great Britain or the United States would be remarkable in such an out-of-the-way place, and their long trek would suggest their view of the local miracles as an important story. The news of the miracles and the detail Josh provides in his comment that U.S. scientists are "trying to isolate some of the toxins and give them to stroke victims. To combat paralysis," suggest the story takes place in the 1970s or early 1980s, when research into the medicinal use of cone shell venom was getting underway in the United States.

Characterization

The blindness of the shell collector restricts descriptions of him and others to the senses he does have. The collector hears and feels rather than sees and so description of others in the story often comes through his available senses. For example, that the Jims are not used to the heat comes through to the collector via their handshakes, which are "slick and hot." When they sleep the first night in their bags, the collector hears "siafu feasting on the big men." The next day, when they follow behind him to the shore, the collector hears how out of shape the New Yorkers are as they huff "to keep up." They rely on their eyesight, watching the thorns along the path, but the agile collector feels his way familiarly and confidently. Similarly, when the Muslims arrive, eager to persuade the collector to use the cone shell to heal the mwadhini's daughter, the collector determines how many of them are present by the distinctive sounds made by their clothing, "these ocean Muslims in their rustling kanzus and squeaking flip-flops." He also identifies the scent of their professions, "each stinking of his work—gutted perch, fertilizer, hull-tar." The mwadhini is characterized by his voice, which bears "an astonishing faith, in the slow and beautiful way it trilled sentences, in the way it braided each syllable." The shock to the collector of having his son living in the kibanda is reported through the sensory details the collector picks up: It was strange "to hear him unzip his huge duffel bags, to come across his Schick razor . . . [hear him] chug papaya juice, scrub pans, wipe down counters." When the three boys are invited to eat dinner in the kibanda, the collector observes: "they shifted and bobbed in their chairs and clacked their silverware against the table edge like drummers." Hashish dangerously dulls the collector's senses, turns him around, gets him confused. In this dulled and thus especially vulnerable state, he gets the sting he would have easily avoided if sober. Coming to his senses, feeling the shells beneath his toes again and knowing Seema's presence without seeing her, marks his return to health. Blind, yes, but at the end, the collector is in full command of his other exquisitely trained modes of perception.

In addition to perceiving the world through his available senses, the collector's perceptions are filtered through his formal education and career in North America and his experience in Kenya. He is shaped by his knowledge and understands the world in terms of it. Moreover, in a strange way the collector has come to be like the subject he studies. "A stone fish sting corroded the skin off the sole of the shell collector's own heel, years ago, left the skin smooth and printless." Like a "printless" snail, the collector moves carefully across the lagoon, not disturbing the coral reef, aware of the dangerous creatures around him. Like a shelled creature, the collector is armored and withdrawn, keenly aware in some ways and overall quite self-protective and defensive. The so-called miraculous cures draw strangers to this place. Yet they come also to examine the collector, believing him to be some rare type of nature healer, one who heals with poison. They are drawn, it seems, by something more insidious, something growing "outward from the shell collector himself, the way a shell grows, spiraling upward from the inside, whorling around its inhabitant." In this sense, the collector is tempted to wonder if something in him has drawn Josh to this place, too, some inevitable force that the collector in all his knowledge is unable to forestall and whose tragic outcome the collector with all of his warnings is unable to avoid.

HISTORICAL CONTEXT

The History of Lamu, Kenya

The Swahili town of Lamu on Lamu Island, just off the northeastern coast of Kenya, is the oldest East African settlement. According to some sources, Arabs arrived on the island as early as the eleventh century, bringing their culture, language, and religion, Islam. During the 1500s, after the Portuguese arrived, the island town became a busy port from which timber, various spices, ivory, and slaves were exported to Europe and the Far East. By the eighteenth century, the export of slaves was the dominant source of income. When slavery was abolished in the nineteenth century, the Lamu economy suffered. By the middle of that century, the area became a subject of the sultanate of Zanzibar, which controlled the coastal areas until Kenya attained independence from Britain in 1963. In the late twentieth century, Lamu remained virtually a nineteenth-century place, without most modern technologies. There are no cars on the island, which is populated by about four thousand people. It is strictly Islamic, and visitors to the island are advised to comply with conservative dress codes. English, Swahili, and Arabic are used on Lamu. (There are forty-two native languages in Kenya as a whole.)

Medicinal Uses of Cone Venom

Historically, the meat of cone shells was considered a delicacy. People the world over collected cone shells for food. In the twentieth century, many scuba divers knew they should not pick up cone-shaped shells on the ocean floor since these creatures have a harpoon-like striking apparatus that can inject paralyzing venom into their enemies or prey. Since cone shells are so slow moving, they evolved this mechanism to paralyze their prey, giving them time to ingest the tranquilized victim. If a diver is stung, the venom can paralyze the person's hand and, in the worst cases, can ultimately cause respiratory paralysis and death. However, in the 1970s, U.S. pharmacological researchers began analyzing the cone shell venom in search of some chemical that might be medically beneficial. Throughout that decade and the two decades following, this research sought to isolate certain chemicals, called conotoxins, in the venom. These chemicals prevent nerve cells from communicating, so they cause paralysis. Medical researchers see conotoxins as having painkilling properties. In the 1980s and 1990s, many medical and pharmacological articles were published about different types of conotoxins and their probable medicinal applications. In 2004, ziconotide, a drug derived from a conotoxin, was approved by the FDA for the treatment of intractable pain. This drug is the synthetic form of the conotoxin derived from the cone snail *Conus magus*. Researchers claimed this drug is a thousand times more potent than morphine. Pharmacological research continued in the early 2000s to produce other synthetic pain-killers based on cone shell venom. Ziconotide and similar drugs are injected directly into the spinal cord. They are used to treat chronic pain, epilepsy, seizures, and in some cases schizophrenia. Peptides in the venom work on the gateways that control the action of nerves and muscles. Collectors of shells seek a perfect cone shell for its beauty, but pharmacology experts know the beauty of this creature lies, ironically, in its deadly venom.

CRITICAL OVERVIEW

The Shell Collector: Stories garnered a remarkable number of awards and was similarly well-received by reviewers. Called a "skillful first collection," in the *New York Times Book Review*, the book was praised in *Library Journal* for its characters that "are limned by the things around them." *Library Journal* compliments Doerr for his "subtle linguistic self-consciousness [and] fluid and eddying plots." A reviewer for *Publishers Weekly* adds that "Nature, in these eight stories, is mysterious and deadly, a wonder of design and of nearly overwhelming power." The *Publishers Weekly* reviewer notes too that this "delicate balance" is sustained in the title story about the discovery of a poisonous snail that can both "kill and . . . effect a rapid recovery from malaria." The attention that this event brings to the protagonist, the reviewer writes, disrupts "the carefully ordered universe that he has constructed to manage both his blindness and his temperament." Also commenting on the title story, a reviewer in *Kirkus Reviews* points out that the collector's accidental cure leads him to be "mistaken for a great healer." The reviewer concludes that Doerr's collection is "the best new book of short fiction since Andrea Barrett's *Ship Fever*."

Similarly impressed was Tim Appelo, writing for *Seattle Weekly*. Appelo begins his review by stating, "It's easy to see why Anthony Doerr was crowned king of last year's literary debutants, showered with cash and raves by the NEA, the *Times* of New York, L.A., and Seattle, the O. Henry and New York Public Library Young Lions Awards, and *Entertainment Weekly*." This is a different brand of writing, Appelo explains: "Instead of trendily transgressive coming-of-age-

Many people enjoy gathering seashells at beaches all over the world, some even make a living at it
© Robert Holmes/Corbis

as-a-cool-kid-like-me tales, [Doerr] gives us a whirlwind tour of the world." Comparing Doerr to one of the greatest American naturalists, Henry David Thoreau, Appelo asserts that Doerr reels "in nature imagery with the deft hand of a poet and the eye of a mystic." Appelo criticizes the "plotting" and thinks Doerr can be "too pat," but he still concludes, "his fiction is an exotic specimen well worth collecting."

CRITICISM

Melodie Monahan

Monahan has a Ph.D. in English and operates an editing service, The Inkwell Works. In the following essay, she explores the central theme of how knowledge is obtained and how it is handled in "The Shell Collector."

Anthony Doerr's "The Shell Collector" explores how people learn about nature and what factors determine how they react to and interpret what they come to know. The story also suggests how print and broadcast news media change information by interpreting it in certain ways and shrinking it to fit their delivery

WHAT DO I READ NEXT?

- *About Grace* (2004) is Doerr's first novel, which tells the story of a man whose dreams foretell the future and who attempts to avert the fruition of a dream about the death by drowning of his infant daughter. Readers who enjoy *The Shell Collector: Stories* will enjoy how Doerr handles this Cassandra theme with a twist.

- Caldecott Medal winner *Snowflake Bentley* (2004), by Jacqueline Briggs and illustrated by Mary Azarian, tells the story of the photographer Wilson Bentley, who set out to record snowflakes on film. One of Doerr's science heroes, Bentley had an interest in the fine details of the natural world that is similar to Doerr's own.

- The eight stories in the National Book Award winner *Ship Fever* (1996), by Andrea Barrett, tell stories that braid together a fascination with science and the natural world with an examination of the professional and private lives of people who study them. The stories are set in the eighteenth, nineteenth, and twentieth centuries. In an interview, Doerr remarked that Barrett's writing showed him how to write.

- *The Sea around Us* (1951), by Rachel Carson, introduces readers to marine life and topographical features. This poetic and scientific book inspired an award-winning documentary and stayed on the *New York Times* bestseller list for thirty-one weeks.

formats, and how preexisting belief systems can impose meaning, too. The events of the story highlight the risks of living in a remote natural environment and how learning can occur through accidental injury. The story raises questions about the price involved in the acquisition of knowledge and who is responsible for its mismanagement. In all, the story addresses how these characters learn about the saltwater shell

> THE COLLECTOR'S DELIBERATE, CONSCIENTIOUS WAYS OF LEARNING ARE CONTRASTED WITH THE WAYS INFORMATION TRAVELS AND TRANSFORMS THROUGH GOSSIP AND NEWS MEDIA."

creatures, what happens as a result of the information they gain, and how that information affects those who acquire it.

At the center of the story is the unnamed protagonist, who at the age of twelve meets an intuitive ophthalmologist, who knows he can do nothing medically for the boy's blindness and yet who knows enough about shells to introduce the boy to mollusks. Though the child gets only a vague idea of beach and sea, "the blurs that were waves . . . the smudged yolk of sun," he perceives acutely the mouse cowry in his hand, "the sleek egg of its body, the toothy gap of its aperture." So much information comes to the child through handling the shell that he concludes, "He'd never seen anything so clearly in his life." As the world available through sight closes for him, the world of conchology opens brightly. The boy learns Braille and studies books on shells. He adds to this book learning the firsthand experience of working as a sailboat crewmember, traveling through the tropics. During these formative years, "his fingers, his senses . . . obsessed over the geometry of exoskeletons." Blindness heightens the young man's other senses, making him all the more able to perceive through touch and smell because of the one disability. Through the following years, during which he acquires a B.A. in biology and Ph.D. in malacology, the protagonist gains much theoretical knowledge of shell creatures. He has an academic career, his scholarship based on his discoveries of "new species of bivalves, a new family of tusk shells, a new *Nassarius*, a new *Fragum*." After his marriage dissolves, he retires to an extremely remote and shell-rich location on the Kenyan seashore near Lamu, where he lives like a hermit.

The retirement to Kenya and daily work collecting shells presents the protagonist with what he does not know; "malacology only led him downward, to more questions." In this practically pure natural setting, he faces with wonder "the endless variations of design" and ponders what factors cause different types of shell formation. Studying the diverse, beautiful shell creatures in solitude is a privilege, bringing him face-to-face with the "utter mystery," which elicits in him "a nearly irresistible urge to bow down." The protagonist is slow-paced, diligent, mindful of what he does not know and in awe of nature's complexity. Alone, working quietly and methodically, he is able to maintain an inner equilibrium. However, this peaceful solitary life is disrupted when newcomers arrive.

The collector's deliberate, conscientious ways of learning are contrasted with the ways information travels and transforms through gossip and news media. The sensational report of cone shell venom being used to cure malaria in Lamu spreads through "the daily gossip of coastal Kenyans," who know full well the constant threat of malaria. Always in a rush to get the most recent news, journalists report from a distance and through brief interviews on the newsworthy incidents. The *Daily Nation* covers the occurrences in "a back-page story," and KBC radio devotes a "minute-long . . . spot" to them, which includes "sound bites" of Dr. Kabiru's boasts that he has done research on this new application of cone venom and is "confident" of its efficacy. The actual events suggest a different interpretation of the local doctor's role, however. As the events unfold, Dr. Kabiru concludes that medically he can do nothing to save Nancy and is surprised by her inexplicable recovery after he pronounces her case terminal. The doctor's involvement in the second case amounts only to his acquiescence in bringing the mwadhini to the collector. As he is quoted on the radio, the doctor suggests the credit for these events belongs to him; in the safe after-the-fact glow of the positive outcomes, he claims to have researched the venom and anticipated the cures. In actuality, Nancy's sting was accidental; her recovery a complete surprise. The mwadhini's insistence that his daughter be stung comes out of the father's desperate leap of faith in the face of his daughter's imminent death and Nancy's surprising recovery. But these aspects of the events are not reported in the local news. The third incident regarding the collector's son, Josh, is omitted entirely.

The first round of reportage is picked up by global news services: "A BBC reporter came, and a wonderful-smelling woman from the *International Tribune*." The protagonist advises them and other people who collect around his kibanda that cone venom can injure and kill. Though the journalists are "more interested in miracles than snails," he begs them "to write about the dangers of cones." Still, the media emphasize the cures and give no space to the venom's danger. The protagonist's son, Josh, comments on a U.S. journal, *The Humanitarian*. This publication prints a blurb "about the miracles [the collector has] been working." One accident and one desperate experimentation based on it are transformed in this publication (whose title suggests its slant) as ongoing miraculously effective philanthropic work performed by an altruistic scientist. The truth of the actual events, along with the motives of those involved, is distorted as the report is slanted toward the sensational conclusion. Ironically, as the news media and its readers jump to conclusions about a miracle cure, the collector himself becomes more focused on the risks, worrying about the pilgrims who follow him into the lagoon and who may be stung or fall against the fire coral and be injured. He even worries about his son's safety and that of the boys who go along the shore with him.

Perhaps the most striking contrast to the collector's slow-paced, sustained, and respectful acquisition of knowledge is made by the "two big Jims" sent by a New York tabloid to get the scoop on the miracle cure. These men blunder into the seashore environment of Lamu with no preparation or understanding but well equipped with foregone conclusions. They have ten thousand dollars to offer for an interview and assume the money gives them the right to spend a couple nights in the collector's kibanda and traipse after him out onto the coral reef. The proverbial bulls in a china shop, they lumber and huff after him, irritated by siafu and pricked by thorns.

In contrast to the superficiality of the journalists, the shell collector's knowledge of his environment runs deep. He is at one with it, but always aware of its dangers. As he searches for shells while "the Jims" look on, he thinks of the venom of various nematocysts (jellyfish) and their acute and immediate effect on humans stung by them, how the "weeverfish bite bloated a man's entire right side." He finds a cone shell and lifts it up for the Jims to see. One of the journalists dismisses the cone, after all his "pinkie's bigger," as though size determines strength. The collector informs him: "This animal . . . has twelve kinds of venom in its teeth. It could paralyze you and drown you right here." These city men observe the water through their snorkeling masks, while the collector inches his way, barefoot, finding the undersea world through the immediacy of touch.

The following night, under the dulling intoxication of hashish, the Jims carelessly wonder how the sting of a cone shell feels, and the collector, led astray by them and similarly intoxicated, thinks temporarily that their dying that way would not be such a bad idea. People see the world differently in drug-induced states and while natural beauty comes through, the dulled senses increase human vulnerability. Ironically, the stoned Jims make it back to the kibanda, but the collector becomes disoriented and is stung by the cone he holds while being tempted to satisfy the journalists' dangerous curiosity. The Jims leave with enough of what they came for to write the marketable lurid story; the collector is left to struggle through the effects of the sting.

Nancy's naïve quest into this region, seeking the elusive "inner peace and equilibrium" promoted by some "neo-Buddhist," and Josh's idealistic Peace Corps sojourn to Africa suggest two other ways the unknown world is experienced and interpreted. Seattle-born Nancy, urban, moneyed, with husband and children yet in midlife crisis, wanders along some self-referential mission into Africa, placing herself at risk and quickly acquiring sunstroke and malaria. Josh, even at thirty, is in some ways a child at heart. The Peace Corps appeals to his patronizing altruism, and clouded by both his American culture and a distorted view of his father's work, he comes to Kenya ready to see his father's miraculous deeds. Josh's uninformed enthusiasm, untempered idealism, and careless efforts to help put at risk the boys who follow him about the lagoon and ultimately cost him his life when he foolishly picks up a cone because it is pretty.

Add to these inexperienced Americans, the local Muslims who confront the ravages of malaria, cholera, and other physiological problems, and find that community-wide prayers are unhelpful. The faithful mwadhini is so afraid for his acutely ill daughter, he is willing to jump to the conclusion that if one person can recover from malaria after being stung by a cone then perhaps his terminally ill daughter can, too. To the extent that these local people are uneducated about their environment and without the necessary medicines to treat injury and disease, they are daily at risk. The irony here is that the blind faith of the mwadhini brings about the lucky cure of his daughter, literally restoring her to health within a day.

What is the shell collector's responsibility in all of this and what is the story's ultimate message? The first question is raised yet left unanswered. As the shell collector goes about his reclusive work, collecting shells and boxing them up to be sent off to universities, events happen which he does not design or control. Nancy and then Josh come to him; one recovers inexplicably by accident, the other gets a lethal sting and dies though he has been warned repeatedly. The shell collector has to wonder if these events inevitably swirl around him like a shell forms, creating out of its own nature an enclosed world to armor the shelled creature inside. It seems to be a spiral of events "at once inevitable and unpredictable." A hermit by choice and profession, the collector wants to be left alone. Yet for awhile all the world finds a way to his door, locals plagued with disease and seeking cure and journalists bent on reading in his crusty, sinewy nature and lifestyle the sensational story that sells yet unwilling to provide space for the cautionary note. Josh's death serves as a warning for those who take time to hear the meaning in this story. One point to Doerr's story is that people in this kind of environment need to tread gently, acquire information objectively without preformed belief or agenda, and take the necessary time to learn. Still, accidents happen for good and for ill. The same substance that can paralyze and kill in a moment may in another application have medical benefits. Science explores, and sometimes accidents confirm that investigation or redirect it.

Source: Melodie Monahan, Critical Essay on "The Shell Collector," in *Short Stories for Students*, Thomson Gale, 2007.

Penguin Group

In the following interview, Doerr discusses his prevalent theme of humanity's interaction with nature and his use of magic and the supernatural in his stories.

The Shell Collector, Anthony Doerr's first collection of stories, ranges from Liberia and

Tanzania to Montana and Maine. Traversing the vast terrain of the world, Doerr shows an extraordinary empathy in stories that most often concern themselves with the interaction between humans and nature. He writes with delicious specificity about natural science and displays a talent for evoking landscape through poetic language. In these stories, the call of nature—to know its wildness and bow before it—is inseparable from the need to capture and tame it through activities like gardening, fishing, photography, or hunting. He describes the communion that seems to come through the interaction between people—eager, suffering, and full of desire—and a nature that is cruel and unmanageable but also an extravagant conveyor of the divine. As grounded as Doerr's stories are in the physical world, magic and the supernatural appear as powerful forces in many of the stories. In the O'Henry Award-winning "The Hunter's Wife," nature's ferocious and awesome powers are matched by the truly unexplainable gifts of the title character. Doerr traces the briefly intersecting paths of a hunter in Montana and the young magician's assistant who first becomes his wife and then learns that she is a kind of medium between life and death, a link to the supernatural. As the hunter's wife struggles to understand her gift, the couple finds a rift between what each is willing to accept is possible in the world. In the extraordinary epic "The Caretaker," a Liberian man survives terrifying carnage in his homeland and flees to the United States. As the caretaker for a summer home of rich people who have "something to do with computers," Joseph witnesses the beaching of five whales on the Oregon coast. In an astonishing act of guilt and repentance, the refugee buries the hearts of the dead whales; even those gigantic organs do not seem large enough to encompass the vastness of his grief. Joseph loses his job but stays to cultivate the plot of land atop the hearts, befriending the deaf and depressed daughter of the house's owners. Together they search for redemption in the garden and through their tentative new friendship. The title story is a lyrical and somber tale constructed of achingly beautiful, precise language. The shell collector is a blind former professor who is attempting a retreat from the human world by retiring to the coast of Tanzania to live out his days wading in a quiet lagoon and collecting shells with fingers that seem to see. His world is simple and empirical: "Ignorance was, in the end, and in so many

ways, a privilege: to find a shell, to feel it, to understand only on some unspeakable level why it bothered to be so lovely. What joy he found in that, what utter mystery." Yet the world intrudes on the shell collector, asking him to be a father, a guide, and a savior; reluctantly, and with devastating and then surprisingly hopeful consequences, he is drawn in. Doerr's greatest gift is to see an equal humanity in people belonging to all ages, cultures, and countries. He applies his empathy to a retired professor ("The Shell Collector") and a Latina high school girl ("So Many Chances"), to a morally questionable African immigrant ("The Caretaker") and an average American suburbanite ("For a Long Time This Was Griselda's Story"). He demonstrates how immersion in the natural world, far from limiting the scope of these lives, allows them to be truly free individuals, to be themselves in the purest sense. His characters seem to find comfort in necessity, in simplicity, and in isolation. The hunter says damningly of cities: "There is no order in that world." Yet even as Doerr evokes the lure of the natural world and seems to espouse its virtues over those of civilization, he also subtly advocates for the irreplaceable value of human relations, however fragile and ephemeral those might be. In this dazzling collection, Doerr achieves a humane resonance for his haunting and original stories. His characters trip over the line between nature and magic, between what we can collect, catalogue, and know and what lies beyond the human capacity to understand, to which we can only surrender. In taking us around the planet with these intriguing and thoroughly modern characters, Doerr insists on nature's relevance in a fractured world, reveling in the one experience that all human beings across the planet have in common: the rapturous apprehension of nature.

An Interview with Anthony Doerr

[Penguin Group:] *There are so many locations in this book, in Europe, Africa, and America. Have you been to each of these places, and how much do particular locales inspire your stories?*

[Anthony Doerr:] I've been to all of them but Liberia, where the first half-dozen pages of "The Caretaker" takes place, and Belorussia, where maybe a page of "July Fourth" occurs. In many ways, though, the locales didn't quite inspire the stories: I think maybe the stories and their settings came to me simultaneously. That

"I'D SAY I WANTED TO EMPHASIZE THAT HUMAN EXPERIENCES—THE TRULY IMPORTANT ONES, LIKE FALLING IN LOVE, HAVING YOUR HEART BROKEN, AND DYING—ARE SHARED BY ALL PEOPLE; THAT IS, INDEPENDENT OF CULTURE."

is, the landscapes and the narratives grew out of each other. Like real human beings, fictional characters make marks on their respective environments, but environments make marks on their characters, too, and I tried to present each character's story as inseparable from the place(s) where it occurs. In terms of my process, I didn't write "The Shell Collector" in Kenya, and "The Caretaker" in Oregon, or anything like that. But as I wrote the story, I'd look back through my journals, or look at photos, or Web sites, or travel brochures, or naturalists' accounts, or whatever else I could use to help me evoke the places I was writing about. So in the end the settings are products of memory, research, imagination, and of course the psyche of the point-of-view character.

You have also lived abroad, though you currently live in Idaho. How does travel and firsthand experience with different cultures affect you as a writer? Do you consciously cultivate this expansive lens?

Travel definitely affects me as a writer. Whatever limited observational skills I have, I use them best and most when I find myself in a strange place, slightly uncomfortable. Especially if the people around me aren't speaking in English. It helps me remember that the United States is just a small, isolated, wildly privileged corner of the world. In many ways travel is the easiest way to get myself out of the routine and commonplace, but it's not the only way. I mean, you can go out into your backyard right now and peer into the grass and witness a dozen unfamiliar, astounding things in ten minutes: ants ambushing each other, worms aerating the soil, beetles having sex in your rosebushes. So yes, I consciously cultivate it. But if we can't afford the time or the plane ticket at the moment, I try to get outside and find something unfamiliar, some tiny miracle a half-mile from the front door.

Do you fish or hunt? Why do you think there is this connection between fishing and philosophical rumination? Will you keep writing about it?

I don't hunt. I do fish. I think there is a connection between thinking and fishing mostly because you spend a lot of time up to your waist in water without a whole lot to keep your mind busy. You're alone (even if you're with someone, you're usually far apart, or standing quietly) and you either turn inward, to your thoughts, or you turn outward and look at things: light on the river, a gnat on your sleeve, clouds all lit up with sunlight. For me fishing is, in a lot of ways, an excuse to go to a river or a lake or the ocean and just spend a whole day seeing. I don't know if I'll keep writing about it; I probably will.

"For a Long Time This Was Griselda's Story" is particularly interesting because it follows two characters—Duck and Rosemary—who find a normal, good life in the suburbs; they don't seem to have the desperate need to commune with the natural that most of your other characters have. The heroine turns out to be not the dramatic magician's assistant with the glamorous life, but her dull, plain sister. Can you tell us a little bit about writing this story and about why you decided to shift your focus with these characters? Does the title itself reveal something of the process?

The title does indeed very much reveal the process; for a long time, it was Griselda's story, and I was stuck on it. The plot seemed too fanciful, the ending was horrific, and I nearly abandoned it. But around that time a student of mine asked me about all the places I'd lived since leaving high school, and she seemed so impressed with my brief travel history and dissatisfied with her own "mundane" life in comparison. I told her that my life thus far sure didn't seem very glamorous, and that I wasn't sure I learned anything very special just because I had traveled a bit. My feeling is that you can learn just as much (or more!) and have just as rewarding and important a life (or more important!) if you never leave the confines of your hometown. As I talked with her, I realized that was the key to revising my story: of the two sisters, Rosemary's life was the truly interesting one, not Griselda's. After that the revisions sort of fell into place.

The hunter's wife also has a mysterious gift that can only be described as magical; what exactly do you imagine this gift to be? Can you describe it for us? And did you intend to suggest that the gift is as costly to her as it is precious to others?

I suppose I'd describe her gift as an extremely sensitive empathy. Does that sound about right? And, sure, I think her gift was costly to her. It thrilled her, of course, and broadened her understanding of the world, but it also destroyed her marriage. I'm fascinated by the idea that any supernatural gift—flying, say, or being able to predict the future—must also carry with it a balance, an antigift. Often, I'd think, it would be the curse of isolation. I mean, think about it: If you were the only twelve-year-old in the world who could fly, at first it would be so exhilarating, absolutely incredible, drifting over the rooftops. But after a while, say a year or so, of drifting among the clouds, maybe playing pranks on your friends, wouldn't you get tired of it? Wouldn't you feel lonely? Wouldn't you wish, more than anything, that someone else could fly with you? Or that you never learned to fly at all?

Many of your characters face dangers, even death, through the happenstance events of nature and its creations. In "The Hunter's Wife," the couple comes close to death in a hard winter. The shell collector lives in a world filled with incipient danger, in part because of his blindness but also because of the facts: just as the cone shells promise ecstasy and healing, they also kill. One gets the sense that nature threatens as much as it enthralls. Were you conscious of trying to get this across, and was it hard to write about both? Was it tempting to simply vaunt the glories of the natural world, especially at a time when it is so threatened?

I was conscious of trying to get that idea across, yes. For me it wasn't tempting to hype the glory of wilderness without balancing it, without trying to emphasize how small one human is in the face of the evolution of the entire planet. Anyone who has spent a few nights in a tent during a storm can tell you: The world doesn't care all that much if you live or die. But then, in the morning, the weather lifts, and you see new snow everywhere, and you feel the utter glory of being allowed to stand there and look at it. Or just walk outside some clear night and look up at the stars. All that ancient, huge energy up there—it's gorgeous, but the scale is so humbling, too.

Dorotea, Joseph, and even Seema, the little girl saved by the shell collector, are each able to find some peace through experiences with the physical world. Were you aware of emphasizing, over the course of these stories, the fact that all people from all backgrounds, experience nature in similar ways? Do you see this is an important political or moral point?

I'd say I wanted to emphasize that human experiences—the truly important ones, like falling in love, having your heart broken, and dying—are shared by all people; that is, independent of culture. I thought a short-story collection was particularly well suited to making this point, since by nature it can range more widely than a novel. I certainly believe that there are commonalities that supercede culture, so, yes, I feel it is a very important political and moral point—probably the most important one. But as you sit down to write, you don't really think consciously: "Now I'll design a group of stories that emphasize a continuum of human emotion across a range of possible experiences." You just try to write a story and make it plausible, moving, and cleanly told. In many ways any political element takes care of itself: in the design of the narrative, in what I'm interested in writing about to begin with. We're all political creatures, so the stories we tell will be inescapably political.

How do you balance your interactions with civilization—and your writing life—with encounters with nature? Do you get to spend as much time outdoors as you like? What are some other things that inspire you?

I have a fairly normal life: I go to the grocery store; I watch SportsCenter. I do try to get outdoors as much as possible, and a few times a year my wife and I feel the travel lust coming on and start searching the Internet like crazy for cheap plane tickets. Because I teach as well as write, I don't spend as much time away from a desk as I would like, but compared to many of my friends I get out a fair amount. Living in Idaho is, in many ways, a gift, because there are dazzling, roadless mountains literally in our front yard.

What writers have been most important to you? Can you tell us something about the novel you are writing?

Gosh, so many writers have been important to me: J. M. Coetzee, Rick Bass, Joseph Conrad, Andrea Barrett, Denis Johnson, Cormac McCarthy. Each of them continues to expand my ideas about what is possible in fiction. Thanks for asking about my novel. I haven't said much about it because I routinely change it pretty drastically, but let's see ... I can tell you that it's set, for the most part, in the Caribbean and in Alaska. The main character is a hydrologist who studies snow, so there's lots of snow and ice in the book. Early in the story he dreams he will inadvertently drown his infant daughter, and he begins to believe that his dream will come true, so he, of course, fights like heck to stop it from happening. I probably ought to stop there.

Source: Penguin Group, "Interview with Anthony Doerr," in *Penguin Group*, 2006, pp. 1–12.

Collectanea

In the following interview, Doerr talks about the influence an environment has on his writing, the importance of writing as if he were a native of that environment and the influence of other artistic mediums on his work.

[*Collectanea:*] *Tony, you've lived in some spectacular places, from Maine to Kenya, Alaska to New Zealand—and let's not forget Idaho and New Jersey. Most recently you were in Rome, Italy, for the Joseph Brodsky Rome Prize Fellowship and we were reading your articles for* The Morning News *all summer— swept away in your experiences with Italian culture, living* La Dolce Vita *(or so we liked to imagine). All of us at* COLLECTANEA *are fascinated by the influence environment has on writing and the creative process, and we'd like to focus this craft interview in that direction.*

Many writers feel that they cannot write about their environment while "living it" since the material is too close to home. Do you find that the influence of a location immediately takes hold of your writing or that it resonates later, after there's some distance?

[Anthony Doerr:] Both. I agree, any place in its full-throated reality incessantly bombards you with so many details that you tend to get overwhelmed. I especially think of Manhattan like that; you see enough on one city block to fill a thousand-page novel, so how are you supposed to whittle that down into a couple of paragraphs?

That problem is present with every city: Nairobi, London, Rome. Your filter has to be extremely fine, always discarding sensory input, or you'd never make it through a day. So I agree with Hemingway, et al, that sometimes it's easier to write about a place once you have some distance from it.

For example, I didn't write "The Shell Collector" in Kenya, or "The Caretaker" in Liberia and Oregon. But as I wrote those stories, as I write any piece of fiction, I look back through my journals, which were written while I was in the grips of a place, and all its whirling details. That's my raw material. Then I quarantine myself in some quiet place, a library or my office, and I'll look at photos, or Web sites, or travel brochures, or naturalists' accounts, or whatever else I can use to help me evoke the setting.

In the end, my settings are products of memory and research, buttressed by imagination, and tinted by the psyche of the point-of-view character. They are places you could find in an atlas, true, but they are as much products of imagination as anything else.

So many of your stories elicit a strong, almost palpable setting. How do you come to know—and fully experience—a new location once you have arrived? And how do you let a location work its magic on you?

I'm not sure I ever "know" or "fully experience" a place. I'm not sure a person who lives in the same town for seventy years ever fully knows a place. (I think of John Ames in Marilynne Robinson's *Gilead*.)

When I'm traveling, two things help me pay attention: being alone, and being obsessive about keeping a journal.

I love traveling with people, of course, especially my wife, but it's easiest for me to forget my own situation—if I'm comfortable, if whoever I'm with is comfortable, etc.—when I'm alone. I sort of try to become one big eye, roaming across the bridges, peering between trees. Looking outward, I find, is always easiest to do alone.

And then, whenever I can, on trains, or in the tent, or wherever, I write down what I can in a journal. Trying to turn experience into sentences forces you to pay keener attention than you might otherwise. It focuses your concentration on your memories, on what is happening around you. It forces you to hunt for the nuances of a place, for the details that—you hope—will offer a reader what Robert Penn Warren called that "stab of actuality."

I don't mean to suggest that there is a set of certain objective details hidden beneath the texture of a place that one ought to go hunting for;

every person will find his or her own details. It is always a matter of instinct and, finally, laborious trial and error.

How does immersion in another language and culture influence your writing? Have you noticed any subtle or obvious characteristics of a given language influencing your writing style—such as sentence structure, word choice, rhythm, etc.?

That is a difficult question to articulate. I highly doubt my sledgehammer-command of three hundred Italian or Kiswahili words has affected how I use English. If it has, I'm unaware of it.

Culture is an even more complex and invisible thing. I do know that whatever limited observational skills I have, I probably use them best and most when I find myself in a strange place, slightly uncomfortable. Especially if the people around me aren't speaking in English. It helps me remember that the United States is a mostly isolated, wildly privileged corner of the world, that English is just one language among thousands, albeit one that has global hegemony.

Strangely enough, whatever book I happen to be reading seems to have the most effect on the rhythm in my own sentences. When I read *The Shipping News* I kept dropping the subjects off my own sentences. When I read Saramago's *Blindness* I kept joining independent clauses together with commas instead of periods.

Have you attempted to write in another language? If so, which one and if not, which would you like to write in?

Wow. I've never attempted it, no, excepting the cover letter for my Italian visa application. Writing well in two languages seems like the province of minds greater than my own.

Which one would I like to write in? Since I'm wishing, I might as well wish for Mandarin Chinese. I'd love to be able to fathom a language poles apart from English. And I'd love to be able to travel through China and talk to people.

I remember when I first received a copy of the Japanese translation of *The Shell Collector* and remembered it had to be read top-to-bottom and right-to-left. It was a wonderful reminder of how arbitrary the conventions of language are, how a language exists only because a group of people all agree that "tree" signifies a tree and that an "i" is a little line with a dot on top of it.

Having little kids is another nice reminder of that. Last night I chopped up a piece of bacon and gave it to my sons and they spread out the pieces on their little trays and started counting them. "One bacon, two bacons, three bacons..." I thought: Why don't we call three pieces of bacon 'three bacons' anyway?

Has a location ever directly affected the course of a story or novel in any way, e.g. caused changes in plot, birthed or killed characters?

In my fiction, setting and narrative usually grow out of one another. The landscape moves across the characters as much as they move across it. So, in many, many senses, locations determine *everything* that will happen in a story or novel, not just who lives or dies, but who they are at all. The plot of *About Grace*, for example, would be entirely different if it took place in other locations. So, location is sort of inseparable from the course of a story.

When you're searching for creative direction, what other mediums inspire your work, whether film, photography, theater, design, music? Any artists in particular?

All sorts of mediums/media amaze me. Music, always. Architecture, sometimes. I am in awe of Chris Ware lately, the cartoonist (or graphic novelist?) who made *Jimmy Corrigan* and just released a prelude to a new book, *Rusty Brown*. The painstaking hours he must spend on each drawing, even his smallest panels, appeals to me a great deal; it is the same mixture of meticulousness and generosity I'm trying to pour into my own work.

In Rome, in a little library inside the Villa Farnese, I got to hold a couple Dürer etchings and look at them with a magnifying glass. It's not his confidence or his choice of subject that appeals to me as much as his breathtaking level of hyper-precision. I mean, there's a tiny billy goat in the upper right hand corner of "Adam and Eve," peering off a cliff, no bigger than the nail of your pinkie finger, and you look at that goat with a magnifier and realize Dürer has etched fur into its coat, cracks into its horns. And he's doing this in 1504, with handmade tools and no electrical lights.

During your travels, were you ever surprised to find yourself drawn to or relying upon another artistic medium for self-expression?

Drawing, I suppose. I'm an awful draftsperson, but I so, so wish I was better at it. It's hard for me to sit in a church like Sant' Ivo alia Sapienza in Rome, or in the Pantheon, and not want to draw it.

One of the many reasons we find your work compelling is your ability to evoke a world which the reader positively believes and lives in, not merely as a fleeting tourist, but as one with all the experience and expertise of a native. How do you "research" your stories to lend them their authenticity?

If I do pull it off, it's with old-fashioned research. Botany books, the Internet and trips to the library. I think you have to be deeply curious about something to write about it. Or at least to write well about it. If you're really interested in something, whether it's venomous snails or how bicycles are made, your enthusiasm will travel from your heart through the page and enter the reader's heart.

Using a somewhat technical language is part of that, too. I love the language that rises up around devotion to things, the language of heart surgeons, the language of horse racers, the language of radio repairmen in the 1930s. A lot of that stuff is only a few Google searches away, and it helps make the dream that is fiction more convincing. It helps prevent your reader from waking up and realizing she's just reading black letters on a white page.

The late John Fowles once wrote that he was often inspired first by an extraordinary image that haunted him. Others have said that a single isolated sentence has ignited them. If it's possible to generalize, in what form does your inspiration come?

Probably from finding those things which interest me most deeply. Usually these are things that simultaneously seem both accessible and deeply mysterious. Snowflakes. Seashells. Radio waves. I latch on to something and want to learn more about it, and sometimes, maybe three times of ten, I'm able to start building a narrative and characters up out of that. All of that has to do with wonder, I think: finding things that elicit a sense of wonder about the world. If a beginning writer wants advice from me, I ask her, "What *amazes* you?" All the best artists are at some level wildly in love with the world.

Which work of literature has been significantly influential or formative for you and your writing?

Moby Dick. Rick Bass's *The Watch.* And Cormac McCarthy's *Suttree.*

Along the lines of generating work, Jenefer Shute said that the most important thing a writer can do is to learn how he/she works—is it at night or in the morning, through revision or slowly crafted sentences. If you don't mind sharing it, how do you work best?

Mornings. Get up with the babies, change their diapers, put them in their high chairs with a waffle or something, then tag out with my wife and start working. My brain is too tired in the evenings.

And the million-dollar question, what we all want to know: What are your first drafts like? And could you give us an example of a first-draft sentence followed by its final form?

It's complicated in my case because I am always revising, eternally revising. There must be a first draft in there, engraved invisibly beneath all the revisions, but really the first draft is just a single sentence I've written down and immediately begun altering. Before adding a second sentence, I'm already revising the first one. It's hard to give an example of that, but I guess I can try. Here's an early description of the village in a story/novella, "Village 113" that'll be published in *Tin House* this summer.

> "Sometimes, during storms, rocks shear away from the walls of the gorge and careen down through the trees toward the village, and people shuffle into cellars as if waiting out a bombardment. Other days the avenue of sky above the river glows so white it seems to fuse with light, the rooftops glazed with light, the gutters spilling over, light splashing onto the streets."

And here's the description that made it finally into the story, in roughly the same place.

> "Here is the Park of Heroes; here are the gingko trees, a procession in the dark. Here are the ancient lions, their backs polished from five centuries of child-riders. On the full moon, her mother used to say, the lions come to life and pad around the village, peering in windows, sniffing at trees."

Can you give us a taste of what your second novel is about? (We're chomping at the bit here.)

Right now it's about the Nazi occupation of Kiev, and about a veterinarian and his blind daughter who—illegally—build a transmitter and begin risking their lives to broadcast music. But it's big and complicated and some parts are from the perspective of a young German soldier. Most days it feels like a big puddle of mud I'm trying to hold in my hands and carry around the house.

About four weeks ago, though, I took a break from the novel. I'm trying to put together a short manuscript about my time in Rome, a memoir about being American overseas, changing diapers in Piazza Navona, seeing the pope die, eating ravioli, etc. So I'm sort of working on two books right now. And also thinking about putting together a book of long stories, maybe three or four. Maybe my second novel will be part of that, a book of three novellas, say.

Please tell us something, anything, that we haven't asked you about and that you'd like to share with COLLECTANEA.

I wish you a thousand successes. Trying to be an artist is hard and lonesome sometimes, but getting up in the morning and trying to create something is the most wonderful thing you can do with your time.

Source: Collectanea, "Interview with Anthony Doerr," in *Collectanea*, Vol. 1, No. 1, Winter 2006, pp. 1–7.

Thomson Gale

In the following essay, the critic gives an overview of Anthony Doerr's work.

With his first collection of short stories, Anthony Doerr at age twenty-eight achieved immediate recognition from coast to coast. "Doerr's prose dazzles," wrote Nancy Willard in the *New York Times*, "his sinewy sentences blending the naturalist's unswerving gaze with the poet's gift for metaphor." Tamara Straus, a reviewer for the *San Francisco Chronicle*, characterized Doerr's literary ancestry as a combination of "Henry David Thoreau (for his pantheistic passions) and Gabriel García Márquez (for his crystal-cut prose and dreamy magic realism)."

The publication of *The Shell Collector: Stories* not only earned Doerr comparisons with Flannery O'Connor, a master of the short story, but also resulted in his being credited with the revival of the American short story itself. "In his first collection of short stories, young Anthony Doerr shows the big kids how it's done," Nancy Connors wrote in the *Plain Dealer*. "And he goes a long way toward cleaning up the bad reputation some of his elders have given the short story." Connors observed in her review of *The Shell Collector* that the genre had of late given way to stories that were "pretentious, silly, or meaningless." Doerr's stories, however, "are polished jewels," she continued.

Doerr, who grew up in Cleveland, Ohio, lived in Africa and New Zealand before moving to Boise, Idaho. All these landscapes come into play in this collection. In the title story, a blind man, self-exiled to an African archipelago, discovers a potential cure for blindness in a poisonous snail. In "The Caretaker," set in Liberia, a man leaves home to search for his mother, who is late coming home from the market, only to stumble into a nightmarish world where he is forced to kill a man. Eventually, he escapes to Oregon, where he finds work as a caretaker, but he cannot escape the torment of his memories until five whales become beached nearby and his response to them redeems him. "The Hunter's Wife," set in Montana, tells the story of a relationship between an outdoorsman and a woman whose supernatural abilities allow her to commune with dying animals.

No matter where these stories are set, they are all grounded in nature. Straus wrote, "This Nature, with a capital N, is what marks Doerr's people. The thick green forests and whispering shores, cold rivers and jungles offer refreshment away from the pressures of contemporary society and popular culture. In their place are starker universal confrontations with fellow man and the self." Nature is the main theme in all of Doerr's tales. They are set outdoors and revolve around themes of hunting and collecting, gathering and letting go, and living as an outsider. His characters are exiles and refugees, people living on the fringe of society, like the woman who follows the sideshow metal-eater in "For a Long Time This Was Griselda's Story." *The Shell Collectors* "is a paean to the exquisite universe outside ourselves," wrote Gail Caldwell for the *Boston Globe*. "Perilously beautiful, as precise and elegant as calculus, that wider place of Doerr's imagination is so commanding, so poetically rendered, that it informs and even defines the characters who wander across its stage."

Doerr also seems to understand America's predominant and yet excluded place in the world. In "July Fourth" he tells of a challenge posed by a group of wealthy American fishermen to a group of British anglers. The contest is to see which group can catch the largest freshwater fish on each continent. The losing team must walk through Times Square naked. The Americans aren't really up to the challenge but remain relentlessly optimistic. "They would map out routes and make contingency plans," Doerr wrote, "and the boundless resources of America, its endless undulant swale, its nodding wheat and white silos gone lavender in the twilight, its vast warehouses and deft craftsmen, would unfurl to help them. They would not lose, they could not lose; they were Americans, they had already won."

The elements that recur in Doerr's short stories are also present in his first novel, *About Grace*. The protagonist, David Winkler, is a hydrologist and meteorologist whose career is dependent on the structure and rhythm of nature, which he understands and with which he seems to be at peace. In his personal life, however, Winkler is frightened by his gift for premonition; he is able to see the future but not to fix it. He foresaw his marriage and accepted it. When he foresees the accidental death of his baby daughter Grace by his own hand, he flees the country, hoping to avert the tragedy. After many years of self-imposed exile, Winkler returns home, unable to resist the need to learn of his daughter's fate. His "loneliness, regret, and guilt are painfully palpable," wrote a *Kirkus Reviews* contributor. Though the critic found the conclusion less than satisfying, the reviewer concluded that the novel "possesses a seductive symbolic intensity, and abounds with gorgeous descriptions and metaphors," In the *Spectator*, reviewer Robert Edric found this novel of the wandering outsider "compelling, balanced and anchored to the solid ground of the story being told; and yet with a finesse, flair and precision equally suited to its grander themes."

Source: Thomson Gale, "Anthony Doerr," in *Contemporary Authors Online*, Thomson Gale, 2005.

SOURCES

Appelo, Tim, Review of *The Shell Collector: Stories*, in *Seattle Weekly*, July 9, 2003, http://www.seattleweekly.com/arts/0328/arts-books.php (accessed November 1, 2006).

Doerr, Anthony, "The Shell Collector," in *The Shell Collector: Stories*, Scribner, 2002, pp. 9–39.

Review of *The Shell Collector: Stories*, in *Kirkus Reviews*, Vol. 69, No. 220, November 15, 2001, p. 1566.

Review of *The Shell Collector: Stories*, in *Library Journal*, Vol. 127, No. 1, January 2002, p. 156.

Review of *The Shell Collector: Stories*, in *New York Times Book Review*, Vol. 107, No. 10, March 10, 2002, p. 22.

Review of *The Shell Collector: Stories*, in *Publishers Weekly*, Vol. 248, No. 48, November 26, 2001, p. 39.

FURTHER READING

Erdman, Sarah, *Nine Hills to Nambonkaha: Two Years in the Heart of an African Village*, Holt, 2003.

This book gives a portrait of an African village in Ivory Coast, where Sarah Erdman lived for two years. She describes a place where sorcerers still conjure magic and where expected installments of electricity never occur, a place ravaged by AIDS. Erdman was the first Caucasian in the village since the time of the French colonialists.

Lytle, Mark, *Gentle Subversive: Rachel Carson, Silent Spring and the Rise of the Environmental Movement*, Oxford University Press, 2006.

This biography of Rachel Carson maps out her development as a scientist, her love of the sea, and her growing awareness of the environment and what was needed to protect it, culminating with her landmark, Silent Spring, which began the environmental movement in the United States.

Romashko, Sandra D., *The Shell Book: A Complete Guide to Collecting and Identifying*, Windward Publishing, 1992.

This popular book serves as a guide for collectors and helps them identify shells by presenting color photographs of shells found in various shorelines, including the Atlantic Coast, the Gulf of Mexico, the Caribbean, the Bahamas, and the West Indies.

Sill, Cathryn P., *About Mollusks*, Peachtree Publishers, 2005.

Written by an elementary school teacher and intended for young readers, this book describes mollusks, their environment, and their behavior. It is beautifully illustrated by the author's husband, John Sill.

Thomsen, Moritz, *Living Poor: A Peace Corps Chronicle*, University of Washington Press, 2003.

At the age of forty-eight, Thomsen joined the Peace Corps and went to live in Ecuador. His story is touchingly comic and sad by turns and includes wonderful descriptions of the Ecuadorian landscape.

Trick or Treat

PADGETT POWELL

1993

"Trick or Treat," a short story by Padgett Powell, originally appeared in *Harper's* magazine in November 1993 and later was included in the author's collection of short stories, *Aliens of Affection* (1998). "Trick or Treat" is a brief glimpse into the life of a frustrated and lonely housewife, Mrs. Hollingsworth, who allows herself to be seduced by a smart-mouthed twelve-year-old boy named Jimmy Teeth. Mrs. Hollingsworth is not only at odds with her life, but she also has a love/hate relationship with the South, where she lives. "Trick or Treat" won a 1995 O. Henry Award and was anthologized in the award publication, *The O. Henry Prize Stories 1995*.

Powell is a renowned southern writer, having lived most of his life in Florida. Some would argue that Florida is not *southern* the way Georgia or Alabama are, but one reading of Powell's fiction may change their minds. He imbues his characters and settings with a distinctly southern tang which is not overdone but at the same time is impossible to ignore. Powell's work is both funny and emotionally evocative. Many critics have described his use of language as lush. His characters are just fantastical enough to entertain without being entirely unbelievable or unsympathetic.

AUTHOR BIOGRAPHY

Padgett Powell was born in Gainesville, Florida, on April 25, 1952, to Albine Batts Powell and

Padgett Powell © *Jerry Bauer. Reproduced by permission*

Bettyre Palmer Powell, a brewmaster and a schoolteacher, respectively. He grew up in various cities in Florida and South Carolina. In college, Powell struggled with his English classes, opting for chemistry as a major. He graduated from the College of Charleston with a bachelor's degree in chemistry in 1975 and went on to graduate school at the University of Tennessee. Powell lost interest in school and left before he finished. He moved to Texas and became a roofer.

Powell enrolled in the University of Houston's Master of Fine Arts program in fiction writing in hopes of meeting women. He studied under post-modernist author Donald Barthelme, and while a student, he developed and wrote his first novel, *Edisto*. Powell graduated in 1982 and, in 1984, an excerpt of *Edisto* appeared in the *New Yorker*. Later that year, the novel was published separately. The esteemed American author Saul Bellow praised Powell as a promising new writer. *Edisto* won recognition as a National Book Award nominee for first novel in 1984 and was listed as one of the five best books of 1984 by *Time* magazine, and the novel garnered the Whiting Foundation Writer's Award for Powell. The author also received an American Academy and Institute of Arts and Letters' Rome Fellowship in literature for two years, 1986 and 1988.

Also in 1984, Powell took a job teaching writing at the University of Florida, back in his birth home of Gainesville. His next two books, short story collections *Typical* and *A Woman Named Drown*, were not as successful as Powell's first novel. Powell kept writing; however, his struggling writing career and alcoholism brought him to an all-time low. He made a bargain with himself that he would not drink any more alcohol until he made a million dollars, and the same night *Harper's* magazine called him about the purchase of "Trick or Treat," which went on to win an O. Henry Award and be published in the O. Henry Award collection for best short fiction. Powell later included "Trick or Treat" in his own collection, *Aliens of Affection* (1998). In 1996, Powell returned to the main character of *Edisto* in the sequel, *Edisto Revisited*.

In 2000, Powell published *Mrs. Hollingsworth's Men*, an atypical novel based on one of the characters in "Trick or Treat." This work uses an avant-garde style that plays with the narrative line, using a series of vignettes to illustrate this unusual character rather than a standard plot of rising action, climax, and resolution.

As of 2006, Powell continued to teach writing at the University of Florida in Gainesville, where he lived with his wife, poet Sidney Wade, and their two daughters.

PLOT SUMMARY

"Trick or Treat" takes place in the southern United States. It begins with Mrs. Hollingsworth walking to the grocery store dressed in lizard-skin cowboy boots and other unspecified strange clothes that she calls her "costumes." She has attracted the attention of a twelve-year-old boy, who has been watching her walk by for weeks from his yard. He is attracted to her and wants to make a pass at her. He finally takes the risk of talking to her. Mrs. Hollingsworth philosophizes about her relationship with the South, and the boy asks her if she is crazy. Offended, Mrs. Hollingsworth stalks off, and the boy is dismayed at having upset her and possibly ruined his chances at having sex with her.

The boy turns up at her house with a lawn mower at a later date. Mrs. Hollingsworth opens the door and looks him over in his tee-shirt and cut-off, frayed shorts which makes the boy self-conscious and defensive. He asks her if she wants him to cut her lawn. Meanwhile he is thinking of the lascivious things he would rather say to her. Mrs. Hollingsworth says, "No . . . But you can cut it anyway," and she shuts the door, testing him for worthiness by seeing whether he will cut her lawn without discussing terms. The boy whips across the front lawn, cutting the grass quickly. Mrs. Hollingsworth lets him into the backyard and recognizes his determination as a "sexual mission."

She is intrigued. While he finishes the back-yard, she makes *the* lemonade" and brings it to the backyard where she expects him to make his first true advance, setting "the lunacy of his early need and her late fatigue in motion." The sound of a police radio nearby sends the boy over her six-foot privacy fence before she realizes he is gone. The policeman, Sergeant Garcia, asks Mrs. Hollingsworth about the lawn mower, which turns out to have been stolen from a nearby hardware store. Mrs. Hollingsworth points out the boy's fleeing footprint in the mud but cannot help him any further than that. The boy calls her later that day and says, with a disguised voice, that he will take a rain check on the lemonade then hangs up without getting an answer. Later that day, Mr. Hollingsworth comes home, and Mrs. Hollingsworth goes through her ritual kiss and welcoming, all the while thinking of the boy and what it will be like to kiss him. She thinks of their impending affair as "an act of survival" because she is "anonymous" to her family, but not to the boy.

Two weeks later Halloween takes place, a holiday that Mrs. Hollingsworth dislikes for its stupid costumes and paranoia about candy that drives some people to use a metal detector to check for dangerous inclusions. The boy turns up on her porch in a suit and fedora and asks to be let in before he is spotted. He is afraid that his father and older brother are going to try and keep him away from Mrs. Hollingsworth's house. She lets him into her house and is struck by his likeness to Mickey Rooney's character Andy Hardy. But rather than hang his hat, the boy tosses his suit and hat into the trash compactor, revealing the same tee-shirt and cut-off shorts. The boy reveals that the suit and hat were

a disguise to hide from his father and brother, not a Halloween costume. This makes Mrs. Hollingsworth laugh, but she stops herself, afraid that she will offend the boy. She asks him if he steals a lot and if he has been arrested. He avoids the questions, teasing her that she talks too much. Then he confesses that the only time he was caught was, ironically, when he took a red WD-40 straw, an item which is very small and costs nothing by itself.

Mrs. Hollingsworth asks him what his name is and he tells her it is Jimmy. He wants it to be first names only, "like a hot line," but Mrs. Hollingsworth insists on full names. His name is Jimmy Teeth. She decides he must not be lying about his name because it is so unusual. She introduces herself to him as Janice Halsey, which he knows is not her name but does not catch on that it is her maiden name.

They sit in companionable silence for a while. Jimmy finally asks her if she does like the South after all, harkening back to their first conversation. They both agree that they like the South. Then Mrs. Hollingsworth tells him that the South is "a vale of tears that were shed a long time ago. It's a vale of *dry* tears." She tries to explain it further when Jimmy just sits there nodding in agreement. Jimmy is worried his plan is not going to work, that she is too "square," but then Mrs. Hollingsworth takes his hand. They look at each other over their clasped hands, nearly in tears from unspeakable emotions. Jimmy suddenly worries how to explain himself if someone walks in on them, and he laughs out loud when he realizes his lawn mower and his disguise clothes are gone. He worries that his laugh is inappropriate but then realizes that "nothing was inappropriate." Mrs. Hollingsworth decides that in entering this affair she cannot be an authority figure over Jimmy because that would make their relation-ship immoral.

Mrs. Hollingsworth tells Jimmy she will pay him eight dollars for the lawn mowing rather than five if he promises not to tell her husband. He agrees. Then she asks him if he still goes trick-or-treating. "No'm, I quit that." Mrs. Hollingsworth is pleased with his answer, and the matter is settled. She will have sex with him. Mrs. Hollingsworth likens herself to Orpheus, ascending "from the underworld with instructions to not look back, with some comical but not ungratifying sex mixed in."

CHARACTERS

Sergeant Garcia

Sergeant Garcia comes to Mrs. Hollingsworth's yard to investigate a report of a stolen lawnmower. His arrival causes Jimmy Teeth to run away because the lawn mower he used was indeed stolen. Mrs. Hollingsworth, having just been interrupted in her role of being seduced by Jimmy, looks at Garcia and thinks, "*sex with cops.*"

Janice Halsey

See Mrs. Hollingsworth

Mr. Hollingsworth

Mr. Hollingsworth has been married to Mrs. Hollingsworth for fifteen years. He works all day long. Their marriage is not unhappy, but on some level Mrs. Hollingsworth is upset by how perfect everything is. It is not clear if Mr. Hollingsworth is aware of her feelings.

Mrs. Hollingsworth

Mrs. Hollingsworth, the protagonist of "Trick or Treat," is a thirty-seven-year-old unhappy housewife who starts an affair with a twelve-year-old neighborhood boy. She has three children, one older than twelve and two younger. She has been married for fifteen years and leads a life of soap operas and tropical vacations, but she is dissatisfied with it all. Mrs. Hollingsworth enters into her affair with Jimmy Teeth as a means of survival, a way to be a person again rather than just a wife and mother. There are allusions to Mrs. Hollingsworth's fine education: her classical reference to the myth of Orpheus, who descends into the underworld to retrieve his wife Eurydice; her comment that she can read *Madame Bovary* in the original French; and her cryptic ponderings about the South as a vale of dry tears.

When the story opens, Mrs. Hollingsworth is walking down the street, dressed in odd clothes, and talking to herself about the South. She has a love/hate/love relationship with the South. She tells Jimmy that she likes the South, but its inconsistencies also make her crazy, and she cannot ignore them: "stray pets collected and neutered by alcoholics, unless it rains; automotive mechanical intelligence in inverse proportion to dental health; and *Halloween*." Out of boredom, she thinks of going insane, as if it were a choice. Jimmy's arrival in her life spares

TOPICS FOR FURTHER STUDY

- How does your family celebrate Halloween? How is Halloween celebrated in the United Kingdom, Australia, Canada, and other observant countries? Write a story that takes place during Halloween and exhibits unusual customs, whether real or fictional.

- The southern United States has a rich cultural tradition. Pick one aspect, such as music, literature, food, or pastimes, and research it thoroughly. Present your findings to your classmates in a creative fashion. You could make a poster or a diorama, write a song or create a dish to pass, or make up a game to play, for example.

- Mickey Rooney is mentioned in the story by Mrs. Hollingsworth when she compares Jimmy Teeth in his suit and hat disguise to this Hollywood actor. Watch one of Rooney's Andy Hardy movies and write a one-page response to the film, explaining why Mrs. Hollingsworth compares Jimmy to Mickey Rooney. Do they look similar? Behave similarly? Something else?

- In the United States, there have been a few high-profile cases of older women convicted of statutory rape because they conducted a sexual relationship with a minor male. Mary Kay Letourneau and Debra Lafave are two examples. From a different perspective, although fictional, is the cult classic film, *Harold and Maud*. Watch the movie as well as research a case of statutory rape, involving an older woman and a young boy. Write an essay that compares the movie, the case, and Powell's short story, concluding with your opinions on age of consent and statutory rape.

her from that path, and instead Mrs. Hollingsworth takes up with the young boy, a decision that many people would revile as statutory rape.

Jimmy Teeth

Jimmy Teeth is a twelve-year-old boy who is fixated on having sex with Mrs. Hollingsworth, a woman who is old enough to be his mother. He eventually gets up the nerve to talk to her and then visit her house. Jimmy has a freckled face that is round, like an uncarved pumpkin. His thoughts are full of profanities although he never says them aloud. He likes to wear tee-shirts with inappropriate sayings on them with the idea that Mrs. Hollingsworth will be impressed with his wit. He has young stringy legs but acts as mature as he can, given his age and inexperience.

At the beginning of the story, Jimmy does not know how to talk to women and starts off badly with Mrs. Hollingsworth, offending her by asking her if she is crazy, which is not far from the truth. Skipping school and stealing a lawn mower, Jimmy tries to initiate the affair by mowing her lawn and nearly succeeds. Despite his tribulations in getting close to Mrs. Hollingsworth, she is actually an easy catch because she is looking for something new or different to lend interest to her life. At the end of the story, Jimmy comes into her house, brave, determined, and mostly assured of success. Mrs. Hollingsworth accepts his swagger and his implicit invitation. Jimmy worries a little about being caught in her kitchen, but it does not stop him from his mission.

THEMES

Sexuality

Sexuality is a central theme in Powell's short story. Jimmy, at twelve years of age, is beginning puberty, a time when the human body matures from childhood to adulthood. An important aspect of this maturation is that the body readies itself for reproduction. Teenagers, full of new hormones from puberty, become interested in sex. Jimmy's pursuit of an older woman is daring and unusual, but his thoughts about sex, while still immature, are not. Since the story is told largely from Mrs. Hollingsworth's point of view, the reader does not learn directly why Jimmy is attracted to the housewife who is old enough to be his mother.

Contemporary society does not condone sex between adults and minors—people under the age of eighteen. Mrs. Hollingsworth deliberates whether to enter into a relationship with Jimmy, but she barely considers the question of pedophilia, a deviant behavior in which an adult engages in sex or sexual activity with a child. She recalls worrying about it with her own children but lets that thought go immediately and does not dwell on it. Mrs. Hollingsworth, in the final scene of the story, sees Jimmy as mature in some ways which in her view makes it okay for them to enter into a sexual relationship. Dissatisfied with her life and her family, including her husband, she looks forward to a relationship with Jimmy, "with some comical but not ungratifying sex mixed in."

Ennui

Ennui (pronounced awn-WEE), a word borrowed from French, denotes a feeling of continual weariness or melancholy which is not easily relieved. In Powell's short story, the character of Mrs. Hollingsworth exhibits ennui. Mrs. Hollingsworth attributes her sense of ennui to her boring husband and children as well as to her troubled relationship with the South. This ennui about the South is identified at the beginning of the story: "It loves me, it loves me not. I love *it*, I love it not." Mrs. Hollingsworth wears ridiculous clothes when she goes grocery shopping in an attempt to shake off her melancholy. But it is Jimmy Teeth who rescues her with his underage bravado and unusual—and risky—proposition. Although the end of the story pushes the boundaries of socially acceptable behavior, it is weirdly uplifting within its own terms because the point-of-view character, Mrs. Hollingsworth, is finally fighting to be free of her ennui.

Machismo

Machismo (pronounced ma-KEYS-mo), a word borrowed from Spanish, denotes an exaggerated sense of masculinity. Jimmy Teeth overcomes his young age with machismo to appeal to Mrs. Hollingsworth and attract her attention. He tries to talk to her (and thinks of even dirtier things to say that he believes are grown up perhaps because they are crass) but comes across as smart-mouthed. He mows her lawn as a way to spend time with her and get her to notice him but has to run away when the police come to reclaim the stolen lawnmower. Last, he appears on her doorstep dressed in a suit and fedora, like an old fashioned movie star, but the costume is really just a disguise to hide from his father and older brother. With confidence borrowed from machismo, Jimmy stuffs the disguise into the trash compactor and sits down at Mrs. Hollingsworth's kitchen table. This last visit finally wins her over as Jimmy appears to her to be more than just a boy from the neighborhood.

Escape

Escape is sought by both Mrs. Hollingsworth and Jimmy Teeth. Mrs. Hollingsworth is dissatisfied and bored and wants some kind of change, although she does not directly face and try to solve her problems. Instead, she turns outward from her dissatisfaction with her family life and toward a neighborhood boy. Jimmy Teeth wants to escape his youth and be grown up enough to date older women like Mrs. Hollingsworth. This combination of desires makes Jimmy's proposition of a sexual relationship to Mrs. Hollingsworth possible rather than ridiculous. Together, in their illicit union, Mrs. Hollingsworth and Jimmy anticipate being able to escape temporarily from the confining aspects of their separate lives. But escapism never provides a permanent resolution from the problems one avoids.

STYLE

Setting

"Trick or Treat" is set in the contemporary American South, although the specific state and city are not given. The time period is established by present-day references, such as Jimmy's tee-shirt advertising bubblegum which says "JUST BLOW ME," Volvos, a Lawn-Boy mower, Saran Wrap, WD-40, and running a metal detector over bags of Halloween candy. The South as a region is clearly established by Mrs. Hollingsworth, who talks about the South throughout the story, wondering at her mixed feelings about her environment. The South has a rich literary history because many fiction writers who grew up there, like Powell, use it as the setting for their stories.

Motif

A motif is a recurring image, idea, or detail. Motifs often support or underscore a theme, and they lend cohesion to the structure. In Powell's story, pumpkins are a reoccurring motif, which suggest innocence. When Mrs. Hollingsworth first notices Jimmy standing in his yard watching her, she describes him as "an uncarved, unlit pumpkin" and "a portrait of innocence." At the end of the story, after Mrs. Hollingsworth has decided to accept Jimmy's proposition, she recalls that "speaking pumpkin head on a fence." The distinction is made between a jack-o'-lantern (which is a pumpkin carved with a face and lit from the inside with a candle) and a regular pumpkin. Jack-o'-lanterns have a semblance of intelligence (the face) and life (the candle). Featureless, a pumpkin is unassuming and blank. Jimmy must fight past her perception of his young pumpkin-head to be noticed and taken seriously as a "suitor, or whatever he was."

Title

Given that "trick or treat" is the call children use on Halloween to bring adults to their doors with gifts of one sort or another, the title of this story seems to be used in an ironic or lurid way. Effective titles are always significant, drawing readers' attention to the essence or main idea of a work. On the surface, Jimmy comes to the door with a trick or treat for Mrs. Hollingsworth, a reversal of the holiday custom. Moreover, Mrs. Hollingsworth's willingness to engage the boy sexually, giving him the "treat" of sexual experience, may well turn out to be a sordid "trick," conditioning the boy to become a child molester as an adult and turning Mrs. Hollingsworth into a prostitute (of sorts) if this sexual encounter can be called a "trick," the common expression for a sexual encounter between a prostitute and someone who pays for her services.

HISTORICAL CONTEXT

Generation Y

Generation Y is an American cultural reference to people born between the late 1970s through the 1990s. As a term, it correlates to Generation X, known also as the post-baby boom generation. Generation Y as a group is a little difficult to categorize because it is still developing; those who fall within this cultural generation include high school students, college students, and people in their early thirties who are just getting started with their careers and families. Also, with this generation there is no catalyzing event, such as was World War II for the baby boomers.

What is understood about Generation Y is that members of this group experienced their

COMPARE & CONTRAST

- **1990s:** Following the recession of the 1970s and the 1980s, the United States experiences an economic boom. This boom is largely tied to the explosive growth of personal computers, the Internet, and related technologies.

  Today: After the September 11, 2001, terrorist attacks, the U.S. economy stalls, and Americans experience an economic recession. Corporations cut back staff, gas prices rise, and the real estate market in many parts of the country goes soft.

- **1990s:** Iraq invades Kuwait on August 2, 1990, the beginning of the Persian Gulf War. The United Nations comes to Kuwait's defense, led by U.S. forces. Most of the actual conflict takes place during January and February 1991. Kuwait is liberated, and the war won by February 28, 1991.

  Today: The United States invades Iraq on March 20, 2003, intending to overthrow Iraqi president Saddam Hussein, who is captured on December 13, 2003, and put on trial by the interim Iraqi government for crimes against humanity. Iraq meanwhile is torn apart by civil strife, and U.S. forces are unable to withdraw and ensure the safety of Iraqi citizens. The U.S. occupation receives strong criticism from all over the world, but a solution for stability is not readily apparent.

- **1990s:** Grunge culture, propagated by Seattle garage bands, such as Nirvana, is popular among American youth. It is characterized by loose-fitting, layered worn clothes. Alternative rock music, an outgrowth of punk and indie rock, is at its height. Generation X is associated with grunge culture.

  Today: Hip hop music and fashion are in the mainstream, following the popularity of gangsta rap styles in the 1990s. Hip hop fashion for men is characterized by baggy, low-slung pants, expensive sneakers, a durag (pronounced DOO-rag, a kerchief tied on the head), and heavy gold or platinum jewelry. Women also wear prominent jewelry, but their clothing tends to be close-fitting and revealing, especially at the waist.

---

formative years during a millennial rollover and the September 11, 2001, terrorist attacks on the United States. They have no significant memories of the cold war between the United States and the U.S.S.R. Generation Y was the first generation to grow up using personal computers, and thus its members have been given many other nicknames associated with technology such as the Net Generation and the Google Generation. Generation Y constituents grew up in an age of economic expansion, diversity, and expanding gay rights, although as of 2006 they appear not necessarily more liberal than their predecessors. Powell's character Jimmy probably belongs to Generation Y to judge by his obscene tee-shirt, a fashion style that became more culturally acceptable after the 1990s.

Bull Market of the 1990s

The 1990s was a period of speedy economic growth, during which the stock market was described by economists as bullish. A bull market describes a long-term trend when investor confidence is high and when the economy is good for many consumers. A bear market, by contrast, refers to a period when investors are pessimistic. A famous and extreme bear market in U.S. history occurred during the Great Depression of the 1930s.

The bull market of the 1990s was due in large part to the dot-com boom. Personal computers and Internet technologies grew exponentially as computers found their way into almost every aspect of life, including schools, businesses, and homes. People became concerned that the dot-com bubble would eventually burst because stock speculation and excessive confidence over-inflated the value of many dot-com companies. That bubble burst in the spring of 2000. The burst was a complicated process which included a ruling against Microsoft by the U.S. Supreme Court on April 3, 2000; a drop in business spending following the millennial rollover; and a market correction in March 2000. The deflation of the dot-com bubble turned this bull market into a bear market. Mrs. Hollingsworth's family is doing well financially, which may be because of the 1990s bull market economy in which they are living. She acknowledges the costly landscaping of her property and their annual vacations abroad. Also, her husband is making enough money so that Mrs. Hollingsworth can afford to stay home even after her children are in school full-time.

Halloween

Halloween is a secular holiday celebrated in the United States on October 31. The name of this holiday is derived from All Hallows Eve, or the night before All Hallows Day, which is also called All Saints' Day. All Saints' Day, a religious holiday for Catholics, is observed on November 1. Pope Gregory III moved All Saints Day to November 1 in the eighth century so as to coincide with the holidays already being celebrated by pagans. One of these pagan holidays, the one celebrated in Ireland, was Samhain (pronounced SOW-in), the beginning of winter. This holiday marked a time when the boundaries between the living and dead were permeable.

In modern tradition, children dress up in fantastical costumes on Halloween and visit their neighbors, calling out "trick or treat," a cheerful threat which earns the child a treat (often a piece of candy) as a bribe for their not playing a trick. Some people, reacting to reports of poison, razor blades, and other dangerous inclusions in this candy taken from strangers, go to extreme measures to check their children's treat bags. Mrs. Hollingsworth's neighbors, who run a metal detector over their kids' bags, express this cautionary attitude. In reality, many parents find a cursory examination for unwrapped or unusual pieces of candy to suffice. Incendiary reports about candy that has been tampered with say more about modern paranoia and isolation from one's neighbors than they do about what this secular holiday means to its celebrants.

The television show Desperate Housewives included a storyline in which a teenage boy becomes involved with an older woman, much like the characters in "Trick or Treat" ABC-TV/The Kobal Collection/Tom, Ron

CRITICAL OVERVIEW

When Powell's first novel, *Edisto* (1984), was reviewed by critics, many praised Powell. For example, Ron Loewinsohn of the *New York Times* praises him as "an extravagantly talented writer." Once a student of the post-modernist author Donald Barthelme, Powell incorporates occasional experimental methods, which are both admired and criticized. Overall though, he is regarded as a southern writer with a flair for lush language, southern dialect, humor, and original ideas. T. Coraghessan Boyle, in a review of *A Woman Named Drown* for the *New York Times Book Review*, admires Powell's "distinctive, understated humor." A *People Weekly* review by Campbell Geeslin of the same novel agrees, calling Powell "very funny." In a review

WHAT DO I READ NEXT?

- *City Life* (1970) is Donald Barthelme's third book of short stories. Barthelme was Powell's writing mentor when Powell was studying for his Master of Fine Arts degree in creative writing.

- *The Sound and the Fury* (1929), by William Faulkner, is a southern Gothic novel about the decline of the Compson family from southern nobility to vice-riddled tragedy, told in the stream-of-consciousness style.

- Set in South Carolina, *Edisto* (1984) is Powell's first novel, a coming-of-age story about Simons Manigault. *Edisto* garnered Powell much critical acclaim and remains a popular book.

- *Typical* (1991) is Powell's first collection of short stories. It features Powell's humor, lush language, and weird characters. The title story was selected for *The Best American Short Stories 1990*.

- *The Adventures of Tom Sawyer* (1876), by Mark Twain, is a novel about a young boy and his friends and their childhood adventures while growing up in the nineteenth-century American South. Twain is famous for his use of dialect in his writing; Powell also uses southern dialect and idioms to ground his stories in their southern settings.

- *Cat on a Hot Tin Roof* (1955), by Tennessee Williams, is a Pulitzer Prize-winning play about a wealthy southern family being torn apart by illness, alcoholism, greed, and despair.

- *Ferris Beach* (1991), by Jill McCorkle, is a novel about a young woman who struggles with her identity while caught between her own self-consciousness and her admiration for the wild women in her life. The novel takes place in McCorkle's home state of North Carolina.

- *Copacetic* (1984) is Yusef Komunyakaa's debut collection of poetry. Komunyakaa's style imbeds striking images into jazz rhythms. Komunyakaa grew up in pre–civil rights era Louisiana, and this southern upbringing influences his poetry.

---

of *Typical*, Powell's first collection of short stories, Amy Hempel, praises Powell's command of the short form, as well as his "almost unequaled ability to bring Southern colloquial speech to the page." Stefan Kanfer, reviewing *Typical* for *Time* magazine acclaims Powell's "unique gift for regional American comedy" as well as his "vigorous imagination." However, Michiko Kakutani's *New York Times* review of *Typical* was less positive. He protested that half of the collected stories were "brittle" and "seemingly unfinished," failing to "do justice to a writer as gifted as Mr. Powell." Scott Spencer, though, gave a glowing review of *Edisto Revisited*, describing Powell's style in terms that have become familiar. He enjoys Powell's "almost disorientingly dazzling turns of phrase," the "lushness of the writing," and his "brilliant prose."

Aliens of Affection, the book in which "Trick or Treat" appeared, was no less warmly received by critics than Powell's other works. A reviewer for *Publishers Weekly* describes Powell's writing as "hyperactive"—but in a good way; in other words, "hip, sexy and playful." The reviewer also nominated "Trick or Treat" as the best story in the collection. A. O. Scott gives a qualified but generally positive review of *Aliens of Affection* in the *New York Times Book Review*: "Powell is an inordinately gifted writer whose stylistic inventiveness has temporarily overwhelmed his perceptive acuity." Francis Hwang focuses on Powell's southern affinity in his review of the collection and describes the stories as "refreshingly vulgar, deeply humane." Elizabeth Brunazzi agrees that "Trick or Treat" is the best story in *Aliens of Affection*, but suggests a limitation in her opinion that this story is the only one "in which Powell successfully defines a female character." Brunazzi's review is mostly positive, celebrating Powell's book as "provocative" and "entertaining."

Powell focuses on the character Mrs. Hollingsworth from "Trick or Treat" in his slim novel, *Mrs. Hollingsworth's Men*. Reviews of this book are mixed. Critics still favor Powell's language, but some are puzzled by his unconventional approach. The book lacks a typical plot, called a "book of poems disguised as a novel" by *New York Times Book Review* critic Robert Kelly. Scott, writing about *Aliens of Affection*, sums up Powell's literary career so far: "In all of the stories there is the good humor and humane intelligence that make Powell's work so appealing."

CRITICISM

Carol Ullmann

Ullmann is a freelance writer and editor. In the following essay, she examines the southern Gothic elements in Powell's short story.

"Trick or Treat," by Padgett Powell, belongs to the southern Gothic subgenre of fiction. Southern Gothic is an offshoot of Gothic literature which is a genre that uses weird or supernatural elements in a story that examines social issues. Gothic is a type of romantic literature and borrows heavily from romanticism. Southern Gothic uses Gothic elements in conjunction with issues peculiar to the southern United States. The South has its own regional identity comprised of shared history, mythology, food traditions, and dialect. Predecessors to Powell in the southern Gothic subgenre include Flannery O'Connor, William Faulkner, Tennessee Williams, Harper Lee, and Eudora Welty—to name only a few. Powell uses Gothic elements in his story to raise it above the ordinary. Instead of being a simple tale of adolescent sexuality and mid-life disillusionment, "Trick or Treat" is a story of more mythic proportions, replete with talking pumpkins heads, adulterous lemonade, and costumed housewives walking to and from the grocery store.

Characters in Gothic stories exhibit a combination of sympathetic and grotesque elements such that the reader is intrigued but uncomfortable. "Trick or Treat" offers a glimpse into the life of a happily married but enraged housewife, Mrs. Hollingsworth. She both loves and hates the South. She is bored; she is lonely despite having a family. To counter her ennui, Mrs.

> THE EXCESS OF EMOTION AND THE DARK THEMES OF POWELL'S STORY MARK IT AS A GOTHIC IN A SOUTHERN SETTING, RESPLENDENT WITH THE ABSURD, THE GROTESQUE, AND THE PSYCHOLOGICALLY DISTURBING."

Hollingsworth dresses strangely and talks to herself while she walks. The finishing Gothic touch on this character is her justification for entering into a sexual relationship with a twelve-year-old boy, supposedly as a way to save her sanity. Insane women are also a common feature in Gothic stories.

> She was toying with the idea of losing herself. She did not want her mind to depart . . . she wanted the little craft of things that were considered *her*, that she considered her, to get loose and drift and turn just a little off-line.

Like Mrs. Hollingsworth, her young suitor Jimmy Teeth also combines the normal and the weird. It is not unusual for him, at twelve years old, to feel aroused around women whom he finds attractive; however, it *is* unusual for him to pursue a relationship with someone outside his age group, especially a woman old enough to be his mother. In the course of the story, Jimmy never mentions his mother although he does talk about his father and brother. Jimmy's mother may be missing from his life, either dead or absent, therefore complicating the reasons for Jimmy's interest in Mrs. Hollingsworth.

Jimmy's intense emotions and unusual, even absurd, behavior are components of a Gothic story. Another mark of absurdity is Jimmy's luck at stealing the lawnmower, leaping the six-foot fence to escape the police, and finally getting Mrs. Hollingsworth alone on Halloween night. He is a mixture of maturity and innocence, working hard to sell himself as old enough to be worth Mrs. Hollingsworth's notice. At the very end of "Trick or Treat," Mrs. Hollingsworth asks Jimmy if he still goes trick-or-treating. "No'm, I quit that," an answer which satisfies Mrs. Hollingsworth, as if giving up trick-

or-treating were a measurable milestone for maturity. When they exchange names, Mrs. Hollingsworth is struck by Jimmy's strange last name, Teeth, concluding that it is too weird to be made up. Jimmy's last name, Teeth, is another grotesque component. The name conveys images that are both sensual and aggressive.

Gothic stories seek to establish a certain atmosphere—brooding, ruined, lonely—which Mrs. Hollingsworth invokes at the beginning of the story while she ponders her love for the South, and its love for her. "Trick or Treat" is set in the southern United States just before and on Halloween. Halloween is the perfect time of year for a Gothic story because of its natural associations with the grotesque and morbid, a time when Gothic motifs are commonly used. The fact that Mrs. Hollingsworth and Jimmy finally commit to going ahead with their relationship on Halloween night is no coincidence. The southern setting enhances the Gothic character of Powell's story. Jimmy, still unclear about the regional history, asks Mrs. Hollingsworth what she means by the "south."

> "This," Mrs. Hollingsworth said, indicating with her arm the trees and air and houses and suspiring history and ennui and corruption and meanness and bottomland and chivalric humanism and people who are smart about money and people who don't have a clue and heroism and stray pets around them.

The arrival of Jimmy Teeth in Mrs. Hollingsworth's life is just the sort of grotesque event one can expect in a southern Gothic story. Her first, unnerving description of him is of "an uncarved, unlit pumpkin" peering over a picket fence and talking to her. The pumpkin head may be an allusion to Washington Irving's short story, "The Legend of Sleepy Hollow," a frightening American Gothic tale of a headless horseman who uses a pumpkin in place of his missing head. The pumpkin head also alludes to a jack-o'-lantern, which is a pumpkin that has been hollowed out, carved with a face, lit with a candle, and thus temporarily given an impression of life.

Jimmy later calls Mrs. Hollingsworth "Bonnie" and refers to himself as "Clyde," a reference to infamous criminals Bonnie Parker and Clyde Barrow who were in love and lived life on the run as they robbed their way across the Texas countryside in the 1930s. Bonnie and Clyde are tragic, romantic figures, who pursued lives of love and revenge that eventually killed them. This reference, therefore, casts Mrs. Hollingsworth and Jimmy as larger than life and destined for each other. Jimmy is also referred to as "Lolito," a reference to Vladimir Nabokov's novel *Lolita*, a tragic and comic story about an older man sexually obsessed with a twelve-year-old girl. Jimmy is Mrs. Hollingsworth's Lolito, and, as in Nabokov's novel, Powell has infused his story with as much potential for comedy as calamity.

The absurd and disturbing subject matter further defines Powell's story as Gothic. The most disturbing element of "Trick or Treat" is the sexual relationship that develops between Mrs. Hollingsworth and Jimmy Teeth. "It was hysterical, she was hysterical, it was perfect." In western culture it is not as common for younger men to date older women as it is for younger women to date older men; however, the twenty-five year disparity in their ages is the least upsetting aspect. No matter how she tries to justify the relationship or how mature and confident Jimmy behaves, if Mrs. Hollingsworth has sex with Jimmy she will have committed statutory rape. Even though Jimmy is consenting, the law denies him the ability to make the choice to consent until he is eighteen years of age. Legally and psychologically, Mrs. Hollingsworth is not considered a pedophile (an adult who is sexually attracted to children) but instead an ephebophile (an adult who is sexually attracted to adolescents). They are mutually exclusive terms. Mrs. Hollingsworth, loosened from the moorings of her safe and boring southern landing, lets herself drift out into these dark waters.

The excess of emotion and the dark themes of Powell's story mark it as a Gothic in a southern setting, resplendent with the absurd, the grotesque, and the psychologically disturbing. The characters of Mrs. Hollingsworth and Jimmy Teeth are at once familiar and yet twisted, discomforting. They turn to each other, as unlikely a pairing as they seem: a smart-mouthed youth and a well-educated housewife. For Mrs. Hollingsworth, this may just be the love that she has long sought from the South. For Jimmy, Mrs. Hollingsworth is both his conquest and his conqueror. Seeing no farther into their relationship than the first moment of its formation, the reader understands the Gothic tragedy of this story is the formation of that relationship itself.

Source: Carol Ullmann, Critical Essay on "Trick or Treat," in *Short Stories for Students*, Thomson Gale, 2007.

Brian J. Barr

In the following interview, Powell discusses the writing process, writing about the South, teaching, and the influence Donald Barthelme has had on him.

Padgett Powell has written some of the most lyrical and hilarious stories to emerge from the Southern literary tradition, and his characters are some of its rowdiest and most unforgettable. Powell embraces the stereotypical pickup trucks, cheap booze, and Piggly Wigglys that crowd the genre with an irascible, pessimist's wit, proving what a wonderful and silly thing it is to be Southern, and, ultimately, human. In a story titled "Typical," his character John Payne examines the circumstances that led him to realize he is "a piece of shit." In another, "Scarliotti and the Sinkhole," a brain-damaged man in a trailer perched atop a sinkhole watches *The Andy Griffith* Show, avoids his medication, and wonders what life will be like when his trailer finally goes underground ("The sinkhole was the kind of thing he realized that other people had when they had Jesus. He didn't need Jesus. He had a hole, and it was a purer thing than a man").

A student of Donald Barthelme, Powell first rose to national attention with his debut novel, *Edisto* (1984), the story of ten-year-old Simons Manigault and his wild adolescence in coastal South Carolina. It was nominated for the American Book Award for best first novel. Soon after, he began teaching at the University of Florida in his hometown of Gainesville, where he now serves as director of the MFA program. He has written three novels in addition to *Edisto—A Woman Named Drown, Mrs. Hollingsworth's Men, Edisto Revisited*—as well as two collections of short fiction, *Typical* and *Aliens of Affection*.

This conversation took place over a three-month span. Powell preferred that the interview take place via email because, in his words: "I rather despise the phone. Poets like the phone."

I. "What is one doing in a classroom finally but peddling his biases?"

[*Brian J. Barr:*] *A line from your short story "Chihuahua" won't leave my head. Your character*

says: "A man is supposed to be a kind of diversified portfolio of modest interest in things, none of which is to get out of hand." Obviously this was meant in jest by you as the writer, considering the character was undergoing psychiatric treatment for "winder-peekin." But I'm curious—do you feel our society places too much emphasis on turning us into well-rounded people?*

[Padgett Powell:] I think the pique I feel hasn't to do with well-roundedness, per se, which after all might make little Renaissance men of us, or at least a good Boy Scout. "Diversified portfolio" refers more to custodialism in life, which has irked me to no end. We are to be a clan of choosers among our "options," each of which to greater or lesser degree aggrandizes us into more and more secure positions. I have a number of dubious heroes in my writing who have renounced this custodializing, or who have not had the opportunity to renounce it (Wayne, say). As a result of my own repudiation, I am these days having to ask people the difference between term and universal life insurance, etc.

Your characters also seem to be wrangling with their own insignificance in life. Is this a reflection of your own struggle?

No. My insignificance is not to be contested.

You were a roofer in Texas for quite a few years before enrolling in the University of Houston. Because roofing is such a blue-collar work environment, did you feel a need to keep it secret from your coworkers that you wanted to write stories for a living?

I did not declare to anyone that I wanted to write any more than one would declare he wants to be President. They of course knew something was wrong with me, but I was usually the boss so not much was made of it.

I'm only asking this because I remember working on house-painting crews in Pennsylvania and they'd all laugh and shake their heads when I'd jot down story ideas in a notebook.

I was once caught reading James Dickey when I was not out at the strip club with them and there was some head shaking over this.

Do you find any sort of parallel between hard labor and the writing life?

I believed at the time I came out of that (labor) that I would be a better writer for having done it, and for being in physical shape. I still subscribe to this idea. I am suspicious of a soft body.

Is there anything about hard labor you miss?

After thirty, working for a living with your body is contraindicated. You always miss being around hard people without imaginary issues.

You've been employed at the University of Florida for twenty-plus years. In that time, have you developed any sound philosophy on the teaching of writing?

In the beginning one admits he knows not what he is doing and is possibly effective. In the end one gets tired, begins to believe he knows what he is doing, and is not possibly effective. My regular approach these days is usage instruction followed by begging for coherence. If we get past those hurdles, we might look at what I call The Rules, and at Miss O'Connor's dictum (in a letter to Hawkes): "The higher the fantasy of action, the more precise the writing, and that is the way it ought to be."

The Rules? I'm intrigued . . .

Rule 1 is The Gosling Rule. The story concerns the first thing the reader sees move. Rule 2 is that the problem, or the apparent and necessarily related problem, must appear soon, in the first paragraph if not the first sentence. Rule 3 is a complex function [wh = f(c1,c2,c3 . . . + e + t)] involving withholding. Rule 4 is the bar test: everything must be said more or less as if you might say it to a stranger in a bar. Rule 5 is the doozie quotient. Rule 7 is the 3 Questions: Did it, could it, should it happen? Before any of these rules apply the writing must place itself unmurkily on the spectrum of credulity.

These rules are not of course actually in this or any other order. Twain's early count of nineteen rules, some say twenty-two, etc., is a pretty good count that still holds up. Rules beget rules and you need to make sure some of them are sterile or you'll have overcrowding and chaos in the pen.

I've always imagined that because your voice is so strong, young writers in the MFA program at U of F find it easy to slip into mimicry, sort of aping your dialogue and characters. Do you see a lot of mini-Padgetts coming through your classroom?

One hopes not. Either it does not happen, or I am blind to it. There was some talk, I think, of Chris Bachelder's having been after me somewhat;

I did not see it. I encouraged him in what he was doing. Perhaps he was. What is one doing in a classroom finally but peddling his biases?

II. "Them southern dogs is hell, ain't they?"

Since you write largely about the South, were there any writers early on that influenced you in writing about where you're from?

Yes: I read the celebrity writers of the day like Mailer and Vidal and Capote, and I regard two of those as Southern. Then I graduated to what I thought of as more serious writers, and these were Southern: Faulkner, O'Connor, Tennessee Williams, and [Walker] Percy. I regard those four writers as a family of sorts: Percy is directly out of O'Connor by Faulkner. Then I met Don Barthelme and had to adjust my view some to include him and Beckett and so forth. I think Barthelme is Southern in the extreme—he knows who lost the Civil War and how, for example. Texas is the South, one with its own little secession ongoing.

When you say Faulkner, O'Connor, and Percy are "more serious" than Gore Vidal & Co., what distinguishes them for you?

"More serious" will not win friends; arguably Vidal is about as serious as it gets. What I intended to suggest was that I had been drawn to certain writers partly owing to their celebrity: you could see Mailer and Vidal fighting on *Dick Cavett*.

MAILER: "I would not hit anyone here, you're all too small."

CAVETT: "Smaller?"

MAILER: "Intellectually smaller."

CAVETT: "Perhaps you'd like another chair to help contain your giant intellect."

MAILER: I'll accept the chair if you'll accept fingerbowls.

CAVETT: Fingerbowls? Fingerbowls. I don't get that. Does anyone on our team [Vidal and Janet Flanner] want that one?

MAILER: Think about it.

CAVETT: Fingerbowls.

MAILER: Why don't you just read another question off your list, Cavett?

CAVETT: Why don't you just fold it five ways and put it where the moon don't shine?

Capote on Carson, I think, telling Jacqueline Susann that she looked like a truck driver in drag, saying elsewhere he was an alcoholic, a drug fiend, a homosexual, and a genius. This looked like fun. Then I discovered there was an off-TV stratum: behind a Mailer was a Bellow, a Roth, and behind Vidal and Capote was a Faulkner and an O'Connor. In a sense I came to think these behind-the-scenes fellows were real writers, or more real, because they were less celebrated; they were harder, quieter, and so forth. It's just how a boy discovers the terrain. Of course it keeps going: behind all these is Shakespeare, behind him Chaucer, and so forth.

It seems that in the world of Southern lit, all writers are direct descendants of Faulkner and O'Connor and, maybe more recently, Barry Hannah. Do you find it stifling that no matter how wildly different a Southern writer's voice may be, a parallel will always be drawn to the Grandmother and Grandfather of Southern lit?

Not stifling—exhilarating, if one is going to react to the nonsense at all. It's a good bloodline, and one must be from a bloodline. To paraphrase a dogfighter I know, them Southern dogs is hell, ain't they?

Your prose is also quite dependent on rhythm and your sense of timing very powerful. On top of these writers, are you a fan of music? Does it figure into your work?

Short answer: yes. Who don't like rhythm? Even the people who can't catch a beat on the dance floor fancy that they like rhythm and are unpersuaded that they don't have a clue, which is why they are so dangerous out there.

Long answer: the second live band I heard, in 1966, after a set of pure garbage from some high school boys in a battle of the bands that confirmed everything one's parents said about the badness of rock and roll, was a band calling itself the 1% with my schoolmates Allen Collins and Bob Burns in it. We were fourteen. They transfixed us, with correct guitar, want of clutter, clean bass, and rhythm. They became Lynyrd Skynyrd. I took Latin at the same time; Latin is rhythm on the page. Latin also teaches you English in a way that you will not learn it otherwise. I kick myself today for never having done a profile of Allen Collins before he died. We were in homeroom in the tenth grade at Nathan Bedford Forrest High and he'd come in dead-tired from playing until three in the morning. They were bar none the best band anybody ever heard. I was up to Virgil at that point. When you went and saw the 1% on Saturday night, about all you could say was "mirabile dictu."

III. "I just naturally got tired or empty of the purely realistic utterance"

How long were you writing before Edisto *was published? Can you remember some of the things you were working on?*

I wrote figments of *Edisto* in college as early as 1972. Scruff Taurus wrote a column called "Fighting About Writing" in the school newspaper I edited. I did sketches of him beating up members of the English department there, and used them to try to charm the professor I eventually would model the Doctor on. It worked. She said the writing was good. I said the things were a joke, cartoons. She said she knew that but the prose was strong. Here was the birth of the literary mother. She soon found out I had not read Faulkner and, appalled, gave me her copy of *Absalom, Absalom!* That is the birth of the literarily mothered boy.

This writing and some more that would become the early stuff of *Edisto* was stolen in a roofing truck in San Antonio around 1976. I envisioned my pages blowing about the desert at Eagle Pass, Texas, where I imagined the truck being taken into Mexico. I think I had about forty pages, the first three chapters of the book, when I met Barthelme in 1981. He said, "You've thought about this a bit." "Yes." "You'll settle down. You're just nervous. Give me all you've got." He was referring to a certain ersatz-Faulkner alignment things had taken. The book was then taking more literally the Doctor's desire that her son sound like a writer, perhaps specifically like those whose books she had given him.

Simons was in fact named Huck early on.

Am I to assume Scruff Taurus was your pseudonym in the college paper? Seems too perfect a name.

I wrote the column and all the other articles in the paper, about ten pseudonyms altogether. Scruff Taurus was the son of Norman Mailer by a black girl from the Carolina coast who could sing jazz—he was, thus, the prototypical White Negro of Mailer's fevered fancy. This offspring was perhaps suggested by Mailer's having a white hero not unlike himself in *American Dream* who was sleeping with a black jazz singer. I was just localizing things a bit, and by having in my mind Mailer as the father I could have the son do some Mailer parody, which I could do. This figure, Taurus, toned down a good deal, was a secure armature to take into *Edisto*. I had to get Taurus out of the heroic position because he was a cartoon; I replaced him with another cartoon, Simons, but a more cuddly cartoon. The matter of race could be reduced to Simons's boyish speculations, where it would be safe.

Do you feel fiction affords one the opportunity to address race more openly than, perhaps, essays or journalism?

Any address of race is subject to a charge of racism. I suppose fiction affords some sheathing armor, but the bull is coming nonetheless.

This college professor you mention, could she be considered your literary mother? Did she mother you, literarily?

She did. She said, "The prose is strong," she said, "I've had intelligent students before, but not brilliant," and she dropped that Modern Library copy of *Absalom, Absalom!* in my lap, with her maiden name in the flyleaf. At that moment I had a literary mother and a woman interested in my literariness. It was working. Cf. Faulkner about all writing having to do with getting in someone's pants.

Could Barthelme be considered your literary father? He played a significant role in the shaping of Edisto, yes?

Barthelme edited the book, cutting for cleanliness and strength. In terms of my overall development as a writer, he lamented that he had found me already "fully formed." By this he meant that I was, then, formed by my vision of realistic writing as more or less an amalgam of Faulkner and O'Connor and Williams and Percy and, say, Mailer.

I could not at the time make sense of Barthelme and Beckett and so forth. I never would have had I not, in knowing Don personally, seen that he was a red-blooded normal dude, not a wacko that the writing might suggest. Before I met him in fact I anticipated a Warhol kind of beast. He showed up in jeans and a yoked cowboy shirt a little drunk and introducing himself as Don and shaking hands firmly. We had not had a teacher to that point in our tour in Houston who would deign shake hands.

I referred to Don, as did many of the students, as Uncle Don. He did not shape *Edisto* beyond cleaning up, with considerable deftness, what I gave him. He could have been a professional editor of the highest caliber. He did in fact select the ten non-consecutive chapters that were sent to the *New Yorker*. They admitted later that they would not have seen that excerpt had they been given the entire book at first.

I assumed some influence from Don along what we'll call surreal lines only later. Either that or I just naturally got tired or empty of the purely realistic utterance. I've swung so far in this direction now that I'm virtually unpublishable. Don himself at this age was swinging back to realism; he was a man of sense.

So, are your usual outlets not receptive to your surreal work? Would you say a story like "Manifesto" is exemplary of the direction you've swung?

The larger commercial venues do not receive wacky mode. "Manifesto" is about halfway out on the surreal moonshot, I'd say. It's a dialogue between two men who appear to be one man, for the convenience of smooth flux. That is one of the entertaining things about it, to me—a dialogue that is a monologue. I have thinner and weirder action than that, I'm afraid.

What sort of publishing snags have you run into with this kind of work?

Snags? Just, you know, "We pass, we pass, we pass . . ."

I think it's admirable that you refuse to lasso your creative potential for the simple sake of commercial viability. It seems you just let your writing fly and if that means nobody wants what comes of it, so be it.

Nothing to admire. No sacrifice involved, but rather an enfeeblement that prevents any other kind of writing than that which one does. I used to ask Don why he did not write a blockbuster and cash in, to which he'd say, "Can't." I thought he meant can't violate my pure vision, my self. He meant "can't," as hard as that is to believe, given his range (to wit, his satires). By the way, on the subject of his Southernness, folk should have a look at "The Sea of Hesitation." Only a Southerner at heart knows that much about the Wawer off the top of his head, and can write "Proceed with your evil plan, sumbitch."

IV. "I try to assault what passes for southernness if I can"

*Is it true you view writing as a spoiling of
paper? Can you expound?*

I take this phrase from Barthelme, who was
always two-wording the world. We were, he
averred, but spoiling paper. Similarly, once
when I asked him if he wasn't, after eleven
books, satisfied, he said, with a little backhand-
ing of the space near him, as if dismissing something, "Oh, I have my ... *little things.*" I was
aghast, somewhat. I am not so aghast now,
beginning to get it.

*By "little things," did Barthelme mean he had
only a few things he was satisfied with in his writing? It's a terrifying thought, if so.*

He meant that his things were little things.
He was equally dissatisfied by all of them. Here's
the actual conversation:

[Padgett Powell:] Are you satisfied?

[Donald Barthelme:] Of course I'm not
satisfied!

[Padgett Powell:] You have eleven books—

[Donald Barthelme:] Oh, I have my [*batting
them away*] *little things.*

*When you say you are beginning to get it, are
there only a few things you are satisfied with in
your past work? Can you single them out?*

No, it is not a discriminatory dissatisfaction;
it is a realizing that the work is not large.

*Do you have an approach in creating
characters?*

No approach. Unless one's talent is large,
characters are a portion or aspect of oneself, a
generally inexcusable facet, which is where the
mantel of "fiction" comes in handy.

*I've been thinking about this business of
Southernness. I know of a West Virginia writer,
Ann Pancake, who spoke of a "responsibility" she
feels in representing "her people" in her fiction. Do
you take similar precautions with characters?*

I try to assault what passes for Southernness
if I can. This puts me a tad outside the good-old-
boy network, I like to think. This thinking might
be more hopeful than accurate. Actually, the
idea of having a position at all with respect to
characters or Southernness or to characters and
Southernness strikes me as the wrong thing to
do. Having a position at all, of any sort, seems
contraindicated. I wish it weren't too late to go
to chiropractic school.

*Yeah, you're definitely outside the good-old-
boy network. Even though I place* Aliens of
Affection *on the same pedestal of short fiction as*
Airships *and* Everything That Rises Must
Converge, *something about you and your work
overall does reek of a general outsiderism, as if
there is no easy category yet for what you do.*

I would never have thought that those two
books could be twinned in any way beyond that
they are Southern. She was our Hera. Barry
Hannah is a full mortal with his ear to the oracle
hole in the ground. The ground has a little whis-
key moistening it. Barry has to brush this moist
dirt from his ear and run home and write down
what he's heard. He is very good at that. I think I
inhabit a liquid fey interface between "believing"
in the South and making fun of folk who believe.
But, as I say, I think it even feyer to ponder one's
position in all this. I pitch for a softball team of
grad students tonight. Feeling primed. We are
the Sinkholes, which we like to pronounce in the
Spanish way.

*This balance between believing and making
fun of those who believe, do you think you'd be
able to achieve it if you were living and working in,
say, Montana, or some other region of the US?*

Well, sure, but it takes time to develop the
sense of the local game. It might take a lifetime in
fact. I have lived in Montana, by the way, long
enough to begin to at least appreciate that it is
not Civil War ground. It is the ground of our
greatest genocide. What bastards we were.
Arguably worse bastards than we were on Civil
War ground, but very refreshing to be off Civil
War ground and free of that particular debate.

V. "It is very hard for us to comprehend
what we are"

*You're a big fan of buffalo. Can you tell me
how you came to buffalo and why you appreciate
them so?*

Yes. There were sixty million buffalo on the
Plains; some conservative estimates are as low as
only thirty million. Apparently you could see
herds that went beyond the horizon, the ground
appearing to ripple as they moved. We got them
down to about three hundred head in one notable last herd that was offered to the US government for sale, which declined. Canada bought it.
Canada, to where we'd chased the Nez Percé.
Today, there is a federal buffalo reserve outside
of Missoula that great fanfare is made of; it is
only 1800 acres and it has on it from three

hundred to five hundred buffalo. I like them because they seem gently wild, as opposed to violently wild, and they have the huge rump-like hump, the giant head, the eyeball the size of a billiard ball. What is not to like? We killed them all.

And of course the Indians today are still in a world of hurt, where we put them, after killing their meat. It is very hard for us to comprehend what we are. The details of our history are so repellent, once you start to get the fine print, that you fall back dazed and fail to retain what you've just read. Chief Joseph alone will appall.

Did you only come to love buffalo when you saw one up close in Montana, or was it just a general admiration that came from reading about them or seeing them on television?

I saw one quarantined for brucellosis here on a prairie in Florida about twenty years ago, a big bull that was apparently going to live out his days alone. He was resting on the ground, upright, like a dog. Then in Montana I saw them close enough to almost touch, in Yellowstone, trotting in the snow. You could hide and they'd come by, close. You want to tousle them.

Have you ever thought of writing a book of naturalism on the buffalo? Something like Rick Bass's The Ninemile Wolves? *Do you have any interest in nonfiction?*

Nonfiction is exhausting. I agreed recently with an agent to consider doing a book on a Shaolin kung fu priest in New York, and got all bothered up in thinking about camping out in NYC for a year and penetrating the wude in a big-time Capotean/Wolfeish way, and never heard back from the agent. So, no. My little piece on the world-champion armwrestler took two months and more work than two books of fiction. But if I could get up with some whorigi-nal beeves and talk to Ted Turner, I'm there. I want to have a buffalo you can saddle up and ride. I am afraid of horses but I would not be sore afraid of a buffalo. A man with a buffalo would not need anything else.

Source: Brian J. Barr, "Interview with Padgett Powell," in *The Believer*, Vol. 4, No. 7, September 2006, pp. 1–15.

Thomson Gale

In the following essay, the critic gives an overview of Padgett Powell's work.

> PADGETT POWELL IS 'A TOUGH WRITER, REMARKABLY RESISTANT TO DEMOCRATIC NOTIONS OF RIGHT AND WRONG, WHAT'S FAIR AND WHAT'S UNFAIR,' CONCLUDED SCOTT SPENCER. . . ."

Padgett Powell burst onto the literary scene in 1984 with his first novel, *Edisto*. A college chemistry major turned day-laborer and roofer, Powell nurtured his literary aspirations by reading American novelist William Faulkner's works in his spare time and eventually enrolled in the University of Houston's creative writing graduate program. In the words of *Time* critic R. Z. Sheppard, *Edisto*, which was adapted from Powell's master's thesis, showed that its author had "all the literary equipment for a new career: a peeled eye, a tuning-fork ear, and an innovative way with local color and regional dialect."

Critics have compared Powell's technique to that of the great U.S. regional writers, including Mark Twain, Tennessee Williams, J. D. Salinger, Flannery O'Connor, and Faulkner. Although he has been influenced by the styles of past writers, Powell's mode of expression remains distinctive. Reviewing *Edisto* for the *Washington Post Book World*, Jonathan Yardley commented that much of the book is "so fresh and original; Padgett Powell clearly knows what he is doing, and he does it very well." In a piece for the *New York Times Book Review*, Ron Loewinsohn similarly praised Powell, calling him "an extravagantly talented writer."

Named for the predominantly black, rural, backwater section of undeveloped South Carolina coastline near what the narrator calls the "architect-conceived, Arab-financed" Hilton Head, *Edisto* is a young man's episodic account of his unusual coming of age. Simons (pronounced "Simmons") Manigault, the book's narrator, is a precocious, prepubescent twelve-year-old trapped in a seemingly incomprehensible world—that of adults. Simons's parents are separated and his college-professor mother, known among the local blacks as "the Duchess," has decided that her only son should be a writer.

Simons is no ordinary child. He is, stated Sheppard in *Time*, "one of the most engaging fictional small fry ever to cry thief: sly, pungent, lyric, funny, and unlikely to be forgotten." In a review in *Newsweek*, Peter Prescott pointed to the "great comic effect" the author manages in his treatment of Simons: Powell endows his protagonist with a sophisticated sort of innocence that is at once poignant and amusing.

In return for his pursuit of literary knowledge, Simons's mother gives him free reign to do virtually anything he pleases. Simons frequents the Baby Grand, a predominantly black local bar whose clientele has dubbed the youth something of a folk hero. Simons explains, "I am a celebrity because I'm white, not even teenage yet, and possess the partial aura of the Duchess." The Duchess's aura, however, is informed by her drinking and her promiscuity, both of which figure in her son's development.

It is not until Taurus, the Duchess's mysterious lover and Simons's substitute father, enters the story that the boy, in a sense, becomes a man. Sybil Estess, writing in *Southwest Review*, dubbed Taurus a "blessed intruder into [the] story," who teaches Simons how to live fully in the present. Taurus inspires in Simons the courage to move on without knowing what might happen in the future. "Something is happening, happening all the time," Simons learns, and a life in Edisto is not what lies ahead for the boy. Taurus's influence allows Simons to willingly accept the changes he is about to encounter. By the end of the novel, Simons's parents reunite and the family moves to the cardboard world of Hilton Head. Taurus, having fulfilled his role as teacher in the story, exits Simons's life as unexpectedly as he had entered it.

Powell's pages are filled with the symbolism, colorful characters, and precise vernacular of past regionalist giants, but the young writer, as pointed out by Jonathan Yardley in his review in *Washington Post Book World*, has added "a new twist, and a most agreeable one." Avoiding the trap of sentimentality, Powell addresses the highly developed and commercial "new" South of the 1980s, "finds it imperfect—but accepts it anyway." An air of honesty permeates the author's advice to readers living on the brink of the twenty-first century: the "best thing to do," Powell tells us through Simons, "is to get on with it."

Edisto is ironic in its implication that one must learn the ways of the world in spite of one's parents. But more than an examination of a youth's rite of passage, the book, explained Peter Ross, writing in *Detroit News*, is "a masterwork of invention, and even more of intelligent feeling, of emotion tempered by sound thinking." Robert Towers's evaluation of *Edisto* echoed Ross's enthusiastic response. Towers wrote in the *New York Times Review of Books* that he was "charmed by the book's wit and impressed by its originality. Some turn of phrase, some flash of humor, some freshly observed detail, some acutely rendered perception of a child's pain or a child's amazement transfigures nearly every page."

Powell's follow-up to *Edisto* is the novel titled *A Woman Named Drown*. Like its predecessor, Powell's second book explores conventional occurrences in unconventional terms. Al, the narrator of *A Woman Named Drown*, has been called a grown-up version of *Edisto*'s Simons Manigault. Al is working on his Ph.D. in inorganic chemistry when he receives a surprising good-bye letter from his girlfriend of six years. In reaction, he quickly moves in with a woman whom he hardly knows: an aging actress named Mary Constance Baker, whose last role was the lead in a play titled *A Woman Named Drown*. Mary uses Al as a substitute for her late husband, and after they roam around Florida together for a while, she leaves him in a motel to continue, in Powell's words, his "little downside sabbatical"—alone. Paul Gray of *Time* suggested that the book's hero "arrives back where he started a mildly wiser fellow." *A Woman Named Drown*, as T. Coraghessan Boyle noted in the *New York Times Book Review*, recreates "the distinctive, understated humor that is Mr. Powell's signature. He presents a terrific, hyperreal dialogue in quick, bludgeoned pieces, and his narrator's phrasing and dialect are always surprising and inventive."

In 1996 Powell returned to the character of Simons Manigault in the novel *Edisto Revisited*. The narrative begins just after Simons has graduated from architectural school. Gripped by a profound malaise, he has no desire to design anything. Then he meets his beautiful cousin Patricia and, according to *Tribune Books* contributor Alexander Theroux, "wastes no time in laying the foundation for an illicit, passionate affair in good Southern Gothic tradition with this eye-catching relation of his. But this is a novel about chronic drift," added Theroux, "and our wandering protagonist is not about to find salvation in the arms of a woman. Within a month he goes off to Texas. . . . Drift embraced as lifestyle frees him from the suffocating exigencies of life. Drifting allows Simons to a degree to become attuned to the small poetries of everyday existence, at least so he believes in his self-indulgent, overly romantic belief that work robs you of your soul."

Although *Edisto Revisited* did not draw the lavish praise that its predecessor had, reviewers still found much to like in the book. Theroux noted: "Powell is blessed with a quirky, thoughtful prose style. There are deftly drawn, image-filled passages. . . . Powell paints a spare yet vivid portrait of a seedy South in a novel concerned with giving up on the battles of life before they begin. . . . [*Edisto Revisited*] is cynical and yet oddly compassionate." Writing in *Washington Post Book World*, Valerie Sayers described the book as "frustrating and exhilarating, dark and light, willful and mysterious. I wish there were more of it."

Padgett Powell is "a tough writer, remarkably resistant to democratic notions of right and wrong, what's fair and what's unfair," concluded Scott Spencer, a reviewer in *New York Times Book Review*. "In the intricacies of his brilliant prose, he conceals a stunning stubbornness, a disdain for nostalgia, spirituality, sobriety and, finally, even identity." Spencer went on to call *Edisto Revisited* "a puzzling work of high style, a rendering of haplessness that seems to poeticize passivity. While his novel may make you wonder if it has much of what is called meaning, Mr. Powell finally overpowers such doubts with his countless quotable passages, his humor and his seductive evocation of the romance of giving up." Also in the *New York Times Book Review*, A. O. Scott called *Edisto* and *Edisto Revisited* "two of the smartest and most affecting recent fictional treatments of young Southern manhood."

Southern manhood is the informing theme of *Mrs. Hollingsworth's Men*. As the novel commences, the eponymous Mrs. Hollingsworth is sitting down to make a grocery list. What is drawn from her pen, however, is not a list of vegetables but rather a series of reflections on men, quickly evolving into fictions peopled by Confederate general Nathan Bedford Forrest, a shady businessman named Roopit Mogul, and two bumbling criminals, Oswald and Bundy. Mrs. Hollingsworth also details her take on the world, her prejudices, and her dissatisfaction with the mundane pursuits of her "Tupperware" daughters and inattentive husband. In his *New York Times Book Review* piece on the novel, Robert Kelly wrote that *Mrs. Hollingsworth's Men* "is a slim, sly deceiver of a book, full of mirth and wickedness . . . At the core of the novel, something rings true: a woman thinks her thoughts. And they create a tumultuous narrative, full of the rancorous prejudices involved in responding to the world around you."

A *Publishers Weekly* reviewer called *Mrs. Hollingsworth's Men* an "evocative daydream of a novel," adding: "This challenging but highly inventive narrative is just quirky enough to hit plenty of literary funnybones." *Booklist* correspondent Neal Wyatt found the vignettes "loosely connected, sometimes incoherent, but beautifully written and oddly appealing." And Kelly deemed the work "indeed a spare book, slender yet full of excitements and dubious desires."

Critics suggest that part of Powell's appeal as a writer lies in his honest treatment of universal themes. His rare ability to attach an intangible moment of insight to a single, concrete experience adds intimacy and credence to his words. A. O. Scott observed that the author is noted for "his devotion to characters who reject the bland conformity of contemporary life: to spirited eccentrics and losers of all kinds. This affection may be a legacy of the South's defeat in the Civil War, or it may have a more general, more strictly contemporary relevance."

In "Hitting Back," an essay Powell published in *A World Unsuspected*, a collection of childhood memoirs edited by Alex Harris, the author remembers an incident that sparked a transformation in the way he looked at the world: disapproving little Don, a so-called "friend," put dog excrement on the author's Sunday best. As Powell puts it, "I recall this as my very first instance of moral outrage." In the same essay, Powell mourns the tainting of his southern junior high school innocence by the mindset of ignorant whites in positions of power. He and his friend were punished for breaking their school's segregated sex rule on the bus, considered an indirect but effective way of keeping black boys away from white girls. Powell recollects with a sense of loss the naivete that inspired his befuddlement when asked if he knew why this rule existed. "That was precisely it," he recalls. "We couldn't begin to know."

In a phone interview with Andrea Stevens in *New York Times Book Review*, Powell reflected: "I couldn't fit in ten years ago. I couldn't fit in twenty years ago. My interest remains with those who fail deliberately and those who can't help it." The author also once explained to *CA:* "Bad luck at fishing and worse with women made me what little writer I am. Had things turned out a bit differently, I'd be Doug Flutie. Reading William Faulkner's *Absalom! Absalom!* did it."

Source: Thomson Gale, "Padgett Powell," in *Contemporary Authors Online*, Thomson Gale, 2006.

Brad Vice

In the following essay, Vice gives a critical analysis of Padgett Powell's work.

Padgett Powell is one of the most linguistically inventive American authors and one of the fiction writers of the contemporary South who follows the tracks laid by William Faulkner, the man Flannery O'Connor once described as the "big train." "The first thing I ever wrote was bad Faulkner," admits Powell in his contributor's note in a 1997 issue of *The Oxford American* magazine, which featured his autobiographical essay "On Coming Late to Faulkner". In the article Powell addresses his former self, the unpublished neophyte, in relation to Faulkner: "[You] with your two-cylinder syntax are a mule and cart being borne down by the Dixie Limited. Fond mocking is, actually, all that you can do, given the roar of the train that blasts you from the track." One might say the same of the mature and successful Powell, whose "fond mocking" is not always easy to digest, with his goofy, white-trash sensibility mixed with an ornate, almost Latinate syntax. Since finding Faulkner, Powell has, in his own words, "made" six books of fiction: four novels, *Edisto* (1984), *A Woman Named Drown* (1987), *Edisto Revisited* (1996), and *Mrs. Hollingsworth's Men* (2000); and two collections of short stories, *Typical* (1991) and *Aliens of Affection* (1998). *Typical* comprises twenty-two short stories, most of them thematically connected vignettes scattered among a few longer, more traditional short stories. *Aliens of Affection* comprises two novellas, "Wayne" and "All Along the Watchtower", and five full-length short stories. Powell is also a prolific nonfiction essayist; his articles and book reviews have appeared in many literary magazines and newspapers, including *The New York Times Book Review* and *Esquire*.

THESE STORIES DISPLAY A FURTHER RENOVATION OF POWELL'S STYLE AND AN INTENSIFICATION OF HIS LINGUISTIC PLAYFULNESS. HE USES EXTRAVAGANT LANGUAGE AS A TOOL TO CREATE FURTHER IRONIC SPACE BETWEEN AUTHOR AND CHARACTERS AS WELL AS BETWEEN CHARACTERS AND READERS."

Powell was born in Gainesville, Florida, on 25 April 1952. His father, Albine Batts Powell, was a brewmaster, and his mother, Bettyre Palmer Powell, taught school. The family relocated to South Carolina when Powell was a young boy. His first love was not literature but science, and in 1975 he graduated from the College of Charleston, in Charleston, South Carolina, with a B.A. in chemistry. His scientific training may be responsible for the precision of his prose. Soon after graduation Powell became a graduate student at the University of Tennessee in Knoxville to work toward a master's degree in chemistry, but he soon found himself spending more time reading than studying chemistry. Having lost interest in school, he spent a few years drifting around the Southeast and working as a freight handler, household mover, and orthodontic technician.

Powell worked for almost six years as a roofer in Texas, writing in his spare time, before he eventually entered the prestigious M.F.A. program at the University of Houston, where he studied with the legendary fiction writer Donald Barthelme. In an interview Powell described his former teacher as a kind, caring man who took Powell under his wing because he saw something of himself in his student's determination. Powell recalls that "We had similar tastes. We liked the same things, the same bars, the same books, the same women. The only thing we differed on was music. I only like rock and roll. He always wanted to talk about jazz. He really wasn't so much a writer as a jazz painter on the page." Powell received his master's degree in 1982. During his time in Houston, Powell met his future wife, the poet Sidney

Wade, whom he married on 22 May 1984. Both Powell and Wade are now professors at the University of Florida in Powell's hometown of Gainesville. They have two daughters, Amanda Dahl and Elena, both born in the same hospital as their father and grandfather.

Powell burst onto the literary scene with the publication in 1984 of *Edisto*, a book Walker Percy praised as "a truly remarkable first novel, both as a narrative and in its extraordinary use of language. It reminds one of *Catcher in the Rye*, but it's better—sharper, funnier, more poignant." Named for a largely undeveloped strip of South Carolina coast, "too small for the Arabs to bother to take," *Edisto* is narrated by a precocious twelve-year-old boy, Simons Manigault. Simons's mother, separated from his father and called "the Duchess" by Edisto's native black population because of her status as a displaced member of the local gentry, desperately wants her son to grow up to be a writer. Because of the Duchess's lofty aspirations for him, Simons's narration is one of the most unusual voices in recent literary history. Similar to Mark Twain's Huckleberry Finn, Simons is a wild creature, fond of skipping school, fishing, and hanging out at the Baby Grand, a local juke joint where the patrons, largely black, slip him beer. For the most part, he is as completely "unsivilized" as Twain's protagonist describes himself to be, except for the heavy doses of Greek and Latin classics Simons's mother force-feeds him daily. As long as Simons continues his literary pursuits, the Duchess turns a blind eye to his truant behavior and allows him to do as he pleases. Simons's mixture of puerile freedom and erudition leads to a literary style that is both philosophically penetrating and winsomely charming.

By the end of the novel Simons's parents have reconciled and his family moves to the plastic world of Hilton Head, South Carolina, a resort island full of condominiums, golf courses, and, worst of all, prep schools. Forced to leave the wildness of his former existence behind, Simons finds himself in a hollow new world where he no longer feels like an individual. *Edisto* is a bildungsroman, not only of one boy, but of a whole way of life in the South. As the sleepy agrarian past disappears in favor of a new commercial landscape, there is no room for sentimentality or regret. "It's the modern world. I have to accept it," Simons declares in the final chapter of the novel. "I'm a pioneer."

In 1984 *Edisto* was nominated for a National Book Award and was selected for inclusion in *Time* magazine's list of the year's best fiction, along with works by Norman Mailer, Saul Bellow, John Updike, and Milan Kundera. These honors helped Powell to return to his hometown of Gainesville as a professor of creative writing. He proved to be a dynamic teacher both in and out of class. Not only did Powell show his students how to construct well-made stories, but he would also throw wild parties where the former chemist would instruct his students on how to make homemade bombs out of bottles of Aqua Velva and balloons filled with hydrogen. In 1986, shortly before the publication of his second novel, *A Woman Named Drown*, Powell received the Whiting Foundation Writers' Award.

Like Powell's first novel, *A Woman Named Drown* fared well with critics, using the same combination of ordinary circumstances mixed with extraordinary prose. The protagonist, Al, is a Ph.D. student of inorganic chemistry who, like Simons in *Edisto*, is desperate to avoid responsibility. Al studies chemistry not because he is a "true scientist" like his friend Tom, another student in the same doctoral program, but a "scientist by default." Al sees science as a dodge, an excuse to keep from taking over his millionaire father's pipe business. As the novel opens, Al receives a Dear John letter from his longtime girlfriend, who has left him for a "famous crystallographer." Depressed, he drops out of the doctoral program and, on the rebound, moves in with an older woman he hardly knows, a down-and-out actress named Mary Constance Baker whose last role was in a play titled *A Woman Named Drown*. After the tumultuous affair ends, Al decides to visit Tom in Alabama, where he has taken a new job. Al finds that his friend has become disappointingly middle-class. Since Tom has abandoned "true" science for money, Al gives in as well and returns to school to complete his degree, knowing that the upcoming year will be his last before he is forced to become the custodian of his father's pipe empire.

In a review of *A Woman Named Drown* published in the 7 June 1987 issue of *The New York Times Book Review*, T. Coraghessan Boyle writes that "All of these adventures are enlivened by the distinctive, understated humor that is Mr. Powell's signature. He presents a terrific, hyperreal dialogue in quick bludgeoned pieces, and his narrator's phrasing and dialect are always surprising and inventive."

In an interview published with Boyle's review of *A Woman Named Drown*, Powell discussed his work thus far and his plans for the future with journalist Alex Ward. "I don't want to be thought of as a six-bout fighter," said Powell, who, like his character Al, is fond of boxing metaphors. "I'd rather be considered for what I do over the long haul." Being valued for the long haul means showing a certain amount of variance and growth. According to Powell, *Edisto* is based on a real person, while *A Woman Named Drown* is "pure fiction." His second novel began as a dream he had while enrolled in a writing workshop taught by Barthelme at the University of Houston. The dream was so vivid that Powell wrote it down quickly and read it to the class. "They thought it was horrible," he recalled, "But you always feel embarrassed with a story at first." Powell added, "the story goes through a gestation period in your mind and you know you have to write it. So you do, and then you really embarrass yourself." This insight into the writing process referred not only to his previous work but also to a new book he was in the middle of writing, tentatively titled "Mr. Irony." At the time of the interview, Powell described the book as being about two women from Texas who take an incredibly cheap world tour with two gentlemen, one of whom is the title character. "I'm not sure what I've got here," he said about the manuscript, "except that it's supposed to be humorous, and it needs work."

"Mr. Irony" underwent significant revision over the next three years. Some of this time Powell spent traveling. In 1989 he was a Fulbright fellow in Turkey. Upon his return "Mr. Irony" was published, not as a novel but as a densely packed short story, in *The Paris Review*. It was a landmark story for Powell's career, for it marked a complete departure from his previously realistic fiction and served as a sort of *ars poetica*. "Mr. Irony" is a dazzling piece of metafiction.

Even in Powell's first two novels, one can easily see that he was attempting to adopt the humor and linguistic playfulness that Barthelme engineered in short-story collections such as *Come Back, Dr. Caligari* (1964) and novels such as *The Dead Father* (1975). But neither *Edisto* nor *A Woman Named Drown* pushed the boundaries of fiction as much as Powell's next work, the 1991 short-story collection *Typical*, in which "Mr. Irony" was republished. With this book he proved that he was approaching the kind of postmodern assault on form that had made his mentor famous.

The arch-absurdist Barthelme is thinly disguised as the title character in "Mr. Irony", the longest story and the centerpiece of the collection. Powell himself appears in the story as Mr. Irony's "student of low-affected living edged with self-deprecating irony." Teacher and student embark on the "Man-at-His-Best World Tour," via "unspecified variable means of transport," with two Texas women found at the International Hostelry for Available Traveling Women. The two couples dive from the cliffs in Acapulco, ride elephants in Lanxang (Laos) and join a Rocky Mountain goat safari. Toward the end of the tour, Mr. Irony's student narrator decides to withdraw himself from the narrative in hopes of making the story better: "I had in fact picked up my self-deprecating ironic ways from Mr. Irony, whose student I allegedly was.... I could serve the tale best, I thought, and finally not without considerable self-deprecation and irony, by removing myself from it, and deciding thereupon to do so, and hereby pronounce myself expunged from this affair as teller—." The narration is saved by Mr. Irony himself, who assures his student that he should not make himself "scarce" because he has the ability and talent to finish the tale. Powell's statement concerning the nature of art is clear. Irony, self-doubt, and self-deprecation are tools the writer must use to prevent his ego from getting ahead of the work, but these should never be used as an excuse for quitting. "Things need you, son," Mr. Irony tells his protégé near the end of the story.

Typical begins with an epigraph from Barthelme asserting that the virtue of desire is greater than the virtue of honesty: "Truth is greatly overrated, volition where it exists must be protected, wanting itself can be obliterated, some people have forgotten how to want." Of the characters that populate the stories of *Typical*, some are more honest than others, but all somehow deal with a reduced capacity to want; most of them have become emotionally paralyzed by their dreary, everyday lives.

The metafictional "Mr. Irony" spawned a series of "Mister" stories that are featured in *Typical*, including "Mr. Nefarious", "Miss Resignation", "Dr. Ordinary", "General Rancidity", and "Mr. Irony Renounces Irony". They are mostly amusing, lyrical vignettes, one- or two-page portraits of characters whose personalities seem to be wholly dependent on the habits or emotional states indicated by their names. Many of these stories seem as if they could have been written by Barthelme himself. Like his mentor, Powell appears to prefer short fiction that explores the limits of language rather than stories that rehash tired plots and draw their power from a simple conflict. In this way the series of "Mister" stories that occupy much of *Typical* are anything but typical.

In other stories from the collection, such as "The Winnowing of Mrs. Schuping" and "Letter from a Dogfighter's Aunt, Deceased", Powell melds his postmodern training with his Southern gothic upbringing to forge a style that is completely his own. Reminiscent of Carson McCullers's work, "The Winnowing of Mrs. Schuping" is a portrait of a feisty spinster who has decided to simplify her life by divesting herself of responsibilities and possessions. The occupation of winnowing away her life requires a new name, and she arbitrarily renames herself Mrs. Schuping. Unlike Mr. Irony, who loves to travel and wax philosophical about the nature of narrative, Mrs. Schuping gives up travel and reading altogether. She has come to distrust reality completely, and this distrust immobilizes her. She is content to preside serenely over the deterioration of her house, until her winnowing plans are interrupted by a local sheriff, a fat, amorous man who, "in the river of life's winnowing," acts as a "big boulder in the bed of the dwindling stream."

"Letter from a Dogfighter's Aunt, Deceased" is a ghost story told from the perspective of the ghost, an unusual narrative point of view that is both first person and omniscient. This meditative perspective comes from one long dead, but not too long. Aunt Humpy, formerly a stuck-up librarian maniacally intent on correcting her family's grammar, now lovingly watches over Brody, a nephew she helped run away from home so that he could become a breeder of fighting dogs. From her vantage point in Heaven she looks kindly on her fierce nephew, who is now a nonchurchgoer and career criminal. Brody lives on the margins of society, a rogue white male determined to be free of middle-class mores. Aunt Humpy is proud of her nephew because she is now free of the "myriad

prejudices and passions and myopias that made us the human being we mortally became." She appreciates the purity of Brody's lawless existence in the same way that he appreciates the purity of the thoroughbred dogs he conditions "to a point suggesting piano wires and marble, reduced by another sculpted cat to a soft red lump resembling bloody terry cloth." In a sense Aunt Humpy is an apologist for the Southerners about whom Powell writes best: tough, mean, yet often sweet boys and men such as Simons and Al, whose self-determined sense of right and wrong often comes into conflict with those in the mainstream.

In the title story, "Typical", Powell proves that he has not lost his ear for the way white, blue-collar Southern males talk and carry themselves. "Typical" is a loosely structured interior monologue filtered through the consciousness of an unemployed steel-mill worker, John Payne. Payne's observations concerning the nature of money, sex, marriage, and race are both comic and narrow-minded, yet his insights into his own limitations and shortcomings are nothing short of remarkable: "I'm not nice, not too smart, don't see too much point in pretending to be either. Why I am telling anyone this trash is a good question.... There are many mysteries in this world. I should be a better person, I know I should, but I don't see that finally being up to choice. If it were, I would not stop at being a better person. Who would?" Payne is a "typical" white male, frustrated by his lot in life. Depressed by his inability to control his life, Payne has lost the desire to do anything but drink. As Barthelme warned in the epigraph to the book, Payne has "forgotten how to want." Now he is merely another victim of social and economic forces beyond his control, and rather than continue to combat these indiscriminately, he has given in to a sort of blue-collar fatalism.

"Typical" was selected for inclusion in the 1990 edition of *The Best American Short Stories* and also won a Pushcart Prize that year. Several other pieces from *Typical* were selected for inclusion in other prize-winning anthologies. "Letter from a Dogfighter's Aunt, Deceased" was selected for inclusion in the anthology *The Literary Ghost: Great Contemporary Ghost Stories* (1991) under the title "Voice from the Grave". "The Winnowing of Mrs. Schuping" was anthologized in the 1992 edition of *New Stories From the South* and was later selected by novelist Anne Tyler for inclusion in *Best of the South: From Ten Years of New Stories from the South* (1996).

In 1996 Powell returned to the novel genre as well as to his most popular character, Simons Manigault, with *Edisto Revisited*. The narrative begins just after Simons has graduated from architecture school. No longer is he a wild creature of the Carolina coast. His education has caused him, like many of the characters in *Typical*, to give up hope. Profoundly depressed, Simons finds that he has no desire to do anything but consume alcohol. He is momentarily saved by a passionate love affair with his cousin Patricia. The novel wastes little time in laying the foundations of an incestuous romance in the Faulknerian tradition. But even this relationship becomes too much responsibility for Simons to handle, and eventually he flees back to Edisto to find his old friends. Although *Edisto Revisited* did not draw the lavish praise that *Edisto* did, reviewers still found much to like in the book, calling it a tour de force of style. Near the end of *Edisto Revisited* Simons, determined to grow up, renounces the self-defeating indulgences of alcohol, just as Powell himself decided around this time to stop drinking.

There is always a hint in Powell's writing that his fiction is really just autobiography cast into a multitude of masks and personae. Powell has indicated in interviews that Simons is based on a "real person," while the chemistry-student protagonist of *A Woman Named Drown* pursues Powell's abandoned study of science. "Typical" and "Mr. Irony" reflect two different aspects of Powell's personality. The unemployed Payne is a realistic character reminiscent of the kind of men that Powell would have worked with closely as a day laborer in Texas, while "Mr. Irony" depicts Powell's relationship with his teacher Barthelme and employs the artful fictional techniques that Barthelme practiced.

The fictive positions in "Typical" and "Mr. Irony" seem to be mixed in "Wayne's Fate", another of the stories in *Typical*. Wayne is a half-intoxicated roofer who loses his balance atop a high building and is decapitated during the fall. His severed head lands in a five-gallon bucket of mastic. The story concludes with the reattachment of his head and the semiresurrection of his corpse. At the end the reader discovers that Wayne is not fully functional but is capable of making lewd comments. He convinces the narrator of the story, a fellow roofer, to make a few lewd comments to the owner of the home they are repairing while they await the paramedics.

Several other Wayne stories were published in Powell's 1998 short-story collection, *Aliens of Affection*. These stories display a further renovation of Powell's style and an intensification of his linguistic playfulness. He uses extravagant language as a tool to create further ironic space between author and characters as well as between characters and readers. Unlike Powell's previous writings, in which he seemed rather intimate with his characters, in the aptly titled *Aliens of Affection* he holds his characters at arm's length. Not only are they emotionally alienated from the reader, they are alienated from themselves. Few characters in these stories speak with the clarity or coherence of Payne in "Typical". Most of them are psychotic, drug-addled, and even brain-damaged. In essence, Powell has abandoned realism for a fictional world filtered through a myriad of unusual psychological states.

In the other Wayne stories in *Aliens of Affection* Wayne has not prospered since his decapitation in *Typical*. He is now out of work, and his teeth are falling out. His wife, Felicia (Wayne refers to her simply as "Ugly"), kicks him out of their home for being selfish. As it turns out in the course of the Wayne stories, he is a harmless, irresponsible drunk who drifts from one episode to the next, pointlessly rotating among women, bars, and menial jobs. The last section of "Wayne" is told by an intrusive narrator who explains that Wayne's lack of psychological depth is worthy of study: "Wayne isn't afraid of anything because he knows he is afraid. I, by contrast, think myself fearless, and when something scares me, *it scares the shit out of me*." These moments of fear force the narrator to "undergo a little private analysis the likes of which have never troubled Wayne." Wayne's cowardice, meanness, low intelligence, and lack of motivating psychology are actually assets. The narrator editorializes the ending of the sequence by again comparing Wayne to himself, lamenting, "For all my teeth! Muscles! College!" The narrator is plagued by a sense of self-doubt that never hinders Wayne: "Wayne may be roofing, but I am afraid."

A trilogy of stories in *Aliens of Affection* appears under the title "All Along the Watchtower". The stories feature a nameless pseudohero resembling Wayne-perhaps the same protagonist in all three stories, perhaps not-who negotiates the indistinct boundaries of personality. In "Chihuahua" the narrator, a former mental patient, sets off on an arbitrary quest to locate a fifty-pound Chihuahua. This takes him south of the border to Mexico, where he finds not only the freakish dog but also a local nurse who supplies the narrator with pills, sex, and the illusion that life can be simple and even pastoral. The narrator of "Stroke" also seems to have diminished mental capacity. The narrative unfolds with all the unimpeded honesty of a stroke victim who cannot edit his thoughts. In the forty-page title story, "Aliens of Affection", the last in the trilogy, the narrator inhabits yet another haze of delusion in which metaphors become literal and the actual world is lost in a fog of language. But readers are still sure they are in the South, or at least the literary South, because of the presence of a devil-may-care Southern belle, Dale Mae.

The departure from traditional narrative and plot in *Typical* is extended to a radical reinvention of the concept of characters in *Aliens of Affection*. Many readers might accuse Powell's later characters of flatness, but what they lack in depth they make up for in originality. Because several of the characters in *Aliens of Affection* are mentally deficient and are incapable of articulating the futility of their own lives as perceptively as Payne in "Typical", or as eloquently as Simons in *Edisto* and *Edisto Revisited* and Al in *A Woman Named Drown*, they are more content to let the absurdity of the world they live in speak for itself. When commentary is needed, the author must make it directly himself, as he does at the end of the Wayne stories.

Another of Powell's schizoid characters, Rod, takes on the persona of Scarliotti in "Scarliotti and the Sinkhole", also from *Aliens of Affection*. Rod is a trailer-park resident who has been struck in the head by the side mirror of a moving truck. Because he refuses to take his medication, he develops a split personality disorder and creates a new persona to act out his more heroic side. Rod names this more heroic and dangerous alter ego Scarliotti. As Scarliotti, Rod manages to seduce a gas station attendant who really only sleeps with him in order to drink his beer and take his medication. The story ends with a sinkhole threatening to swallow up Rod's trailer. It is difficult to determine whether this sinkhole is a literal danger or an absurdist metaphor for Rod's increasingly dismal existence. He cannot combat the sinkhole as Scarliotti, nor even escape from it as Rod. The story ends with a babbling monologue that shifts between a meditation on dogfighting and an analysis of the Confederate general J. E. B. Stuart.

It is difficult to decide whether Powell's Southern absurdism is a tool for social commentary or simply a tool to poke fun at his characters. To some extent, the radical assault on character in the stories of *Aliens of Affection* seems to be another attempt to comment upon the changing nature of the South, which is described as a "vale of dry tears" in the story "Trick or Treat". In contrast to colorful, realistic characters such as Simons and Al, who follow in a long line of disaffected Southerners mourning the loss of the old, aristocratic South, Powell's more recent characters are simply incapable of fitting in. They are victims of insanity, stroke, and brain damage, failing to adjust to contemporary life but still clinging to fragmented memories of the old South, to such things as dogfights and Civil War heroes. In an essay titled "Whupped Before Kilt", originally appearing in a 1998 issue of *The Oxford American* magazine and later republished as the preface to the 1998 edition of *New Stories From the South*, Powell points out that since the South lost the Civil War, Southern literature has been a literature focused on failure. Quoting Faulkner's Wash Jones in *Absalom, Absalom!* (1936)-" Well, Kernel, they mought have kilt us, but they ain't whipped us yit, air they?"-Powell asserts that the "literature of the South is full of people running around admitting or denying their whippedness." In contrast to the state of "whippedness," he sees integrity to be "the denial of whippedness." The various figures that populate Powell's later short stories display the unusual characteristic of being "whupped," but because they do not know they are whipped they retain a certain amount of integrity. The reader knows that characters such as Wayne and Rod are victims of circumstance. As victims they will inevitably be bested in their personal dogfights with the world at large. Wayne and Rod, however, do not know that they are underdogs. Their ignorance to their plight causes them to be fearless, and in this fearlessness readers may find a small but deep reservoir of integrity. As with *Typical*, the stories in *Aliens of Affection* brought Powell awards for the power and insight of his writing. "Aliens of Affection", the final story in the trilogy "All Along the Watchtower", was selected for the 1998 edition of *New Stories from the South*. That same year, "Wayne in Love" was selected by Garrison Keillor for inclusion in *The Best American Short Stories*.

Throughout his career, Powell has attempted to reinvent the literature of the old South by paying particular attention to the aspects of the Southern literary tradition that make it unique, primarily the language of the region. From *Edisto* to *Aliens of Affection*, Powell's adept use of inventive syntax, coupled with his finely tuned ear for dialect, has drawn favorable comparisons with such masters of regionalism as Twain and Faulkner. Powell is not, however, a writer lost in the past; his subject matter is that of the contemporary South, a new urban landscape that threatens to erase the identity of the old South as the region gives in to commercial forces from beyond its borders. The traditional theme of defeated Southerner is consistent throughout Powell's body of work. The author's nonconformist "whupped" characters, from Simons to Wayne, are used to critique a culture that has given itself over to the vapid worship of success.

As a writer of short fiction, Powell is one of the few writers who have successfully managed to combine postmodern absurdism with the gothic and grotesque traditions of Southern regionalism. In this sense, his short stories appear to be the direct heir to the work of Barthelme and O'Connor. Like his teacher Barthelme, Powell frequently abandons traditional narrative for fictions that seem to exist in a pure realm of language. Much of his work is unencumbered by realistic plots, and even in his more straightforward stories the settings and characters can only be described as odd or idiosyncratic. Like O'Connor, Powell endeavors to create memorable misfits, his most notable creations being the meditative Mrs. Schuping and the crazed roofer Wayne. Many of Powell's characters seem to be allegorical in nature, with personalities invented to question conventional notions of individuality or even philosophical notions of free will; others are just plain funny.

Source: Brad Vice, "Padgett Powell," in *Dictionary of Literary Biography*, Vol. 234, *American Short-Story Writers Since World War II, Third Series*, edited by Patrick Meanor and Richard E. Lee, The Gale Group, 2001, pp. 250–56.

SOURCES

Boyle, T. Coraghessan, "A Better Class of Fools," in *New York Times Book Review*, June 7, 1987, p. 9.

Brunazzi, Elizabeth, "Southern Stories Map Social Boundaries and Emotional Territory," in *San Francisco Chronicle*, May 31, 1998, p. RV-9, http://sfgate.com/cgi-bin/article.cgi?file = /chronicle/archive/1998/05/31/RV3439.DTL (accessed October 30, 2006).

Geeslin, Campbell, Review of *A Woman Named Drown*, in *People Weekly*, Vol. 27, June 15, 1987, p. 14.

Hempel, Amy, "'A Lesson in Hard-Boil,'" in *New York Times*, July 21, 1991, p. 6.

Hwang, Francis, Review of *Aliens of Affection*, in *City Pages*, Vol. 19, No. 897, February 11, 1998, http://www.citypages.com/databank/19/897/article4339.asp (accessed October 30, 2006).

Kakutani, Michiko, "A Potpourri of Characters and Their Stories," in *New York Times*, August 16, 1991, p. C21.

Kanfer, Stefan, Review of *Typical*, in *Time*, Vol. 137, No. 26, July 1, 1991, p. 71.

Kelly, Robert, "The New Southern Male," in *New York Times Book Review*, November 5, 2000, p. 28.

Loewinsohn, Ron, "Age 12 and Burning with Questions," in *New York Times*, April 15, 1984, p. 14.

Powell, Padgett, "Trick or Treat," in *Prize Stories 1995: The O. Henry Awards*, edited by William Abrahams, Doubleday, 1995, pp. 52–63.

Review of *Aliens of Affection*, in *Publishers Weekly*, Vol. 244, No. 40, September 29, 1997, p. 62.

Scott, A. O., "Southern Comfort," in *New York Times Book Review*, February 1, 1998, p. 27.

Spencer, Scott, "Carolina Slacker," in *New York Times Book Review*, March 31, 1996, p. 14.

FURTHER READING

Ayers, Edward L., and Bradley C. Mittendorf, eds., *The Oxford Book of the American South: Testimony, Memory, and Fiction*, Oxford University Press, 1998.

This book is a collection of essays, memoirs, diaries, and letters covering the colonial period up through the twentieth century. The editors have attempted unity in their book rather than a mere catalogue of texts, bringing together history, philosophy, and social issues to illustrate a subculture alive within its own historical context.

Cocca, Carolyn E., *Jailbait: The Politics of Statutory Rape Laws in the United States*, State University of New York Press, 2004.

Cocca's book is the first to look in-depth at the history and application of U.S. legislation enacted to protect and punish adolescents who are having sex. The author uses case studies as well as statistics in her examination of statutory rape laws.

Martin, Robert K., and Eric Savoy, eds. *American Gothic: New Interventions in a National Narrative*, University of Iowa Press, 1998.

This collection of essays celebrates the revival and reinvention of Gothic literature in North America with focus on theory, history, psychoanalysis, racial politics, and women's writing.

Nabokov, Vladimir, *Lolita*, Vintage Books, 1989.

First published in 1955, this famous, controversial novel is about a man who lusts after a twelve-year-old girl whom he calls Lolita. Mrs. Hollingsworth refers to Jimmy as "Lolito."

What I Saw from Where I Stood

MARISA SILVER

2001

When Marisa Silver's short story collection *Babe in Paradise* appeared in print in 2001, it received enthusiastic reviews, many of which singled out "What I Saw from Where I Stood" as one of its best stories. The story chronicles one week in the lives of young couple, Charles and Dulcie, who a year earlier had miscarried after six months of pregnancy. Charles, the "I" of the title, tells their story from his perspective, from "where [he] stood," as he struggles to help his wife deal with the baby's death and to gain enough strength to face the future. Through his narrative that subtly details his observations and responses to his wife's pain, Silver presents a poignant study of the healing influence of compassion and support, and the resilience of the human spirit.

AUTHOR BIOGRAPHY

Marisa Silver was born on April 23, 1960, in Shaker Heights, New Jersey, to Raphael Silver, a film director and producer, and Joan Micklin Silver, a director. While taking classes in the early 1990s at Harvard University, Silver began writing short stories, but her interest in film turned her attention to directing and editing documentaries, including with Peter Davis, the Emmy-nominated "A Community of Praise," a segment of the *Middletown* series for PBS, which profiled Christian fundamentalists. In 1992, she directed an episode of *L. A. Law* and *Indecency*, a film for television. She gained fame,

Marisa Silver The Kobal Collection. Reproduced by permission

however, at age twenty-four for her work in film, beginning with *Old Enough*, which she wrote and co-produced with her sister Dina in 1984. The film won the Grand Jury Prize at the Sundance Film Festival that year. Her directorial success continued with *Permanent Record* in 1988, *Vital Signs* in 1990, and *He Said, She Said* in 1991, with Ken Kwapis who later became her husband.

Silver turned to fiction writing toward the end of the decade when she decided that she did not have enough creative control over her work in films. During this period, she attended creative writing workshops, and in 2001, she had a collection of short stories, *Babe in Paradise* published. In 2005, her novel *No Direction Home* appeared. Both works received positive reviews. Silver has also contributed articles to various periodicals, including the *New Yorker*, *American Film*, *Hollywood Reporter*, *Interview*, *People*, and *Working Woman*. As of 2005, she lived with her husband and two sons in Los Angeles.

PLOT SUMMARY

Charles, a young telephone repairman who narrates the story, explains at the beginning of

"What I Saw from Where I Stood" that his wife Dulcie, a second-grade teacher, is afraid of the Los Angeles freeways. He remembers that she had to drive home from a party that they went to the previous week after he got drunk. Her touch as she took the keys from his pocket excited him, especially since he admits that she has not been touching him very much lately. Dulcie sank lower in the driver's seat when they passed the hospital where she had miscarried their baby a year earlier after being pregnant for six months.

During the drive home, they were rear-ended. As he and Dulcie got out of the car to inspect the damage, which was minor to such an old car, four or five men emerged from the van that hit them and started posturing. One then pulled a gun. After Dulcie screamed, "Don't shoot," another demanded her keys, which she immediately threw on the ground. Charles calmly picked up the keys and handed them to one of the men along with money from his wallet. When the man with the gun did not move, Charles panicked, grabbed Dulcie's hand, and ran down a side street. They made it to the police station where Dulcie expressed her fears about the men getting their keys and address, but the police gave them "their heartfelt assurance" that there was nothing the police could do for them. They tried to convince Dulcie that carjackers showing up at the homes of their victims "almost never happened," but she was not reassured and so spent a sleepless night going over the details of the crime.

She grew more agitated as she tried and failed to find any logical explanation for what happened. Charles notes that she did the same thing when they lost their baby a year before, as she struggled to find some reason for it or someone to blame even though she had been told that what had happened was no one's fault. As they laid there in bed, Charles told her not to think about what could have happened during the carjacking, but Dulcie insisted, "How can you not think about it?"

When Charles came home from work the next day, he noticed that Dulcie had obviously been crying for a long time. She also had moved the mattress from their bedroom to the middle of the living room to get away from the rat that had nested in the bedroom wall and had been waking them up for the past month with its scratching. When the janitor refused to do anything about it, Charles had patched every hole in the apartment so that the rat would not be able to get in, which reassured Dulcie. After the carjacking, though, her fears returned, and she became convinced that the rat would find a way into the apartment. She also insisted that Charles put his voice on the answering machine so that callers know that there is a man living there.

That night, they slept with the lights on so that, Dulcie insisted, people knew they were home and would not break in. She then, however, considered the possibility that anyone would assume they were out of town if the lights were on at four in the morning. When she wondered whether she should get an inflatable man to put in the seat beside her while driving alone and insisted that there was a good chance that any man driving next to her would have a gun, Charles tried to calm her. He explains how difficult it was for Dulcie when her milk came in two days after their baby died. She had exclaimed, "What a waste."

The next evening, Charles was startled by someone throwing an egg at his car until he realized that it was Halloween. He notes that normally Dulcie enjoys decorating for the holiday and greeting children at the door, but this night he found no decorations and a dark apartment. Dulcie refused to open the door to anyone, afraid that teenagers would be out, "looking for trouble."

When the doorbell rang, Charles waved away Dulcie's protests and opened the door to a boy wearing a cowboy outfit. Charles tried to give him some cookies, but the boy would not take them, insisting that he was only allowed to take things that are wrapped. After he heard other children trick-or-treating on the floor below, Charles insisted to Dulcie that they could not live like this any longer, but she replied, "I can."

Three days after the carjacking, Dulcie returned to work. Charles explains how much she loves teaching. Later that day, however, she showed him a new rule at the school that forbids teachers to touch their students and declared, "this is a f——up town." The two then tried to make jokes about the city.

The following Saturday, Dulcie called the exterminator after she read that rats could carry airborne viruses. When the exterminator arrived, he told them that rats come inside houses to get warm and to have babies, which visibly upset Dulcie.

Charles explains that a month after the baby died, they received the ashes in the mail. When Dulcie realized what they were, she began to giggle uncontrollably. They decided to scatter the ashes in the ocean. After Charles waded out into the water and dumped the contents of the small bag into the ocean, Dulcie told him, "I think that's the bravest thing I've ever seen a person do."

One week after the carjacking, the police told them that their car was found, and it was being held in South Central Los Angeles, a dangerous part of town. The officer warned Charles to go there early in the morning. When they got to the car, they discovered that it had been stripped of everything, including the steering wheel, and so they had to leave it at the pound. Dulcie begged Charles not to make her go with him to the police lineup to pick out the men who robbed them.

Charles dropped Dulcie off at school and walked for hours on a path up into the mountains, thinking about whether he should leave her. He admits that he had been looking forward to the baby and remembers how he felt during its birth, acknowledging that he felt like he would die if anything happened to Dulcie. When he got home, he took the mattress back into the bedroom. Dulcie did not say anything to him about it when she returned, realizing that he had made up his mind to get things back to normal. When he turned to her in bed, she did not move away as he expected she would. As they began to make love, Dulcie got nervous and mentioned getting her diaphragm, but Charles insisted that it would be okay without it. The two were very frightened at the prospect of facing another pregnancy, but they did not stop.

CHARACTERS

Charles

Charles is a young repairman for the telephone company who, although he likes to get drunk at parties, proves himself to be very responsible, supportive, and caring with his wife Dulcie. He presents the details of their lives in a matter of fact manner, yet these qualities emerge in bits of dialogue and through often subtle gestures. During the carjacking, he acts with a cool head, calmly handing over money to one of the men. But when one of the carjackers starts to wave a gun in his face, he acts quickly, grabbing Dulcie's hand and running away from them. He takes seriously the warning about venturing into South Central Los Angeles only in the morning when he has to pick up their car.

Charles does everything that he can to ease Dulcie's fears after the carjacking, agreeing to sleep in the living room with all of the lights on. He notices the pain she experiences whenever she is reminded of the death of their child as when she shrinks down in the driver's seat when they pass the hospital. After they receive the baby's ashes in the mail, Charles tenderly describes the package, "nestled inside [a Styrofoam] hole, like a tiny bird." He then takes the remains, wades out into the ocean, and scatters them into the water, an act that Dulcie insists is "the bravest thing [she had] ever seen a person do."

His patience has its limits though. Realizing that Dulcie's fears have caused them to live "like some rat trapped in [their] own wall," he begins to gently force Dulcie to accept the messiness of everyday life and to have enough courage to regain a measure of hope for the future.

Dulcie

Dulcie is a second-grade teacher in a Los Angeles public school and is married to Charles. Since their baby died a year ago, she has withdrawn from the world and from Charles, refusing to allow herself to be vulnerable to another disaster. The carjacking only increases her withdrawal as she begins to fear everyone around her: men in cars who might point guns at her, teenagers at Halloween who may be looking for trouble, and Charles when he wants to become intimate with her, which could result in another disastrous pregnancy.

Dulcie, however, still has the capacity for trust, especially in Charles who determines that she cannot continue being so fearful of the world. When he pulls the mattress back into the bedroom, "she climb[s] into bed like a soldier following orders." While she is still afraid of the dark and of the consequences of another pregnancy, she eventually lets Charles lead her back into the world of the living.

THEMES

Lack of Control

Dulcie becomes afraid of things that she cannot control. She is afraid of freeways because she cannot always get off of them when she wants. She is afraid of having another baby because she

TOPICS FOR FURTHER STUDY

- Research the psychological effects that losing a child can have on a parent. Prepare a PowerPoint demonstration of your findings, including what most often happens to parents who face this kind of loss. Prepare to lead a discussion on what other ways Charles and Dulcie could have coped with their loss.

- Silver uses flashbacks to provide crucial information about the loss of the couple's child. How would you film a version of the story that would include the information gained in the flashbacks? Write a screenplay of a scene from the text that includes at least one flashback.

- Read one or two stories in the collection that contains this story and compare and contrast them with "What I Saw from Where I Stood." Write an introduction for the collection that specifically addresses these stories.

- Write a story or a poem that focuses on the frustrations or dangers of urban living.

cannot make sure that it will live. In an effort to regain a sense of order and control, she tries to find logical explanations for the terrible things that have happened to her. Charles notes: "Dulcie needs things to be exact. You have to explain yourself clearly when you're around her." When their baby died, she kept trying to find a reason, thinking that it must have been her fault. She needed someone to take the blame, and if it turned out to be her, she could accept that because at least she would have an answer, something that she could fix in order to prevent the same thing from happening again.

When their car is stolen, Dulcie stays up all night going over what happened, wondering why their car was picked and why the men had not shot them. She finally concludes that nothing about the incident makes sense. Since she cannot find a logical explanation for the carjacking and for their getting away unhurt, she feels that she does not have any control over her own safety and so tries to do everything she can to make herself more safe. She leaves the lights on so burglars will think they are at home, and she wants to buy an inflatable man to put in the passenger seat so other motorists will think she is with a man and then will not attack her. Charles goes along with her desperate need for control until he realizes that she will never be able to attain it. In an effort to break them out of the cage she has put them in, he gently persuades her to take a chance on the future without knowing what may happen. By the end of the story, Dulcie begins to accept the fact that she cannot control all of the aspects of her life and that knowledge causes her to reconnect with Charles and to take a chance on getting pregnant again.

Disillusionment

Dulcie and Charles are repeatedly disillusioned about the difference between the way the world should and does work. Babies should not die because of a "fluke thing," and a car should not be stolen in the city where dreams come true. They had also believed that there were people who could help fix problems, but they soon discover that they are on their own. After the carjacking, the police give them "their heartfelt assurance that there was nothing at all they could do." When they hear a rat scratching behind their bedroom wall, they inform the landlord who insists, "he would get on it right away," but they eventually learn that his words really mean, "You'll be living with that rat forever, and if you don't like it there're ten other people in line for your apartment." After their expectations are continually dashed, Charles tries to encourage Dulcie to come to an acceptance of the daily injustices of their world. Silver suggests that this acceptance is a necessary part of survival.

STYLE

Setting as Metaphor

Los Angeles becomes a metaphor for the clash between expectation and reality in the story. On their way home from a party, Charles and Dulcie drive through Santa Monica with its "nice houses. Pretty flowers. Volvos" before they pass the Hollywood boulevards where scantily dressed teenagers club hop while others wait to

sell their bodies in back alleys and in cars. Couples like them move to Los Angeles in the hope that they can find the beautiful landscapes and happy endings they see in film, but most newcomers learn they must settle for the shabby, rat-infested apartments and dangerous sections such as South Central where one dares not venture alone. Dulcie and Charles cannot afford to live in Santa Monica; they must struggle instead to cope with their limited and ordinary lives, which for them includes the death of a child and a carjacking.

Narrative Flashbacks

The story focuses on one week in the past. Charles relates the events during this week through dialogue between the two of them and through additional details about the setting. Since Dulcie cannot talk about the death of their child, Charles must provide the information through flashbacks, which he weaves into the dialogue in order to illustrate the devastating significance of this event. The first time a flashback occurs, it takes place right before they get rear-ended. As they pass by the hospital where Dulcie lost the child, Charles explains the details of the death and then comes back to the present, noticing that as Dulcie looked at the building, "she sank behind the wheel." This flashback, occurring immediately before they are threatened by the carjackers, reinforces Dulcie's sense that the world is a terrifying place that cannot be understood. It also juxtaposes the two losses, the car and the baby a year earlier. Later, when Charles remembers how he scattered the baby's ashes in the sea, he illustrates his concern and support for Dulcie, which eventually help her cope with the death.

HISTORICAL CONTEXT

Crime in Los Angeles

In 1992, violent and property crimes committed in Los Angeles hit a record high. Although the numbers declined thereafter, violent crime remained a serious problem in the city, much of which, including carjackings and drive-by shootings, has been attributed to the city's gangs, which numbered over a thousand. This atmosphere of violence is noted by Charles and Dulcie, and they try to turn it into a joke, suggesting that if they turn on the television, they would probably "catch a freeway chase . . . Or a riot."

The year 1992 experienced a record high due to the riots that took place after the verdict was read for four police officers on trial for beating black motorist Rodney King. King had led them on a high speed chase through the streets of Los Angeles, and after resisting arrest, he was tackled and beaten with nightsticks by the four officers. The beating had been caught on video tape and gained widespread media coverage before the trial. The verdicts that acquitted the four for most of the counts were broadcast live on April 29, 1992. Soon after, thousands of residents, mostly young black, Asian, and Latino males, crowded into the South Los Angeles streets in protest. Other factors that contributed to the tensions included high unemployment in the area and the belief that L.A. police profiled suspects and treated minorities with excessive force.

The protest soon turned violent as stores were looted and burned, bystanders were beaten, and police were shot at. The worst violence continued for three days and prompted mayor Tom Bradley to impose a curfew and close businesses and schools. California governor Pete Wilson called out 4,000 National Guard troops and later federal troops to help restore order. By May 4, the riots had ended. Over 50 people had been killed; more than 4,000 were injured; 12,000 were arrested; and there was an estimated one billion dollars in property damage.

The beating and trial generated criticism of the Los Angeles Police Department along with police chief Daryl Gates, who were all accused of racism and brutality. A year later, after mounting pressure from the public, the four officers were charged with civil rights violations. Two of them were subsequently found guilty, and the other two were acquitted. This time, the verdicts did not cause a violent public outburst.

CRITICAL OVERVIEW

Reviews for *Babe in Paradise* were quite strong, with "What I Saw from Where I Stood" being singled out as one of the best stories. Jonathan Yardley, in his review in the *Washington Post* determines that the setting is the "most interesting and rewarding" aspect of these stories: "The

private dramas confronted by Silver's mostly rather luckless men and women are often noteworthy and occasionally revealing, but it's the sense of entering an unknown world that gives [the collection] its strongest appeal." He also applauds Silver's characterizations, concluding that "The compassion and sympathy Silver feels for these people are given deeper meaning by the good-humored affection with which she regards them" and that "she resists the temptation to take cheap shots at the oddities of life there. She understands that like people everywhere else, Los Angelenos of all kinds and classes are pursuing happiness, they're just doing it in their own way."

In her review of the collection for the *Los Angeles Times*, Michelle Huneven finds that "occasionally, Silver hits a wrong note" and that her "prose could also use a good tidying up: there are too many stray words and phrases and gratuitous explanations, and some stories are overly long, with too much dramatized or explained." Yet, she points out that "the stories are ambitiously and successfully well-structured," especially in Silver's juxtaposition of flashbacks and present time. Huneven also praises her "in focus" characterizations, her use of "myth and fact," and her observations of the southern California landscape, a "dark, desperate, down-and-out world . . . where the elusive instances of human connection and hope are all too rare, and therefore all the more luminous."

Bernard Cooper, in his review for the *New York Times Book Review*, echoes many of his colleagues' sentiments, insisting that "each story in the collection develops by way of careful unrushed narrative," which "allows for an abundance of acute observation and for traces of optimism to develop in the most stifling circumstances." He suggests that Silver's "considerable gifts" are revealed in her ability to retain the "sting" of misery in each story and "to pinpoint the surprising ways that even the most disaffected among us are brought together, if only provisionally." David Uhlin, in his review for the *Atlantic Monthly*, claims that "not all the stories are successful. But when it comes to small moments—the frustrations and regrets of daily living—Silver's work is powerful and heartfelt."

Reviewers who singled out "What I Saw from Where I Stood" for special attention include one writing for *Publishers Weekly*. This reviewer finds

A woman is dragged from her vehicle during a demonstration of a carjacking, like the one that begins this story © Eleanor Bentall/Corbis

the collection as a whole "uneven but promising" with "painfully real characters and strikingly inventive writing." While, the reviewer claims, "too often an exciting premise leads to a dead end, and characters metamorphose in ways that go unexplored," "What I Saw from Where I Stood" stands out as "one of the more powerful and taut entries." Megan Harlan, in *Entertainment Weekly*, concludes that while "some tales feel Hollywood-flashy and a little forced," most of them, including "What I Saw from Where I Stood" "are deft montages of disillusionment."

CRITICISM

Wendy Perkins

Perkins is a professor of American and British literature and film. In the following essay, she examines the story's focus on the transforming effects of compassion and support.

Marisa Silver's "What I Saw from Where I Stood" opens with Charles's announcement that his wife, Dulcie, is afraid of Los Angeles freeways. He soon discloses that freeways are only the first in a long list of things that frighten her—feelings that she has been able to express to Charles. Her greatest fear, however, is something that she cannot voice—that if they try to get pregnant again, the child may die just as the first one has. Charles recognizes how much losing their child has damaged Dulcie and has caused her withdrawal from the world and from him. In her sympathetic portrait of Charles's struggle to help ease Dulcie's suffering, Silver dramatizes how compassion and patient support can help promote a wary acceptance of the vagaries of fate and of the possibilities of the future.

Events have not been kind to Dulcie. One year after she lost her baby, she and Charles were rear-ended by a group of men in a van, one of whom pointed a gun at them and then stole their car. This incident reinforced Dulcie's suspicion

WHAT DO I READ NEXT?

- "Babe in Paradise," the title story of Silver's 2001 collection, focuses on a young woman and her troubled relationships in Los Angeles.
- Silver's *Direction Home* (2005) chronicles the experiences of two boys and a teenaged girl who travel to Los Angeles where they come to understand the complexities of family dynamics as they find a new home.
- *Understanding the Riots: Los Angeles before and after the Rodney King Case* (1992), by Coffey Shelby III, explores the tensions that contributed to the riots, including problems in the Los Angeles Police Department, changes in immigration patterns in south Los Angeles, as well as the Rodney King verdict.
- *Beloved* (1987), by Toni Morrison, explores the devastating effects that the loss of a child has on its mother. The novel's main character, Sethe, kills her newborn in order to save it from a life of slavery, but her feelings of guilt overwhelm her and push her toward insanity.

---

that the world is a dangerous place and that she cannot prevent terrible things from happening to her. When the police are unable to allay her fears that the men who stole the car will try to break into their apartment, she stays up all night, trying to determine why they were targeted and what prevented them from being shot. Charles notes that Dulcie tried to make sense of the loss of her child in the same way, but then, as now, she failed. She was told that her baby's death was "a fluke," which plunged her into a harsh, random world that she could not understand or explain or from which she could not gain a sense of security.

Charles tried to protect her, however, physically when he grabbed her hand and started to run away from the car, and emotionally when he

> "... ALL HE COULD THINK OF WAS THAT HE WOULD DIE IF ANYTHING EVER HAPPENED TO HER. THE REALIZATION OF HIS DEEP LOVE FOR HER PROMPTS HIM TO SEE ANOTHER OPTION—TO GENTLY ASSERT THAT LIFE WITH ALL OF ITS DANGER AND PROMISE CAN AND SHOULD BE FACED."

---

tries to ease her fears that the men will come after them. When Dulcie points out that the two of them know what the men look like, he tells her that the men are thieves not killers, trying to convince her that they are safe now.

He does this several times during the next week, as Dulcie's fearful state causes her to think that the rat that scratches behind their bedroom wall will get out and spread airborne diseases and that male drivers who stop next to her at traffic lights most likely have a gun in their car. Charles patiently patches all of the holes in the apartment and agrees to move the mattress into the living room and to leave the lights on so that people will think that they are home and so not break in, all in an effort to help Dulcie get some sleep.

Charles tries other tactics to calm her, but they do not work as well. Humor falls flat as when she insists he put his voice on the answering machine, and he responds, "You're worried about the rat hearing your voice on the machine?" Dulcie is serious about her fears and refuses any suggestion that she might be overreacting. She also refuses Charles's attempts to physically comfort her. He admits, "Since the baby, we've had a hard time getting together." At this point, Dulcie is too afraid that another baby may have the same fate as her first, so she avoids any suggestive or sexual contact with Charles that might lead to a pregnancy or even remind her of the possibility of one.

Charles's compassion and patience have calmed Dulcie's momentary fears, but they have not been able to help her accept their past and generate hope for their future. Charles feels that he is being pulled down into her world of fear and mistrust. One night as he is driving

---

home, he is shocked by an egg thrown at his car and he starts to choke, almost losing control of the car. His sense of entrapment is symbolized by a fly he notices that is caught between the lamp and the Tee-shirt hanging over it. As he listens to Dulcie reciting statistics about how many people now have guns, he watches it "darting frantically back and forth until, suddenly, it was gone."

Charles's growing frustration finally causes him to refuse to give into Dulcie's fears. When he comes home and discovers that she will not open their door to children on Halloween, a holiday that she had previously loved, he gently takes her hands in his and tries to explain that children are ringing the bell, not teenagers "looking for trouble." But when she still refuses to answer the door, Charles insists, "this is ridiculous," grabs a box of cookies and tries to give them to the young "cowboy" in the hallway. When the boy refuses the offer because they are not "wrapped," Charles is reminded of the dangers that really do exist in their world. When he looks down at the other children on the floor below, however, who are enjoying the holiday, he cannot contain his frustration and declares to Dulcie, "We can't live like this." But Dulcie replies that she can.

Charles recognizes that both of them are "living like some rat trapped in our own wall." He takes a long walk up into the mountains to clear his head and think about his future. He sees only two options: "I could stay with Dulcie and be as far away from life as a person could be, or I could leave." As he walks, he thinks about the death of their child, but realizes that during that time, all he could think of was that he would die if anything ever happened to her. The realization of his deep love for her prompts him to see another option—to gently assert that life with all of its danger and promise can and should be faced.

While he is walking, he sees trash amid the vegetation in the canyon and decides that all of it might just be "fighting for a little space." He carries that sense of acceptance of the things that make up his world back to the apartment, where he drags the mattress back into the bedroom. When he turns off the light, Dulcie gasps in the darkness, but he waits patiently while she gets used to it. This time, when he turns to her, she does not pull away, and after a few awkward moments, "things became familiar again." When she grows fearful as their lovemaking intensifies, Charles assures her that "it's okay."

> **THE RAT DOES NOT FIT INTO DULCIE'S IMAGINED WORLD, WHERE BABIES ARE BORN HEALTHY, STREETS LEAD SAFELY HOME, AND RATS LIVE IN GARBAGE CANS OR IN SOMEONE ELSE'S HOME."**

Charles's love for Dulcie has enabled him to create a safe environment for her where she can heal after the death of their child and gain the strength necessary to eventually confront and accept the illogical nature of experience. Through his generous and compassionate support, he shows her how even the most damaged person can find a way to open up to the promise of life.

Source: Wendy Perkins, Critical Essay on "What I Saw from Where I Stood," in *Short Stories for Students*, Thomson Gale, 2007.

Joyce Hart

Hart is a freelance writer and published author. In the following essay, she examines the personality differences in the two main characters by studying what they each see from where they stand.

Marisa Silver's short story "What I Saw from Where I Stood" is, as one can tell from the title, an account of limited point of view. It is Charles's view of what happened to him and his wife following her miscarriage, and Charles narrates the story. The story illustrates how people read their environment differently depending on their point of view. To each person, some details stand out more than others, depending on the person's experience and his or her makeup. When two people experience loss, they may come away finding separate meanings in their shared experience. The significance of those details is determined by a person's perception. So while one person might be filled with fear and pessimism, as the wife Dulcie is, another person might focus on other details and be filled with awe and excitement, as Charles is.

In Silver's short story, the narrator begins by describing Dulcie's fear. She is afraid of freeways because she feels she cannot control where she is going as well as she can when she drives along side roads with regular intersections and streetlights. Later, the narrator explains that Dulcie likes to analyze everything. She needs to know the cause of her circumstances, needs to know why she miscarried the baby, what she did wrong to have the car stolen, why the rats come to their apartment wall to make scratching noises behind their bed. For Dulcie, believing that she is in control gives her courage; she can accept their circumstances as long as they do not disrupt her sense of how things should be. Unfortunately, their circumstances constantly show her she is not in control, and so they frighten her. She continually anticipates something dreadful may happen. Suddenly vulnerable after the baby's death, Dulcie begins to dread the worst. Her life and her thoughts are constantly distracted by possibilities of doom. Why else would she be fearful of being on the freeway and having limited options of escape? It is because she expects the worst to happen and needs a quick exit in order to avoid it. Ironically, her avoidance of freeways made her choose a side street where their car was hijacked.

Looking back on the months following the baby's death, Charles begins the story the evening they drove home from a party: he was drunk, and Dulcie was driving. He sits in the passenger seat, looking out the window, watching the scenery change from suburb to urban setting then watching how the people change from guys with "pudgy girlfriends" to "boys strutting the boulevard, waiting to slip into some one's silver Mercedes and make a buck." He is leaning back, somewhat dazed, and taking in the details. Even when the guys who eventually steal his car bump into the back of them, the narrator simply reacts to the slight dent in the fender rather than immediately wanting to accuse anyone for the damage. The incident happened; it was not big thing, and the narrator is ready to move on. Having been drinking, Charles takes things in stride, does not need to justify or explain them. But when he sees that one of the carjackers has a gun, Charles admits that he is scared. Now he reacts. He pulls Dulcie, and together they run away. As they consult with police, Charles is more able that Dulcie to get over this experience.

Dulcie, by contrast, will not let go. She attempts to gather all the details like someone piecing together a jigsaw puzzle. She wants the incident to make sense. In the process, she feeds her fear. The youths have the narrator's keys. If they look at the car registration papers, they will know where Charles and Dulcie live. Dulcie does not stop there. She imagines. If the youths who robbed their car know where Dulcie lives, she automatically assumes that they will come after her. If they come to the house, what will they do? Dulcie may imagine that they will steal their things. She may imagine that they will rape her, hurt her, and maybe even kill her. Fear knows no end. Dulcie obsesses about these possibilities. This mental movie keeps her awake and agitated and away from her job. Now when she drives down the road, she thinks about guns. She reads articles and memorizes statistics about how many people own guns. The man in the car next probably has one, Dulcie imagines. The woman at the market most assuredly carries one in her purse. Guns are everywhere, at least in Dulcie's mind.

Charles reports that he goes to work the day after the car hijacking. He has removed himself from the incident with the youths. When he comes back home, however, he discovers that Dulcie has moved things around. She can no longer sleep in the bedroom because there is a rat that makes scratching noises on the other side of the wall, and Dulcie cannot make it go away. The rat does not fit into Dulcie's imagined world, where babies are born healthy, streets lead safely home, and rats live in garbage cans or in someone else's home. Since Dulcie cannot remove the rat from their bedroom, she removes the bed. Charles says that Dulcie had been okay with the rat for a while. She even gave the rat a name, as if it were a pet. But since the incident with the car hijackers, Dulcie has lost it. She has too much to think about now. Her fears from the hijacking are all consuming. Now the rat is a vermin that can kill. Dulcie's perceptions are changing. Now everything is out to get her.

Charles views the rat differently. He does not like it any better than Dulcie, but he patched up all the holes that might give it access to their apartment. This assures him that the rat will not harm them. He feels like he fixed the situation, but Dulcie insists on their finding an exterminator. Dulcie is horrified when she sees the Rod, the rat-removing guy, put on surgical gloves. In Dulcie's mind this confirms her greatest fears, that rats are carriers of disease. In contrast, Charles comments, "This was a guy who dealt with rats every day of his life, and it didn't seem to faze him." Here there are three different people experiencing the same circumstances, with at least two different interpretations. When Dulcie learns that the rat might have come into the apartment because it is a warm, safe place in which to have babies, she reacts outside her fears of infection. However, then, Dulcie takes another negative turn. Now she feels guilty for causing the rat's death. This thought takes her back to the death of her own baby, the miscarriage that she suffered. So the cycle not only continues; it expands. She blames herself for the baby; now, she starts to blame herself for not just the rat's potential death but for the death of the rat's babies. Readers can begin to imagine what it must be like to live inside Dulcie's head, to see the world as she sees it. Her perception is full of remorse and fear; her muscles are clenched, her heart beats fast and hard, and she dreads another incident that proves that the world is a dangerous place.

There is a brief respite in Dulcie's fears, which occurs when the baby's ashes are delivered to her apartment from the mortuary. The narrator is concerned that the ashes will upset Dulcie, but she remains calm. She even says something positive after watching Charles scatter the baby's ashes into the ocean: "I think that's the bravest thing I've every seen a person do." For Dulcie, dispersing the ashes was even braver than facing the youth with a gun and running away from him, which the narrator did just a few days before. Facing death at the point of a gun is different, in Dulcie's mind, than handling the baby's ashes. The loss of her baby strikes deeper into her psyche than the potential loss of her own life or that of her husband's. Maybe the difference comes from the fact that the baby has died, whereas the threat to their own lives is only a possibility. For whatever reason, for the first time in the short story, Dulcie appears to be a bit more at ease. The birth and death of their child has gone full circle. The story is complete. As she leaves the beach behind, Dulcie picks up a smooth stone and places it in her pocket, as if she wants a souvenir. However, she has second thoughts and takes the stone out of her pocket and lets it drop to the ground. It is possible that at this point even Dulcie is learning to let things go.

The story about their stolen car also comes full circle, when the police find it. When they go to reclaim the car, they find it is a mess. Even the steering wheel is missing. The trash the youths left behind is now scattered all over the floor. The car is not worth salvaging. The car is like the couple's history. What they were before they met, before their baby died, before their car was stolen is not what they are now. They cannot reclaim what they were. They must go forward. It makes no sense to attempt to redo the past by going over it piece by piece; it makes no sense to fix their car. They would be throwing away money on the car if they bought new parts, just like they would be throwing away the present, fresh moments of their lives, if they were to keep trying to relive the past.

Toward the end of the story, something happens that makes it look as if Charles and Dulcie have switched places. Dulcie tells him that life, in many ways, is like "a self-fulfilling prophecy. Everybody expected things to be bad, so people made them bad." It is as if she is talking to herself. But from this point, Dulcie seems to be shifting her perceptions. She does not want to identify the youths who stole her car because she is not ready to confront them. She does not want to reawaken all those fears they caused.

Some change occurs in Charles, too. For example, when he drops Dulcie off at work, he reports that she turns to wave to him, "as if it were any regular day, as if we weren't living like some rat trapped in our own wall." Now it is a regular day for Dulcie, but Charles is some place else. He is the one who feels trapped by his perceptions, and he is the one who has to take a day off work. It is possible that Dulcie merely reacted sooner than the narrator to what happened to them. Charles might have had similar reactions of fear and anxiety, but they surfaced more slowly in him. Whatever the reason, he suddenly feels as if he might go crazy if he has to face other people's problems. He has enough problems.

So Charles goes for a hike and looks down at the canyon and watches the darkness lift off the land "as if someone were sliding a blanket off." Here, on the top of the hill, he views his ordinary life from a distance and glimpses what is really happening. What does he find? He sees things he has never noticed before, trees and plants, animals and trash, all mixed together. While the garbage might have distracted him previously, on this day it does not bother him at all. Instead of his wanting to go clean up the wilderness, to remove what he thinks does not belong in the landscape, he thinks now that every piece of trash as well as every stem of vegetation has a place. "For all I knew, this was one of those mountains that was made of trash, and it was nature that didn't belong. Maybe the trash, the dirt, the plants, bugs, condoms—maybe they were all just fighting for a little space." Charles has caught himself doing what Dulcie used to do, trying to sort out all the things he thought were good from the things he perceived were bad. It was a tiresome, unending task that had worn him down. What a difference it made to look at the mountain as one built from trash with nature trying to reclaim it, instead of looking at the mountain as being contaminated by the refuse. All things, in the narrator's new view, belong exactly where they are. The mixture of trash and the natural elements are not intruding on one another, as he had thought of the rat, but are merely trying to coexist.

So when he goes home, Charles attempts to reclaim his and Dulcie's relationship. He is not sure if there is enough left to salvage. Is it like their trashed car and not worth the effort? Or is there one strong element left that makes it worth the effort? He places the mattress back in the bedroom, a symbol of change that will greet Dulcie as soon as she steps into the apartment. The mattress also symbolizes the more intimate part of their relationship, one that has been missing ever since they lost the baby. Can they make love again?

Dulcie comes home and everything appears normal. She does not mention the mattress having been moved. They eat, watch television, go about their normal routine until it is time to go to bed. First, they listen for the rat, the symbol of their past fears. If the rat is there, it is not making any scratching sounds, is not distracting them. The couple relaxes into the silence. Maybe life is starting over for them, but they are both still afraid. What do they fear? They are afraid of opening to one another, afraid of allowing their hearts to be unprotected. Neither of them wants to endure more pain. However, they have come to realize that closing one's heart is just as painful as having one's heart broken. So they start slowly. Maybe they can love again. Maybe they can even open themselves to the possibility of creating a new life.

Source: Joyce Hart, Critical Essay on "What I Saw from Where I Stood," in *Short Stories for Students*, Thomson Gale, 2007.

Thomson Gale

In the following essay, the critic gives an overview of Marisa Silver's work.

Novelist and short story writer Marisa Silver is also a director of feature films. As the daughter of a director mother and a director/producer father, she came to moviemaking in her early twenties when she and her sister made an independent film entitled *Old Enough*. Silver asked her sister, Dina, to produce the script she had written, and Dina agreed. Silver's early filmmaking efforts were tinged with controversy, however. When she applied to the filmmaking workshop held by Robert Redford's nonprofit Sundance workshop and was accepted, there were charges of favoritism because her father had taught marketing at the workshop and introduced his daughter with a personal letter. However, Silver responded to her critics by pointing out that at the prestigious Sundance workshop, having a famous parent does not guarantee acceptance; she was accepted on her own merits and not through cronyism, she maintained.

"Still," wrote John Stark in *People*, "there's no denying the sisters had a head start. Marisa conferred with Hollywood screenwriters and Redford even helped her direct a scene of her movie. Dina (who accompanied her sister to Sundance) tackled the business end, taking workshops on how to produce and distribute films. When the month-long workshop was over, the Silver sisters headed to Hollywood, hoping to sell their movie. Hollywood wasn't buying, so they returned to New York where Dina formed a limited partnership called Silverfilm to raise an additional 400,000 dollars to be used on the film." The possibility of a sale to Hollywood was encouraging as the Sundance Film Festival had awarded sisters' movie the Grand Jury Prize.

The film was ultimately released by Orion. David Denby wrote in a *New York* article that it "has some shrewd moments, but I wish it had been bolder." It is the story of the friendship between two girls living on Manhattan's Lower East Side. Lonnie (played by Sarah Boyd) is the twelve-year-old daughter of wealthy parents, and Karen (played by Rainbow Harvest) is the fourteen-year-old streetwise daughter of an Italian janitor. *New Statesman* writer John Coleman described the film's detail as "exquisite" and called *Old Enough* "unassuming and not to be missed."

Silver next directed *Vital Signs*, a film about third-year medical students. The movie stars Jimmy Smits as the dean and chief of surgery. Other cast members include Laura San Giacomo, who plays a waitress putting her husband through medical school, William Devane as a surgeon, and Norma Aleandro as a cancer patient. Unfortunately, critics of the film complained that it is not very original. "The film's very basic problem is that it contains no surprising turns, and that its characters are familiar through and through," commented Janet Maslin in a *New York Times* review. *People* contributor Ralph Novak wrote that "by the time the romantic subplots are resolved and the predictable medical crises have been dealt with, this experience seems too much like a long hospital stay."

Silver and her husband, Ken Kwapis, codirected the more well-received *He Said, She Said*, starring Kevin Bacon and Elizabeth Perkins as columnists who fall in love despite their opposing viewpoints. Writing again in *People*, Novak called Bacon's character, Dan, "a womanizer" and Perkins's character, Lori, "marriage-minded, and always the twain shall meet. The only real difference between them is that Perkins gets away with throwing a coffee mug at Bacon's head, a bit of ostensible comedy that would not be regarded as at all funny if it were a man throwing a hard object at a woman." Bacon eventually throws over Sharon Stone to settle down with Perkins. For this project, Silver and Kwapis shared the directing responsibilities along gender lines, with Kwapis responsible for Bacon's lighter role as a marriage resistor and Silver for Lori's side of the relationship story. Maslin called Lori's characterization "more sincere and much more heavily fraught with emotion."

In addition to her movie work, Silver has also published a short story collection and a novel. The title character in Silver's story collection, *Babe in Paradise*, is Babe Ellis, a young woman trying to find her place in the city of Los Angeles. She appears in three of the nine stories set in the City of Angels. The characters here are not the movers and shakers of Los Angeles and Hollywood, but rather the people who live on the periphery of the fast lane. *Atlantic Monthly* reviewer David Uhlin felt that "when it comes to small moments—the frustrations and regrets of daily living—Silver's work is powerful and heartfelt." Uhlin further found this

to be particularly true in her depictions of the relationships between children and parents. *New York Times Book Review* reviewer Bernard Cooper wrote that in Silver's collection "trouble comes thick and fast: wildfire, carjacking, robbery, drug addiction, panic disorder. It is an indication of Silver's considerable gifts that rather than being melodramatic or numbing, this onslaught of misery retains its sting story after story."

In Silver's first novel, *No Direction Home*, the author "deftly tells the stories of three families whose struggles to survive are made tougher by depression, dementia, and traumatic separation," commented Deborah Donovan in *Booklist*. Themes of abandonment, family breakup, and responsibility underlie Silver's plot. When Caroline's husband becomes so depressed that he leaves her, she moves herself and her ten-year-old twin sons to her parents' home in Los Angeles. Her mother, Eleanor, is suffering from dementia, and her father, Vincent, has hired Mexican immigrant Amador to be her caretaker. However, Amador has also recently left his own family in Mexico to work in America. Seeking to reconnect with his father, teenager Rogelio sets out from Mexico to locate Amador and bring him back home. Meanwhile, teenager Marlene, an illegitimate half-sister to Caroline's sons and daughter of the father who recently left them, also sets out to find her father, whom she has never known. Caroline and Vincent must also deal with emotional issues left over from when he abandoned her and her mother decades earlier. The three families' lives merge and intersect as old wounds reopen and healing begins.

"Silver has a knack for creating flawed but sympathetic characters," observed Christine DeZelar-Tiedman in a *Library Journal* review of *No Direction Home*. She "proves herself a deft juggler of plot lines and an effective realist; she conjures an aching world of half-truths, physical need and emotional frustration," remarked a *Publishers Weekly* contributor. "Silver's prose is insightful, deeply empathetic and nonjudgmental, focused on individual struggles and the all-too-human face of suffering, her language charged with grace," concluded Luan Gaines on the *Curled Up with a Good Book* Web site.

Source: Thomson Gale, "Marisa Silver," in *Contemporary Authors Online*, Thomson Gale, 2006.

Michelle Huneven

In the following review, Huneven comments on the grim world in Silver's short story collection Babe in Paradise.

Marisa Silver's debut collection of short stories, *Babe in Paradise*, is peopled by housebreakers, eavesdroppers, carjackers, baby sellers, pornographers, bad parents and others who consider the social contract optional. And that's just the humans. Nature adds other transgressors: birds that nest inside houses, rats that hide inside walls, fires that devour homes. In other words, boundary problems abound.

The paradise of the title is Los Angeles, a Los Angeles that's haunted by the unattainable physical beauty and happy endings of Hollywood yet as populated by ordinary strugglers: a public school teacher, a man who rents out equipment, Hollywood wannabes. Their homes are ill-constructed, flimsy: shabby apartments; a "pitiable warren of rooms"; an advertised "hillside aerie" turns out to be a pale pink shoebox with walls cracked at the seams.

The human body is no more substantial, reliable or well tended; babies are miscarried or born with holes in their hearts or dropped in infancy or transported for sale in suitcases. Bones break, lungs give out, addictions take over, panic overwhelms. In other words, Silver's world is just like life, only grimmer.

Personal feelings are routinely smothered, ignored or brutalized. In fact, most of the characters in these stories have been so ill-treated by fate, their fellows and/or themselves that they're understandably skittish, if not completely shut down.

Silver's women in particular foster no illusions about sex, intimacy or any other human connection—although they often exhibit a dark humor. "Romeo's here," says a woman about to go on her first date in years. "Let's just hope he's not a complete psycho." Their relations with men tend to be a confusing mix of desire and revulsion; in love, the female characters are often harsh, dissociated and given to cruelty. In "Gunsmoke," Alice sleeps with an old boyfriend: "Neither one of us makes a noise, or looks the other in the eye," she says. Mariana in "The Missing" keeps an eye on her beeper during sex. In "Statues," a young actress, whose boyfriend admires a former porn actress-turned-movie star, impulsively makes her own short porn film—in front of him. At 16, Babe, who

appears in three of the nine stories, sleeps with the man who drives the Goodwill truck: "[S]he knew the emotions she had for him were not love, and that someone who encouraged such feelings of disgust and petulant wanting did not love her either." Later, she'll kick him in the head with the hard toe of her boot.

Men are often absent, and their absences shape and define many of the other characters' lives. Babe of the title does not know who her father is, and her mother will not say. In "Gunsmoke," Alice's father left his family to become a desert hermit. In "The Missing," Mariana's father died when she was young. In "Falling Bodies," an infant's father is dead from a rock-climbing accident. These absences, and the silences surrounding them, become irretrievable, missing pieces of the self: Babe, on remembering a man she and her mother mysteriously met in a coffee shop, muses, "I really have no idea about the things that went on in my life."

On the other hand, several of Silver's characters redeem themselves by willingly and generously taking on the job of parenting, often for other people's children—these are the heroes of the collection.

In "Two Criminals," a dying man adopts the two stepdaughters he's raised; his younger brother, we understand, will take over for him in the future. The older man in "Falling Bodies," initially dubious about his alleged grandchild's paternity, ultimately commits to the child whether the blood bond is real or a lie. In "What I Saw From Where I Stood," a young couple suffer the trauma of a miscarriage, and it is the husband, Charles, who decides it's time to try for another child.

Like Denis Johnson's angelic miscreants, some of these raw, damaged characters are redeemed by the surprising and timely surfacing of compassion, affection or self-knowledge. Babe, in particular, engenders hope and respect: Fatherless, with a mentally ill mother and a knack for finding the worst possible boyfriends, she nevertheless negotiates trying circumstances with liveliness if not always grace.

At times, Silver's eye can be as cold and judgmental as a casting director's. She's hard on physical imperfections, detailing the varicose veins and wrinkles and hollow cheeks of older (45-to 50-year-old) women. Other women have "pancake batter folds of flesh," nipples "as wide and dark as pancakes" and ill-fitting bras. A man's age spots are described as "dollops of chocolate," and "his skin looks like it's about to peel off in big leathery plates."

Occasionally, Silver hits a wrong note—a character teaches in "a rough part of Glendale," for example; where, exactly, could that be? Silver's prose could also use a good tidying up: There are too many stray words and phrases and gratuitous explanations, and some stories are overly long, with too much dramatized or explained.

That said, the stories are ambitiously and successfully well-structured; Silver is adept at weaving flashbacks into the present action. And at her best—in "The Missing," "The Passenger" and "Gunsmoke," the characters are in focus, myth and fact play off each other and the Southern California landscape is convincingly observed.

Other times, Silver's Los Angeles, with its drug crimes, brush fires and Hollywood desperation, seems too typically apocalyptic, a city borrowed from *Boogie Nights* and *Dragnet* and less familiar—thank God—to those of us who inhabit it day by day.

Silver's vision cumulatively amounts to a dark, desperate, down-and-out world, a Los Angeles of her own making, where the elusive instances of human connection and hope are all too rare, and therefore all the more luminous.

Source: Michelle Huneven, "The Seduction of Place: *Babe in Paradise,* fiction by Marisa Silver," in *Los Angeles Times,* August 5, 2001, p. 1.

Jonathan Yardley

In the following review, Yardley contends that it is "the sense of entering an unknown world" that makes Babe in Paradise *appealing, and regards Silver's compassion and sympathy for her characters noteworthy.*

Peter and Janie, newly married, decide on impulse to leave home in Ohio and move to California. He wants to be a screenwriter, and she has acting ambitions. They toss "their wedding money and everything they owned" into their Volkswagen and head west. When they get there, it is a revelation of sorts:

> "Los Angeles, at first glance, seemed nothing like what Janie had imagined it to be. She anticipated wide streets lined with giraffe-necked palm trees, lawns as plush as carpets topped with wide, complacent houses. She expected a kind of sheen to bathe the city, as

if glamour were a weather condition. But all they could see from the freeway were the flat, dusty roofs of sunstroked buildings, many of which were topped by billboards advertising refried beans and strip clubs. . . . Finally, Peter spotted the sign for the Hollywood Freeway. They were relieved. Now they could stop looking for Los Angeles, which seemed to be everywhere and nowhere at the same time."

This Los Angeles, which shares the same physical space as Sunset Boulevard and Santa Monica yet scarcely seems in the same universe, is the setting for the nine short stories collected in *Babe in Paradise,* the first book by Marisa Silver, who also has worked as a movie director. As the narrator of one of these stories says about this place: "People think Los Angeles is the same everywhere—all palm trees and swimming pools. But some nights you need a passport and a two-way dictionary just to get from Hancock Park to Koreatown."

It is this aspect of these stories that is most interesting and rewarding. The private dramas confronted by Silver's mostly rather luckless men and women are often noteworthy and occasionally revealing, but it's the sense of entering an unknown world that gives *Babe in Paradise* its strongest appeal. Other writers—Raymond Chandler, Nathanael West, Kenneth Anger, Joan Didion, John Rechy—have given us glimpses of other parts of Los Angeles, but Silver shows us a different place. In this she displays a kinship with certain writers—Edward F. Jones, Patricia Griffith, Marita Golden, Gary Krist, George Pelecanos—who write about aspects of Washington that rarely find their way into the corridors-of-power schlock fiction the city usually inspires, just as Los Angeles usually inspires casting-couch schlock fiction.

The title story is about a 16-year-old girl whose eccentric mother has found her way to the Coast because "Los Angeles held out the possibility of paradise," but Babe quickly learns there's precious little of that for her. Instead she and her mother discover "that the world was an unwelcoming place, and that their life was barely hinged to its periphery." For them as for almost everyone else in these stories, Los Angeles offers not paradise but loneliness and isolation and in some cases fear. "We can't live like this," says a young husband whose marriage is troubled for many reasons; a few pages later, in the story cited above, Peter tells Janie, "We just can't live like this anymore." Yet they have little choice except to struggle on. "You get by," a young woman tells her suicidal mother. "You do okay."

The compassion and sympathy Silver feels for these people are given deeper meaning by the good-humored affection with which she regards them. Unlike many who have written about Los Angeles, she resists the temptation to take Cheap shots at the oddities of life there. She understands that like people everywhere else, Los Angelenos of all kinds and classes are pursuing happiness, they're just doing it in their own way. Take, for example, a good-hearted woman named Jenna:

> "She talks about the spirit like it's a kindly neighbor you might run into at the grocery store. She eagerly embraces whatever is alternative and unscientific. She's been channeled, visualized, rolfed, and aromatherapied. She's hennaed her hair and her hands, shaved her head in order to free herself of vanity, grown dreadlocks to accomplish the same goal. Cynicism makes her sad.... [Her husband] loves it all—her potions and her faith that there is something else going on while we go about what we mistakenly consider our lives."

From time to time Silver teeters at the edge of literary slumming—putting on public display her empathy for the lower social orders—but passages such as that one pull her out of it. There are, fortunately, many of them in this book, which is as good-hearted as Jenna herself, albeit far less giddy.

Source: Jonathan Yardley, "The Hidden Corners of L.A.," in *Washington Post*, August 9, 2001, p. C02.

SOURCES

Cooper, Bernard, "City of Angels," in *New York Times Book Review*, August 26, 2001, p. 25.

Harlan, Megan, Review of *Babe in Paradise*, in *Entertainment Weekly*, No. 607, August 3, 2001, p. 62.

Huneven, Michelle, "The Seduction of Place," in *Los Angeles Times*, August 5, 2001, p. 1.

Review of *Babe in Paradise*, in *Publishers Weekly*, Vol. 248, No. 22, May 28, 2001, p. 45.

Silver, Marisa, "What I Saw from Where I Stood," in *Babe in Paradise*, Norton, 2001, pp. 59–80.

Uhlin, David, Review of *Babe in Paradise*, in *Atlantic Monthly*, Vol. 288, No. 1, July–August 2001, p. 163.

Yardley, Jonathan, "The Hidden Corners of L.A.," in *Washington Post*, August 9, 2001, p. C02.

FURTHER READING

Fulton, William, *The Reluctant Metropolis: The Politics of Urban Growth in Los Angeles*, Johns Hopkins University Press, 2001.
> In this collection of twelve essays, Fulton explores the political and financial development of the city in the last thirty years of the twentieth century.

Kennedy, Marla Hamburg, Ben Stiller, and David L. Ulin, eds., *Looking at Los Angeles*, Metropolis Books, 2005.
> The editors collected photographs and pictorial representations of Los Angeles from the early part of the twentieth century to the twenty-first. The collection presents a visual history of the city as revealed in its architecture, culture, and people.

Marx, Robert J., and Susan Wengerhoff Davidson, *Facing the Ultimate Loss: Coping with the Death of a Child*, Champion Press, 2003.
> The authors have worked extensively in the field of grief counseling and in this book suggest ways to cope with the death of a child.

Rosof, Barbara D., *The Worst Loss: How Families Heal from the Death of a Child*, Owl Books, 1995.
> Rosof, a California psychotherapist who counsels families who have lost a child, explains how grieving is an important part of the recovery process and how barriers to this process can be broken down.

Glossary

A

Aestheticism: A literary and artistic movement of the nineteenth century. Followers of the movement believed that art should not be mixed with social, political, or moral teaching. The statement "art for art's sake" is a good summary of aestheticism. The movement had its roots in France, but it gained widespread importance in England in the last half of the nineteenth century, where it helped change the Victorian practice of including moral lessons in literature. Oscar Wilde and Edgar Allan Poe are two of the best-known "aesthetes" of the late nineteenth century.

Allegory: A narrative technique in which characters representing things or abstract ideas are used to convey a message or teach a lesson. Allegory is typically used to teach moral, ethical, or religious lessons but is sometimes used for satiric or political purposes. Many fairy tales are allegories.

Allusion: A reference to a familiar literary or historical person or event, used to make an idea more easily understood. Joyce Carol Oates's story "Where Are You Going, Where Have You Been?" exhibits several allusions to popular music.

Analogy: A comparison of two things made to explain something unfamiliar through its similarities to something familiar, or to prove one point based on the acceptance of another. Similes and metaphors are types of analogies.

Antagonist: The major character in a narrative or drama who works against the hero or protagonist. The Misfit in Flannery O'Connor's story "A Good Man Is Hard to Find" serves as the antagonist for the Grandmother.

Anthology: A collection of similar works of literature, art, or music. Zora Neale Hurston's "The Eatonville Anthology" is a collection of stories that take place in the same town.

Anthropomorphism: The presentation of animals or objects in human shape or with human characteristics. The term is derived from the Greek word for "human form." The fur necklet in Katherine Mansfield's story "Miss Brill" has anthropomorphic characteristics.

Anti-hero: A central character in a work of literature who lacks traditional heroic qualities such as courage, physical prowess, and fortitude. Anti-heroes typically distrust conventional values and are unable to commit themselves to any ideals. They generally feel helpless in a world over which they have no control. Anti-heroes usually accept, and often celebrate, their positions as social outcasts. A well-known anti-hero is Walter Mitty in James Thurber's story "The Secret Life of Walter Mitty."

Archetype: The word archetype is commonly used to describe an original pattern or model from which all other things of the same kind are made. Archetypes are the literary images that grow out of the "collective unconscious," a theory proposed by psychologist Carl Jung. They appear in literature as incidents and plots that repeat basic patterns of life. They may also appear as stereotyped characters. The "schlemiel" of Yiddish literature is an archetype.

Autobiography: A narrative in which an individual tells his or her life story. Examples include Benjamin Franklin's *Autobiography* and Amy Hempel's story "In the Cemetery Where Al Jolson Is Buried," which has autobiographical characteristics even though it is a work of fiction.

Avant-garde: A literary term that describes new writing that rejects traditional approaches to literature in favor of innovations in style or content. Twentieth-century examples of the literary avant-garde include the modernists and the minimalists.

B

Belles-lettres: A French term meaning "fine letters" or" beautiful writing." It is often used as a synonym for literature, typically referring to imaginative and artistic rather than scientific or expository writing. Current usage sometimes restricts the meaning to light or humorous writing and appreciative essays about literature. Lewis Carroll's *Alice in Wonderland* epitomizes the realm of belles-lettres.

Bildungsroman: A German word meaning "novel of development." The *bildungsroman* is a study of the maturation of a youthful character, typically brought about through a series of social or sexual encounters that lead to self-awareness. J. D. Salinger's *Catcher in the Rye* is a *bildungsroman*, and Doris Lessing's story "Through the Tunnel" exhibits characteristics of a *bildungsroman* as well.

Black Aesthetic Movement: A period of artistic and literary development among African Americans in the 1960s and early 1970s. This was the first major African-American artistic movement since the Harlem Renaissance and was closely paralleled by the civil rights and black power movements. The black aesthetic writers attempted to produce works of art that would be meaningful to the black masses. Key figures in black aesthetics included one of its founders, poet and playwright Amiri Baraka, formerly known as Le Roi Jones; poet and essayist Haki R. Madhubuti, formerly Don L. Lee; poet and playwright Sonia Sanchez; and dramatist Ed Bullins. Works representative of the Black Aesthetic Movement include Amiri Baraka's play *Dutchman*, a 1964 Obie award-winner.

Black Humor: Writing that places grotesque elements side by side with humorous ones in an attempt to shock the reader, forcing him or her to laugh at the horrifying reality of a disordered world. "Lamb to the Slaughter," by Roald Dahl, in which a placid housewife murders her husband and serves the murder weapon to the investigating policemen, is an example of black humor.

C

Catharsis: The release or purging of unwanted emotions—specifically fear and pity— brought about by exposure to art. The term was first used by the Greek philosopher Aristotle in his *Poetics* to refer to the desired effect of tragedy on spectators.

Character: Broadly speaking, a person in a literary work. The actions of characters are what constitute the plot of a story, novel, or poem. There are numerous types of characters, ranging from simple, stereotypical figures to intricate, multifaceted ones. "Characterization" is the process by which an author creates vivid, believable characters in a work of art. This may be done in a variety of ways, including (1) direct description of the character by the narrator; (2) the direct presentation of the speech, thoughts, or actions of the character; and (3) the responses of other characters to the character. The term "character" also refers to a form originated by the ancient Greek writer Theophrastus that later became popular in the seventeenth and eighteenth centuries. It is a short essay or sketch of a person who prominently displays a specific attribute or quality, such as miserliness or ambition. "Miss Brill," a story by Katherine Mansfield, is an example of a character sketch.

Classical: In its strictest definition in literary criticism, classicism refers to works of ancient Greek or Roman literature. The term may also be used to describe a literary work of recognized importance (a "classic") from any time period or literature that exhibits the traits of classicism. Examples of later works and authors now described as classical include French literature of the seventeenth century, Western novels of the nineteenth century, and American fiction of the mid-nineteenth century such as that written by James Fenimore Cooper and Mark Twain.

Climax: The turning point in a narrative, the moment when the conflict is at its most intense. Typically, the structure of stories, novels, and plays is one of rising action, in which tension builds to the climax, followed by falling action, in which tension lessens as the story moves to its conclusion.

Comedy: One of two major types of drama, the other being tragedy. Its aim is to amuse, and it typically ends happily. Comedy assumes many forms, such as farce and burlesque, and uses a variety of techniques, from parody to satire. In a restricted sense the term comedy refers only to dramatic presentations, but in general usage it is commonly applied to nondramatic works as well.

Comic Relief: The use of humor to lighten the mood of a serious or tragic story, especially in plays. The technique is very common in Elizabethan works, and can be an integral part of the plot or simply a brief event designed to break the tension of the scene.

Conflict: The conflict in a work of fiction is the issue to be resolved in the story. It usually occurs between two characters, the protagonist and the antagonist, or between the protagonist and society or the protagonist and himself or herself. The conflict in Washington Irving's story "The Devil and Tom Walker" is that the Devil wants Tom Walker's soul but Tom does not want to go to hell.

Criticism: The systematic study and evaluation of literary works, usually based on a specific method or set of principles. An important part of literary studies since ancient times, the practice of criticism has given rise to numerous theories, methods, and "schools," sometimes producing conflicting, even contradictory, interpretations of literature in general as well as of individual works. Even such basic issues as what constitutes a poem or a novel have been the subject of much criticism over the centuries. Seminal texts of literary criticism include Plato's *Republic,* Aristotle's *Poetics,* Sir Philip Sidney's *The Defence of Poesie,* and John Dryden's *Of Dramatic Poesie.* Contemporary schools of criticism include deconstruction, feminist, psychoanalytic, poststructuralist, new historicist, postcolonialist, and reader-response.

D

Deconstruction: A method of literary criticism characterized by multiple conflicting interpretations of a given work. Deconstructionists consider the impact of the language of a work and suggest that the true meaning of the work is not necessarily the meaning that the author intended.

Deduction: The process of reaching a conclusion through reasoning from general premises to a specific premise. Arthur Conan Doyle's character Sherlock Holmes often used deductive reasoning to solve mysteries.

Denotation: The definition of a word, apart from the impressions or feelings it creates in the reader. The word "apartheid" denotes a political and economic policy of segregation by race, but its connotations—oppression, slavery, inequality—are numerous.

Denouement: A French word meaning "the unknotting." In literature, it denotes the resolution of conflict in fiction or drama. The *denouement* follows the climax and provides an outcome to the primary plot situation as well as an explanation of secondary plot complications. A well-known example of *denouement* is the last scene of the play *As You Like It* by William Shakespeare, in which couples are married, an evildoer repents, the identities of two disguised characters are revealed, and a ruler is restored to power. Also known as "falling action."

Detective Story: A narrative about the solution of a mystery or the identification of a criminal. The conventions of the detective story include the detective's scrupulous use of logic in solving the mystery; incompetent or ineffectual police; a suspect who appears guilty at first but is later proved innocent; and the detective's friend or confidant—often the narrator—whose slowness in interpreting clues emphasizes by contrast the detective's brilliance. Edgar Allan Poe's "Murders in the Rue Morgue" is commonly regarded as the earliest example of this type of story. Other practitioners are Arthur Conan Doyle, Dashiell Hammett, and Agatha Christie.

Dialogue: Dialogue is conversation between people in a literary work. In its most restricted sense, it refers specifically to the speech of characters in a drama. As a specific literary genre, a "dialogue" is a composition in which characters debate an issue or idea.

Didactic: A term used to describe works of literature that aim to teach a moral, religious, political, or practical lesson. Although didactic elements are often found inartistically pleasing works, the term "didactic" usually refers to literature in which the message is more important than the form. The term may also be used to criticize a work that the critic finds "overly didactic," that is, heavy-handed in its delivery of a lesson. An example of didactic literature is John Bunyan's *Pilgrim's Progress.*

Dramatic Irony: Occurs when the reader of a work of literature knows something that a character in the work itself does not know. The irony is in the contrast between the intended meaning of the statements or actions of a character and the additional information understood by the audience.

Dystopia: An imaginary place in a work of fiction where the characters lead dehumanized, fearful lives. George Orwell's *Nineteen Eighty-four,* and Margaret Atwood's *Handmaid's Tale* portray versions of dystopia.

E

Edwardian: Describes cultural conventions identified with the period of the reign of Edward VII of England (1901–1910). Writers of the Edwardian Age typically displayed a strong reaction against the propriety and conservatism of the Victorian Age. Their work often exhibits distrust of authority in religion, politics, and art and expresses strong doubts about the soundness of conventional values. Writers of this era include E. M. Forster, H. G. Wells, and Joseph Conrad.

Empathy: A sense of shared experience, including emotional and physical feelings, with someone or something other than oneself. Empathy is often used to describe the response of a reader to a literary character.

Epilogue: A concluding statement or section of a literary work. In dramas, particularly those of the seventeenth and eighteenth centuries, the epilogue is a closing speech, often in verse, delivered by an actor at the end of a play and spoken directly to the audience.

Epiphany: A sudden revelation of truth inspired by a seemingly trivial incident. The term was widely used by James Joyce in his critical writings, and the stories in Joyce's *Dubliners* are commonly called "epiphanies."

Epistolary Novel: A novel in the form of letters. The form was particularly popular in the eighteenth century. The form can also be applied to short stories, as in Edwidge Danticat's "Children of the Sea."

Epithet: A word or phrase, often disparaging or abusive, that expresses a character trait of someone or something. "The Napoleon of crime" is an epithet applied to Professor Moriarty, arch-rival of Sherlock Holmes in Arthur Conan Doyle's series of detective stories.

Existentialism: A predominantly twentieth-century philosophy concerned with the nature and perception of human existence. There are two major strains of existentialist thought: atheistic and Christian. Followers of atheistic existentialism believe that the individual is alone in a godless universe and that the basic human condition is one of suffering and loneliness. Nevertheless, because there are no fixed values, individuals can create their own characters—indeed, they can shape themselves—through the exercise of free will. The atheistic strain culminates in and is popularly associated with the works of Jean-Paul Sartre. The Christian existentialists, on the other hand, believe that only in God may people find freedom from life's anguish. The two strains hold certain beliefs in common: that existence cannot be fully understood or described through empirical effort; that anguish is a universal element of life; that individuals must bear responsibility for their actions; and that there is no common standard of behavior or perception for religious and ethical matters. Existentialist thought figures prominently in the works of such authors as Franz Kafka, Fyodor Dostoyevsky, and Albert Camus.

Expatriatism: The practice of leaving one's country to live for an extended period in another country. Literary expatriates include Irish author James Joyce who moved to Italy and France, American writers James Baldwin, Ernest Hemingway, Gertrude Stein, and F. Scott Fitzgerald who lived and wrote in Paris, and Polish novelist Joseph Conrad in England.

Exposition: Writing intended to explain the nature of an idea, thing, or theme. Expository writing is often combined with description, narration, or argument.

Expressionism: An indistinct literary term, originally used to describe an early twentieth-century school of German painting. The term applies to almost any mode of unconventional, highly subjective writing that distorts reality in some way. Advocates of Expressionism include Federico Garcia Lorca, Eugene O'Neill, Franz Kafka, and James Joyce.

F

Fable: A prose or verse narrative intended to convey amoral. Animals or inanimate objects with human characteristics often serve as characters in fables. A famous fable is Aesop's "The Tortoise and the Hare."

Fantasy: A literary form related to mythology and folklore. Fantasy literature is typically set in non-existent realms and features supernatural beings. Notable examples of literature with elements of fantasy are Gabriel Gárcia Márquez's story "The Handsomest Drowned Man in the World" and Ursula K. Le Guin's "The Ones Who Walk Away from Omelas."

Farce: A type of comedy characterized by broad humor, outlandish incidents, and often vulgar subject matter. Much of the comedy in film and television could more accurately be described as farce.

Fiction: Any story that is the product of imagination rather than a documentation of fact. Characters and events in such narratives may be based in real life but their ultimate form and configuration is a creation of the author.

Figurative Language: A technique in which an author uses figures of speech such as hyperbole, irony, metaphor, or simile for a particular effect. Figurative language is the opposite of literal language, in which every word is truthful, accurate, and free of exaggeration or embellishment.

Flashback: A device used in literature to present action that occurred before the beginning of the story. Flashbacks are often introduced as the dreams or recollections of one or more characters.

Foil: A character in a work of literature whose physical or psychological qualities contrast strongly with, and therefore highlight, the corresponding qualities of another character. In his Sherlock Holmes stories, Arthur Conan Doyle portrayed Dr. Watson as a man of normal habits and intelligence, making him a foil for the eccentric and unusually perceptive Sherlock Holmes.

Folklore: Traditions and myths preserved in a culture or group of people. Typically, these are passed on by word of mouth in various forms—such as legends, songs, and proverbs—or preserved in customs and ceremonies. Washington Irving, in "The Devil and Tom Walker" and many of his other stories, incorporates many elements of the folklore of New England and Germany.

Folktale: A story originating in oral tradition. Folk tales fall into a variety of categories, including legends, ghost stories, fairy tales, fables, and anecdotes based on historical figures and events.

Foreshadowing: A device used in literature to create expectation or to set up an explanation of later developments. Edgar Allan Poe uses foreshadowing to create suspense in "The Fall of the House of Usher" when the narrator comments on the crumbling state of disrepair in which he finds the house.

G

Genre: A category of literary work. Genre may refer to both the content of a given work—tragedy, comedy, horror, science fiction—and to its form, such as poetry, novel, or drama.

Gilded Age: A period in American history during the 1870s and after characterized by political corruption and materialism. A number of important novels of social and political criticism were written during this time. Henry James and Kate Chopin are two writers who were prominent during the Gilded Age.

Gothicism: In literature, works characterized by a taste for medieval or morbid characters and situations. A gothic novel prominently features elements of horror, the supernatural, gloom, and violence: clanking chains, terror, ghosts, medieval castles, and unexplained phenomena. The term "gothic novel" is also applied to novels that lack elements of the traditional Gothic setting but that create a similar atmosphere of terror or dread. The term can also be applied to stories, plays, and poems. Mary Shelley's *Frankenstein* and Joyce Carol Oates's *Belle fleur* are both gothic novels.

Grotesque: In literature, a work that is characterized by exaggeration, deformity, freakishness, and disorder. The grotesque often includes an element of comic absurdity. Examples of the grotesque can be found in the works of Edgar Allan Poe, Flannery O'Connor, Joseph Heller, and Shirley Jackson.

H

Harlem Renaissance: The Harlem Renaissance of the 1920s is generally considered the first significant movement of black writers and artists in the United States. During this period, new and established black writers, many of whom lived in the region of New York City known as Harlem, published more fiction and poetry than ever before, the first influential black literary journals were established, and black authors and artists received their first widespread recognition and serious critical appraisal. Among the major writers associated with this period are Countee Cullen, Langston Hughes, Arna Bontemps, and Zora Neale Hurston.

Hero/Heroine: The principal sympathetic character in a literary work. Heroes and heroines typically exhibit admirable traits: idealism, courage, and integrity, for example. Famous heroes and heroines of literature include Charles Dickens's Oliver Twist, Margaret Mitchell's Scarlett O'Hara, and the anonymous narrator in Ralph Ellison's *Invisible Man*.

Hyperbole: Deliberate exaggeration used to achieve an effect. In William Shakespeare's *Macbeth*, Lady Macbeth hyperbolizes when she says, "All the perfumes of Arabia could not sweeten this little hand."

I

Image: A concrete representation of an object or sensory experience. Typically, such a representation helps evoke the feelings associated with the object or experience itself. Images are either "literal" or "figurative." Literal images are especially concrete and involve little or no extension of the obvious meaning of the words used to express them. Figurative images do not follow the literal meaning of the words exactly. Images in literature are usually visual, but the term "image" can also refer to the representation of any sensory experience.

Imagery: The array of images in a literary work. Also used to convey the author's overall use of figurative language in a work.

In medias res: A Latin term meaning "in the middle of things." It refers to the technique of beginning a story at its midpoint and then using various flashback devices to reveal previous action. This technique originated in such epics as Virgil's *Aeneid*.

Interior Monologue: A narrative technique in which characters' thoughts are revealed in a way that appears to be uncontrolled by the author. The interior monologue typically aims to reveal the inner self of a character. It portrays emotional experiences as they occur at both a conscious and unconscious level. One of the best-known interior monologues in English is the Molly Bloom section at the close of James Joyce's *Ulysses*. Katherine Anne Porter's "The Jilting of Granny Weatherall" is also told in the form of an interior monologue.

Irony: In literary criticism, the effect of language in which the intended meaning is the opposite of what is stated. The title of Jonathan Swift's "A Modest Proposal" is ironic because what Swift proposes in this essay is cannibalism—hardly "modest."

J

Jargon: Language that is used or understood only by a select group of people. Jargon may refer to terminology used in a certain profession, such as computer jargon, or it may refer to any nonsensical language that is not understood by most people. Anthony Burgess's *A Clockwork Orange* and James Thurber's "The Secret Life of Walter Mitty" both use jargon.

K

Knickerbocker Group: An indistinct group of New York writers of the first half of the nineteenth century. Members of the group were linked only by location and a common theme: New York life. Two famous members of the Knickerbocker Group were Washington Irving and William Cullen Bryant. The group's name derives from Irving's *Knickerbocker's History of New York*.

L

Literal Language: An author uses literal language when he or she writes without exaggerating or embellishing the subject matter and without any tools of figurative language. To say "He ran very quickly down the street" is to use literal language, whereas to say "He ran like a hare down the street" would be using figurative language.

Literature: Literature is broadly defined as any written or spoken material, but the term most often refers to creative works. Literature includes poetry, drama, fiction, and many kinds of nonfiction writing, as well as oral, dramatic, and broadcast compositions not necessarily preserved in a written format, such as films and television programs.

Lost Generation: A term first used by Gertrude Stein to describe the post-World War I generation of American writers: men and women haunted by a sense of betrayal and emptiness brought about by the destructiveness of the war. The term is commonly applied to Hart Crane, Ernest Hemingway, F. Scott Fitzgerald, and others.

M

Magic Realism: A form of literature that incorporates fantasy elements or supernatural occurrences into the narrative and accepts them as truth. Gabriel Gárcia Márquez and Laura Esquivel are two writers known for their works of magic realism.

Metaphor: A figure of speech that expresses an idea through the image of another object. Metaphors suggest the essence of the first object by identifying it with certain qualities of the second object. An example is "But soft, what light through yonder window breaks? / It is the east, and Juliet is the sun" in William Shakespeare's *Romeo and Juliet*. Here, Juliet, the first object, is identified with qualities of the second object, the sun.

Minimalism: A literary style characterized by spare, simple prose with few elaborations. In minimalism, the main theme of the work is often never discussed directly. Amy Hempel and Ernest Hemingway are two writers known for their works of minimalism.

Modernism: Modern literary practices. Also, the principles of a literary school that lasted from roughly the beginning of the twentieth century until the end of World War II. Modernism is defined by its rejection of the literary conventions of the nineteenth century and by its opposition to conventional morality, taste, traditions, and economic values. Many writers are associated with the concepts of modernism, including Albert Camus, D. H. Lawrence, Ernest Hemingway, William Faulkner, Eugene O'Neill, and James Joyce.

Monologue: A composition, written or oral, by a single individual. More specifically, a speech given by a single individual in a drama or other public entertainment. It has no set length, although it is usually several or more lines long. "I Stand Here Ironing" by Tillie Olsen is an example of a story written in the form of a monologue.

Mood: The prevailing emotions of a work or of the author in his or her creation of the work. The mood of a work is not always what might be expected based on its subject matter.

Motif: A theme, character type, image, metaphor, or other verbal element that recurs throughout a single work of literature or occurs in a number of different works over a period of time. For example, the color white in Herman Melville's *Moby Dick* is a "specific" motif, while the trials of star-crossed lovers is a "conventional" motif from the literature of all periods.

N

Narration: The telling of a series of events, real or invented. A narration may be either a simple narrative, in which the events are recounted chronologically, or a narrative with a plot, in which the account is given in a style reflecting the author's artistic concept of the story. Narration is sometimes used as a synonym for "storyline."

Narrative: A verse or prose accounting of an event or sequence of events, real or invented. The term is also used as an adjective in the sense "method of narration." For example, in literary criticism, the expression "narrative technique" usually refers to the way the author structures and presents his or her story. Different narrative forms include diaries, travelogues, novels, ballads, epics, short stories, and other fictional forms.

Narrator: The teller of a story. The narrator may be the author or a character in the story through whom the author speaks. Huckleberry Finn is the narrator of Mark Twain's *The Adventures of Huckleberry Finn.*

Novella: An Italian term meaning "story." This term has been especially used to describe fourteenth-century Italian tales, but it also refers to modern short novels. Modern novellas include Leo Tolstoy's *The Death of Ivan Ilich,* Fyodor Dostoyevsky's *Notes from the Underground,* and Joseph Conrad's *Heart of Darkness.*

O

Oedipus Complex: A son's romantic obsession with his mother. The phrase is derived from the story of the ancient Theban hero Oedipus, who unknowingly killed his father and married his mother, and was popularized by Sigmund Freud's theory of psychoanalysis. Literary occurrences of the Oedipus complex include Sophocles' *Oedipus Rex* and D. H. Lawrence's "The Rocking-Horse Winner."

Onomatopoeia: The use of words whose sounds express or suggest their meaning. In its simplest sense, onomatopoeia may be represented by words that mimic the sounds they denote such as "hiss" or "meow." At a more subtle level, the pattern and rhythm of sounds and rhymes of a line or poem may be onomatopoeic.

Oral Tradition: A process by which songs, ballads, folklore, and other material are transmitted by word of mouth. The tradition of oral transmission predates the written record systems of literate society. Oral transmission preserves material sometimes over generations, although often with variations. Memory plays a large part in the recitation and preservation of orally transmitted material. Native American myths and legends, and African folktales told by plantation slaves are examples of orally transmitted literature.

P

Parable: A story intended to teach a moral lesson or answer an ethical question. Examples of parables are the stories told by Jesus Christ in the New Testament, notably "The Prodigal Son," but parables also are used in Sufism, rabbinic literature, Hasidism, and Zen Buddhism. Isaac Bashevis Singer's story "Gimpel the Fool" exhibits characteristics of a parable.

Paradox: A statement that appears illogical or contradictory at first, but may actually point to an underlying truth. A literary example of a paradox is George Orwell's statement "All animals are equal, but some animals are more equal than others" in *Animal Farm.*

Parody: In literature, this term refers to an imitation of a serious literary work or the signature style of a particular author in a ridiculous manner. A typical parody adopts the style of the original and applies it to an inappropriate subject for humorous effect. Parody is a form of satire and could be considered the literary equivalent of a caricature or cartoon. Henry Fielding's *Shamela* is a parody of Samuel Richardson's *Pamela.*

Persona: A Latin term meaning "mask." Personae are the characters in a fictional work of literature. The persona generally functions as a mask through which the author tells a story in a voice other than his or her own. A persona is usually either a character in a story who acts as a narrator or an "implied author," a voice created by the author to act as the narrator for himself or herself. The persona in Charlotte Perkins Gilman's story "The Yellow Wallpaper" is the unnamed young mother experiencing a mental breakdown.

Personification: A figure of speech that gives human qualities to abstract ideas, animals, and inanimate objects. To say that "the sun is smiling" is to personify the sun.

Plot: The pattern of events in a narrative or drama. In its simplest sense, the plot guides the author in composing the work and helps the reader follow the work. Typically, plots exhibit causality and unity and have a beginning, a middle, and an end. Sometimes, however, a plot may consist of a series of disconnected events, in which case it is known as an "episodic plot."

Poetic Justice: An outcome in a literary work, not necessarily a poem, in which the good are rewarded and the evil are punished, especially in ways that particularly fit their virtues or crimes. For example, a murderer may himself be murdered, or a thief will find himself penniless.

Poetic License: Distortions of fact and literary convention made by a writer—not always a poet—for the sake of the effect gained. Poetic license is closely related to the concept of "artistic freedom." An author exercises poetic license by saying that a pile of money "reaches as high as a mountain" when the pile is actually only a foot or two high.

Point of View: The narrative perspective from which a literary work is presented to the reader. There are four traditional points of view. The "third person omniscient" gives the reader a "godlike" perspective, unrestricted by time or place, from which to see actions and look into the minds of characters. This allows the author to comment openly on characters and events in the work. The "third person" point of view presents the events of the story from outside of any single character's perception, much like the omniscient point of view, but the reader must understand the action as it takes place and without any special insight into characters' minds or motivations. The "first person" or "personal" point of view relates events as they are perceived by a single character. The main character "tells" the story and may offer opinions about the action and characters which differ from those of the author. Much less common than omniscient, third person, and first person is the "second person" point of view, wherein the author tells the story as if it is happening to the reader. James Thurber employs the omniscient point of view in his short story "The Secret Life of Walter Mitty." Ernest Hemingway's "A Clean, Well-Lighted Place" is a short story told from the third person point of view. Mark Twain's novel *Huckleberry Finn* is presented from the first person viewpoint. Jay McInerney's *Bright Lights, Big City* is an example of a novel which uses the second person point of view.

Pornography: Writing intended to provoke feelings of lust in the reader. Such works are often condemned by critics and teachers, but those which can be shown to have literary value are viewed less harshly. Literary works that have been described as pornographic include D. H. Lawrence's *Lady Chatterley's Lover* and James Joyce's *Ulysses*.

Post-Aesthetic Movement: An artistic response made by African Americans to the black aesthetic movement of the 1960s and early 1970s. Writers since that time have adopted a somewhat different tone in their work, with less emphasis placed on the disparity between black and white in the United States. In the words of post-aesthetic authors such as Toni Morrison, John Edgar Wideman, and Kristin Hunter, African Americans are portrayed as looking inward for answers to their own questions, rather than always looking to the outside world. Two well-known examples of works produced as part of the post-aesthetic movement are the Pulitzer Prize–winning novels *The Color Purple* by Alice Walker and *Beloved* by Toni Morrison.

Postmodernism: Writing from the 1960s forward characterized by experimentation and application of modernist elements, which include existentialism and alienation. Postmodernists have gone a step further in the rejection of tradition begun with the modernists by also rejecting traditional forms, preferring the anti-novel over the novel and the anti-hero over the hero. Postmodern writers include Thomas Pynchon, Margaret Drabble, and Gabriel Gárcia Márquez.

Prologue: An introductory section of a literary work. It often contains information establishing the situation of the characters or presents information about the setting, time period, or action. In drama, the prologue is spoken by a chorus or by one of the principal characters.

Prose: A literary medium that attempts to mirror the language of everyday speech. It is distinguished from poetry by its use of unmetered, unrhymed language consisting of logically related sentences. Prose is usually grouped into paragraphs that form a cohesive whole such as an essay or a novel. The term is sometimes used to mean an author's general writing.

Protagonist: The central character of a story who serves as a focus for its themes and incidents and as the principal rationale for its development. The protagonist is sometimes referred to in discussions of modern literature as the hero or anti-hero. Well-known protagonists are Hamlet in William Shakespeare's *Hamlet* and Jay Gatsby in F. Scott Fitzgerald's *The Great Gatsby*.

R

Realism: A nineteenth-century European literary movement that sought to portray familiar characters, situations, and settings in a realistic manner. This was done primarily by using an objective narrative point of view and through the buildup of accurate detail. The standard for success of any realistic work depends on how faithfully it transfers common experience into fictional forms. The realistic method may be altered or extended, as in stream of consciousness writing, to record highly subjective experience. Contemporary authors who often write in a realistic way include Nadine Gordimer and Grace Paley.

Resolution: The portion of a story following the climax, in which the conflict is resolved. The resolution of Jane Austen's *Northanger Abbey* is neatly summed up in the following sentence: "Henry and Catherine were married, the bells rang and every body smiled."

Rising Action: The part of a drama where the plot becomes increasingly complicated. Rising action leads up to the climax, or turning point, of a drama. The final "chase scene" of an action film is generally the rising action which culminates in the film's climax.

Roman a clef: A French phrase meaning "novel with a key." It refers to a narrative in which real persons are portrayed under fictitious names. Jack Kerouac, for example, portrayed various friends under fictitious names in the novel *On the Road*. D. H. Lawrence based "The Rocking-Horse Winner" on a family he knew.

Romanticism: This term has two widely accepted meanings. In historical criticism, it refers to a European intellectual and artistic movement of the late eighteenth and early nineteenth centuries that sought greater freedom of personal expression than that allowed by the strict rules of literary form and logic of the eighteenth-century neoclassicists. The Romantics preferred emotional and imaginative expression to rational analysis. They considered the individual to be at the center of all experience and so placed him or her at the center of their art. The Romantics believed that the creative imagination reveals nobler truths—unique feelings and attitudes—than those that could be discovered by logic or by scientific examination. "Romanticism" is also used as a general term to refer to a type of sensibility found in all periods of literary history and usually considered to be in opposition to the principles of classicism. In this sense, Romanticism signifies any work or philosophy in which the exotic or dreamlike figure strongly, or that is devoted to individualistic expression, self-analysis, or a pursuit of a higher realm of knowledge than can be discovered by human reason. Prominent Romantics include Jean-Jacques Rousseau, William Wordsworth, John Keats, Lord Byron, and Johann Wolfgang von Goethe.

S

Satire: A work that uses ridicule, humor, and wit to criticize and provoke change in human nature and institutions. Voltaire's novella *Candide* and Jonathan Swift's essay "A Modest Proposal" are both satires. Flannery O'Connor's portrayal of the family in "A Good Man Is Hard to Find" is a satire of a modern, Southern, American family.

Science Fiction: A type of narrative based upon real or imagined scientific theories and technology. Science fiction is often peopled with alien creatures and set on other planets or in different dimensions. Popular writers of science fiction are Isaac Asimov, Karel Capek, Ray Bradbury, and Ursula K. Le Guin.

Setting: The time, place, and culture in which the action of a narrative takes place. The elements of setting may include geographic location, characters's physical and mental environments, prevailing cultural attitudes, or the historical time in which the action takes place.

Short Story: A fictional prose narrative shorter and more focused than a novella. The short story usually deals with a single episode and often a single character. The "tone," the author's attitude toward his or her subject and audience, is uniform throughout. The short story frequently also lacks *denouement*, ending instead at its climax.

Signifying Monkey: A popular trickster figure in black folklore, with hundreds of tales about this character documented since the 19th century. Henry Louis Gates Jr. examines the history of the signifying monkey in *The Signifying Monkey: Towards a Theory of Afro-American Literary Criticism,* published in 1988.

Simile: A comparison, usually using "like" or "as," of two essentially dissimilar things, as in "coffee as cold as ice" or "He sounded like a broken record." The title of Ernest Hemingway's "Hills Like White Elephants" contains a simile.

Socialist Realism: The Socialist Realism school of literary theory was proposed by Maxim Gorky and established as a dogma by the first Soviet Congress of Writers. It demanded adherence to a communist worldview in works of literature. Its doctrines required an objective viewpoint comprehensible to the working classes and themes of social struggle featuring strong proletarian heroes. Gabriel García Márquez's stories exhibit some characteristics of Socialist Realism.

Stereotype: A stereotype was originally the name for a duplication made during the printing process; this led to its modern definition as a person or thing that is (or is assumed to be) the same as all others of its type. Common stereotypical characters include the absent-minded professor, the nagging wife, the troublemaking teenager, and the kindhearted grandmother.

Stream of Consciousness: A narrative technique for rendering the inward experience of a character. This technique is designed to give the impression of an ever-changing series of thoughts, emotions, images, and memories in the spontaneous and seemingly illogical order that they occur in life. The textbook example of stream of consciousness is the last section of James Joyce's *Ulysses.*

Structure: The form taken by a piece of literature. The structure may be made obvious for ease of understanding, as in nonfiction works, or may obscured for artistic purposes, as in some poetry or seemingly "unstructured" prose.

Style: A writer's distinctive manner of arranging words to suit his or her ideas and purpose in writing. The unique imprint of the author's personality upon his or her writing, style is the product of an author's way of arranging ideas and his or her use of diction, different sentence structures, rhythm, figures of speech, rhetorical principles, and other elements of composition.

Suspense: A literary device in which the author maintains the audience's attention through the buildup of events, the outcome of which will soon be revealed. Suspense in William Shakespeare's *Hamlet* is sustained throughout by the question of whether or not the Prince will achieve what he has been instructed to do and of what he intends to do.

Symbol: Something that suggests or stands for something else without losing its original identity. In literature, symbols combine their literal meaning with the suggestion of an abstract concept. Literary symbols are of two types: those that carry complex associations of meaning no matter what their contexts, and those that derive their suggestive meaning from their functions in specific literary works. Examples of symbols are sunshine suggesting happiness, rain suggesting sorrow, and storm clouds suggesting despair.

T

Tale: A story told by a narrator with a simple plot and little character development. Tales are usually relatively short and often carry a simple message. Examples of tales can be found in the works of Saki, Anton Chekhov, Guy de Maupassant, and O. Henry.

Tall Tale: A humorous tale told in a straightforward, credible tone but relating absolutely impossible events or feats of the characters. Such tales were commonly told of frontier adventures during the settlement of the west in the United States. Literary use of tall tales can be found in Washington Irving's *History of New York,* Mark Twain's *Life on the Mississippi,* and in the German R. F. Raspe's *Baron Munchausen's Narratives of His Marvellous Travels and Campaigns in Russia.*

Theme: The main point of a work of literature. The term is used interchangeably with thesis. Many works have multiple themes. One of the themes of Nathaniel Hawthorne's "Young Goodman Brown" is loss of faith.

Tone: The author's attitude toward his or her audience maybe deduced from the tone of the work. A formal tone may create distance or convey politeness, while an informal tone may encourage a friendly, intimate, or intrusive feeling in the reader. The author's attitude toward his or her subject matter may also be deduced from the tone of the words he or she uses in discussing it. The tone of John F. Kennedy's speech which included the appeal to "ask not what your country can do for you" was intended to instill feelings of camaraderie and national pride in listeners.

Tragedy: A drama in prose or poetry about a noble, courageous hero of excellent character who, because of some tragic character flaw, brings ruin upon him- or herself. Tragedy treats its subjects in a dignified and serious manner, using poetic language to help evoke pity and fear and bring about catharsis, a purging of these emotions. The tragic form was practiced extensively by the ancient Greeks. The classical form of tragedy was revived in the sixteenth century; it flourished especially on the Elizabethan stage. In modern times, dramatists have attempted to adapt the form to the needs of modern society by drawing their heroes from the ranks of ordinary men and women and defining the nobility of these heroes in terms of spirit rather than exalted social standing. Some contemporary works that are thought of as tragedies include *The Great Gatsby* by F. Scott Fitzgerald, and *The Sound and the Fury* by William Faulkner.

Tragic Flaw: In a tragedy, the quality within the hero or heroine which leads to his or her downfall. Examples of the tragic flaw include Othello's jealousy and Hamlet's indecisiveness, although most great tragedies defy such simple interpretation.

U

Utopia: A fictional perfect place, such as "paradise" or "heaven." An early literary utopia was described in Plato's *Republic,* and in modern literature, Ursula K. Le Guin depicts a utopia in "The Ones Who Walk Away from Omelas."

V

Victorian: Refers broadly to the reign of Queen Victoria of England (1837-1901) and to anything with qualities typical of that era. For example, the qualities of smug narrow-mindedness, bourgeois materialism, faith in social progress, and priggish morality are often considered Victorian. In literature, the Victorian Period was the great age of the English novel, and the latter part of the era saw the rise of movements such as decadence and symbolism.

Cumulative Author/Title Index

Cumulative Nationality/Ethnicity Index

African American

Baldwin, James
The Rockpile: V18
Sonny's Blues: V2
Bambara, Toni Cade
Blues Ain't No Mockin Bird: V4
Gorilla, My Love: V21
The Lesson: V12
Raymond's Run: V7
Butler, Octavia
Bloodchild: V6
Chesnutt, Charles Waddell
The Sheriff's Children: V11
Ellison, Ralph
King of the Bingo Game: V1
Hughes, Langston
The Blues I'm Playing: V7
Slave on the Block: V4
Hurston, Zora Neale
Conscience of the Court: V21
The Eatonville Anthology: V1
The Gilded Six-Bits: V11
Spunk: V6
Sweat: V19
Marshall, Paule
To Da-duh, in Memoriam: V15
McPherson, James Alan
Elbow Room: V23
Toomer, Jean
Blood-Burning Moon: V5
Walker, Alice
Everyday Use: V2
Roselily: V11
Wideman, John Edgar
The Beginning of Homewood: V12
Fever: V6

*What We Cannot Speak About
We Must Pass Over in Silence:*
V24
Wright, Richard
Big Black Good Man: V20
Bright and Morning Star: V15
The Man Who Lived Underground:
V3
The Man Who Was Almost a Man:
V9

American

Adams, Alice
Greyhound People: V21
The Last Lovely City: V14
Agüeros, Jack
Dominoes: V13
Aiken, Conrad
Silent Snow, Secret Snow: V8
Alexie, Sherman
*Because My Father Always Said
He Was the Only Indian Who
Saw Jimi Hendrix Play "The
Star-Spangled Banner" at
Woodstock:* V18
Allen, Woody
The Kugelmass Episode: V21
Anderson, Sherwood
Death in the Woods: V10
Hands: V11
Sophistication: V4
Asimov, Isaac
Nightfall: V17
Baida, Peter
A Nurse's Story: V25

Baldwin, James
The Rockpile: V18
Sonny's Blues: V2
Bambara, Toni Cade
Blues Ain't No Mockin Bird: V4
Gorilla, My Love: V21
The Lesson: V12
Raymond's Run: V7
Barrett, Andrea
The English Pupil: V24
Barth, John
Lost in the Funhouse: V6
Barthelme, Donald
The Indian Uprising: V17
*Robert Kennedy Saved from
Drowning:* V3
Beattie, Ann
Imagined Scenes: V20
Janus: V9
Bellow, Saul
Leaving the Yellow House: V12
A Silver Dish: V22
Bender, Aimee
The Rememberer: V25
Benet, Stephen Vincent
An End to Dreams: V22
Berriault, Gina
The Stone Boy: V7
Women in Their Beds: V11
Bierce, Ambrose
The Boarded Window: V9
*An Occurrence at Owl Creek
Bridge:* V2
Bisson, Terry
The Toxic Donut: V18
Bloom, Amy
Silver Water: V11

Subject/Theme Index